An Introduction to Computer Graphics and
Creative 3-D Environments

Barry G. Blundell

An Introduction to Computer Graphics and Creative 3-D Environments

 Springer

Barry G. Blundell
MInstP CPhys CSci MBCS CEng CITP MRSNZ
Auckland University of Technology
Auckland
New Zealand

ISBN: 978-1-84800-041-4   e-ISBN: 978-1-84800-042-1
DOI 10.1007/978-1-84800-042-1

British Library Cataloguing in Publication Data
A catalogue record for this book is available from the British Library

Library of Congress Control Number: 2008930127

Please note that glasses must be included with all returned books. Springer will not accept any returns if the glasses have been separated from the book.

Printed on acid-free paper

9 8 7 6 5 4 3 2 1

Springer Science+Business Media
springer.com

This book is dedicated to
Jandy, Alys, Quintus, Jasper, Gryphon

and also

To the mists of Avalon

What if you slept? And what if, in your sleep, you dreamed?
And what if, in your dream, you went to heaven
and there plucked a strange and beautiful flower?
And what if, when you awoke, you had the flower in your hand?
Ah, what then?

Samuel Taylor Coleridge (1772–1834)

"A little lowly hermitage it was,
Down in a dale, hard by a forest's side,
Far from resort of people, that did pass
In travel to and fro: a little wide
There was an holy chapel edifyde,
Wherein the Hermit duly wont to say
His holy things each morn and eventide:
Thereby a crystal stream did gently play,
Which from a sacred foundation welled forth alway".

Edmund Spenser (c1522–1599),
'The Faerie Queene'

Contents

Preface

'. . . a fierce delight in the soft glow of leaves, in the white birch stems and tracery of sparse twigs against blue sky, in the scents of sap and grass and gum and heather flowers; stivers the hair on him with keenness for interpreting each sound, and fills the very fern or moss he kneels on, the very trunk he leans against, with strange vibration.'

This book is designed to be a course text for students studying computer graphics and related subjects at the introductory level within the context of an undergraduate or graduate degree programme. The content is presented in such a way as to ensure that it is accessible to the widest possible audience and wherever feasible a trans-disciplinary approach is adopted, thereby making the subject matter accessible to students of both the traditional Arts and Sciences. The book is designed to support the infusion of research content within the course curriculum. Coverage includes:

1. An introduction to computer graphics – both two and three-dimensional image depiction. Here we primarily focus on fundamental techniques and methodologies that underpin the formation and manipulation of image scenes.
2. Basic mathematical techniques employed in computer graphics. Only an elementary knowledge of maths is assumed – our primary objective is to ensure that the contents are accessible to students with diverse backgrounds. At the same time, the introductory coverage of maths is structured in a way that enables students who have previously studied this material to easily verify their skills and, if appropriate, skip material with which they are already familiar.
3. Discussion in relation to key aspects of the human visual system and the suitability of the traditional computer display to optimally interface with our complex sense of sight. In this context we consider a range of pictorial, oculomotor, and parallax depth cues and discuss facets of 3-D image depiction.
4. Computer graphics provides the primary means by which we visualise the results of the computational process and also underpins our interaction with the digital domain. With this in mind, we consider aspects of the human-computer interaction process and the synergy that exists between the visual image and interaction tools. This includes discussion of haptic technologies and bi-manual interaction.

5. Various 'creative' 3-D display system technologies (including stereoscopic, multi-view, volumetric, varifocal and holographic techniques) are introduced. Here, we consider characteristics of the displayed image, discuss interaction opportunities, and highlight key strengths and weaknesses.

Anaglyph, stereo, and Pulfrich viewing glasses are supplied with this book. These are intended to provide the reader with the opportunity to experiment with 3-D images. The anaglyph glasses can be used to view images reproduced in the text. A number of stereograms are also provided and these can be easily viewed using the stereo glasses or, after a little practice, they can be fused directly. The Pulfrich glasses provide an interesting insight into characteristics of the human visual system and can be used when viewing dynamic computer generated images or television scenes – enabling a scene to appear to reside within a 3-D space rather than within the confines of the 2-D screen on which it is actually displayed. In addition, if you are interested in obtaining a simple interactive program that will enable you to create line drawings in stereo form (and so experiment with 3-D image formation) please contact the author directly at the e-mail address given below.

The book has been designed to enable some flexibility in the order in which content is studied. For example, Chapter 5 (Interfacing with the Visual System), Chapter 9 (Creative 3-D Display Systems) and Chapter 10 (Interaction and Haptic Feedback) are, in the main, independent of the other chapters and can therefore be read out of sequence.

To aid the learning process a number of 'Over to You' (OTU) exercises are presented within the body of each chapter. These are designed to reinforce and/or extend discussion. Feedback on selected exercises is provided towards the end of the book. In addition, chapters are accompanied by review questions (and possible solutions) which are intended to give an opportunity for revision.

At the beginning of each chapter a fragment of text and an image are presented. These are reproduced from the outstanding book, 'Memories' by John Galsworthy, the illustrations being created by Maud Earl (see also Figure 1.8). This book was first published in 1911 and provides an excellent example of the synergy that can exist between two mediums of expression – both of which impinge on our imagination and equally support a 'suspension of disbelief' (see related discussion in Chapter 1). In fact, as the reader will note, the images created by Maud Earl have a number of remarkable attributes – not the least of which is their 'kinetic' form. Although we are presented with a single static image (corresponding to an image frame) we can anticipate the dog's (Chris's) motion.

Despite the care that has been taken in the preparation of this book, errors and omissions will undoubtedly have occurred. The author would very much appreciate feedback from readers, especially concerning ways in which future editions could be improved, and in relation to any work that has been omitted or incorrectly attributed. It has been a privilege to have had the opportunity to write this book. It is hoped that you will enjoy perusing its contents and that having done so you will feel encouraged to study computer graphics (and related subjects) at a more advanced level.

Barry G. Blundell
Barry.blundell@physics.org

Acknowledgements

'. . . there was much in him yet of the cave
bear – he dug graves on the smallest
provocations, in which he never buried
anything.'

It has taken some 18 months to turn the original outline for this book into a completed manuscript. Although planned during a brief period spent in Wales (did it really rain *every* day?), the main part of the work has been carried out in an ancient Orangerie located in the grounds of a château in central France. Certainly a tranquil and idyllic setting in which to write and as the months and seasons passed this book began to take shape. During this time many people provided both direct and indirect assistance and I should like to begin by acknowledging the staff at Springer (London) for their invaluable support and encouragement. Particular thanks to my editor, Beverley Ford, and also to Helen Desmond and Joanne Cooling – it continues to be a pleasure to work with the Springer team. My thanks also to Claire Annals for the work that she has carried out in copy-editing this manuscript. I should like to express my thanks to B. Gokulnathan and the team in Delhi who have done invaluable work in developing the page proofs.

I should like to thank our many friends in France who have accepted us into their community and have provided a great deal of practical help and encouragement. Particular thanks to Mme and Mlle de V, who have welcomed us into their home for many years, and have provided a setting that has never failed to inspire the author. My thanks to Jean-Pierre (for his friendship, constant good humour, and practical help), and Jeannine, and to many people in the local community – particularly Guy and Maïte Beaufils, Dominique Laborde (for his wise counsel – a true French philosopher), Christelle and Gildas Bréchard; not forgetting Mireille and Jacky Philippe ('*salut poilu*'). A special thanks to the Mayor of Chambon-sur-Voueize for permission to reproduce the image of the Execution of Sainte-Valérie (Figure 1.8(a)).

I have been privileged to know Professor Rüdiger Hartwig for some years. His encouragement, support, wise counsel and friendship have been a tremendous help and I sincerely thank him for all he has done.

In connection with permissions relating to the reproduction of material in this book, I should like to express my gratitude to the following people: Professor Nicholas Wade, University of Dundee for permission to reproduce Figure 9.9; Dr Gregg Favalora of Actuality Systems for supplying the two images presented in Chapter 9 of the Perspecta display (Figure 9.22, and Table 9.4), along with the accompanying brief technical specification; Laura Wallace on behalf of SensAble Technologies for providing the illustrations reproduced in Figure 10.5, along with Table 10.1; the IET (formerly IEE) for permission to reproduce Figure 1.18; the Optical Society of America for permission to reproduce Figure 9.29; Reachin Technologies for supplying Figure 9.7; Dr Peter Morse (University of Melbourne) and Mark Pharoah (Museum of South Australia) for providing the wonderful stereo photographs taken by Frank Hurley during the 1911–1914 Mawson Antarctic Expedition; Figure 9.4 is reproduced from a book written by A.M. Low in 1933. Despite every effort it has not proved possible to contact the author's family or the publisher. My thanks also to Dr Mark Bolas for providing the stereograms reproduced in Figure 9.32, and to Professor Shree Nayar for the images depicted in Figure 9.33. Professor Henry Fuchs has been kind enough to provide scans of his original images which are shown in Figure 9.34, together with the content that forms the basis of OTU Exercise 9.14.

The photograph reproduced in Figure 6.5(a) was originally supplied some years ago by A.V. Roe (of AVRO fame – aircraft pioneer extraordinaire). The writing that appears on this photograph is a personal note by Mr Roe which reads '*I think there will be a big future for flying ships when the money system has been reformed*'. The Italian Ministry of Cultural Goods and Activities gave permission to reproduce Figure 1.8(b); Miss Jocelyn Galsworthy was kind enough to give permission for the reproduction of material from John Galsworthy's book, 'Memories'. Figure 1.17 is reproduced from a book by Keith Geddes and Gordon Bussey – despite every effort it has not proved possible to contact the authors or publishers of this work. The remarkable anaglyph images presented in this book were created by A.G.J. Davies in the 1960s [Davies 1967]. Despite extensive efforts, it has proved impossible to contact Mr Davies. If any reader can shed light on his whereabouts please do let me know.

This is the last section of the book that remains to be written prior to the submission of the completed manuscript and is being drafted in a somewhat surreal setting – an early morning sailing of a fast catamaran brashly plying its way between Waiheke Island in the Hauraki Gulf and Auckland. The bright sunlight, shimmering sea and brooding backdrop of Rangitoto Island greatly contrast with the setting in France where, up until a short time ago, I was working. Here, in New Zealand, I should particularly like to acknowledge Mr Richard Wood for his vision and keen enthusiasm for this work (not forgetting Tiger!). Indeed I look forward to future projects on which we shall work. My sincere thanks to Professor Ajit Narayanan, and Dr Kathy Garden at AUT University. I should also like to express my gratitude to the library staff who in recent months have provided a great deal of help, particularly those who work in the Interloans section; their assistance has been invaluable. Thanks also to colleagues in various countries who have given invaluable advice concerning the content of this book and who have read and have provided most helpful comments in relation to a number of sections.

Authorship is a time-consuming, obsessive and somewhat addictive occupation. As the character of a book begins to develop it becomes the focal point of an author's existance, and distractions involving practical aspects of day to day life are cast to one side as so much irritating trivia. And so I should like to thank all my family for their patience and understanding – especially Jandy, Alys and Quintus (not to forget Gryphon for the chaos that he causes each and every day) who have supported me and have helped with my 'addictive occupation'. I sincerely appreciate their quest to locate for me an 'authors' rehab centre'. . .

Finally, I should like to thank Jasper who has gently snored by my side as each and every page has been written (with the exception of the 30 days he has had to pass once again in New Zealand quarantine). Often during the last long winter Jasper must have been sorely tempted to remain at the side of the blazing log fire rather than once again traverse the deep snow covered path to the Orangerie, with hard frost painting rich fractal patterns on all windows. Even the computer (to say nothing of fingers and toes) objected to the constant sub-zero temperatures – but Jasper was always there – neither knowing nor understanding why so many hours were spent at that desk. For his unquestioning and uncomplaining companionship I am indeed indebted.

Barry G. Blundell
May 2008

Setting the Scene 1

1.1 Introduction

In this chapter, we provide general background discussion and introduce various concepts relating to computer graphics techniques. Not only does computer graphics provide us with a window onto the digital world by which we are able to intuitively view the results of computational processes but it also underpins interaction activities. Consequently, we begin by considering the crucial role played by computer graphics in the implementation of the modern interactive computer interface. To highlight the diverse demands that we place upon computer graphics systems, we briefly consider three indicative areas of application. These are flight simulation/entertainment (for which realism is a vital concern), medical diagnosis (in which facilitating the process of accurate information extraction is paramount) and electronic computer aided design (where attention is especially directed towards accuracy and support for simple and intuitive interaction).

Over the centuries, techniques have been developed that make it possible for us to accurately render views of 3-D objects and scenes on 2-D media (such as the artists canvas, paper or, in more recent times, the flat screen computer display). In Section 1.3, we turn our attention to aspects of this evolutionary process and begin by describing important advances made during the Renaissance period that flourished in Italy between the 14th and 16th centuries. It was during this time that the techniques needed to permit a 3-D space to be geometrically mapped onto a 2-D surface were derived and disseminated. Our account includes a brief description of a demonstration of accurate mathematically based perspective techniques in painting. It is generally believed that Filippo Brunelleschi was the first to make such a demonstration (in the early 15th century) – but as we will see, there is some mystery overshadowing this event... Indeed, more than 1000 years earlier artists proved themselves to be able to craft superbly realistic images on 2-D media but to what extent they understood and utilized geometric constructs or simply relied on their own, often remarkable talents, is a matter for debate.

Because of the spatial separation of our two eyes, each receives a slightly different view of our surroundings. Differences (disparities) in these views are identified by the visual system and are used to provide a strong sense of three-dimensionality. This cue to depth is known as binocular parallax (or stereopsis). Unfortunately, when we view an image that is depicted in a conventional manner on a 2-D medium, the two eyes are presented with identical views and so binocular parallax is absent. As we discuss, in the first half of the 19th century, Charles Wheatstone and David Brewster made great progress in harnessing this cue and developed stereoscopic techniques able to effectively support binocular parallax.

In Section 1.3 we describe several milestones in the development of electronic displays able to depict perspective views and this paves the way for a discussion of general principles that underpin the modern computer display. In Section 1.4 we briefly consider the vector graphics and bitmapped (pixmapped) display paradigms. During the 1960s and 1970s, the former approach played a dominant role in computer graphics applications. However, advances in technologies resulted in a transition to the generally superior bitmapped technique. Although vector graphics displays are no longer in use, we include coverage of this display modality to highlight (by way of comparison) the advantageous characteristics offered by the bitmapped approach. Additionally, bear in mind that the underlying principle of operation of the vector display is used (in modified form) by some emerging 'creative'[1] 3-D systems.

The implementation of the traditional Cathode Ray Tube display together with thin panel technologies based on plasma, liquid crystal and field emission techniques are outlined in Section 1.5. Finally, in Section 1.6 we introduce several techniques that may be used to encode binocular content within images depicted on a 2-D tableau thus enabling the visual system to effectively extract this information and so support a strong sensation of 3-D *relief*. In this section we focus on general issues and provide a number of exemplar images that can be viewed using the simple glasses included with this book.

Here, and in other chapters, you will find a number of 'Over To You' (OTU) exercises. These are placed within the body of the chapter to most readily link to local content and will assist in reinforcing subject matter. For some OTU exercises feedback is provided towards the end of the book so enabling you to conveniently verify your responses. Additionally, at the end of each chapter you will find a number of 'Review' questions intended to assist in revision and self-assessment. These are accompanied by brief summaries of possible responses – but these should not be viewed as representing 'model' answers!

---

[1] For the present we will use this term loosely and simply say that it refers to 3-D display technologies that may more naturally interface with the human visual system than does the widely used conventional flat screen computer display. It embraces forms of virtual reality systems, multi-view, holographic, volumetric and stereoscopic systems.

Key Learning Outcomes: At the end of this chapter you should be able to:

- *Discuss the pivotal role played by interactive computer graphics in modern computing and appreciate that different types of application place different demands on computer graphics systems.*

- *Discuss milestones in the evolution of modern computer graphics that enable 3-D images to be accurately portrayed on a 2-D screen.*

- *Describe several characteristics of the flat-screen display, and contrast the vector graphics and bit-mapped (pixmapped) graphics approaches.*

- *Discuss technologies used in the implementation of flat-screen displays.*

- *Delineate various techniques that may be used to support the binocular parallax depth cue and which therefore enable images to appear to exist in 3-D space.*

1.2 The Nature of Computer Graphics

'I think there is a world market for maybe five computers.'[2]

Computer graphics techniques provide the primary means by which we are able to view the results of wide ranging computational processes. Additionally, these techniques play a pivotal role in our interaction with the digital word. As indicated in Figure 1.1, computer graphics underpins the modern human-computer interface. Here, we indicate a collection of hardware and software (which we loosely refer to as 'graphics elements') that provide a vital interface between underlying digital data and the human operator. These elements support the synthesis and depiction of pictorial imagery that is presented to the complex human visual system. Although visual stimuli provide an extremely powerful means by which we visualise our surroundings (i.e. gain insight and understanding), other senses also play a crucial role. With this in mind, in Figure 1.1 we indicate that human visualisation processes may take input not only from the computer display but also from other interface mechanisms (such as the generation of sound and in the case of a growing number of applications, haptic feedback[3]). These sources of input to the human sensory systems are used to support the cognitive process of visualisation whereby we are able to form some type of mental image and thereby extract information, understand, and decide upon any appropriate responses that should be made.

---

[2] Attributed to Thomas J. Watson (1874–1956) former chairman of IBM.
[3] Haptic feedback is discussed in Chapter 10 and for the present we will simply note that it encompasses both touch and force feedback.

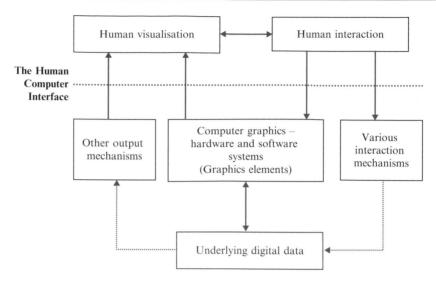

Figure 1.1 Aspects of the human-computer interface. Computer graphics techniques play a vital role in providing a window onto the digital world and in supporting interaction.

Real time interaction is critical to modern computing. For example, in the case of a video game, flight simulator or the like, we anticipate true real time performance and perceptible delays (latencies) that may occur as a result of the computational tasks that must be performed in order to execute an interactive operation, detract from the sense of immersion and are likely to negatively impact on the experience. Consequently, we cannot simply consider computer graphics software in isolation but must also bear in mind the architecture of the underlying hardware and interactions that occur between the graphics software and other elements within the system.

In other situations small delays that follow the initiation of an interactive operation and the system's response to it may be more readily tolerated. For example, when presented with some form of image (perhaps a graph indicating the change of one or more quantities with time), we may zoom on a feature of particular interest or manipulate image characteristics so as to facilitate the extraction of information. Here, slight pauses that can occur between the initiation of an operation and its completion may be deemed tolerable.

For the purposes of this book we will coin the following general description in relation to the scope of computer graphics (here, we use the word 'pictorial' in its widest possible sense):

> Computer graphics embraces all aspects of the synthesis, depiction and manipulation of pictorial representations by computational machines together with their presentation to the human visual system.

In Figure 1.2, we indicate some of the areas which (to a greater or lesser extent) influence the design and implementation of graphics systems and which must therefore be embraced by the computer graphics developer.

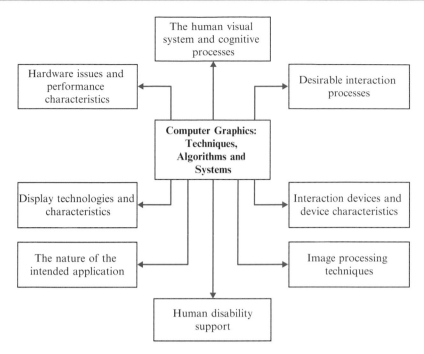

Figure 1.2 Seldom can the computer graphics system be considered in isolation – it usually forms part of a highly integrated and often complex environment. Here, we indicate some areas which are likely to influence the implementation of such a system and that must therefore considered by the designer.

The underlying purpose and demands placed on a graphics system vary greatly according to the nature of the application. In the subsections that follow we briefly consider three applications in which computer graphics plays a pivotal role.

1.2.1 Flight Simulation and Computer Games Applications

Such applications seek to immerse the user within a synthetic computer generated environment and so place stringent demands on the graphics system. In this context:

'...we rely on the recipient entering willingly into the experience and augmenting synthetic images with their imagination, which can lead to the viewer becoming completely absorbed or immersed ...' [Blundell and Schwarz 2006].

Within this context the expression 'suspension of disbelief' is often used and refers to the presentation of content in such a manner that the participant(s) become immersed within the synthetic world. It is often incorrectly claimed that this term was first coined in Hollywood in the 1930s. In fact, it actually dates back to the late 18th century and appears to have been first employed by the English poet Samuel Taylor Coleridge in the context of poetry[4]. Certainly

---

[4] 'During the first year that Mr. Wordsworth and I were neighbours, our conversations turned frequently on the two cardinal points of poetry, the power of exciting the sympathy of the reader by a faithful adherence to the truth of nature, and the power of giving the interest of novelty by the modifying colours of imagination. The sudden charm, which accidents of light and shade, which moon-light or sun-set diffused over a known and

poets such as Coleridge, William Wordsworth and many others have succeeded in creating verse that is able to directly impinge on the 'minds eye' or rather that intangible part of the mind in which our imagination enables us to visualise tantalising ephemeral images. For example, in 1804 Wordsworth wrote 'Daffodils' a part of which is reproduced in Figure 1.3(a). The Rime of the 'Ancient Mariner' was written by Wordsworth's fellow poet Samuel Taylor Coleridge – see Figure 1.3(b).

Such verse is extremely evocative – although it may appear to be far removed from today's state of the art computer games and flight simulators. However, a key point to note is that the actual medium via which synthetic content is conveyed is often of secondary importance – as long as it does not act in a manner that is contrary to a suspension of disbelief[5] – and so enables us to become engrossed in a synthetic world created by others (provided that the medium of expression does not act as an obtrusive interface). Certainly, the tremendous benefits that are derived from expensive flight simulation systems would be greatly eroded if participants were unable to become engrossed simply as a result of obtrusive cues that provide continuous reminders that the experience is wholly artificial. In this respect computer graphics and associated display system technologies play a pivotal role by presenting to the human visual system images which 'augment realism'[6] and do not break the thread of mental immersion. In this respect, image quality and real time response to interactive operations are critical concerns.

As a further example of evocative verse which transcends the medium of expression it is appropriate to quote the Rev. George Gilfillan (1813–1878) who when discussing the work of Edmund Spenser (1552–1599) – the author of 'The Faerie Queene' writes:

'Whereas to Spenser was given all power over the fairy lands of imagination – to satisfy that 'thirst for a wilder beauty than earth supplies', which has been called the essence of poetry – to 'lay us on the lap of a lovelier nature, by stiller streams and greener meadows' – to change all substances into shadows, and all realities into dreams – to create, by the sheer force of his fancy, ideal wildernesses and worlds grander and richer than all the

---

familiar landscape, appeared to represent the practicability of combining both. These are the poetry of nature. The thought suggested itself (to which of us I do not recollect) that a series of poems might be composed of two sorts. In the one, the incidents and agents were to be, in part at least, supernatural; and the excellence aimed at was to consist in the interesting of the affections by the dramatic truth of such emotions as would naturally accompany such situations, supposing them real. And real in this sense they have been to every human being who, from whatever source of delusion, has at any time believed himself under supernatural agency. For the second class, subjects were to be chosen from ordinary life; the characters and incidents were to be such, as will be found in every village and its vicinity, where there is a meditative and feeling mind to seek after them, or to notice them, when they present themselves.

*In this idea originated the plan of the 'Lyrical Ballads'; in which it was agreed, that my endeavours should be directed to persons and characters supernatural, or at least romantic, yet so as to transfer from our inward nature a human interest and a semblance of truth sufficient to procure for these shadows of imagination that willing **suspension of disbelief** for the moment, which constitutes poetic faith. Mr. Wordsworth on the other hand was to propose to himself as his object, to give the charm of novelty to things of every day, and to excite a feeling analogous to the supernatural, by awakening the mind's attention from the lethargy of custom, and directing it to the loveliness and the wonders of the world before us; an inexhaustible treasure, but for which in consequence of the film of familiarity and selfish solicitude we have eyes, yet see not, ears that hear not, and hearts that neither feel nor understand. With this view I wrote the 'Ancient Mariner,"* Biographia Literaria (first published in 1817 – see Coleridge [1985]).

[5] In the next section we will refer to related discussion that took place some 750 years ago concerning the creation of pictorial images.

[6] Within this context realism does not necessarily refer to photorealistic images – visual content may take the form of any abstraction that we may wish to consider.

I WANDER'D lonely as a cloud

That floats on high o'er vales and hills,
When all at once I saw a crowd,
A host, of golden daffodils;
Beside the lake, beneath the trees,
Fluttering and dancing in the breeze.

Continuous as the stars that shine

And twinkle on the Milky Way,
They stretch'd in never-ending line
Along the margin of a bay:
Ten thousand saw I at a glance,
Tossing their heads in sprightly dance...

(a)

The Jabberwocky

'Twas brillig, and the slithy toves
Did gyre and gimble in the wabe:
All mimsy were the borogoves,
And the mome raths outgrabe.

"Beware the Jabberwock, my son!
The jaws that bite, the claws that catch!
Beware the Jubjub bird, and shun
The frumious Bandersnatch!"

He took his vorpal sword in hand:
Long time the manxome foe he sought-
So rested he by the Tumtum tree,
And stood awhile in thought.

And, as in uffish thought he stood,
The Jabberwock, with eyes of flame,
Came whiffing through the tugey wood,
And burbled as it came!

One, two! One, two! And through and through
The vorpal blade went snicker-snack!
He left it dead, and with its head
He went galumphing back.

"And hast thou slain the Jaberwock?
Come to my arms, my beamish boy!
O frabjous day! Callooh! Callay!"
He chortled in his joy.

'Twas brillig, and the slithy toves
Did gyre and gimble in the wabe:
All mimsy were the borogoves,
And the mome raths outgrabe

(c)

Down dropt the breeze, the sails dropt down,
'Twas sad as sad could be;
And we did speak only to break
The silence of the sea!

All in a hot and copper sky,
The bloody Sun, at noon,
Right up above the mast did stand,
No bigger than the Moon.

Day after day, day after day,
We stuck, nor breath nor motion;
As idle as a painted ship
Upon a painted ocean.

Water, water, every where,
And all the boards did shrink;
Water, water, every where,
Nor any drop to drink.

(b)

(d)

Figure 1.3 In (a) an extract from 'Daffodils' – written by William Wordsworth and in (b) verse from 'The Rime of the Ancient Mariner' by Samuel Taylor Coleridge. As with other mediums of expression, poetry is able to catalise vivid ephemeral images within the 'mind's eye'. Also see Footnote 4. In (c) we reproduce Lewis Carroll's remarkable poem 'The Jabberwocky'. This is best understood when read out loud! The image depicted in (d) provides us with one person's perception of the poem's content. See text for discussion. (Image (d) is reproduced from Lewis Carroll's 'Alice Through the Looking Glass'.)

mythologies of the past, or than all the fantasies of the combined Arabian genius in the 'Thousand and One Nights' – to plant and nourish to maturity a great forest of poetry, in which all men have since delighted to lose themselves, and as they plunged into its divine darkness, chequered with gleams of intense light, have forgot earth, their own identity, everything, wandering on in sweet bewilderment, and wishing everything, that they might awake and return to common life no more for ever! 'Shak[e]speare in his "Tempest" and "Midsummer-Night's Dream", and Milton in his 'Comus', have performed feats of creative fancy similar in kind, and equally beautiful; but, while their structures are comparatively small, Spenser's is vast – theirs are but turrets, while 'The Faerie Queene' is a 'castle in the clouds', complete in every part of its aerial architecture, with drawbridge, battlements, moat, arches, court-yard, and all – complete, we mean, so far as plan is concerned, for, owing to its author's premature death, it is in point of execution a great fragment.[7]

In Figure 1.3(c), we reproduce Lewis Carroll's remarkable verse 'Jabberwocky' (which appears in the well known story 'Through the Looking-Glass'). Here, you will notice that Carroll uses a range of verbs, adjective and nouns not normally encountered in an English language dictionary. These are often referred to as 'nonsense words' – which is indeed an odd title as the words directly inpinge on our sense of imagination and stimulate vivid, although perhaps fleeting images. Certainly, from the perspective of our imagination, the words generally make sense and therefore for the purposes of this book we will avoid refering to them as nonsense words but will coin the term 'intangibles'.

The action of such 'intangibles' is perhaps best understood by quoting Alice's[8] reaction to this verse:

'... "It seems very pretty," she said when she had finished reading it, "but rather hard to understand!" (You see she couldn't confess, even to herself, that she couldn't make it out at all.) "Somehow it seems to fill my head with ideas – only I don't exactly know what they are!"...'

Intangibles act directly on the imagination and individually they have no singularly defined form. For example, neither a Jabberwocky nor a Bandersnatch can be assigned a single representation – each reader is left to visualise these surreal, dreamscape creatures, within the limitless bounds of their own imagination – see Figure 1.3(d). (Nonetheless, perhaps we would all agree that it would be inadvisable to poke either creature with a stick ...)

By weaving together 'intangibles', Lewis Carroll employs a powerful tool able to directly impinge on the imagination, and which strongly promotes a suspension of disbelief. Many artists who seek to create works that convey feelings and stimulate human emotions use the same type of approach – often such images do not make recourse to the confines of a perspective framework.

> **Where possible, the content and interaction opportunities should transcend the medium of expression.**

1.2.2 Medical Applications

In the case of the flight simulation and computer games applications referred to above, it is vitally important that the computer graphics and display system technologies support a strong

---

[7] Reverence George Gilfillan, from 'The Genius and Poetry of Spenser', in *The Poetical Works of Edmund Spenser*, Vol. III, James Nichol, Edinburgh (1859).
[8] Alice is best known within the context of Lewis Carroll's famous work 'Alice in Wonderland'. She plays a similar role in 'Through the Looking-Glass', from which the above quotation is taken.

sense of realism. In contrast, systems developed for medical applications are generally intended to facilitate the extraction of information. For example, a clinician undertaking treatment planning may wish to view the form and extent of a cancerous tumour and accurately determine its position. In this case, the graphics system will usually be responsible for processing very large data sets and for supporting interactive operations so that images may be presented to the operator in a way that facilitates the information extraction process. Although delays (latencies) that occur between the initiation of an interactive operation and the system's response may be frustrating, these are unlikely to be as critical as similar latencies that may occur in applications of the type referred to in the previous subsection.

1.2.3 Electronic Computer Aided Design (ECAD)

Computers play a pivotal role in all aspects of the engineering design and manufacturing processes. Users can perform highly interactive operations by means of the graphics oriented interface:

'... the emphasis is on interacting with a computer-based model of the component or system being designed in order to test, for example, its structural, electrical or thermal properties. Often the model is interpreted by a simulator that feeds back the behaviour of the system to the user for further interactive design and test cycles.' [Foley et al. 1990]

Basic elements within a simple and traditional ECAD system used for the development of digital circuits are summarised in Figure 1.4. Here, schematic capture software provides an interactive graphical interface by means of which a user is able to design circuits. Such an environment will enable the user to undertake various important tasks. For example:

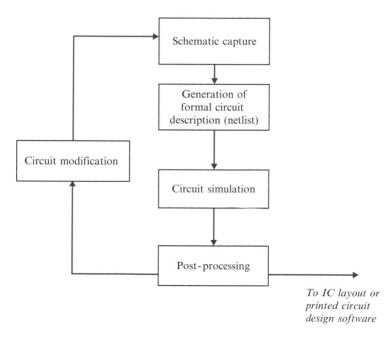

Figure 1.4 Basic elements within a traditional ECAD system intended for use in the development of electronic circuits.

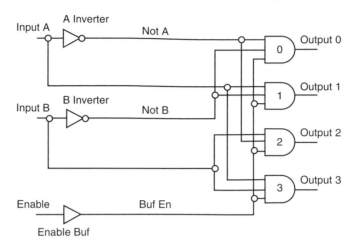

Figure 1.5 The circuit for a simple decoder. A formal description of this circuit (and of far more complex circuits) may be readily formed by means of graphical schematic capture software. (Reproduced from Blundell *et al.* [1987].)

1. To select components (such as logic gates) from a library and place these within a design space.
2. To enable the user to specify additional components (including behavioural models).
3. To enable the user to connect components in the required manner.
4. To enable components and connections to be labelled.
5. To support hierarchical design techniques so that a circuit may be presented at different levels of abstraction. Thus, for example, at the highest level the circuit may simply be represented as a rectangular box with various labelled inputs and outputs.

Once a circuit has been designed, the schematic capture software enables a formal description of the circuit to be generated. By way of an example, consider the simple circuit depicted in Figure 1.5 which represents a decoder with two inputs (A and B), an 'enable' input and four outputs (0–3). A 'gate level' description of the circuit would have the general form illustrated in Figure 1.6.

The decoder circuit illustrated in Figure 1.5 comprises only seven logic gates and provides a trivial example of the sort of circuit that we may wish to simulate during a training exercise. For actual applications, circuits that are designed using ECAD software are usually far more complex. Manually creating circuit descriptions for complex circuits is not a trivial undertaking and is prone to error. The use of a graphical environment for the design of circuits and the production of a formal circuit description can greatly facilitate aspects of the design process.[9]

As indicated in Figure 1.4, once a netlist has been generated, the circuit may be simulated and a post-processor used to show its response to both static and time varying input signals. Here again, through the adoption of an interactive graphics environment the process of interpreting electrical waveforms is greatly facilitated.

This simple ECAD design example is based on the use of 2-D graphics. However, there are many situations in which CAD applications demand the depiction of images that span (or

---

[9] When dealing with complex circuits, mechanical designs etc. the somewhat restricted area of the display screen that is available for interactive design can negatively impact on the design activity. Generally only parts of a circuit can be displayed on the screen at any one time.

```
                          ** Circuit Header
CCT <Logic type>             ** Specification of logic family
Decoder                      ** Name of circuit
(Output0, Output1,           ** Identify the inputs and outputs
Output2, Output3,
InputA, InputB, Enable)

                          ** Declaration of Circuit Elements
NOT (5,5)                    ** Gate Propagation delays
AInverter (NotA,InputA)      ** Instance of inverter
BInverter (NotB,InputB)      ** Instance of inverter
;
BUF (5:6:8,3:5:8)
EnableBuffer
(BufEn,Enable)
;
NAND (5,5)
Gate0 (Output0,NotA,NotB,BufEn)
Gate1 (Output1,InputA,NotB,BufEn)
Gate2 (Output2,NotA,InputB,BufEn)
Gate3 (Output3,InputA,InputB,BufEn)
;
WIRE


NotA NotB  BufEn
Output0 Output1Output2 Output3
;
INPUT
InputA InputB Enable
.                            **End of circuit description
```

Figure 1.6 A gate level description of the circuit illustrated in Figure 1.5.

at least appear to span) three dimensions (see related discussion in Section 7.7 concerning constructive solid geometry techniques). In the next section we briefly outline aspects of the evolutionary process that has culminated in modern computer graphics, and emphasise issues relating to the techniques employed to enable 3-D scenes to be depicted on a 2-D tableau such as the flat screen display.

1.3 The Evolution of Computer Graphics

> 'Bees . . . by virtue of a certain geometrical forethought . . .
> know that the hexagon is greater than the square and the triangle
> and will hold more honey for the same expenditure of material.'[10]

Since the earliest times people have sought to use pictorial images as a means of communication, as an aid to scientific understanding and as an outlet for creative expression. However, many of

---

[10] Attributed to Pappus of Alexandria ~320 AD. Quoted in Boyer [1991].

Figure 1.7 This fresco fragment was uncovered in Pompeii and dates back to the 1st Century AD (the eruption of Mount Vesuvius which caused the destruction of Pompeii occurred in 79 AD). The artist demonstrates the ability to capture detailed imagery and realistic perspective upon a 2-D tableau. The facial expressions are captivating and transcend the passage of time.

the works created prior to the period of the Renaissance (which flourished in Italy between the 14th and 16th centuries) fail to accurately convey the inherent three-dimensionality that we associate with our view of the physical world – although there are many remarkable exceptions (see, for example, the image depicted in Figure 1.7). In the case of such images, the incorporation of natural 'perspective' and other cues that provide a sense of depth (see Chapter 5) may well have been achieved by highly gifted individuals working on the basis of intuition rather than by conscious consideration of the physical and geometrical processes that give rise to the visible image scene.

The Renaissance (rebirth) denotes a period of great intellectual and cultural enlightenment – a time when artistic, scientific and mathematical thinking appears to have coalesced and so fuelled rapid progress. It is a period renowned for remarkable artistic works which possess, surpass and even transcend photorealism.

Surviving images rendered on two-dimensional (2-D) surfaces during the European Dark Ages tend to lack realism – the natural perspective that we perceive when viewing our surroundings is often distorted, objects (such as figures) are twisted in unnatural ways and angles often seem to be somewhat peculiar – see, for example Figure 1.8(a). However, during the Renaissance period the techniques needed to enable images to exhibit a natural sense of realism were derived and disseminated. To what extent the great pioneers of the Renaissance discovered or re-discovered these techniques is a matter of debate.

OTU Exercise 1.1: Realism in Early Painting

Using library or Internet facilities, locate early (pre-Renaissance) images rendered on 2-D tableaux. Discuss ways in which these images convey a natural sense of three-dimensionality. To what extent do the artists manage to capture facial expressions and so convey an individual's character or the events taking place? Additionally, examine images which originate from other cultures during the same period.

In literature, it is generally recognised that an architect named Filippo Brunelleschi (1377–1446) provided the first demonstration of the use of mathematically based geometrical techniques to capture a 3-D scene on a 2-D medium. This belief is based on two demonstrations that he gave early in the 15th century concerning the use of mathematical techniques for the production of painted works. Unfortunately, neither of these paintings appears to have survived – although one of the demonstrations is described in some detail by Brunelleschi's biographer (Antonio de Manetti) – apparently from first hand knowledge. However, this account leaves a number of questions unanswered and the demonstration given by Brunelleschi has an air of mystery – especially when we consider the technique employed for viewing the completed work.

   The demonstration described by de Manetti concerns the creation of a painting of a Florentine Baptistery in relation to which he writes:[11]

'The necessary conditions for viewing were that the spectator should peep from the back of the panel through a small hole at a mirror, in such a way that the painted surface was visible in reflection ... The peep-show system was used because the painter needs to presuppose a single place from which the painting must be viewed ...'

The panel referred to is the tableau on which the painted work was created and the general viewing arrangement is summarised in Figure 1.9. Before proceeding, it is instructive to briefly consider the manner in which a simple perspective projection of a 3-D scene onto a 2-D tableau is achieved. As we know from our everyday experience, as an object is moved so as to become more distant from the eye, it appears to become smaller (see Figure 1.10). Two examples of this illusion are shown in Figure 1.11 and it arises because of the finite separation of the eye's focusing system and the retina onto which the image is cast. Let us suppose that, as depicted in Figure 1.10, an object of height h_o lies at a distance u from the eye. Given that the focusing system of the eye and retina are separated by a distance v, then on the basis of similar triangles, we can write:

$$\frac{h_i}{v} = \frac{h_o}{u}$$

Thus the size of the image formed on the surface of the retina (h_i) depends on the height of the object and its distance from the eye (we can assume that v is the same for all observers).

---

[11] Quoted in Kemp [1978].

(b)

(a)

(c)   **(d)**

Figure 1.8   Prior to the Italian Renaissance period, images created on a 2-D tableau often failed to convey a natural sense of perspective. In (a) a painting (depicting the execution of Sainte Valérie) is reproduced. This dates back to the fifteenth Century. Although there is a lack of natural perspective, shadows and shading (*chiaroscuro*), the clarity of the facial expressions associated with the figures (e.g. of Sainte Valérie and her executioner) reveal emotions and testify to the artist's overall skill. In (b) Piero della Francesca demonstrates a superlative ability to compose a scene within a natural perspective framework. Notice, for example, that the egg (which is suspended vertically) is clearly shown as being located to the rear of the figures. This work (Virgin and Saints with Federigo da Montefeltro) is rich in symbolism and was created in ∼ 1470. It exemplifies the rapid progress that was made during the Renaissance period. In (c) a painting by Maurice Greiffen-Hagen (1862–1931) – 'Miss Mamie Bowles'. This is described in GPIPG [1905] as follows: *'This work, by reason of its intrinsic artistic qualities, is removed from the ordinary category of mere portraiture, and becomes, by its significant grace and spontaneous action, a picture of interest to any lover of art, independently of the person portrayed. No set attitude is detected, and no posing for effect. So skilfully has the painter wrought in seizing the individuality of his fair sitter that all he seems to have done is to paint her just as she is, in a momentary pause. For a few brief moments the sands of life cease to run, that her image may be left indelibly recorded; then they run on, leaving for after years a sense of the spirit and grace, without which portraiture is bereft of its most essential attributes.'* The image reproduced in (d) is also highly kinetic – the artist has captured a fleeting instant and the realism is such that we may well expect (or anticipate) the dog's movement. (Figure (a) is reproduced by kind permission of the Mayor of Chambon-sur-Voueize, La Creuse, France and is located in the Abbatiale Ste-Valérie. Image (b) is reproduced under licence from Italian Ministry of Cultural Goods and Activities and (c) from GPIPG [1901]. Image (d) by Maud Earl and is reproduced from 'Memories' by John Galsworthy [1912].)

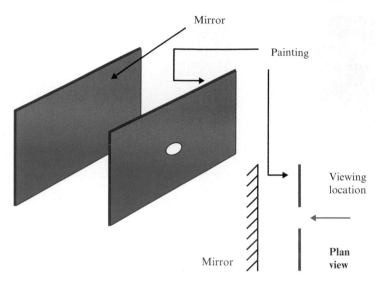

Figure 1.9 The arrangement described by di Manetti that was used by Brunelleschi when allowing his painting to be viewed. A hole is cut through the centre of the painted tableau. The observer places an eye to this hole and so is able to see the painted image reflected by the mirror.

Consider the case that we have a collection of objects in a 3-D space and that we wish to depict them on a 2-D tableau in a natural perspective framework. The relative size that we assign to each of the objects will be determined by their actual physical size and their relative depths within the scene. In Figure 1.12 we illustrate a single object and locate a 'projection

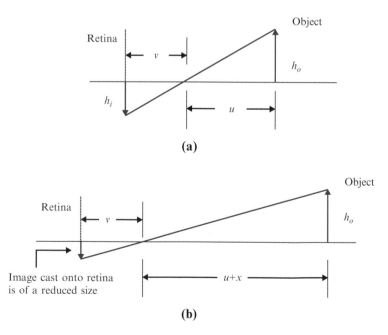

Figure 1.10 In (a) we illustrate an object of height h_o that is located at a distance u from the eye and which casts an image of height h_i on the retina. In (b) the same object is moved to a distance $u + x$ and this results in the formation of a smaller retinal image.

Figure 1.11 The linear perspective cue to depth. As a result of the finite separation of the focusing system within the eye and the retina onto which images are cast, parallel objects appear to converge in the distance. Additionally, at a greater distance, objects appear to be of a reduced size.

plane' ('view plane') between the object and the observer. This plane represents the tableau (e.g. artist's canvas or computer display) on which we wish to depict the object. To determine the size at which the object should be displayed on the tableau, we simply draw construction lines from the two endpoints of the object to the viewing location. The points at which

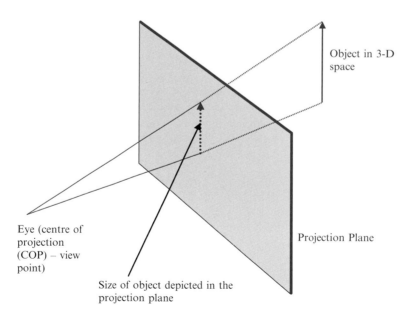

Object in 3-D space

Projection Plane

Eye (centre of projection (COP) – view point)

Size of object depicted in the projection plane

Figure 1.12 A simple perspective projection. The size of an object that resides within a 3-D space and which is to be depicted on a 2-D surface can be readily determined by locating a 'projection plane' between the object and the observer. Construction lines are then projected from the object's end points to the chosen viewing location. The points at which the two lines intersect the projection plane denote the size at which the object should be represented. The process is repeated for all the lines that comprise the scene. Interesting results can be obtained by employing a non-planar projection surface.

these lines pass through the projection plane indicate the size at which the object should be drawn.[12]

If the image scene comprises a set of objects, then we can obtain the perspective projection by repeating this process for each object. Naturally, the size that we assign to each will depend on:

1. The depth of the object behind the projection plane.
2. The location of the selected viewpoint relative to the projection plane.
3. The physical size of each object.

> It is important to note that a perspective projection of a set of objects in a 3-D space onto a 2-D surface assumes a certain viewing location.

Let us now return to that day in the early 15th century when Filippo Brunelleschi is said to have demonstrated his ability to depict a Florentine Baptistery within a geometrically accurate framework. Recall the 'peep hole' method which he employed for viewing the completed work – as summarised in Figure 1.9. By providing a single hole through which the completed painting was to be viewed, Brunelleschi (deliberately or otherwise) achieved three important goals:

1. He constrained (defined) the viewpoint from which the completed work was to be observed and as we have seen this is an important consideration in the production of accurate perspective.
2. He ensured that the observer could only view the painting with a single eye – thereby eliminating binocular input to the visual system.[13]
3. By judicious choice of the diameter of the viewing hole, Brunelleschi could have ensured that only the painting was visible to the observer – all peripheral scenery could have been occluded. This would have provided a greater sense of immersion.

The indirect viewing technique employed by Brunelleschi (whereby the observer viewed the painting's reflection in a mirror) is somewhat puzzling. The image produced by such an arrangement would have been laterally inverted, thus anybody viewing the painting via Brunelleschi's apparatus and comparing this view with the actual scene would have been likely to have immediately identified differences between the two. However, as suggested by Lynes [1980] Brunelleschi may have judiciously selected a viewpoint from which the Baptistery exhibited considerable symmetry. Alternative suggestions are:

1. Brunelleschi may have created his picture by viewing the reflection of the Baptistery in a mirror (rather than by viewing the building directly). The painting would therefore have been laterally inverted and the system devised for viewing the completed work would have cancelled out this effect. Additionally, although creating the painting using the image

---

[12] A straight line segment is fully described by the position of its two endpoints. Therefore determining the location of these two points defines the location of the entire line.

[13] This is an important consideration and appears to be something that even very young children instinctively make use of. For example, when at play with a model train set, children will often view the advancing or receding train from a vantage point that is close to the track. Invariably, they will close one eye. Should they use both eyes, the binocular parallax cue will strongly suggest the actual distance of the train. On the other hand, by employing only a single eye, the powerful binocular cue is disabled and it is therefore more difficult for the visual system to judge actual distances – models take on greater realism!

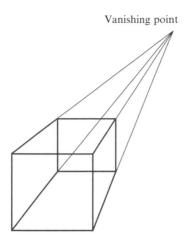

Vanishing point

Figure 1.13 A perspective view of a cube using a single vanishing point. Compare this with the view depicted in Figure 1.14.

depicted in the mirror would not have been easy (see, for example, Kemp [1978]) this may have facilitated the process of obtaining an accurate perspective view.

2. There is the *possibility* that Brunelleschi created his painting directly on the mirror's surface (see Lynes [1980] for interesting discussion). If this were the case, then it would undermine the widespread belief that Brunelleschi was the first to demonstrate the use of an accurate mathematically based perspective technique.

Edgerton [1976] provides an alternative suggestion:

'*The shrewd master may have realised something which has received attention from perceptual psychologists in recent times: that perspective illusion is strong only when the observer's awareness of the painted picture surface is dispelled. When the viewer loses his "subsidiary awareness" as the phenomenon is now called, he tends to believe the picture surface does not exist and that the illusionary space depicted is actually three-dimensional.*'

In this respect the use of a mirror by means of which the completed painting was viewed (and here it is important to realise that 15th century mirrors were of poor quality) may well have enhanced the observer's sense of realism and perhaps the mirror's reflection characteristics would have also caused some mild blurring of the image thereby reducing the visibility of defects in the painting!

Subsequent to Brunelleschi's demonstration, Leon Battista Alberti played an important role in the development and dissemination of perspective techniques. In a book produced in ~1435 ('*Della Pittura*'),[14] Alberti outlines a methodology to be used in the production of geometrically accurate images. Discussion centres on the use of a single point perspective technique in which, as indicated in Figure 1.13, there is one 'vanishing point'. This contrasts with the two and three point perspective techniques – an example of the former is provided in Figure 1.14.

—————————

[14] *Della Pittura* ('On Painting') is the title of the Italian version of this book. It was also produced in Latin (*De Pictura*). Some small differences in content exist.

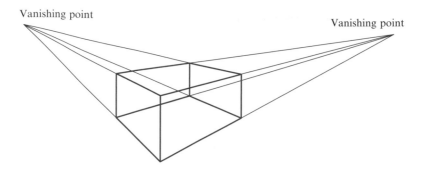

Figure 1.14 A perspective view of a cube using two vanishing points.

Piero della Francesca (∼1410–1492) also played a key role in the development of perspective techniques[15] (one of his works is illustrated in Figure 1.8(b)). Contrasting the contribution of Alberti with that of Piero, Boyer [1991] writes:

'... *Piero handled the more complicated problem of depicting on the picture plane objects in three dimensions as seen from a given station point* [viewing location].'

OTU Exercise 1.2: The Three Point Perspective Technique

Re-draw the cube illustrated in Figure 1.14 to produce a view that employs three vanishing points.

Over the subsequent years, techniques such as those described by Alberti coupled with an understanding of ways in which shading and colour can be effectively employed ultimately enabled photorealistic renditions of 3-D scenes to be created on the 2-D tableau. By drawing on the techniques that have evolved, the artist can transcend and surpass photorealism – the world created by the artist embracing both imagination and emotion:

'*The artist is responsible for every detail depicted on the canvas – the finished work represents the coalescence of the artist's ability to accurately observe a 3-D scene and to properly map these observations onto a 2-D space. Indeed the window created by the artist has a profundity that surpasses photographic recording, for the artist depicts a perspective corresponding to the scene as it is perceived after being processed by the human visual system – as it appears in the 'mind's eye'. The rendered scene therefore not only encodes imagery within a perspective framework but is also likely to contain detail of the artist's cognitive processes.*' [Blundell 2007]

---

[15] He wrote several books including *De Prospective Pingendi* (∼1478).

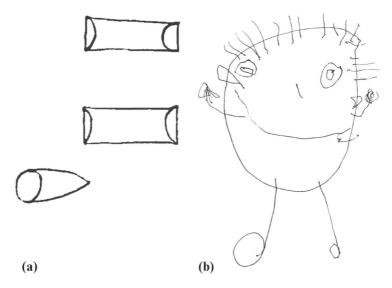

Figure 1.15 In (a) early medieval drawings of a cylindrical object are illustrated. In this context Edgerton [1991] writes: '. . . *early geometers could signify three-dimensional forms only by drawing them "squashed". . . Readers. . . were expected not to visualise the cylinder empirically but rather to reason it intellectually. Sicut haec figura docet.'*[16] In (b) a portrait of the author drawn by a four year old – again *Sicut haec figura docet*!

OTU Exercise 1.3: Capturing 3-D Images on a 2-D Tableau

Consider the two images depicted in Figure 1.15. Discuss their form and content. Do you consider that the use of a perspective framework within which we are able to enhance the realism of 3-D images that are rendered on a 2-D surface always provides us with a natural and intuitive means of creative expression?

> Computer graphics extends the creative opportunities that can be derived from traditional image rendering techniques enabling the production of animated image content and support for interactive operations.

A further important landmark in the use of the 2-D tableau for the depiction of 3-D objects relates to the work of Gaspard Monge (1746–1818) who developed drafting techniques that play a vital role in engineering design. In support of teaching students 'descriptive geometry' (which would have considered many of the 3-D geometrical issues that are of importance in today's computer graphics) he produced a book – 'Geometrie Descriptive' – in which he describes the use of a double orthographic projection technique enabling 3-D objects to be depicted by means

---

[16] *Sicut haec figura docet*: As this figure teaches.

Elevation views

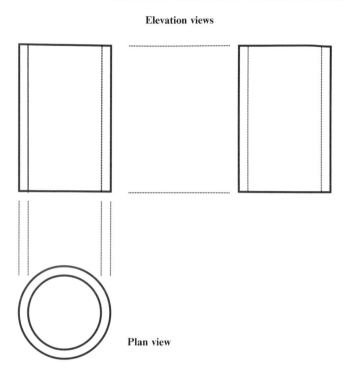

Plan view

Figure 1.16 Orthogonal views of a hollow cylinder. From these views we are able to reconstruct the 3-D shape. However, the reconstruction process can be greatly assisted by the inclusion of a 3-D rendition of the object. In fact the orthogonal and 3-D views are complementary. The former provides a convenient means of including quantitative information (such as component dimensions) whilst the latter assists in the visualisation (reconstruction) process.

of elevation and plan views.[17] A simple example showing the use of front, side and plan views to depict a hollow cylinder is provided in Figure 1.16.

This approach is based on the parallel projection technique in which a 3-D object is mapped onto a 2-D plane by means of a series of parallel lines. In the general case, (referred to as the 'oblique parallel projection' technique) the projection lines are not perpendicular to the surface (a traditional tableau or computer screen) onto which the projection is being made. However, in a more restricted scenario, the parallel projection lines lie perpendicular to the surface and this is referred to as orthographic projection – the approach pioneered by Gaspard Monge.

In the 19th century a number of important developments took place and these continue to have a profound effect on the way in which we depict and visualise information. One major milestone was the development of the stereoscope by Charles Wheatstone and David Brewster.

---

[17] This book was produced a time when France was in a state of great social and political turmoil and the techniques that he describes were viewed as having considerable military significance. As a result, for a time the book was 'classified'. Following the restoration of the French monarchy, Monge – a remarkable mathematician and superb teacher – was stripped of all his titles and banished. '...it broke the spirit of Monge, who died shortly afterwards'. [Boyer 1991].

These two great scientists (working independently of each other) made this breakthrough: the former first demonstrating a stereoscope in 1838 and the latter in 1849. Subsequently, there was considerable and rather heated debate as to the actual inventor – see, for example, Wade [1983] and Blundell [2006]. The operation of the stereoscope is outlined in Sections 1.6 and 9.3 – for the present it is sufficient to note that stereoscopic images incorporate the powerful depth cue of binocular parallax and so images possess a remarkable sense of *relief* – appearing to exist within three spatial dimensions. (By way of example, try viewing the stereoscopic images presented in Figures 1.32 and 9.8 using the simple stereoscopic viewing glasses that are provided with this book.) Since the pioneering work of Wheatstone and Brewster, numerous display technologies able to support binocular parallax have been proposed, prototyped and developed (see Chapter 9) and we will refer to these as 'creative' display paradigms.

The invention of photographic techniques greatly advanced the accuracy and ease with which images could recorded. Unfortunately, as with the artist's canvas, the conventional photographic image presents each of the two eyes with an identical view and therefore the binocular disparities that occur when we directly view a physical 3-D scene are absent. This can make it difficult to accurately determine absolute and relative distances (and in the cases of images depicted on the conventional computer display can limit interaction opportunities). However, this difficulty can be greatly ameliorated through the use of stereo photography, stereo computer graphics etc. As we discuss in Section 1.6, the creation of a photographic stereo image involves taking two separate photographs of an image scene – each from a slightly different vantage point. When correctly viewed such a pair of images (called a stereopair) can be fused and the visual system interprets slight differences (disparities) in the two images as providing a powerful cue to depth. This has three key advantages:

1. As noted above, the image appears to reside in three spatial dimensions and this enhances the realism of an image scene.
2. Absolute and relative distances can be judged more accurately.
3. The extraction of information from the scene under observation is often greatly facilitated.

The enhanced realism offered by stereo photographs led to the stereoscope becoming widely popular as a source of entertainment. Additionally (on the basis of (2) and (3) above), the stereoscope became an important tool in scientific and military applications.

Throughout the second half of the 19th century, the stereoscope (and associated stereo photographic techniques) gained great popularity. It was during this period that the quest for television began to gain attention. At that time, highly creative individuals sought techniques that would enable the development of an electronic (or electromechanical) 'telescope' via which audiences would be able to view distant events – *in real time*. A broad range of techniques were proposed and a variety of wonderful names were coined for these largely impractical devices (e.g. Phantascope, Phoroscope and Telectroscope).[18] However, it appears that it was not until 1911 that a reasonably feasible fully electronic television system was proposed. This system was mooted by Alan Archibald Campbell Swinton in a speech to the Röntgen Society and interestingly this included the suggestion that a Cathode Ray Tube (CRT – see Section 1.5.1)

---

[18] It appears that the term 'television' was first publicly used by Constantin Perskyi at the International Electricity Conference (25th August 1900) [Abramson 1987].

(a)   (b)

(c)   (d)

Figure 1.17 In the 1930s television developed rapidly. In (a) John Logie Baird demonstrates TV at Selfridges in April 1925. In (b) a 1938 demonstration by the Baird Company of a TV (the screen is reported as measuring 8 by 6 feet!). Illustration (c) shows a 1938 marketing poster advertising large screen projection TV developed by Scophony employing the remarkable Jeffree supersonic light control. A TV developed by Philips in the late 1930s is depicted in (d). (Images reproduced from Geddes and Bussey [1991].)

be used for the depiction of images. In fact, some 20 years were to pass before an all electronic television system was implemented and in the intervening years, that remarkable individualist and pioneer John Logie Baird was able to develop and demonstrate practical television using an electromechanical image capture and display system. This demonstration took place in January 1926 (for interesting discussion, see Kamm and Baird [2002]). During the next two decades Baird demonstrated high resolution colour television, a colour television system able to support the binocular parallax depth cue (without any need for viewing glasses/viewing apparatus) and pioneered the volumetric display technique (see Section 9.5) whereby 3-D images are depicted within a transparent volume so enabling them to naturally occupy a 3-D space.

Developments in the late 1920s and 1930s led to television broadcasting (although range was somewhat restricted) and so enabled the depiction of physically remote events in real-time – the 'electronic telescope' that had been sought for so long – see Figure 1.17. In contrast *traditional* cinema does not support simultaneity – events are recorded and played back at a later time.

The next, rather natural development was the production of hardware systems enabling user interaction with electronically processed images. Work in this area was given impetus by the urgent and ever increasing needs of the military in WWII, and in the UK, the Royal Signals and Radar Establishment (RSRE) which was then based in Malvern played an important role. In an extensive publication (which continues to retain much of its relevance) Parker and Wallis [1948] discuss the use of an analog calculation system able to map radar data onto a flat screen display to create a perspective view – see Figure 1.18. In this illustration the perspective view of a volume corresponds to the region that is swept-out using a rectangular scan. Two reference planes are added to provide greater clarity in relation to the location of points representing airborne objects within the volume, and two cross-wires may be seen. The inclusion of cross-wires suggests their use for interactive operations within the image scene – although this is not explicitly discussed in the publication. However, the authors do refer to a system that permitted an operator to interact with the overall image. This was accomplished by means of controls supported by the analogue calculation system and which allowed the displayed volume to be rotated on the screen (in real time) – so enabling it to be viewed from any vantage point. This is the earliest electronic display system the author has located to date that is able to generate a perspective view on a 3-D scene and moreover, which permits operator interaction with the displayed image.

It is interesting to note that to enhance the apparent three-dimensionality of the displayed image, Parker and Wallis also employed shading. They write:

'In addition to perspective, the brilliance of the display can be modulated according to Z [meaning depth], *so that the nearer portions of the volume are always brighter. This will be called 'perspective shading'.'* [Parker and Wallis 1948]

In this context it is perhaps an opportune moment to mention the 'spontaneous reversal' in spatial orientation that can occur when viewing wire-frame images. Consider the cube illustrated in Figure 1.19(a). When viewed for a little time, the spatial orientation of the cube is seen to switch – it will appear as either projecting upwards or downwards in depth. This same effect occurs with the staircase depicted in Figure 1.19(b). This arises because the depth cue information included in the drawing suggests two possible spatial orientations – we need to provide additional information to reinforce one particular state and this may be achieved through the incorporation of the 'perspective shading' referred to above.

Figure 1.18 The formation of a perspective view as described by Parker and Wallis in their 1948 publication (it appears that this work was carried out several years before their paper was published). Despite the poor quality of the photograph, the volume indicated (which corresponds the region swept-out by a 'rectangular' radar scan) may be seen together with two reference planes and a pair of cross-wires. By means of controls provided within the analogue calculation system (used to form the perspective view) the image depicted on the screen could be rotated and so the volume could be observed from different vantage points. This is perhaps the earliest example of an interactive graphics display system. (Image reproduced by kind permission from Parker and Wallis [1948] © IET (formerly IEE).)

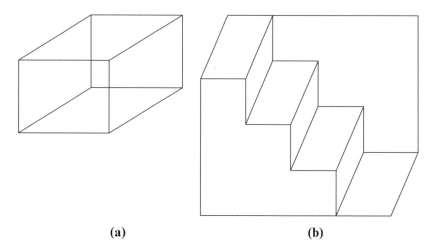

(a)   (b)

Figure 1.19 In (a) when the wire-frame drawing of a cube is viewed for a brief time, its spatial orientation will appear to switch. This is because the drawing suggests two possible orientations – additional depth cue information needs to be included in order to define which of these orientations is actually intended. This is commonly referred to as the Necker cube (after L.A. Necker 1832). Similarly, in (b) the staircase will switch to become an overhanging cornice (attributed to H. Schroder 1858). For further discussion see, for example, Schiffman [1990].

OTU Exercise 1.4: Figure Stability

By means of either reinforcing the lines drawn in the illustrations presented in Figure 1.19, or through the inclusion of shading, ensure that each of the drawings has only one stable orientation. Additionally, using one point or two point perspective diagrams, redraw the illustration presented in Figure 1.19(b) and observe the stability of the perspective rendition.

During the 1940s several other researchers published descriptions of displays able to produce perspective views of 3-D image data on flat screen electronic (CRT based) displays (see, for example, Berkley [1948], MacKay [1949] and summary discussion presented in Blundell [2006, 2007]). Researchers achieved the mapping between a 3-D image space and the 2-D screen using fairly complex analogue calculation systems. Such circuits were somewhat difficult to design and could not be reprogrammed. Naturally, the development of programmable digital technologies greatly facilitated the development of graphics engine hardware and during the 1950s basic graphics displays were produced for use with computer systems.

As far as the development of the principles and applications of computer graphics is concerned, the 1960s denoted a period in which great progress was made. In 1962 Morton Heilig [Heilig 1962] filed a patent describing an immersive virtual reality system known as the Sensorama. Through the use of an immersive graphical display coupled with stereo sound and airflow/vibrational stimuli, this provided a 'virtual theatre' experience. At about the same time, Ivan Sutherland developed a graphics based computer interface called 'Sketchpad'. This is described in the following way:

'The Sketchpad system makes it possible for a man and a computer to converse rapidly through the medium of line drawings. Heretofore, most interaction between man and computer has been slowed down by the need to reduce all communications to written statements that can be typed; in the past we have been writing letters to rather than conferring with our computers.' [Sutherland 1963]

Sutherland goes on to describe the operation of his display system through the use of various examples that show how image primitives may be directly manipulated. For example:

'If we point the light pen at the display system and press a button called "draw", the computer will construct a straight line segment which stretches like a rubber band from the initial to the present location of the pen . . .'

This system therefore supported a high degree of interaction and enabled the user to directly manipulate graphics components by means of devices such as the light pen.

Throughout the 1960s and early 1970s, the electronic display system used for image depiction was largely based on the 'vector graphics' technique. Eventually, this was superseded by the bitmap approach which forms the basis for the modern computer display paradigm. In the next section we briefly discuss aspects of these two techniques and thereby provide an insight into various display characteristics that are of importance in the design and development of computer graphics applications.

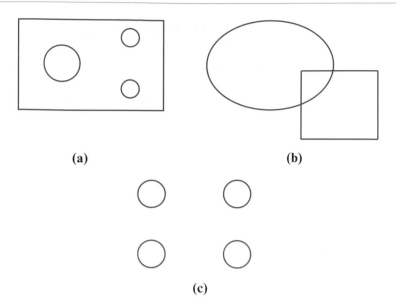

Figure 1.20 Which of these three diagrams represent cross-sections of physical objects? See OTU Exercise 1.5.

OTU Exercise 1.5: Cross-Sections

In the design and depiction of 3-D objects, cross-sectional drawings are often used. Consider the three diagrams presented in Figure 1.20. Identify which of these drawings could represent a cross-section. For each of the diagrams that you believe could correspond to a cross-section, suggest a physical object that it may represent.

1.4 Vector and Bitmapped Graphics: Image Refresh

In the last section we presented background discussion in relation to several events and milestones that have influenced the evolution of modern computer graphics. Our brief chronology ran as far as the early 1960s when Ivan Sutherland demonstrated the placement and manipulation of image primitives by means of an intuitive graphical user interface. Although, the 1960s and 70s denote a period of rapid advance in computer graphics, systems were expensive (in terms of both hardware and applications software) and this tended to limit their general proliferation. Consequently, high performance interactive graphics systems were mainly limited to more specialised applications such as areas of computer aided design, simulation etc. In this context, Herbert Freeman writing in Boff et al. [1986] explains:

'Not until the late 1970s did all these barriers suddenly break away and permit computer graphics to expand into one of the largest and most rapidly growing fields of computer technology. Of course, time was also in its [interactive computer graphics] favour as year after year the cost of graphics equipment kept dropping and the cost of human labour kept increasing. Computer graphics offers enormous possibilities for increased *productivity in every activity in which a picture can facilitate understanding, be it the creation of a design, the monitoring of a manufacturing process, or the display of scientific or business data.'*

One of the major advances that enabled the widespread proliferation of affordable computer graphics systems was the transition from the vector graphics approach to the bitmapped technique. In this section we briefly described aspects of these two display modalities. However, before examining their underlying principles of operation, it is necessary to briefly refer to several issues relating to the refresh of images depicted on some forms of display and to introduce a little associated terminology.

Consider an image that is output to a display – we will refer to this as an 'image frame'. The characteristics of the display hardware may be such that once the image is 'written' to the display screen it will continue to remain visible (without any diminution of brightness) until a new image scene is output. We will refer to such a display system as offering 'steady state light output' (SSLO). Alternatively, in the case of, for example, displays based on the traditional Cathode Ray Tube technology, once the image has been written to the screen, light output rapidly decays and such a display is said to demonstrate 'transient light output' (TLO).

In the case that a system exhibits TLO, it is necessary to continually refresh the display at a rate that is sufficient as to ensure that the image does not appear to flicker. Thus, even if we do not wish to make any modification to the content of the displayed image, identical frames must still be continually re-written to the display.

A display that exhibits TLO must be refreshed at a frequency of at least 30 Hz. However, although when we view a display that is refreshed at this frequency, we may not be conscious of flicker, the transient nature of the light output may still be subliminally evident. When such a display is used for long periods of time, this can be problematic and cause headaches or other discomfort. As a result, when designing a TLO computer display, it is highly desirable to considerably increase the refresh frequency. In fact, higher-end CRT based displays now commonly employ a 120 Hz refresh frequency. Additionally, it is important to note that flicker becomes increasingly evident as image brightness is increased (even when refreshed at 60 Hz, flicker may still be apparent in a highly illuminated image).

> **Critical Flicker Frequency (CFF): The minimum temporal refresh frequency at which an image that is subject to rapid TLO is consciously perceived as being free from flicker. This is also referred to as the 'flicker fusion frequency'.**

The dependence of CFF on image illumination (more correctly termed 'luminance' (L)) is given by the empirically determined Ferry-Porter Law:

$$CFF = a + b \log L$$

where a and b are constants. This relationship has been shown to be valid over a wide range of image 'brightness'.

Even in the case of systems that exhibit SSLO (and that are to be used for the depiction of animated image scenes), it is necessary to update the display at regular intervals. In this context, changes in an image scene (corresponding to, for example, a person walking or an aircraft flying over a landscape) must be output with sufficient regularity as to ensure that the animation appears to progress smoothly. This can be supported by a refresh (update) frequency ~10 Hz i.e. somewhat lower than the demands placed on the graphics engine by the need to ensure that images depicted on a display that exhibits TLO are both consciously and subconsciously perceived as being flicker free. We will use the terms 'image refresh frequency' and 'image update frequency' as follows:

> **Image Refresh Frequency (f_r):** The frequency at which images must be written to a display that exhibits TLO so as to ensure that both conscious and subliminal flicker are avoided.
>
> **Image Update Frequency (f_u):** The frequency at which images must be written to a display so as to permit smooth image animation.

For the reasons given above, in the case of a display that exhibits TLO, $f_r > f_u$, whereas for displays exhibiting SSLO image refresh may be avoided.

From the perspective of the designer who is involved in the development of computer graphics applications, the image update frequency is of particular importance. This is because, in the case of real time applications, the image update period ($T_u = 1/f_u$) determines the time that is available to compute an image frame and pass this to the hardware responsible for interfacing with the display (video memory).

1.4.1 The Vector Display

Although it is most unlikely that you will actually encounter a vector graphics display (outside a technology museum . . .), it is instructive to consider their general principle of operation. Such a discussion not only provides an additional insight into the evolution of modern computer graphics but also (and perhaps more importantly) provides additional understanding of the strengths and weaknesses of the bitmapped graphics technique that almost universally underpins the operation of today's computer display.

In the case of the vector graphics technique, objects depicted on the display are represented as a series of lines or polylines. Each line segment is referred to as a vector.

> **The Vector:** A vector has both magnitude and direction. Thus a line segment that is drawn from one spatial location to another has not only a magnitude (indicated by the length of the line) but also a direction – which is determined by the relative location of its two endpoints and our choice of the endpoint from which we start to draw the line. In contrast a scalar quantity has only an associated magnitude.

OTU Exercise 1.6: Vector and Scalar Quantities

For each of the following, indicate whether it is regarded as a scalar or vector quantity:
Mass, Velocity, Distance, Density, Time, Temperature, Acceleration, Force.

In the case of an image component comprising a single line (vector), it is necessary to define both the start and end coordinates – see Figure 1.21(a). Alternatively, in the case of an image component that takes the form of a polyline, the endpoints of all vectors (other than the last

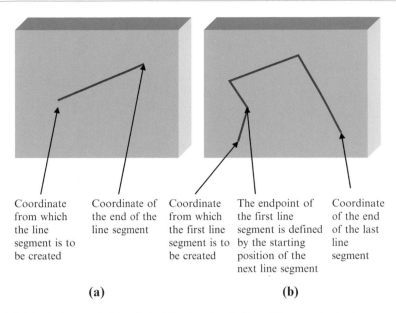

Coordinate from which the line segment is to be created

Coordinate of the end of the line segment

Coordinate from which the first line segment is to be created

The endpoint of the first line segment is defined by the starting position of the next line segment

Coordinate of the end of the last line segment

(a)   **(b)**

Figure 1.21 In (a) we indicate the depiction of a single line (vector) and in (b) a polyline comprising four line segments (vectors).

one to be drawn) are defined by the starting point of the next vector that is to be created (see Figure 1.21(b)).

An image to be drawn on a vector graphics display is stored in a computer's memory as a 'display list'. For each polyline, the starting coordinates of each line segment (vector) are specified – the end coordinates of each line segment being defined by the starting coordinates of the next line segment which is to be drawn. In the case of the last line segment that is drawn when creating the polyline, both its start and end coordinates are defined. Additional information associated with each polyline are the level of illumination and colour (although traditional vector graphics displays had only limited colour capability). A display list together with a simplified model of the graphics engine hardware is illustrated in Figure 1.22.

Vector graphics displays were based on Cathode Ray Tube technology, and here a focused electron beam is directed towards a phosphor-coated screen. When the electron beam impinges upon the phosphor, visible light is produced (as a consequence of a process known as 'cathodoluminescence'). Using magnetic or electrostatic deflection (in fact vector graphics displays employed the latter), the electron beam can be directed to any location on the screen. By way of a simple example, consider the creation of the single line segment illustrated in Figure 1.21(a). Here, the electrostatic deflection signals would be set up in such a way that when the electron beam is turned on, it will be directed to the starting location of the line segment. Subsequently, the electrostatic deflection signals are modified to direct the beam to the end point of the line. The beam will therefore rapidly move from its starting location to this new position. Whilst moving it will excite the phosphor coating on which it impinges, thus giving rise to a visible line. In the case of the polyline illustrated in Figure 1.21(b), the process that we have just outlined would in essence be repeated for each line segment.

Key points to note about the vector graphics method are as follows:

1. The time taken to output a complete image is determined by the complexity of the image. The more line segments (vectors) that are to be drawn, the longer the process will take.

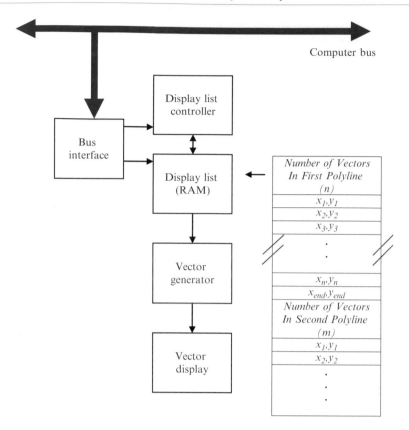

Figure 1.22 Conceptualised diagram showing key elements in a vector graphics display system. The display list stores the coordinate values that are needed to create the lines and polylines on the display screen together with illumination and colour information (not indicated in the illustration). As may be seen, the starting coordinates of the first line within a polyline are supplied and the end coordinates for all other line segments (other than the last in the polyline) can be deduced. An additional final entry for each polyline (x_{end}, y_{end}) indicates the end coordinates of the last vector to be drawn. Additional processing may be performed – for example to remove the bright spots that can occur when two vectors cross.

2. The time taken to output a complete image is also dependent on the order in which lines and polylines are drawn on the screen. In principle, therefore, the time taken to output an entire image can be reduced by drawing the lines and polylines in an optimal order. Unfortunately, obtaining the optimal order is a computationally expensive process and rapidly becomes impractical as image complexity is increased. However, approximate solutions may be adopted and can improve display performance (for related discussion see Schwarz and Blundell [1997]).

3. The screen is not exhaustively scanned. The electron beam simply draws lines in accordance with the contents of the display list (a process which resembles completing the dot-to-dot drawings found in puzzle and activity books for children). As we will see in the next subsection, this represents a major difference between the vector and bit-mapped approaches.

So far we have considered only the depiction of a series of lines and polylines on a vector graphics display. Very frequently we wish to draw 'solid' shapes such as, for example, a filled rectangle. The filling of shapes to give them a solid appearance is, in the case of the vector graphics display, achieved by using a set of lines/polylines to illuminate the region occupied by the shape. The filling process can be very demanding in terms of the number of lines and polylines which

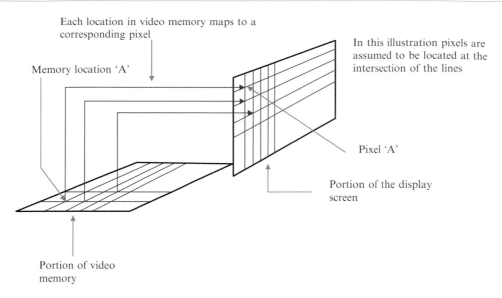

Each location in video memory maps to a
corresponding pixel

Memory location 'A'

In this illustration pixels are
assumed to be located at the
intersection of the lines

Pixel 'A'

Portion of the display
screen

Portion of video
memory

Figure 1.23 The display screen comprises an array of individually addressable 'dots' (pixels). There is a one-to-one mapping between locations in video memory and screen pixels. Thus changing the value stored in a memory location will result in a change in the colour/illumination of a corresponding pixel. All screen pixels are identical in size and shape.

must be drawn to give the impression of uniform illumination. Vector graphics displays were therefore best suited to the depiction of wireframe images in which there was no necessity to depict filled geometric shapes.

1.4.2 The Bitmapped Approach

'There is no reason anyone would want a computer in their home.'[19]

In the case of this technique, the screen comprises a 2-D array of image elements (these can be treated as small dots – each dot being referred to as a pixel (short form of 'picture element')) – see Figure 1.23. There is a one-to-one mapping between screen pixels and video memory (RAM) and by changing the contents of a memory location, an appropriate visible change can be produced in the corresponding pixel. Thus, referring to Figure 1.23 (in which for convenience we conceptualise the video memory as a 2-D array) modifying the contents of memory location 'A' will, when the display is refreshed, directly impact on the visual properties of pixel 'A' – and will effect no other pixels.

Key points to note in connection with this approach are as follows:

1. During a screen refresh or update, each and every pixel is addressed. This contrasts with the vector graphics approach in which the time taken to depict an image (frame) is determined by the number of vectors, the order in which they are drawn and their spatial distribution. In this sense the bitmapped approach is predictable – during an image refresh or update, all screen pixels are written to – and therefore the time taken to refresh or update the image is independent of image content/complexity.

---

[19] Attributed to Ken Olson founder and president of Digital equipment Corporation (DEC). Quoted in Eberly [2004].

2. A display screen may comprise, for example ~1280 pixels horizontally and 1024 pixels vertically. A corresponding number of memory locations are required for the storage of an image frame. If we assume a screen that measures 40cm horizontally, then the inter pixel spacing is ~0.3 mm.

3. The term 'bitmapped display' specifically refers to display technologies in which each pixel is represented by a single bit in video memory. Thus the pixel may be turned on (illuminated) or otherwise. Such a system does not support grey scale (levels of pixel illumination) or mixtures of colour. Today's displays provide support for these vital attributes by representing each pixel by, for example, 24 bits. Displays that support grey scale and colour are generally referred to as pixmapped (rather than bitmapped) displays. However, in practise, the two terms are often used interchangeably. Additionally, it should be noted that video memory is often referred to as the 'frame buffer'.

Although the pixmapped approach denotes an elegant and straightforward technique, it was not widely adopted until the early 1980s. A major issue was the high cost and relatively low storage capacity of suitable memory devices (RAM chips). Additionally, the bitmapped/pixmapped approach requires rapid memory access times. Consider a display that supports the depiction of n_h (horizontal) by n_v (vertical) pixels and for which the refresh frequency is f_r. Then (in the case that pixel values are read directly from the video memory one at a time (sequentially), the system must support a memory access time (T_a) given by:

$$T_a = \frac{T_r}{n_h \cdot n_v},$$

(1.1)

where T_r denotes the refresh period and $T_r = 1/f_r$.

OTU Exercise 1.7: Video Memory Access Time

Suppose that we assume the use of a bitmapped display comprising 1000 by 800 pixels and exhibiting TLO. Assuming a refresh frequency of 70 Hz and that pixel values stored in the frame buffer are read sequentially, calculate the time available for accessing each pixel value from memory.

1.5 Display Hardware

'Nothing exists in the intellect before it is in the sense . . .
and of our senses, as the wise men conclude,
that of seeing is the most noble.
Hence, [it] is commonly said not without reason
that the eye is the entrance portal
through which intellect perceives . . .'[20]

In the main, computer graphics applications are designed to operate upon fairly standard computer platforms. These systems have well-defined characteristics and there is often no

---

[20] Attributed to Fra Luca Pacioli from *Divina proportione*. Quoted in Edgerton [1991].

requirement for those involved in the development of applications programs to have an in-depth understanding of the architecture of either the graphics hardware, or the display. Normally it is sufficient to simply be able to interpret the parameters by which the graphics systems are characterised. For example, in the case of the display we may consider the refresh/update frequency, the total number of display pixels (both vertically and horizontally) and characteristics relating to the depiction of colour.

However, there is a growing interest in the development of 3-D display technologies which have the ability to support alternative (and perhaps more natural/synergistic) interaction tools and that interface more naturally with the human visual system. Clearly, in order for the designer to be able to accurately assess the potential of such systems, architectural issues must be well understood. In turn, this enables computer graphics applications to be developed in such a way that they can utilise the display technology in an optimal manner. In Section 1.6, we briefly introduce several general techniques that can be used to enable displays to support the binocular parallax depth cue (also see Chapter 9). It is likely that in the short to medium term future, there will be greater scope for developing computer graphics applications for use with emerging 'creative' 3-D display systems. In this case it is important to have a clear understanding of key issues relating to hardware operation and in turn, this provides the opportunity to see how such display modalities can be improved and further developed. With this in mind, in this section we briefly summarise the operation of the conventional flat-screen display paradigm – this provides us with a convenient basis on which we can assess alternative display modalities.

Traditionally the computer display has been almost exclusively based upon Cathode Ray Tube (CRT) technology. In recent years, however, we have seen the rapid proliferation of thin panel displays and these are now rapidly taking over from the CRT. In the subsections that follow, we briefly review the operation of CRT, gas plasma, liquid crystal and field emission displays. In addition we provide historical discussion concerning the so-called 'direct view storage device'.

For additional discussion see, for example, Sherr [1998] and also MacDonald and Lowe [1997]. Although these books are a little dated, they remain excellent sources and contain much useful information.

1.5.1 Cathode Ray Tube Based Displays

There is a tendency to assume that displays based upon the Cathode Ray Tube (CRT) are archaic – a technology that is soon to be extinct. However, an understanding of the CRT can be helpful in several respects:

1. The operating principles are perhaps a little more intuitive to grasp than those of the thin-panel display that is able to support full colour image depiction.
2. To a certain extent, both field emission and gas plasma displays can be regarded as thin panel renditions of the CRT – they share key operating principles.
3. The visual characteristics of thin-panel displays were derived from those supported by the CRT. In this sense, the visual characteristics of the CRT retain their relevance.
4. From a cost-performance perspective, CRT-based displays remain very competitive and, whilst undoubtedly they will be superseded, it is unlikely that they will move into extinction for some time to come.

It is for these reasons that brief discussion of CRT-based displays is included in this book.

The principles that underpin the operation of the CRT date back to the late 19th century. As mentioned in Section 1.3, in 1911 Archibald Campbell Swinton proposed the use of the

CRT for television [Campbell Swinton 1912] and by the 1930s this technology was pivotal in the implementation of wholly electronic television systems. In the 1940s, the CRT was not only playing a role in the depiction of electronically processed data, but also hybrid technologies were providing a means of storing and rapidly switching electronic signals (for discussion on the latter, see Blundell and Schwarz [2000]). Given the proven record of the CRT, it was quite natural that it would become the standard computer display. After all, the CRT industry was well established and displays of this type could be produced in a cost-effective manner.

The modern computer display based upon CRT technology employs the 'raster' scanning of electron beams. For a moment, we will put to one side the issue of generating colour images and simply consider the monochrome (single colour) display. In this case, the raster scan works in the following manner:

1. The electron beam is initially directed towards the top left-hand corner of the display screen.
2. Electro-magnets are used to move the electron beam horizontally across the screen. As the electron beam travels from the left to the right-hand side of the screen, it excites the phosphor coating (which is bonded to the rear of the screen) and this gives rise to the production of a visible line.
3. The electron beam is rapidly moved back to the left-hand side of the screen – to a position slightly below its original location indicated in (1) above. Since the electron beam is moved so quickly to this position, it does not have the chance to significantly excite the phosphor, and therefore does not give rise to a visible line.
4. From this new position the electron beam is again swept horizontally across the screen. This gives rise to another visible line, which is slightly below the first line referred to above.
5. The process is repeated and as indicated in Figure 1.24, this gives rise to a set of horizontal lines drawn on the display screen.
6. When the electron beam finally reaches the bottom right-hand corner of the screen, it is rapidly returned to the top left-hand corner. This is known as the 'vertical flyback'. If the deflection occurs quickly enough then this vertical flyback does not give rise to a visible diagonal line across the screen.
7. The technique outlined above enables the entire screen to be scanned, and a set of horizontal scan lines are produced. The light output from the excited phosphor rapidly decays and therefore so as to avoid the flicker problems discussed in the previous section, the display must be regularly refreshed (this involves rapidly repeating steps (1) to (6)). In terms of the terminology used in the last section, the display is said to exhibit 'transient light output' (TLO). To generate an image, it is necessary to modulate the beam as it travels across the screen. In Figure 1.25 we illustrate (in a simplified way) the manner in which a rectangle can be produced by turning the electron beam on and off at the appropriate times.

The generation of colour images is somewhat more complex and is underpinned by the fact that we can generate any colour within the visible spectrum by mixing together sources of red, green, and blue light in appropriate proportions. The colour CRT employs three electron beams that are simultaneously scanned across the surface of the screen in the manner outlined in points 1 to 7 above. Three different types of phosphor are deposited on the surface of the screen. One of these gives rise to the emission of red light, the second green, and the third blue. We can consider each pixel to comprise three sub-pixels – each of a particular primary colour. Complexity in the implementation of the colour CRT arises when we consider how we can lay

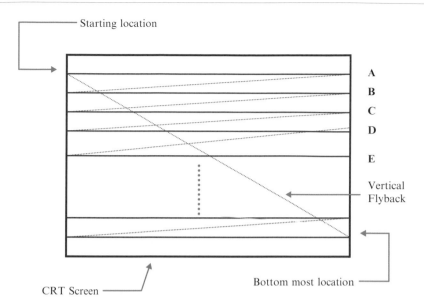

Figure 1.24 A simple raster scan – see text for details (the separation of the scan lines is exaggerated for clarity). Note: this scan is non-interlaced. In the case of the interlaced scan, the electron beam moves down the screen drawing, for example lines, A, C, E etc. Subsequently it is returned to the upper left of the screen and sweeps out lines B, D etc. This interlaced approach is well suited for use in television. For discussion on the interlaced scan technique see, for example, Clements [2006].

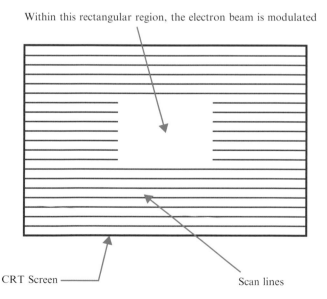

Figure 1.25 The production of an image is achieved by modulating the electron beam in accordance with its instantaneous screen location. Here, we illustrate the production of a rectangle. As the beam travels across the region in which the rectangle is to be depicted it is either turned off (to produce a black rectangle) or simply reduced in strength to generate a rectangle with shading.

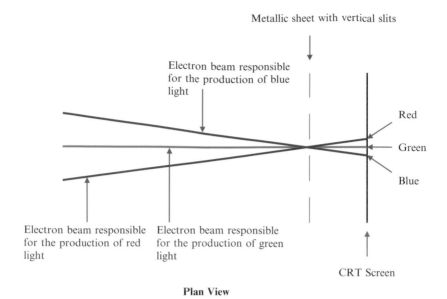

Plan View

Figure 1.26 A simplified plan view of a part of the Trinitron tube (distances and slit sizes have been greatly exaggerated for clarity). The three beams cross in the region of the slits and subsequently impinge on the CRT screen. On the inner face of the CRT, the red, green and blue phosphors are arranged in strips — each group of three strips being aligned with a slit in the metallic plate.

out these three phosphors on the screen's surface and ensure that each can only be 'addressed' by a single electron beam (e.g. the electron beam responsible for the production of red light should only be able to address the red phosphor). This is achieved by inserting a thin sheet of metal which lies just below the CRT screen. As depicted in Figure 1.26, in the case of the Trinitron tube, this sheet of metal comprises a set of narrow, vertical strips, and the phosphors deposited on the inner face of the CRT are arranged as a series of vertical stripes. The trajectory of the electron beams is such that they intersect and cross over in the region of the slits and subsequently impinge on the screen. By accurately aligning the location of the slits with the stripes of the three phosphors it is possible to ensure that each electron beam is only able to 'write' to a phosphor of a certain colour.

The three electron beams are individually modulated and this permits different proportions of red, green and blue light to be mixed — enabling the production of colours throughout the visible spectrum. Unfortunately, the insertion of the metallic sheet results in a significant loss of beam current (electrons that strike the sheet cannot reach the screen and are therefore unable to contribute to the production of light output).[21]

---

[21] The use of a sheet comprising a set of slits superseded a previous technique employing a 'shadow mask'. The shadow mask again took the form of a metallic sheet located just behind the face of the CRT. However, rather than employing a set of slits, the shadow mask comprised a set of holes and the phosphor coatings were deposited as dots rather than stripes. Each pixel was generated using three phosphor dots – one for the production of red light, another for green and a third for blue. The slit approach is superior to the shadow mask technique since it significantly reduces the amount of beam current that is lost. Additionally, the Trinitron tube can be produced at lower cost.

1.5.2 The Direct View Storage Device (DVSD)

'You couldn't see it in a brightly lit room.
You couldn't selectively erase lines that had been drawn on it.
In fact, it had all the disadvantages in the world except one:
It was cheap.'[22]

As we have discussed, the CRT exhibits TLO and so even static (non-animated) images have to be continually refreshed. Additionally, in Section 1.4.1 we explained that in the case of the vector graphics approach, the time needed to depict an image frame is dependent on the content of the image. Thus in the case of more complex images, the image refresh period would be greater and ultimately this may exceed the refresh requirements that must be met in order to ensure the production of a flicker-free image. Alternatively, our wish to avoid image flicker determines the number (and spatial distribution) of vectors that can comprise an image scene. During the 1960s and 1970s memory devices offered quite low performance (in terms of access speed) and this also limited the number of vectors that could be drawn within the refresh period.

So as to overcome these difficulties the 'Direct View Storage Device' (DVSD) was developed and played a dominant role in the implementation of vector graphics displays. This represented a specialised form of CRT and its principle of operation is outlined in a number of text dealing with computer graphics (see, for example, Freeman writing in Boff et al. [1986]). Here, it is sufficient to note that this type of display exhibited SSLO over a considerable period. Thus images created on such a display would remain visible (without diminution of light output) for a significant time after their formation and this circumvented the need for regular image refresh (at least from the perspective of offering flicker-free image depiction).

This device had several weaknesses and by today's standards was relatively expensive to manufacture. Weaknesses included limited colour capability. Additionally, vectors within an image scene could not be individually erased. Consequently, to modify an image it was first necessary to erase the image in its entirety and subsequently output the modified image.

1.5.3 Plasma Thin Panel Displays

The operation of the thin panel plasma display is underpinned by the production of a gaseous discharge – a physical process that was extensively researched in the 19th century. Interestingly, the generation of a gas discharge using an appropriate electric field pre-dates the discovery of cathode rays and the subsequent development of early forms of CRT. Although we may view plasma display panels as representing state-of-the-art technologies, it is amusing to note that they actually operate according to a physical process that was researched even before the discovery of cathode rays!

In Figure 1.27(a), we illustrate a sealed glass tube containing an inert gas such as neon whose pressure is somewhat less than that of the surrounding atmosphere. An electrode is located at either end of the tube and a voltage (v) is applied between these electrodes. This creates an electric field within the gas – the field strength (E) being given by:

$$E = \frac{v}{d},$$

---

[22] Attributed to Carl Machover (who was a manufacturer of these displays) – quoted in Rivlin [1986].

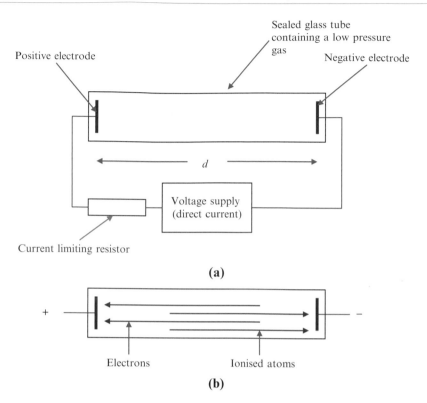

Figure 1.27 In (a) we illustrate a discharge tube. This contains a gas that is at a reduced pressure. Two electrodes (separated by a distance d) are used to create an electric field. The results of this field are indicated in (b) – positive ions are attracted towards the negative electrode (the cathode) and electrons towards the positive electrode (the anode). Collisions with gas atoms results in the formation of other ion-electron pairs or atomic excitation. In this latter case subsequent decay to the 'ground state' results in the emission of electromagnetic radiation.

where d denotes the separation of the electrodes. Thus increasing the voltage or reducing the separation of the electrodes will increase the strength of the field. In the absence of any electric field or other stimulus, the gas within the tube will contain a number of positive ions (atoms that have lost electrons) and free electrons. Under the influence of the electric field, the positive ions will be attracted towards the negative electrode and the free electrons to the positive electrode.

As they gravitate towards the respective electrodes, the ions and electrons accelerate (thereby gaining kinetic energy) and will be in continuous collision with non-ionised atoms of the gas. During such collisions, the charged particles may impart energy to atoms such that the following occur:

(a)   **Excitation**: A ground state electron will be excited to a higher energy level.
(b)   **Ionisation**: In the case that enough energy is transferred, an electron may gain sufficient energy to escape from the atom – thus forming a further ion-electron pair.

These two scenarios are summarised in Figure 1.28 where we also indicate the result of each process. In the case that an electron is excited from a lower to a higher energy level, the atom will subsequently return to the ground state and when this happens electromagnetic radiation is released. A simplified model of this process is provided in Figure 1.29. Here, a ground state

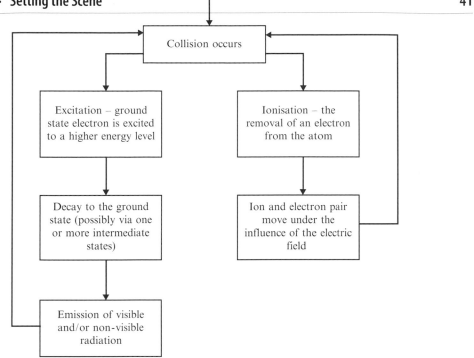

Figure 1.28 Summary of the basic physical processes that result in a discharge within a gaseous media – these underpin the operation of thin panel plasma displays.

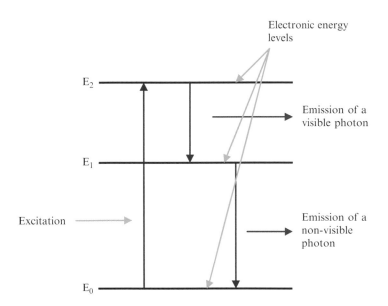

Figure 1.29 Here we provide a simple model illustrating three electronic energy levels. We assume that a collision causes the excitation of an electron from the ground state $< E_0 >$ to energy level $< E_2 >$. Subsequently the atom decays – firstly to a metastable state $< E_1 >$ and then to the ground state. We assume that the first of these decays results in the emission of a visible photon and the second the emission of a non-visible photon (in the ultraviolet part of the electromagnetic spectrum).

electron (with energy E_0) is excited to the energy level E_2. Subsequently, we assume that a decay occurs to a metastable state (energy level E_1) and a photon is released with energy $E_2 - E_1$ such that:

$$E_2 - E_1 = \frac{hc}{\lambda},$$

where h denotes Planck's constant, c the speed of light in a vacuum (free space) and λ the wavelength of the emitted radiation. This wavelength may, for example, be in the visible portion of the electromagnetic spectrum (see Figure 5.5). A further radiative decay is also indicated in Figure 1.29 and this may result in the emission of visible or non-visible (e.g. ultraviolet) radiation. In summary, the excitation process may give rise to the emission of visible light, non-visible radiation – or both.

In the case that the collision imparts sufficient energy to ionise the atom, an electron-ion pair are formed. These then contribute to the current flowing in the discharge tube – the electron moving towards the anode and the positive ion to the cathode. In turn, these particles are likely to excite or ionise other atoms.

> The 'cathode' is the name of the negative electrode.
> The 'anode' is the name of the positive electrode.

Back in the 19$^\text{th}$ century, research pioneers found the discharge process both fascinating and intriguing. Returning to Figure 1.27(a) let us suppose that we begin with a glass tube filled with air and connected to this tube is a pipe attached to some form of vacuum pump. We apply a voltage between the two electrodes, darken the room and begin the pumping process. Gradually as the pressure is reduced, thin streamers ('wisps') of light appear in the tube. As the pressure is further reduced, a glow begins to extend throughout the tube – although, most intriguingly, close to the cathode and some way along the tube there are regions of darkness (which are respectively called 'Crookes' dark space' and the 'Faraday dark space'). Gradually, as the pressure falls further, the extent of the dark spaces increases until we reach a point at which the gas no longer glows and, if the voltage difference between the electrodes is sufficient, the walls of the glass tube begin to fluoresce. It was this fluorescence that directly led to the discovery of cathode rays and the subsequent development of the Cathode Ray Tube.

So much for our brief review of the basic physics associated with the process of gaseous discharge. Let us now turn our attention to the use of this process in the implementation of display technologies. One of the first and certainly the most well known devices able to provide a numeric readout was known as the 'Nixie tube' – a special form of valve which, through until the early 1970s, was widely used as an alpha-numeric display. In addition the gas discharge process underpins the operation of neon signs and fluorescent lights.

Central to the development of thin panel displays is support for full colour image depiction. The colour of light emanating from a gaseous discharge relates to the gas (or mixture of gases) that are employed – for example, neon (the gas most widely used in neon advertising signs) gives (under appropriate conditions) a strong orange discharge. By judiciously selecting appropriate gases, it is possible to generate the three primary colours and so form a display comprising a 2-D matrix of cells with triads of cells operating together to generate the red, green and blue colours that comprise a pixel. Unfortunately, this would make the fabrication process extremely difficult – adjacent cells would need to be filled with a different gas or gas mixture (and sealed from each other to prevent gas mixing). Researchers have therefore

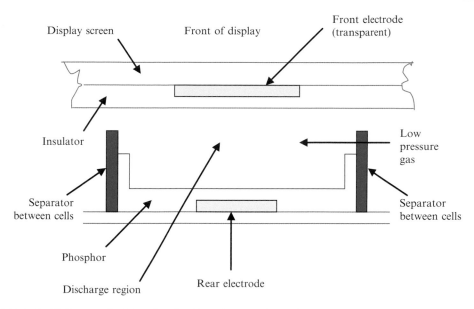

Figure 1.30 A simplified cross-sectional view of a cell used in a plasma panel. Here, the gaseous discharge is initiated by applying a voltage (alternating current (AC)) between the two electrodes. The gas mixture is designed to maximise the production of non-visible (ultraviolet) radiation. This stimulates the emission of visible light from the phosphor and this light radiates from the cell.

sought and implemented the thin panel plasma display using alternative techniques. In essence the gas discharge gives rise to non-visible (ultraviolet) radiation and phosphor materials are then used to convert from ultraviolet to visible light. A simplified diagram showing the basic components that comprise a cell is illustrated in Figure 1.30 – its operation is summarised below:

1. As with the CRT, each pixel comprises three sub-pixels – one red, one green and one blue. By controlling the level to which each triad of sub-pixels are activated, each overall pixel is perceived as being able to demonstrate a 'full colour' capability. In the case of a plasma screen, each sub-pixel has an associated cell – the light output from which can be controlled.
2. Through the application of a voltage between the rear and front electrodes shown in Figure 1.30, a gaseous discharge occurs. The low pressure gas mixture is designed to maximise the emission of non-visible ultraviolet radiation (with a wavelength of $\sim$ 147 nm). A mixture of helium and xenon or neon and xenon may be used for this purpose.
3. The ultraviolet radiation impinges on the phosphor (which is deposited towards the rear of each cell). This causes the phosphor to emit visible radiation and this emerges from the front of each cell. Each of the three sub-pixels within a group employs a different phosphor and this supports the production of red, green and blue light.
4. The arrangement illustrated in Figure 1.30 represents a cell driven by an alternating voltage (AC). An essential difference between the AC and DC (direct current) approaches concerns the location of the electrodes. In the case of the former, the electrodes are insulated from the gas whereas in the case of the latter, the electrodes are in direct contact with the gas.

1.5.4 Liquid Crystal Thin Panel Displays

As their name implies, liquid materials exhibit characteristics that are common to both the liquid and solid states. As with a liquid, the molecules are able to move freely (as long as they remain in close proximity to each other). However, in addition, there is a strong degree of molecular alignment. Liquid crystal molecules are rod-like in shape and so we can envisage a collection of molecules that have no defined position but which exhibit some form of preferred alignment.[23] This alignment may be influenced by the application of an electric field or by the physical nature of the surfaces with which the liquid crystal material is in contact.

Suppose that we sandwich a *thin* layer of liquid crystal material between two glass plates which have been specially prepared as follows:

1.   We score a set of fine parallel ridges onto the inner surface of each plate. The direction of ridges on one plate is orthogonal to those on the other. Thus we can consider one set of ridges to be horizontal and the other set to be vertical. The rod-like liquid crystal molecules that are directly in contact with the two plates will tend to line up with the adjacent ridges. As the set of ridges in the two plates are orthogonal, this means that at one boundary the molecules will be aligned in a 'horizontal' direction and at the other boundary in a 'vertical' direction. This will influence the orientation of the molecules within the bulk of the material – from one surface to the other. Here we can conceptualise a stack of 'sheets' of molecules whose orientation will gradually rotate through 90° (provided that the two surfaces are in close proximity).
2.   We coat both glass plates with a transparent conductive material (using for example, indium oxide). These coatings form electrodes and enable us to apply an electric field across the liquid crystal material. When an appropriate field is applied, the molecules align themselves in the direction of the field – no longer does their orientation gradually spiral from one glass plate to the other – see Figure 1.31.

As may be seen from the illustration, we add two polarizing filters and illuminate the arrangement from the rear. When the unpolarized (randomly polarized) light impinges on the first filter only light polarized in a certain direction is able to emerge. This then passes through the liquid crystal material – which acts as an optical waveguide. In the case that no field is applied, the gradually twisting molecules rotate the plane of the lights polarization through 90°. The light then encounters the second polarizing filter and if we have arranged that the planes of polarization of the two filters are crossed (orthogonal to one another), then the light will emerge and be visible to the observer. However, if we now apply an electric field across the liquid crystal material, the molecules are rearranged and no longer rotate the light's plane of polarization by 90°. The second filter now prevents the light from emerging.

In short, this display technique is based on our ability to control the orientation of the liquid crystal molecules and hence the polarization of light passing through the material. Note that the CRT and plasma displays (together with the field emission approach – see the next subsection) are fundamentally based upon the controlled production of light (e.g. by electrons impinging on a phosphor) whereas the liquid crystal approach is based on the controlled modulation of incident light.

A liquid crystal flat panel display provides a rectangular array of pixels. Generation of colour images is made possible by forming each pixel from three subpixels (one being responsible for

---

[23] In this discussion we assume the use of nematic liquid crystal material and confine ourselves to a simple display embodiment.

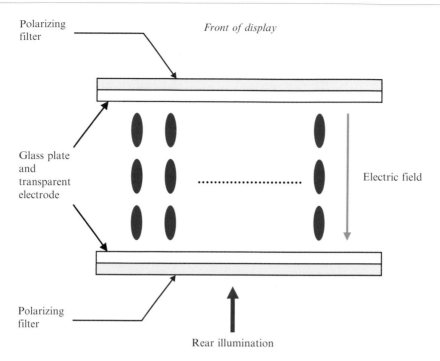

Polarizing filter

Front of display

Glass plate and transparent electrode

Electric field

Polarizing filter

Rear illumination

Figure 1.31 An electric field is applied between the glass plates and the rod-like molecules align themselves with this field. This is a cross-sectional view of the display panel.

the generation of red content, one the generation of green content, and the other, blue content). Colour emission is achieved by equipping each subpixel with a filter of a suitable colour. Given a display comprising 10^6 or more pixels, individually addressing each pixel via its own dedicated electrical connection is impractical[24] and a row and column addressing technique is used. In this case a display comprising n by n pixels can be addressed using only $2n$ connections (these being vertical and horizontal strips of the transparent electrode coating). Thus 10^6 pixels can be addressed by 2000 connections. In the case of a so-called 'passive matrix' display we address a particular pixel by applying a voltage difference to the appropriate row and column connections – when we remove the signal, the pixel reverts to its 'natural state'. Such an approach necessitates the regular refreshing of each pixel and parallels the TLO characteristic of the CRT. Overall, liquid crystal displays of this type offer limited performance, have a limited viewing angle and are likely to exhibit a poor contrast ratio.

An alternative 'active matrix' approach provides superior characteristics. Here, an individual transistor is associated with each pixel/subpixel. This transistor can serve several purposes – for example it can be used to define a clear threshold in relation to changes in the characteristics of the pixel and to maintain the drive signal to a pixel so that regularly refreshing the display (to avoid image flicker) is unnecessary (the SSLO paradigm). The transistors are fabricated directly on the display structure and must not block the transmission of the light through the panel. Their fabrication is by no means a simple task! Also note that since all thin panel

---

[24] This also applies to the plasma display panel.

display technologies employ individually addressable pixels display hardware failure can result in irritating 'dead pixels'.

1.5.5 Field Emission Thin Panel Displays

The field emission approach closely mimics the CRT – visible light output is achieved by means of electrons that are accelerated towards a phosphor coated display screen. However, these electrons are generated using 'cold cathodes' which emit electrons as a consequence of the high fields produced at their sharp tips. These electrons are accelerated towards the phosphor coated screen with one or more cold cathode electron sources being responsible for the production of each pixel/subpixel (recall that the CRT employs electron beam scanning techniques whereas in the case of the field emission approach each pixel is formed via its own dedicated electron beam). This technique offers to combine the high performance characteristics of the CRT with the benefits of the thin panel display paradigm. However, the extent to which this technique will succeed will ultimately be governed by commercial considerations – manufacturing costs, strength of competitive approaches etc.

1.6 Encoding the Third Dimension

'Somewhere he remembered the soft glow of candlelight,
The scratching quill.
Resolutely he put them aside for security;
Bright screen fluorescent lights
Words marched before him, orderly and presentable.
But once, the screen went down and they streamed from his fingers,
Flickered and danced like ancient promises,
Half forgotten light.' [25]

In section 1.3 we briefly referred to the binocular parallax depth cue and its critical role in providing a strong sense of 3-D *relief*. In this section we extend this discussion and provide several exemplar images that contain binocular information. Subsequently, we briefly introduce four techniques that may be used to encode binocular information within images (e.g. photographs, drawings and computer graphics scenes) in such a way as to enable this information to be made available to the visual system in an appropriate manner.

Here, we confine our discussion to techniques that are underpinned by the general stereoscopic approach and postpone until Chapter 9 consideration of the volumetric, varifocal and holographic paradigms.

1.6.1 Exemplar 3-D Images

As previously mentioned, when we view our surroundings our two eyes each receive a slightly different view on the scene under observation. This is caused by their physical separation and is particularly apparent when we view scenes that are in fairly close proximity and where there is considerable spatial separation of components within the scene. This effect may be readily

---

[25] Patricia Blundell (1959–).

observed by looking at our surroundings and closing one eye and then the other. As you will note, the two images that we see are a little different. The differences (disparities) in the two views obtained by the eyes are interpreted by the visual system as providing a sensation of three-dimensionality.[26]

Before we begin to consider ways in which we can encode this information in images that are portrayed on a flat surface, it is instructive and interesting to take a look at a few examples. Using the viewing glasses provided with this book and which comprise two different coloured filters, take a look at the section of 'anaglyph images'. When correctly viewed these images exhibit a remarkable three-dimensionality – the figures no longer appear to reside on the page, but instead stand out from it. Here, the left and right hand views of the stereopair are printed using different colours and with the help of the filtered glasses, one view may be seen by the left eye and the other view by the right eye. This is commonly known as the 'anaglyph technique'.

In section 1.3 we briefly mentioned the pioneering research of Charles Wheatstone and David Brewster in the 19th century and their work on the development of the stereoscope. Figure 1.32 depicts several stereopairs (generally referred to as stereograms) and in each case an image scene is photographed from two slightly different locations. To observe the three-dimensionality that can be derived from stereopairs, it is necessary to fuse the two images. With a little practice this can be achieved by converging the eyes, and in fact the use of a stereoscope to view such images is not a requirement. However, in the case that you have not previously practiced directly fusing stereo images, stereo viewing glasses are provided with this book (these are the glasses comprising 2 transparent eye pieces). You may need to move them either closer to the page or a little further away from it in order to properly observe the three-dimensionality of each image scene. These viewing glasses simply assist in the process of fusing the images comprising each pair. Once you have practiced viewing the images using the glasses, it is likely that you will find it quite easy to view the images directly simply by converging your eyes. Additional stereograms are included elsewhere in this book – see for example Figure 9.8.

In the next subsection, we briefly outline four basic methods by which stereo images can be encoded and correctly presented to the visual system.

1.6.2 Coding Techniques

In this sub-section, we briefly introduce four general techniques that can be used in the implementation of flat-screen display systems able to support the binocular parallax depth cue. These four techniques are summarised in Figure 1.33 and are outlined below:

1. *Chromatically Coded Images*

This is the technique used in the formation of the anaglyph[27] images referred to above. Here, the left and right views which form the stereo pair are each depicted in a different colour (for example, green and red). Filter glasses are used to present each eye with a different view. Thus, for example, the left eye may be presented with a view depicted in red, and the right eye with a view depicted in green – only one view being seen by each eye.

---

[26] Note the images cast onto the retinae of the eyes contain both vertical and horizontal disparities.

[27] Anaglyph – from the Greek: 'To carve in relief'.

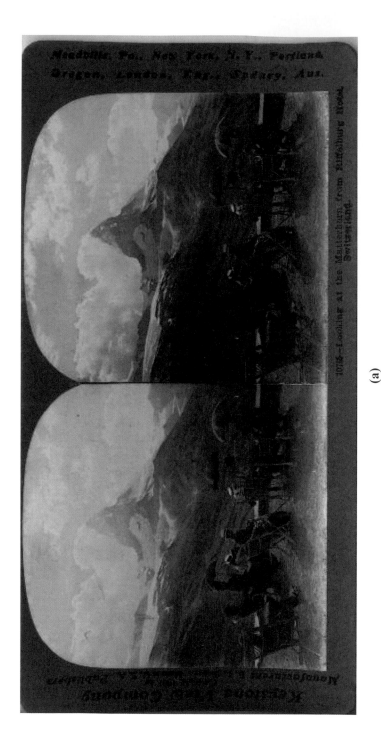

(a)

Figure 1.32 Examples of stereopairs (stereograms). With practice, these can be viewed directly – by slightly crossing the eyes, the two images can be fused. Alternatively, donning the simple stereo glasses that accompany this book facilitates the viewing process. Stereo photographs (h) through to (j) were taken by Frank Hurley during the 1911–1914 Mawson Antarctic Expedition.[28] Original titles are (h) 'Pacing the after deck. Capt. J.K. Davis and Skipper Davis, the whaling expert from Hobart. En route to Hobart from West Base Station,' (i) 'Adelie penguin rookery on ridge west of Main Base Hut,' and (j) 'The northern extremity of the Mertz Glacier Tongue'. (Image (d) kindly supplied by and reproduced with the permission of Robin Ramsey. Images (h) through to (j) kindly supplied by and reproduced with the permission of the South Australian Museum Mawson Mawson Collection. These images are © Mawson Collection, South Australian Museum.)

[28] If you are interested in further information concerning the superb stereo images crafted by Frank Hurley, the following URL is recommended: http://www.antarcticavirtua.net

Figure 1.32 *Continued*

(b)

Figure 1.32 *Continued*

(c)

(d)

Figure 1.32 *Continued*

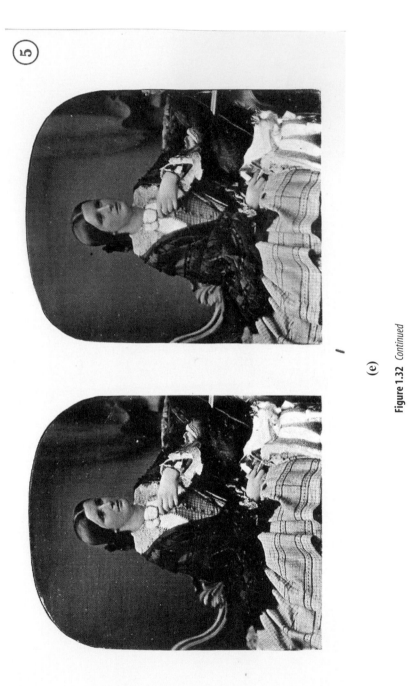

Figure 1.32 *Continued*

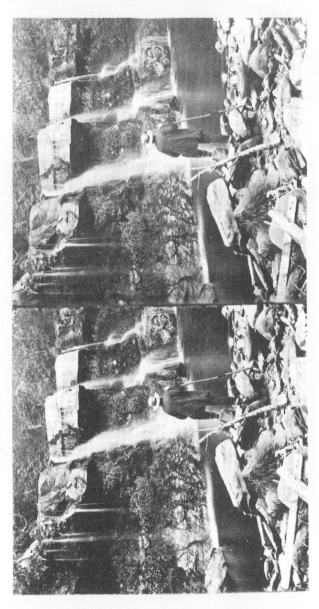

Figure 1.32 *Continued*

(f)

(g)

Figure 1.32 *Continued*

(h)

Figure 1.32 *Continued*

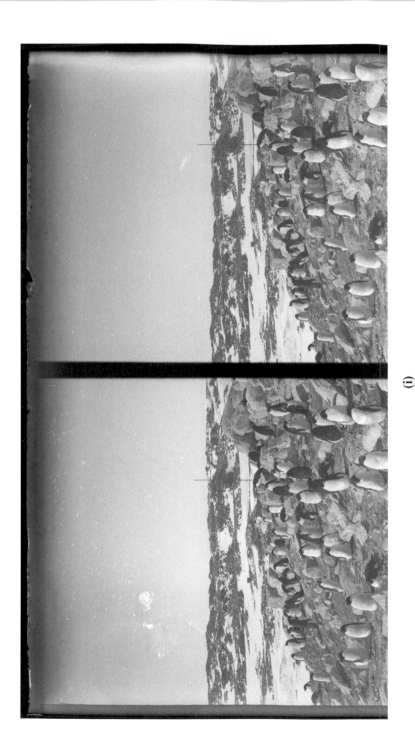

Figure 1.32 *Continued*

(i)

Figure 1.32 *Continued*

(j)

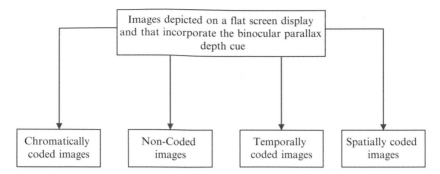

Figure 1.33 Four general techniques that may be used to encode stereoscopic views within an image depicted upon a screen or other 2-D tableau. The terminology used here is taken from Blundell [2007].

This represents a very simple but effective technique and the viewing glasses are inexpensive. Unfortunately as with all 3-D display paradigms, it does not provide a Utopian solution and has several weaknesses:

(a)   It is important to ensure that 'cross-talk' is avoided/minimised. In this context, cross-talk occurs when the left eye is presented with content intended for the right eye, and vice versa. In the case of the anaglyph display we can avoid cross-talk by ensuring that the optical characteristics of the filters used in the viewing glass are sufficiently well-defined so that the red light is not transmitted through the green filter, and the green light is not transmitted through the red filter. Additionally, we can select colours that are well separated in wavelength – thereby facilitating the decoding of the two colours. Most commonly, red and green or red and blue are used.

(b)   By employing chromatic (colour) coding our ability to depict images comprising multiple colours is somewhat restricted. That is not to say that this technique is limited solely to the depiction of two-colour images, although there are restrictions on the range of colours that can be accommodated – for interesting discussion see Girling [1990].

The anaglyph technique dates back to the mid 19th century and is generally attributed to Joseph D'Almeida and Louis Du Hauron who employed this approach for 'magic lantern' slide shows. The technique gained popularity in the 1950s for 3-D cinema and is frequently used in both advertising and comics.

2. *Non-Coded Images*

As we have seen, in the case of the stereoscopic technique, invented by Charles Wheatstone and David Brewster, the left and right views of the stereo pair are depicted side by side (recall Figure 1.32). Each image is then directed to the appropriate eye. In this scenario, coding of the images is unnecessary because they are kept apart and presented to the visual system separately. This technique underpins immersive virtual reality headsets. Here, two separate display screens are employed: one for the left eye, and one for the right. Thus the left and right views of the stereo pair are fed directly to the two eyes. Cross talk is avoided because each eye can only see a single screen. In the case of a head-mounted display of the type used in immersive virtual reality, a lightweight and physically compact form of headgear is required. However, if the display screens are located in close proximity to the eyes it is not possible to focus on the images that they depict. In fact, as you will observe by moving a finger, pen, or the like – held vertically – towards one eye it is possible to readily identify the least distance of distinct vision. This is known as the 'near point', and is ~25 cm for the emmetropic ('normal') eye. In implementing a virtual reality headset, it is therefore necessary to interpose an optical arrangement between each eye and the corresponding display screen. This allows the eyes to focus on the display screens despite their close proximity and the image is able to occupy a wide field of view (100 to 140° horizontally and 40 to 60° vertically).

We tend to think of immersive virtual reality as a state-of-the-art technology, but it is interesting to note that from a visual perspective the basic idea has been around for some time. In 1930, Joseph Bayer filed a patent [US Patent Number 1,876,272] concerning a system intended to act as an aid to aircraft flying in conditions of poor visibility (he named this system 'A Fog Penetrating Televisor'). This purported to capture stereo images using a pair of infrared detectors. These images were then depicted on a stereoscopic display by means of which each eye was presented with the appropriate image. Although the underlying techniques used for data collection were somewhat flawed, the inventor appears to have had a sound understanding of the benefits to be derived through the use of stereoscopic imaging techniques. A similar stereoscopic display is described by Otto Schmitt [1947]. More recently, in the 1960s, Ivan Sutherland (who we have already mentioned in relation to the development of an interactive computer graphics interface) developed a head-mounted display that employed two miniature Cathode Ray Tubes and an associated optical arrangement. These two CRT's were located just above either ear and pointed forwards. An optical arrangement was then used to direct the images depicted on the CRT's into the eyes [Sutherland 1968, Blundell 2007].

3. *Temporal Coding*

Here, the left and right-hand views of the stereo pair are depicted as alternate frames on a flat screen display. Thus, for example, the first, third, and fifth frames etc. depict one of the images of the stereo pair, and the second, fourth, and sixth etc. frames correspond to the other. In this way a stereopair is temporally coded (i.e. coded in time). In order to correctly perceive the stereo content, a user must wear special purpose viewing glasses which may be either 'active' or 'passive'. These two forms of glasses are summarised below:

(a) **Active Glasses**: Active glasses receive a synchronisation signal from the computer which controls the optical properties of the two eye-pieces. Typically these comprise liquid crystal-based shutters and can be switched between transparent and opaque states. When, for example, a frame intended for the left eye is depicted on the display, the eyepiece for this eye would be transparent, while the other would be opaque. When the next image refresh occurs, the optical states of the two eye-pieces switch. In short, only one eyepiece is transparent at any one time, and this ensures that the alternate images depicted on the display screen can only be seen by the appropriate eye. Traditionally, active glasses were linked to a computer via a cable; the modern rendition typically employs an ultrasound link and therefore a physical connection is unnecessary.

(b) **Passive Glasses**: Typically, these employ polarising filters and are used in conjunction with an active polarising filter that is fitted to the front of the display screen. As with (a) above, the objective is to ensure that each of the two images of a stereopair is directed to the appropriate eye – and cannot be seen by the other eye. In the simplest case, the active linearly

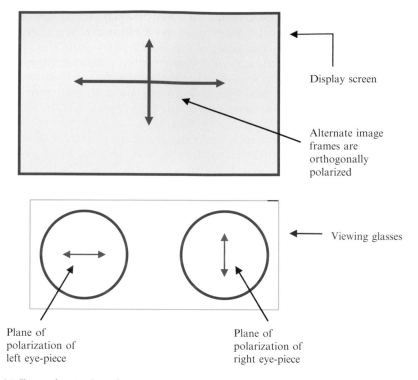

Display screen

Alternate image frames are orthogonally polarized

Viewing glasses

Plane of polarization of left eye-piece

Plane of polarization of right eye-piece

Figure 1.34 The use of passive glasses for viewing images depicted using the temporal coding technique. See text for discussion.

polarising filter fitted to the display screen is able to switch between two orthogonal[29] planes of polarisation – as illustrated in Figure 1.34. The filters fitted to the viewing glasses are arranged so that, for example, the right eye filter will pass only the vertically polarised light and the left eye filter only the light polarised in the horizontal direction.

No 3-D display provides a perfect solution – and the temporally coded approach is no exception. Problematic areas that need careful considerations are as follows:

- Alternate frames are presented to each eye. Therefore if, for example, we were to use a display that is refreshed at (say) 50 Hz, then the frequency at which images are presented to each eye would be 25 Hz. This exacerbates the problem of image flicker and so this technique should only be used with display hardware able to operate at a high update frequency (i.e. ≥ 100 Hz).

---

[29] That is, the planes of polarization are at $90°$ to each other.

- When this approach is implemented with a CRT-based display, it is important to remember that the light output following a frame refresh or update from the three phosphor materials responsible for generating the red, green, and blue light, does not decay at the same rate (this is also the case with plasma and field emission based displays). When active viewing glasses are employed, this can lead to undesirable cross-talk (recall from above that in this context cross-talk refers to the left or right-hand views of the stereo pair being partially visible to the unintended eye (i.e. 'ghosting')).
- As with the anaglyph technique, this approach necessitates the use of viewing glasses. Although in some situations the need to wear these may be tolerable, in other applications this may not be appropriate.

4. Spatial Coding

This technique can be implemented in various ways but is essentially based on the projection of the left and right images that form the stereopair into two separate regions such that when an observer is correctly positioned, each eye is presented with one of these views. Perhaps the simplest approach to the implementation of such a display is the 'parallax stereogram' technique proposed by F.E. Ives in 1903. This method is illustrated in Figure 1.35(a). Here, the left and right

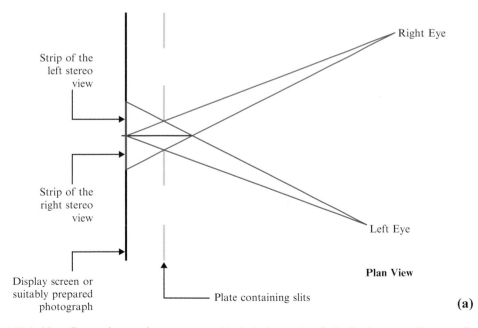

Figure 1.35 In (a) we illustrate the general arrangement used in the implementation of a Parallax Stereogram. Here, a small section of the screen and slit plate are shown and sizes have been exaggerated for clarity. In (b) and (c) overleaf, we illustrate the preparation of the interleaved stereogram. As indicated in (b) the two stereo images are divided into a set of vertical strips and these are then interleaved – as shown in (c).

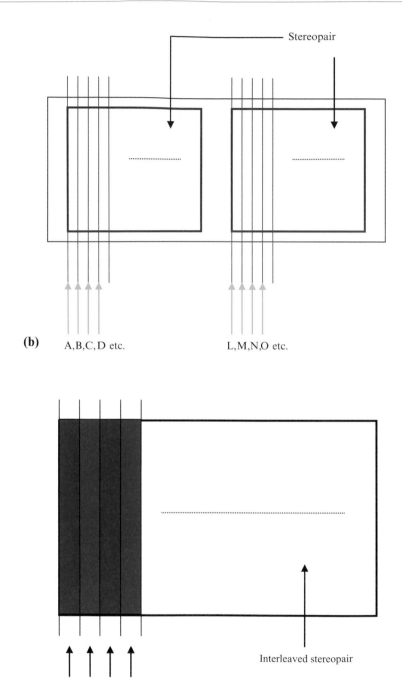

(b) A,B,C,D etc. L,M,N,O etc.

(c) A, L, B, M, etc.

Figure 1.35 *Continued*

views on the stereopair are each divided into a set of vertical strips and these are displayed in an interleaved manner – see Figures 1.35(b) and (c). A plate comprising a set of vertical slits lies between the displayed image and the viewer. The pitch of the slits (i.e. the distance between the centres of adjacent slits) is arranged to be approximately the same as the pitch of the interleaved image strips and so when an observer is correctly positioned, the right eye is able to see only one set of strips and the left eye the other set.

This approach is advantageous in as much as the observer does not need to don any viewing glasses – however, there are several weaknesses. For example:

- An appreciable amount of the light output by the display is lost – its passage being blocked by the opaque portions of the slit plate. However, this problem can be addressed in a number of ways such as through the use of a lenticular sheet.
- Freedom in viewing position is somewhat restricted.

In Chapter 9, we further discuss the above display techniques and introduce several other approaches.

1.7 Discussion

'The sleep of reason brings forth monsters.'[30]

In this chapter, we have introduced a broad range of background material and have emphasised the pivotal role played by computer graphics in the implementation of the human-computer interface. As discussed, different types of application impose different demands on graphics hardware and software systems. Furthermore, computer graphics techniques can seldom be implemented in isolation and so it is desirable to consider their operation within highly integrated environments.

We have identified a number of important milestones in the development of geometrical techniques that enable a 3-D scene to be accurately rendered on a 2-D tableau. As we have seen, great progress was made in this area during the Italian Renaissance – concepts that were discovered and re-discovered during this period play a vital role in the depiction of 3-D images on the conventional computer display. For convenience, in Figure 1.36 we summarise some of the historical events referred to in this chapter (see also Blundell [2006]).

Finally, we have considered various display system techniques. Here, we distinguished between the vector and bitmapped (pixmapped) approaches used in the implementation of the conventional flat screen computer display and have commented on the lack of support that this display modality provides for the binocular parallax depth cue (stereopsis). We have also briefly outlined several 'creative' display techniques that advance the flat screen display and enable the inclusion of binocular parallax.

---

[30] Attributed to Goya. Quoted in Taylor, F., 'Dresden, Tuesday 13 February 1945', Bloomsbury Publishing, (2004).

Filippo Brunelleschi: Generally considered to have provided the first demonstration of an accurate mathematically based perspective technique	~1415
Leon Battista Alberti: *Della Pittura*	~1435
Piero della Francesca: De prospective pingendi	~1478
Gaspard Monge: Geometrie Descriptive (publication delayed)	~1795
Samuel Taylor Coleridge: Biographia Literaria (the concept of 'suspension of disbelief')	1817
Charles Wheatstone: Demonstration of the Stereoscope	1838
David Brewster: Demonstration of the Stereoscope	1849
Joseph D'Almeida and Louis Du Hauron: The Anaglyph technique	~1850
F.E. Ives Invention of the Parallax Stereogram	1903
Alan Archibald Campbell Swinton: Proposal for all-electronic TV – employing the CRT	1911
John Logie Baird: First demonstration of practical TV (electro-mechanical)	1926
Joseph Bayer: Electro-mechanical stereoscopic display	1930
Otto Schmitt: Electronic Stereoscopic Display (immersive using CRT's)	1947
Parker and Wallis: Seminal publication on perspective displays and 3-D paradigms. Also around this time – Carl Berkley and Otto Schmitt	1948
Morton Heilig: Sensorama – an immersive virtual reality environment	1962
Ivan Sutherland Sketchpad – an interactive graphics system	1963

Figure 1.36 A summary of some early events that have influenced the evolution of modern computer graphics. Note that events listed here are limited to those specifically referred to in this chapter.

1.8 Review Questions

1. Distinguish between screen update frequency and screen refresh frequency.
2. Distinguish between the terms 'bitmapped' and 'pixmapped' as used in the context of a display.
3. What is a pixel?
4. State one important depth cue that is absent from images depicted on a *conventional* flat screen display.
5. Consider the use of a perspective projection technique that enables a 3-D scene to be projected onto a 2-D tableau. State one critical assumption that is made.
6. State one major weakness of the vector graphics approach.
7. In the context of flat screen display techniques, name four general techniques that may be used for the encapsulation (and presentation to the visual system) of the binocular parallax depth cue.
8. Briefly describe the source of binocular parallax.
9. State your understanding of the scope of modern computer graphics.
10. What is meant by the term 'critical flicker frequency'?

1.9 Investigations

1. In Section 1.2 we outlined three general areas of application and identified different demands that they impose on computer graphics based applications software. Identify two other exemplar areas where computer graphics plays an important role. In each case, compare and contrast the demands that are place on the graphics hardware and software systems.
2. Investigate and discuss the contribution made by Leonardo da Vinci to the development of techniques that enabled the creation of photorealistic images.
3. When stereopairs such as those depicted in Figure 1.32 are correctly viewed (either by means of a stereoscope or by slightly crossing the eyes), the two images are fused into a single image. In this situation, comment on the positioning of the two views on the retinae – what, for example, is the result of crossing the eyes as far as the positioning of the retinal images is concerned?
4. Obtain a copy of the seminal paper published by Parker and Wallis [1948]. Examine and discuss the descriptions that are provided of 3-D display techniques. Identify techniques that you feel could be of use today within the context of the modern human-computer interface.
5. Discuss how you could use two digital cameras to produce stereopairs (of the type illustrated in Figure 1.32). You are encouraged to put your ideas into practice!
6. In Section 1.2 we indicate that '*Where possible, the content and interaction opportunities should transcend the medium of expression*'. Discuss this notion.

1.10 Feedback to Review Questions

1. In the case that a display screen exhibits transient light output then, so as to avoid image flicker, it must be refreshed at regular intervals. The minimum frequency at which it must

be refreshed is referred to as the screen refresh frequency. The screen update frequency corresponds to the minimum frequency that a sequence of image frames must be depicted in order to provide the sense of smooth animation.

2. In the case of a bitmapped display each pixel is represented by single bit in memory. The pixmapped approach allows the state of each pixel to be represented by a plurality of bits. A pixmapped display is able to support both grey scale and multi-colour image depiction.

3. A pixel is the fundamental element from via which computer processed images are formed. The word 'pixel' is derived from the term 'picture element'.

4. Binocular parallax – also referred to as stereopsis.

5. The location of the viewpoint is assumed.

6. The time needed to output an image frame depends on the number of vectors within the frame, their spatial distribution and the order in which they are drawn.

7. Chromatic coding, temporal coding, spatial coding and non-coded images.

8. Because the two eyes are physically separated (by a distance of $\sim$6.5 cm), when we view a 3-D scene each eye is presented with a slightly different view. Small differences between these views (disparities) are interpreted by the visual system as providing a strong sense of depth. However, if the disparities are too great, a double image is perceived.

9. For the purposes of this book, the following description is assumed: Computer graphics embraces all aspects of the synthesis, depiction and manipulation of pictorial representations by computational machines together with their presentation to the human visual system.

10. This is the minimum frequency at which image frames that are subject to transient light output (TLO) must be refreshed so that a flicker free image is perceived. This frequency is influenced by various factors such as image illumination. Furthermore, although an image may be consciously perceived as being free of flicker, subliminal perception of flicker may still be a problem.

A Maths Primer 2

'We took him out – soft, wobbly, tearful;
set him down on his four, as yet not quite
simultaneous legs, and regarded him.'

2.1 Introduction

In this chapter, we introduce some of the basic mathematical techniques that underpin aspects of modern computer graphics. We focus on practical issues and for a more rigorous treatment several textbooks are recommended. Students entering introductory courses in computer graphics often have wide-ranging mathematical backgrounds. Consequently, although some readers will already be familiar with the material presented here, others may not have previously studied some or all of the topics. In order to ascertain your degree of familiarity with the chapter contents, and so determine sections that should be studied, we suggest that you attempt the OTU Exercises within the chapter and also the Review Questions (located at the end of the chapter).

This chapter largely focuses on the basic maths which underpins the representation and manipulation of images within a 2-D space. In other parts of this book we extend this discussion to embrace three spatial dimensions. In the next section, we briefly introduce Cartesian, Polar and Homogeneous coordinate systems. This leads on to discussion in Section 2.3 about the representation of a line using Cartesian and parametric equations. Section 2.4 focuses on vectors – these play a key role in computer graphics and it is therefore important that you have a basic understanding of techniques that can be employed in their manipulation and of the ways in which they can be used in defining points lines and curves. Subsequently, in Section 2.5 we turn our attention to matrices and describe various operations that can be performed upon them. In Section 2.6 we consider the parabola, circle, spiral and ellipse. Finally, in Section 2.7 we outline the de Casteljau Algorithm which enables us to create a parabola using three 'control' points.

Key Learning Outcomes: At the end of this chapter you should be able to:

- *Discuss the use of Cartesian, Polar and Homogeneous coordinate systems and convert between these systems.*

- *Describe a line in terms of either the Cartesian and parametric forms of representation.*

- *Use and manipulate vectors. This includes the description of a line using a vector equation and the use of the scalar (dot) product.*

- *Perform basic operations on matrices. This includes the multiplication of matrices and the calculation of the inverse matrix.*

- *Discuss characteristics of the parabola, circle, rose curve, Archimedes spiral and ellipse.*

- *Outline the operation of the de Casteljau Algorithm for the creation of a parabola.*

2.2 Cartesian, Polar and Homogeneous Coordinate Systems

> *'I read that when archaeologists dug down into the ancient cemetery,*
> *they found fragments of human bones!*
> *What kind of barbarians were these people, anyway?'* [1]

In order to place and manipulate image components (such as points, lines and geometrical shapes), it is necessary to have a means of specifying (in an unambiguous manner) their location relative to some point of reference. In this section we review the use of rectangular and polar coordinate systems for defining the location of a point on a plane. Additionally we briefly describe homogeneous coordinates.

2.2.1 The Cartesian Plane

By means of a vertical and a horizontal line, we are able to develop a 'Cartesian plane'. The two lines are called axes (the vertical line is often referred to as the y-axis and the horizontal line as the x-axis) and divide the plane into four quadrants. This enables us to establish a 'rectangular

---

[1] Attributed to Jack Handey (1949–).

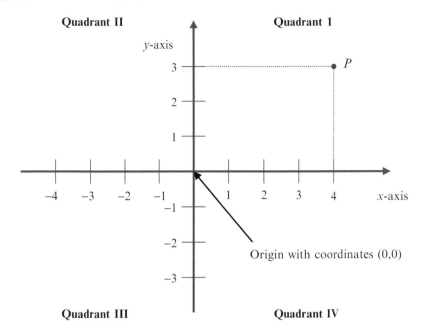

Figure 2.1 A rectangular coordinate system. This divides the Cartesian plane into four quadrants. Notice the arrows on the horizontal and vertical axes denote increasingly positive directions.

coordinate system' by means of which the location of any point on the plane can be specified.[2] The point at which the lines intersect is referred to as the 'origin' and it is from this location that the horizontal and vertical distances of points on the plane are measured – see Figure 2.1. As may be seen from this illustration, both axes are provided with a linear scale where both positive x and y values increase in the direction indicated by the arrows located on the two axes (i.e. positive x values increase to the right and positive y values increase vertically).

In Figure 2.1, a point (P) is indicated and its location can be defined by measuring its horizontal and vertical displacement from the origin (in this case 4 units horizontally and 3 units vertically). These distances are expressed as an ordered pair. Here, the horizontal distance is, by convention, assumed to be the first member of the pair and the vertical distance comes second:

$$(horizontal\ distance,\ vertical\ distance).$$

Which is usually written as (x, y). The x coordinate is referred to as the abscissa and the y coordinate as the ordinate. Returning to the point P indicated in Figure 2.1, its location may be specified as (4,3).

2.2.2 Polar Coordinates

Consider point P indicated in Figure 2.2. Rather than specifying the location of this point according to its horizontal and vertical displacement from the origin, we now specify:

---

[2] For the moment, we confine our discussion to a plane or 2-D space. See Section 6.2 for reference to a 3-D space and Figure 5.25 which illustrates left and right-handed coordinate systems.

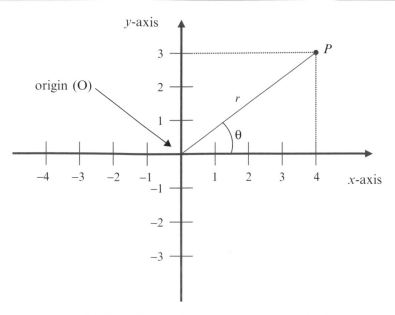

Figure 2.2 The use of polar coordinates to represent the location of a point.

- The magnitude of the point's displacement from the origin (O) i.e. the distance OP. We will denote this distance as r.
- The angle of the line OP as measured from the positive x-axis in an anticlockwise (counter clockwise) direction. We will denote this angle as θ.

Thus in the case of point P, the magnitude of its distance (r) from the origin is given by Pythagoras' Theorem such that $\sqrt{4^2 + 3^2} = 5$ units and the angle is calculated by:

$$\tan \theta = \frac{y}{x},$$

thus,

$$\vartheta = \arctan\left(\frac{y}{x}\right), \tag{2.1}$$

which for point P is: $\arctan(\frac{3}{4}) \sim 37°$.

Polar coordinates are represented in the form (r, θ) and so point P could be represented as $(5, 37°)$. Each and every point on the Cartesian plane may be defined by a single and unique pair of coordinate values (x, y). In contrast, when polar coordinates are used, different values of θ may be used to define the location of a particular point. For example, in the case of the point P referred to above we have determined that $\theta \sim 37°$. However, as indicated in Figure 2.3, if we add 360° to this value we will still define the location of point P. In fact, adding (or subtracting) any integer multiple of 360° to θ (whilst at the same time not making any change to r) will continue to define the location of point P.

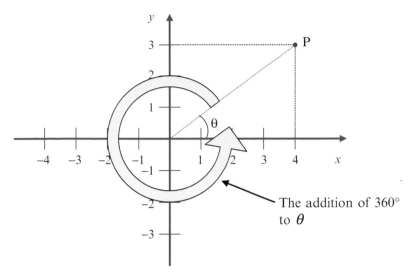

Figure 2.3 Adding (or subtracting) any integer multiple of 360° to θ (whilst at the same time not making any change to r) will continue to define the location of the point P. (An integer is a positive or negative whole number.)

OTU Exercise 2.1: Conversion from Rectangular to Polar Coordinates

Convert the following rectangular coordinates for a point P to polar coordinates:

a.   (3,3)
b.   (−3,3)

Hint: recall that θ is measured in the anticlockwise direction from the positive x-axis.

2.2.3 Homogeneous Coordinates

Homogeneous coordinates are frequently used in computer graphics and greatly facilitate various geometrical operations (see, for example, Section 3.5). In essence homogeneous coordinates are based on rectangular Cartesian coordinates and a point (x, y) located in a 2-D space is represented in homogeneous form by a triple:

$$[wx \quad wy \quad w].$$

Where w is a non-zero value and is referred to as the scale factor or the 'homogeneous coordinate'. For example, consider a point P whose rectangular coordinates in a 2-D space are (2,6). To represent this point in homogeneous form we simply select a value for w (let us arbitrarily use the value of 4) and can then express the point P as:

$$[8 \quad 24 \quad 4]$$

In fact, we can select any (nonzero) value for w. For example, the point P could also be expressed as [2 6 1] ($w = 1$), [4 12 2] ($w = 2$) etc. Thus it follows that a point in 2-D space can be represented by an infinite set of homogeneous coordinates – there is no single (unique) representation. However, we recognise that two sets of homogeneous coordinates represent the same point if (and only if) one is a multiple of the other.

A homogeneous point $[a\ b\ w]$ can be converted back to Cartesian coordinates by simply dividing the first two terms by w. Thus $[a\ b\ w] \rightarrow (a/w, b/w)$.

In this book we will employ homogeneous coordinate representations as a convenient means of supporting various geometrical operations and will not overly concern ourselves with underlying theory. However, it is interesting to note that by taking a pair of Cartesian coordinates corresponding to the location of a point in 2-D space and representing these as a triple, we are effectively adding another dimension – the point in 2-D space being represented as a point on an associated line in 3-D space.

2.3 The Line

'The greatest task before civilization at present is to make machines what they ought to be, the slaves, instead of the masters.'[3]

Recall from elementary coordinate geometry that an infinite straight line located on a 2-D plane may be defined in terms of its gradient (m) and the point (c) at which it crosses the y-axis (the 'y-intercept')[4]:

$$y = mx + c. \tag{2.2}$$

Verifying this equation provides us with a convenient opportunity to undertake a brief 'workout' with simple algebra (what joy ...).[5] Consider the line depicted in Figure 2.4(a) which passes through the point A located at (x, y) and the point B at (x_1, y_1). On the basis of similar triangles we can write:

$$\frac{y_1 - y}{x_1 - x} = \frac{y - c}{x}.$$

The gradient (m) of a straight line is given by:

$$m = \frac{y_1 - y}{x_1 - x}. \tag{2.3}$$

Thus:

$$m = \frac{y - c}{x},$$

and so:

$$mx = y - c.$$

Hence:

$$y = mx + c.$$

---

[3] Attributed to Havelock Ellis (1859–1939).
[4] In the case of a line which is parallel to the y-axis (and which therefore has an infinite gradient) it is represented by $x = a$ where a denotes the point at which the line crosses the x-axis.
[5] This is an 'explicit' form of equation in that given a value for x, the value of y may be directly calculated. In contrast, an 'implicit' form of equation equals zero – e.g. $y - mx - c = 0$

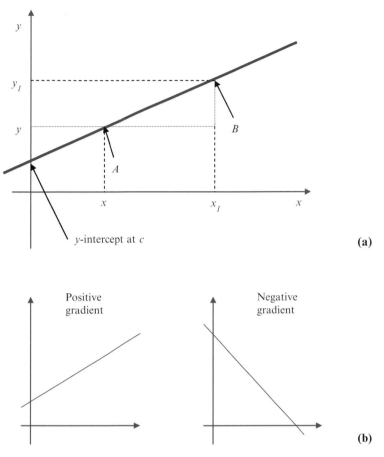

Figure 2.4 In (a) the equation for a straight line may be obtained by considering similar triangles that are indicated in red. See text for discussion. In (b) we illustrate lines with positive and negative gradients.

OTU Exercise 2.2: The Equation of a Line

Determine the equation of an infinite straight line that passes through the points (2,1) and (3,2).

Hint: It is helpful to begin by sketching the line.

2.3.1 A Finite Line: The Parametric Description

The above discussion enables us to describe the location of an infinite line in a 2-D space. However, we are often concerned with finite lines – that is, line segments that are of a certain length. Here, it is convenient to employ parametric equations in which, rather than providing a single expression that relates x and y (as is the case in Eq. 2.2), we express x and y separately in terms of a third independent variable. For example, consider the line segment illustrated in Figure 2.5 which connects points P_1 (located at (x_1, y_1)) and P_2 (at (x_2, y_2)). We define a

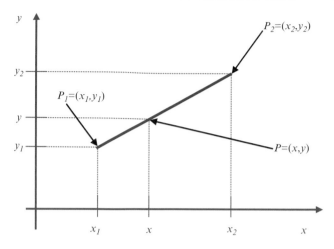

Figure 2.5 The location of a point $P = (x, y)$ on a line segment can be conveniently expressed using parametric equations – see text for details.

parameter (t) that represents the fractional distance that we have moved along the line (i.e. t varies between 0 and 1). From inspection of Figure 2.5 it is apparent that the coordinates of an arbitrary point (x, y) which is located on the line segment may be expressed by:

$$x = x_1 + (x_2 - x_1)\, t \tag{2.4}$$

$$y = y_1 + (y_2 - y_1)\, t \tag{2.5}$$

In the case that $t = 0$, then $x = x_1$ and $y = y_1$ – in which case, the point (x, y) is located at P_1. Alternatively when $t = 1$, $x = x_2$ and $y = y_2$ in which case (x, y) is located at the other end of the line segment (i.e. at P_2). For other values of t, we can reach any point on the line. Eq.'s 2.4 and 2.5 are known as parametric equations and the variable t is referred to as the 'parameter'

OTU Exercise 2.3: The Parametric Form

Show that the two parametric equations given above for a straight line may be used to obtain Eq. 2.3.

As indicated in the above OTU Exercise, converting the parametric representation of a line (or curve) into an expression that directly relates the x and y variables is readily achieved by eliminating the parameter (t). By way of a simple example, consider the parametric equations $x = 2t$ and $y = t + 4$. From the first equation, we can write $t = x/2$. Substituting this into the second equation for t gives: $y = x/2 + 4$. By comparison with Eq. 2.2, it is apparent that this represents a straight-line graph with a gradient of 0.5 and with a y intercept of 4.

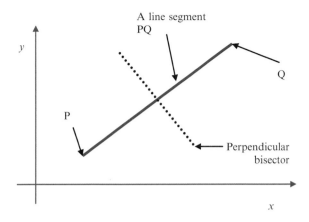

Figure 2.6 A line segment PQ and its perpendicular bisector. See text for discussion.

OTU Exercise 2.4: Parametric Form and Mid-Point of a Line Segment

Consider a line segment whose end points are at (1,2) and (3,4). Represent this line segment in parametric form. Using the parametric equations, determine the coordinates of the mid-point of the line.

2.3.2 The Perpendicular Bisector

Consider the line segment illustrated in Figure 2.6 with end-points P (located at (x_1, y_1)) and Q (at (x_2, y_2)). In this diagram we also illustrate the perpendicular bisector of PQ.[6]

> In the case of two orthogonal lines, the product of their gradients is equal to -1.

Thus, if, for example, the line segment PQ has a gradient of 4, then a line that is perpendicular has a gradient of $-1/4$.

The coordinates of the mid-point of the line segment PQ may, for example, be found as follows:

1. In the case that PQ is expressed using parametric equations, we simply insert the values of the line's endpoints into Eq. 2.4 and 2.5 and set t to 0.5.
2. Alternatively we can intuitively write:

$$(x_{mid}, y_{mid}) = \left(\frac{x_2 + x_1}{2}, \frac{y_2 + y_1}{2} \right).$$

Here, we are calculating the average of the end-point coordinate values.

---

[6] The perpendicular bisector is a line that crosses the mid-point of PQ – the angle between the two lines is $90°$.

OTU Exercise 2.5: The Perpendicular Bisector

Consider a line segment whose end-points are located at (1,1) and (4,3). Obtain an equation for the perpendicular bisector to this line.

2.4 Vectors in a 2-D Space

> *'O sleep! O gentle sleep!*
> *Nature's soft nurse, how have I frighted thee,*
> *That thou no more wilt weigh my eyelids down*
> *And steep my senses in forgetfulness.'*[7]

In Section 1.4.1 we briefly distinguished between scalar and vector quantities (recall that a scalar quantity (such as mass) has only an associated magnitude (size) whereas a vector quantity (such as velocity) has both magnitude and direction). As we will see, vectors are widely used in computer graphics and in this section we briefly overview some elementary vector techniques.

Since vectors have both magnitude and direction, they are represented graphically by means of 'directed line segments' – the length of a line providing the magnitude representation and the orientation (coupled with the direction of the arrow that is drawn on the line) indicating the vector's direction. In Figure 2.7 three vectors are illustrated. The vectors shown in (a) and (b) are of the same size and are parallel – thus they are equal in both magnitude and direction. However, although the vector illustrated in (c) is equal in magnitude to the vectors in (a) and (b) it is not parallel to them. Thus the vector in (c) is not equal to vectors depicted in (a) and (b).

2.4.1 Vector Notation

Vector quantities are usually denoted by underlining the symbol used to represent the vector (e.g. '$\underline{a}$'), by the use of an overhead arrow (e.g. $\vec{op}$) or by means of bold typeface. In this book we will use the latter approach. A vector from point A to point B will be indicated as '**AB**' or may, simply be labelled as, for example, **a**. The vectors **AB** and **BA** (see Figure 2.8(a)) are of the same magnitude. However, they point in opposite directions and are therefore not equal.

2.4.2 'Free' and 'Position' Vectors

A 'free' vector is simply indicated by a directed line segment (as in Figure 2.7) and is not 'anchored' to any particular location. Consequently, its absolute position is not defined. In contrast, a position vector is 'anchored' in as much as it has a fixed starting point – see Figure 2.8(b) where a position vector is indicated. This shows the absolute location of point P relative to the origin (O) – the vector is denoted **OP**.

---

[7] From 'Henry IV' by William Shakespeare. The reader is left to judge whether or not he may have been referring to the after effects of mathematics . . .

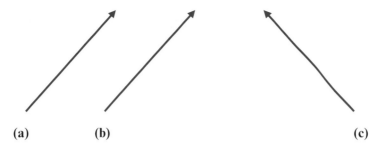

(a)   (b)   (c)

Figure 2.7 Three vectors in 2-D space. Here, the vectors illustrated in (a) and (b) have the same magnitude and direction and are therefore said to be equal. However, although the length of the vector depicted in (c) is the same as those shown in (a) and (b) (i.e. they are equal in magnitude), the vector in (c) has a different orientation. Therefore, this vector does not equal the other two.

2.4.3 Specifying Vectors

An arbitrary vector in 2-D space may be defined by means of two orthogonal 'unit' vectors (a unit vector is one unit in length (i.e. has a magnitude of unity)). As indicated in Figure 2.9(a), one of these vectors is oriented parallel to the x-axis and the other parallel to the y-axis. The former is commonly assigned the symbol '**i**' and the latter the symbol '**j**' (note the use of bold typeface to indicate that both are vector quantities). Consider the vector **OP** illustrated in Figure 2.9(b). We may 'travel' from O to P by moving 3 units along the x-axis and 2 units along the y-axis. This corresponds to placing 3 instances of the vector **i** and 2 instances of the vector **j** end to end. Thus, we can express the vector **OP** as:

$$\mathbf{OP} = 3\mathbf{i} + 2\mathbf{j}.$$

OTU Exercise 2.6: Expressing a Vector in Terms of Orthogonal Unit Vectors

Consider a point Q that is located at (6,9). Express the position vector **OQ** in terms of unit vectors **i** and **j**.

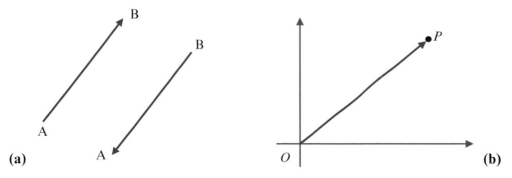

(a)   (b)

Figure 2.8 In (a): a vector from point A to point B is not equal from one that 'travels' from B to A. Diagram (b) shows a position vector that identifies the distance and location of a point P measured from the origin (O).

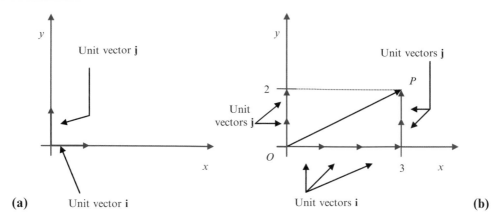

Figure 2.9 In (a) we illustrate the two unit vectors **i** and **j**. The former lies parallel to the x-axis and the latter is parallel to the y-axis. In (b) we demonstrate that the vector **OP** can be represented by placing three instances of **i** and two instances of **j** end to end.

Many texts denote a unit vector by placing a 'hat' above the symbol used to represent the vector. Thus the unit vectors **i** and **j** could be represented as $\hat{\mathbf{i}}$ and $\hat{\mathbf{j}}$. However, when referring to these standard unit vectors, we will simply use the symbols **i** and **j**.[8] In the case of other unit vectors, we will include the 'hat' symbol.

Note: The representation of a vector by means of unit vectors **i** and **j** (e.g. **a** = 4**i** + 2**j**), is commonly referred to as the 'component form'. Alternatively we can describe the vector in row or column form. In row vector notation the vector **a** would be given by **a** = [4 2]. Using this notation, we can express the unit vectors **i** as [1 0] and **j** as [0 1].

2.4.4 The Magnitude (Modulus) of a Vector

We can use Pythagoras' Theorem to find the magnitude (length (also referred to as the modulus)) of a vector. Consider the vector **OP** illustrated in Figure 2.9(b). The length of this vector is given by:

$$|\mathbf{OP}| = \sqrt{3^2 + 2^2} = \sqrt{13}.$$

Notice the use of the two vertical line segments that are placed on either side of **OP**. These indicate that we are referring to the magnitude of the vector **OP**.

2.4.5 Addition of Vectors

The process of adding two vectors may be most readily understood by reference to a simple example. Suppose that we wish to add together the vectors **p** and **q** indicated in Figure 2.10(a). The process may be accomplished in the manner used above in connection with the unit vectors **i** and **j** – we simply relocate either **p** or **q** so that 'tail' of one vector is placed at the 'head' of the other – see Figure 2.10(b) where we have relocated **q**.

---

[8] When we extend our discussion to a 3-D space, we will use the symbols **i**, **j** and **k** to denote the standard unit vectors. Thus for vectors within a 2-D space we employ two unit vectors and for 3-D we include an additional unit vector.

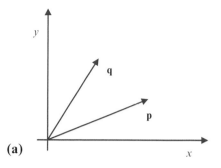
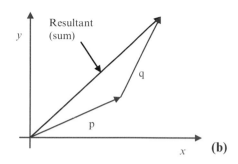

Figure 2.10 The addition of vectors **p** and **q**. In (a) the two vectors are depicted. So as to find their sum (**p** + **q**) we relocate one of the vectors (ensuring that we do not change either its length or direction) and place the 'tail' of this vector on the 'head' of the other. The sum (resultant) is indicated in (b).

When vectors are specified in terms of the orthogonal unit vectors (**i** and **j**), their addition is a simple process. For example, suppose that we want to add two vectors – **p** and **q** where **p** = 3**i** + 4**j** and **q** = 2**i** + 6**j**. We simply add together each pair of orthogonal components. Thus we add 3**i** and 2**i** (giving 5**i**) and 4**j** and 6**j** (giving 10**j**). Hence, **p** + **q** = 5**i** + 10**j**.

By way of a further example, suppose that we wish to add together **a** and **b**: where **a** = **i** + 2**j** and **b** = 2**i** + **j**. Adding the two orthogonal pairs gives us: **a** + **b** = 3**i** + 3**j**. This process is illustrated in Figure 2.11.

OTU Exercise 2.7: Addition and Subtraction of Vectors

Assume that **p** = 2**i** + 9**j** and **q** = 4**i** + 5**j**.

1.   Calculate **p** + **q**.
2.   Calculate **p** − **q**.

Note: The process of subtraction is carried out by subtracting each of the two orthogonal pairs.

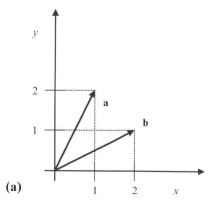
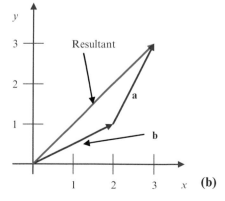

Figure 2.11 The addition of two vectors: **a** = **i** + 2**j** and **b** = 2**i** + **j**. As can be seen from (b) the resultant (sum) is found by adding the two pairs of orthogonal components. As indicated, this gives 3**i** + 3**j**.

2.4.6 Reversing the Direction of a Vector

In Figure 2.12 we illustrate the vector $\mathbf{a} = 2\mathbf{i} + 3\mathbf{j}$. If we wish to create a vector that has equal magnitude but that points in the opposite direction, we simply change the sign of both orthogonal components. In the case of vector $\mathbf{a}$, this will produce a new vector (we will refer to this as $\mathbf{b}$ (where $\mathbf{b} = -\mathbf{a}$)). The vector $\mathbf{b}$ is given by: $\mathbf{b} = -2\mathbf{i} - 3\mathbf{j}$ – see Figure 2.12.

OTU Exercise 2.8: Reversing the Direction of a Vector

Consider the vector $\mathbf{c}$ that is shown in Figure 2.12: where $\mathbf{c} = -4\mathbf{i} + 2\mathbf{j}$. On the diagram draw the vector $\mathbf{d}$ (where $\mathbf{d} = -\mathbf{c}$). Express this vector in terms of $\mathbf{i}$ and $\mathbf{j}$.

2.4.7 Changing the Magnitude of a Vector

We can increase or decrease the magnitude (length) of a vector (i.e. scale the vector) by multiplying the vector by a positive number – a positive scalar value. For example, consider the vector $\mathbf{a} = 2\mathbf{i} + 3\mathbf{j}$. To increase the length of this vector by a factor of three, we simply multiply by 3 – i.e. $3\mathbf{a} = 6\mathbf{i} + 9\mathbf{j}$. However, as indicated in Section 2.4.6, changing the sign of the two orthogonal components reverses the direction of the vector. This is equivalent to multiplication by $^-1$. Hence, if we multiply a vector by any negative number we will not only reverse the direction of the vector but also (in the case of all negative numbers other than $^-1$) increase or decrease the vector's magnitude. For example, if we multiply a vector by $^-2$, we will create a new vector which points in the oppose direction and is twice the length of the original.

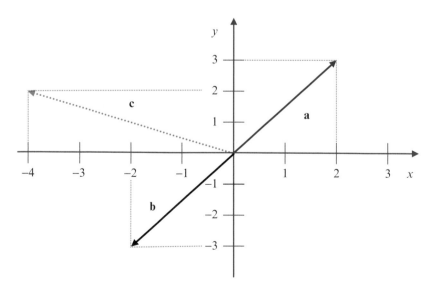

Figure 2.12 Here, we depict a vector $\mathbf{a} = 2\mathbf{i} + 3\mathbf{j}$. To create a vector which has the same magnitude but that points in the opposite direction, we change the sign of the two orthogonal components that define the vector. This results in a vector that is given by $-2\mathbf{i} - 3\mathbf{j}$. This vector is labelled $\mathbf{b}$ (where $\mathbf{b} = -\mathbf{a}$). **Note**: changing the sign of the two components is the same as multiplying by -1. Regarding vector $\mathbf{c}$ – see OTU Exercise 2.8.

2.4.8 The Unit Vector

Consider a vector **a**. If we wish to produce a unit vector (recall this is a vector of unit length) which points in the same direction as **a**, then we determine the magnitude of **a** and divide the two orthogonal components that define **a** by this value. In short:

$$\hat{\mathbf{a}} = \frac{\mathbf{a}}{|\mathbf{a}|}.$$

Recall that the 'hat' symbol is used to indicate a unit vector and that $|\mathbf{a}|$ denotes the magnitude of **a**. For example, consider the vector $\mathbf{a} = 3\mathbf{i} + 4\mathbf{j}$. The magnitude of this vector is found using Pythagoras' Theorem – see Section 2.4.4: $|\mathbf{a}| = \sqrt{3^2 + 4^2} = 5$. Thus the unit vector $\hat{\mathbf{a}}$ is given by:

$$\hat{\mathbf{a}} = \frac{3\mathbf{i} + 4\mathbf{j}}{5} = \frac{3\mathbf{i}}{5} + \frac{4\mathbf{j}}{5}.$$

2.4.9 The Scalar Product

The scalar product provides us with a convenient way of determining the angle between two vectors. Consider the vectors **a** and **b** where $\mathbf{a} = a_1\mathbf{i} + a_2\mathbf{j}$ and $\mathbf{b} = b_1\mathbf{i} + b_2\mathbf{j}$ (here, a_1, a_2, b_1 and b_2 represent real numbers). The scalar product of these two vectors is given by:

$$\mathbf{a}·\mathbf{b} = (a_1\mathbf{i} + a_2\mathbf{j})·(b_1\mathbf{i} + b_2\mathbf{j}).$$

Notice the use of the period to denote the scalar product (because of this, it is also commonly referred to as the 'dot' product). To increase clarity, when indicating a scalar product we will use a period in bold typeface – a non-bold period between two terms will signify conventional multiplication. To calculate the scalar product, we multiply the terms in the brackets:

$$\mathbf{a}·\mathbf{b} = (a_1\mathbf{i} + a_2\mathbf{j})·(b_1\mathbf{i} + b_2\mathbf{j}) = (a_1 b_1)\mathbf{i}·\mathbf{i} + (a_2 b_2)\mathbf{j}·\mathbf{j} + (a_1 b_2)\mathbf{i}·\mathbf{j} + (a_2 b_1)\mathbf{j}·\mathbf{i}. \qquad (2.6)$$

This expression may easily be simplified. However, before we can do so we need to introduce a further result which relates the scalar product to the angle between the associated vectors. Consider the two vectors **a** and **b** in a 2-D space as depicted in Figure 2.13. Assuming that θ is the angle between the vectors such that $0 \leq \theta \leq 180°$, we can write:

$$\mathbf{a}·\mathbf{b} = |\mathbf{a}||\mathbf{b}| \cos \theta. \qquad (2.7)$$

A derivation of this equation is provided in Appendix C. Now consider the scalar product of the unit vectors **i** and **j** (specifically $\mathbf{i}·\mathbf{i}, \mathbf{j}·\mathbf{j}, \mathbf{i}·\mathbf{j}$ and $\mathbf{j}·\mathbf{i}$). For $\mathbf{i}·\mathbf{i}$, using Eq. 2.7 we can write:

$$\mathbf{i}·\mathbf{i} = |\mathbf{i}||\mathbf{i}| \cos \theta.$$

In this case we know that $|\mathbf{i}| = 1$ (**i** is a vector of unit length) and also that the angle (θ) referred to here is zero (hence $\cos \theta = 1$). Thus $\mathbf{i}·\mathbf{i} = 1$ and similarly $\mathbf{j}·\mathbf{j} = 1$ Now consider the scalar product of two orthogonal unit vectors[9] ($\theta = 90°$ and so $\cos \theta = 0$):

$$\mathbf{i}·\mathbf{j} = |\mathbf{i}||\mathbf{j}| \cos 90 = 0.$$

---

[9] The terms 'orthogonal', 'perpendicular' and 'normal' all refer to entities that meet at right-angles. In mathematics, when dealing exclusively with vectors we tend to use the term 'orthogonal' to signify an angle of $90°$ between two vectors.

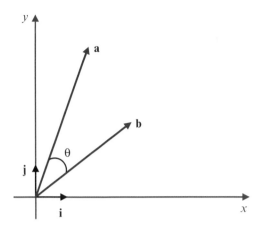

Figure 2.13 The angle θ between the two vectors **a** and **b** may be readily determined by use of the scalar (dot) product. See text for discussion.

> When two vectors are orthogonal, their scalar product is zero.

We can now use these results to simplify Eq. 2.6 and so:

$$\mathbf{a\cdot b} = (a_1\mathbf{i} + a_2\mathbf{j})\cdot(b_1\mathbf{i} + b_2\mathbf{j}) = (a_1b_1)\mathbf{i\cdot i} + (a_2b_2)\mathbf{j\cdot j} + (a_1b_2)\mathbf{i.j} + (a_2b_1)\mathbf{j\cdot i} = a_1b_1 + a_2b_2. \quad (2.8)$$

Equating Eq.'s 2.7 and 2.8 gives the following important result:

$$\mathbf{a\cdot b} = a_1b_1 + a_2b_2 = |\mathbf{a}||\mathbf{b}| \cos\theta \quad (2.9)$$

To illustrate a use of this result consider two vectors **a** and **b** in a 2-D space where **a** = **i** + 3**j** and **b** = 4**i** + 6**j** and let us calculate the angle between these vectors. We begin by calculating their magnitudes: $|\mathbf{a}| = \sqrt{1^2 + 3^2} = \sqrt{10}$ and $|\mathbf{b}| = \sqrt{4^2 + 6^2} = \sqrt{52}$. We also calculate **a·b** and find this to equal 22. On the basis of Eq. 2.9 we can write:

$$\mathbf{a\cdot b} = 22 = \sqrt{10}\sqrt{52}\cos\theta,$$

and so,

$$\cos\theta = \frac{22}{\sqrt{10}\cdot\sqrt{52}}.$$

Hence $\theta \sim 15°$.

> Note that the scalar product gives a result that is a scalar rather than a vector quantity. This is in contrast to the 'vector product' (see Section 6.3) which (as the name implies) produces a result that is a vector quantity.

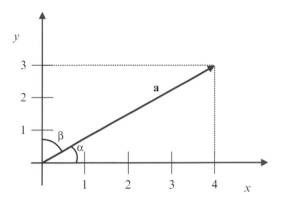

Figure 2.14 The direction cosines are given by cos α and cos β. See text for discussion.

OTU Exercise 2.9: Using the Scalar Product

1. Find the angle between the vectors **a** = 2**i** + 3**j** and **b** = 4**i** + **j**.
2. Determine whether or not the vectors **p** = 2**i** + **j** and **q** = −**i** + 2**j** are orthogonal.

2.4.10 Direction Cosines

> 'Writers seldom choose as friends those self-contained characters
> who are never in trouble, never unhappy or ill,
> never make mistakes and always
> count their change when it is handed to them.'[10]

Consider the vector **a** = 4**i** + 3**j** depicted in Figure 2.14. The symbols α and β respectively denote the angles between this vector and the positive x and y axes. The cosines of these angles (cos α and cos β) are referred to as the vectors 'direction cosines'. These can be easily determined:

$$\cos\alpha = \frac{4}{|\mathbf{a}|}, \text{ and } \cos\beta = \frac{3}{|\mathbf{a}|}.$$

Since $|\mathbf{a}| = \sqrt{4^2 + 3^2} = 5$ it follows that cos α = 4/5 and cos β = 3/5. In the case that two vectors are parallel, they will have the same direction cosines.

2.4.11 The Vector Equation of a Line

Vectors provide a means of unambiguously defining the location of a point on a 2-D plane relative to some fixed location. For example, the position vector 3**i** + 4**j** (which we assume is 'anchored' to the origin) defines a point that is 5 units in distance from the origin and which is located in a specific direction.

---

[10] Attributed to Catherine Drinker Bowen (1897–1973).

Table 2.1 Exemplar values of t are used to create the line depicted in Figure 2.15.

t	$\mathbf{a}$
0	$2\mathbf{j}$
1	$\mathbf{i} + 3\mathbf{j}$
2	$2\mathbf{i} + 4\mathbf{j}$
3	$3\mathbf{i} + 5\mathbf{j}$

A straight line may be defined by specifying the location of two points through which the line passes. In fact, it is convenient to view a line as comprising a locus of points – indeed a line or other graphics primitive that is depicted on a bitmapped (pixmapped) display is formed from a set of illuminated points (pixels)) and vectors can be used to define the location of each of these points. In the previous subsections we have considered vectors to have the general form $a_1\mathbf{i} + a_2\mathbf{j}$ – both a_1 and a_2 representing real numbers that, for a particular vector, have a fixed value. However, we can represent a vector in a more general way by allowing both a_1 and a_2 to vary in some related manner. For example, consider the vector $\mathbf{a}$ which we will express as:

$$\mathbf{a} = x\mathbf{i} + y\mathbf{j}, \tag{2.10}$$

where, for example, x and y are related by: $y = x + 2$ (recall that this is a particular instance of the general equation for a straight line that we provided in Eq. 2.2 and has a gradient of unity and y intercept of 2). Following previous discussion in Section 2.3.1, it is often convenient to express x and y in terms of an independent variable (which for the present we will represent using the symbol t) and so, we can specify our exemplar line by the parametric equations $x = t$, $y = t + 2$. Thus we can write Eq. 2.10 as:

$$\mathbf{a} = t\mathbf{i} + (t + 2)\mathbf{j}.$$

By inserting values for t, we can generate a set of vectors that define points that lie on the line given by the Cartesian equation $y = x + 2$. This is demonstrated in Table 2.1 and Figure 2.15. In the table we use four exemplar values for t (0, 1, 2, 3) and for each, we determine $\mathbf{a}$ using the above expression. In the illustration, we plot these vectors and as can be seen, the points that they specify lie on a straight line that has a gradient of unity and a y intercept of 2.

Note: Different parametric equations can give rise to the same graph. By way of an example, consider the Cartesian equation for a line $y = 4x + 3$. We may assign the parameter (t) to form the parametric equations $x = t$, $y = 4t + 3$. Substituting these parametric equations into Eq. 2.10. we obtain:

$$\mathbf{a} = t\mathbf{i} + (4t + 3)\mathbf{j}.$$

Alternatively, we could assign t so that $x = t/4$ in which case, y would simply equal $t + 3$. Substituting these parametric equations into Eq. 2.10, we obtain:

$$\mathbf{a} = (t/4)\mathbf{i} + (3 + t)\mathbf{j}.$$

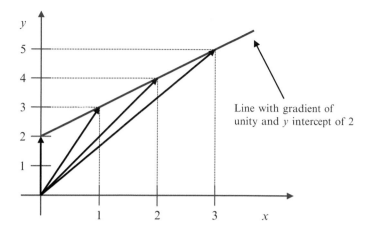

Figure 2.15 The use of a vector equation for plotting a line. The four vectors given in Table 2.1 are plotted and give rise to a set of points that lie on a line which has a gradient of unity and a y intercept of 2.

OTU Exercise 2.10: Plotting Lines Using the Vector Equation

In relation to the two vector equations presented above (i.e. $\mathbf{a} = t\mathbf{i} + (4t + 3)\mathbf{j}$ and $\mathbf{a} = (t/4)\mathbf{i} + (3 + t)\mathbf{j}$) show that when plotted they both give rise to the same line.

So far we have considered the use of a vector equation to enable us to determine the location of points that form a line. However, we can also specify a line using an alternative vector technique. Consider the scenario illustrated in Figure 2.16.

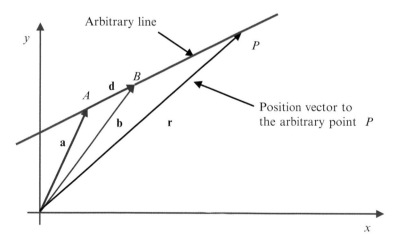

Figure 2.16 An alternative approach to the vector representation of a line. Here, we specify a vector **a** that defines a point on the line together with a second vector (**d**) that gives the direction of the line (slope).

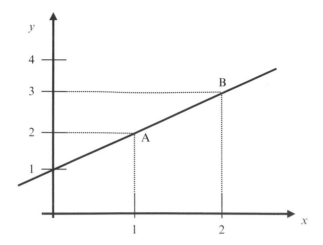

Figure 2.17 A line that passes through the points (1,2) and (2,3). See text for discussion concerning the representation of this line by means of a vector equation.

Here, we can define all points on the line by means of two vectors. Firstly we employ a vector that defines the location of a point on the line (in the illustration we employ a vector labelled **a**). Secondly, we use a vector that defines the direction (gradient) of the line – this is labelled vector **d** in the diagram. The position vector (**r**) of any arbitrary point (P) on the line may then be expressed as:

$$\mathbf{r} = \mathbf{a} + u\mathbf{d}, \tag{2.11}$$

where u is a real number (positive or negative) which scales the vector **d** and therefore enables us to reach any point on the line. For example, in Figure 2.16, the position vector to the point P would be given by: $\mathbf{r} = \mathbf{a} + 3\mathbf{d}$. The vector **r** is commonly written as $\mathbf{r}(u)$ – so indicating that **r** is a vector that is a function of a parameter (u). In Figure 2.16, we also indicate a vector **b** such that $\mathbf{d} = -\mathbf{a} + \mathbf{b}$. Consequently we can rewrite Eq. 2.11 as:

$$\mathbf{r}(u) = \mathbf{a} + u(\mathbf{b} - \mathbf{a}). \tag{2.12}$$

In the case that $0 < u < 1$, then P lies between points A and B. If $u > 1$ then P lies to the right of B and if u is negative then P lies to the left of A.[11]

To further illustrate this general approach, consider the line depicted in Figure 2.17 which passes through the points (1,2) and (2,3). In this case the vector **a** may be expressed as $\mathbf{a} = \mathbf{i} + 2\mathbf{j}$ and the vector **b** as $\mathbf{b} = 2\mathbf{i} + 3\mathbf{j}$. Thus using Eq. 2.12 we obtain:

$$\mathbf{r}(u) = (\mathbf{i} + 2\mathbf{j}) + u((2\mathbf{i} + 3\mathbf{j}) - (\mathbf{i} + 2\mathbf{j})).$$

This can be simplified to give:

$$\mathbf{r}(u) = (1 + u)\mathbf{i} + (2 + u)\mathbf{j}.$$

---

[11] Recall that multiplying a vector by a negative number will not only scale the vector's magnitude, but will also reverse its direction.

As we know, a vector in 2-D space can be represented as $\mathbf{r} = x\mathbf{i} + y\mathbf{j}$ and by comparison, in the case of our exemplar line $x = 1 + u$ and $y = 2 + u$. Eliminating the parameter u, we obtain $y = x + 1$ which is the Cartesian equation for this line.

OTU Exercise 2.11: Locating the Point at which Two Lines Intersect

Consider two lines that are given by the vector equations: $\mathbf{r}_1(t) = \mathbf{i} + 3\mathbf{j} + t(-\mathbf{i} + 2\mathbf{j})$ and $\mathbf{r}_2(s) = \mathbf{i} - 2\mathbf{j} + s(2\mathbf{i} + \mathbf{j})$. Note that here, we have used the letters t and s to represent the two parameters.

1. Show that these two lines are not parallel.
2. Obtain the position vector to the point of their intersection.

Note: We have not explicitly considered these two issues – a little lateral thinking is needed (perhaps supported by coffee)!

2.5 Matrices

'Taking mathematics from the beginning of the world
to the time of Newton,
what he has done is much the better half.' [12]

In this section, we take a break from our discussion of vectors and introduce some elementary concepts in relation to matrices. A matrix takes the form of a rectangular array of elements and by convention these are placed within 'square' brackets. Thus a matrix A may be given by:

$$A = \begin{bmatrix} 1 & 2 & 3 \\ 5 & 9 & 3 \\ 7 & 2 & 4 \end{bmatrix}.$$

This would be referred to as a 3×3 matrix [13] (comprising 3 rows and 3 columns of elements). A matrix that comprises the same number of rows and columns is referred to as a 'square' matrix whereas if the number of rows and columns are not equal, the matrix is said to be rectangular. In generalised form, a matrix comprising m rows and n columns may be represented as:

$$A = \begin{bmatrix} a_{11} & a_{12} & \dots & a_{1n} \\ a_{21} & a_{22} & \dots & a_{2n} \\ \cdot & \cdot & \cdot & \cdot \\ a_{m1} & a_{m2} & \dots & a_{mn} \end{bmatrix}. \tag{2.13}$$

---

[12] Attributed to Gottfried Wilhelm Leibniz (1646–1716).
[13] This is commonly referred to as the 'dimensions' or 'order' of the matrix.

In an excellent book devoted to matrices Bickley and Thompson [1964], write:

'*Mathematical notation is a language: it conveys information by means of symbols used in accordance with certain conventions. In it brevity is a virtue, provided it is not achieved at the expense of doubt or ambiguity. But if the notation were no more than a shorthand, its usefulness would be very limited.*'

As we shall see here and in subsequent chapters, matrices provide us with a powerful tool and are an excellent example of a mathematical notation that facilitate the representation and efficient manipulation of numerical values. In fact operations on matrices underpin the depiction of both static and dynamic image scenes and also our interaction with computer graphics applications. In the following subsections, we briefly summarise various operations that can be performed on matrices.

2.5.1 Addition and Subtraction of Matrices

We can add and subtract matrices that are of the same order (dimensions). For example consider the following example:

$$\begin{bmatrix} 2 & 3 \\ 1 & 4 \end{bmatrix} + \begin{bmatrix} 5 & 1 \\ 2 & 4 \end{bmatrix} = \begin{bmatrix} 7 & 4 \\ 3 & 8 \end{bmatrix}.$$

As may be seen, addition is carried out by summing corresponding elements within the two matrices. Thus, for example, we add the top left most elements in the two matrices (2 and 5) and place the result (7) in a corresponding position within the matrix which represents the sum. Subtraction is carried out using the same approach:

$$\begin{bmatrix} 2 & 3 \\ 1 & 4 \end{bmatrix} - \begin{bmatrix} 5 & 1 \\ 2 & 4 \end{bmatrix} = \begin{bmatrix} -3 & 2 \\ -1 & 0 \end{bmatrix}.$$

However, we *cannot* perform the following addition and subtraction operations – the matrices are not of the same order:

$$\begin{bmatrix} 1 \\ 2 \end{bmatrix} + \begin{bmatrix} 1 & 3 \\ 4 & 5 \end{bmatrix} \qquad \begin{bmatrix} 1 & 7 \\ 5 & 2 \end{bmatrix} - \begin{bmatrix} 1 & 3 \end{bmatrix}$$

Note that the addition of two matrices is commutative ($A + B = B + A$) whereas subtraction is not commutative ($A - B \neq B - A$).

2.5.2 Multiplication of Matrices

The multiplication of two matrices is not quite as simple as the addition and subtraction processes described above. Here, each element within the matrix that represents the result is *not* obtained by multiplication of corresponding elements. Furthermore in order that two matrices can be multiplied, it is not necessary for them to have the same dimensions:

> **Two matrices can be multiplied if the number of columns in the first matrix equals the number of rows in the second.**

Thus, for example the following two matrices can be multiplied:

$$\begin{bmatrix} 1 & 2 & 3 \\ 2 & 5 & 4 \end{bmatrix} \times \begin{bmatrix} 1 & 2 & 3 \\ 3 & 1 & 5 \\ 2 & -1 & 4 \end{bmatrix},$$

whereas the following two matrices *cannot* be multiplied:

$$\begin{bmatrix} 2 & 1 \\ 1 & 6 \end{bmatrix} \times \begin{bmatrix} 2 & 3 \\ 1 & 2 \\ 6 & 4 \end{bmatrix}.$$

To illustrate the way in which matrices are multiplied, let us consider a simple example:

$$\begin{bmatrix} 1 & 2 \\ 3 & 4 \end{bmatrix} \begin{bmatrix} 5 & 6 \\ 7 & 8 \end{bmatrix}.$$

Notice that it is usual to omit the multiplication sign – the lack of a sign between two matrices is assumed to indicate multiplication. Consider the diagram presented in Figure 2.18. In order to obtain element a in the result matrix, we use the first row of the first matrix and the first column of the second matrix (the latter is shown as being arranged as a row and placed above the first matrix). We then multiply the two pairs of elements and add the result (so obtaining 19). This result provides us with element a in the solution matrix.

We then repeat this process using the second row of the first matrix and the first column of the second. Thus we calculate $3 \times 5 + 4 \times 7 = 43$ and this provides element c in the solution matrix.

Having operated on both rows of the first matrix using the first column of the second, we now repeat the process – but this time we make use of the second column in the second matrix. In Figure 2.19, we show the generation of element b in the solution matrix. Element d is obtained by using the second column of the second matrix and the second row of the first.

When first encountered, the multiplication process can seem complicated and perhaps confusing. However, the key is to remember that we take each of the columns of the second matrix and use these to operate in turn on each row of the first. Returning to the above example, the

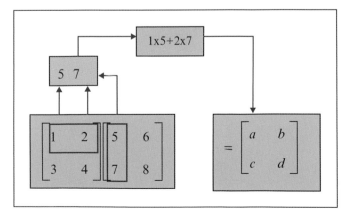

Figure 2.18 To multiply matrices we bring together columns of the second matrix with rows of the first. Here, we illustrate the operation performed using the top row of the first matrix with the first column of the second. This provides element a in the solution matrix.

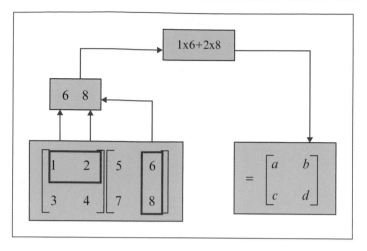

Figure 2.19 Continuing with the example depicted in Figure 2.18, here we generate element *b* in the solution matrix using the top row of the first matrix and the second column of the second matrix.

actual operation that are performed are as follows:

$$\begin{bmatrix} 1 & 2 \\ 3 & 4 \end{bmatrix}\begin{bmatrix} 5 & 6 \\ 7 & 8 \end{bmatrix} = \begin{bmatrix} 1 \times 5 + 2 \times 7 & 1 \times 6 + 2 \times 8 \\ 3 \times 5 + 4 \times 7 & 3 \times 6 + 4 \times 8 \end{bmatrix} = \begin{bmatrix} 19 & 22 \\ 43 & 50 \end{bmatrix}.$$

OTU Exercise 2.12: The Multiplication of Matrices

Undertake the following multiplications (in the case of (3), what do you notice):

1. $\begin{bmatrix} 1 & 2 \\ 2 & 3 \end{bmatrix}\begin{bmatrix} 1 & 1 \\ 3 & 2 \end{bmatrix}.$

2. $\begin{bmatrix} 2 & 1 \\ 3 & 2 \end{bmatrix}\begin{bmatrix} 2 \\ 1 \end{bmatrix}.$

3. $\begin{bmatrix} 1 & 2 \\ 3 & 4 \end{bmatrix}\begin{bmatrix} 1 & 0 \\ 0 & 1 \end{bmatrix}.$

The multiplication of larger matrices is achieved in a similar manner – although as the size (order) of the matrices increase, the manual multiplication process becomes increasingly laborious. By way of a simple example, let's consider the multiplication of two 3 by 3 matrices:

$$\begin{bmatrix} 1 & 2 & 3 \\ 2 & 1 & 2 \\ 3 & 1 & 0 \end{bmatrix}\begin{bmatrix} 2 & 0 & 1 \\ 1 & 3 & 2 \\ 0 & 1 & 1 \end{bmatrix}.$$

We begin by using the top row of the first matrix and the first (left most) column of the second and calculate $(1 \times 2) + (2 \times 1) + (3 \times 0)$. The result (4) is the top left most element in the result matrix. We then repeat this process – the pattern can be seen in the calculation that follows:

$$\begin{bmatrix} 1 & 2 & 3 \\ 2 & 1 & 2 \\ 3 & 1 & 0 \end{bmatrix} \begin{bmatrix} 2 & 0 & 1 \\ 1 & 3 & 2 \\ 0 & 1 & 1 \end{bmatrix}$$

$$= \begin{bmatrix} (1 \times 2) + (2 \times 1) + (3 \times 0) & (1 \times 0) + (2 \times 3) + (3 \times 1) & (1 \times 1) + (2 \times 2) + (3 \times 1) \\ (2 \times 2) + (1 \times 1) + (2 \times 0) & (2 \times 0) + (1 \times 3) + (2 \times 1) & (2 \times 1) + (1 \times 2) + (2 \times 1) \\ (3 \times 2) + (1 \times 1) + (0 \times 0) & (3 \times 0) + (1 \times 3) + (0 \times 1) & (3 \times 1) + (1 \times 2) + (0 \times 1) \end{bmatrix}$$

$$= \begin{bmatrix} 4 & 9 & 8 \\ 5 & 5 & 6 \\ 7 & 3 & 5 \end{bmatrix}.$$

In computer graphics, we sometimes encounter situations in which we need to multiply three matrices. By way of a simple example, let's consider the multiplication of three 2 by 2 matrices denoted A, B and C where:

$$A = \begin{bmatrix} 2 & 3 \\ 0 & 1 \end{bmatrix}, \quad B = \begin{bmatrix} 1 & 4 \\ 0 & 2 \end{bmatrix} \text{ and } C = \begin{bmatrix} 4 & 1 \\ 0 & 2 \end{bmatrix}.$$

We assume that we wish to calculate the product $A \cdot B \cdot C$ – that is:

$$\begin{bmatrix} 2 & 3 \\ 0 & 1 \end{bmatrix} \begin{bmatrix} 1 & 4 \\ 0 & 2 \end{bmatrix} \begin{bmatrix} 4 & 1 \\ 0 & 2 \end{bmatrix}.$$

To calculate this product, we need to decide which pair of matrices we will initially multiply. Do we begin by multiplying A and B or do we first multiply B and C? The former will lead to our calculating $(A \cdot B) \cdot C$ and the latter $A \cdot (B \cdot C)$. Below we illustrate both of these scenarios:

- **Determining $(A \cdot B) \cdot C$:**
  We begin by multiplying A and B:

$$A \cdot B = \begin{bmatrix} 2 & 3 \\ 0 & 1 \end{bmatrix} \begin{bmatrix} 1 & 4 \\ 0 & 2 \end{bmatrix} = \begin{bmatrix} 2 & 14 \\ 0 & 2 \end{bmatrix},$$

  and now perform the multiplication with C:

$$\begin{bmatrix} 2 & 14 \\ 0 & 2 \end{bmatrix} \begin{bmatrix} 4 & 1 \\ 0 & 2 \end{bmatrix} = \begin{bmatrix} 8 & 30 \\ 0 & 4 \end{bmatrix}.$$

  Thus:

$$(A \cdot B) \cdot C = \begin{bmatrix} 8 & 30 \\ 0 & 4 \end{bmatrix}.$$

- **Determining $A \cdot (B) \cdot C$:**
  In this case we begin by multiplying B and C:

$$B \cdot C = \begin{bmatrix} 1 & 4 \\ 0 & 2 \end{bmatrix} \begin{bmatrix} 4 & 1 \\ 0 & 2 \end{bmatrix} = \begin{bmatrix} 4 & 9 \\ 0 & 4 \end{bmatrix}.$$

We now multiply this result with matrix A:

$$\begin{bmatrix} 2 & 3 \\ 0 & 1 \end{bmatrix} \begin{bmatrix} 4 & 9 \\ 0 & 4 \end{bmatrix} = \begin{bmatrix} 8 & 30 \\ 0 & 4 \end{bmatrix}.$$

Thus:

$$A \cdot (B \cdot C) = \begin{bmatrix} 8 & 30 \\ 0 & 4 \end{bmatrix}.$$

Hence both approaches give the same answer. This is a general property of matrices, and we would say that the multiplication of three matrices is 'associative'. However, it is important to note that matrix multiplication is not 'commutative' – that is:

$$A \cdot B \neq B \cdot A.$$

Therefore, although in determining $A \cdot B \cdot C$, we can first multiply A and B, and subsequently perform the multiplication with C or multiply B and C and then perform the multiplication with A, we must not change the order of the matrices within the individual multiplications. For example:

$$A \cdot (B \cdot C) \neq A \cdot (C \cdot B) \neq (B \cdot C) \cdot A \neq (C \cdot B) \cdot A$$

2.5.3 The Inverse of a Matrix

In OTU Exercise 2.12, you will have noticed that in the case of (3), multiplication by $\begin{bmatrix} 1 & 0 \\ 0 & 1 \end{bmatrix}$ has no effect – it does not change the 'identity' of the matrix on which it operates. For this reason, it is referred to as the 'identity matrix' for multiplication of 2 by 2 matrices. Consider the case that two 3 by 3 matrices are multiplied. Here, the identity matrix is:

$$\begin{bmatrix} 1 & 0 & 0 \\ 0 & 1 & 0 \\ 0 & 0 & 1 \end{bmatrix}. \tag{2.14}$$

OTU Exercise 2.13: An Identity Matrix

Perform the following multiplication and hence verify that the second (right hand) matrix acts as an identity matrix.

$$\begin{bmatrix} 1 & 2 & 1 \\ 2 & 1 & 0 \\ 2 & 0 & 3 \end{bmatrix} \begin{bmatrix} 1 & 0 & 0 \\ 0 & 1 & 0 \\ 0 & 0 & 1 \end{bmatrix}.$$

In the case that we perform simple numerical multiplications, the identity element is 1 (multiplication by 1 has no effect). Furthermore we know that:

$$a \times a^{-1} = I.$$

Here a represents any number, a^{-1} is the inverse of a and I is the identity element (which in this case is unity). For example, consider the case that $a = 3$, the inverse is 1/3 and the result of their multiplication is 1. Similarly, multiplying a matrix by its inverse gives the identity matrix.

In order to find the inverse of a matrix, we must first find the 'determinant' – this is often simply abbreviated to 'det'. Below we briefly consider this process for both 2 by 2 and 3 by 3 matrices:

1. **The Determinant of a 2 by 2 Matrix**: Consider a matrix A given by:

$$A = \begin{bmatrix} a & b \\ c & d \end{bmatrix}.$$

The determinant of A (det A) is given by ad-bc. For example, consider the following case:

$$A = \begin{bmatrix} 2 & 4 \\ 3 & 1 \end{bmatrix}.$$

Then:

$$\det A = \begin{vmatrix} 2 & 4 \\ 3 & 1 \end{vmatrix} = (2) \cdot (1) - (4) \cdot (3) = -10.$$

Notice the use of two parallel lines to signify the determinant.

2. **The Determinant of a 3 by 3 Matrix**: Finding the determinant of a 3 by 3 matrix is a little more complicated. Consider the matrix A given by:

$$A = \begin{bmatrix} a_{11} & a_{12} & a_{13} \\ a_{21} & a_{22} & a_{23} \\ a_{31} & a_{32} & a_{33} \end{bmatrix}.$$

The determinant of A is given by:

$$\det A = a_{11}(a_{22}a_{33} - a_{23}a_{32}) - a_{12}(a_{21}a_{33} - a_{23}a_{31}) + a_{13}(a_{21}a_{32} - a_{22}a_{31}).$$

A brief inspection of this equation reveals that the bracketed terms are in fact 2 by 2 determinants. Thus we can re-write this in a more convenient way:

$$\det A = a_{11} \begin{vmatrix} a_{22} & a_{23} \\ a_{32} & a_{33} \end{vmatrix} - a_{12} \begin{vmatrix} a_{21} & a_{23} \\ a_{31} & a_{33} \end{vmatrix} + a_{13} \begin{vmatrix} a_{21} & a_{22} \\ a_{31} & a_{32} \end{vmatrix} \tag{2.15}$$

Returning to the issue of finding the inverse of a matrix. Here, we simply consider the case of a 2 by 2 matrix. The general technique is illustrated in Figure 2.20.

In this example, the value of the determinant ($ad - bc$) is 11. We now draw a diagonal line as indicated in the illustration. The elements on either side of this line are swapped and the sign of the two elements that lie on the diagonal are changed. Finally we divide each element by the determinant.

Recall our previous comment that when we multiply a matrix by its inverse, we obtain the identity matrix. This provides us with a convenient way of checking the calculated inverse. Continuing with the example used in Figure 2.20 – let's verify the inverse that we calculated:

$$\begin{bmatrix} 1 & 4 \\ -2 & 3 \end{bmatrix} \begin{bmatrix} 3/11 & -4/11 \\ 2/11 & 1/11 \end{bmatrix} = \begin{bmatrix} 3/11 + 8/11 & -4/11 + 4/11 \\ -6/11 + 6/11 & 8/11 + 3/11 \end{bmatrix} = \begin{bmatrix} 1 & 0 \\ 0 & 1 \end{bmatrix}.$$

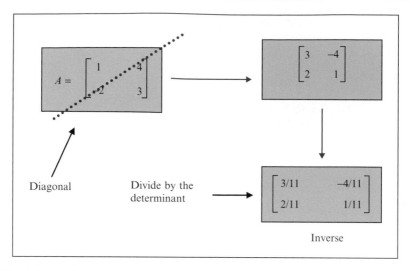

Figure 2.20 Finding the inverse of a matrix. We begin by calculating the determinant which, in this example, is 11. The elements on either side of the diagonal of the original matrix are swapped and the signs of the two elements on the diagonal are changed. We then divide each element in this new matrix by the determinant.

OTU Exercise 2.14: Calculating an Inverse Matrix

Find the inverse of the following matrix:

$$\begin{bmatrix} 2 & 4 \\ 3 & 1 \end{bmatrix}.$$

Verify that the identity matrix is obtained when you multiply the above matrix by the calculated inverse.

2.5.4 Multiplication by a Constant

We can multiply a matrix by a constant (scalar) value. Consider a matrix A that we wish to multiply by a constant k. Then:

$$kA = \begin{bmatrix} ka_{11} & ka_{12} \\ ka_{21} & ka_{22} \end{bmatrix}. \tag{2.16}$$

For example, suppose that $k = 3$ and A is given by:

$$A = \begin{bmatrix} 1 & 2 \\ -4 & 3 \end{bmatrix},$$

then:

$$kA = 3A = \begin{bmatrix} 3 & 6 \\ -12 & 9 \end{bmatrix}.$$

2.5.5 Concerning Row and Column Vectors

In Section 2.4 we considered issues relating to the manipulation and use of vectors and as discussed, a point in a 2-D space may be represented by $a\mathbf{i} + b\mathbf{j}$ where $\mathbf{i}$ and $\mathbf{j}$ represent orthogonal unit vectors that are aligned with the horizontal and vertical axes.

As mentioned previously, it is often convenient to employ a notation for the representation of such vectors and in this respect we can use either column or row vectors. Thus, for example, we can represent the vector $3\mathbf{i} + 4\mathbf{j}$ in the following ways:

$$3\mathbf{i} + 4\mathbf{j} = \begin{bmatrix} 3 \\ 4 \end{bmatrix},$$

which is referred to as a column vector. Alternatively we can use a row vector representation:

$$3\mathbf{i} + 4\mathbf{j} = \begin{bmatrix} 3 & 4 \end{bmatrix}.$$

As we will discuss in Chapter 3, matrices are used for geometric operations such as scaling (enlargement or reduction in size) and for the rotation of graphics elements. In this context we employ matrices that act on vectors and here it is instructive to consider a simple example. Suppose that we have a point P in 2-D space whose location is defined by the vector $3\mathbf{i} + 4\mathbf{j}$ and that we want to apply a scaling factor such that both the horizontal and vertical components of the vector are scaled by the same amount – lets assume a factor of 2 – so giving rise to a vector P'. We can achieve this goal by representing the point P as either a row or column vector. Below we briefly examine these two approaches:

1. **The Use of a Row Vector**: Here, we could multiply the horizontal and vertical components of P by a matrix S where S is given by:

    $$S = \begin{bmatrix} 2 & 0 \\ 0 & 2 \end{bmatrix}.$$

    Thus:

    $$\begin{bmatrix} 3 & 4 \end{bmatrix} \begin{bmatrix} 2 & 0 \\ 0 & 2 \end{bmatrix} = \begin{bmatrix} 6 & 8 \end{bmatrix}.$$

    The points P and P' are illustrated in Figure 2.21.

2. **The Use of a Column Vector**: In this case, we change the order of multiplication – the matrix S being located to the left of the column vector:

    $$\begin{bmatrix} 2 & 0 \\ 0 & 2 \end{bmatrix} \begin{bmatrix} 3 \\ 4 \end{bmatrix} = \begin{bmatrix} 6 \\ 8 \end{bmatrix}.$$

As can be seen from this simple example, in (1) the matrix responsible for the transformation acts on the point P to produce the scaled result. On the other hand, when we use a column vector, the point acts on the transformation matrix – a scenario that is somewhat less intuitive. For simplicity, in this book we will usually employ the row vector approach.

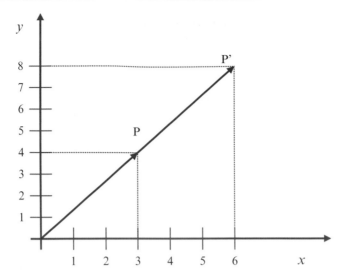

Figure 2.21 The use of a scaling factor whereby both the horizontal and vertical components are scaled by the same amount. Here, a scaling factor of 2 is used on the position vector that defines the location of a point *P*.

2.5.6 Using Matrices to Solve Equations

Let us suppose that we have two unknown quantities (which we will denote as x and y) that are related by a single equation. For example:

$$2x + y = 10.$$

We can determine solutions to this equation by 'inspection' – simply a process of trial and error. For example $x = 1$ and $y = 8$ satisfies the equation, $x = 2$, $y = 6$ provides another solution etc. Depending on the significance of x and y, we are not necessarily restricted to integer values and so there are an infinite number of possible solutions. However, if we have a second equation that provides us with an alternative way of relating x and y, then we can employ the two equations 'simultaneously' and thereby determine a unique solution (recall from elementary maths that these are commonly referred to as 'simultaneous equations').

For example, consider the two simultaneous equations:

$$2x + y = 10$$
$$3x + 2y = 17$$

Here, we can use one equation to eliminate an 'unknown' from the other. For example, we know from the first equation that:

$$y = 10 - 2x.$$

We can now insert this into the second equation and so write:

$$3x + 2(10 - 2x) = 17.$$

From which it follows that $x = 3$. Inserting this into either of the above equations yields y: in this case $y = 4$. We often encounter situations in which we have more than two unknown quantities – for example, we may have three 'unknowns' whose values are related by three equations.

Indeed, in scientific problem solving and in engineering, we commonly face situations in which there are a large number of unknown quantities which are related by an equally large set of equations. Finding solutions by means of the algebraic approach used above rapidly becomes time consuming and tedious. Fortunately, we can employ matrices in solving such equations and the technique may be readily implemented in software. Below we briefly describe the use of matrices to solve the pair of simultaneous equations presented above and in Section 7.4.1 extend this discussion to determining three quantities by means of three equations.

We can re-write the pair of simultaneous equations using matrix notation:

$$\begin{bmatrix} 2 & 1 \\ 3 & 2 \end{bmatrix} \begin{bmatrix} x \\ y \end{bmatrix} = \begin{bmatrix} 10 \\ 17 \end{bmatrix}.$$

This can be easily verified – simply multiply the two left-hand matrices. If we denote the left most matrix as K, the central matrix as L and the right-hand matrix as M then we can represent this equation as:

$$K \cdot L = M.$$

If we now multiply through by the inverse of K (K^{-1}), we obtain:

$$L = K^{-1} \cdot M.$$

This is because when we multiply K by its inverse, we obtain the identity matrix (recall Section 2.5.3) and the multiplication of L by the identity matrix leaves L unchanged. To solve the simultaneous equations, we must simply determine the inverse matrix (K^{-1}) and multiply by M. In Section 2.5.3 we outlined the technique used to obtain the inverse matrix – in the case of the example that we are using, the determinant is unity and so the inverse of K is given by:

$$\begin{bmatrix} 2 & -1 \\ -3 & 2 \end{bmatrix}.$$

Thus:

$$\begin{bmatrix} x \\ y \end{bmatrix} = \begin{bmatrix} 2 & -1 \\ -3 & 2 \end{bmatrix} \begin{bmatrix} 10 \\ 17 \end{bmatrix} = \begin{bmatrix} 3 \\ 4 \end{bmatrix}.$$

This agrees with the result that we previously obtained. The key advantage to the matrix technique is that it is readily extensible to solving for a larger set of unknown quantities.

2.6 Concerning Curves

'Willingly would I burn to death like Phaeton,
were this the price for reaching the sun
and learning its shape, its size and its substance.'[14]

In this section we briefly turn our attention to curves and begin our discussion by considering the parabola. Subsequently we review the circle and ellipse. These are examples of conic sections (or simply 'conics') and in Section 2.6.3 we consider the so called rose curves and Archimedes' Spiral.

---

[14] Eudoxus of Cnidus.

OTU Exercise 2.15: Conic Sections

As their name implies, conic sections represent the family of the cross-sections of a cone. Draw a cone and indicate on your diagram a cross-section that is circular, one that is elliptical and one that is parabolic.

2.6.1 The Parabola

Consider the development of a simulator or game in which a pictorial representation is used to show the path followed by a projectile such as a heavy calibre shell fired from a gun or a cricket ball in flight. Discounting any secondary influences (e.g. air turbulence), such objects follow a 'parabolic' trajectory. A parabola may be defined as:

'... the set of points (x,y) that are equidistant from a fixed line (directrix) and a fixed point (focus) not on the line. The midpoint between the focus and the directrix is the vertex.' [Larson et al. 1998]

Consider a simple parabola given by the explicit Cartesian equation $y = x^2$. This curve is illustrated in Figure 2.22. The focus is located at (0,0.25) and the directrix is 0.25 units below the x-axis. Thus, if we consider an exemplar point on the curve (2,4), it is apparent that this point is 4.25 units above the directrix and its distance from the focus is $\sqrt{2^2 + 3.75^2} = 4.25$.

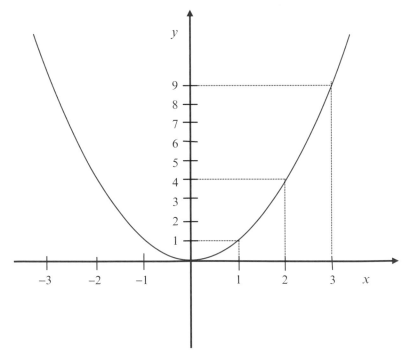

Figure 2.22 A parabola – each point on the curve lies at an equal distance from the focus and from the directrix. This parabola is symmetrical about a vertical axis. The vertex lies midway between the directrix and the focus. In the case of the parabola that is given by $y = x^2$, the focus is at (0,0.25).

The general equation for a parabola is of the form:

$$(x - h)^2 = 4p\,(y - k),\qquad(2.17)$$

where the vertex is located at (h, k) and p denotes the vertical distance of the focus from the vertex. The reader may be unfamiliar with this equation and if so, it is sufficient to note that a parabola is created when we graph an equation of the form:

$$y = ax^2 + bx + c,$$

where a, b and c are real numbers and $a \neq 0$. Recall from elementary maths that the right-hand side of this equation is a quadratic function.

Considering the parabola given by $y = x^2$, we can represent this by means of a vector equation. Using the parametric equations $x = u$ and so $y = u^2$, we can express the position of a point on the curve by the position vector $\mathbf{r}(u)$ as:

$$\mathbf{r}(u) = u\mathbf{i} + u^2\mathbf{j}.$$

Substituting values for u into this equation enables us to obtain a set of vectors which define points on the parabola.

Consider the case that a parabola is symmetrical about a horizontal axis (as opposed to the situation depicted in Figure 2.22 in which the parabola is symmetrical about a vertical axis). The general equation is:

$$(y - k)^2 = 4p\,(x - h).\qquad(2.18)$$

Again, (h, k) denotes the location of the vertex and the focus is p units from this point in a horizontal direction.

OTU Exercise 2.16: The Parabola

The explicit Cartesian equation for a parabola that is symmetrical about the x-axis, whose vertex lies on the origin and that has a focus at (0.25,0) is given by:

$$y^2 = x.\qquad(2.19)$$

Here, we assume that the parabola lies to the right of the y-axis (i.e. positive x). Obtain an expression for the position vector $\mathbf{r}(u)$ to points on this curve. By selecting suitable values for the parameter (u), draw vectors to points on the curve and so sketch its shape.

2.6.2 The Circle

A circle is defined as a locus (collection) of points that are equidistant from a fixed point. The general explicit Cartesian equation for a circle of radius R and which is centred on the point (a, b) is:

$$(x - a)^2 + (y - b)^2 = R^2.\qquad(2.20)$$

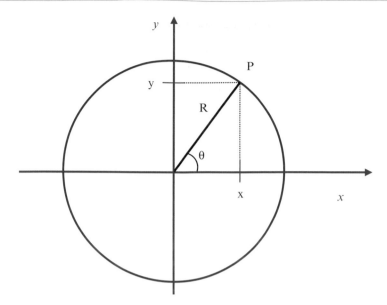

Figure 2.23 A circle of radius R that is centred on the origin. The point P with coordinates (x, y) lies on the circle as shown. As discussed in Section 2.2.2, such a point may be represented in polar coordinates. See text for discussion.

For example, consider a circle of radius 3 units and that is centred on the origin. The Cartesian equation for this circle would be:

$$x^2 + y^2 = 9. \tag{2.21}$$

We can represent a circle using a vector equation and, as we will see, this has certain advantages. Consider a circle of radius R and that for simplicity we assume is centred on the origin – see Figure 2.23. The angle between a line connecting a point P with coordinates (x, y) to the origin and the x-axis is denoted by θ.

From the illustration it is apparent that:

$$\cos\theta = \frac{x}{R}, \text{ and } \sin\theta = \frac{y}{R}.$$

Thus:

$$x = R\cos\theta, \text{ and } y = R\sin\theta.$$

We can use these two parametric equations to represent points on the circle by means of a position vector $\mathbf{r}(\theta)$. (Notice that here we express $\mathbf{r}$ as a function of the parameter θ (previously we have expressed $\mathbf{r}$ as a function of a parameter u)). Thus:

$$\mathbf{r}(\theta) = R((\cos\theta)\mathbf{i} + (\sin\theta)\mathbf{j}).$$

2.6.3 The Archimedes' Spiral and Rose Curves

It is instructive to briefly digress and consider the generation of the two curves that are commonly referred to as the 'Archimedes' spiral' and the 'Rose curve'. As its name suggests, the former takes the form of a line that spirals around a fixed point (in a manner akin to the track of a vinyl record or CD). Such a curve may be represented by the parametric equations:

$$x = k\theta\cos\theta$$

$$y = k\theta\sin\theta.$$

Here, k is a positive number that determines the size of the spiral and θ the angle relative to, for example, the x-axis. The spiral may also be represented by the equation:

$$r = b - \frac{a}{2\pi}\theta.$$

In this case, b and a respectively denote the outer and inner radii and h the track width. Thus $(b-a)/h$ represents the number of revolutions of the spiral (N). The angle θ is measured from a reference position and runs from $0°$ to $2N\pi$.

A Rose curve may be generated using parametric equations of the form:

$$x = k\cos(n\theta)\cos\theta$$

$$y = k\cos(n\theta)\sin\theta$$

OTU Exercise 2.18: Archimedes Spiral and the Rose Curve

Using graphing software, a graphing calculator or by manual calculation, generate an Archimedes spiral and also a Rose curve. The more adventurous reader may choose to write a simple graphics program that is able to do this!

2.6.4 The Ellipse

Consider a coffee cup. When we look directly down on the cup, the shape of its rim is correctly perceived as being circular. However if we now look at the cup from a more oblique location, the rim no longer appears to be circular but is elliptical (why?). In fact, when viewing our surroundings, we often look at circular objects from off-axis locations and are adept at judging (usually subconsciously) whether an object that has an elliptical outline is in fact elliptical in shape or rather corresponds to a distorted view of a circular object.

An ellipse that is centred on the origin is represented by the Cartesian equation:

$$\frac{x^2}{a^2} + \frac{y^2}{b^2} = 1. \tag{2.22}$$

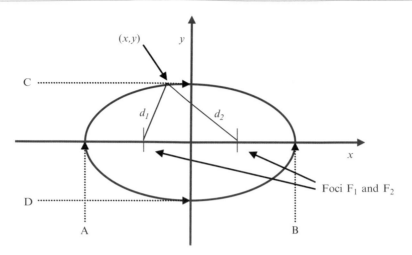

Figure 2.24 An ellipse centred on the origin. Consider a point (x,y) whose distance from F_1 is d_1 and from F_2 is d_2. Let $L = d_1 + d_2$. An ellipse comprises the set of points for which L is constant. An ellipse has a major axis (AB) and a minor axis (CD).

An ellipse is illustrated in Figure 2.24 and is defined as the locus of points the sum of whose individual distances from two fixed points (called foci) is constant. A line passing through the foci is said to intersect the ellipse at its two vertices (denoted as A and B in the illustration) and a line (cord) connecting these vertices is referred to as the major axis (the major axis denotes the greatest extent of the ellipse). The mid-point of this line is the centre of the ellipse and a cord that passes through this centre and that is perpendicular to the major axis is referred to as the minor axis.

The Cartesian equations for an ellipse with a centre at (h, k) and with major and minor axes of lengths $2a$ and $2b$ are given below:[15]

1. In the case that the major axis is horizontal:

$$\frac{(x - h)^2}{a^2} + \frac{(y - k)^2}{b^2} = 1. \tag{2.23}$$

2. In the case that the major axis is vertical:

$$\frac{(x - h)^2}{b^2} + \frac{(y - k)^2}{a^2} = 1. \tag{2.24}$$

The vector equation for an ellipse that is centred on the origin is given by:

$$\mathbf{r}(\theta) = (a \cos \theta)\mathbf{i} + (b \sin \theta)\mathbf{j}. \tag{2.25}$$

This indicates the use of the parametric equations:

$$x = a \cos \theta$$

$$y = b \sin \theta$$

---

[15] Larson *et al.* [1998].

Thus:

$$\cos\theta = \frac{x}{a}, \text{ and } \sin\theta = \frac{y}{b}.$$

We can obtain the Cartesian equation for an ellipse (as given in Eq. 2.22) by squaring and adding these two equations:[16]

$$\left(\frac{x}{a}\right)^2 + \left(\frac{y}{b}\right)^2 = \cos^2\theta + \sin^2\theta = 1$$

2.7 Forming a Parabola Using Three Points: de Casteljau Algorithm

In this section we briefly outline a simple technique that enables a parabola to be generated using three 'control points'. Before considering the underlying maths, it is instructive to manually construct a parabola using this technique. The approach is outlined in the following OTU Exercise.

OTU Exercise 2.19: Forming a Curve using Three Control Points

In Figure 2.25, we indicate three 'control' points that are labelled A, B and C. These are arbitrarily positioned. A line connects points A and B and a second line connects points B and C. In this example, we begin by marking the mid-points of lines AB and AC. We then draw a line between these two points (labelled *m* and *n* in the diagram) and mark the mid-point of this line.

We now mark a point on the lines AB and BC that lies at, say, one-quarter way along each line (these points are marked in the illustration). Connect these two points together with a line segment and mark a point that lies one quarter way along this line. Repeat this process for other fractional values. (For example, mark a point that lies three-quarters the way along AB and one that lies three-quarters along BC. Draw a line that connects these two points together and mark a point that lies three-quarters the way along this line.)

Finally, draw a curve that connects the points that you have indicated on the various line segments that you have drawn (this curve should also pass through points A and C).

Recall that in Section 2.3.1 we considered an arbitrary point on a line segment (see Figure 2.5) and expressed the location of this point by means of two parametric equations (see Eq.'s 2.4 and 2.5). Here, the parameter t denotes the fractional distance of the point along the line segment. With reference to Figure 2.26, we can easily write an equivalent vector equation that defines the location ($\mathbf{p}(t)$) of any point P on the line segment:

$$\mathbf{p}(t) = (1-t)\,\mathbf{p}_0 + t\mathbf{p}_1. \tag{2.26}$$

Consider now the three points indicated in Figure 2.27 and that are located in a 2-D space. We will assume that the location of the points are respectively given by the vectors $\mathbf{p}_A$, $\mathbf{p}_B$ and $\mathbf{p}_C$.

---

[16] Here we use: $\cos^2\theta + \sin^2\theta = 1$.

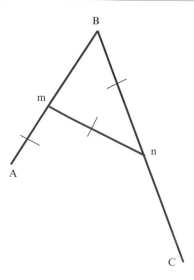

Figure 2.25 Constructing a curve using three control points (A, B and C). See text for discussion.

From Eq. 2.26, we can express the location of a point on the line AB as:

$$\mathbf{p}_A^B(t) = (1 - t)\,\mathbf{p_A} + t\mathbf{p_B}. \tag{2.27}$$

Similarly, the location of a point on the line connecting B and C may be expressed as:

$$\mathbf{p}_B^C(t) = (1 - t)\,\mathbf{p_B} + t\mathbf{p_C}. \tag{2.28}$$

If, as in Figure 2.25, we now connect these two points by a line segment, then a point (q) lying the same fractional distance along this new line segment will be at a position ($\mathbf{q}(t)$) given by:

$$\mathbf{q}(t) = (1 - t)\,\mathbf{p}_A^B + t\mathbf{p}_B^C. \tag{2.29}$$

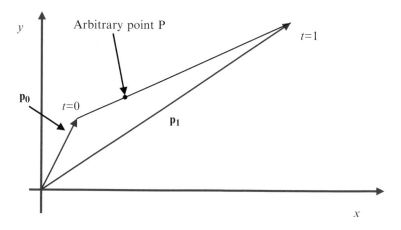

Figure 2.26 An arbitrary point P lies on the line segment illustrated. The location of this point can conveniently be expressed as a vector equation – see Eq. 2.26. When $t = 0$, this equation places the point at one end of the line segment and when $t = 1$, at the other end.

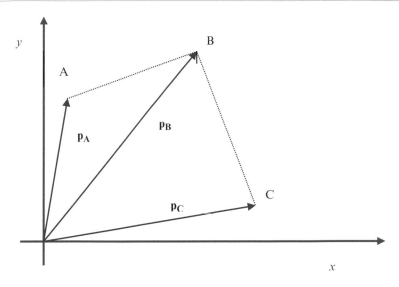

Figure 2.27 The location of the three points A, B, and C are defined respectively by the vectors $\mathbf{p_A}$, $\mathbf{p_B}$ and $\mathbf{p_C}$. See text for discussion.

To obtain a vector equation that shows how the point q moves as we vary the parameter t, we simply substitute Eq.'s 2.27 and 2.28 into Eq. 2.29 for $\mathbf{p_A^B}$ and $\mathbf{p_B^C}$. This gives:

$$\mathbf{q}(t) = (1 - t)\left((1 - t)\,\mathbf{p_A} + t\mathbf{p_B}\right) + t\left((1 - t)\,\mathbf{p_B} + t\mathbf{p_C}\right) = (1 - t)^2\,\mathbf{p_A} + 2t\,(1 - t)\,\mathbf{p_B} + t^2\mathbf{p_C}.$$

This is a quadratic equation in t and hence corresponds to a parabolic curve. The approach is generally referred to as the de Casteljau algorithm. Certainly the use of control points provides a convenient technique for the creation of curves and also for their manipulation – a key issue in interactive design – simply changing the location of a control point changes the shape of the curve. Unfortunately, curves generated using three control points are of little practical value in creative design – however this technique is interesting because it provides a simple introduction to curve formation by means of control points. In Chapter 4 we consider alternative approaches which extend this discussion.

2.8 Discussion

> *'In times of change, the learner will inherit the earth*
> *while the learned are beautifully equipped*
> *for a world that no longer exists.'*[17]

A broad range of mathematical tools and techniques underpin the development of computer graphics applications. In this chapter we have laid various foundations and in subsequent sections we will build on this material to provide a stronger basis for working within the graphical world. In the next chapter we turn our attention to techniques used in the formation of 2-D images and particularly demonstrate the application of both vectors and matrices.

---

[17] Attributed to Eric Hoffer (1902–1983).

2.9 Review Questions

The questions that follow are intended to provide the opportunity to revise the material covered in this chapter. Some questions relate to content directly covered in this chapter – others require the application of material to slightly new situations.

2.9.1 Coordinate Systems

1. Express the Cartesian coordinates (1,2) in polar form.
2. Express the Homogeneous coordinates [2, 6, 2] as rectangular Cartesian coordinates.
3. Express the polar coordinates (5, 60°) as rectangular Cartesian coordinates.

2.9.2 The Line

1. Consider the line given by $y = 4x + 3$. State the gradient (slope) and the coordinates of the y intercept.
2. Give an example of an 'explicit' equation and also of an 'implicit' equation.
3. Express the equation stated in (1) above in parametric form.
4. State the gradient of the line which is perpendicular to $y = 5x - 6$.
5. A line passes through the points (2,3) and (4,6). Determine the Cartesian equation for this line.
6. Determine the coordinates of the point at which the line $y = 3x + 6$ crosses the x-axis.

2.9.3 Vectors

1. Find the magnitude of the vector $4\mathbf{i} + 6\mathbf{j}$.
2. Find the angle between the vectors $2\mathbf{i} + 3\mathbf{j}$ and $\mathbf{i} + 4\mathbf{j}$.
3. Consider a line that passes through the points (1,2) and (5,6). Represent this line using a vector equation.
4. What is the scalar product of two orthogonal vectors?

2.9.4 Matrices

1. The matrices A and B are given by:

$$A = \begin{bmatrix} 1 & 3 \\ 4 & 2 \end{bmatrix}, \text{ and } B = \begin{bmatrix} 2 & 1 \\ 1 & 0 \end{bmatrix}.$$

   Determine: $A + B$, $A - B$ and AB.
2. State the identity matrix for multiplication of (a) a 2 by 2 matrix (b) a 3 by 3 matrix.
3. The matrix A is given by:

$$A = \begin{bmatrix} 1 & 3 \\ 4 & 2 \end{bmatrix}.$$

   Find det A.
4. Multiply the row vector [3 2] by the matrix A (as given in Question 3).

2.9.5 Curves

1. A parabola has a Cartesian equation $y = 2x^2 + 1$. Express this in parametric form.
2. State the Cartesian equation for a circle that is centred on the origin and that has a radius of 9 units.
3. Find the coordinates of the points at which the parabola $y = 2x^2 - 3$ crosses the x-axis.
4. Find the coordinates of the points at which the line $y = x + 2$ intersects with the parabola $y = x^2$.

2.10 Feedback to Review Questions

2.10.1 Coordinate Systems

1. Magnitude$= \sqrt{1^2 + 2^2} = \sqrt{5}$. The angle relative to the x-axis is given by $\theta = \arctan\left(\frac{2}{1}\right) \approx 63°$. Thus the point may be represented as $(\sqrt{5}, \ 63°)$.
2. Here, the scale factor (homogeneous coordinate) is 2. Thus the Cartesian coordinates are $(2/2, 6/2) = (1,3)$.
3. Using Figure 2.28, $\cos 60° = \frac{x}{5}$. Thus $x = 2.5$ units. Also, $\sin 60° = \frac{y}{5}$, and so $y \sim 4.3$ units. Thus the Cartesian coordinates are $(2.5, 4.3)$.

2.10.2 The Line

1. Compare the equation with Eq. 2.2. The gradient$= 4$ and the y intercept is 3.
2. An explicit equation is one in which, for example y is expressed in terms of x (e.g. Eq. 2.2). An example of an implicit equation is $y + x - 3 = 0$.
3. $x = u/4, \ y = u + 3$.
4. In the case of two orthogonal lines, the product of their gradients is equal to -1. The line given has a gradient of 5, consequently the orthogonal line must have a gradient of $-1/5$.

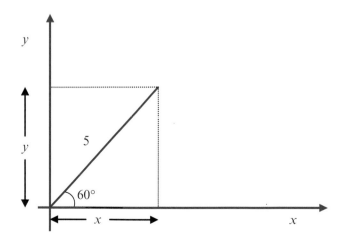

Figure 2.28 See Feedback to Review Question 2.10.1(3).

5. Substituting these two pairs of coordinates into Eq. 2.2 we obtain:

$$3 = 2m + c \text{ and } 6 = 4m + c.$$

Solving for m and c, we obtain $m = 3/2$ and $c = 0$. Thus the Cartesian equation is:

$$y = \frac{3}{2}x.$$

6. At the point at which a line crosses the x-axis, $y = 0$. Substituting this into the Cartesian equation, we obtain $x = -2$. Thus the line crosses the x-axis at $(-2, 0)$.

2.10.3 Vectors

1. Magnitude= $\sqrt{4^2 + 6^2} = \sqrt{52} \approx 7.2$.
2. Here, we use the scalar product. Firstly calculate the magnitude of each vector. We obtain magnitudes of $\sqrt{13} \approx 3.6$ and $\sqrt{17} \approx 4.1$. Using Eq. 2.9:

$$2 \times 1 + 3 \times 4 = 3.6 \times 4.1 \times \cos\theta.$$

Thus:

$$\theta \approx \cos^{-1}\left(\frac{14}{14.76}\right) \approx 18°.$$

3. These two points may be represented by the vectors $\mathbf{i} + 2\mathbf{j}$ and $5\mathbf{i} + 6\mathbf{j}$. We can now use Eq. 2.12 such that:

$$\mathbf{r}(u) = (\mathbf{i} + 2\mathbf{j}) + u((5\mathbf{i} + 6\mathbf{j}) - (\mathbf{i} + 2\mathbf{j})).$$

Thus:

$$\mathbf{r}(u) = (1 + 4u)\mathbf{i} + (2 + 4u)\mathbf{j}.$$

4. The scalar product of two orthogonal vectors is zero.

2.10.4 Matrices

1. $A + B = \begin{bmatrix} 3 & 4 \\ 5 & 2 \end{bmatrix}$, $A - B = \begin{bmatrix} -1 & 2 \\ 3 & 2 \end{bmatrix}$, $AB = \begin{bmatrix} 5 & 1 \\ 10 & 4 \end{bmatrix}$.
2. For a 2 by 2 matrix: $\begin{bmatrix} 1 & 0 \\ 0 & 1 \end{bmatrix}$. For a 3 by 3 matrix: $\begin{bmatrix} 1 & 0 & 0 \\ 0 & 1 & 0 \\ 0 & 0 & 1 \end{bmatrix}$.
3. Det A $= ad - bc = -10$.
4. As follows:

$$\begin{bmatrix} 3 & 2 \end{bmatrix} \begin{bmatrix} 1 & 3 \\ 4 & 2 \end{bmatrix} = \begin{bmatrix} 11 & 13 \end{bmatrix}.$$

2.10.5 Curves

1. Use, for example, $2x^2 = u$ and $y = u + 1$.
2. Equation of the circle is given by:

$$x^2 + y^2 = 81.$$

3. At the point(s) at which the parabola crosses the x-axis, $y = 0$. Thus:

$$0 = 2x^2 - 3.$$

Hence $x \approx \pm 1.2$. The coordinates of the point of intersection are $(1.2,0)$ and $(-1.2,0)$.

4. At the points of intersection both equations have the same x and y values. Thus we can equate the equations and so: $x^2 = x + 2$. Rearranging and factorising, gives: $(x - 2)(x + 1) = 0$. Thus $x = 2$ or $x = -1$. Substituting these values into either of the original Cartesian equations enables us to determine the y values. Thus when $x = 2$, $y = 4$ and when $x = -1$, $y = 1$. The coordinates of the points of intersection are: $(2,4)$ and $(-1,1)$.

Images in a 2-D Space 3

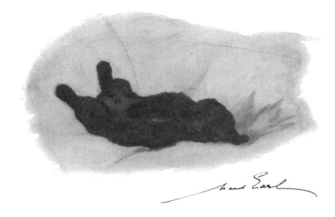

*'Keeping me too warm down my back,
and waking me now and then with
quaint sleepy whimperings.'*

3.1 Introduction

Having briefly reviewed some key mathematics, we now turn our attention to issues that arise when we create and manipulate 2-D images. As with other chapters in this book, we place particular emphasis on basic principles and lay important foundations on which the reader will be able to build. We begin by making some general remarks in relation to the formation of 2-D images and introduce the concepts of a 'viewport' and screen addressing. Subsequently, in Sections 3.3 and 3.4 we describe the use of 2 by 2 matrices for the manipulation of image components. Here, we demonstrate that we can encapsulate multiple transformations within a single matrix operator. In Section 3.5 we consider the application of Homogeneous transformations but as with other sections in the chapter confine our discussion to their use in a 2-D space.

In Section 3.6 we make some introductory remarks in relation to 'graph theory' in which representations take the form of a set of nodes connected by edges. Within this context we discuss two simple ways in which we can identify the location of a point relative to an object's boundary. The remainder of the chapter focuses on the process of clipping – particularly the clipping of line segments and polygons relative to a rectangular window or clipping boundary. We introduce several clipping algorithms: the Cohen-Sutherland and Liang-Barsky Algorithms which enable a collection of line segments to be individually clipped together with the Sutherland-Hodgman algorithm that enables both concave and convex polygons to be clipped against a convex clipping boundary.

Key Learning Outcomes: At the end of this chapter you should be able to:

- *Understand the nature of a viewport and basic issues relating to screen addressing.*

- *Employ and understand the limitations of using 2 by 2 matrices for effecting transformations.*

- *Employ homogeneous matrices for effecting transformations.*

- *Encapsulate several transformations within a single matrix.*

- *Determine the location of a point relative to an object's boundary.*

- *Understand several techniques that can be employed in the clipping of line segments and polygons.*

3.2 Some Basic Considerations

'It is not the result of scientific research that ennobles humans and enriches their nature, but the struggle to understand while performing creative and open-minded intellectual work.'[1]

In computer graphics a view of a 2-D scene may be constructed using image primitives such as lines, curves, rectangles, circles and the like. These may be amalgamated with other content such as the output from some form of medical scanner, digitised images or data that is generated by some computational process (e.g. the results of a simulation). Consequently, we commonly encounter situations in which image primitives and point form data coexist within the image scene that we wish to display. Naturally, the use of high-level primitives is advantageous as they may be efficiently and readily manipulated. For example, to change the size of a circle we simply define a new radius whereas if the circle were specified in terms of a set of discrete points then a change in radius would require computational operations to be carried out on each and every point. As discussed in Chapter 1, the computer display supports a rectangular 2-D array of picture elements (pixels) each of which can be individually addressed. Therefore, before an image can be depicted it is necessary to decompose it into point form data – each data element being mapped to an appropriate pixel. However, because of the efficiency with which we are able to manipulate higher-level image primitives, it is desirable that image decomposition into a point form representation is deferred as long as possible.

---

[1] Attributed to Albert Einstein (1879–1955).

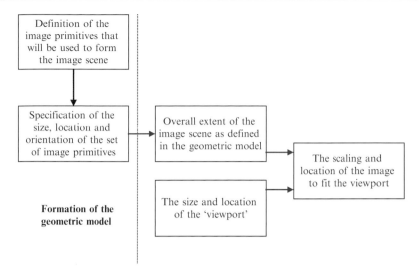

Figure 3.1 Key issues that may arise in the formation of a simple 2-D image that comprises a set of high-level graphics primitives.

In constructing an image scene, we must define the size and location of image primitives. Moreover, we need to consider changes that are to occur in the scene with time (so supporting animation) and the way in which the scene is to react to interactive operations. In terms of animation we may, for example wish to depict a bouncing ball. Here, a circle could be used to depict the ball, a line to depict the ground and equations of motion used to compute the location of the circle over time.

In Figure 3.1 we summarise several key tasks that must in some way be dealt with during the creation of a computer graphics scene. These are briefly discussed in the following subsections.

3.2.1 Model Formation

Languages used for the creation of computer graphics images provide primitives that may be used to specify components within an image scene. Thus, for example, if we wish to draw a circle, it is not necessary to become involved in the algorithm needed to accomplish this goal – we can simply specify that we wish to create a circle with a certain radius at a particular location. Additionally, we can indicate that the circle is to be filled (thereby forming a 'solid' circle of a certain colour or containing a certain pattern) – or otherwise. As indicated above, using primitives that enable us to specify image components at a high level greatly facilitates the creation of image scenes.

3.2.2 The Extent of the Image scene and its Relation to the Viewport

Typically, we define the image scene within a 2-D Cartesian space. The location and orientation of points and objects within this space are defined numerically and here, we are able to use both integer and non-integer values. Additionally, we must define a 'viewport' – this being the region of the display screen into which we are to map the image.

In the simplest case, we may choose to allow the whole image scene to exclusively occupy the entire screen. Alternatively, we may wish to limit the extent of the viewport to part of the display

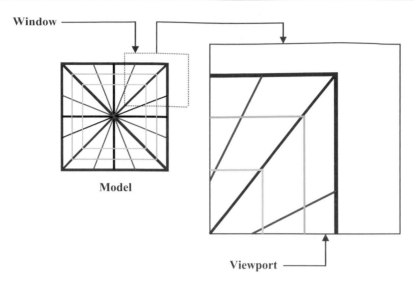

Figure 3.2 The relation between the model, the window onto this model and the screen viewport.

screen (for example, the viewport may be restricted to a portion of a 'window') or depict only a portion of the geometric model within the viewport. Additionally, it is important to remember that interaction is a vital ingredient in modern computer graphics and we frequently encounter situations in which we wish to carry out interactive operations such as 'pan' and 'zoom'. This necessitates adjusting both the location of the viewport relative to the Cartesian space via which we have defined a scene and the extent of this space that is depicted within the viewport.

In Figure 3.2, we provide a simple illustration showing the positioning of the viewport relative to the overall model. On the left-hand side of this illustration we show a simple line drawing that represents the image defined by the geometric model and specify a 'window' which indicates the portion of the modelled image that we wish to display. This content is then mapped to the viewport and depicted on the screen. Naturally, mapping all or part of the model to the viewport will require scaling and here the choice of scaling factors used in both the horizontal and vertical directions should ensure that unwanted image distortion is avoided.

Let us assume that the 2-D space in which the image is located is described by a rectangular Cartesian coordinate system – with a horizontal axis (labelled x) and vertical axis (labelled y) – as indicated in Figure 3.3(a). By convention, the location of pixels on the display screen is defined in terms of their horizontal and vertical distances *from the screen's top left-hand corner*. Thus if we assume that the screen comprises an array of m pixels horizontally and n pixels vertically (i.e. a total of mn pixels), then the top left most pixel would be indexed as (0,0) and the bottom right hand pixel as $(m - 1, n - 1)$ – see Figure 3.3(b). More generally, we can index any screen pixel as (p_h, p_v) where $0 \leq p_h \leq m - 1$ and $0 \leq p_v \leq n - 1$. Here, it is important to note that in defining the location of points and components that are contained in the image scene, we can (and usually do) employ non-integer coordinates. However, the actual values of p_h and p_v which are used to index (address) individual pixels are positive integers.

It is instructive to consider a simple example in which we take an image component (in this case our model will be a square constructed from four line segments) and map this into a viewport – which, for the sake of simplicity will be assumed to occupy the full extent of the computer screen. In Figure 3.4(a), we assign some arbitrary Cartesian coordinates to the

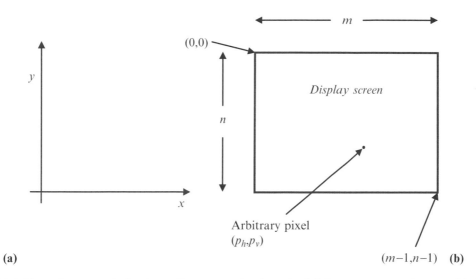

(a)   **(b)**

Figure 3.3 In (a) we assign a rectangular Cartesian coordinate system to the 2-D space in which the image is represented. In terms of the display screen, pixels are traditionally indexed from their location relative to the top left hand corner This is indicated in (b). Here, the top left most pixel is denoted as (0,0) and the bottom right most pixel as $(m - 1, n - 1)$. An arbitrary pixel is indexed as (p_h, p_v) – where p_h and p_v are measured from the upper left hand side of the screen. Note that whereas the points and components that represent the 2-D image scene may be assigned non-integer coordinates, the values of p_h and p_v are positive integers

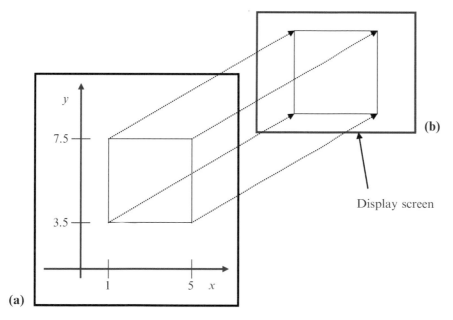

Figure 3.4 In (a) we depict a square comprising four line segments – this represents a simple model that is to be displayed. We assume that the viewport corresponds to the entire screen and that we wish to display the square so that it is located centrally and that its horizontal extent is 50% of the screen width. See text for discussion.

endpoints of the four line segments that form a square. Let us suppose that we wish this square to be depicted centrally on the display screen (Figure 3.4(b)) and to occupy 50% of the screen width. Furthermore, we will assume that the display comprises an array of 1024 pixels in the horizontal direction and 768 pixels vertically.

(a)　In this simple example, we require the square to be depicted centrally on the screen – and its horizontal extent is to occupy 50% of the screen width. Thus the left and right-hand sides of the square should be drawn one-quarter and three-quarters of the way across the screen respectively. This corresponds to one quarter of 1024 (=256) and three-quarters of 1024 (=768). Since we have assumed that the first (left-hand) column of pixels has a horiziontal address of zero (rather than one), it follows that in order to correctly specify the horizontal address, we must subtract one from both of these numbers – giving 255 and 767.

(b)　Horizontal pixel addresses (p_h) are related to the x coordinates of the model by a linear relationship in which we employ a scaling factor (S) and position shift (offset) (p):

$$P_h = Sx + p.$$

(c)　We know that the x coordinates of the model (which are 1 and 5) respectively map to pixel columns 255 and 767. By inserting these pairs of values into the above equation we can form simultaneous equations and so determine S and p:

$$255 = S + p$$
$$767 = 5S + p$$

Thus $S = 128$ and $p = 127$, and we can now write down an equation that will map any other x coordinates associated with the model into the appropriate pixel columns:

$$P_h = 128x + 127.$$

(d)　For simplicity, we assume that the application of the same scaling factor in the vertical and horizontal directions will result in the depiction of a square rather than a rectangle. In this case we can write an expression that relates y coordinates in the model to the pixel row addresses:

$$P_v = -128y + p'.$$

Notice the inclusion of a negative sign – this takes into account that screen coordinates increase with their position relative to the top, rather than the bottom, of the screen.

(e)　Our original brief was to depict the model so that it lies in the centre of the screen – consequently, it follows that the average y coordinate (given by $y_{max} + y_{min}$ divided by two (which equals 5.5)) should be placed in pixel row 383 (remember that the pixels must be referenced by integer values). Hence we can write:

$$383 = -704 + p',$$

where 704 is the product of 128 and 5.5. Thus p′ equals 1087 and so:

$$P_v = -128y + 1087.$$

(f)　In summary we have established that:

$$P_h = 128x + 127 \text{ and } P_v = -128y + 1087.$$

We could now use these equations to map any other points comprising the model into pixel addresses. However, as mentioned above, all pixel addresses are integer values and this results in the approximation of ideal point locations to the closest physical pixel position. For further related discussion see Section 8.5.

A developer may choose not to directly map the image coordinates to pixel locations but may employ an intermediate stage. In this case 'normalised device coordinates' (NDC) may be specified. Here, as the name implies, image coordinates are mapped into a normalised system comprising a square with sides of unit length. Thus the minimum coordinates are (0,0) and the maximum (1,1). This coordinate system provides a simple standard to which manufacturers can readily interface their hardware and software systems.

3.3 Transformations Using 2 by 2 Matrices

> 'I detest the man who hides one thing in the depths of his heart
> and speaks forth another.'[2]

Motion is often a vital aspect of an image scene. It may be an inherent attribute (e.g. the depiction of a ball bounding) or may arise in response to user input (e.g. in the case of a flight simulator, video game or creative design exercise). Consequently, the designer must not only focus on issues such as the form and placement of objects that comprise the scene but also on the ways in which these objects interact and may be manipulated. This demands the regular use of techniques that allow objects to be efficiently re-sized and relocated. In this section, we consider the application of 2 by 2 matrices for effecting object scaling, object rotation and object reflection about some axis. Additionally, we examine the issue of object relocation. This leads on (in Section 3.4) to discussion concerning combining such 'transformations'. As with other sections of this chapter, we confine ourselves to objects within a 2-D space – see Chapter 6 for related discussion concerning objects that are defined within three spatial dimensions.

3.3.1 Scaling an Image Component

In Section 2.4.7 we indicated that the magnitude of a vector may be changed by multiplying its vertical and horizontal components by an appropriate value. For example, to increase the magnitude of the vector $2\mathbf{i} + 3\mathbf{j}$ by a factor of four, we simply calculate $4(2\mathbf{i} + 3\mathbf{j}) = 8\mathbf{i} + 12\mathbf{j}$. Since both components are multiplied by the same value, only the vector magnitude has been changed – there is no alteration in vector direction. As we noted in Section 2.5.5, matrices can be used to manipulate vectors and this includes scaling. In the case that position vectors are used to define the vertices of an object (e.g. a triangle or rectangle), then matrices can be used to change the magnitude of these vectors and so enlarge or reduce the extent of the shape.

By way of a simple example, consider the vector $\mathbf{a} = 2\mathbf{i} + 3\mathbf{j}$ and let us suppose that we want to increase the vector's magnitude by a factor of four. This may be accomplished as follows:

$$\begin{bmatrix} 2 & 3 \end{bmatrix} \begin{bmatrix} 4 & 0 \\ 0 & 4 \end{bmatrix} = \begin{bmatrix} 8 & 12 \end{bmatrix}.$$

---

[2] Attributed to Homer ($\sim$800–850 BC).

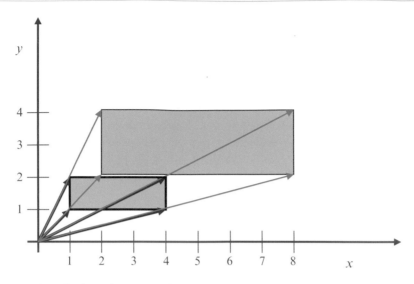

Figure 3.5 Here, we apply a scaling factor of two to the smaller rectangle and so achieve enlargement. Note that this also results in a change in location.

Here, we have expressed **a** as a row vector and the scaling factor is encapsulated in the top left and bottom right elements of the 2 by 2 matrix. Now consider the smaller of the two rectangles illustrated in Figure 3.5. and let us suppose that we wish to apply a scaling factor of 2. We simply, operate on the position vectors that define the location of each vertex using the matrix $\begin{bmatrix} 2 & 0 \\ 0 & 2 \end{bmatrix}$

OTU Exercise 3.1: Scaling the Dimensions of a Shape

Determine the effect of applying the scaling matrix $\begin{bmatrix} 2 & 0 \\ 0 & 3 \end{bmatrix}$ to the rectangle depicted in Figure 3.5.

3.3.2 Object Rotation

Consider the position vector **a** indicated in Figure 3.6 that lies at an angle ϕ with respect to the x-axis. We will assume that this vector is given by $\mathbf{a} = x\mathbf{i} + y\mathbf{j}$. Suppose that we now operate on this vector so as to produce a second vector **b** which has the same magnitude as **a** but is rotated by an angle θ (where, as usual, θ is measured in an anti-clockwise direction). This vector is also illustrated in Figure 3.5 and we will assume that it is given by $\mathbf{b} = x'\mathbf{i} + y'\mathbf{j}$. We can write:

$$x = |\mathbf{a}| \cos \phi \tag{3.1}$$

$$x' = |\mathbf{a}| \cos (\theta + \phi) = |\mathbf{a}| [\cos \theta \cos \phi - \sin \theta \sin \phi] \tag{3.2}$$

$$y = |\mathbf{a}| \cos (90 - \phi) = |\mathbf{a}| \sin \phi \tag{3.3}$$

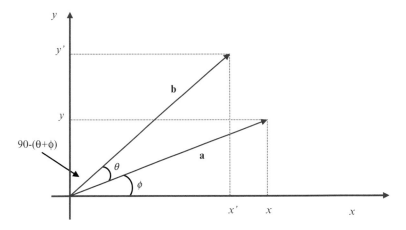

Figure 3.6 The rotation of a vector about the origin. See text for discussion.

$$y' = |\mathbf{a}| \cos\left(90 - (\theta + \phi)\right) = |\mathbf{a}| \sin\left(\theta + \phi\right) = |\mathbf{a}| \left[\sin\theta \cos\phi + \cos\theta \sin\phi\right]. \qquad (3.4)$$

Here, we are making use of the so-called 'sum and difference' formulas (i.e. for $\sin(\theta + \phi)$, $\cos(\theta + \phi)$, $\cos(90° - \theta)$ and $\cos(90° - (\theta + \phi)))$ – see Appendix A for a summary of these equations. In addition, we know that $|\mathbf{a}| = |\mathbf{b}|$ – the vectors differ only in their orientation. Through the use of Eqs. 3.1 and 3.3, we can now eliminate ϕ from Eqs. 3.2 and 3.4. Therefore, we can write the following simultaneous equations:

$$x \cos\theta - y \sin\theta = x'$$
$$x \sin\theta + y \cos\theta = y'$$

We can express these in matrix form:

$$\begin{bmatrix} x & y \end{bmatrix} \begin{bmatrix} \cos\theta & \sin\theta \\ -\sin\theta & \cos\theta \end{bmatrix} = \begin{bmatrix} x' & y' \end{bmatrix}. \qquad (3.5)$$

By way of an example, suppose that we wish to rotate the vector a = 3**i** + 2**j** through an angle of 30° thereby giving a vector **b**. Then:

$$\begin{bmatrix} 3 & 2 \end{bmatrix} \begin{bmatrix} \cos 30 & \sin 30 \\ -\sin 30 & \cos 30 \end{bmatrix} = \mathbf{b}.$$

Thus

$$\begin{bmatrix} 3 & 2 \end{bmatrix} \begin{bmatrix} 0.87 & 0.5 \\ -0.5 & 0.87 \end{bmatrix} = \mathbf{b}.$$

And so the vector **b** is approximately equal to 1.6**i** + 3.2**j**.

OTU Exercise 3.2: Rotation About the Origin

1. Write down the 2 by 2 matrix that will give a 90° rotation of a vector about the origin. You should assume that the angle is measured in an anti-clockwise direction.
2. Write down the 2 by 2 matrix that will give a 180° rotation of a vector about the origin.

3.3.3 Object Reflection

In Figure 3.7 we illustrate a vector labelled **a** together with its reflection in the x-axis – this is denoted as vector **b**. Vector **c** represents the reflection of vector **a** in the y-axis. Additionally, we depict vector **d** that corresponds to the reflection of vector **a** in both the x and y-axis.

Consider the case that vector **a** is reflected in the x-axis. This causes no change to the vector's horizontal component – the vertical component simply changes in sign. For example, if vector **a** = 3**i** + 2**j**, then vector **b** would be given by **b** = 3**i** − 2**j**. Similarly, if the vector **a** is reflected in the y-axis, then the sign of the vector's horizontal component would change – and the vertical component would not be effected (vector **c** being given by **c** = −3**i** + 2**j**). Finally, if vector **a** is 'simultaneously' reflected in both axes, then the signs of both the horizontal and vertical components are changed (giving **d** = −3**i** − 2**j**). These reflections can be achieved using a 2 by 2 matrix such that:

$$[x \ \ y] \begin{bmatrix} +1 \ or \ -1 & 0 \\ 0 & +1 \ or \ -1 \end{bmatrix} = [x' \ \ y']. \tag{3.6}$$

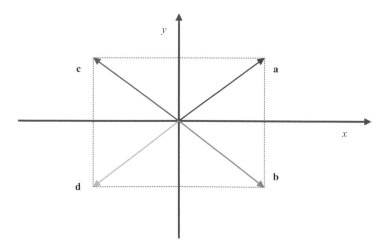

Figure 3.7 Here, we depict the reflection of vector **a** in the x-axis (giving vector **b**), in the y-axis (giving vector **c**) and its 'simultaneous' reflection in both the x and y-axes (vector **d**).

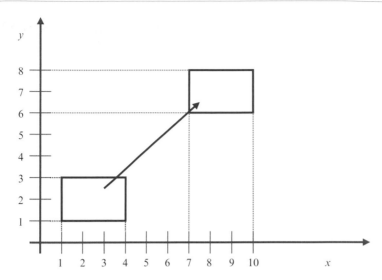

Figure 3.8 Here the lower rectangle is shifted (a translation operation) six units horizontally and five units vertically. This type of operation cannot be achieved through multiplication with a 2 by 2 matrix operator.

For example, in the case that the vector $4\mathbf{i} + 3\mathbf{j}$ is reflected in the y-axis, the resulting vector would be given by:

$$[4 \ \ 3]\begin{bmatrix} -1 & 0 \\ 0 & 1 \end{bmatrix} = [-4 \ \ 3].$$

3.3.4 Object Translation

The location of a point defined by a vector can be readily shifted using vector addition. For example, consider the rectangle depicted in Figure 3.8. Suppose that we wish to relocate this shape by 6 units in the horizontal direction and 5 units vertically. We simply add [6 5] to the vectors that define the locations of the vertices. Unfortunately, we cannot achieve object translation using a 2 by 2 matrix multiplication operation. This causes difficulty when we seek to combine transformations.

3.4 Combined Transformations Using 2 by 2 Matrices

We frequently encounter situations in which we wish to 'simultaneously' perform more than a single transformation on a point or object. The implementation of transformations by means of matrix multiplication operations enables multiple transformations to be encapsulated within a single matrix operator and this increases efficiency. However, as we indicated above, translation cannot be accomplished though multiplication with a 2 by 2 matrix operator and so for the present we will put translation to one side and focus on scaling, rotation and reflection operations.

When we apply two or more dissimilar transformations (e.g. a reflection and a rotation operation), the order in which they are applied usually determines the result that is obtained.

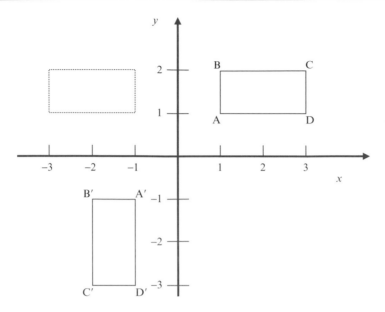

Figure 3.9 Here, we reflect the rectangle ABCD in the y-axis and then apply a rotation through 90° about the origin. This rotation is in the anticlockwise direction.

By way of an example, consider the rectangle ABCD depicted in Figure 3.9 where we illustrate the effect of first reflecting this rectangle in the y-axis and subsequently performing an anti-clockwise rotation through 90° about the origin.

OTU Exercise 3.3: Order of Transformation Application

Re-draw Figure 3.9 so as to show the effect of first rotating the rectangle through 90° about the origin and then reflecting this rectangle in the y-axis (i.e. reverse the order in which the transformations are applied). Does this impact on the final result?

As may be seen by comparing Figure 3.9 with the result obtained in the above OTU Exercise, changing the order in which the two dissimilar transformations are applied leads to different results.[3] We can combine transformations within a single matrix operator and so in effect 'simultaneously' apply more than one transformation. This is a point that can cause confusion and the issue is summarised in Figure 3.10. Here, we indicate that when forming a matrix able to apply two or more dissimilar transformations (such as reflection and rotation), we embed within the matrix a transformation order (even though the transformations will be carried out via a single matrix operation). Thus, the matrix operator is created so that it achieves the overall transformation that we would associate with carrying out first one of the transformations, and then the other.

By way of example, let's consider the creation of a matrix operator that achieves a reflection in the y-axis followed by a rotation of 90° about the origin (i.e. we follow the order used in

---

[3] In short – the multiplication of matrices is not commutative.

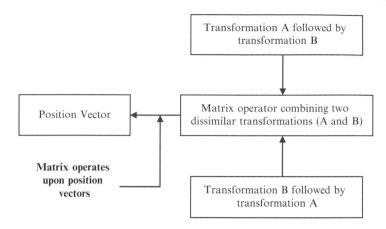

Figure 3.10 Several transformations may be carried out by a single matrix operator. In this way transformations may be accomplished 'simultaneously'. However, in defining the elements within the operator we must encapsulate the overall result that we wish to obtain – i.e. the result of applying transformation A followed by transformation B or *vice versa*.

Figure 3.9). From Section 3.3.3, we know that the 2 by 2 operator able to achieve reflection in the y-axis is given by:

$$\begin{bmatrix} -1 & 0 \\ 0 & 1 \end{bmatrix}.$$

Further, using Eq. 3.5, a rotation through $90°$ about the origin can be achieved with the 2 by 2 matrix:

$$\begin{bmatrix} 0 & 1 \\ -1 & 0 \end{bmatrix}.$$

We now combine these matrices (by multiplication) – placing the first operation before the second. In this case we wish to achieve the result of a reflection followed by a rotation and so the reflection matrix comes first:

$$\begin{bmatrix} -1 & 0 \\ 0 & 1 \end{bmatrix}\begin{bmatrix} 0 & 1 \\ -1 & 0 \end{bmatrix} = \begin{bmatrix} 0 & -1 \\ -1 & 0 \end{bmatrix}. \tag{3.7}$$

If we now apply this matrix to the four position vectors defining the vertices of rectangle ABCD illustrated in Figure 3.9, it is apparent that we obtain rectangle A′B′C′D′.

OTU Exercise 3.4: Combining Transformations

Obtain a single 2 by 2 matrix operator that will give the overall result of firstly a rotation through $90°$ followed by a reflection in the y-axis. Verify your answer by applying the operator to the position vectors that define the vertices of rectangle ABCD illustrated in Figure 3.9 and demonstrate that you obtain the same result as given in your response to OTU Exercise 3.3.

3.4.1 Combining Three or More Transformations

Suppose that we wish to obtain a 2 by 2 matrix operator able to achieve the overall result of firstly a rotation through an angle θ about the origin, followed by a reflection in the y-axis and finally a further rotation by an angle ϕ (again about the origin). Drawing on Eq.'s 3.5 and 3.6 we would determine the operator by the following multiplication:

$$\begin{bmatrix} \cos\theta & \sin\theta \\ -\sin\theta & \cos\theta \end{bmatrix} \begin{bmatrix} -1 & 0 \\ 0 & 1 \end{bmatrix} \begin{bmatrix} \cos\phi & \sin\phi \\ -\sin\phi & \cos\phi \end{bmatrix}.$$

If we now multiply the two right most matrices, we obtain:

$$\begin{bmatrix} \cos\theta & \sin\theta \\ -\sin\theta & \cos\theta \end{bmatrix} \begin{bmatrix} -\cos\phi & -\sin\phi \\ -\sin\phi & \cos\phi \end{bmatrix}.$$

We now multiply these two matrices:

$$\begin{bmatrix} -\cos(\theta-\phi) & \sin(\theta-\phi) \\ \sin(\theta-\phi) & \cos(\theta-\phi) \end{bmatrix}.$$

Here, we have made use of the 'sum and difference' formulas (see Appendix A). Consider the case in which $\theta = \phi$, then the matrix reduces to $\begin{bmatrix} -1 & 0 \\ 0 & 1 \end{bmatrix}$ – recall that this corresponds to a reflection in the y-axis. Thus the initial and final rotations have cancelled each other out. This can be readily confirmed by drawing an appropriate diagram in which the transformations are applied to an arbitrary vector.

3.5 Homogeneous Transformations in a 2-D Space

As discussed in the previous section, a series of rotation, reflection and scaling operations can be readily combined within a single 2 by 2 matrix. However, translation requires a matrix addition (rather than a multiplication) operation. This prevents a translation operation being encapsulated with other transformations within a single 2 by 2 matrix operator. Fortunately, this problem can be readily resolved by expressing vectors in a homogeneous coordinate system (recall Section 2.2) and using 3 by 3 (rather than 2 by 2) matrix operators.

Before we consider encapsulating a series of transformations into a single matrix operator, it is helpful to consider the way in which 3 by 3 matrices can be applied to 'homogeneous vectors' to effect single transformations:

1. **Rotation**: In order to achieve a rotation through an angle θ about the origin, we use a matrix of the form:

$$\begin{bmatrix} \cos\theta & \sin\theta & 0 \\ -\sin\theta & \cos\theta & 0 \\ 0 & 0 & 1 \end{bmatrix}. \tag{3.8}$$

Notice that the four elements on the upper left side are the same as those used in the equivalent 2 by 2 matrix (see Eq. 3.5). To demonstrate the use of this matrix, let us suppose that we wish to rotate the position vector $2\mathbf{i} + 3\mathbf{j}$ through an angle of $30°$ about the origin.

We can express the coordinates (2,3) in homogeneous form as [2 3 1] (recall that a point in 2-D space is not represented by a unique homogeneous coordinate value – for example, (2,3) could also be represented as [4 6 2], [6 9 3] etc.). The transformation is achieved as follows:

$$\begin{bmatrix} 2 & 3 & 1 \end{bmatrix} \begin{bmatrix} \cos 30 & \sin 30 & 0 \\ -\sin 30 & \cos 30 & 0 \\ 0 & 0 & 1 \end{bmatrix} \approx \begin{bmatrix} 0.23 & 3.6 & 1 \end{bmatrix}.$$

Thus following the rotation operation the vector $0.23\mathbf{i} + 3.6\mathbf{j}$ is formed.

2. **Reflection in the x and y axes**: Reflection in the x-axis may be achieved using the matrix operator:

$$\begin{bmatrix} 1 & 0 & 0 \\ 0 & -1 & 0 \\ 0 & 0 & 1 \end{bmatrix}, \tag{3.9}$$

and for reflection in the y-axis we use:

$$\begin{bmatrix} -1 & 0 & 0 \\ 0 & 1 & 0 \\ 0 & 0 & 1 \end{bmatrix}. \tag{3.10}$$

Note that the upper left hand four elements of these two matrices are those used in the equivalent 2 by 2 matrix (see Eq. 3.6).

3. **Scaling**: To enlarge or reduce the size of a vector we can employ the matrix operator:

$$\begin{bmatrix} k & 0 & 0 \\ 0 & l & 0 \\ 0 & 0 & 1 \end{bmatrix}. \tag{3.11}$$

Here, the value of k determines the scaling applied in the x direction and l in the y direction. For example, consider the position vector $2\mathbf{i} + 3\mathbf{j}$ and suppose that we wish to scale this by a factor of 2 in both the horizontal and vertical directions. We simply form the homogeneous vector (see (1) above) and multiply by the matrix operator:

$$\begin{bmatrix} 2 & 3 & 1 \end{bmatrix} \begin{bmatrix} 2 & 0 & 0 \\ 0 & 2 & 0 \\ 0 & 0 & 1 \end{bmatrix} = \begin{bmatrix} 4 & 6 & 1 \end{bmatrix}.$$

Thus the result of the enlargement is the vector $4\mathbf{i} + 6\mathbf{j}$.
When the scaling factors applied in the x and y directions are the same ($k = l$), it is convenient to define an overall scaling parameter s – such that $s = 1/k = 1/l$. We can then multiply Eq. 3.11 by s, and so:

$$s \begin{bmatrix} k & 0 & 0 \\ 0 & l & 0 \\ 0 & 0 & 1 \end{bmatrix} = \begin{bmatrix} 1 & 0 & 0 \\ 0 & 1 & 0 \\ 0 & 0 & s \end{bmatrix}. \tag{3.12}$$

This provides a convenient matrix operator for scaling. However, it is important to note that when s is greater than 1, the application of the matrix operator causes a reduction in size and when s is less than 1 the operator will provide enlargement. This is in contrast to the use of k and l in Eq. 3.11. Here, when k, $l > 1$ enlargement occurs and when k, $l < 1$ size reduction takes place.

By way of an example consider the application of a matrix operator as given in Eq. 3.12 where $s = 2$ to the position vector $2\mathbf{i} + 3\mathbf{j}$. Thus:

$$\begin{bmatrix} 2 & 3 & 1 \end{bmatrix} \begin{bmatrix} 1 & 0 & 0 \\ 0 & 1 & 0 \\ 0 & 0 & 2 \end{bmatrix} = \begin{bmatrix} 2 & 3 & 2 \end{bmatrix}.$$

To convert to Cartesian coordinates we must divide by two (recall Section 2.2.3). Thus, [2 3 2] corresponds to the Cartesian coordinates (1, 1.5) which is defined by the position vector $\mathbf{i} + 1.5\mathbf{j}$. Hence when $s = 2$, the magnitude of the vector is *reduced* by a factor of 0.5.

4. **Translation**: By multiplying homogeneous vectors by an appropriate 3 by 3 matrix, we can perform translation operations in a 2-D space (recall this is not possible when 2 by 2 matrix operators are employed). The matrix operator has the form:

$$\begin{bmatrix} 1 & 0 & 0 \\ 0 & 1 & 0 \\ D_x & D_y & 1 \end{bmatrix}. \tag{3.13}$$

Where, D_x denotes the shift in the x direction and D_y the shift in the y direction.

OTU Exercise 3.5: A Translation Operation

Consider the line segment PQ that is illustrated in Figure 3.11. Express vectors **p** and **q** in homogeneous form and apply a suitable 3 by 3 matrix operator to shift line segment PQ by 4 units horizontally and 2 units vertically thus obtaining P′Q′.

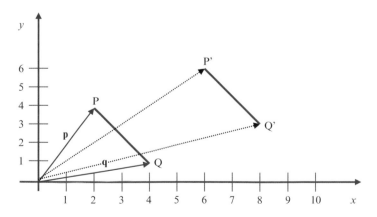

Figure 3.11 A translation operation using a 3 by 3 matrix operator. See OTU Exercise 3.5.

3.5.1 Incorporating Multiple Transformations in a Single Matrix

Suppose that we need to perform a rotation operation followed by a translation (shift) and finally a scaling. We can combine Eq.'s 3.8, 3.11 and 3.13 but must do so in a way that matches the transformation sequence that we wish to apply. Hence we obtain the single matrix operator as follows:

$$\begin{bmatrix} \cos\theta & \sin\theta & 0 \\ -\sin\theta & \cos\theta & 0 \\ 0 & 0 & 1 \end{bmatrix} \begin{bmatrix} 1 & 0 & 0 \\ 0 & 1 & 0 \\ D_x & D_y & 1 \end{bmatrix} \begin{bmatrix} k & 0 & 0 \\ 0 & l & 0 \\ 0 & 0 & 1 \end{bmatrix} = \begin{bmatrix} k\cos\theta & l\sin\theta & 0 \\ -k\sin\theta & l\cos\theta & 0 \\ kD_x & lD_y & 1 \end{bmatrix}.$$

In the case that the scaling factors k and l are identical (we denote this overall scaling factor as s – recall previous discussion), then this result may be re-written:

$$\begin{bmatrix} \cos\theta & \sin\theta & 0 \\ -\sin\theta & \cos\theta & 0 \\ D_x & D_y & s \end{bmatrix}. \tag{3.14}$$

However, if we change the order in which the rotation, translation and scaling operations are applied, the form of the resulting matrix operator is not quite as simple. For example, consider the case in which we apply the transformations in the order translation, scaling and then rotation. Here we have:

$$\begin{bmatrix} 1 & 0 & 0 \\ 0 & 1 & 0 \\ D_x & D_y & 1 \end{bmatrix} \begin{bmatrix} k & 0 & 0 \\ 0 & l & 0 \\ 0 & 0 & 1 \end{bmatrix} \begin{bmatrix} \cos\theta & \sin\theta & 0 \\ -\sin\theta & \cos\theta & 0 \\ 0 & 0 & 1 \end{bmatrix} = \begin{bmatrix} k\cos\theta & k\sin\theta & 0 \\ -l\sin\theta & l\cos\theta & 0 \\ D_x k\cos\theta - D_y l\sin\theta & D_x k\sin\theta + D_y l\cos\theta & 1 \end{bmatrix}$$

3.5.2 Rotation about any Point

So far we have limited our discussion to situations in which we wish to rotate a vector about the origin. However, in many situations (e.g. when animating an image scene or performing interactive operations) we may need to effect rotation about an arbitrary point. We may easily determine a matrix operator able to achieve this goal by employing the standard transformations that we have already discussed. Specifically, we use two translation operations and one rotation about the origin operation. This process may be most easily understood by means of a simple example. Consider the point P illustrated in Figure 3.12(a) and let us suppose that we wish to rotate this about the point A through an angle θ so obtaining point Q. In Figure 3.12(b) we indicate the order of the three standard transformations that we must carry out to achieve this goal. The overall matrix operator is therefore obtained as follows:

$$\begin{bmatrix} 1 & 0 & 0 \\ 0 & 1 & 0 \\ -D_x & -D_y & 1 \end{bmatrix} \begin{bmatrix} \cos\theta & \sin\theta & 0 \\ -\sin\theta & \cos\theta & 0 \\ 0 & 0 & 1 \end{bmatrix} \begin{bmatrix} 1 & 0 & 0 \\ 0 & 1 & 0 \\ D_x & D_y & 1 \end{bmatrix} = \begin{bmatrix} \cos\theta & \sin\theta & 0 \\ -\sin\theta & \cos\theta & 0 \\ \alpha & \beta & 1 \end{bmatrix},$$

where:

$$\alpha = D_x(1 - \cos\theta) + D_y\sin\theta$$
$$\beta = D_y(1 - \cos\theta) - D_x\sin\theta.$$

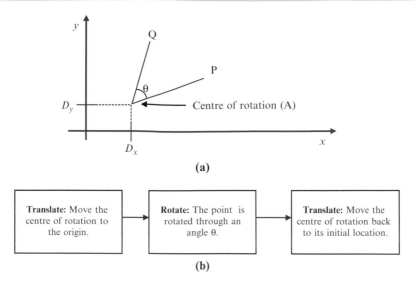

(a)

| Translate: Move the centre of rotation to the origin. | → | Rotate: The point is rotated through an angle θ. | → | Translate: Move the centre of rotation back to its initial location. |

(b)

Figure 3.12 Rotation about an arbitrary point. In (a) we indicate point P that is to be rotated through and angle θ about point A. In (b) we summarise the order of the three transformations that are applied.

3.6 Concerning Graph Theory

'Passed years seem safe ones, vanquished ones,
while the future lives in a cloud, formidable from a distance.
The cloud clears as you enter it.
I have learned this, but like everyone, I learned it late.'[4]

The graphs that we briefly consider in this section are not ones that depict the relationship between two or more variables (so illustrating a mathematical function) but rather comprise a set of points (called 'nodes' or vertices) that are connected by lines (generally referred to as 'edges' or arcs). An example of a simple graph of this type is given in Figure 3.13. Such a graph can be defined thus:

'Formally, a graph G is defined to be a pair [N(G), E(G)], where N(G) is a non-empty finite set of elements called nodes, and E(G) is a finite family of unordered pairs of elements of N(G) called edges.' [Cooley, 2001]

The degree of a node (vertex) is given by the number of edges that meet at the node. In Figure 3.13, there are nodes at which one, two and three edges meet. A node at which three edges meet is said to have a degree of three (a '3-node'). The set of nodes is generally referred to as the 'node set' or 'node list' and the set of edges as the 'edge list'. The sequence of edges that are traversed in getting from one node to another is called a 'path' and if the starting and ending nodes of a path are the same then this is referred to as a 'circuit'.

_____
[4] Attributed to Beryl Markham.

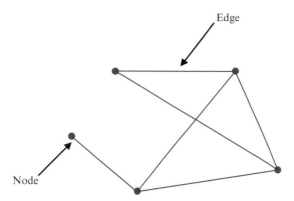

Figure 3.13 A simple graph comprising a set of points (nodes) and lines (edges) that in some way connect these nodes.

Consider the graph depicted in Figure 3.14(a) comprising two disjoint circuits (with nodes denoted ABCD and EFGH) We may describe this in terms of a connectivity list – as depicted in Figure 3.14(b).

A matrix can be used to indicate connectivity (adjacency) and in the case of the elementary example illustrated in Figure 3.14(a), this would have the form:

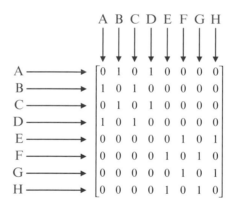

Here, a single bit is used to indicate the presence (or otherwise) of an edge between nodes in the graph. In computer graphics it is convenient to employ graphs to represent objects and, we may assign coordinates to the nodes thereby representing a physical shape (for example, see Figure 3.14(c)).

We may assign to each edge a direction (such directed edges are referred to as 'di-edges' and the overall graph a 'di-graph') – see for example Figure 3.15.

The approach of treating edges as vectors enables us to use the vector directions of circuits to define the inside and outside of an object. For example, we may use the convention that when we are pointing in the direction of the vector, the left hand side denotes the inside of an object and so the outside is to the right – or *vice-versa*. This may be readily understood from the simple example provided in Figure 3.15. Let us suppose that this represents a rectangular object (ABCD) within which a square hole (EFGH) has been cut. As may be seen from the illustration the direction of the di-edges connecting nodes A, B, C and D is such that when

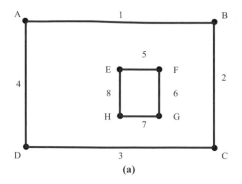

Edge	Node	Node
1	A	B
2	B	C
3	C	D
4	D	A
5	E	F
6	F	G
7	G	H
8	H	E

(b)

Node	x-coordinate	y-coordinate
A	1	5
B	8	5
C	8	1
D	1	1
E	5	4
F	7	4
G	7	2
H	5	2

(c)

Figure 3.14 In (a) we show a simple graph comprising 2 disjoint circuits. In (b) a connectivity list is presented which summarises the interconnection of nodes. It is often convenient to assign coordinates to the locations of nodes and thereby represent the geometrical shape of objects – as illustrated in (c).

looking along each, the interior of the rectangle lies to the left. Similarly, in the case of the hole, the vectors are arranged so that again the interior of the rectangle is to the left of each vector. Alternatively we can adopt the opposite convention – all that matters is that we should exercise consistency.

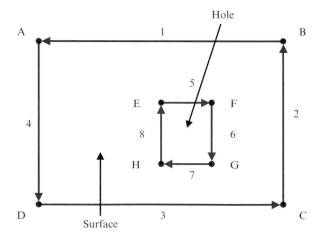

Figure 3.15 A simple example of a di-graph. Here, a direction is associated with each edge. This can be used to indicate the location of a surface and any holes.

Note that when a di-graph is used, this changes the entries within the connectivity matrix. For example in the case of the di-graph presented in Figure 3.15, the connectivity matrix is as follows:

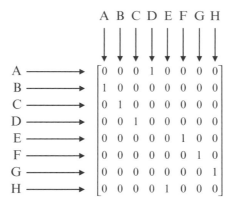

3.6.1 The Location of a Point Relative to a Boundary

Referring to Figure 3.14, let us suppose that we wish to determine if a point P lies inside the rectangle ABCD, inside the hole EFGH or is elsewhere. We can adopt two simple approaches to this problem – the first of which is based on the use of directed edges (vectors). These approaches are outlined below:

(1) **The use of Vectors**: This technique assumes that all edges are straight lines and are represented as vectors. To demonstrate the method, we will consider the three cases indicated in Figure 3.16:

- Here, we assume the situation illustrated in Figure 3.16(a) in which point P lies outside the rectangle ABCD and for the moment we will ignore the hole EFGH. We begin by drawing a line from the point P to a node (vertex). Suppose that we choose node A (an arbitrary choice). We then draw a line from P to the next node in the circuit (following the direction indicated by the vector). Thus we connect P with node D and measure the angle between the two lines that we have drawn. Next we connect P with node C and add the angle between lines PD and PC to the angle already measured (between lines PA and PD). We now connect P with the next node in the circuit – node B. Again we measure the angle between the last line drawn and the line just created (PB). In this case we note that the angle turns in the opposite direction and so we subtract this angle from that previously accrued. Finally we complete the circuit by measuring the angle between lines PB and PA. We add this to the total In the case that the point P lies outside the boundary of a shape, the total accrued angle will be zero.

- Turning to the scenario indicated in Figure 3.16(b) in which P lies within the boundary of the rectangle ABCD. Here, we follow the same technique that was used above. We connect P to one of the nodes (here we have chosen node A – as indicated by the broken line). We then follow the direction of the circuit as shown by the vectors and accrue the angle turned through until we return to the starting point. In the case that the point lies within the circuit, the total angle turned through will be +360°.

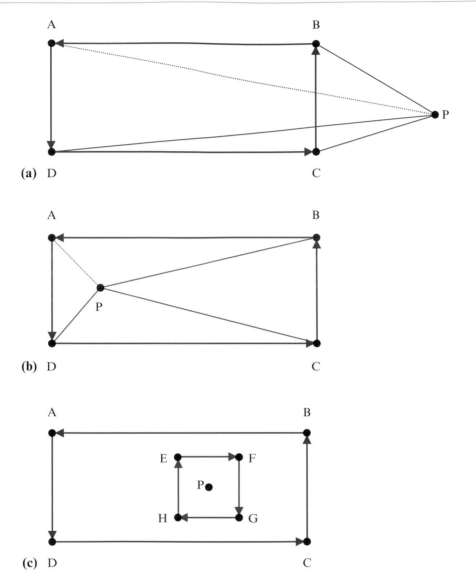

Figure 3.16 In (a) and (b) we test the location of point P relative to a rectangular shape. In (c) P lies within a hole cut into the rectangle.

- Finally, consider the case depicted in Figure 3.16(c). As may be seen from the illustration the direction of circuit ABCD and circuit EFGH lie in opposite directions and so when we repeat the process outlined above, we will turn through a total angle of $-360°$.

The technique outlined above is quite straightforward and the total angle turned through provides us with a simple means of finding whether a point lies inside or outside a shape. In the OTU Exercise that follows we provide a further example. Remember that at each stage we are measuring the angle turned through – which may

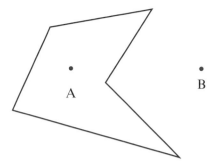

Figure 3.17 Verification of a technique for determining if a point lies within or outside a shape. See OTU Exercise 3.6.

be either positive or negative (hence we may need to add or subtract each new angle from the total previously accrued).

OTU Exercise 3.6: Identifying the Location of a Point Relative to a Shape

Consider the polygon indicated in Figure 3.17. Using the convention that the region to the left of a vector is within the boundary of the shape, draw arrows on each edge to signify vector direction. Using the approach described above verify that the angle turned through as each node is connected to point A is +360° (indicating that A is within the boundary of the shape). Using a protractor, repeat the exercise for point B (for which the total angle turned through should be zero).

The above approach requires that all edges are straight lines. Additionally, before this method can be put into practice, the data must have been sorted so as to delineate a series of separate circuits with contiguous edges. The test is then carried out on one or more circuits as required.

(2)   **The Half-Line Test**: To demonstrate this approach we will continue to employ the simple example used above – a rectangle ABCD within which there is a square hole (EFGH). In Figure 3.18, we illustrate this shape and indicate three points denoted K, L and M. Point K is located within the rectangular shape, point L lies in the hole and point M is outside and to the left of the rectangle.

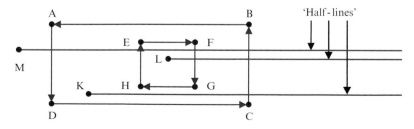

Figure 3.18 Testing if a point resides within the boundary of a shape. See text for discussion.

From each of these points we draw a line that extends horizontally to the right (in the positive x direction) and count the number of times that each of these lines crosses an edge. Thus the 'half line' from point K crosses one edge, the line from point L crosses two edges and the one from point M crosses four edges. In the simplest case (i.e. ignoring various exceptional situations) if the half line from a point crosses an odd number of edges, then it lies within a boundary. This test can be employed even when the edges are not necessarily straight lines and unlike the vector-based approach discussed above, the data does not have to be sorted to delineate a series of separate circuits with contiguous edges.

3.7 Clipping Points and Lines

'Dreamers can find their way by moonlight
and their only punishment
is that they see the dawn
before the rest of the world.' [5]

As discussed in Section 3.2, we may define a 'viewing window' that specifies the portion of an image scene which is to be depicted. Image entities that lie outside this window are then discarded. This process may be compared to the use of scissors to cut out a rectangular or circular portion of a photograph (e.g. the view of a person's face for insertion into a small frame or locket). In the context of computer graphics, the elimination of image components that lie outside the viewing window is referred to as 'clipping'. Comninos [2006] describes clipping in the following, more general, way:

'Clipping is a process that subdivides each element of a picture to be displayed into its visible and invisible parts, thus allowing us to discard the invisible parts of the picture. In 2-D, the clipping process can be applied to a variety of graphics primitives ... Clipping can be performed with respect to a clipping boundary, which may be a convex or concave polygonal boundary.'

In the subsections that follow we confine our discussion to the basic techniques that can be used in clipping points, lines and objects that are located within a 2-D image scene to a rectangular viewing window (rectangular clipping boundary) and in Chapter 8, consider clipping in the context of a 3-D image scene.

3.7.1 Clipping Image Points

Determining whether or not points within a 2-D image scene lie inside or outside a rectangular viewing window represents a trivial task. Consider the viewing window depicted in Figure 3.19 with sides located at x_{min}, x_{max}, y_{min} and y_{max}. In the illustration, two arbitrary points (denoted P_1 and P_2) are indicated. We assume that the function of the clipping algorithm is to determine whether or not these points lie within or outside the viewing window. In the case that either point lies within this window then it will be depicted in the display screen viewport – otherwise it will not form part of the displayed image.

---

[5] Attributed to Oscar Wilde (1854–1900).

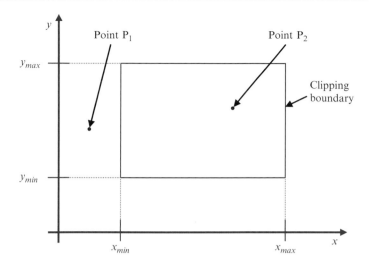

Figure 3.19 A rectangular viewing window has sides at x_{min}, x_{max}, y_{min} and y_{max}. Two points – P_1 and P_2 are defined. The clipping algorithm must determine whether or not these points lie within the viewing window – see text for discussion.

From Figure 3.19, it is readily apparent that for a point to lie within the viewing window, its x coordinate must lie between the x coordinates of the two vertical sides of the rectangle **and** its y coordinate must lie between the y coordinates of the two horizontal sides of the rectangle. Thus a point's x coordinate must be between x_{min} and x_{max} and the y coordinate between y_{min} and y_{max}. We can express this using the inequalities:

$$x_{min} \leq x \leq x_{max}, \qquad y_{min} \leq y \leq y_{max}.$$

If a point with coordinates (x, y) satisfies both of these inequalities, then it is inside the clipping boundary – otherwise it is eliminated from the displayed scene.

3.7.2 Clipping Line Segments: The Cohen Sutherland Algorithm

As we have seen, determining whether or not a point lies within the viewing window is a trivial undertaking – dealing with lines is slightly more complicated. Consider the four line segments illustrated in Figure 3.20. It is apparent that segment S_1 lies entirely within the viewing window and will therefore not affected by the clipping process. On the other hand, since segment S_2 is completely outside the viewing window, it will be culled. In the case of segment S_3, a portion of the line is within the viewing window. The clipping algorithm will retain this part of the line and cull the remainder. Finally, in the case of segment S_4, as this crosses the clipping window it is necessary to cull both ends of the line – leaving only the part that is entirely within the window. In fact, in the case that lines are completely inside or outside the clipping window (as is the case with S_1 and S_2) the clipping process is readily undertaken – we need only check the end points of each line segment in relation to the coordinates of the clipping boundary. Even when a line segment crosses one clipping boundary (as is the case with S_3) the process is again straightforward – the point at which the line intersects the boundary becomes the new

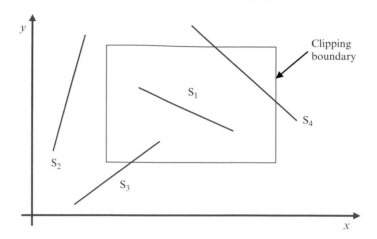

Figure 3.20 Here, we illustrate four line segments and their positions relative to the clipping boundary. During the clipping process, line segment S_1 remains wholly intact, S_2 is culled and both S_3 and S_4 are partially clipped.

endpoint for the line segment. However, for a rectangular viewing window, we must also cater for the possibility that a line crosses two clipping boundaries (naturally, in the case of curves, they may in principle cross clipping boundaries any number of times).[6]

The Cohen Sutherland algorithm provides one approach to the clipping of line segments relative to a rectangular viewing window. This algorithm provides a rapid means by which we can deal with lines that lie entirely within the window (such as S_1 which is accepted without modification) or some of the lines which lie entirely outside the window (such as S_2 which is to be culled). Hence we are able to quickly deal with various lines within the image scene and those remaining are subjected to further tests which may result in line segments being wholly or partially culled.

The operation of the algorithm is underpinned by extending the sides of the viewing window to create a number of regions within the 2-D image plane – see Figure 3.21. The location of each of the nine regions that are now formed is defined by a 4-bit binary code – the meaning attributed to each of the bits is indicated in Figure 3.22. As may be seen from the example provided in this illustration, setting a bit to one is used to define region placement. By way of a further example, consider the code 0101. The two bits that are set to a value of one indicate that the region lies below and to the left of the viewing window. The region within the viewing window is assigned the code 0000.

In terms of the operation of the Cohen Sutherland algorithm, we begin by assigning region codes to the end-points of line segments. This is easily achieved by comparing the end-point coordinates to the locations of the extended sides of the viewing window. We can now easily deal with two specific classes of line:

1. In the case that the two endpoints of a line have region codes 0000, we know that the line lies entirely within the viewing window (e.g. the case of line segment S_1 in Figure 3.20). The line is therefore not clipped but is left fully intact. This is known as the 'trivial acceptance' case.

---

[6] Naturally, the shape of the window against which we are clipping will also determine the maximum number of times that a line segment can potentially cross a boundary.

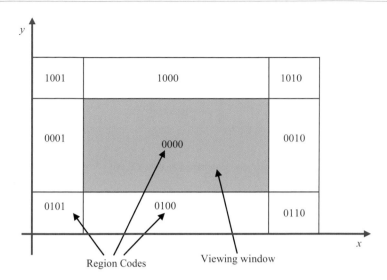

Figure 3.21 The operation of the Cohen Sutherland algorithm is underpinned by extending the sides of the viewing window across the plane that contains the image scene. This results in the formation of nine regions. Each region is identified by means of a 4-bit binary code. The values of individual bits within each code specifies the location of the region relative to the viewing window (above, below, to the right and to the left). The viewing window itself is assigned the code 0000.

2. For each of the remaining line segments, we perform a bit-wise logical 'and' operation on their endpoint region codes. For example consider a line segment that has one endpoint in region 0101 and for which the other endpoint is in region 1001 (see Figure 3.21 for the location of these two regions). If we perform an 'and' operation[7] on the corresponding bits in these region codes, we obtain 0001. Since the result is *not* 0000, we conclude that the line segment is completely outside the viewing window and so the line is culled. This is referred to as the 'trivial rejection' case. By way of a further example consider a line segment that has endpoints in regions 0101 and 1010. The logical 'and' operation of the corresponding bits in these two codes yields 0000. When this result is obtained (i.e. all bits are zero), we conclude that the line cannot be 'trivially rejected' and must be considered further.

The 'trivial rejection' case that we have just described does not identify all lines that lie completely outside the viewing window. For example, consider the line segment S_5 indicated in Figure 3.23. This line has endpoints in regions 0100 and 0010 and is entirely outside the viewing window. If we perform a bit-wise logical 'and' operation on these two codes, we obtain 0000. This indicates that the line cannot be trivially rejected. This is indeed a prudent decision for as may be seen in Figure 3.23 line S_6, which has the same endpoint region codes, passes through the viewing window. Thus without more definite information concerning the location of the endpoints, we cannot be sure whether or not the line passes through the window.

Having dealt with the cases of 'trivial acceptance' and 'trivial rejection' we can now consider dealing with two exemplar lines indicated in Figure 3.24. As may be seen from the illustration, one of these (S_7) has endpoint region codes that correspond to those of the line segment discussed in the previous paragraph. We will label these endpoints as P_1 and P_2. Beginning at point P_1, we locate the point at which the line intersects one of the region boundaries – in

---

[7] In the case of this operation, if either of the bits are zero, then this results in a zero.

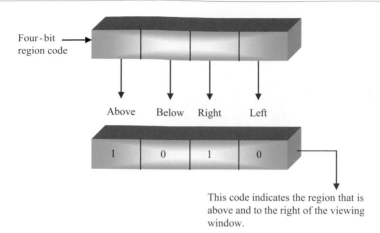

Four-bit region code

Above   Below   Right   Left

| 1 | 0 | 1 | 0 |

This code indicates the region that is above and to the right of the viewing window.

Figure 3.22 The use of region codes by the Cohen Sutherland algorithm. By setting individual bits to one, we are able to define the locations of regions relative to the viewing window. Note that the code 0000 is used to define the region within the viewing window.

Figure 3.24 this point is labelled P_i. We can now cull the part of the line between P_1 and P_i. Examination of the region codes for the remaining part of the line segment (i.e. undertaking the bit-wise logical 'and' operation) results in the value 0010 – a non-zero value indicating that the remainder of the line may be culled.

Let us now consider the line segment S_8 depicted in Figure 3.24. Beginning with endpoint P_3, and knowing that this point lies outside the viewing window, we identify the first intersection of the line with a region boundary. In Figure 3.24, this is labelled P_j. We cull this portion of the line and then perform the bit-wise 'and' operation on the region codes of the endpoints

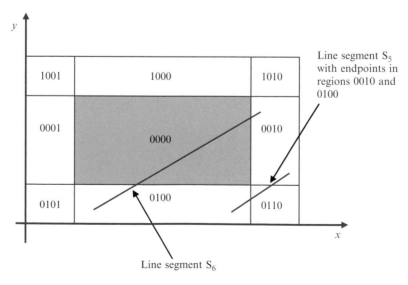

Line segment S_5 with endpoints in regions 0010 and 0100

Line segment S_6

Figure 3.23 Here we illustrate two line segments – both of which have identical endpoint region codes (0100 and 0010). However although line S_5 is completely outside the viewing window, line S_6 passes through the window. Such line segments cannot therefore be 'trivially rejected'.

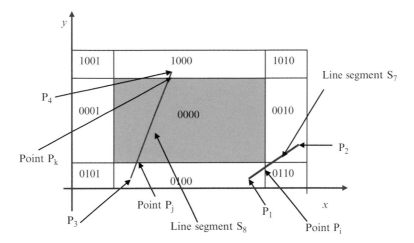

Figure 3.24 Two exemplar line segments. Here, we indicate the labels used in the text for their endpoints and for the points at which the lines intersect region boundaries.

of the remaining portion of the line segment. These are 0000 and 1000 – and so we obtain a result in which all bits are zero. This indicates that we cannot assume that the remainder of the line can be culled. We then turn our attention to the line's other endpoint – P_4. Again we determine that this lies outside the viewing window and identify the point at which the line crosses a region boundary (point P_k in Figure 3.24). We cull the portion of the line between P_4 and P_k. Examination of the region codes for the endpoints of the remainder of the line indicates that they are both 0000 and so the remainder of the line is within the viewing window.

Finally in relation to this clipping algorithm, it is instructive to consider the manner in which we may determine the coordinates of the point at which a line intersects a region boundary. Consider the line segment S_9 that is illustrated in Figure 3.25 and which has endpoint coordinates (x_1, y_1) and (x_2, y_2). In this diagram we also show the left hand boundary of the viewing window which is given by $x = x_{\min}$ and assume that the line segment intersects the boundary at $(x_{\min}, y_i)$. For our current purposes, we assume that the length of the line segment is such that it does cross the boundary and therefore we will overlook its finite length. Recall Eq. 2.2 – in which the general equation for a line is given by:

$$y = mx + c,$$

where m denotes the gradient and c the intercept with the y-axis. For the line shown in Figure 3.25, the gradient is given by:

$$m = \frac{y_2 - y_1}{x_2 - x_1}.$$

Thus:

$$y = \left[\frac{y_2 - y_1}{x_2 - x_1}\right] x + c. \qquad (3.15)$$

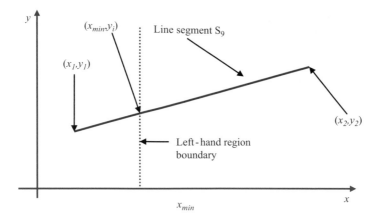

Figure 3.25 Here, we consider a line segment with end-points (x_1, y_1) and (x_2, y_2). We assume that the line intersects the left-hand side of the viewing boundary window at (x_{min}, y_i).

We now determine the y intercept (c) by making use of coordinates through which the line passes (e.g. (x_1, y_1)) – so that we can write:

$$y_1 = \left[\frac{y_2 - y_1}{x_2 - x_1}\right] x_1 + c.$$

Consequently:

$$c = y_1 - \left[\frac{y_2 - y_1}{x_2 - x_1}\right] x_1.$$

Inserting this into Eq. 3.15 and simplifying the expression we obtain:

$$y = y_1 + \left[\frac{y_2 - y_1}{x_2 - x_1}\right] (x - x_1). \tag{3.16}$$

Having obtained the equation for the line passing through (x_1, y_1) and (x_2, y_2), we determine the intersection of this line with the left-hand boundary by simply equating x to x_{min}. Thus the y coordinate of the point of intersection (y_i) is given by:

$$y_i = y_1 + \left[\frac{y_2 - y_1}{x_2 - x_1}\right] (x_{min} - x_1).$$

Naturally, if we are interested in determining the coordinates of the point of intersection with the right-hand boundary, we simply insert $x = x_{max}$ into Eq. 3.16 (where x_{max} denotes the location of this boundary in the horizontal direction). Similarly, when dealing with the upper and lower boundaries, we substitute for y in Eq. 3.16 (e.g. for the lower boundary $y = y_{min}$).

3.7.3 The Liang and Barsky Algorithm

The Cohen Sutherland algorithm for line clipping represents only one of a number of possible techniques that, over the years, have been developed. It is instructive to briefly consider one of the alternative approaches. Here, we have chosen to summarise aspects of a technique developed by Liang and Barsky [1984] and which operates on lines represented in parametric form.

As we have seen, an arbitrary point (x, y) located on a line segment with endpoints (x_1, y_1) and (x_2, y_2) can be represented by the following parametric equations[8]:

$$x = x_1 + (x_2 - x_1)\,u$$
$$y = y_1 + (y_2 - y_1)\,u$$

where the parameter u has values in the range $0 \le u \le 1$. Thus when $u = 0$, the point (x, y) is located at (x_1, y_1) and when $u = 1$, it lies at (x_2, y_2). These represent the two extreme positions and for intermediate values of u, the point (x, y) will be at other locations on the line segment.

It is convenient to let $x_2 - x_1 = \Delta x$ and $y_2 - y_1 = \Delta y$. Thus we can re-write the above parametric equations as:

$$x = x_1 + \Delta x \cdot u$$
$$y = y_1 + \Delta y \cdot u \qquad (3.17)$$

Recall Figure 3.19 in which we defined the location of the clipping boundaries for a rectangular region. As we indicated in Section 3.7.1, for a point (x, y) to lie within the rectangular viewing window, it must satisfy the following inequalities:

$$x_{min} \le x \le x_{max}$$
$$y_{min} \le y \le y_{max}$$

If we substitute Eq. 3.17 into these inequalities, we obtain:

$$x_{min} \le x_1 + \Delta x \cdot u \le x_{max}$$
$$y_{min} \le y_1 + \Delta y \cdot u \le y_{max}$$

It is instructive to split these into four separate equations:

$$x_{min} \le x_1 + \Delta x \cdot u$$
$$x_{max} \ge x_1 + \Delta x \cdot u$$
$$y_{min} \le y_1 + \Delta y \cdot u$$
$$y_{max} \ge y_1 + \Delta y \cdot u$$

It is evident that each of these inequalities corresponds to the limits set by each particular clipping boundary (i.e. the first equation corresponds to the left hand boundary, the second to the right, the third to the lower boundary and the fourth to the upper). We can express these four inequalities as:

$$p_k u \le q_k, \qquad (3.18)$$

where k is an integer such that $1 \le k \le 4$. We define p_k and q_k as indicated in Table 3.1.

---

[8] For summary discussion on parametric equations see Section 2.3.1.

Table 3.1 Defined values of p_k and q_k for $1 \leq k \leq 4$

$k = 1$	$p_1 = -\Delta x$	$q_1 = x_1 - x_{min}$
$k = 2$	$p_2 = \Delta x$	$q_2 = x_{max} - x_1$
$k = 3$	$p_3 = -\Delta y$	$q_3 = y_1 - y_{min}$
$k = 4$	$p_4 = \Delta y$	$q_4 = y_{max} - y_1$

If we take each pair of values given in this table, insert them into Eq. 3.18 and slightly rearrange the result, we obtain the four inequalities listed above. For example consider $k = 1$. In this case, by our definition:

$$p_1 = -\Delta x$$
$$q_1 = x_1 - x_{min}$$

Inserting these into Eq. 3.18, we obtain:

$$-\Delta x \cdot u \leq x_1 - x_{min}.$$

Rearranging this gives:

$$x_{min} \leq x_1 + \Delta x \cdot u.$$

This is identical to the first of the four inequalities listed above and corresponds to the limits set by the left-hand clipping boundary.

OTU Exercise 3.7: Verifying the Values Presented in Table 3.1

Insert each of the lower three pairs of values provided in Table 3.1 into Eq. 3.18 and hence confirm that these give the lower three inequalities presented in the above text.

From the above discussion it is apparent that $k = 1$ corresponds to the contribution made by the left hand boundary, $k = 2$ to that of the right hand boundary, $k = 3$ to the lower boundary and $k = 4$ to the upper. Let us now consider the case of a vertical line segment (i.e. a line that lies parallel to the pair of boundaries denoted by $k = 1$ and $k = 2$). For such a line $x_1 = x_2$ and so $\Delta x = 0$. Hence, $p_{1,2} = 0$. Similarly for a horizontal line $y_1 = y_2$ and so $\Delta y = 0$. Consequently in this case $p_{3,4} = 0$.

Consider the horizontal line S_9 depicted in Figure 3.26. In relation to the lower boundary ($k = 3$), $p_3 = 0$ and furthermore q_3 is negative (this indicates that the line is on the outside of the boundary). Conversely, in the case of S_{10}, again $p_3 = 0$ but now q_3 is positive – indicating that the line is on the inside of the boundary.

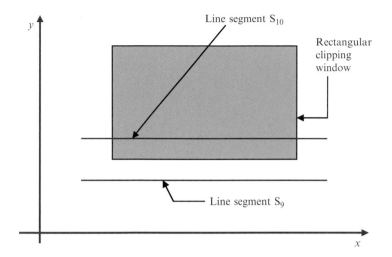

Figure 3.26 Two horizontal line segments. For these lines, and in relation to the lower clipping boundary ($k = 3$), $p_3 = 0$. In addition, for S_9, q_3 is negative – indicating that the line is completely outside the boundary. On the other hand, for line S_{10}, q_3 is positive indicating that the line is on the inside of the lower boundary.

Let us now turn our attention to considering the intersection of a line segment with a boundary. Here we distinguish between a line segment that goes from the outside to the inside of a boundary and the converse. These two cases are illustrated in Figure 3.27. In this diagram we have extended the left and right hand clipping boundaries and line S_{11} crosses the left-hand boundary just above the clipping rectangle.

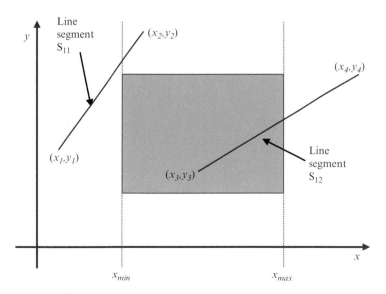

Figure 3.27 Here we extend the left and right-hand boundaries. Line S_{11} is shown crossing from the outside to the inside of the left-hand boundary whereas line S_{12} crosses from the inside to the outside of the right-hand boundary. See text for discussion.

The parameter u is zero at the end point whose coordinates are (x_1, y_1) and unity at the other endpoint and so, for increasing u, the line passes from the outside to the inside of the extended boundary. In the case of line segment S_{12}, u is zero at the end-point with coordinates (x_3, y_3) and so, for increasing u, the line passes from the inside to the outside of the right-hand boundary. Recall from Table 3.1, that for the two vertical sides of the clipping boundary (corresponding to $k = 1$ and $k = 2$), $p_1 = -\Delta x$ and $p_2 = \Delta x$ (where $\Delta x = x_2 - x_1$). For line S_{11}, the difference between the x coordinates of the endpoints is positive and hence p_1 is negative and for S_{12}, p_2 is positive.

> In general if p_k is positive, a line progresses from the inside to the outside of the associated boundary (i.e. the boundary associated with the particular value of k being used). Conversely a negative value of p_k indicates that the line progresses from the outside to the inside of the associated boundary. This provides a convenient means of determining whether or not a portion of a line should be culled or retained.

Determining the point at which a line intersects with a boundary is quite simple. Consider the intersection of the line segment S_{11} with the left-hand boundary – as illustrated in Figure 3.27. For this boundary $k = 1$ and at the point of intersection both the line and the boundary have the same x and y coordinates. We know that for this boundary the x coordinate is equal to x_{min}. Substituting this value into the parametric equation for x given in Eq. 3.17, we can write:

$$x_{min} = x_1 + \Delta x \cdot u.$$

Hence:

$$\frac{x_{min} - x_1}{\Delta x} = u.$$

Recall from Table 3.1 that for $k = 1$, by our definition, $p_1 = -\Delta x$ and $q_1 = x_1 - x_{min}$. Hence we can write:

$$\frac{x_{min} - x_1}{\Delta x} = \frac{-q_1}{-p_1} = \frac{q_1}{p_1} = u.$$

In general:

$$u = \frac{q_k}{p_k}. \tag{3.19}$$

To see how the above ideas can be effectively used, let us turn to Figure 3.28 in which we illustrate a line segment S_{13} and a rectangular clipping window. The clipping boundaries that comprise this window are extended (to 'infinity'). We assume that we have confirmed that this line does not lie parallel to any of these boundaries and so cannot be most readily dealt with. Consequently, we identify whether the line crosses each boundary in order to progress from the outside of the boundary to the inside or *vice-versa*. As discussed above, this is based on the sign of each calculated value of p_k.

We compute p_k for each value of k. Although this would normally be done in numerical order, it is instructive for us to use the order in which the line shown in the illustration is seen to cross the various boundaries. As may be seen, the line first crosses the lower boundary ($k = 3$).

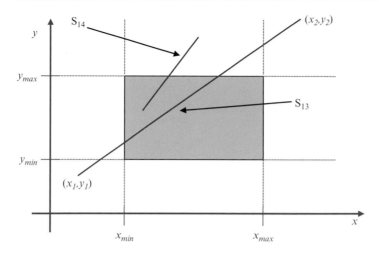

Figure 3.28 Here, we have extended the bounding sides of the rectangle to which a line segment S_{13} is to be clipped. In relation to line segment S_{14} see OTU Exercise 3.8.

From Table 3.1 we know that in relation to this boundary, $p_3 = -\Delta y$, where $\Delta y = y_2 - y_1$. Thus p_3 is negative indicating passage from the outside to the inside of the boundary (this is readily confirmed from the illustration). The line subsequently crosses the left hand boundary ($k = 1$) for which $p_1 = -\Delta x = -(x_2 - x_1)$. Hence, at this boundary p_1 is again negative and so once more the line is passing from the outside to the inside of the boundary.

The line next crosses the top boundary ($k = 4$) and here we find that p_4 is positive – indicating a transition from the inside to the outside of the boundary. Finally, the line crosses the right-hand boundary ($k = 2$): for which p_2 is also positive.

For each of the above intersections, we now compute the parameter u – using Eq. 3.19 – and so we have two values of u for outside to inside intersections and two values of u for the converse.

> In the case of the set of values of the parameter u calculated for inter-sections from the outside of boundaries to their inner sides, we take the highest value (let's call this u_a) as corresponding to the point at which the line enters the clipping window. Conversely, in the case of the set of values of u calculated for intersections from the inner sides of boundaries to their outer sides we take the smallest value (u_b) as indicating the point at which the line emerges from the clipping window.

In the case that $u_a > u_b$, the line segment lies completely outside the clipping window and can be culled. Alternatively, if $u_a < u_b$, we simply substitute these two parameters into the parametric equations for the line (Eq. 3.17) and so find the actual coordinates of the endpoints of the clipped line segment.

For further details relating to this line clipping algorithm see Liang and Barsky [1984]. Also see the work undertaken by Cyrus and Beck [1978].

3.8 Clipping Polygons

'There is a thin line between genius and insanity.
I have erased this line.'[9]

Consider the polygon depicted in Figure 3.29(a) whose shape is defined by a set of line segments. This is clipped against the rectangular window shown in the illustration – the result is indicated in Figure 3.29(b). In this case, clipping can be carried out by processing each individual line segment in the manner described in the previous section. The result of this process is to generate a series of disconnected edges which no longer form a closed polygon. However, when dealing with a polygon that defines a fill area (a region comprising a certain colour or texture) we need to employ a closed polygon and so it is necessary to piece together the disconnected edges generated by the line segment clipping program or adopt an alternative strategy. In the next subsection we outline the Sutherland-Hodgman algorithm which provides a means of clipping a concave or convex polygon against a convex clipping polygon (such as a rectangular viewing window). This algorithm avoids the formation of disjoint edges and ensures the retention of the closed polygon.

3.8.1 The Sutherland-Hodgman Polygon Clipping Algorithm

This algorithm can be used to clip both concave and convex polygons against a convex clipping polygon. As with the Liang-Barsky algorithm introduced in the previous section, use is made of the 'inside-outside test'. Within this context, we infinitely extend each edge of the clipping polygon – each edge then defining an 'inside' and an 'outside' half-space. The manner in which each vertex (comprising the polygon that is being clipped) is treated is determined according to the half-space in which it resides (i.e. inside or outside) or according to any transition in half space that occurs during the processing of adjacent vertices. This can be readily clarified by considering a simple example – as indicated in Figure 3.30. Here we show a rectangular clipping window the four sides (edges) of which are extended. Each edge therefore defines an inside and an outside half-space and the region in which the four inside half-spaces coincide defines the clipping rectangle. A point P survives the clipping process as it lies within the inside half-spaces of all four edges. In contrast, point Q lies within the inside half-spaces of the left, right and

---

[9] Attributed to Oscar Levant (1906–1972).

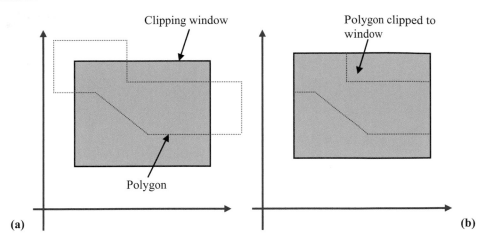

Figure 3.29 In (a) we depict a rectangular clipping window and a polygon (indicated by the broken line) that is to be clipped to the window. In (b) we illustrate the results of the clipping process.

upper edges of the rectangle but is in the outside half space of the lower edge. Consequently it is culled.

The shape of a convex polygon can be defined as being the region in which the inside half-spaces of the edges from which the polygon is formed coincide. This is an important aspect of the Sutherland-Hodgman polygon clipping algorithm and it is for this reason that the algorithm is limited to use with a convex (rather than concave) clipping polygon.

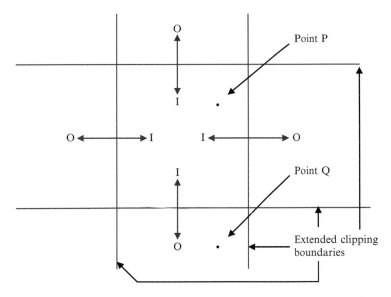

Figure 3.30 Here, we define a rectangular clipping window and extend its four sides. Each of these sides (edges) defines an inside and an outside half-space. In the diagram these are denoted by 'I' and 'O' respectively. The clipping rectangle corresponds to the region in which the four inside half-spaces coincide. During the clipping process a point P which is located within all four inside half-spaces is retained whereas point Q is culled (it is within three inside half-spaces but is in the outside half-space of the lower horizontal edge).

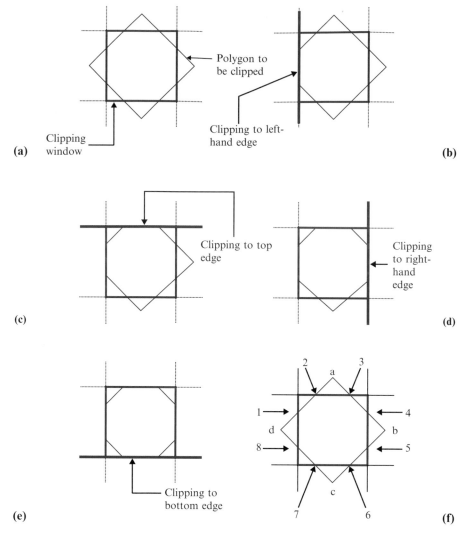

Figure 3.31 Illustrating the operation of the Sutherland-Hodgman polygon clipping algorithm. Here, we employ a simple example – a quadrilateral is clipped to a rectangular window. In (f) we assign symbols to the vertices of the quadrilateral and to the points at which it crosses the extended clipping boundaries. See text for discussion.

Let us now turn our attention to the basic technique employed by this algorithm and here, we will make use of the simple example depicted in Figure 3.31. In (a) we show a rectangular clipping window whose edges have been extended to 'infinity' – and so each edge has associated inside and outside half-spaces. A quadrilateral is also shown – this is to be clipped to the window. As may be seen in Figures 3.31(b)–(e) the quadrilateral is clipped in turn against each edge of the clipping window – for example in (b) it is clipped against the left hand edge – only the portion of the quadrilateral lying within the inside half-space of this edge is retained.

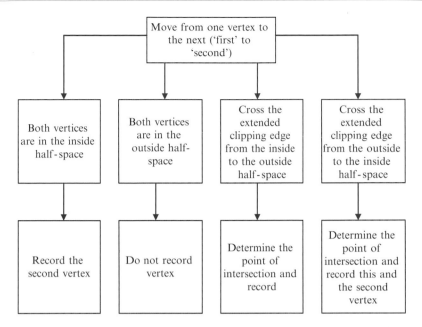

Figure 3.32 The four possibilities and the actions associated with each when clipping a polygon using the Sutherland-Hodgman polygon algorithm. See text for discussion.

To readily understand the operation of this algorithm, we can consider that we 'walk' around the edges of the polygon to be clipped and as we travel from one vertex to the next, we act on one of four possibilities. These are:

- *The last vertex and the next vertex are both within the inside half-space of a clipping boundary.*
- *The last vertex and the next vertex are both within the outside half-space of a clipping boundary.*
- *We have moved across a clipping boundary – the last vertex being in the inside half-space and the next vertex in the outside half space.*
- *We have moved across a clipping boundary – the last vertex being in the outside half-space and the next vertex in the inside half space.*

In the case of Figure 3.31(b) in which we are clipping against the left had edge, we make a circuit of the polygon and the actions we take are summarised in Figure 3.32. Having completed our circuit of the polygon, we then repeat the process for another clipping edge – and so the process continues until we have clipped to all edges of the clipping window.

In Figure 3.31(f) we label the four vertices of the quadrilateral as *a* to *d* and the points at which this object crosses the clipping boundaries as 1 to 8. Thus the unclipped polygon has a vertex list *a, b, c, d*. Let us (arbitrarily) suppose that we start our first circuit by travelling from *d* to *a* and that we are clipping against the left-hand clipping edge (again this is an arbitrary choice). As we 'walk' around the quadrilateral we keep notes in relation to the clipping process – these 'notes' represent a new vertex list that ultimately defines the clipped polygon.

Bear in mind that on this first circuit we are clipping against the left-hand edge (for the moment we may ignore all other clipping boundaries).

- The first point of interest that we encounter relates to our crossing the left-hand boundary (point 1 in Figure 3.31(f)). This corresponds to our crossing from an outside to an inside half-space. As indicated in Figure 3.32, we determine the location of point 1 – make a note of this and also note the location of the next vertex −a.[10]

- Moving from vertex a to vertex b – both are in the inside half space *of the left-hand edge* and so, in accordance with Figure 3.32, we simply add vertex b to the list. So far, this list will read 1, a, b.

- Continuing with our scenic tour – this time along the edge connecting vertices b and c. Thus we simply add vertex c to our list.

- Finally, we 'walk' along the edge connecting vertices d and a. At the point denoted as 8 in Figure 3.31(f) we cross the left-hand clipping boundary – from the inside to the outside half-space. As indicated in Figure 3.32, we determine the location of this point and add it to our list.

Our first tour (which relates only to the left-hand clipping boundary) is now complete and we have created a new vertex list which reads 1, a, b, c, 8. The above process is then repeated for the top, right-hand and bottom clipping boundaries – each time we use the vertex list that was created during the previous tour as the input.

OTU Exercise 3.9: The Sutherland-Hodgman Polygon Clipping Algorithm

Continue the above discussion by undertaking a second, third and fourth 'tour' of the polygon illustrated in Figure 3.31 so clipping against the top, right-hand and bottom clipping edges. Hence confirm that this results in the formation of a polygon with vertices 1,2,3,4,5,6,7,8.

As illustrated in Figure 3.33, the clipping of a concave polygon may result in the production of two or more polygon 'fragments'. In the case of the Sutherland-Hodgman algorithm these fragments are in fact not isolated, but are connected by 'extraneous' edges (also referred to as 'bridging' edges). This can be easily verified by applying the algorithm to the polygon depicted in Figure 3.33.

For further discussion on this algorithm see, for example, Sutherland and Hodgman [1974], Comninos [2006], Hill [1990], Hearn and Baker [1986] and most standard computer graphics texts. It is recommended that the interested reader also examine the operation of the Weiler-Atherton clipping algorithm. This is somewhat more powerful – both concave and convex polygons can be clipped against concave and convex clipping boundaries – even when one or other contains holes. For details see, for example, Comninos [2006], Weiler and Atherton [1977] and most standard computer graphics texts.

---

[10] As we proceed to a, we also cross the top clipping boundary – however, for the moment we ignore this boundary – we are only concerned with the left-hand boundary.

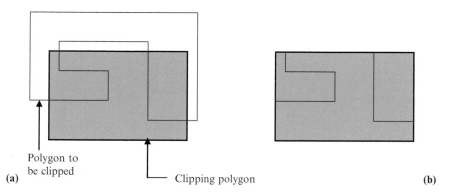

Figure 3.33 In (a) we show a concave polygon and its location relative to a rectangular clipping boundary. The result of the clipping process is depicted in (b). Here, we appear to have generated two disconnected polygon fragments. However, in the case that the Sutherland-Hodgman algorithm is employed, these two fragments are actually connected together via extraneous 'bridging' edges that lie along the clipping window boundary.

3.9 Discussion

'Concern for man and his fate
must always form the chief interest of all technical endeavours.
Never forget this in the midst of your diagrams and equations.'[11]

In this chapter we have introduced some of the basic techniques associated with the creation of simple computer graphics images. In this context we have introduced the use of a viewport and screen coordinate system. Subsequently we considered transformations for manipulating points and vectors within a 2-D space. Here, we demonstrated that several transformations can be encapsulated within a single matrix operator and in this context identified a difficulty associated with 2 by 2 matrices – specifically in relation to translation operations. This led to discussion concerning the use of homogeneous transformations.

The second part of the chapter introduced some simple ideas concerning the use of graphs and di-graphs (comprising a set of nodes and edges) for the representation of 2-D objects. The determination of the location of a point relative to an object boundary has been briefly outlined and we have reviewed some basic issues relating to clipping.

Throughout this chapter our focus has been upon the manipulation of points, straight line segments and polygons. In the chapter that follows we turn our attention to the formation and manipulation of curves within a 2-D space.

3.10 Review Questions

1. As far as the display screen is concerned, from what point are the locations of pixels usually referenced?
2. State a 2 by 2 matrix that causes an anticlockwise rotation through an angle of θ degrees.

---

[11] Attributed to Albert Einstein (1879–1955).

3. State a transformation that cannot be accomplished through multiplication with a 2 by 2 matrix operator.
4. State a homogeneous transformation matrix that will cause an anticlockwise rotation through an angle of θ degrees.
5. State a homogeneous transformation matrix that will cause a reflection in the x-axis.
6. What is a 'di-edge'?
7. State the parametric equations that define the location of a point (x,y) on a line segment.
8. The Sutherland-Hodgman polygon clipping algorithm can be used to clip both _____ and _____ polygons against a _____ clipping polygon.
9. What does the acronym NDC stand for?
10. Suppose that we wish to effect rotation about an arbitrarily positioned point. What basic transformations would you combine to achieve this goal?

3.11 Feedback to Review Questions

1. From the upper left-hand corner.

2. $\begin{bmatrix} \cos\theta & \sin\theta \\ -\sin\theta & \cos\theta \end{bmatrix}.$

3. Translation.

4. $\begin{bmatrix} \cos\theta & \sin\theta & 0 \\ -\sin\theta & \cos\theta & 0 \\ 0 & 0 & 1 \end{bmatrix}.$

5. $\begin{bmatrix} 1 & 0 & 0 \\ 0 & -1 & 0 \\ 0 & 0 & 1 \end{bmatrix}.$

6. The term 'di-edge' refers to directed edges that are used to form 'di-graphs'. Here each edge has an associated direction and this can be used to, for example, define the inside and outside of a polygon.

7. $\begin{aligned} x &= x_1 + (x_2 - x_1)\,u \\ y &= y_1 + (y_2 - y_1)\,u \end{aligned}$

8. The Sutherland-Hodgman polygon clipping algorithm can be used to clip both *concave* and *convex* polygons against a *convex* clipping polygon.

9. NDC is an acronym for 'normalised device coordinates'.

10. Translation – move the centre of rotation to the origin, rotation through the required angle, translation – thereby 'undoing' the previous translation operation.

Curves in 2-D Space 4

'...he cherished the hope that he would reach the cat, but never did; and if he had, we knew that he would only have stood and wagged his tail ...'

4.1 Introduction

We now turn our attention to the formation of curves within a 2-D space and begin by reviewing aspects of elementary Calculus – specifically in relation to differentiation. Here, we do not introduce differentiation techniques from first principles but rather outline procedures that may be adopted in order to achieve certain goals. As in other chapters, a number of 'OTU' exercises are presented and provide the opportunity of gaining some experience in applying the techniques which are discussed.

In Section 4.3 we introduce 'interpolation' – a set of methods that are frequently used in the formation of both static and dynamic images. For example, in the case of the former, interpolation enables us to connect together two or more points using either straight line segments or curves and in the case of dynamic scenes, these techniques enable us to create a set of image frames that 'interpolate' between initial and final states. Thus we can interpolate ('fill in the gaps') either spatially or temporally.

Bézier curves are briefly introduced in Section 4.4. This approach was pioneered by Paul de Faget de Casteljau working for the French car manufacturer Citroën in 1959 and independently by Pierre Bézier (at Rénault) in ~1962. However, it appears that as a result of Citroën's commercial confidentiality policy, some years passed before de Casteljau's activities in the area were published and in the interim Bézier's work had become well known. As a result the technique is almost universally associated with Bézier rather than with de Casteljau.

Having identified key strengths and weaknesses of the Bézier curve generation technique, in Section 4.5 we consider uniform and non-uniform B-splines for curve formation. As we will see, B-splines offer a powerful method for creating and manipulating curves and permit curve segments to be seamlessly connected together. Finally in Section 4.6 we discuss issues relating to the smooth and seamless connection of curve segments and introduce 'orders of continuity'. As we will discuss, zero-order continuity ensures that two curve segments actually join – the coordinates of the end-point of one curve segment coinciding with the coordinates of the starting point of another. First-order continuity ensures that the gradients of two curve segments are, at the point at which the curves connect, identical. Second-order continuity relates to the rate of change of gradient at the point at which two curve segments meet (this is often of importance when dealing with animation).

Although this chapter deals with curve formation in a 2-D space, many of the techniques that are introduced can be extended to support 3-D curve generation.

Key Learning Outcomes: At the end of this chapter you should be able to:

- *Use differentiation techniques to find the gradient and turning points of curves represented in Cartesian and parametric forms.*

- *Understand basic interpolation techniques and distinguish between linear and non-linear forms.*

- *Discuss the characteristics of Bézier curves and obtain the equation for a Bézier curve based on the location of a set of control points.*

- *Describe the use of uniform and non-uniform B-splines for curve formation and manipulation.*

- *Discuss key issues in relation to the seamless interconnection of curve segments and distinguish between different 'orders of continuity'.*

4.2 A Little Calculus

'It is a miracle that curiosity survives a formal education.'[1]

In this section we summarise some mathematical tools and methods that are directly relevant to our subsequent discussions. For students who have studied Calculus it is likely that you will be already familiar with the material outlined here and can therefore skip this section. However, before doing so it may be a good idea to look at the associated OTU Exercises and check

---

[1] Attributed to Albert Einstein (1879–1955).

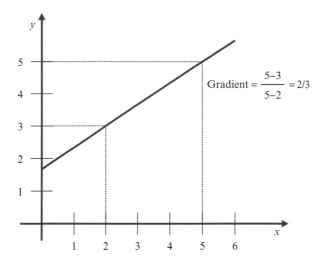

Figure 4.1 A line has constant gradient (m). In the case of this example, the gradient is calculated using Eq. 4.1 and equals 2/3.

that you are in fact able to undertake the calculations. In the case of students who have not previously studied Calculus, the methods described here are presented without derivation and it is suggested that you augment this chapter with a standard maths text such as Larson *et al.* [1998].

Often, we encounter situations in which we are interested in finding the gradient (slope) of a line or curve. In the case of the former and as indicated in Section 2.3, the gradient (m) is given by:

$$Gradient = \frac{y_2 - y_1}{x_2 - x_1}, \tag{4.1}$$

and is easily remembered as the '*change in y divided by the change in x*'. For example in the case of the line illustrated in Figure 4.1, the gradient is calculated as shown. As is apparent from the diagram, in the positive x direction, the line goes 'uphill' – and so by definition is said to have a positive gradient (recall Figure 2.4(b)). On the other hand, if as x increases, a line or curve goes 'downhill' then it is said to have a negative gradient.

A straight line has constant gradient – however, in the case of a curve, the gradient is continually changing. For example, consider the parabola illustrated in Figure 4.2. Here, the gradient is given by the slope of the tangent to the curve at the point of interest. One simple approach to finding the gradient of a curve at a particular point is to plot the curve, draw the tangent to the curve at the point of interest and measure the slope of the tangent using Eq. 4.1. Unfortunately, it is not possible for us to visually estimate the *exact* tangent and so the value that we obtain for the gradient will be subject to error.

Fortunately, the process of differentiation provides a technique by which we can determine the *exact* gradient[2] of a curve at any point.

---

[2] This is also referred to as a functions 'rate of change'. For example, suppose that we have a function that indicates an object's speed (velocity) with respect to time. The differential of this function yields an equation that indicates the rate of change of speed with respect to time – and of course, the rate of change of speed with respect to time corresponds to an object's acceleration.

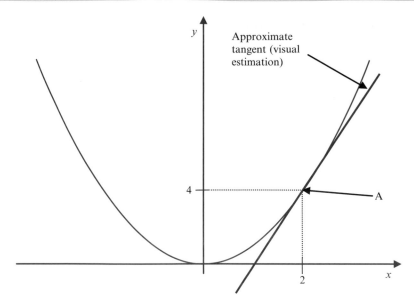

Figure 4.2 Here, we illustrate the curve $y = x^2$. The gradient at A (2,4) may be found by estimating the slope of the tangent to the curve at this point. However, this will only provide an approximate value. In contrast, differentiation provides an exact value.

> **The derivative of a function gives an expression for the function's gradient – its 'rate of change'.**

Below we consider by means of several examples the way in which the derivatives of various functions are obtained. In Section 4.2.2, we extend this discussion to show how we can obtain the gradient of a curve (specified by a Cartesian equation) at a specific location. Subsequently, we turn our attention to dealing with parametric equations.

4.2.1 The Differentiation Process

In this subsection we discuss the process of differentiation and provide a number of examples that demonstrate how the derivatives of various exemplar functions are obtained.

1. **Notation:** Suppose that we have a function $f(x)$ and that we differentiate this function with respect to the variable x. The derivative is then generally indicated as $f'(x)$. This is referred to as the 'first derivative' of the function. If we were then to differentiate $f'(x)$, we would indicate this 'second derivative' as $f''(x)$. Alternatively, consider a function such as $y = 3x + 4$. In this case the first derivative of this function with respect to x would be indicated by: $\frac{dy}{dx}$. This reads '*the derivative of y with respect to x*'. The second derivative would be indicated by: $\frac{d^2y}{dx^2}$.

   In summary two general forms of notation can be used:

   $$f(x) \rightarrow f'(x) \rightarrow f''(x)$$

   $$y \rightarrow \frac{dy}{dx} \rightarrow \frac{d^2y}{dx^2}$$

2. **Differentiating Simple Functions**: Consider the function $f(x) = ax^n$ where a and n are constants. The differential of this function is given by:

$$f'(x) = anx^{n-1}. \tag{4.2}$$

This process can easily be remembered as:

> **Multiply by the power and decrement the power.**

Let us consider some examples:

- The first differential of the function $f(x) = 3x^5$ is given by:

$$f'(x) = 15x^4.$$

- The first differential of the function $f(x) = 3x$ may be obtained following the same procedure (but recall that $x^0 = 1$):

$$f'(x) = 3x^0 = 3.$$

- The differential of any constant is zero.

Bringing together these procedures, we can find the first and second differentials of slightly more complex equations. For example, consider the quadratic equation:

$$f(x) = 3x^2 + 4x + 6.$$

The first and second derivatives are given by:

$$f'(x) = 6x^1 + 4x^0 + 0 = 6x + 4, \quad f''(x) = 6x^0 + 0 = 6.$$

Similarly, consider the equation:

$$y = 5x^2 + 9x + 4.$$

The first and second differentials are:

$$\frac{dy}{dx} = 10x + 9, \quad \frac{d^2y}{dx^2} = 10.$$

OTU Exercise 4.1: Derivatives

Find the first and second derivatives of the following:

1. $f(x) = 3x^3 + 6x^2 - 4x + 7$.
2. $y = 9x^4 - 4x^3 + 2x^2 + 5x - 8$.
3. $y = x(4x + 3)$.
4. $y = \sqrt{x}$.   Hint: $\sqrt{x} = x^{1/2}$.

3. **Differentiating a Function of the Form** $(ax + b)^n$: Consider a function that has the general form:

$$(ax + b)^n, \qquad (4.3)$$

where a, b and n are constants. We may find the differential by expanding this equation and then apply the procedures used above. For example, given the equation $y = (3x + 4)^2$. Expanding this equation we obtain:

$$y = 9x^2 + 24x + 16,$$

and so the first derivative is given by:

$$\frac{dy}{dx} = 18x + 24.$$

However, expanding brackets that are raised to higher powers is tedious (e.g. consider the case of $y = (4x + 3)^{20}$) and fortunately, the derivative can be obtained without the need for expansion. Here, we adopt the following procedure:

> **Multiply by the power, decrement the power and then multiply by the differential of the contents of the bracket.**

Although at first sight this may sound confusing (!), in practise the process is quite straightforward. For example, consider the equation $y = (3x + 4)^2$ (which we differentiated above). Following the above procedure, we begin by multiplying by the power (2) and decrement the power (this gives $y = 2(3x + 4)^1$). We then find the differential of the contents of the bracket (which is 3) and multiply by this value. Thus:

$$\frac{dy}{dx} = 6(3x + 4) = 18x + 24.$$

Note that this is the same result as the one obtained above and that was determined by expanding the bracket prior to differentiating. By way of a further example, consider the equation $y = (4x + 3)^{20}$. The first differential of this equation is:

$$\frac{dy}{dx} = 80(4x + 3)^{19}.$$

4. **The Product Rule**: Consider the case that we wish to differentiate an equation that comprises the product of two functions that we will refer to as u and v. For example:

$$y = 3x^3(1 + x)^{10}$$

Here, we could represent $3x^3$ as u and $(1 + x)^{10}$ as v. We can directly differentiate such an equation by using the 'Product Rule' which indicates that:

$$\frac{dy}{dx} = u\frac{dv}{dx} + v\frac{du}{dx} \qquad (4.4)$$

In the case of the above example, we would obtain:

$$\frac{dy}{dx} = 3x^3 \cdot \frac{d}{dx}(1+x)^{10} + (1+x)^{10} \cdot \frac{d}{dx}3x^3 = 30x^3(1+x)^9 + 9x^2(1+x)^{10}$$

OTU Exercise 4.2: Further Derivatives

Find the first differential of each of the following:

1. $y = (6x + 3)^5$.
2. $y = 3(1 - 3x)^2$.
3. $y = 3x(1 - x)^2$.

4.2.2 Finding the Gradient of a Curve Described by a Cartesian Equation

The approach that we adopt in order to determine the gradient of a curve at a particular point is summarised in Figure 4.3. We begin by obtaining the first derivative – this equation gives us the rate of change of, for example, y with respect to the variable x. (This corresponds to the gradient of the curve). To find the gradient at a particular point, we simply insert the x-coordinate of the point of interest into the equation (for the first derivative). For example consider the curve depicted in Figure 4.2 and whose Cartesian equation is: $y = x^2$.

The point A (with Cartesian coordinates $(2,4)$) indicated on this parabola has a gradient that corresponds to that of the tangent to the curve at this point. Following Figure 4.3 we first obtain

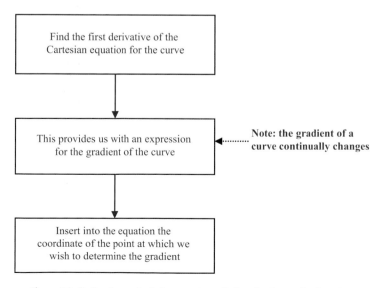

Figure 4.3 Finding the gradient of a curve at a particular point. See text for discussion.

an expression for the gradient of the curve. Thus:

$$\frac{dy}{dx} = 2x = gradient.$$

We substitute the x-coordinate of the point of interest (point A) into this equation and so the gradient at A is 4. Below we provide an additional example to illustrate the use of this general approach:

Example: Find the coordinates of the turning point of the curve $y = 3x^2 + 4x + 2$. Note that at a turning point, the gradient is zero[3]. We begin by finding the first derivative:

$$\frac{dy}{dx} = 6x + 4 = gradient.$$

At the turning point this equation equates to zero. Thus $6x + 4 = 0$ and rearranging, we obtain $x = -2/3$. To find the y coordinate of the turning point, we substitute this x value into the Cartesian equation for the curve – that is:

$$y = 3x^2 + 4x + 2 = 3\left(\frac{-2}{3}\right)^2 + 4\left(\frac{-2}{3}\right) + 2 = \frac{2}{3}.$$

Thus the turning point has Cartesian coordinates $(-2/3, 2/3)$.

OTU Exercise 4.3: Determining the Coordinates of a Turning Point

Consider the curve whose Cartesian equation is given by: $y = 6x^2 - 6x - 2$. Determine the coordinates of the turning point.

4.2.3 Dealing with Parametric Equations

Consider a curve represented by the following parametric equations:

$$y = t + 4$$
$$x = \sqrt{t}$$

Let us suppose that we are asked to find the gradient of this curve at a point A with coordinates (2,8). Here, we are faced with a slight difficulty as neither one of the two equations provides us with a relationship showing how x and y are related. Therefore we cannot 'differentiate y with respect to x' – x and y are not contained within the same equation. One obvious approach to dealing with this situation is to eliminate the parameter t and so obtain an equation that directly relates y and x (in this case: $y = x^2 + 4$). We could then use the approach described above – namely determine dy/dx and insert into this equation the x coordinate of point A. An alternative approach is to differentiate the two parametric equations with respect to the parameter (t). Thus using the first of the two parametric equations we can differentiate y with

---

[3] For example, in the case of the curve illustrated in Figure 4.2, the turning point is at $(0,0)$.

respect to t ($\frac{dy}{dt}$) and in the case of the second equation we can differentiate x with respect to t ($\frac{dx}{dt}$) – as follows:

$$y = t + 4, \quad \frac{dy}{dt} = 1.$$

$$x = \sqrt{t} = t^{1/2}, \quad \frac{dx}{dt} = \frac{1}{2}t^{-1/2} = \frac{1}{2t^{1/2}}.$$

To bring these two equations together and obtain an expression for dy/dx, we make use of the 'Chain Rule'. In the problem that we are discussing, y is a function of t and since $t = x^2$, we can also say that t is a function of x. The Chain Rule indicates that:

$$\frac{dy}{dx} = \frac{dy}{dt} \cdot \frac{dt}{dx}. \tag{4.5}$$

Thus, we can write:

$$\frac{dy}{dx} = (1) \cdot (2)t^{1/2} = 2\sqrt{t}.$$

Since $x = \sqrt{t}$, we can re-write this as $dy/dx = 2x$. Recall, that the original Cartesian equation was $y = x^2 + 4$ and if we differentiate this we obtain $dy/dx = 2x$. Hence the two approaches yield the same result.

4.3 Interpolation

> 'We shall not cease from exploration, and
> the end of all our exploring
> will be to arrive where we started and
> know the place for the first time.'[4]

Interpolation techniques are frequently used in computer graphics and enable the calculation of intermediate values (spatially or temporally) between two or more defined states. This is readily understood by considering example situations:

1. **Dynamic Scenes**: Here, for example, we may wish to depict changes in an object's shape with time (e.g. a square that gets progressively larger or smaller), the trajectory of an object (e.g. projectile fired from a cannon), changes in an object's position (e.g. a car travelling along a straight road) or changes in object attributes with time (such as the transition across a range of shades of colour). Typically, we may start by defining two or more key states (e.g. the starting and ending positions of a car). Subsequently, to achieve a smooth animation we need to interpolate between these key states and generate a number of image frames which, when depicted in sequence, will provide the visual system with a sense of smooth and continuous dynamics. We may, for example, decide to generate these 'interpolated frames' in such a manner that they represent (capture) the state of the system at regular intervals in time or alternatively at intervals that reflect the extent of the changes that have taken place within the scene (e.g. in the case that a car moves with a non-uniform velocity profile).

---

[4] T. S. Eliot.

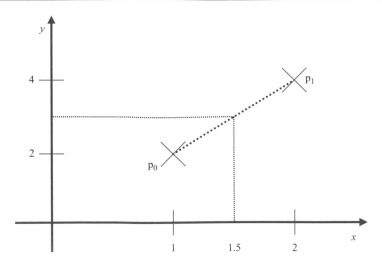

Figure 4.4 The use of interpolation to generate a set of points that lie on the straight line between points p_0 and p_1.

2. **Connecting Points**: Suppose that we have a collection of points that define the geometry of an object (e.g. the vertices of a box). The process of interpolation can be used to fill in the gaps between these points (and so generate the edges of the box). Creating a set of points that lie on a straight line between two defined locations is a straightforward undertaking. However, we are often faced with the more demanding task of connecting points by means of some form of curve (or by using a set of curve segments which are joined together). This facilitates the production of realistic and aesthetic shapes.

In this section, we briefly outline some of the basic principles used in interpolation and begin by considering the generation of a set of uniformly spaced points that lie on a straight line between two defined end-points.

4.3.1 Linear Interpolation

Here, we introduce the use of 'linear interpolation' (this is also referred to by the more imaginative title of 'Lerping'[5]). Consider the elementary example depicted in Figure 4.4 where we have defined two 'key' end-points (p_0 and p_1) that are located at (1,2) and (2,4).

Let us suppose that we wish to generate a set of points that lie on the straight line connecting p_0 and p_1. The simplest case is the point whose x coordinate lies mid-way between those of the end-points (i.e. at $x = 1.5$). Clearly, the y coordinate of this point will lie mid-way between the y coordinates of the end-points (i.e. at $y = 3$). We can use the same approach to determine the y coordinates for each chosen value of x. If we assign to point p_0 the coordinates (x_1, y_1) and to point p_1 the coordinates (x_2, y_2), then:

$$\left(\frac{x_n - x_1}{x_2 - x_1}\right)(y_2 - y_1) + y_1 = y_n, \tag{4.6}$$

where (x_n, y_n) denotes the coordinates of an arbitrary point on the straight line connecting p_0 and p_1. For example, in the case of the end points indicated in Figure 4.4, we can generate

---

[5] Lerping: **L**inear int**ERP**olation.

Table 4.1 Interpolated values for the line segment illustrated in Figure 4.4.

x_n	1.0	1.1	1.2	1.3	1.4	1.5	1.6	1.7	1.8	1.9	2.0
y_n	2.0	2.2	2.4	2.6	2.8	3.0	3.2	3.4	3.6	3.8	4.0

values on the line connecting p_0 and p_1 at increments of 0.1 units in x_n. These values are given in Table 4.1.

Notice that we have made uniform changes to x_n (in this case increasing the value in steps of 0.1 units) and this has resulted in uniform spacing of the points generated along the straight line connecting p_0 and p_1. This process is known as 'linear interpolation'.

It is convenient to express the interpolation process using the parametric form of equation:

$$x_n = x_1 (1 - t) + x_2 t, \qquad y_n = y_1 (1 - t) + y_2 t. \tag{4.7}$$

Here, the parameter t varies between zero (at x_1) and unity (at x_2). For convenience, we will let $1 - t = f_1$ and $t = f_2$. Therefore Eq. 4.7 becomes:

$$x_n = f_1 x_1 + f_2 x_2, \qquad y_n = f_1 y_1 + f_2 y_2. \tag{4.8}$$

The functions f_1 and f_2 are illustrated in Figure 4.5. For each value of the parameter t, the relative values (strengths) of these two functions define the influence that the two key points (p_0 and p_1) have in determining the location of points (x_n, y_n). As a consequence functions f_1 and f_2 are referred to as 'blending functions' (we will be talking about blending functions quite a lot in this chapter and so it is important to understand this simple description of their action). As can be seen from the illustration, at $t = 0$ only function f_1 is non-zero (it has a value of unity) and so from Eq. 4.8 it is clear that (x_n, y_n) lies at p_0: point p_1 has no influence. At the other extreme ($t = 1$) the situation is reversed – only function f_2 is non-zero and so it is apparent that (x_n, y_n) will lie at p_1. Now consider the position mid-way between the two key points ($t = 0.5$). Here both f_1 and f_2 have the same value (0.5) and make an equal contribution to determining the location of (x_n, y_n). Here, we can imagine that points p_0 and p_1 exert an attraction – each 'pulling' in an opposite direction – the strength of the 'attraction' decreasing with distance from each of the two key points. Thus at the half-way position they both exert an equal 'pull' and

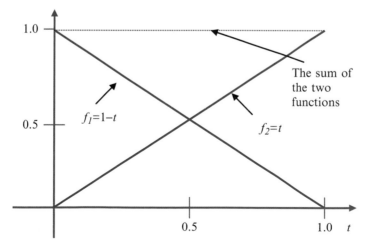

Figure 4.5 The two 'blending' functions f_1 and f_2 used in Eq. 4.8. Note that these sum to unity.

at other positions one key point will exert a larger attraction than will the other. This analogy provides a useful way of conceptualising the way in which blending functions operate.

To gain a further insight into the way in which blending functions operate, recall from elementary maths the 'weighted average'. Here for example, suppose that we need to find the average weight of a collection of objects. Let us assume that in a collection of 20 objects, 2 weigh 1kg, 10 weigh 2kg and the remaining 8 weigh 3kg. Then the average weight would be:

$$Average = \frac{(2) \cdot (1) + (10) \cdot (2) + (8) \cdot (3)}{20} = 2.3kg.$$

This is known as a weighted average calculation and in general terms:

$$Average = \frac{K \cdot a + L \cdot b + M \cdot c + \cdots}{K + L + M + \cdots}. \tag{4.9}$$

Here, K, L and M represent the weights that we ascribe to the quantities a, b, c etc. However, if we are only dealing with two quantities and if their weights sum to unity, this equation becomes:

$$Average = K \cdot a + L \cdot b.$$

This has the same form as Eq. 4.8 and so it is apparent that (x_n, y_n) is simply a weighted average of (x_1, y_1) and (x_2, y_2)! It is useful to note that Eq. 4.8 can be expressed in a more compact form:

$$x_n = f_1 x_1 + f_2 x_2 = \sum_{i=1}^{2} f_i x_i, \qquad y_n = f_1 y_1 + f_2 y_2 = \sum_{i=1}^{2} f_i y_i. \tag{4.10}$$

Here, 'Σ' indicates a summation operation and the values appearing below and above this sign define the range over which this summation is to be carried out. In the above case, 'i' can take on the values 1 and 2 (integer values are used). These two values are inserted into the subscripts of the terms appearing within the summation. By way of a further example, consider the following:

$$x = \sum_{i=1}^{5} (i + 2).$$

In this case the information provided above and below the summation symbol indicates that i can have the values 1, 2, 3, 4, 5. We then insert these values and add the terms:

$$x = \sum_{i=1}^{5} (i + 2) = (1 + 2) + (2 + 2) + (3 + 2) + (4 + 2) + (5 + 2) = 25.$$

Although there is little to be gained in expressing an equation as simple as Eq. 4.8 in this compact form, we will see in subsequent sections that this type of notation can be very useful.

Note that we can express Eq. 4.7 in matrix form:

$$\begin{bmatrix} (1 - t) & t \end{bmatrix} \begin{bmatrix} x_1 \\ x_2 \end{bmatrix} = x_n, \qquad \begin{bmatrix} (1 - t) & t \end{bmatrix} \begin{bmatrix} y_1 \\ y_2 \end{bmatrix} = y_n. \tag{4.11}$$

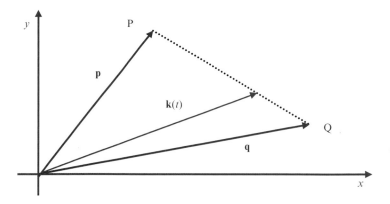

Figure 4.6 Interpolating points ($\mathbf{k}(t)$) along the vector **PQ**. See text for discussion.

OTU Exercise 4.4: Summation Notation

Evaluate the following expression:

$$x = \sum_{j=2}^{6} 2^j$$

Let us now briefly extend the above ideas to encompass vectors. Consider the diagram presented in Figure 4.6. Here, we have two vectors **p** and **q** that define the location of key points P and Q. As we have seen, the vector **PQ** may be represented as $-\mathbf{p} + \mathbf{q}$ and so a fractional distance along this vector is given by $t(\mathbf{q} - \mathbf{p})$, where the parameter t has values in the range $0 \leq t \leq 1$. Thus the position vector $\mathbf{k}(t)$ to any point on the line connecting P and Q is:

$$\mathbf{k}(t) = \mathbf{p} + t\,(\mathbf{q} - \mathbf{p})\,.$$

We can rearrange this equation so that:

$$\mathbf{k}(t) = \mathbf{p}\,(1 - t) + t\mathbf{q}. \tag{4.12}$$

This is the vector form of Eq. 4.7. In the case that, for example, $t = 0.5$, then $\mathbf{k}(t) = 0.5\mathbf{p} + 0.5\mathbf{q}$.

4.3.2 Non-Linear Blending Functions

The blending functions employed in the previous subsection (denoted by f_1 and f_2) ensured that uniform changes in the parameter t give rise to uniformly spaced interpolated values. Within the context of computer graphics this is known as 'linear interpolation'. In many situations this is highly desirable and in other cases the generation of interpolated values that are not uniformly spaced can be advantageous. By way of a simple example suppose that we wish to generate a series of image frames that show an object (e.g. a rectangle) moving in a straight line across the computer screen. We may have defined two key points corresponding to the initial and final positions of the object and we now need to interpolate frames between these two extreme positions. In the case that the object is to travel with constant speed (velocity), we would simply create a series of frames using the linear interpolation technique outlined above and depict these frames at an appropriate rate on the display. Alternatively, let us suppose that the object's velocity is non-uniform – perhaps the object moves slowly at first and subsequently accelerates. In this case, we may use non-linear interpolation – generating a series of frames whose temporal spacing is a function of the object's velocity.

OTU Exercise 4.5: Linear and Non-Linear Interpolation

(a) Consider that we wish to depict the motion of a projectile fired from a cannon. We may define three key points – the initial location of the projectile as it emerges from the cannon, the point at which it returns to the ground and the point of maximum height. In this scenario, what form of interpolation would you employ for the capture of intermediate positions. Discuss your answer.

(b) Discuss situations in which you would employ non-linear interpolation.

Non-linear interpolation involves the use of non-linear blending functions. By way of a simple example, we may define blending functions f_1 and f_2 as:

$$f_1 = \sin^2 t, \quad f_2 = \cos^2 t. \tag{4.13}$$

As with the two blending functions used in the previous subsection, they sum to unity (recall that $\cos^2 \theta + \sin^2 \theta = 1$). The parameter t is now expressed in degrees ($0 \le t \le 90°$) or in radians such that $0 \le t \le \pi/2$.

Concerning Radians: Angles are generally expressed in terms of degrees (including fractions of a degree (minutes and seconds)) or in radians. An angle of 360° is equivalent to 2π radians. Therefore, π radians is equivalent to 180° and $\pi/2$ radians to 90° etc.

1. **Conversion of degrees to radians:** Suppose that we wish to convert 30° to radians. $360° \equiv 2\pi$ radians. Therefore 1° is equivalent to $2\pi/360$ radians and so 30° is equivalent to $30 \times 2\pi/360 = \pi/6$ radians.

2. **Conversion of radians to degrees:** Suppose that we wish to convert $\pi/8$ radians to degrees. $360° \equiv 2\pi$ radians. Hence 1 radian is equivalent to $360/2\pi$ degrees. Thus $\pi/8$ radians $\equiv 22.5°$.

Note the use of the symbol '$\equiv$'. This indicates that one quantity is equivalent to another – radians and degrees are different units and are therefore not equal to each other. However, they are equivalent.

Table 4.2 Here we assume that the two key-points are located at (1,2) and (2,4). Non-linear blending functions are used (see Eq. 4.14) and (x_n, y_n) coordinates are calculated for different values of t.

t (degrees)	0	10	20	30	40	50	60	70	80	90
x_n	2	1.97	1.88	1.75	1.59	1.41	1.25	1.12	1.03	1
y_n	4	3.94	3.77	3.50	3.17	2.83	2.50	2.23	2.06	2

If we assume the use of these blending functions, Eq. 4.8 can now becomes:

$$x_n = x_1 \sin^2 t + x_2 \cos^2 t, \quad y_n = y_1 \sin^2 t + y_2 \cos^2 t. \tag{4.14}$$

Assuming by way of an example that two key points (p_0 and p_1) are located at the positions indicated in Figure 4.4, we can tabulate (x_n, y_n) coordinates for different values of t – see Table 4.2.

OTU Exercise 4.6: Non-Linear Interpolation

By drawing a graph, determine whether or not the (x_n, y_n) coordinates presented in Table 4.2 lie on the straight line connecting the two key-points. Note that although these points are calculated using regular steps of t, on your graph they are not uniformly spaced, thereby providing us with an example of non-linear interpolation.

In computer graphics we frequently encounter situations in which we wish to interpolate between two or more points that are located in a 2-D or 3-D space. As illustrated in Figure 4.7, connecting points using a series of straight-line segments does not yield pleasing and smooth contours. The alternative and generally desirable approach is to connect the points using a smooth curve. Here, a curve may interpolate the points (meaning that it passes through the points) or otherwise. In the following sections we discuss issues relating to the generation of curves the shape of which is defined by the location of a set of 'control points'. Typically, these curves do not interpolate all of these points.

Figure 4.7 Here, a set of points are connected using a series of straight-line segments. A more pleasing effect can be achieved by using one or more curve segments. Try sketching a smooth curve that interpolates these points. In this context, a curve which interpolates the set of points passes through all points.

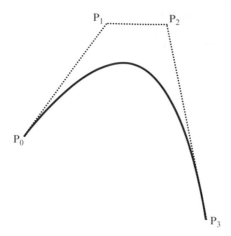

Figure 4.8 An example of a Bézier curve. Note the end-points P_0 and P_3 and also the control points P_1 and P_2.

4.4 Bézier Curves

'A rock pile ceases to be a rock pile
the moment a single man contemplates it,
bearing within him the image of a cathedral.'[6]

Bézier curves were developed by Paul de Faget de Casteljau working for the French car manufacturer Citroën in 1959 and independently by Pierre Bézier (at Rénault) in $\sim$ 1962. However,
it appears that as a result of Citroën's corporate confidentiality policy, some years passed
before de Casteljau's work became widely known and, as a result, this important technique is
attributed to Bézier. In this section we briefly consider Bézier curves within the context of a
2-D space.

A Bézier curve is formed using control points – the location of these points relative to the two
end-points defines the shape of the curve and so they support interaction – moving a control
point changes the shape of the curve. An example of a Bézier curve is provided in Figure 4.8
and as may be seen, the curve passes through points P_0 and P_3 (the 'end points') but does not
pass through the other two (P_1 and P_2) – these being known as the 'control points'. It is as if the
control points exert a force on the curve – drawing it towards them and so changing its shape in
a predictable and well-defined manner.

In the text that follows, we aim to provide an insight into Bézier curves and indicate key
strengths and weaknesses of this technique.

Let's begin by assigning to each point Cartesian coordinates such that P_0 is located
at (x_0, y_0), P_1 at (x_1, y_1), P_2 at (x_2, y_2) and P_3 is at (x_3, y_3). In this case the location
of an arbitrary point (x, y) on the Bézier curve may be expressed using the following

---

[6] Attributed to Antoine de Saint-Exupery (1900–1944).

parametric equations:

$$x = x_0 (1-t)^3 + 3x_1 (1-t)^2 t + 3x_2 (1-t) t^2 + x_3 t^3$$
$$y = y_0 (1-t)^3 + 3y_1 (1-t)^2 t + 3y_2 (1-t) t^2 + y_3 t^3 \tag{4.15}$$

where the parameter t varies between 0 and 1. As we would expect, substituting $t = 0$, into this pair of equations gives $x = x_0$ and $y = y_0$ and substituting $t = 1$ results in $x = x_3$, $y = y_3$ – thus indicating the coordinates of the endpoints of the curve correspond to the location of points P_0 and P_3. Hence the curve interpolates the endpoints.

Let us now determine the gradient of the curve at the two endpoints. We begin by differentiating the above pair of parametric equations with respect to t:

$$\frac{dx}{dt} = -3x_0 (1-t)^2 + 3x_1 \left[(1-t)^2 - 2t(1-t) \right] + 3x_2 \left[2t(1-t) - t^2 \right] + 3x_3 t^2$$
$$\frac{dy}{dt} = -3y_0 (1-t)^2 + 3y_1 \left[(1-t)^2 - 2t(1-t) \right] + 3y_2 \left[2t(1-t) - t^2 \right] + 3y_3 t^2 \tag{4.16}$$

Note that in differentiating the middle two terms of each equation we have used the 'Product Rule' that was summarised in Section 4.2. Thus, for example, in the case of the second term of the first equation, $u = (1-t)^2$ and $v = t$, and so the differential is given by:

$$3x_1 \left[u\frac{dv}{dt} + v\frac{du}{dt} \right] = 3x_1 \left[(1-t)^2 \frac{dt}{dt} + t\frac{d}{dt}(1-t)^2 \right] = 3x_1 \left[(1-t)^2 - 2t(1-t) \right].$$

Returning now to the parametric expressions for the gradient of the Bézier curve given by Eq. 4.16. We can determine the gradient at the start and end-points of the curve (P_0 and P_3) by setting the parameter t to zero for the former and t to one for the latter. Thus for control point P_0 we obtain:

$$\frac{dx}{dt} = -3x_0 + 3x_1,$$

$$\frac{dy}{dt} = -3y_0 + 3y_1.$$

Using the Chain Rule that was summarised in Section 4.2.3, we can write:

$$\frac{dy}{dx} = \frac{dy}{dt} \cdot \frac{dt}{dx} = (-3y_0 + 3y_1) \cdot \frac{1}{(-3x_0 + 3x_1)} = \frac{y_1 - y_0}{x_1 - x_0}. \tag{4.17}$$

Similarly, for point P_3 we can write:

$$\frac{dy}{dx} = \frac{y_3 - y_2}{x_3 - x_2}. \tag{4.18}$$

Referring to Figure 4.9, the gradient of the line connecting P_0 and P_1 is given by:

$$Gradient = \frac{y_1 - y_0}{x_1 - x_0}.$$

By comparison with Eq. 4.17, it is apparent that the gradient of the Bézier curve at control point P_0 is equal to the gradient of the line connecting control points P_0 and P_1. Similarly, from

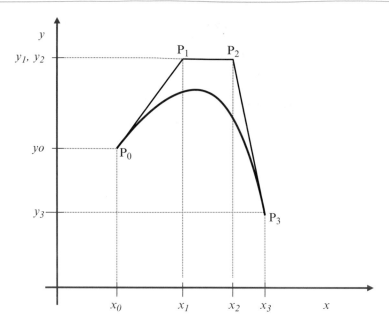

Figure 4.9 The location of the four control points ($P_0 - P_3$). See text for discussion.

Figure 4.9, we can confirm that the gradient of the line connecting points P_2 and P_3 equates to the gradient of the curve at P_3 (see Eq. 4.18).

In summary, the shape of the Bézier curve obtained though the use of the four points indicated in Figure 4.9 is determined by the gradient of the lines connecting each end-point with its adjacent control point. As we interact with the control points and change their location, we change the gradient of these connecting lines and so vary the shape of the curve.

In fact, we are not limited to the use of two control points – additional ones can be added. In this case, the parametric equations for the overall curve follow an easily recognisable pattern. For example, in the case of five points (including the two end-points) we obtain:

$$x = x_0 (1 - t)^4 + 4x_1 (1 - t)^3 t + 6x_2 (1 - t)^2 t^2 + 4x_3 (1 - t) t^3 + x_4 t^4$$
$$y = y_0 (1 - t)^4 + 4y_1 (1 - t)^3 t + 6y_2 (1 - t)^2 t^2 + 4y_3 (1 - t) t^3 + y_4 t^4$$

$$(4.19)$$

And for six points:

$$x = x_0 (1 - t)^5 + 5x_1 (1 - t)^4 t + 10x_2 (1 - t)^3 t^2 + 10x_3 (1 - t)^2 t^3 + 5x_4 (1 - t) t^4 + x_5 t^5$$
$$y = y_0 (1 - t)^5 + 5y_1 (1 - t)^4 t + 10y_2 (1 - t)^3 t^2 + 10y_3 (1 - t)^2 t^3 + 5y_4 (1 - t) t^4 + y_5 t^5$$

$$(4.20)$$

Thus, the number of terms equals the total number of points that are used (this includes the end-points). Additionally the coefficients of each term follow the pattern of binomial coefficients that are given in the famous triangle that bears the name of that well-known French mathematician

Blaise Pascal (1623–1662).[7] The first few rows of Pascal's triangle are given in Appendix A and a brief inspection of these numbers will reveal that the fourth row provides the coefficients used in Eq. 4.15, the fifth row the coefficients used in Eq. 4.19 and the sixth row those appearing in Eq. 4.20.

The values within each row of the triangle (and hence the coefficients within the equations that describe Bézier curves) may be calculated using the equation:

$$B_k = \frac{(n-k)}{k} B_{k-1}. \tag{4.21}$$

Here, n denotes the total number of points that are to be used and k is a pointer to the term in the equation (the first term corresponding to $k = 0$). Thus if, for example we use a total of 5 points ($n = 5$) and assuming that the first term in each row of Pascal's triangle is unity, then the coefficient of the second term ($k = 1$) is $B_1 = ((5-1)/1)1 = 4$. The next coefficient would be given by, $B_2 = ((5-2)/2)4 = 6$ etc.

On the basis of Eq.'s 4.15, 4.19 and 4.20, we can provide a compact vector expression for defining points $\mathbf{p}(t)$ on the curve. Assuming the use of a total of n points, we can write:

$$\mathbf{p}(t) = \sum_{k=0}^{n-1} \mathbf{p}_k B_k (1-t)^{n-k-1} t^k \tag{4.22}$$

Note: Here we assume that by definition $B_0 = 1$ and P_k is the position vector to the kth point.

OTU Exercise 4.7: Bézier Curves

Using Eq.'s 4.21 and 4.22, and assuming the use of a total of 4 points, write down the terms of the vector equation for a Bézier curve.

The functions $B_k (1-t)^{n-k-1} t^k$ are referred to as the Bernstein Polynomials (or blending functions). Table 4.3 summarises the polynomial terms for values of n between 3 and 6. These and subsequent terms can be readily obtained by the expansion of:

$$((1-t)+t)^{n-1}. \tag{4.23}$$

When used in this context, these polynomials are often referred to as 'blending functions'. This is because the curve is a blend of the vectors ($\mathbf{p}_0$, $\mathbf{p}_1$ etc.) – recall previous discussion presented in Section 4.3. Thus for any particular value of t, the terms in the Bernstein Polynomial have certain values. These values are each applied to one of the vectors ($\mathbf{p}_0$, $\mathbf{p}_1$ etc.) and so scale the contribution that the vector makes in defining the shape of the overall curve. In short a weighted sum is calculated in which weightings are applied to the contribution made by each

---

[7] In fact, this pattern of numbers has a much longer history and is recorded in the Chinese work 'Precious Mirror' by Chu Shih-chieh which dates back to the early 14th century [Boyer 1991]. In addition, Cooke [2005] reports knowledge of this pattern of numbers in India some 700 years prior to the efforts of Pascal. Its Sanskrit name is 'Meru Prastara' meaning 'staircase of Mount Meru'.

Table 4.3 The Bernstein polynomial terms (commonly referred to as 'blending functions'). Here, n denotes the number of points used and k provides an index to terms within each polynomial. Note that the coefficients follow the pattern of entries in Pascal's triangle (see Appendix A) and that the terms in each row when added together equal unity.

n	$k=0$	$k=1$	$k=2$	$k=3$	$k=4$	$k=5$
3	$(1-t)^2$	$2t(1-t)$	t^2			
4	$(1-t)^3$	$3t(1-t)^2$	$3t^2(1-t)$	t^3		
5	$(1-t)^4$	$4t(1-t)^3$	$6t^2(1-t)^2$	$4t^3(1-t)$	t^4	
6	$(1-t)^5$	$5t(1-t)^4$	$10t^2(1-t)^3$	$10t^3(1-t)^2$	$5t^4(1-t)$	t^5

control point. Thus we can express Eq. 4.22 as:

$$\mathbf{p}(t) = \sum_{k=0}^{n-1} \mathbf{p}_k h_k(t). \tag{4.24}$$

Where $h_k(t)$ represents the Bernstein polynomials (blending functions).

OTU Exercise 4.8: Bernstein Polynomials

Using Eq. 4.23, or otherwise, obtain the Bernstein Polynomial corresponding to the case that a total of seven points are used ($n = 7$).

4.4.1 Characteristics of Bézier Curves

In this section we briefly consider some of the characteristics of Bézier curves.

1. **The Endpoints**: As may be seen from Eq.'s 4.15, 4.19 and 4.20, all terms (other than the first and last) contain factors in both t and in $(1 - t)$. Consequently, at either endpoint (when the parameter t equals either 0 or 1), these terms equate to zero and so make no contribution to the start and end location of the curve. Thus increasing the number of control points or changing their location does not impact on the coordinates of the curves initial and final coordinates – these are firmly anchored – the curve interpolates the endpoints.

2. **Application of Transformations**: In the case that we wish to translate (shift), rotate or scale a Bézier curve, we do not need to operate upon each point comprising the curve but simply on the end and control points. Once the new locations of these points are found, the curve can be recreated. In this sense Bézier curves are said to exhibit 'affine invariance' – the form of the curve is not changed by affine transformations.

3. **The Convex Hull**: Imagine for a moment that the location of each control point is modelled by a nail that sticks out from a board – as illustrated in Figure 4.10(a). If we then use an elastic band (of appropriate size), and place this around our entire set of pins or nails, it will snap to a shape that is determined by the location of some or all of the pins. This shape defines the 'convex hull' and clearly, the elastic band will not snap to a shape that has 'inward facing' corners.

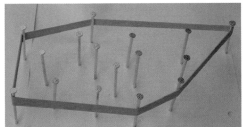

(a)

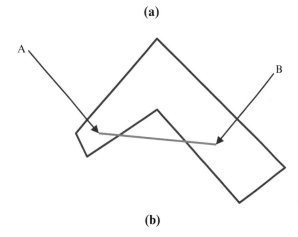

(b)

Figure 4.10 The photograph presented in (a) shows the locations of 16 points – each point being represented using a nail that stands out from a surface. An elastic band has been stretched to encompass this set of points (nails) and when tension is released, the elastic band snaps to a polygon with vertices that are defined by the location of some of the nails. This forms a convex hull. In (b) we illustrate a non-convex set – this has an 'inward facing' corner and so, a line connecting points A and B passes through a region that is outside the set.

Below we briefly define the terms 'convex set' and 'convex hull'.[8]

> 1. **A convex set of points is a collection of points in which a line connecting any pair in the set lies entirely within the set.**
> 2. **Given a collection of points, the convex hull is the smallest convex set that contains the points.**

Thus, for example, points within the region that is defined by the elastic band in Figure 4.10(a) form a convex set. However in the case of the polygon that is depicted in Figure 4.10(b) this does not encompass a convex set – because as may be seen, a line connecting points A and B passes through a region that is external to the polygon.

A Bézier curve lies within the polygon boundary (convex hull) that is defined by the end and control points. Thus, even though the control points may not be positioned in a smooth order (see Figure 4.11), the Bézier curve will remain confined to the convex hull region and of course will always be anchored to the endpoints.

---

[8] Source: Hill [1990].

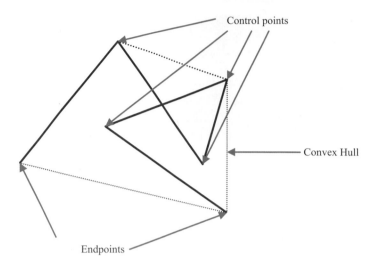

Figure 4.11 Despite the 'jagged' positioning of the control points, the Bézier curve will remain within the convex hull.

4. **Exercising Local Control**: We can form more complex curves by increasing the number of control points. However, consider a situation in which we are interactively creating a curve and that for the most part, the curve has the desired shape. Only in one relatively small region are we not quite happy with its profile and so we modify the location of the nearby control point in an effort to obtain our 'perfect curve'. Unfortunately, movement of this control point will impact on the entire shape of the curve – changing not only the imperfect part on which we are working but also the part that exhibits the desired curvature (recall that all terms within the equation for the Bézier curve are active for all values of the parameter t (other than at the endpoints where t equals zero and one)).

> **The control points are not limited in their scope of effect and this can exacerbate the difficulty of forming more complicated curves via a single set of control points.**

One solution to this problem is to create more complex curves by piecing together separate Bézier curve sections. This process is facilitated by two characteristics:

1. As we have seen Bézier curves pass through the two endpoints and so to connect two such curves, we simply ensure that the location of the endpoint of one section corresponds with the location of the starting point of the next.

2. Matching the starting point of one Bézier curve with the end-point of another will ensure continuity (i.e. no break in the line), but this does not ensure that at the point at which the curves meet there is not an abrupt change in slope. However, recall that at the ends of a Bézier curve, the gradient is equal to that of the line connecting the endpoint with the adjacent control point. Therefore as indicated in Figure 4.12, we can ensure a smooth joining of two curves by arranging that the two intersecting endpoints and their respective adjacent control points lie on a straight line. Thus at the point at which the two sections meet, both will have the same gradient. We discuss this matter in greater detail in Section 4.6.

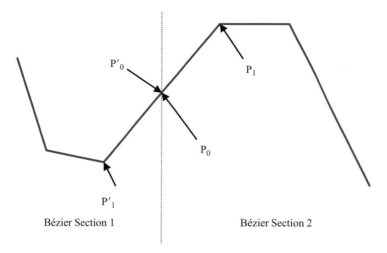

Figure 4.12 Forming a curve by piecing together two Bézier sections. Here we illustrate the control polygons. The starting point of Section 2 coincides with the end-point of Section 1. Additionally so as to ensure a smooth transition in gradient between the two sections, we arrange that points P_0, P_1, P'_0 and P'_1 lie on a straight line. As a result, at the point of intersection the two Bézier curves have the same gradient.

In Chapter 7 we continue our discussion of Bézier curves and show how they can be used to form smoothly curving surfaces.

4.5 Spline Functions and B-Splines

'If you want to build a ship,
do not send your men out to get wood and tools . . .
but teach them a longing for the wide open sea.'[9]

In this section we provide a very brief introduction to 'B-Splines' which are widely used for the formation of curves. Before we begin, it is useful to briefly summarise aspects of the above discussion concerning Bézier curves.

Consider the case of a Bézier curve that employs a single control point (thus a total of three points are used). Referring to Table 4.3, we can write the parametric equations for the curve:

$$x = x_0 (1 - t)^2 + 2x_1 t (1 - t) + x_2 t^2$$
$$y = y_0 (1 - t)^2 + 2y_1 t (1 - t) + y_2 t^2$$

This denotes the quadratic form of Bézier curve. The coordinates of the end-points are given by (x_0, y_0) and (x_2, y_2) and we will arbitrarily locate these at $(1, 1)$ and $(10, 1)$. The above equations then become:

$$x = (1 - t)^2 + 2x_1 t (1 - t) + 10t^2$$
$$y = (1 - t)^2 + 2y_1 t (1 - t) + t^2$$

(4.25)

As can be seen, each equation contains three blending functions.

---

[9] Attributed to Antoine de Saint-Exupery (1900–1944).

OTU Exercise 4.9: Blending Functions

Using a single set of axes, sketch graphs of the three blending functions indicated in Eq. 4.25.

From the graph drawn for the above OTU Exercise, it is apparent that the central term in Eq. 4.25 is non-zero for all values of t (other than 0 and 1 – the end-points) and so contributes to defining the shape of the entire curve. As a result, when we relocate the control point (whose coordinates are given by (x_1, y_1)), we change the shape of the overall curve – although the end-points remain undisturbed. In the case that we increase the number of control points, each influences the profile of the curve – the 'scope of effect' exercised by each control point is not limited. As we have discussed, this can cause problems during an interactive curve creation process.

OTU Exercise 4.10: Sketching a Bézier Curve

Consider the case of a quadratic Bézier curve with end-points at (1, 1) and (10, 1) – as indicated in Eq. 4.25. Assuming that the control point is located at (8, 8), sketch the curve.

Now let us turn our attention to the B-spline approach which enables us to restrict the 'scope of effect' that a control point has in defining the entire shape of the curve. Such curves may be referred to as 'piecewise polynomials' – the overall curve being formed from a series of curve segments that are pieced together in a seamless manner. In the text that follows we loosely follow discussion in Hill [1990].

OTU Exercise 4.11: Sketching a Piecewise Polynomial

Consider the three equations presented below:

$$a(t) = \frac{t^2}{2}$$

$$b(t) = 0.75 - (t - 1.5)^2$$

$$c(t) = 0.5\,(3 - t)^2$$

Sketch the continuous piecewise polynomial that can be constructed using these three equations. Note: For $a(t)$ use values of t in the range $0 \leq t \leq 1$, for $b(t)$ $1 \leq t \leq 2$, and for $c(t)$ $2 \leq t \leq 3$.

The bell shaped curve created in the above exercise is a piecewise function – being formed from separate curve sections. The curve is continuous in the sense that the three sections join together without any breaks. In addition, and at the points of intersection, the segments have the same gradient. This piecewise polynomial is an example of a 'spline function'.

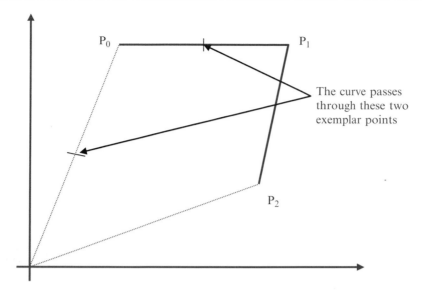

Figure 4.13 Here, we have three points located as shown. We employ a replicated version of the spline function that was considered in OTU Exercises 4.11 and 4.12 to create a curve defined by these points. See text for discussion.

OTU Exercise 4.12: A Spline Function

Referring to the spline function employed in OTU Exercise 4.11:

(a) Show that at the points at which the curves intersect, they have the same gradient.
(b) Determine whether or not, at the points at which the curves meet they have the same rate of change of gradient.

We can replicate this spline function and form a series of blending functions and through the use of a number of control points, we are able to create interesting curves. Recall from our previous discussion that we can represent a Bézier curve using the following notation:

$$\mathbf{p}(t) = \sum_{k=0}^{n-1} \mathbf{p}_k h_k(t). \tag{4.26}$$

Here, we assume the use of n points, k acts as an index, $\mathbf{p}_k$ is the position vector to the kth point and $h_k(t)$ represents the blending functions. Consider the case that we have three points ($n = 3$) as indicated in Figure 4.13.

Suppose that we form blending functions by replicating the spline function as shown in Figure 4.14. Assuming the use of three control points, we create three instances of the function. Using Eq. 4.26, we can now apply these blending functions to the three control points indicated in Figure 4.13. To provide a better insight into the way in which this approach works, it is useful

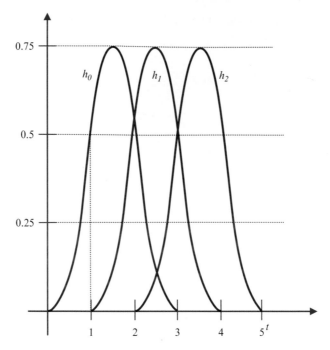

Figure 4.14 Here, three instances of a spline function are shown. These three blending functions are used in conjunction with the three control points depicted in Figure 4.13.

to express Eq. 4.26 in expanded form:

$$\mathbf{p}(t) = \mathbf{p_0}h_0(t) + \mathbf{p_1}h_1(t) + \mathbf{p_2}h_2(t). \tag{4.27}$$

Below we insert some values of t:

- **At $t = 1$:** From Figure 4.14, we see that only the curve $h_0(t)$ is non-zero and at this point it has an amplitude of 0.5.

$$\mathbf{p}(1) = \mathbf{p_0}h_0(1) = 0.5\mathbf{p_0}.$$

Thus the curve passes through a point mid-way between $\mathbf{p_0}$ and the origin. This point is indicated in Figure 4.13.

- **At $t = 2$:** Now two of the functions are non-zero – both $h_0(t)$ and $h_1(t)$ are active and influence the location of the curve. As may be seen from Figure 4.14, at this point, the functions each have an amplitude of 0.5. Thus we can write:

$$\mathbf{p}(2) = \mathbf{p_0}h_0(2) + \mathbf{p_1}h_1(2) = 0.5\mathbf{p_0} + 0.5\mathbf{p_1}.$$

Hence at $t = 2$, both control points exercise an equal influence on the curve. As a result, the curve passes through a point that is mid-way between the two control points. This point is indicated in Figure 4.13.

- **At $t = 3$:** As may be seen from Figure 4.14 $h_0(t)$ has now decayed to zero and so plays no role in influencing the shape of the remainder of the curve. However, $h_1(t)$ and $h_2(t)$ are non-zero – both have amplitudes of 0.5 and exert an equal influence on the location of the curve. Thus at this point, the curve lies mid-way between control points P_1 and P_2. Mark this point in Figure 4.13.

- **At $t = 4$**: Referring to Figure 4.14 we can see that at $t = 4$ only $h_3(t)$ is active and has an amplitude of 0.5.

$$p(4) = p_2 h_3(4) = 0.5 p_2.$$

Consequently, at $t = 4$, the curve passes through a point that is mid-way between the control point and the origin. Mark this point in Figure 4.13.

- **At $t = 0$ and $t = 5$**: As may be seen from Figure 4.14, at both of these points the set of blending functions are zero. Consequently, for example:

$$p(0) = p_0 \cdot 0 + p_1 \cdot 0 + p_2 \cdot 0 = 0.$$

Thus, the curve passes through (0,0) and is therefore 'anchored' to the origin.

OTU Exercise 4.13: Creating a Curve

Using the control points indicated in Figure 4.13 (and the points that you have noted during the above discussion through which the curve passes), sketch the form of curve created by means of the blending functions depicted in Figure 4.14.

The set of blending functions indicated in Figure 4.14 have several key weaknesses. These include:

1. The curve is anchored to the origin.
2. The curve does not pass through (interpolate) the first and last control points and so the coordinates of these points do not correspond to the starting and ending coordinates of the curve.
3. As can be seen from Figure 4.14, for the range of values of t, the blending functions do not sum to unity. For example, at $t = 0$, all blending functions are zero, at $t = 1$, the total amplitude is 0.5 (in fact this is the amplitude of $h_0(t)$ – all other functions are zero). For mid-range values of t, we achieve a constant sum and subsequently, the sum again gradually diminishes until, when $t = 5$, it again returns to zero. As a result, the first and last control points are given a lower weighting and so have less influence on the shape of the curve.

4.5.1 Generating B-Spline Blending Functions

In the example used above, we employed a set of blending functions – each being identical in shape – but shifted from its neighbour by a fixed value. These blending functions ensure that individual control points have only limited influence on the shape of a curve (thus we have addressed the difficulty associated with Bézier curves whereby movement of any control point impacts on the shape of the curve as a whole). On the other hand, as indicated in (1)–(3) above, the approach introduces other difficulties. One way to ameliorate these problems would be to use only a limited portion of the curve – corresponding to mid-range values of t.

Alternatively, we can extend this general technique and thereby create a powerful tool in support of interactive curve design. In this subsection we briefly discuss B-spline functions in general and in Section 4.5.2 comment on the use of a standard 'knot vector' which enables us to create open curves that interpolate the first and last points.

B-spline functions may be generated using a recursive formula [Hill 1990]:

$$N_{k,m}(t) = \left(\frac{t - t_k}{t_{k+m-1} - t_k}\right) N_{k,m-1}(t) + \left(\frac{t_{k+m} - t}{t_{k+m} - t_{k+1}}\right) N_{k+1,m-1}(t). \tag{4.28}$$

This formula (which is in fact much simpler to understand than it may initially appear to be ...) generates the kth B-spline function of order m. Here, we need to distinguish between the terms 'order' and 'degree'. The order of a polynomial is one greater than a polynomial's degree. For example, consider the polynomial:

$$7x^3 + 4x^2 + 5x + 9.$$

This polynomial is of degree three (corresponding to the highest power to which x is raised) and has an order of four (corresponding to the number of terms). A polynomial with a degree of three is referred to as a cubic equation and in the case that the degree is two, the equation is called a quadratic.

OTU Exercise 4.14: Polynomials – Order and Degree

State the order and degree of the following polynomial:

$$6x^5 + 9x^4 + 8x^3 + 3x^2 + 2x + 6.$$

Returning to Eq. 4.28, $N_{k,m}(t)$ represents the kth B-spline blending function of order m and as may be seen, this is obtained using two blending functions of lower order (denoted as $N_{k,m-1}(t)$ and $N_{k+1,m-1}(t)$). Thus, for example the kth blending function of order 4, is obtained using the kth and $k + 1^{th}$ blending functions of order 3 which have been previously calculated.

The simplest way of understanding how this process works is by example and so, in the remainder of this subsection we will briefly use Eq. 4.28 to generate several blending functions. In Section 4.5.2 we continue with general discussion on B-splines and their use in curve generation.

As indicated above, Eq. 4.28 allows us to generate a B-spline function of order m using two functions of order $m - 1$. For such a process to operate we must define the starting point – i.e. the function with order of unity ($N_{k,1}(t)$). (By analogy recall Eq. 4.21 that enables the generation of terms within Pascal's triangle – this also required an initial 'seed' value.) We define our starting value as unity across a fixed range – and as zero elsewhere. Thus:

$$N_{k,1}(t) = 1 \text{ for } t_k < t \leq t_{k+1}$$

$$N_{k,1}(t) = 0 \text{ elsewhere.}$$

For example, if we are dealing with the first ($k = 0$), first order function, then we can write:

$$N_{0,1}(t) = 1 \text{ for } t_0 < t \leq t_1$$

$$N_{0,1}(t) = 0 \text{ elsewhere.}$$

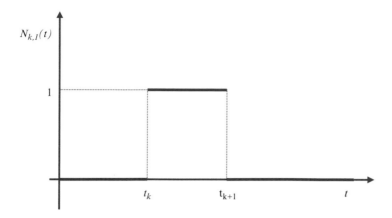

Figure 4.15 Eq. 4.28 is a recursive function by means of which we can generate a B-spline function of order m using two functions of order $m - 1$. Here we indicate the form of the initial function with order of unity ($N_{k,1}(t)$). Note that the actual location of the non-zero portion of this function is determined by the value of k. For example if $k = 1$ then the non-zero portion would occur between t_1 and t_2.

However in the case that we are dealing with the second, first order function, $N_{1,1}(t)$ equals 1 between t_1 and t_2 – and is zero elsewhere. This may appear confusing when encountered for the first time and so in Figure 4.15 we provide further clarification. By using this function in association with Eq. 4.28, we can immediately generate the first ($k = 0$), second-order ($m = 2$) B-spline function. In this subsection, we assume that $t_0 = 0$, $t_1 = 1$, $t_2 = 2$ etc. Thus Eq. 4.28 becomes:

$$N_{0,2}(t) = \left(\frac{t - t_0}{t_1 - t_0}\right) N_{0,1}(t) + \left(\frac{t_2 - t}{t_2 - t_1}\right) N_{1,1}(t) = t N_{0,1}(t) + (2 - t) N_{1,1}(t). \quad (4.29)$$

However, we know that $N_{0,1}(t) = 1$ for $0 < t \leq 1$ (and is zero elsewhere). Similarly, $N_{1,1}(t) = 1$ for $1 < t \leq 2$ (and is zero elsewhere). Thus the first term in the above equation defines the shape of the function between $t = 0$ and $t = 1$ and then the second term contributes the remainder of the function (for $t = 1$ to $t = 2$). The result is the ramp shape depicted in Figure 4.16.

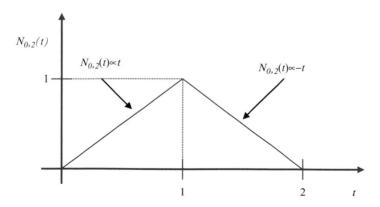

Figure 4.16 The generation of the first ($k = 0$), second-order ($m = 2$) B-spline function.

It is instructive to pause for a moment and consider the form of Eq. 4.29 – which indicates that:

$$N_{0,2}(t) = t N_{0,1}(t) + (2 - t) N_{1,1}(t).$$

The first term increases directly in proportion to t. If we were to plot this relationship we would obtain a straight-line which passes through the origin. By multiplying by $N_{0,1}(t)$ we generate a line segment – when $N_{0,1}(t) = 1$, the multiplication has no effect and elsewhere (where $N_{0,1}(t) = 0$) the graph is eliminated. Similarly, in the case of the second term – although a plot would now reveal a straight-line with a negative gradient and y intercept of 2. Thus we have generated the 'up-ramp' and 'down-ramp' illustrated in Figure 4.16.

Let's continue with the second order function and generate equations for $k = 1$ and $k = 2$. Using Eq. 4.28, we can write for $k = 1$:

$$N_{1,2}(t) = \left(\frac{t - t_1}{t_2 - t_1}\right) N_{1,1}(t) + \left(\frac{t_3 - t}{t_3 - t_2}\right) N_{2,1}(t) = (t - 1) N_{1,1}(t) + (3 - t) N_{2,1}(t). \quad (4.30)$$

Similarly for $k = 2$:

$$N_{2,2}(t) = \left(\frac{t - t_2}{t_3 - t_2}\right) N_{2,1}(t) + \left(\frac{t_4 - t}{t_4 - t_3}\right) N_{3,1}(t) = (t - 2) N_{2,1}(t) + (4 - t) N_{3,1}(t). \quad (4.31)$$

As we can see both of these equations draw upon our definition of the first order function. And we know that:

$$N_{1,1}(t) = 1 \text{ for } t_1 < t \leq t_2$$
$$N_{1,1}(t) = 0 \text{ elsewhere.}$$

$$N_{2,1}(t) = 1 \text{ for } t_2 < t \leq t_3$$
$$N_{2,1}(t) = 0 \text{ elsewhere.}$$

$$N_{3,1}(t) = 1 \text{ for } t_3 < t \leq t_4$$
$$N_{3,1}(t) = 0 \text{ elsewhere.}$$

In Figure 4.17 we illustrate the functions for $k = 0$, $k = 1$ and $k = 2$. As can be seen, changing the value of k does not impact on the shape of the spline generated – it simply produces a shift in location. This is the case for splines of any order – as long as $t_k = k$ (although splines that are of different orders have a different shape).

Let us now turn our attention to the first, third order function. Using Eq. 4.28 we can write:

$$N_{0,3}(t) = \left(\frac{t - t_0}{t_2 - t_0}\right) N_{0,2}(t) + \left(\frac{t_3 - t}{t_3 - t_1}\right) N_{1,2}(t).$$

Which gives:

$$N_{0,3}(t) = \left(\frac{t}{2}\right) N_{0,2}(t) + \left(\frac{3 - t}{2}\right) N_{1,2}(t).$$

This can be expressed as:

$$N_{0,3}(t) = \frac{t}{2} \left[t N_{0,1}(t) + (2 - t) N_{1,1}(t) \right] + \frac{(3 - t)}{2} \left[(t - 1) N_{1,1}(t) + (3 - t) N_{2,1}(t) \right].$$

As we know, the first order values ($N_{0,1}(t)$, $N_{1,1}(t)$ and $N_{2,1}(t)$) define the range over which individual terms in this expression are non-zero. Thus, for example, $t \cdot N_{0,1}(t)$ is non-zero in

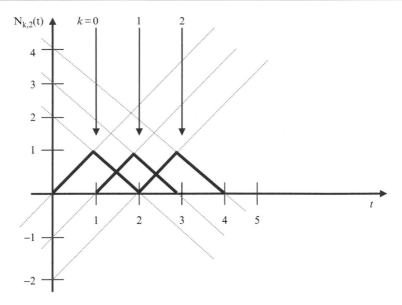

Figure 4.17 The formation of the second-order B-spline functions for $k = 0$, 1 and 2. As may be seen, the functions are identical in shape but each is shifted relative to its neighbours.

the range $t_0 < t \leq t_1$. With this in mind we can write the above expression in terms of a series of piecewise functions:

$$N_{0,3}(t) = \frac{t^2}{2} \text{ for } t_0 \leq t \leq t_1,$$

$$N_{0,3}(t) = \frac{t}{2}(2 - t) + \left(\frac{3 - t}{2}\right)(t - 1) \text{ for } t_1 \leq t \leq t_2,$$

$$N_{0,3}(t) = \frac{(3 - t)^2}{2} \text{ for } t_2 \leq t \leq t_3,$$

and $N_{0,3}(t)$ equals zero elsewhere.

OTU Exercise 4.15: Sketching the First, Third Order Function

By means of the above piecewise expressions, sketch the first, third order function. You should assume that $t_0 = 0$, $t_1 = 1$, etc.

Hint: A sense of *déjà vu* may save time . . .

And so we have turned full circle and have returned to an earlier point in our discussion! However, we are now able to appreciate the way in which B-spline blending functions may be formed. In order to have a powerful tool for interactive curve design, a further ingredient must be added. This is briefly discussed in the next subsection.

OTU Exercise 4.16: Obtaining the First, Fourth Order B-Spline Function

On the basis of the above discussion, obtain piecewise functions that describe the first ($k = 0$), fourth order B-spline function ($N_{0,4}(t)$). You should assume that $t_0 = 0$, $t_1 = 1$, etc. (The cubic B-spline is widely used in computer graphics.)

4.5.2 Non-Uniform B-Splines

In the previous subsection, we outlined the way in which B-spline functions can be generated and following earlier discussion concerning Bézier curves, it is apparent that we can use such blending functions in association with a set of control points to generate a curve whose shape can be readily manipulated. We can express the curve in vector form:

$$\mathbf{p}(t) = \sum_{k=0}^{n-1} \mathbf{p}_k N_{k,m}(t).$$

In the case of the B-splines described in the previous subsection, we arranged for values of t_k to increase in steps of unity – these are referred to as uniform B-splines. However, when we remove the requirement for uniformity, really interesting things happen!

The sequence of values used for t_k is referred to as the 'knot vector'. As we have seen, blending functions comprise a collection of polynomials that form a continuous curve. The point at which two polynomials connect is referred to as a 'joint' and a 'knot' is the value of t at which this happens. Thus, a 'knot vector' denotes the location of joints within a set of blending functions. A 'standard' form of knot vector is used in the formation of B-splines and can ensure that the curve created by using these blending functions in connection with a set of control points will interpolate the first and last points.

The approach adopted is to employ non-uniform knot spacing and this results in the production of sets of non-identical blending functions. Furthermore, we reduce some of the intervals between successive knot values to zero and this is achieved by defining multiple identical knots (the number of identical knot values is referred to as the 'multiplicity'). This can result in discontinuities such that at a particular point all (but one) blending functions are zero. As a result, the curve that is formed can be forced to interpolate control or end points. For example, assuming the use of eight control points, the standard knot vector for a B-spline of order four is:

$$0,0,0,0,1,2,3,4,5,5,5,5$$

Application of this vector results in the formation of a set of blending functions that can be used to create curves that interpolate the first and last control points. Assuming that we have n control points and are employing blending functions of order m, then the entries within the standard knot vector are determined as follows:

1. The number of elements (knots) within the knot vector equals the sum of the number of control points (n) and the order of the B-spline functions to be used. Thus the number of elements equals $n + m$.
2. From left to right elements within the knot vector do not decrease in value. Consequently, $t_k \le t_{k+1}$.
3. For the generation of B-splines of order m, the first m elements within the knot vector are zero.

4. Subsequent to (3), the next $n - m$ elements increase in size in steps of unity. The first of these elements is 1.

5. The last m elements have the same value – this value being $n - m + 1$.

Below we apply these rules so as to form the knot vectors for second, third and fourth order B-splines – we will assume the use of 6 control points:

- **Second-order:** From (1) above the number of elements within the knot vector equals $n + m = 8$. From (3) the first two elements equal zero. In line with (4), the next 4 elements have values 1, 2, 3 and 4 respectively. Finally, from (5), the last two elements each have a value of $n - m + 1 = 5$. Therefore the knot vector is:

$$0, 0, 1, 2, 3, 4, 5, 5$$

- **Third Order (Quadratic):** Following the approach adopted for the second-order case, the knot vector is given by:

$$0, 0, 0, 1, 2, 3, 4, 4, 4$$

- **Fourth Order (Cubic):** Following the same approach as used above, we obtain:

$$0, 0, 0, 0, 1, 2, 3, 3, 3, 3$$

For discussion concerning both uniform and non-uniform B-splines see texts such as Watt [2000], Foley *et al.* [1990] and Jones [2001].

4.6 Continuity

Let us suppose that we wish to connect together two Bézier curves to create a single smooth curve. Naturally, we must ensure that there is no break between curves – the ending point of one curve must coincide with the starting point of the other. Since Bézier curves interpolate their endpoints, we can achieve this goal by simply ensuring that the coordinates of the endpoint of one curve coincide with those of the other curve. However, as we have seen, this does not guarantee that the two curves will seamlessly (smoothly) connect – at the point of intersection, the gradient of one curve may be quite different to that of the other. Recall that at the endpoint, the line connecting the endpoint to the adjacent control point forms the tangent to the curve. Therefore, we can ensure that the two curve segments have the same gradient at the point at which they meet by arranging for the endpoint and adjacent control point of each curve to lie on a straight line – recall Figure 4.12.

In the case that the endpoint of one curve segment is coincident with the endpoint of another curve segment, the curves are said to exhibit 'zero-order' continuity (denoted C^0). When two curve segments share a common tangent at the point at which they meet, they are said to exhibit 'first-order' continuity (C^1). Additionally, in the case that at the point at which two curve segments meet their respective rate of change of gradient (curvature) is the same, they are said to exhibit 'second-order' continuity (C^2).

As indicated above, in the case of compound Bézier curves, attaining C^0 and C^1 continuity is straightforward. However, C^2 continuity is more difficult. In this respect, Newman and Sproull [1981] write:

'Higher-order continuity [beyond C^1] can also be ensured by geometric constraints on control points, but beyond first-order constructions become complex.'

On the same matter, Mortenson [1985] writes:

'... *the advantage of higher order Bézier curves is that they can achieve correspondingly higher orders of continuity between segments of compound curves. For example, a fifth-order, or quintic, Bézier polynomial permits us to specify end-points, end tangents, and curvature at each end. But how do higher degree polynomial functions affect the computation of geometric properties and relationships?'*

Second-order continuity can be particularly important when we are dealing with motion. For example:

- When we wish a fluid to pass smoothly over a surface formed from compound curves.
- In the case that we wish to set up some form of 'virtual camera' which is to travel along a curved path (that is created using compound curves).

> Suppose that we have an equation that defines the position(s) of a moving object with time. We now differentiate this equation with respect to time (i.e. determine ds/dt). This new equation defines the rate of change of position – which corresponds to the object's speed (when speed is represented as a vector quantity, it is referred to as 'velocity'). If we now differentiate the equation that we have obtained for the object's speed – again with respect to time, we obtain an equation for the rate of change of speed (how quickly the object's speed is changing with time). This second differential (denoted d^2s/dt^2) indicates the object's acceleration.

OTU Exercise 4.17: Second-order Continuity

Consider the diagram depicted in Figure 4.18 which shows a road formed from two curve segments. As indicated, the two segments each have a different radius of curvature. Let us suppose that a car travelling at a speed of 140km/h passes through the point at which the two road segments join (labelled A) – how will the dynamics of the car be affected?

Hint: Consider the orders of continuity supported at the point at which the two curves join.

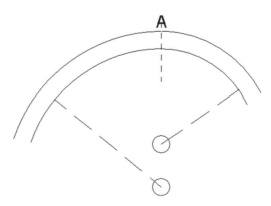

Figure 4.18 Two road segments are indicated. These each have a different radius of curvature and join at point A. See OTU Exercise 4.17 (Reproduced by permission of Professor Rüdiger Hartwig.)

As we have seen, B-splines are formed by connecting piecewise polynomials and below we consider the continuity at the points at which one section 'takes over' from another. Let us briefly consider the piecewise functions given in OTU Exercise 4.11 – these are:

$$a(t) = 0.5t^2 \qquad 0 < t \le 1,$$
$$b(t) = 0.75 - [t - 1.5]^2 \quad 1 < t \le 2,$$
$$c(t) = 0.5\,[3 - t]^2 \qquad 2 < t \le 3.$$

1. **Zero-Order Continuity**: To determine if the endpoint of one curve segment is coincident with the endpoint of the next segment, we need to establish the values of $a(1)$ and $b(1)$ and also $b(2)$ and $c(2)$. From the above equations, we obtain:

$a(1)$	0.5
$b(1)$	0.5
$b(2)$	0.5
$c(2)$	0.5

    Thus $a(t)$ and $b(t)$ join at $(1,0.5)$ and $b(t)$ and $c(t)$ at $(2,0.5)$. Hence these three curve segments exhibit zero-order continuity.[10]

2. **First-Order Continuity**: To determine first-order continuity, we must first differentiate the above equations and hence obtain expressions for the gradient of each curve segment. This gives:

    $$\frac{da}{dt} = t, \qquad \frac{db}{dt} = 3 - 2t, \qquad \frac{dc}{dt} = t - 3. \qquad (4.32)$$

    $$\text{At} \quad t = 1, \quad \frac{da}{dt} = \frac{db}{dt} = 1.$$

    $$\text{At} \quad t = 2, \quad \frac{db}{dt} = \frac{dc}{dt} = -1.$$

    Thus at $t = 1$, $a(t)$ and $b(t)$ share a common tangent. Similarly at $t = 2$. The overall curve therefore demonstrates first-order continuity.

3. **Second-Order Continuity**: Here, we need to obtain expressions for the rate of change of gradient of the three curve segments. Hence we differentiate the three equations given in Eq. 4.32. This gives:

    $$\frac{d^2a}{dt^2} = 1, \qquad \frac{d^2b}{dt^2} = -2, \qquad \frac{d^2c}{dt^2} = 1.$$

    Clearly, the rate of change of gradient of the three curve segments is not equal at the points at which the curves join and so these piecewise functions do not exhibit second-order continuity.

The piecewise curve considered above is a third order (quadratic) B-spline in which the knots are uniformly spaced. It is instructive to briefly consider the continuity demonstrated by the widely

---

[10] Note: Here we are assuming that each of the curve segments is itself continuous. Since the functions are polynomials, this is a valid assumption and so we need only consider possible discontinuities at the knots.

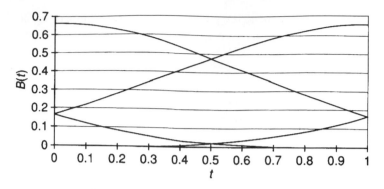

Figure 4.19 The basis functions that are used in the formation of a cubic ($m = 4$) B-spline. See text for discussion. (Reproduced with permission from Vince [2006].)

used cubic B-spline ($m = 4$). Here, the 'basis functions' may be expressed as [Vince 2005]:

$$a(t) = \frac{t^3}{6}$$

$$b(t) = \frac{-3t^3 + 3t^2 + 3t + 1}{6}$$

$$c(t) = \frac{3t^3 - 6t^2 + 4}{6}$$

$$d(t) = \frac{(1-t)^3}{6}$$

In each case we assume that $0 \leq t \leq 1$. The form of these functions is illustrated in Figure 4.19. Below we briefly consider the orders of continuity that are associated with a cubic B-spline:

1. **Zero-Order Continuity**: We anticipate that $a(t)$ joins $b(t)$. Subsequently, $b(t)$ joins $c(t)$ and finally $c(t)$ connects to $d(t)$. For each curve segment, t lies between zero and one. Thus, $a(1)$ should be coincident with $b(0)$, $b(1)$ with $c(0)$ and $c(1)$ with $d(0)$. Inserting these values for t into the above equations we obtain:

$a(1)$	0.167
$b(0)$	0.167
$b(1)$	0.667
$c(0)$	0.667
$c(1)$	0.167
$d(0)$	0.167

   Thus, the curves connect with zero-order continuity.

2. **First-Order Continuity**: Following the approach used above in connection with the quadratic B-spline, by differentiating the basis functions we are able to determine the

gradients of the curve segments at the points at which they connect. Hence, we obtain:

$$\frac{da}{dt} = \frac{t^2}{2}.$$

$$\frac{db}{dt} = -1.5t^2 + t + 0.5.$$

$$\frac{dc}{dt} = 1.5t^2 - 2t.$$

$$\frac{dd}{dt} = \frac{-(1-t)^2}{2}.$$

Inserting the points at which the curve segments intersect enables us to verify C^1 continuity. At the point at which $a(t)$ joins $b(t)$, both curves have a gradient of 0.5. At the point where $b(t)$ meets $c(t)$, both curves have a gradient of 0. Finally at the point at which $c(t)$ and $d(t)$ join, the gradient of both curves equals -0.5. Consequently at the points at which the pairs of curves, they share common gradients and so they demonstrate C^1 continuity.

4. **Second-Order Continuity**: Following the approach used in connection with the quadratic B-spline, we obtain expressions for the rate of change of gradient by determining the second derivatives. Differentiating the above equations gives:

$$\frac{d^2a}{dt^2} = t, \quad \frac{d^2b}{dt^2} = -3t + 1, \quad \frac{d^2c}{dt^2} = 3t - 2, \quad \frac{d^2d}{dt^2} = 1 - t.$$

Inserting $t = 1$ into the first of these equations and $t = 0$ into the second, we obtain the rate of change of gradient at the point at which they join. Here, both equations indicate a rate of change of gradient of 1. Similarly, if we insert $t = 1$ into the second equation and $t = 0$ into the third, we obtain the rate of change of gradient at the point where $b(t)$ and $c(t)$ meet. In both cases the rate of change of gradient is -2. To obtain the rate of change of gradient of the curve segments at the point at which $c(t)$ and $d(t)$, we insert $t = 1$ into the third equation and $t = 0$ into the forth. This indicates that at this point both of these basis functions have the same rate of change of gradient (which is unity). Consequently, at the points at which the curve segments connect, they exhibit second-order continuity. The support provided by cubic B-splines for three orders of continuity ensures that joints are smooth and seamless.

4.7 Discussion

'The best artist has that thought alone
Which is contained within the marble shell;
The sculptor's hand can only break the spell
To free the figures slumbering in the stone.'[11]

In this chapter we have covered some important topics relating to the formation of curves within a 2-D space. In Section 4.3 we focused on interpolation techniques and distinguished between

---

[11] Attributed to Michelangelo di Lodovico Buonarroti Simoni (1475–1564).

linear and non-linear forms. The use of Bézier and B-spline techniques enables a number of control points to be used for the manipulation of curve shape. Interaction is a pivotal part of computer graphics and the use of control points provides an intuitive way of forming curves. However, as discussed in the case of Bézier curves, the movement of one control point impacts on the shape of the entire curve. In contrast, the B-spline approach enables us to limit the scope of effect which the manipulation of individual control points will have on the overall shape of a curve.

As we have discussed, it is often desirable to form more complex curves by piecing together smaller curve segments. This process is facilitated if each individual curve segment interpolates its end-points. Towards the end of the chapter, we have emphasised issues relating to the smooth and seamless joining of curve segments. In this context we introduced zero, first and second orders of continuity.

4.8　Review Questions

1. Differentiate the following expression with respect to the variable x:

$$y = 5\,(2x - 7)^8 .$$

2. What is the order of the following polynomial:

$$3x^4 + 2x^3 - 5x^2 + 2x + 1.$$

3. What is the degree of the polynomial given in (2) above?
4. What is a convex hull?
5. Convert 5π radians to degrees.
6. Indicate one weakness of the Bézier curve drawing technique.
7. Suppose that we have an equation that indicates the distance travelled by an object over time. What is the result of differentiating this equation twice (with respect to time)?
8. When two or more Bézier curves are joined, how do we ensure first order continuity (C^1)?
9. What do you understand by C^2 continuity?
10. Within the context of splines, what is do you understand by the terms 'joint' and 'knot'?

4.9　Feedback to Review Questions

1. The differential is:

$$\frac{dy}{dx} = 80\,(2x - 7)^7 .$$

2. The order of the polynomial is 5.
3. The polynomial has a degree of 4.
4. For a given set of points, the convex hull is the smallest convex set that contains the points.
5. This can be converted as follows: 2π radians $\equiv 360°$. Therefore 1 radian $\equiv 360/2\pi$ degrees. Hence 5π radians $\equiv (360/2\pi)5\pi = 900$ degrees.
6. Several possible responses. For example, changes in the location of one control point will impact on the shape of the entire curve.

Anaglyph Images

These anaglyph images should be viewed using the red and green filter glasses that are supplied with this book. Please note that the red filter should be in front of the right eye, and the green filter over the left eye.

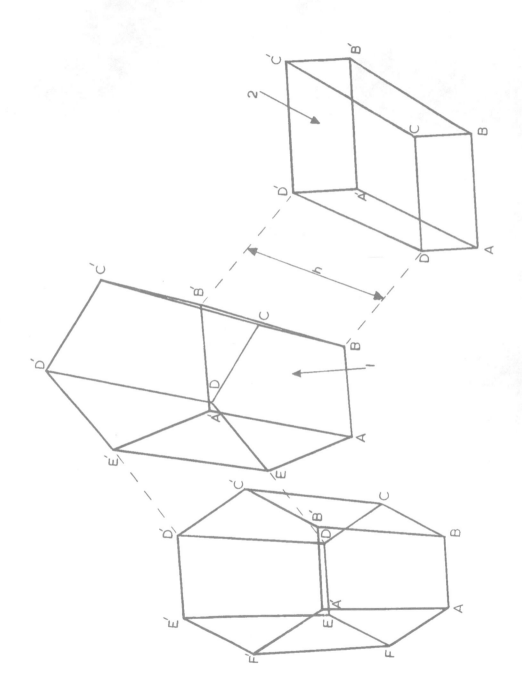

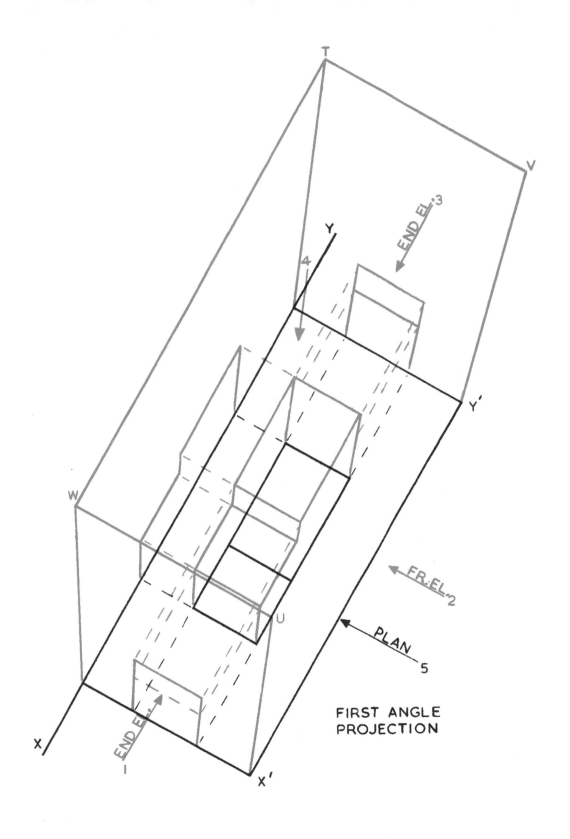

T

V

Y

END EL.3

4

Y'

W

FR.EL.2

U

PLAN

5

X

END EL.

1

X'

FIRST ANGLE
PROJECTION

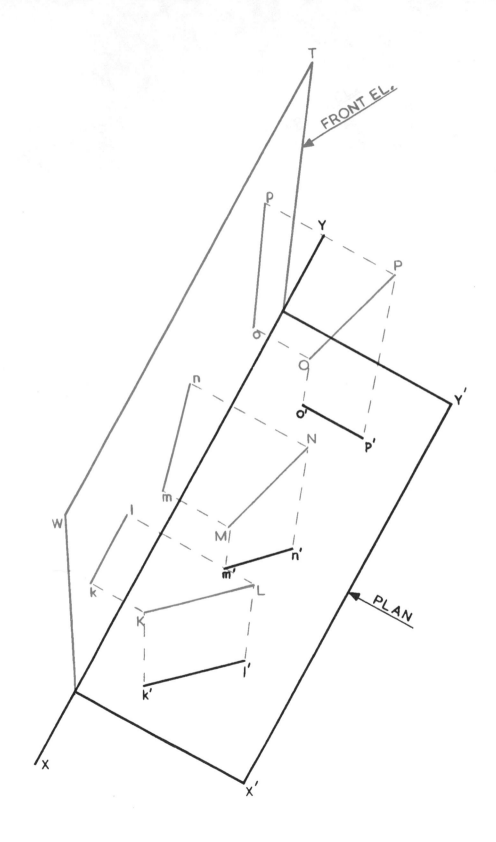

T

FRONT EL.

P

Y

P

o

Q

n

o'

N

P'

m

M

n'

l

m'

W

k

L

K

l'

PLAN

X

k'

Y'

X'

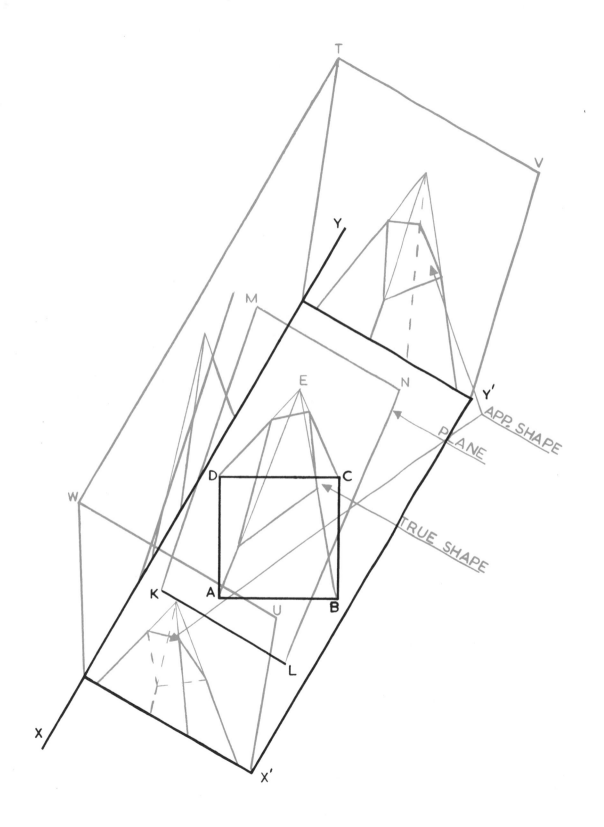

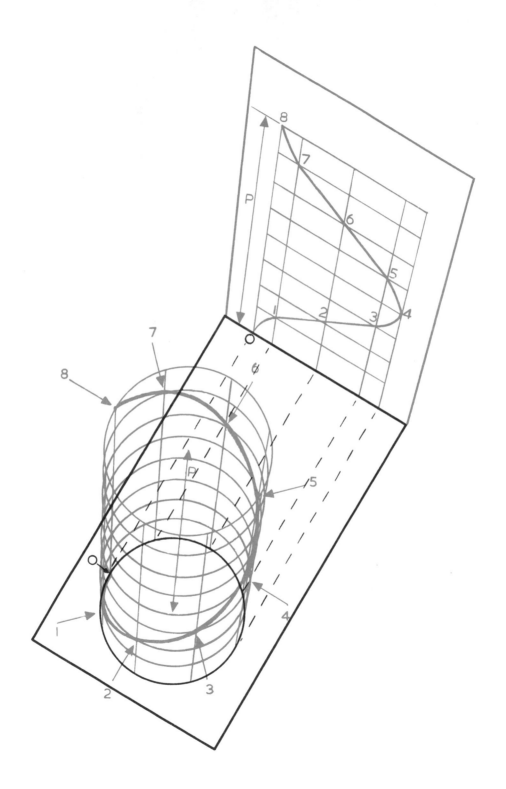

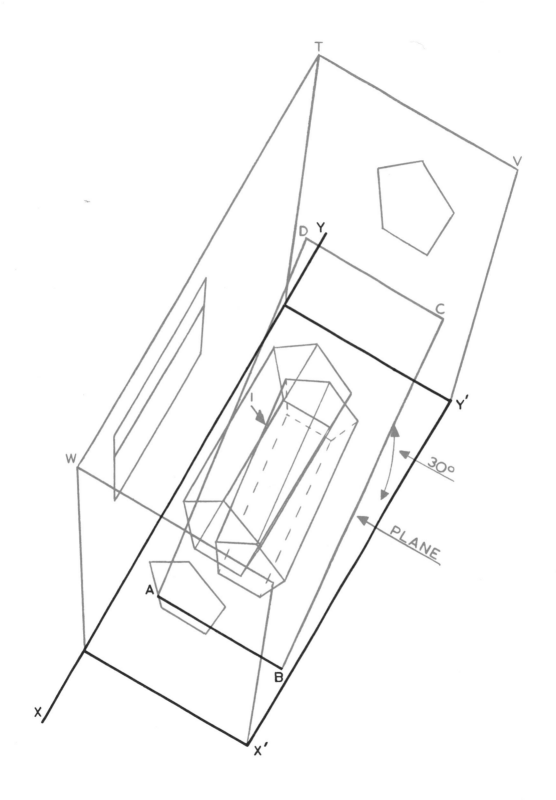

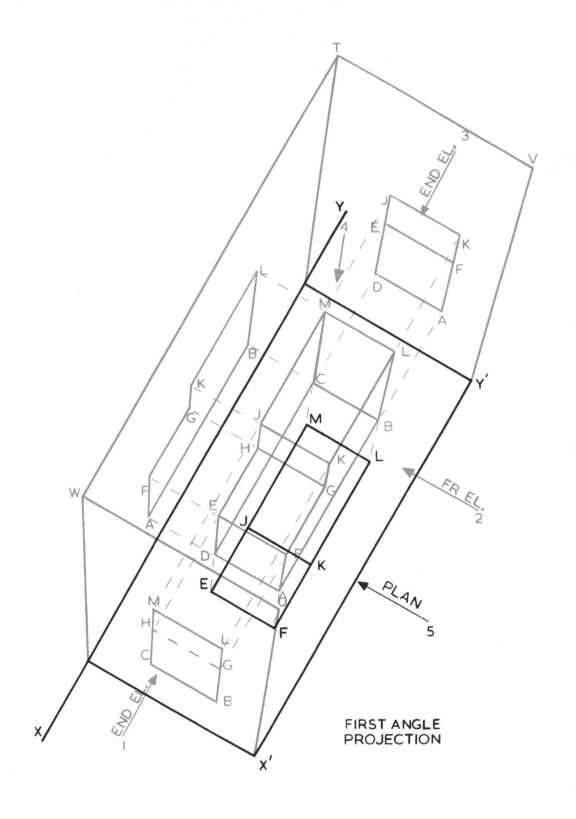

FIRST ANGLE
PROJECTION

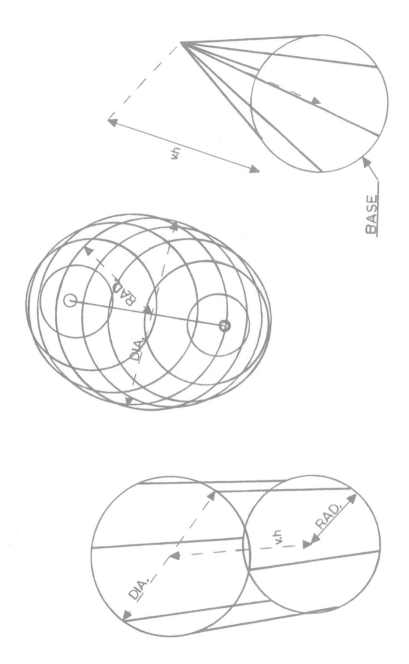

BASE

RAD.

DIA.

h.v

DIA.

h.v

RAD.

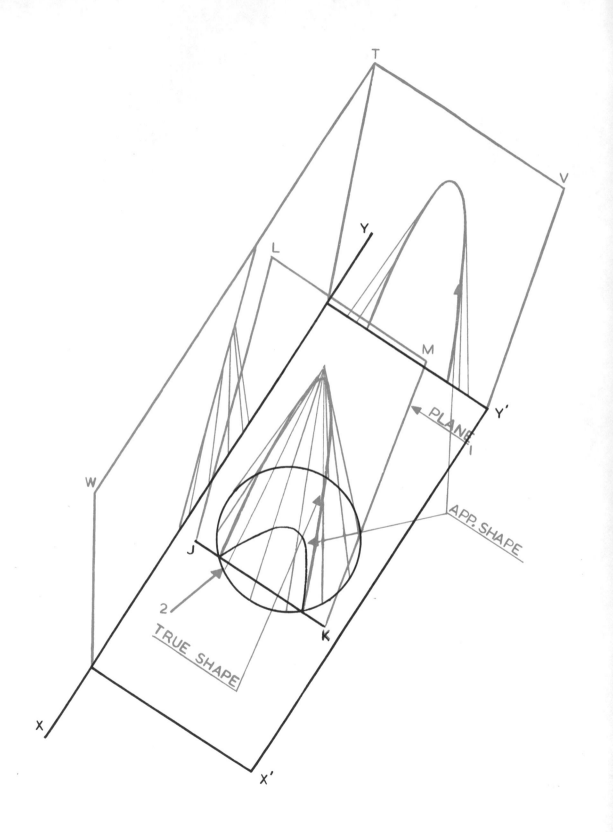

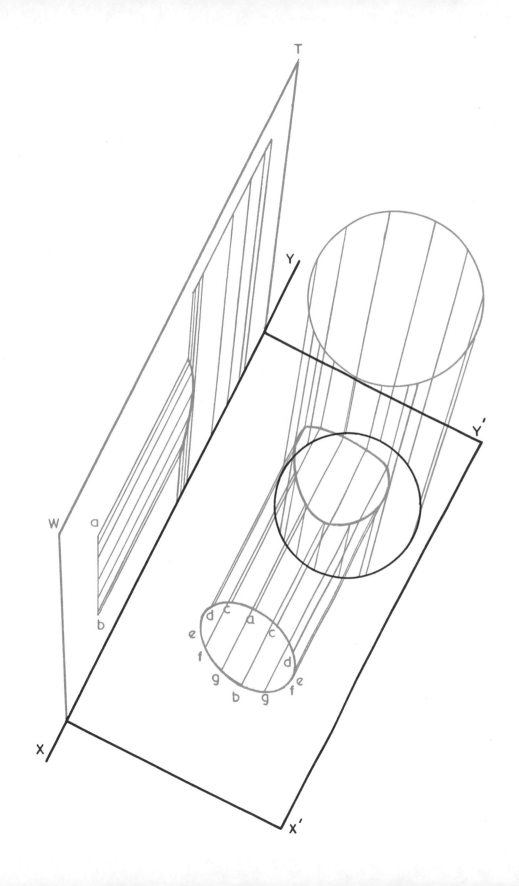

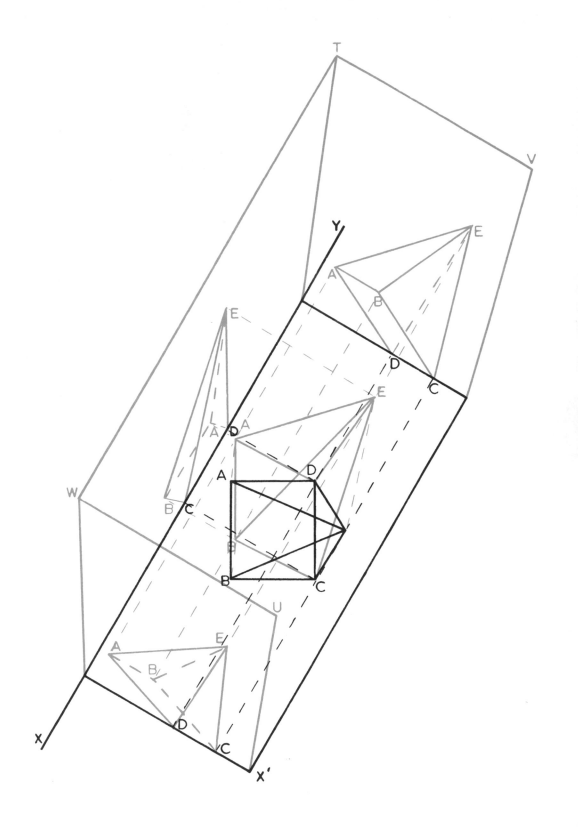

7. We obtain an expression for the rate of change of velocity. This represents the object's acceleration.
8. By ensuring that at the point at which two curves meet, they share a common tangent.
9. When at the point at which two curves meet, their respective rate of change of gradient is the same, they are said to exhibit C^2 (second order) continuity.
10. A joint refers to the point at which two piecewise polynomials connect. A knot is the value of the parameter t at which this happens.

Interfacing with the Visual System 5

'He would never let the harmless creatures pass without religious barks.'

5.1 Introduction

In this chapter we briefly discuss aspects of the human visual system and the cues by which we perceive the three-dimensionality of our surroundings. A number of useful references are supplied and these are strongly recommended to readers interested in gaining a greater understanding of the vitally important processes via which we obtain a visual impression of, and interact with, our surroundings. Unfortunately, computer generated images are often created on the basis of intuition and in many situations such an approach may not yield optimal results (especially when we consider the pivotal role that computer graphics plays in supporting visualisation and in defining interaction opportunities).

Clearly, in order to design a safe and efficient aircraft, designers must have a sound knowledge of the physical characteristics of the atmosphere through which the plane will fly and the conditions that the plane may encounter. Similarly, the design of a ship cannot be undertaken without an in-depth knowledge of the behaviour of the oceans through which the ship will travel. On a more mundane level, the design of a seat which is to offer *sustained* comfort requires that issues relating to human form and posture be taken into account. Certainly, seating designed without a true appreciation of the human frame is unlikely to offer optimal and/or sustained comfort.[1]

These simple examples are intended to demonstrate that the design and engineering of a product cannot (or rather should not) be carried out with reference only to the product itself – many other issues must be considered and, in the case of computer graphics, these include facets of the visual system, cognitive processes, proprioception and the like. In short, in developing high quality interactive computer graphics applications, we should not focus solely on technology but must also consider human attributes and sensory systems. These are increasingly important considerations – particularly when we move to display systems able to effectively support 'true' 3-D imaging, new interaction modalities (including bi-manual interaction) and haptic feedback.

It is interesting to consider the typical interfaces provided by leading commercial vendors. In this context Blundell and Schwarz [2006] write:

'... it is interesting to stand back for a moment and speculate on the number of hours per week that we now spend bound to our computers, attempting to convey our emotionally driven thought processes via imprecise communication skills to machines that operate solely on logic and that are utterly oblivious to the richness of human dialogue.'

In the next section we open this discussion by summarising some key characteristics and features of the eye along with issues relating to our perception of 'visible' radiation. In Section 5.3 we introduce depth cues via which we perceive the three-dimensionality of our surroundings and outline a simple classification scheme. This is used in the following three sections where we consider pictorial, oculomotor and parallax cues.

Key Learning Outcomes: At the end of this chapter you should be able to:

- *Describe the eye in terms of a high performance optical instrument.*

- *Delineate various characteristics and performance metrics of the human visual system.*

- *Understand issues relating to our perception of 'visible' radiation.*

- *Describe a range of pictorial, oculomotor and parallax depth cues.*

- *Appreciate the benefits that can be derived (in terms of our ability to visualise and interact with 3-D data) by properly supporting parallax depth cues.*

---

[1] Aircraft seating perhaps provides an example of seats optimally designed for sustained human *discomfort...*

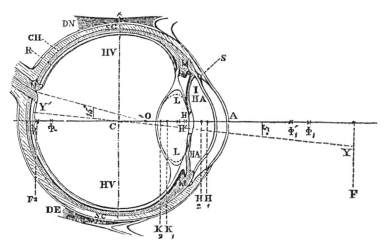

FIG. 2.—Transverse section of an Ideal or Schematique Eye.

A, Summit of cornea; SC, Sclerotic; S, Schlemm's canal; CH, Choroid; I, Iris; M, Ciliary muscle; R, Retina; N, Optic nerve; HA, Aqueous humour; L, Crystalline lens, the anterior of the double lines on its face showing its form during accommodation; HV, Vitreous humour; DN, Internal rectus muscle; DE, External rectus; YY', Principal optical axis; ΦΦ, Visual axis, making an angle of 5° with the optical axis; C, Centre of the ocular globe. *The cardinal points of Listing* ·—H_1H_2, principal points; K_1K_2, nodal points; F_1F_2, principal focal points. *The dioptric constants according to Giraud-Teulon:*—If, Principal points united; $\phi_1\phi_2$, principal foci during the repose of accommodation; $\phi'_1\phi'_2$, principal foci during the maximum of accommodation; O, fused nodal points.

Figure 5.1 The form and major constituents of the human eye. See text for discussion. (Reproduced from 9th edition of the Encyclopaedia Britannica [1879].)

5.2 The Eye

> *Any fool can make things bigger,*
> *more complex, and more violent.*
> *It takes a touch of genius – and a lot of courage –*
> *to move in the opposite direction.[2]*

In this section, we briefly review various characteristics of the human eye which, even when considered in isolation, is a truly remarkable optical instrument. Figure 5.1 illustrates the form and main constituents of the eye and in Table 5.1 we summarise some key characteristics. These are discussed in more detail in the subsections that follow.

5.2.1 Photoreceptors

The human eye contains $\sim 126 \times 10^6$ photoreceptors. These are responsible for the conversion of electromagnetic energy into signals that are passed along the optic nerves. Photoreceptors known as 'cones' operate most efficiently under daylight illumination and support colour

---

[2] Attributed to Albert Einstein (1879–1955).

Table 5.1 Some key characteristics of the eye – see text for discussion.

Characteristic	Description
Number of photoreceptors	~126,000,000
Density of photoreceptors in the *fovea*	~150,000 mm^{-2}
Spectral response	~400–~700 nm
Detection acuity	~0.5″ [3]
Near Point	~25 cm
Peak sensitivity (cones)	~555 nm
Peak sensitivity (rods)	~505 nm

vision.[4] A second type of photoreceptor ('rods') exhibit greater sensitivity and therefore play a greater role under more subdued levels of illumination. Rods and cones have different peak wavelength sensitivities – the former have a peak response at ~500–510 nm and the latter at ~555 nm.

> **The Purkinje Shift:** Johannes Purkinje noticed that at dusk, the apparent brightness of different coloured objects changes. For example, blue objects appear to become brighter and red objects darker. This is caused by the increased reliance placed on the rods at lower levels of illumination (coupled with the corresponding decrease in reliance that is placed on cones). Thus the eye becomes more responsive to shorter wavelengths hence blue objects appearing to become brighter and red objects darker.

The retina (labelled 'R' in Figure 5.1) comprises the vast array of photodetectors together with interconnections that enable the initial processing of detector signals. The distribution of rods and cones on the retina is far from uniform. In fact, the density of rods gradually increases towards the optical axis (the horizontal line indicated in Figure 5.1) and then rapidly falls away. This sudden decrease in the number of rods is accompanied by a very large increase in the number of cones such that the region around the optical axis (the central region of vision) in essence comprises only cones. This region is known as the fovea and supports super-high resolution colour imaging (in this region the density of cones is ~150,000 mm^{-2}). The central part of an image scene (corresponding to our area of fixation) is cast onto the fovea and this enables the part of the image scene that is of greatest interest to be captured at tremendous resolution. Here, there is little point in attempting to improve on the remark made by Hermann Ludwig Helmholtz (1821–1894) in 1873:

'*So that the image that we receive by the eye is like a picture, minutely and elaborately finished in the centre but only roughly sketched at the borders.*' [Helmholtz 1873]

---

[3] Note: $1/60°$ is referred to as '1 minute' (denoted 1′) and $1/3600°$ is referred to a '1 second' (denoted 1″).
[4] Colour vision is supported through the use of three classes of cone – each of which have different peak wavelength sensitivities.

Figure 5.2 The presence of the 'blind spot' can be readily confirmed by means of this simple diagram. Close your left eye and look at the 'X' with your right eye. Adjust the distance of the diagram from the eye until the circle disappears. When this occurs, the circle is being projected onto the blind spot region of the retina. Continue to gaze at the 'X' and note that although the circle cannot be seen, the horizontal line appears to be unbroken. This can take a few moments' practice – as it is important that the 'X' continues to denote the point of fixation. In this situation, the visual system is extrapolating the line across the unseen space.

OTU Exercise 5.1: The Density of Pixels on a Standard Computer Display

(a)   As indicated above in the fovea, the density of photoreceptors in the region of the fovea is $\sim$150,000 mm^{-2}. Compare this to the density of pixels (picture elements) employed in a typical computer monitor.

(b)   Does the fovea represent the part of the retina that is best able to support night-time vision? Explain your answer.

The web of photoreceptor connections and interconnections lie in the path of the incoming light – such that the light must pass through these prior to reaching the photodetectors. Furthermore, and perhaps somewhat surprisingly, the photoreceptors do not point to the incoming light but rather towards the back of the eye. Neither of these features would appear optimal – but they do not negatively impact on the eye's performance as an optical instrument!

There is one region of the retina in which neither rods nor cones are present. This is the area in which the connections from the network of photoreceptors leave the eye and is referred to as the 'blind spot'.

OTU Exercise 5.2: Verifying the Existence of the Blind Spot

Consider the diagram presented in Figure 5.2. Following the instructions given in the figure caption, verify the presence of a blind spot region on your retina. Discuss why, when we view our surroundings, the blind spot is not apparent (even when we use only one eye).

5.2.2   The Focusing System

Two mechanisms are used to bring light that enters the eye to focus on the retina.[5] Firstly, light entering the eye is refracted at the interface between the eye and the cornea (labelled 'A' in Figure 5.1). The focusing action that takes place at this interface is dependent on the difference in refractive index between the surrounding air and the cornea and also on the curvature of this boundary. Approximately two-thirds of the focusing action of the eye is achieved at this

---

[5] The image cast onto the retina is inverted.

interface.[6] However, this represents non-adjustable focusing – adjustments in focal length are the responsibility of the crystalline lens. This comprises layers of crystalline tissue and its shape is controlled by surrounding ciliary muscles (denoted 'M' in Figure 5.1). In the absence of any force, the lens is approximately spherical in shape and as the muscles exert more tension, its thickness (and hence its curvature) decreases. The overall focusing action of the lens is determined by the curvature of its two surfaces and the difference in refractive index between these surfaces and the materials in contact with them. In fact, the region in front of the lens is filled with an aqueous humor (this liquid is used to support the internal pressure of the eye and so maintain its shape and is denoted as 'HA' in Figure 5.1). To the rear of the lens, the eye is filled with a vitreous ('jelly like') humor ('HV' in Figure 5.1) through which light passes before impinging on the retina.

Focusing action (accommodation) is not controlled from within the eye but rather represents a response generated through the processing of an image scene. As we would expect, this occupies a finite time – the reaction time to a stimulus is reported as being ~0.3 seconds with the focusing action being completed in ~0.9 seconds [Boff et al. 1986]. However, this time period is influenced by factors such as the target distance and level of illumination.

The term 'near point' is used to indicate the least distance of distinct vision – i.e. the minimum distance at which an object can be brought to focus. For a 'normal' eye this is ~25 cm.

OTU Exercise 5.3: The Near Point

Cover one eye. Hold a pointer such as a pen or pencil vertically at arm's length and gradually bring this pointer closer to the open eye. Note the least distance at which the pointer remains sharply in focus (you will need to ask somebody to measure this for you). Repeat the process for the other eye.

5.2.3 Perception of Colour

As indicated previously, the human eye is able to detect electromagnetic radiation in the range ~400 to 700 nm – this defines the energy range of photons that may be detected by the visual system. Recall from basic physics the equation:

$$E = h\nu, \tag{5.1}$$

where E represents the photon energy, ν the frequency of the radiation and h Planck's constant.[7] Furthermore, frequency (ν) and wavelength (λ) are related by:

$$c = \nu\lambda. \tag{5.2}$$

Here, c represents the speed of propagation of the radiation, which within a vacuum ('free space') ~3×10^8 ms^{-1}.

OTU Exercise 5.4: Photon Energy

Consider light of wavelength 550 nm. Calculate the photon energy (assume the speed of light (c) is ~3×10^8 ms^{-1} and Planck's constant (h) is ~6.6×10^{-34} J.s).

---

[6] Naturally, when the eye is immersed in water, the focusing action that normally occurs at this boundary no longer takes place.

[7] Planck's constant ~6.626×10^{-34} J.s.

Colour is an attribute ascribed by the visual system and enables us to distinguish between different photon energies.[8] As a result, colour is not a characteristic of light *per se* but is a property that is conceptualised by the visual system and can therefore be regarded as a remarkable form of illusion. In this context Schiffman [1982] writes:

> *'Colour or hue is the psychological correlate to wavelength.'*

The eye is not uniformly sensitive to all wavelengths – the cones (which, as we have already mentioned, operate most efficiently in day light conditions) have a peak sensitivity at ~555 nm (yellow/green) and the rods (operating most efficiently under subdued lighting conditions) have a peak sensitivity at ~505 nm (blue/green). Our perception of the 'brightness' of a light source is therefore determined not only by its light output (indicated by the number of photons entering the eye per unit time interval) but also by the wavelength of the radiation being emitted (which as we have indicated relates to photon energy). In short, a source of radiation that exhibits a high level of light output may not be visible (as the wavelength of the source may lie outside the operating limits of the visual system) or may be only dimly perceived.

When considering the light entering the eye from a source, we can consider the radiative energy per unit time as measured in Watts (1 W = 1 J.s). However, this does not provide us with an indication of the perceived 'brightness' of the source (here for the moment we use the word 'brightness' loosely) – the essential issue is the response of the photodetectors to the radiation. In photometry, measurements are made in terms of the response of the eye to a source of radiation and this takes into account the spectral response profiles of the rods and cones – see Figure 5.3. Note that the response profiles shown in this diagram are normalised and so, although rods and cones are equally sensitive to red light (~650 nm), this is not evident from the diagram.

In considering the response of the eye to incident radiation, photometric units are employed (e.g. the lumen). By definition, 1W of radiative energy at a wavelength of 555 nm corresponds to 680 lumens. Below an example is provided showing the conversion of radiative power output (measured in Watts) to photometric units (measured in lumens).

Conversion of Watts to Lumens: Consider a 200 mW helium-neon laser that emits radiation at a wavelength of 633 nm. Determine the photometric power output in lumens.

By definition, 1 Watt of radiant energy at 555 nm corresponds to 680 lumens. However, the laser is emitting radiation at 633 nm. Consequently, we employ the spectral luminous efficiency curves (see Figure 5.3) and find that at 633 nm, the photopic curve has a value of ~0.25. This value provides the scaling factor that represents the response of the cones to this particular wavelength. Thus the laser has a photometric power output of $200 \times 10^{-3} \times 680 \times 0.25 = 34$ lumens

---

In describing colour, three important parameters are used – brightness,[9] saturation (purity of colour) and hue (colour). These parameters are brought together in the 'colour spindle' – as shown in Figure 5.4. As may be seen from this illustration brightness increases vertically, saturation with distance from the central axis and hue is a function of location on the circumference.

---

[8] The sensation of colour can also be induced by means of a flickering light source.
[9] For the moment we continue to use the term 'brightness' loosely.

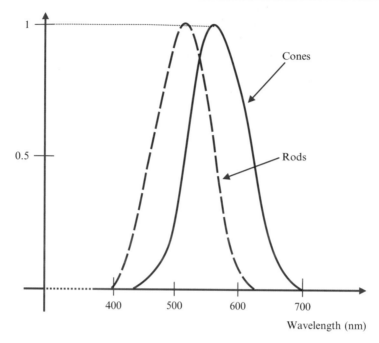

Figure 5.3 Spectral luminous efficiency curves for the human eye. Wavelength is indicated on the horizontal axis and the normalised[10] response of rods and cones is depicted on the vertical axis. The rods (which support 'night' vision) exhibit a peak sensitivity at a wavelength of ~500–510 nm (perceived as blue/green) and the cones which are dominant in 'daylight' vision have a peak sensitivity 555 nm (perceived as yellow/green). The curve relating detection efficiency to wavelength for the rods is known as the 'scotopic curve' and that associated with the cones is the 'photopic curve'.

The shape of the spindle indicates that the highest degree of saturation (corresponding to rich, vibrant colours) can only be achieved at levels of moderate 'brightness'.

OTU Exercise 5.5: Seeing Beyond the 'Visible' Spectrum

As we have indicated, the human eye is sensitive to wavelengths of ~400 to 700 nm. This is referred to as the visible portion of the electromagnetic spectrum. Suppose that this operating range was broader, spanning the ultraviolet and infrared portions of the electromagnetic spectrum (see Figure 5.5). Discuss ways in which this would impact on our perception of our surroundings. In what ways would this assist with, or detract from, our ability to judge spatial relationships and the shape of objects within a scene? In your discussion you may wish to consider ways in which a honey bee's perception of the colour of flowers differs from our own[11].

---

[10] Note that for convenience both curves have been 'normalised' – the peak sensitivity of either curve being indicated as equalling unity. Clearly, in practice rods and cones do not exhibit the same peak sensitivity.

[11] A honey bee is also able to detect the polarisation of light and local magnetic field. Since we have no equivalent senses it is extremely difficult for us to appreciate the sensation that bees experience in respect of these sensory systems.

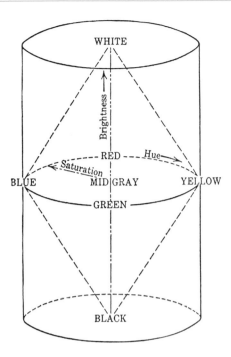

Figure 5.4 The colour spindle that relates 'brightness', saturation and hue. From this diagram it is apparent that the achievable level of saturation is a function of 'brightness'. (Reproduced from Troland [1930].)

5.2.4 The Dynamic Range

As we will discuss shortly, the eye is able to operate across a tremendous range of lighting conditions. In everyday life we frequently refer to the 'brightness' of a light source – the greater the brightness, the greater the light output. However, it is important to remember that the process of gauging 'brightness' is underpinned by the interaction occurring between photons and the photodetectors in the eye. As indicated above, even though a source may emit

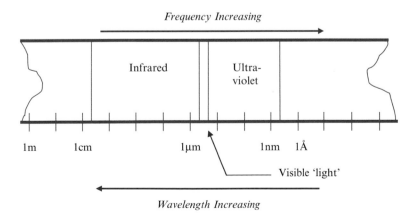

Figure 5.5 A portion of the electromagnetic spectrum – see OTU Exercise 5.5.

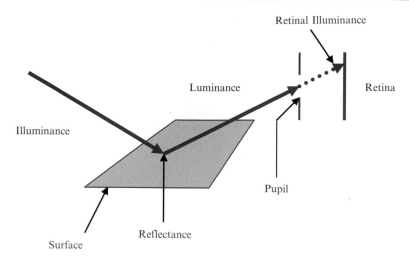

Figure 5.6 Light falling on and being reflected by a surface. The light energy incident on the surface is referred to as the 'illuminance', and that reflected by the surface as the 'luminance'. The retinal illuminance takes into account the restriction that the pupil imposes on the light which reaches the retina.

a high radiant energy, we may perceive the output only dimly (and in fact, if the source is emitting only in the infrared or ultraviolet regions of the electromagnetic spectrum, the *perceived* source output will be zero). Thus our perception of 'brightness' does not necessarily relate to the absolute magnitude of the light output from a source but can be used in a more meaningful way when we compare the appearance of two or more objects or surfaces that are each emitting light of the same wavelength. In short, 'brightness' is a facet of our visual awareness and is therefore not an absolute measurement.

However, it is possible to devise experiments that enable us to gauge how perceived brightness (B) varies as a function of the actual light output (I) by a source. This leads to the approximate relationship:[12]

$$B \propto I^{0.33} \tag{5.3}$$

When referring to the light energy incident on a surface, we will use the term 'illuminance' which may be expressed in units of lumens/m^2. Generally, when we view our surroundings, we do not look directly at light sources but rather at light reflected by surfaces and in this context, we use the term 'luminance'.[13] The illuminance and the luminance are related by the surface 'reflectance' such that:

$$Reflectance(\%) = \frac{Luminace}{Illuminace} \cdot 100. \tag{5.4}$$

These various terms are summarised in Figure 5.6 where we illustrate light falling on and being reflected by a surface.

---

[12] The validity of this relationship is governed by various conditions.

[13] The term 'retinal illuminance' is used to refer to the light energy incident on the retina and is measured in 'trolands' where 1 troland corresponds to 1 cd/m^2 viewed through a pupil with an area of 1 mm^2. See, for example, O'Shea [1985] and Blundell and Schwarz [2006].

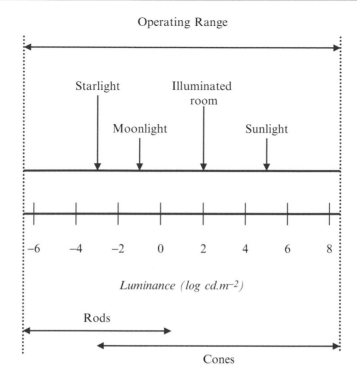

Figure 5.7 The human eye is able to operate across a tremendous range of lighting conditions. Here, the luminance of a sheet of white paper under different lighting conditions is indicated on a logarithmic scale. As may be seen, between starlight and sunlight, the luminance changes by approximately eight orders of magnitude. However, neither of these settings represent extremes of the eyes operating range. In the lower part of the diagram, we indicate the approximate operating range of the rods and cones. Here, it is important to note that neither rod or cone function abruptly ceases but rather that increased reliance is placed on one and less reliance on the other – until ultimately only one form of photoreceptor is in operation.

OTU Exercise 5.6: Perceived 'Brightness'

Suppose that a room is illuminated by means of two lamps and that we wish to double the perceived ambient 'brightness'. How many additional lamps would be needed? You should assume that all lamps have the same light output.

Turning now to the range of luminance over which the eye is able to operate. The photon flux under the night time stars is $\sim 10^{12}$ photons $m^2 s^{-1}$ and on a sunny day is $\sim 10^{20}$ photons $m^2 s^{-1}$. Between these two situations the photon flux varies by some eight orders of magnitude – but the human visual system has no difficulty in coping with such conditions. In Figure 5.7 we illustrate the luminance (on a logarithmic scale) of a sheet of white paper under various conditions. The rods represent the ultimate photoreceptor – a rod can be activated by a single photon – although as a consequence of retinal noise (which is represented by photodetectors randomly 'firing') we cannot perceive the incidence of a single photon.[14]

---

[14] Experiments relating to the ultimate sensitivity of the human eye were carried out in the 1940's and the interested reader is referred to Hecht *et al.* [1942].

The iris (denoted 'I' in Figure 5.1) controls the size of the pupil – the pupil being the hole in the iris through which light enters the eye. The size of the pupil varies with lighting conditions and so this provides a mechanism whereby the eye is able to adapt to different levels of luminance. However, the action of the pupil does not in itself explain the ability of the eye to operate across such a wide range of lighting conditions. Here we need to bear in mind two points:

1. **Reaction Time**: The reaction time of the pupil to changes in luminance is relatively slow. For example, when there is a strong reduction in the level of illumination, it takes $\sim$10 s for the pupil to dilate to 2/3 of its maximum size and up to five minutes for it to fully open. Conversely, when there is a sudden increase in illumination, it takes $\sim$5 s for the pupil to fully contract [Lindsay and Norman 1972].

2. **Change in Size**: In sunlight the diameter of the pupil as $\sim$2 mm and in starlight $\sim$6 mm [Boff *et al.* 1986]. The area of the pupil therefore changes by a factor of:

$$\frac{\pi \cdot 3^2}{\pi \cdot 1^2} = 9.$$

Thus the pupil can only change the level of retinal illumination by a factor of $\sim$9 which is very little when considered within the context of the range of lighting conditions across which the eye is able to operate (see Figure 5.7). It is therefore evident that the photoreceptors must be adaptive to the wide-ranging lighting conditions under which the eye can operate efficiently. As for the actual function of the pupil, Blundell and Schwarz [2006] write:

'...it seems that the principle reason for the changing size of the human pupil is not to finely control the amount of light entering the eye, but rather to achieve the best compromise between resolution and sensitivity under different lighting conditions.'

Although the eye is able to operate across a wide range of lighting conditions, within a typical image scene differences in luminance are quite small. In this context, we often consider the image contrast ratio (C) which may be expressed in terms of the maximum and minimum luminance in an image scene (L_{max} and L_{min} respectively) such that:

$$C = \frac{L_{max} - L_{min}}{L_{max} + L_{min}}. \tag{5.5}$$

Thus the contrast ratio is dependent on the extremes of luminance contained within a scene and is independent of changes in the overall illuminance.

When we talk of the tremendous sensitivity of the human eye it is important to bear in mind that this assumes that the eye has adapted to the conditions under which it is to operate. For example, in order to exhibit maximum sensitivity, the eye must undergo 'dark adaptation' which involves 'immersion' in darkness for a period of $\sim$30 minutes.

5.2.5 Acuities

Measurements in relation to the resolution characteristics of the eye are commonly referred to as acuities. Below, several of these are briefly summarised:

(1) **Vernier Acuity**: Consider two line segments that are drawn end to end (Figure 5.8(a)). Vernier acuity refers to our ability to determine misalignment of one line relative to the other. Detecting the alignment and misalignment of line segments is crucial in accurately

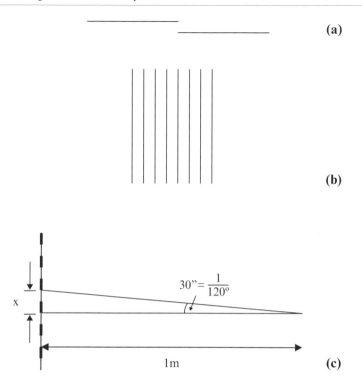

Figure 5.8 In (a) two line segments are shown. Vernier acuity relates to the minimum perceivable misalignment – naturally, this is a function of viewing distance. Grating acuity relates to our ability to resolve discrete elements in a pattern. In (b) a simple grating is illustrated: this type of pattern may be used to measure grating acuity. Diagram (c) shows a plan view of a grating that is located 1 m from the eye. Under suitable conditions the eye is able to resolve lines that have a pitch of ~0.145 mm and that are at a distance of 1 m.

reading measurements indicated by a 'vernier scale' (traditionally used, for example, by microscopes, micrometers, vernier callipers etc) hence the name of this acuity.[15]

(2) **Grating Acuity**: This refers to our ability to resolve discrete elements within a pattern. In Figure 5.8(b) a simple grating comprising a series of light and dark strips is shown. This type of pattern may be used to measure grating acuity – although as with other acuities, measurements are strongly influenced by viewing conditions such as the contrast ratio of the grating, level of illuminance etc. However, under appropriately favourable conditions, the minimum line spacing that can be detected in a grating is ~30''. Consider a grating in which lines are separated by a distance x and that lies at a distance of 1m from the eye (see Figure 5.8(c)). It is apparent that:

$$x = 1 \cdot \tan 30'' = \tan\left(\frac{1}{120}\right) \approx 0.145\,\text{mm}.$$

Thus under appropriate conditions we are able (in principle) to resolve lines that are separated by ~0.2 mm when located at a distance of 1m from the eye.

(3) **Detection Acuity**: Consider, for example, a length of wire that lies at 90° to the visual axis. As this wire is moved further away, the angle that it subtends at the eye will gradually

---

[15] It also referred to as the 'Localisation Acuity'.

decrease, Detection acuity refers to the minimum angle that we are able to detect and typically, we have little difficulty perceiving objects that subtend an angle of $\sim 1'$ [Coren *et al.* 1994].

OTU Exercise 5.7: Detection Acuity

(a) Consider a straight piece of wire that is held vertically, which lies at $90°$ to the visual axis and that is 2m from the eye. Assuming that the horizontal angle subtended at the eye is $1'$, determine the thickness of the wire. Further, if we assume that a distance of 20 mm separates the eye lens and retina, state the horizontal extent of the retinal image.

(b) Estimate the angle subtended at the eye by an image pixel depicted on a conventional flat screen display. You should estimate the diameter of the pixels depicted on your computer monitor and also the typical viewing distance.

(c) View an overhead cable (such as power transmission line or telephone cable) from a distance. Choose a cable that can be seen against the skyline. By changing your location, estimate the maximum distance at which the cable remains visible. On the basis of this, and any other relevant information, determine the *approximate* angle that the diameter of the cable subtends at the eye. Is the clarity of the cable increased or decreased by viewing it (a) against a blue sky, (b) against a cloudy sky?

(d) Under good lighting conditions, what is the maximum distance at which you are able to perceive a thread supporting a spider's web? Estimate the angle that this thread subtends at the eye and the size of the retinal image formed.

Pioneering experimental work was carried out in the 1930s in order to determine the highest detection acuity achievable (under optimal conditions). Hecht and Mintz [1939] report a value of $0.5''$ corresponding to a retinal image of $\sim 0.04 \, \mu m$ – this being smaller than the diameter of individual cones! The publication by Hecht and Mintz is well worth reading. See also summary discussion in Boff *et al.* [1986] and Blundell and Schwarz [2006].

5.3 Cues to Depth

'How far that little candle throws his beams!
So shines a good deed in a weary world.' [16]

Here, and in subsequent sections of this chapter, we briefly discuss various 'depth cues' by means of which we are able to judge spatial relationships within the physical world and that are employed when we create 3-D images using either the traditional flat screen display or emerging creative display technologies.

   In our everyday lives we are remarkably adept at judging spatial relationships and in the main we achieve this complex feat without conscious effort. This applies to both static and dynamic scenes. We briefly consider these two scenarios in the subsections that follow.

---

[16] 'The Merchant of Venice' Act V, Scene I. William Shakespeare (1564–1616).

5.3.1 Static Scenes

We can readily determine the relative location of objects in, for example, a room. It is apparent (perhaps we should say obvious) to us that one chair is closer to us than is another and that the remote control for the TV lies within our reach. In this latter context we are often able to make accurate judgements as to the absolute location of objects. Consider reaching out for that cup of tea or glass of wine while preoccupied by other tasks. These are not processes that involve us in conscious effort – with little (if any) hesitation the hand connects with the handle of the cup or the stem of the glass – seldom do we make an error of subconscious judgement and knock over the cup or glass (unless, of course they are resting on vital papers or in the case that we have recently purchased a new white carpet and are drinking red wine – in which case errors of judgement invariably occur . . .).

The process of reaching out for and interacting with objects within an environment is not only underpinned by visual cues but also by our awareness of the position and orientation of our limbs – these are key aspects of 'proprioception'. As indicated in Blundell and Schwarz [2006]:

'To enable us to interact effectively with our surroundings . . . it is necessary for the CNS [central nervous system] to have an accurate knowledge of the position and orientation of our limbs within 3-D space, together with relevant information concerning their motion and the forces that we exert (or that are exerted on us) during any interaction process. In this context, the terms 'Proprioception' (proprius from the Latin 'own') and 'Kinesthesis' (kine from the Greek 'movement') are both commonly employed.'

Facets of proprioception are summarised in Figure 5.9 (see also Section 10.2). It is important to note that our sense of sight coupled with the intuitive knowledge that we possess in relation to the position and orientation of our limbs, provides an incredibly powerful mechanism for interaction with our surroundings. Since computer graphics techniques provide the primary means by which we visualise and interact with computer-processed data, it is apparent that issues relating to proprioception should be considered when developing computer graphics based applications.

OTU Exercise 5.8: Bi-manual Interaction

Although human dexterity is greatly enhanced through the use of synergistic bi-manual inter-action, conventional computer interaction techniques (typically based on the keyboard and mouse) and computer graphics applications, generally support only uni-manual interaction. The task of threading cotton through the 'eye' of a sewing needle provides a simple example of an interaction task that draws on not only our sense of sight but also on the use of two hands working synergistically. This can be readily demonstrated as follows:

(a) Hold a needle in the non-preferred hand (i.e. if you are right-handed, hold the needle in the left hand) and thread the cotton through the eye of the needle.

(b) Attach the needle to a fixed object (e.g. hold the needle in a vice) and without using the non-preferred hand in any way, again thread the cotton (i.e. use only the preferred hand for the task).

Compare the relative difficulty of these two approaches.

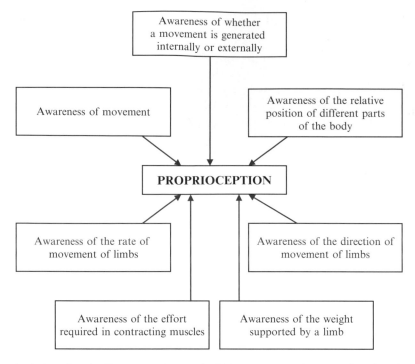

Figure 5.9 Some facets of proprioception. From our current perspective, it is important to note that aspects of proprioception play a vital role in our interaction with computer systems. (Diagram © 2005 Q. S. Blundell.)

5.3.2 Dynamic Scenes

In the context of driving a car, consider the type of judgements that we make in relation to gauging relative and absolute distances and also relative speeds (after a little practice, such judgements are generally made without conscious effort). Perhaps we are driving at speed along a busy motorway and decide to overtake a truck that is in front of us. With only a glance in the rear view mirror we rapidly determine the relative distance and speed of a vehicle approaching in the outside lane. On the basis of this information, we change lanes, accelerate and overtake. Seemingly without effort we again change lanes – a task that relies on our accurate judgement of both the speed and the separation of the vehicles between which we reposition our car. All of these judgements must be made in real time and our visual system must take into account ever-changing geometry – the position of traffic is continually varying with respect to our own coordinate system(s).

When driving a car, we seldom consciously reflect on the nature of information presented to the visual system and upon which often critical decisions are based. Nor (even when first learning to drive) are we consciously selective of the cues that we employ in carrying out manoeuvres. In contrast, when learning to land a light aircraft, there is a need to make a conscious effort – in those final moments before touch-down, our centre of attention should be directed towards the horizon – although instinctively, there is perhaps a feeling that we should be focusing on the ground immediately below the plane and with which we wish to make gentle contact! In this situation, we must consciously adapt and develop our everyday use of depth cue information.

In the next three sections, we briefly outline a range of depth cues that play a pivotal role in our judgement of spatial and absolute distances and of relative speed. Although for convenience, we review each of these cues separately, it is important to note that in practice we seldom employ them in isolation – usually information that we derive in relation to the 3-D nature of our surroundings (and indeed the three-dimensionality of objects depicted within a computer generated scene) is based on our interpretation of a plurality of cues. Furthermore, the relative emphasis and range of effectiveness of cues varies with distance. By way of a simple example consider an aircraft flight. When we look out of the window from an altitude of say 30,000 feet, it seems that we are hardly moving in relation to the terrain far below. As the plane descends, motion eventually becomes more apparent. Perhaps just prior to landing we pass over a city at an altitude of a few thousand feet. From our window, we certainly gain a greater sense of motion – although the buildings and cars over which we pass still appear to be remote and divorced from us. However, once over the runway threshold and moments before touchdown, our considerable speed suddenly becomes apparent and the ground begins to race by (even though we are now travelling more slowly that when in the cruise). In those last moments before wheels meet runway and the reverse thrust is applied our perception of speed is augmented by depth cues that are most effective at short-range distances – these depth cues were unable to assist (or had less value) with our judgement of speed when the ground was further away.[17]

In brief:
1. Depth cues provide the basis by which our visual system makes judgements of absolute distances, relative distances and relative speeds.
2. Judgements are usually made on the basis of a range of depth cue information. Seldom in our everyday lives do we rely on only a single cue.
3. Different depth cues are effective over different distances – some cues are able to provide useful long-range information, whilst others are limited to shorter viewing distances.

OTU Exercise 5.9: Perception of Motion

Determine the minimum speed of motion that you are able to continuously perceive. You may, for example, choose to write a simple program that enables an object such as a rectangle to move across a computer screen. In this case, your program should permit the user to vary the speed of movement (and perhaps provide a readout of speed).

Depth cues may be grouped in various ways and in the discussions that follow we adopt an approach that is most relevant to conventional computer graphics and creative 3-D environments. As indicated in Figure 5.10, cues are grouped into to three possible categories – pictorial, oculomotor and binocular.

---

[17] Here, the speed at which components within the image scene move across the retina plays a major role.

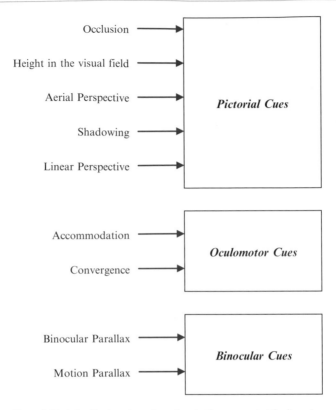

Occlusion ⟶

Height in the visual field ⟶

Aerial Perspective ⟶   *Pictorial Cues*

Shadowing ⟶

Linear Perspective ⟶

Accommodation ⟶   *Oculomotor Cues*

Convergence ⟶

Binocular Parallax ⟶   *Binocular Cues*

Motion Parallax ⟶

Figure 5.10 A classification scheme for various depth cues – see text for discussion.

In the next section we briefly review a number of pictorial cues, in Section 5.5 we consider the oculomotor cues of accommodation and convergence and in Section 5.6 we turn our attention to binocular cues.

5.4 An Overview of Various Pictorial Depth Cues

As their name implies, these cues underpin the depiction of pictorial images of 3-D scenes rendered on a 2-D tableau (such as artist's canvas or computer display). Consequently this set of cues play a pivotal role in the formation of computer generated 3-D images and in the case of the traditional flat screen display, oculomotor and parallax cues are absent. In the subsections that follow, we briefly discuss cues in this category.

5.4.1 Occlusion

One or more opaque objects within an image scene may wholly or partially obscure (occlude) our view of others that lie at greater distances. For example, in Figure 5.11(a) we are likely to assume (in the absence of additional information) that two rectangles are illustrated. Since our view of one of these rectangles is partially obstructed, this indicates that the rectangle on the left is the closer. However, this may be a false assumption – one of the rectangles may have been cut away – as indicated in the right-hand illustration. In (b) we illustrate a more complex

(a)

(b)

Figure 5.11 The depth cue of occlusion. In (a), we assume that one rectangle is partially occluding our view of another and from this we may conclude that the left hand rectangle is the closer of the two. However, this may not be correct – the diagram may not be showing two *complete* rectangles – one may have been cut away as indicated in the right-hand diagram. Thus the occlusion cue is underpinned by assumptions that we make about the shape of objects within the visual scene. In the photograph reproduced in (b), one car partially occludes another, a person partially occludes our view of one of the cars, the cars partially occlude our view of the lawn and a shrub on the left hand side partially occludes our view of one of the cars. This provides us with key information concerning the location of objects with the scene – but as with the simple diagram presented in (a) we make assumptions about the shape and completeness of objects within the image scene. These are usually based on prior experience and image context. Furthermore, additional cues will be available and will assist in (and reinforce) our understanding of the 3-D space. (Photograph © P.J. Blundell (2007).)

scene. Here, occlusion provides us with various information concerning the relative positions of objects within the scene – however, as with the diagram in (a) we must make assumptions as to the shape and completeness of each object. Fortunately, other depth cues are likely to be present and these will help to resolve ambiguities.

5.4.2 Height in the Visual Field

This cue is illustrated in Figure 5.12. As may be seen, the sea appears to ascend towards the horizon and the sky descends until they ultimately meet and so define the position of the horizon. Consequently, for an object located below the horizon, the more distant the object, the higher it appears to lie within the visual field. In contrast for objects that are located above the horizon, the more distant the object, the lower it appears to lie within the visual field.

Figure 5.12 The 'height in the visual field' cue. Here, it *appears* that the sky descends and the sea ascends until they meet at the horizon. Consider objects that are below the horizon. The more distant the object, the higher it appears to lie in the visual field. In contrast, in the case of objects that are located above the horizon, the more distant they are, the lower they appear to lie in the visual field. (Photograph (South Pacific) © P.J. Blundell (2007).)

OTU Exercise 5.10: Height in the Visual Field

(a)   Assume that the two rectangles illustrated in Figure 5.11(a) are located *below* the horizon. Re-draw this diagram so that the information that we derive from the occlusion cue is reinforced by the cue of height in the visual field.

(b)   Add to Figure 5.12, two boats/ships and two birds/planes. Incorporate the height in the visual field cue so as to indicate that each boat and each bird is at a different distance. What other cues could you incorporate so as to reinforce the impression of relative distance?

5.4.3 Aerial Perspective

As light passes through the atmosphere, it impinges upon, and is scattered by, small particles such as dust and water vapour – see Figure 5.13. As a result distant objects appear to be less well defined. In addition, more distant objects take on a bluish hue. This is as a result of the relationship between the extent to which light is scattered by small particles and the wavelength of the light. In this respect:

$$I \propto \frac{1}{\lambda^4}. \tag{5.6}$$

This is referred to as Rayleigh scattering and as can be seen from this relationship, the shorter the wavelength (λ), the greater is the degree of scattering (I). Thus blue light is scattered more than red light and it is as a result of this scattering process that the sky appears blue.

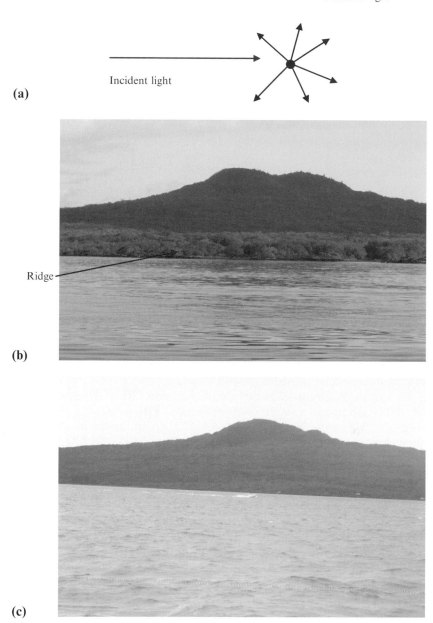

Figure 5.13 In (a) we indicate the scattering of light by a small particle – this process is referred to as Rayleigh scattering. As indicated by Eq. 5.6 the extent to which light is scattered is strongly influenced by wavelength – blue light is more strongly scattered than red light and it is for this reason that the sky is blue (is the sky on Mars blue?). In (b) we illustrate enrichment of visual content as a result of scattering. The image shows Rangitoto Island in the Hauraki Gulf. Notice a ridge in the foreground. This is visible because light emanating from the more distant background is subjected to a greater amount of scattering. Compare this image to (c) which was taken on another day when scattering was less apparent and, as a consequence of the texture and colour of the foliage, the ridge is not so readily discerned. (Photographs © A.R. Blundell (2007).)

On the basis of aerial perspective, objects (such as mountains) which appear to be less distinct or which have a bluish tint, are perceived as lying at greater distances. In this context, Coren [2004] writes:

'*In some geographic regions (such as the prairies of the United States and Canada), this can lead to considerable errors of judgement because the clear, dry air reduces aerial perspective. Thus a plateau that appears to be 1 or 2 miles away on a clear dry day, when looking across a dry sector of Wyoming, may be actually 20 or 30 miles from the observer.*'

He goes on to add:

'*The scattering of light may also cause an overall reduction in the relative contrast* [recall Eq. 5.5]. *In the absence of any other cues, you will tend to see the brighter of two identical objects as closer, and even when other cues are present, reduced contrast is associated with seeing objects as more distant.*'

In fact during the Lunar expeditions in the early 1970s, astronauts reported difficulty in estimating the distance of rock formations. Naturally as the moon possesses no atmosphere, scattering is absent and so even distant objects appear to be bright, exhibit a high relative contrast and do not take on the bluish tint that is the norm here on Earth.

As with other pictorial cues, scattering can be synthetically introduced into graphics images so reinforcing the impression that objects such as mountains lie at different distances.

5.4.4 Familiar Size

We are well aware of the physical size of objects that we encounter in our everyday lives and as a consequence of linear perspective (see below) we know that as an object is placed at a greater distance, it will appear to be of diminished size. Consequently, the perceived size of objects within an image scene provides us with an indication of their distance (both absolute and relative) – for example the two cars depicted in Figure 5.11(b). The significance of this cue can be readily demonstrated by using models of objects (such as playing cards) which are not of the standard size. When these are viewed (within an environment in which other cues are absent), observers usually gauge their distance incorrectly.

5.4.5 Shadows and Shading

Consider the image reproduced in Figure 5.11(b). The shadows cast by the cars, the figure and the trees in the background greatly assist in our interpretation of the layout of the 3-D scene. In addition, smooth and abrupt changes in the luminance provide us with important indications of the shape of objects (see, for example, the rear portion of the car that lies in the foreground in Figure 5.11(b)). Our interpretation of shadows and shading involves an assumption as to the location of the light source – which is generally assumed to lie overhead (see below). By way of a simple example, consider the illustration presented in Figure 5.14. The shading that is associated with each circle provides us with an immediate sensation of 3-D relief – circles appear as domed regions that either stand out from, or are indented into the page. Turning the diagram through 180° reverses the perceived orientation of each dome. Interestingly, rotating the diagram through 90° leads to a less stable condition – and in this case, we are interpreting the effect of shading caused by two light sources – one lying to the left and the other to the right.

As mentioned above, we generally assume that a light source is positioned overhead – specifically above the head – the light source location being assumed relative to a head-centred coordinate system. This is perhaps a little surprising since in our every-day lives, the location of light sources is usually defined relative to our physical surroundings and, as we move the

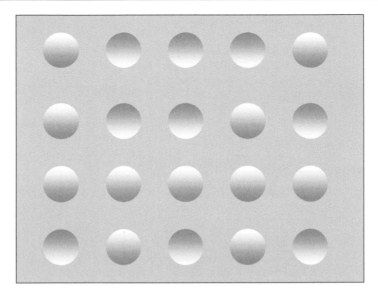

Figure 5.14 We generally assume that the source of illumination is from overhead – relative to a 'head-centred' coordinate system. In this diagram, the use of shading leads to the circles appearing as domed regions – lying out of, or being impressed into, the page. Rotation of the diagram through 180° causes the perceived orientation of each domed circle to reverse (the visual system has responded by continuing to assume an overhead source of lighting and interprets the image scene accordingly). Finally, rotation of the diagram by 90° leads to instability – the shading is no longer consistent with overhead illumination – it now appears that two light sources are present – one to the left-hand side and the other to the right.

location of the head, light source locations continually vary in position relative to the head-centred coordinate system.[18]

Turning to Figure 5.15, we can identify two forms of shadow. Firstly, as indicated in Figure 5.15(a), shading and shadowing may be distributed over the surfaces of an object. Such 'attached shadows' provide information as to the shape of an object. Alternatively, as indicated in Figure 5.15(b), an object may occlude the passage of light and therefore generate a 'cast shadow'. The shape of this shadow generally provides a distorted silhouette of the object from which the shadow is cast. Consequently, in determining the shape of an object, we usually place less reliance on the cast shadow. However, this form of shadow can provide a useful cue as to the distance between the object responsible for shadow formation and the surface on which the shadow lies.

The reflection process underpins the formation of shadows and shading. Below we briefly summarise two forms of reflection – 'diffuse' and 'specular'.

5.4.5.1 *Diffuse Reflection – Lambert's Law*

A diffuse (scattering) reflector (e.g. chalk) possesses a 'rough'[19] surface – as indicated in Figure 5.16(a). As may be seen from this illustration, reflected rays travel in random directions and

---

[18] There are occasional exceptions such as the miner's helmet that is equipped with a torch. In this case, the location of the light source is fixed relative to a head-centred coordinate system.

[19] Within this context, a smooth surface is one in which the surface variations are small compared to the wavelength of incident light.

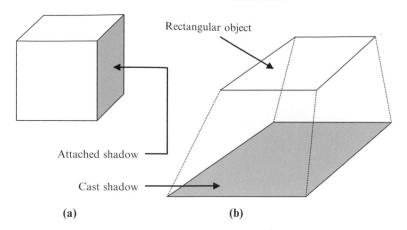

(a)   **(b)**

Figure 5.15 In (a) we indicate an attached shadow associated with a cube. This form of shading assists in our interpretation of the shape of 3-D objects. In (b) a shadow is cast by a rectangular surface. Cast shadows can provide us with an insight into the distance between an object (or collection of objects) and the surface on which shadows lie. For (b), indicate the location of the point light source. What would be the effect of replacing the idealised 'point' light source with a real source that has a finite extent?

as a result, in the case of perfectly diffuse surface, light is reflected uniformly (see Figure 5.16(b)). A reflectance model that assumes that there is no angular variation in the strength of the reflected light is generally referred to as 'Lambertian shading' and provides a simple way of representing surface shape and shading.

Let us assume that a ray emanating from a point light source impinges on the surface at an angle ϕ (measured relative to the surface normal). Further, we assume that the viewing location (again relative to the surface normal) is denoted by θ – as indicated in Figure 5.16(c). Since we have recognised that light is uniformly reflected by the surface, it follows that changes in θ (corresponding to changes in viewing location – or surface orientation relative to the observer) will not impact on luminance. On the other hand, changes in ϕ (corresponding to a change in the position of the point light source or to a change in the orientation of the surface relative to the source) do impact on luminance.

Consider the situation indicated in Figure 5.17 in which a light source Q illuminates the small region of a diffuse surface that is located around a point P. For simplicity, the illustration provides a cross-sectional view – however, in reality, a cone of light emanates from the source and when the axis of the cone lies at right-angles to the surface, a circular region will be illuminated. As the angle between the axis of the cone and the surface normal increases, the extent of the region that is illuminated will increase and will take the form of a section through the cone. Let us suppose that the luminous flux incident on an area A is denoted as F, then:

$$E = \frac{F}{A},\qquad (5.7)$$

where E represents the illuminance (measured in lumens per square metre). We can express F in terms of the emission from the source such that:

$$F = I\omega.\qquad (5.8)$$

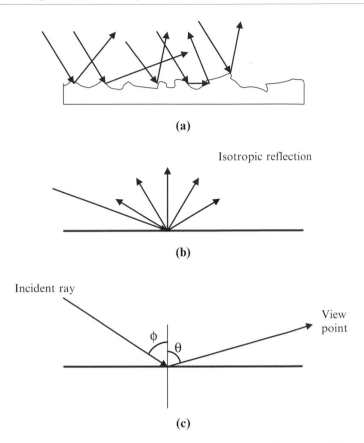

Figure 5.16 In (a) we provide a magnified and conceptualised impression (in cross-section) of the nature of a diffuse surface. The rough (mat) surface causes rays to be reflected in random directions. As a result, a perfectly diffuse surface reflects isotropically – light output does not vary with direction – see (b). In (c) an incident ray impinges on a surface at an angle ϕ to the surface normal. The viewpoint lies at an angle θ to the normal – see text for discussion.

Here, I denotes the luminous intensity of the source in the direction QP and ω the solid angle of the cone of light that illuminates the surface and that is measured at the light source. Thus the luminous intensity is a measure of the 'luminous flux density' in a particular direction.[20] Combining the above two equations we obtain:

$$E = \frac{I\omega}{A}. \tag{5.9}$$

The solid angle (ω) of a cone is defined by the ratio:

$$\omega = \frac{S}{r^2}. \tag{5.10}$$

---

[20] Naturally, we cannot *necessarily* assume that the luminous flux emitted by a source is the same in all directions.

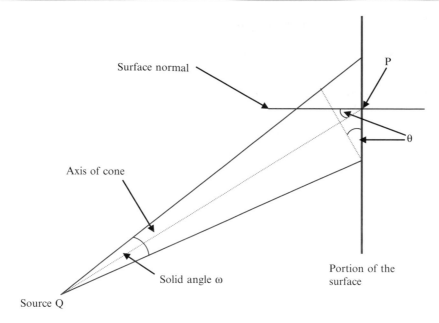

Figure 5.17 A cone of light illuminates a screen within a small region around the point *P*. The area of the screen that is illuminated corresponds to a section through the cone. In our discussions, we assume that this area is denoted by *A* and that the area of the circular 'base' of the cone that lies at 90° to the cone axis is given by *S*.

This is illustrated in Figure 5.18 in which Q denotes the centre of a sphere of radius r. A cone drawn from the centre of the sphere intersects its surface and defines the extent of a circular region of area S. In the case that, for example, the sphere has a radius of 1 m and the area of S is 1 m^2, then ω is unity and this is defined as 1 steradian (sr). The total solid angle all around a

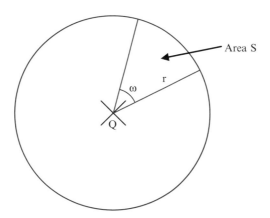

Figure 5.18 Here, *Q* denotes the centre of a sphere of radius *r*. A cone drawn from this centre intersects the surface of the sphere and defines the extent of a circular region of area *S*. In the case that, for example, the sphere has a radius of 1 m and the area of *S* is 1 m^2, then ω is unity and this is defined as 1 steradian (sr).

point (within three dimensions) is given by the area of the surrounding sphere divided by r^2:

$$\omega = \frac{4\pi r^2}{r^2} = 4\pi, \text{ steradians.}$$

Substituting Eq. 5.10 into Eq. 5.9, we obtain:

$$E = \frac{IS}{Ar^2}.$$

The areas S (which lies at right-angles to the axis of the cone) and A (which is the area illuminated on the surface) are related by:

$$S = A\cos\theta,$$

where θ represents the angle between the cone axis and the surface normal. (If, for example, the beam axis is at right-angles to the surface, $\theta = 0$ and therefore S and A are equal.) We can write:

$$E = \frac{I\cos\theta}{r^2}. \tag{5.11}$$

This equation can also be expressed as:

$$E = \frac{I\hat{\mathbf{n}}\cdot\hat{\mathbf{s}}}{r^2}. \tag{5.12}$$

Where $\hat{\mathbf{n}}\cdot\hat{\mathbf{s}}$ represents the scalar product of two unit vectors: $\hat{\mathbf{n}}$ being the unit vector normal to the surface and $\hat{\mathbf{s}}$ the unit vector in the direction of the source of illumination. Recall Eq. 5.4 in which the illuminance and luminance are related by the surface reflectance. Since we are dealing specifically with a diffuse surface, the reflectance characteristic of the surface is usually referred to as the 'coefficient of diffuse reflectance' (k_d) and has a value between zero and unity. Using Eq. 5.4 and Eq. 5.12, we can express the luminance (l) (light flux emanating from the surface) as:

$$l = \frac{IK_d\hat{\mathbf{n}}\cdot\hat{\mathbf{s}}}{r^2}. \tag{5.13}$$

This is generally referred to as Lambert's Law after Johann Heinrich Lambert (1728–1777).[21] In our model, we have employed a point light source and have quite rightly assumed that in this case, the amount of light incident on the illuminated region of the surface decreases with the inverse square of the distance between the light source and the surface. From the perspective of the graphics developer, the inverse square dependence indicated in Eq 5.13 can be problematic as at times, it may be desirable to place the lighting source at 'infinity'. In this case, the level of illumination cast by the source on the surface would be zero (see, for example Eq. 5.11). Additionally, as Hill [1990] comments:

'... experiments have shown that the use of this law directly yields pictures with exaggerated depth effects... The problem is thought to be the model... We model light sources as point sources for simplicity, but most real [physical world] scenes are actually illuminated by additional reflections from the surroundings which are difficult to model.'

---

[21] Speaking of Lambert, Boyer [1991] writes: 'It is said that when Fredrick the Great asked him in which science he was the most proficient, Lambert curtly replied, "All." '!!

One approach to this problem is to adopt a workable solution which provides an appropriate visual effect. In this case we set to one side the physical model (i.e. the inverse square law) and re-cast Eq. 5.13 as:

$$l = \frac{I K_d \hat{\mathbf{n}} \cdot \hat{\mathbf{s}}}{d + \eta}. \tag{5.14}$$

Here, d represents the distance of an object from the centre of projection (recall Figure 1.12) and η is an arbitrary constant.[22] In this way, points within an image scene that are closer to the eye appear to be brighter than those that lie at a greater distance. In this context, Salmon and Slater [1987] write:

'This is very important since surfaces at different distances that have the same colour but which overlay from the viewpoint of the COP [centre of projection] would be otherwise indistinguishable.'

Although this approach provides us with a workable solution, it is important to bear in mind that such a model is not based on the actual physical process.

Typically, a light source such as the one employed above will directly illuminate parts of an object. In addition, ambient (background) light will be present and will add to the amount of light incident on part (if not all) of the object. We can represent this additional illumination (I_a) by including in Eq. 5.14 a term $I_a K_a$ – where K_a represents the proportion of the incident ambient light that is reflected by the surface. In the physical world (e.g. in a room), the level of ambient lighting is not uniform – although for expediency, such an assumption is generally made when creating a 3-D scene. In this context, Ware [2000] writes:

'One of the consequences of modelling ambient light as a constant is that no shape-from-shading information is available in terms of cast shadows.'

5.4.5.2 *Specular Reflection*

Having briefly considered reflection by rough (mat) surfaces (diffuse reflection), we now turn our attention to reflection from smooth surfaces (of which an optically perfect mirror provides us with the ultimate example). Such surfaces exhibit angular directionality in their reflectance of incident light and this process is generally referred to as 'specular reflection'. Consider the diagram presented in Figure 5.19(a) in which a ray of light impinges on a smooth mirrored surface at an angle i with respect to the surface normal. In the case of a true mirror, the reflected light follows the path indicated – such that the angle of incidence (i) equals the angle of reflection (r). However, in the case of other forms of 'shiny' surface that are non-perfect reflectors, not all of the reflected light will follow this exact path. This situation is illustrated in Figure 5.19(b).

Consider, for example a billiard ball or waxed apple that is illuminated with white light. A highlighted region will be seen on the surface of the object – its location being determined by the position of both the light source and viewpoint relative to the object. This highlight occurs due to specular reflection. Note that the colour of this region is not determined by the colour of the object that is being illuminated but rather by the colour of the light source (thus, for example, a white highlight can be produced on the surface of a shiny red apple).

Phong Bui-Tuong developed an illumination model for specular reflection. As indicated above, a ray of light impinging on the surface of an ideal reflector (e.g. a smooth mirrored

---

[22] Alternatively, d can represent the distance from the COP to the source of illumination.

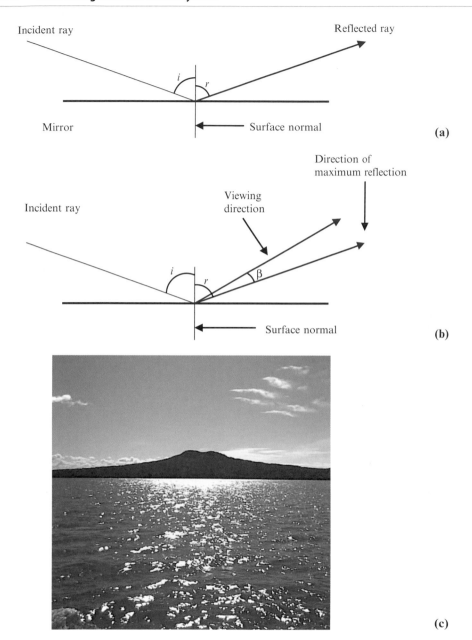

Figure 5.19 Specular reflection. In (a), a ray impinges on a mirrored surface. The angle between this ray and the surface normal is denoted by i and the reflected ray emerges at an angle r (again measured relative to the normal). In the case of a mirror, $i = r$. In (b) a ray impinges on a shiny (non-perfect reflector). Here, the direction of maximum reflection occurs at an angle r – although in the case of the smooth non-perfect reflector, not all of the reflected light will follow this exact path. The viewing direction is assumed to lie at an angle β relative to this path. When $\beta = 0°$ the level of reflected light is greatest. As $|\beta|$ increases, the level of reflected light diminishes. In (c) an example of specular reflection is presented. (Photograph © A.R. Blundell (2007).)

surface) at an angle i relative to the surface normal, will give rise to a reflected ray that lies at an angle r (again measured relative to the normal) such that the angles of incidence and reflection are the same. However, in the case of specular reflection, all the reflected light does not follow this exact path and we can write:

$$i = r \pm \phi, \tag{5.15}$$

where ϕ denotes a deflection range. Typically, very shiny surfaces will exhibit a narrow deflection range whereas in the case of duller surfaces, the reflection range will be wider. A specular reflection model should ensure that the greatest amount of reflected light emerges along the path that we associate with the ideal reflector – such that the angles of incidence and reflection are equal. In addition, the reflection model should take into account the emergence of light within a cone surrounding this path in such a way that as $|\phi|$ increases, the light strength diminishes.

OTU Exercise 5.11: Clouds, Sunsets and Reflection

1. Discuss the underlying reason(s) for the colour of the clouds.
2. Carefully observe and account for the changing colours of the sky around the time at which the sun sets. The book by James Elkins [2000] is recommended to the interested reader. The early riser is also encouraged to consider the dawn sky. . .
3. Examine the highlights that occur on the surfaces of everyday objects as a result of specular reflection. Note that these highlights take on the colour of the source of illumination – rather than the colour of an objects surface. Also notice the effect of varying the location of the source of illumination and/or the viewing location relative to a surface.

To model the strength of reflected light across the deflection range, the Phong model employs a cosine function such that:

Strength of specular reflection $\propto \cos^n \phi$.

Where n denotes the specular reflection exponent for the surface. Although Eq. 5.14 was developed in relation to our previous discussion concerning diffuse reflection, it can be employed to model the situation indicated in Figure 5.19(b) – specifically expressing the light output along the 'direction of maximum reflection' as a function of the angle of incidence of a point source of illumination. We can write:

$$l = I_a K_a + \frac{I}{d + \eta} \left[K_d(\hat{\mathbf{n}} \cdot \hat{\mathbf{s}}) + \omega(\theta) \cos^n \phi \right]. \tag{5.16}$$

The first term in this equation relates to the reflection of ambient light (see previous discussion concerning diffuse reflection). Here, I_a denotes the illumination provided by the ambient light and K_a the proportion of the incident light that is reflected. Expanding the square bracket yields two terms. The first of these takes the form of the Eq. 5.14 and the second term accommodates light emerging within the cone surrounding the 'direction of maximum reflection'. In the case that, for example, we are dealing with an optically perfect mirror, the specular reflection exponent (n) tends to infinity and, since the cosine of any angle lies between 1 and -1, this term tends to zero. Hence, the reflected light emerges along a path such that the angles of incidence and reflection are equal. In the case that we are dealing with a very shiny surface n may take on a value of 200 (or greater) and for a dull surface may be close to unity.

The degree of specular reflection is also influenced by the angle of incidence and this is taken into account in Eq. 5.16 through the inclusion of the reflection function $\omega(\theta)$. In the case of glass, the degree of specular reflection varies considerably with the angle at which the incident light strikes the surface and so the function $\omega(\theta)$ provides us with a means by which we can accommodate this behaviour. Alternatively, for many materials we may assume that ω is essentially independent of θ. In this case, for a particular surface, we employ a fixed value of ω (in the range 0 to 1) – the value being selected to give the most visually satisfactory result.

Eq. 5.16 may be re-written as:

$$l = I_a K_a + \frac{I}{d + \eta} \left[K_d(\mathbf{\hat{n}} \cdot \mathbf{\hat{s}}) + \omega(\theta)(\mathbf{V} \cdot \mathbf{R})^n \right] \qquad (5.17)$$

where vectors $\mathbf{V}$ and $\mathbf{R}$ are assumed to have a magnitude of unity. The former is assumed to point in the direction of the viewer and the latter in the direction of specular reflection.

Hearn and Baker [1986] briefly summarise an alternative approach to modelling light reflection. In this context they write:

'One technique, developed by Torrance and Sparrow [1967] and adapted to graphics applications by Blinn, divides each surface in a scene into a set of tiny planes. Each of the small planes is assumed to be an ideal reflector, and the planes are oriented randomly over the total surface. A Gaussian distribution function is used to set the orientation of each plane. The specular reflection for the surface is calculated as the total contribution from the small planes as a function of the intensity from a distant point source. . .'

5.4.6 Texture

Surface texture and texture gradients strongly support our perception of 3-D space and provide an important mechanism by which we determine the shape of 3-D objects. Furthermore, the judicious use of textures plays a critical role in the formation of realistic and photorealistic images. Below we briefly summarise the use of textures within each of these contexts:

1. **Perception of a 3-D Space**: Consider the simple illustration provided in Figures 5.20(a) and (b). In (a) a set of equally spaced horizontal lines are shown and we can consider this to represent a very simple uniform pattern texture. In contrast, in (b), the horizontal lines gradually become closer and this 'texture gradient' immediately gives an impression of depth. In this context, it is important to note that when we view our surroundings, as distance increases, elements that comprise a texture gradually become smaller and more densely spaced thus a repetitive texture pattern should conform to the linear perspective cue. In fact, J.J. Gibson who was a pioneering researcher in the area of depth perception suggested the use of the texture gradient as a cue able to incorporate both linear perspective and relative size.

2. **Perception of Shape**: Both gradual and abrupt changes (discontinuities) in texture gradient provide a means of gaining information about the shape and orientation of objects within a scene. This is illustrated in an elementary manner in Figure 5.21.

3. **Computer Graphics**: In the physical world, surfaces are often not smooth and to create realistic and photorealistic images, it is often desirable to model different forms of surface

Figure 5.20 In (a) we depict a simple uniform texture that provides no indication of depth. By contrast, in (b) a 'texture gradient' is employed. The elements that comprise the texture gradually become more densely spaced and this provides us with an impression of depth. This impression can be reinforced by making the elements gradually decrease in length (whilst retaining a central vertical axis of symmetry). J.J. Gibson (1904–1977) who was a pioneering leader in the area of depth perception viewed the texture gradient cue as providing a means of combining the linear perspective and relative size cues.

texture. Here, for example we may wish to represent the rough bark of a tree, grass, fur, different forms of fabric or the pile of a carpet. Additionally, in some cases (such as a carpet) we may not only wish to represent the actual texture of the material but also some form of repetitive pattern.

One simple approach to the formation of an irregular surface texture (such as that of a raisin) is to employ a shading model (such as we have outlined above) and allow the surface normal to randomly vary in direction with location on the surface. Texture mapping methods can also be used. In this context Sherman and Craig [2003] write:

'*Simply put, the technique of texture mapping allows one to paste a texture onto a polygon. Textures add the appearance of detail and gradient cues onto what are otherwise simple, flat surfaces. When viewed close up, and especially when viewed stereoscopically, texture-mapped objects begin to reveal their secret of being little more than cardboard cut-outs or the facades of a theatrical set.*'

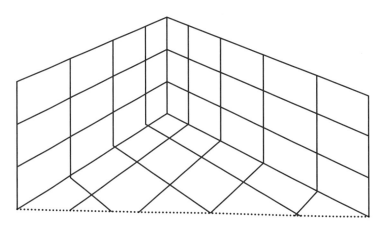

Figure 5.21 Here, abrupt changes in a simple pattern texture can be used to indicate shape – in this case the corner of a room or box.

5.4.7 Linear Perspective

'If the world should blow itself up,
the last audible voice would be that of an expert
saying it can't be done.'[23]

In Section 1.3 we introduced linear perspective and briefly summarised the demonstration of Filippo Brunelleschi who, in the early 15th century, is said to have provided the first demonstration of an accurate mathematical based perspective technique for the capture of a 3-D scene on a 2-D tableau. As indicated in Figure 1.10, linear perspective (by which an object appears to diminish in size as it is moved further away from an observer) occurs as a result of the finite separation between the focusing elements of the eye and the photo-receptors that are located on the retina. It is because of this geometry that the size of the image cast onto the retina depends on the angle it subtends at the eye and in turn this depends on both image size *and* image distance.

Let us now turn our attention to the perspective projection of an object located within a 3-D space onto a 2-D surface. In undertaking such a projection, we endeavour to create an image on the surface that *appears* to be three-dimensional and within the context of our current discussion, we are particularly interested in forming a 2-D rendition of a 3-D object that satisfies the linear perspective cue. Here, we note that in the physical world, when the distance between an observer and an object varies, the visual angle subtended by the object at the eye changes as a direct result of the change in object distance. However, in the case of a perspective projection, when we wish to provide an impression of a change in object distance, we produce a change in the visual angle subtended by the object by manipulating the actual size of the object.

As indicated in Figure 1.12, the surface on which a 3-D image is projected (the projection plane) is assumed to lie between the object and the observer. In this illustration the object is simply represented as an arrow. Lines drawn from the top and bottom of this arrow pass through the projection plane and meet at the centre of projection (COP) – which corresponds to the assumed viewing location. The points at which these two lines intersect the projection plane defines the size of the projection of the object. Consider now the inclusion of a second arrow that is the same size as the original but which lies at a greater distance from the projection plane. If we draw lines from the top and bottom of this arrow to the COP, then at the point at which they intersect the projection plane they will be more closely spaced than were the lines emanating from the original object. This is in line with our desire to incorporate linear perspective within the projected image – the more distant an object, the smaller is the projected rendition.

In Section 1.3 we introduced the use of vanishing points and in Figure 1.13 illustrated the formation of a perspective view of a cube using a single vanishing point (VP). In terms of our current discussion, it is useful to consider the roles played by both the COP and VP and to simplify matters we will limit this discussion to a 2-D model (which may be readily extended to deal with a 3-D space). In Figure 5.22(a), we depict vertical and horizontal axes together with a line segment located on the *y*-axis that represents the projection (viewing) plane. To the right of the projection plane we show a line segment AB that lies parallel to the horizontal axis and on the other side of the projection plane indicate the position of the COP which is at an arbitrary location on the *x*-axis. We extend a line from each end of the line segment to the COP and the location at which these lines cut the projection plane indicates the end points of the projection of the line segment AB. In Figure 5.22(b) we alter the location of the line segment – whilst remaining parallel to the *x*-axis, end point A is now in contact with the projection plane.

---

[23] Attributed to Peter Ustinov (1921–2004).

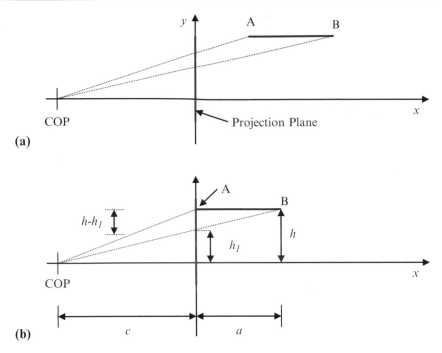

Figure 5.22 In (a) we illustrate a line segment AB that lies parallel to the horizontal axis and is therefore normal to the projection (viewing) plane. Two lines of projection connect the ends of this line to the centre of projection (COP). The perspective projection of AB is therefore a line in the projection plane that spans the gap between the lines of projection. In (b), the line segment is moved so that end-point A touches the projection plane. Here, we note that all points located in the projection plane (such as point A) remain unaltered by the projection. See text for discussion.

As may be seen from this illustration, the projection of point A does not give rise to a new point in the projection plane – in fact in the more general case, all points lying in the projection plane remain unaltered by the projection. In the illustration, we denote the length of the line segment AB as a, the distance of this line from the horizontal axis as h. The distance of the projection of point B (as measured from the origin) is h_1, and we assume that the COP lies at a distance c from the origin. On the basis of similar triangles, we can now write:

$$\frac{h}{c+a} = \frac{h_1}{c},\tag{5.18}$$

and so:

$$h_1 = \frac{ch}{c+a}.\tag{5.19}$$

Now consider the diagram presented in Figure 5.23(a) and that is based on Figure 5.22(b). Here, two horizontal line segments are equally spaced from the horizontal axis and we indicate equidistant points along the two segments by means of a number of vertical lines. This diagram could, for example represent a non-perspective plan view of a railway track (the horizontal lines representing the rails and the vertical lines the wooden or concrete 'sleepers'). This diagram is redrawn in (b) so as to show only three 'sleepers' and the symbols assigned to various

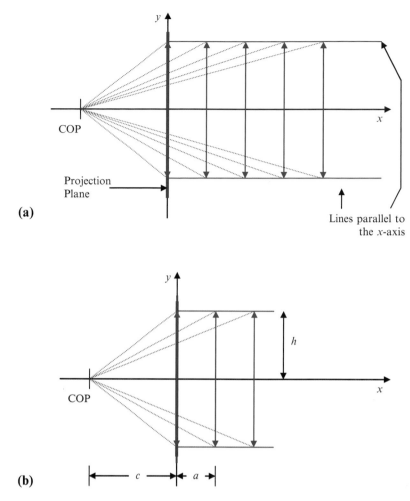

(a)

(b)

Figure 5.23 In (a) two lines that are parallel to and equidistant from the horizontal axis are shown. Between these a number of equally spaced line segments are indicated. The end points of each of these vertical lines are connected to the COP by means of lines of projection. We can conceptualise this diagram as representing a plan view of a section of a railway track. Here, the two horizontal lines represent the steel rails, and the vertical lines the wooden or concrete 'sleepers'. In (b), the top diagram is simplified to show only three 'sleepers' and the symbols used in the text to represent various distances are indicated.

distances are indicated. Lines of projection are included from the ends of each 'sleeper' and the distance between the two projection lines from each sleeper as they intersect the projection plane provides us with each sleeper's perspective projection. In fact, we note that such a perspective projection would be of little value – from this particular orientation the projections for all of the 'sleepers' would be overlayed and so we would not be able to distinguish between them (this being equivalent to looking down a railway track from the absolute ground level – only the nearest sleeper would be visible).

Turning now to Figure 5.24, in which we use the projections in the projection plane of each of the 'sleepers' obtained in Figure 5.23(b) to recreate a perspective view with a single vanishing point. As may be seen from this diagram, the vanishing point (VP) is indicated on the horizontal

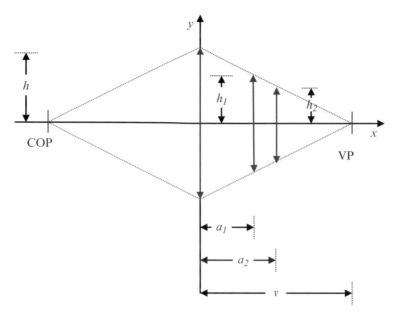

Figure 5.24 Re-creating a perspective view by means of the projections obtained in Figure 5.23. Here, a vanishing point (VP) is indicated and is located at an arbitrary distance along the horizontal axis. In the perspective view, the two horizontal lines depicted in Figure 5.23 merge at the vanishing point. See text for discussion.

axis at an arbitrary distance from the projection plane. (Recall from discussion in Chapter 1 that in the case of this simple projection, lines in the non-perspective view that are parallel to the horizontal axis will merge at the vanishing point.) Thus, in the perspective view, the two horizontal lines (which we conceptualise as representing railway tracks) meet at the VP – as indicated in the illustration. Furthermore, the endpoints of each of the vertical line segments (the 'sleepers') will be located on these lines. In the diagram, we have therefore taken each of the projections of the 'sleepers' and have placed these at locations at which they span the triangle. As may be seen, the three vertical line segments shown in the illustration are no longer equally spaced – as distance from the viewpoint increases, the sleepers become more closely spaced.

By referring to Figure 5.24, we can write an expression for the distance of each vertical line from the origin. For the second line which lies at a distance a_1 from the projection plane, it is apparent (on the basis of similar triangles) that:

$$\frac{h}{v} = \frac{h_1}{v - a_1}.$$

Similarly for the next vertical line:

$$\frac{h}{v} = \frac{h_2}{v - a_2}.$$

Thus for the nth line (where $n = 0, 1, 2 \ldots$) we can write:

$$\frac{h}{v} = \frac{h_n}{v - a_n}. \tag{5.20}$$

On the basis of Figure 5.23, we can write:

$$h_n = \frac{ch}{c + na}.$$

(5.21)

Substituting this into Eq. 5.20 and rearranging gives:

$$a_n = v\left[1 - \frac{c}{c + na}\right],$$

(5.22)

and so, the spacing between vertical lines is given by:

$$a_n - a_{n-1} = vc\left[\frac{1}{c + (n-1)a} - \frac{1}{c + na}\right].$$

(5.23)

OTU Exercise 5.12: A Perspective View

Consider a simple numerical example in which the parameters indicated in Figures 5.23(b) and 5.24 have the following values: $c = 10\,cm$, $a = 2\,cm$, $h = 6\,cm$, $v = 10\,cm$. Using Eq. 5.21, determine the lengths of the projections of the first five vertical lines (illustrated in Figure 5.23(a)) and also calculate the distance of each from the origin when arranged to give a perspective view (as illustrated in Figure 5.24). Using your calculated values, draw a graph (indicate distance from the origin on the x-axis and line length on the y-axis). Confirm that the set of points that you have plotted lie on the line $y = \frac{-h}{v}x + h$.

From the above discission, it is apparent that we create the projections of objects in the projection plane on the basis of a certain COP or viewpoint. As a result, a 3-D image that is projected onto a 2-D surface will be geometrically optimal when viewed from this location. This applies not only to perspective images created by artists on a canvas but also to 3-D images depicted on the conventional computer display.

When we view our physical surroundings, the optical components within the eye create a 2-D projection of the 3-D scene on the retina. Naturally, the geometrical content of this projection changes as we adjust our viewing location. In contrast, when we view a 3-D scene depicted on a conventional computer display or artist's tableau the image cast onto the retina is (to a first approximation) a replica of the scene under observation. Changing our viewpoint will result in changes to the retinal image that do not correspond to the changes that would occur if we were looking directly onto an equivalent and physical 3-D scene. As we have seen, in order to create such an image the computer graphics designer or artist must form the perspective projection on the basis of a certain assumed viewpoint. When viewed from other locations the retinal image will be distorted and will not correspond to the image that would be seen if the 2-D rendition were replaced by the equivalent physical 3-D scene.

However, in this context, Ware [2000] writes:

'It is an obvious fact that most pictures are not viewed from their correct centres of perspective. In a movie theatre, only one person can occupy this optimal viewpoint... When a picture is viewed from an incorrect viewpoint, the laws of geometry suggest that significant distortion should occur... However, while people report seeing some distortion initially when looking at moving pictures from the wrong viewpoint, they become unaware of the distortion after a few minutes... Apparently the human visual system overrides some aspects of perspective in constructing the 3-D world that we perceive...'[24]

Our ability to adapt to (or perhaps ignore) aspects of incorrect perspective provides yet another example of the remarkable capabilities of the human visual system. Within this context it is perhaps worth a brief aside and a return to previous discussion in Section 5.2 concerning the blind spot (recall this arises as a consequence of the absence of photoreceptors in the region in which the connections from the photoreceptive array leave the eye). From our everyday experience, we know that we are not aware of the presence of this blind spot – there is no 'black hole' in the images that we observe. Perhaps we might suppose that this is due to our binocular vision – the part of an image scene that is lost because of the blind spot in one eye is captured by the other eye and *vice versa*. However, closing one eye can immediately dispel this notion – the blind spot remains invisible to us. An alternative scenario is that the blind spot is very small in extent and therefore has an insignificant impact on the image captured by the eye. However, in relation to the size of the blind spot, Helmholtz [1873] writes:

'... it covers an angle equal to 11 full moons placed side by side in the sky.'

Clearly, the extent of the blind spot is by no means insignificant and the ability of the visual system to compensate for its presence is yet another example of the remarkable characteristics of our imaging system!

Finally in this section, we turn our attention to a little mathematics relating to the projection of image components onto the projection plane. We begin by assigning a rectangular coordinate system that is able to represent points within a 3-D space. Here, we make use of three mutually orthogonal axes (labelled x, y and z) as illustrated in Figure 5.25.

The use of a right-handed coordinate system (as in Figure 5.25(a)) can be readily confirmed by employing the thumb together with the first and second fingers of the *right* hand. Arrange these orthogonally and then align the thumb with the x-axis and the first finger with the y-axis. In the case that a right-handed coordinate system is employed, the second finger should point in the positive z direction.[25] Adopting the same approach (but with the *left* hand) confirms the use of a left-handed coordinate system – try this out using Figure 5.25(b)).

OTU Exercise 5.13: Left and Right Handed Coordinate Systems

Consider the diagram presented in Figure 5.26. Does this represent a left handed or right handed coordinate system?

---

[24] For related discussion see Kubovy [1986].
[25] This can require a little practice and may remind readers of high-school physics lessons in which a similar approach is adopted for Fleming's Left and Right Hand Rules in connection with electromagnetism.

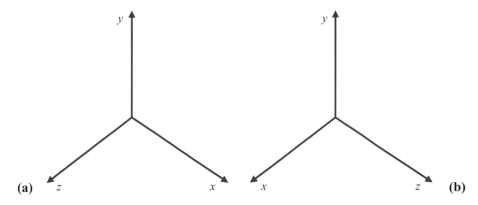

Figure 5.25 In (a) we represent a right-handed rectangular coordinate system and in (b) a left-handed system. To avoid ambiguity that can arise when simple line drawings of 3-D objects are depicted on a 2-D surface, it is convenient to imagine the three lines as representing the corner of a room (e.g. in (a) the x and z axis represent the boundaries between the floor and two walls and the y axis the line along which the two walls meet).

In our previous discussions, we have defined the location of a point on the x–y plane using an ordered pair of the form (x, y). When wishing to represent the location of a point within a 3-D rectangular coordinate system, we extend the 2-D approach and specify a third measurement corresponding to the distance in the 'z' direction – that is we specify a triple (x, y, z).

Let us now turn to the projection illustrated in Figure 5.27. Here, a triangle (with vertices labelled KLM) in 3-D space is projected onto the projection plane. This is achieved by drawing lines from each vertex to the COP – the vertices of the projection of the triangle (labelled K'L'M' in the diagram) are defined by the points at which the lines of projection intersect with the projection plane. Consider vertex K and let us suppose that the coordinates of this point (in 3-D space) are given by (K_x, K_y, K_z). The coordinates of a point Q (given by (Q_x, Q_y, Q_z)) on the line connecting K to the COP may be expressed in

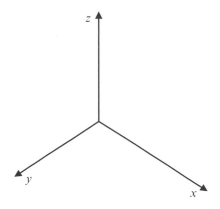

Figure 5.26 Is this a left handed or right handed coordinate system?

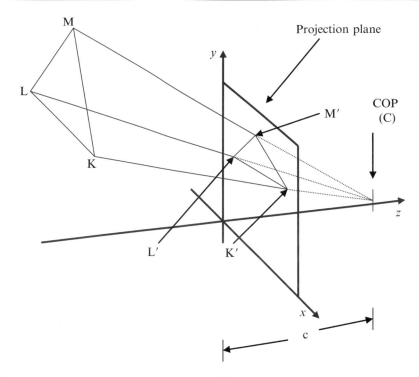

Figure 5.27 The projection of an arbitrary object (in this case a triangle KLM) in 3-D space onto the projection plane. For convenience we define the projection plane as being located in the $z = 0$ plane and assume that the centre of projection (COP) is located on the z-axis. See text for discussion.

parametric form as:

$$Q_x = C_x + u\left[K_x - C_x\right]$$
$$Q_y = C_y + u\left[K_y - C_y\right]$$
$$Q_z = C_z + u\left[K_z - C_z\right],$$

where (C_x, C_y, C_z) denotes the coordinates of the COP and the parameter u represents the fractional distance of the point Q along the line CK ($0 \le u \le 1$). Thus, for example, if $u = 0$ then Q lies at the COP and in the case that $u = 1$, then the three equations show that Q is at the point K.

Our current objective is to determine the coordinates of the vertices of the triangle that is projected onto the projection plane. For the moment we will focus on the projection of vertex K (which is denoted as K' in the diagram). The coordinates of K' are given by:

$$K'_x = C_x + u\left[K_x - C_x\right]$$
$$K'_y = C_y + u\left[K_y - C_y\right]$$
$$K'_z = C_z + u\left[K_z - C_z\right].$$

As may be seen from Figure 5.27, for convenience, we have arranged for the projection plane to coincide with the plane $z = 0$ (i.e. the projection plane lies in the x–y plane). Consequently, the

z coordinate of K' (K_z') must be zero. Thus:

$$C_z + u\,[K_z - C_z] = 0,$$

and so at K', the parameter u is given by:

$$u = \frac{C_z}{C_z - K_z}.$$

We can now substitute this value for u into the equations for K_x' and K_y' and so obtain:

$$K_x' = C_x + \frac{C_z\,[K_x - C_x]}{C_z - K_z}, \quad K_y' = C_y + \frac{C_z\,[K_y - C_y]}{C_z - K_z}, \quad K_z' = 0.$$

Because we have arranged for the COP to lie on the z-axis, both C_x and C_y equal zero and so the above expressions may be simplified:

$$K_x' = \frac{C_z K_x}{C_z - K_z}, \quad K_y' = \frac{C_z K_y}{C_z - K_z}, \quad K_z' = 0. \tag{5.24}$$

Similarly we can represent the coordinates of the projection of vertex L in the projection plane as:

$$L_x' = \frac{C_z L_x}{C_z - L_z}, \quad L_y' = \frac{C_z L_y}{C_z - L_z}, \quad L_z' = 0, \tag{5.25}$$

and for vertex M:

$$M_x' = \frac{C_z M_x}{C_z - M_z}, \quad M_y' = \frac{C_z M_y}{C_z - M_z}, \quad M_z' = 0.$$

In each case we see that the projection of a point onto the projection plane is affected by the distance of the point from the COP and this confirms our previous discussions. Also we note that by locating the coordinates of the projection of each of the triangle's vertices, we are able to completely describe the geometry of the projected shape (each side of the triangle is completely defined by the location of its endpoints). In Section 6.5 we return to discussion on projection and in the next section turn our attention to the oculomotor cues.

5.5 Oculomotor Depth Cues

> 'Real seriousness in regard to writing
> is one of two absolute necessities.
> The other, unfortunately, is talent.'[26]

When we view our immediate surroundings, the focal length of the crystalline lens within each eye is continually modified to ensure that each object within the visual field to which we direct or re-direct our attention is sharply focused on the retina.[27] At the same time the eyes are oriented so that their visual axes meet at the point of fixation thus ensuring that the area of particular

---

[26] Attributed to Ernest Miller Hemingway (1899–1961).
[27] When we view objects that are at a distance of ~3 m or greater, the curvature of the lens does not vary.

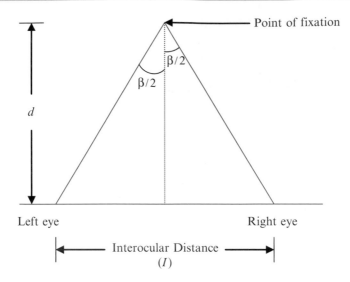

Figure 5.28 By means of triangulation, convergence may (in principle) provide us with information concerning the distance of an object that is the focus of our attention. The angle β is referred to as the angle of convergence.

interest within the visual field is cast onto the fovea of each eye. The former action is referred to as accommodation (see also Section 5.2.2) and the latter as convergence.[28] When we view a 3-D image scene depicted on a conventional computer screen, the focal length of the eyes and the point of convergence are defined by the distance between the display screen and the observer. In this sense, although various pictorial cues employed in the depiction of the scene may provide us with a sense of depth, the focusing and convergence actions of the eyes do not re-adjust – as indeed they would if we were looking at an image that actually occupies a 3-D space.

> The lack of support for the oculomotor and binocular cues denotes a fundamental difference in 3-D images depicted on the conventional flat screen display and their physical counterpart. The extent to which this negatively impacts on the visual system and on our ability to visualise and interact with complex 3-D scenes is a matter of ongoing debate.

Convergence enables us to obtain (at least in principle) distance information on the basis of triangulation. As indicated in Figure 5.28 if in some way the visual system is able to measure the degree of convergence of the eyes, then this information coupled with their finite separation provides a mechanism for measuring the distance of an image component that is the focus of our attention.

---

[28] More accurately, convergence denotes the rotation of the eyes towards the nose and divergence is used when referring to the opposite motion.

On the basis of the diagram we can write:

$$\tan\left(\frac{\beta}{2}\right) = \frac{I}{2d}.\qquad(5.26)$$

Assuming that the angle β is measured in radians, we can use the small angle approximation $\tan \beta/2 \approx \beta/2$ and so:[29]

$$\beta \approx \frac{I}{d}.$$

We can now determine how β varies with changes in d. Recall our earlier discussion in relation to differentiation – the differential $d\beta/dd$ gives us the rate of change of β with respect to changes in d. The differential of the above expression with respect to d is obtained as follows:

$$\beta \approx \frac{I}{d} = Id^{-1}.$$

Thus:

$$\frac{d\beta}{dd} \approx -Id^{-2} = \frac{-I}{d^2},$$

and so:

$$\left|\frac{d\beta}{dd}\right| \approx \frac{I}{d^2} \approx \frac{6.3}{d^2},$$

where $||$ denotes the magnitude and we assume an interocular distance of ≈ 6.3 cm. This equation confirms our intuitive understanding that for more distance objects, the triangulation process rapidly becomes less sensitive to changes in d.

OTU Exercise 5.14: Convergence Angle

Consider an object that is initially at a distance of 4m from the eyes and which is moved to a distance of 5m. On the basis of Eq. 5.26, calculate the change in the convergence angle (β). Now suppose that an object is initially at a distance of 20 cm. What increase in the object's distance would give the same change in the convergence angle? (Assume an interocular distance of 6.3 cm.)

Unfortunately, in the case of the conventional flat screen display, this discussion has little relevance as changes in convergence angles cannot be used to determine the depth of image components within a scene and so this cue cannot be used to support interaction. As we will discuss in Chapter 9, some creative 3-D display technologies support both accommodation and convergence in a natural manner and so this cue is potentially of value. However there is some uncertainty as to the extent to which accommodation and convergence reliably contribute to

---

[29] You may wish to verify this approximation. For example, set your calculator to radians mode and enter a small angle such as $\pi/36$ (which corresponds to $5°$). You should find that $\pi/36 \sim 0.0873$. Taking the tan of this angle, we obtain a result of ~ 0.0875. But be sure that your calculator is set to work with radians rather than degrees!!

our overall perception of relative and absolute distance – see Blundell [2007] for summary discussion.

When we view our physical surroundings, the focusing and convergence actions of the eyes operate in harmony – the eyes focusing on, and their visual axes converging upon the point of fixation. The optical system exhibits a focal length f such that:

$$\frac{1}{u} + \frac{1}{v} = \frac{1}{f}.$$

Here, u denotes the distance of the point of fixation from the eye (the object distance) and v the distance between the eye's optical system and the retina (the image distance).

In the case that we are viewing images depicted on the conventional flat screen display, u denotes the distance between the screen and the eye and of course v is defined by internal dimensions within the eye. In addition the convergence distance of the eyes is also u. In short, the accommodation and convergence of the eyes remain synchronised (although they do not adjust to image content). In contrast, in the case of displays that operate on the principle of the stereoscope (see Sections 9.3 and 9.4) accommodation and convergence become decoupled – this is known as accommodation/convergence (A/C) breakdown. When such displays are continuously viewed for extensive periods of time, this can have negative consequences for the visual system.

Although accommodation and convergence depth cues are often defined in terms of the focusing and convergence actions of the eyes, it is important to note that this is not strictly accurate. When the thickness of the eyes' crystalline lens changes or when the eyes slightly rotate so as to bring together at a certain distance their optical axes, these actions are either consciously triggered or are a result of the conscious (or often subconscious) selection of a point of fixation within a scene. Putting to one side the case in which, for example, we deliberately 'cross' or de-focus the eyes, it is apparent that physical changes in the eyes represent the observable and measurable result of the processing of the image scene coupled with our conscious or subconscious selection of a point of fixation. This leads naturally to the question of how we derive depth information from such stimuli and there are in fact a number of interesting possibilities. In this context Clark and Horch writing in Boff *et al.* [1986] (and quoting the ideas of Helmholtz) write:

'Helmholtz concluded that our perception of eye movement and of the direction of gaze came not from sensory receptors that monitor the position of the eyeballs or the contractions of muscles but from the effort of willing the eyes to move (a sense of "innervation").'

The sense of innervation was considered to underpin not only accommodation and convergence but also many aspects of proprioception. However, with the discovery of the abundance of sensory receptors in muscles, joints and beneath the skin, 'innervationists' gradually lost ground. For summary discussion see Blundell and Schwarz [2006].

5.6 Binocular Cues

Finally in this chapter, we turn our attention to the cues of binocular and motion parallax. By definition binocular cues arise because we are equipped with two spatially separated eyes. In fact, convergence can also be considered to be a binocular cue. However, as discussed in the previous section, when we view our physical surroundings the accommodation and convergence of the eyes operate in harmony and so it is more meaningful (certainly in terms of our current discussions) to consider these two cues alongside each other.

As we have discussed, the conventional flat screen display supports only the pictorial cues. It is inherently unable to satisfy the oculomotor cues but can be modified to support binocular and motion parallax (see Chapter 9). When we are considering standard (traditional) computer graphics, binocular cues usually have little relevance but are pivotal to discussions concerning various forms of creative 3-D display.

Let us begin by briefly returning to Chapter 1 and specifically the stereograms depicted in Figure 1.32. By using the viewing glasses supplied with this book or by consciously 'crossing' the eyes (to change the distance at which their visual axes meet), we can merge the image pairs to form 3-D images that no longer appear to lie in the plane of the page. Such images convey a remarkable sense of *relief* (three-dimensionality) which arises due to the ability of the visual system to process and capitalise on the disparities contained within the image pairs. However, before we proceed, it is instructive to examine an alternative technique that yields (under certain conditions) a similar result.

OTU Exercise 5.15: The Pulfrich Effect

Here is an OTU exercise that everyone is likely to enjoy – it simply involves relaxing and watching one of your favourite films on the TV. The only requirement is that you select a film containing scenes in which there is lots of relative motion. (such as the scenes in 'Dumbo' in which the train is depicted or in 'Armageddon' prior to the landing on the asteroid). Don the Pulfrich glasses that are supplied with this book (these are the cardboard glasses comprising transparent and darkened[30] eyepieces).

After a time you should perceive a strong sense of image three-dimensionality (the *relief* associated with stereoscopic images). In case this doesn't work for you, try changing the ambient level of lighting in the room (dimmed lighting works best for the author) and/or reverse the viewing glasses so that the darkened filter is placed over the other eye. In addition whilst watching the TV, it is best if you do not make a conscious effort to see this effect – just let the visual system relax!

The objective of the above OTU Exercise is to observe the 'Pulfrich Effect' – a visual illusion that is underpinned by reducing the level of light entering one eye relative to the other. Unfortunately, Pulfrich became blind in 1905 – some 22 years before he actually published details of his earlier observations. He attributed this effect to the ability of the visual system to respond more rapidly to brighter input. Thus the darkened filter reduces the level of light entering one eye and so the output from this eye is processed more slowly than the output from the other. This leads to a temporal disparity which is interpreted as providing a strong sense of image depth.[31] However, this denotes only one of several explanations – see Blundell and Schwarz [2006] for summary discussion, or Howard and Rogers [2002] for more in-depth treatment.

---

[30] A neutral density filter.

[31] The classic demonstration of the Pulfrich Effect involves the use of a pendulum. When viewed through 'Pulfrich glasses', the pendulum bob no longer appears to move in a plane but rather seems to follow an elliptical path.

In the next subsection we briefly summarise aspects of the binocular parallax depth cue and in Section 5.6.2 we turn our attention to motion parallax.

5.6.1 Binocular Parallax (Stereopsis)

'Perhaps some day we shall know how to heighten creativity.
Until then, one of the best things we can do
for creative men and women
is to stand out of their light.'[32]

Binocular parallax (stereopsis) provides a remarkably powerful cue to depth and is underpinned by the spatial separation of the two eyes. When we view our physical surroundings, the images cast onto the two retinae contain small differences. We may readily observe differences in the images captured by the two eyes by looking onto a 3-D scene and alternating the closure of the eyes. It is also important to note that when we view our immediate surroundings, the images cast onto the retinae usually contain disparities in both the horizontal and vertical directions.

In the text that follows, we briefly review aspects of the geometry of stereopsis (confining ourselves to the issue of horizontal disparity) and provide references for more in-depth discussion. Consider the diagram presented in Figure 5.29 which shows (in plan view) the optical axes of the two eyes converging at point labelled O. The circle is assumed to pass through the optical node of each eye. A second point (P) is also illustrated and from this point a line is drawn to each of the eyes. Without recourse to geometrical proof, it is apparent from the illustration that the angles α and β (which denote the angles between each of the lines drawn from P and the optical axis of the corresponding eye) are not equal in size.

Putting this another way, the angle which point P subtends at each eye is different. As a consequence, when light from point P is projected onto the retinae, a disparity will exist between the two retinal images. This leads to an obvious question – does a locus (collection) of points exist in 3-D space that will cast identical images onto each of the retina? This question has attracted interest for many centuries (as has binocular vision in general) and in 1613 Father Franciscus Aguilonius[33] coined the term 'horopter' to describe a set of points in 3-D space that produce retinal images in the two eyes which contain no disparity.[34] Below we briefly discuss a theoretical form of horizontal horopter that is known as the Vieth-Müller circle.

> In relation to the discussion that follows, it is important to bear in mind that the theoretical horopter comprises a set of points – each of which subtends the same angle at both eyes.

Let us begin with a little geometry. Consider the diagram presented in Figure 5.30. Here, three points labelled O, x and y are indicated. These lie on the circumference of a circle and each is connected by two lines to a cord (with end points m and n). Recall from elementary geometry that:

---

[32] Attributed to John William Gardner (1912–2002).
[33] Father Franciscus Aguilonius (1567–1617).
[34] There is some confusion in literature concerning the precise definition of the horopter. This arises because we can consider disparity in a number of ways (for related discussion see Blundell and Schwarz [2006]).

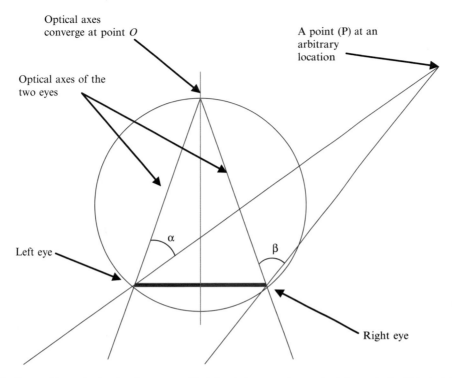

Figure 5.29 Here, we illustrate in plan view the two eyes with their optical axes meeting at point O. A second point (P) is also indicated. It is evident that this point subtends a different angle at either eye – i.e. angle $\alpha \neq \beta$.

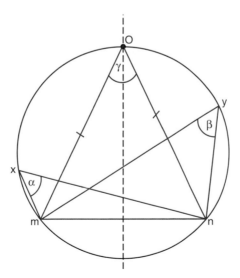

Figure 5.30 A simple rule of geometry – angles on the circumference of the same circle and that are erected on the same cord (in this case the line *mn*) are equal. Thus angles α, β and γ are equal in size. We apply this same rule to the diagram presented in Figure 5.31.

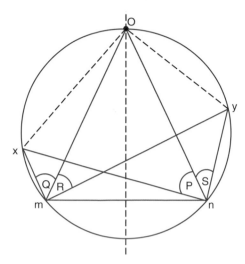

Figure 5.31 Here we extend the diagram presented in Figure 5.29. Points *m* and *n* are located at the optical nodes of the two eyes and the circle passes through these points. Label *O* represents the point of fixation and hence the lines connecting *m* and *n* with *O* correspond to the optical axes of the two eyes. On the basis of the rule summarised in Figure 5.30, it is apparent that angles *P* and *Q* are equal. Similarly angles *R* and *S* are also equal. As a result, it follows that point *x* subtends the same angle at each eye. The same is true for point *y*. In fact all points on the circle subtend equal angles at the two eyes. The circle represents a theoretical horopter known as the Vieth-Müller circle.

> **Angles at the circumference of a circle and that are erected on the same cord are equal in size.**

As may be seen from the illustration, angles α, β and γ lie on the circumference of the circle and are erected on the same cord (with end points *m* and *n*). Thus these angles are equal in size. Let us now turn to the diagram presented in Figure 5.31. As was the case with Figure 5.29, the circle passes through the optical nodes of the two eyes and point *O* represents the point of fixation (i.e. the lines connecting points *m* and *n* to *O* represent the optical axes of the eyes). Bearing in mind the geometry that we have just summarised, it is apparent that angles *P* and *Q* are equal in size (they are both on the circumference of the circle and are erected from the cord with end points *x* and *O*. Similarly angles *S* and *R* are also equal in size (being erected on the cord with end points *y* and *O*).

Bearing in mind that the lines connecting points *m* and *n* to the point of fixation (*O*) represent the optical axes of the two eyes, it is apparent that angles *P* and *Q* represent the angles subtended at each eye by point *x* and similarly angles *S* and *R* represent the angles that point *y* subtends at the two eyes. Thus point *x* subtends the same angle at each eye and for point *y*, this too subtends the same angle at each eye.

In fact, any point on the circle will subtend an equal angle at the two eyes. The circle therefore represents a theoretical horizontal horopter and this is known as the Vieth-Müller circle. However, it is important to note that we have only considered the horopter in cross section[35] and a full treatment would require us to consider disparities in both the horizontal and vertical directions.

---

[35] That is, a cross section of the horopter in the 'equatorial' plane.

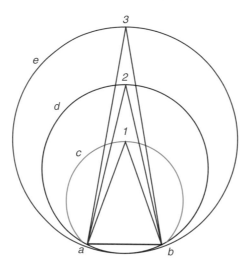

Figure 5.32 In this diagram, the optical nodes of the eyes are at points *a* and *b*. When the point of fixation lies at position 1, the theoretical horopter (the Vieth-Müller circle) is represented (in the horizontal equatorial plane) by circle *c*. Changing the point of fixation to positions 2 and 3 results in horopters *d* and *e* respectively. (Reproduced from Encyclopaedia Britannica, Adam and Charles Black, Edinburgh [1879].)

Given a certain point of fixation, we have now identified a locus of points that will (at least in theory) give rise to retinal images that do not contain disparities and as we change the fixation distance, this set of points also changes – see Figure 5.32. Points on either side of the horopter and which are close to it will give rise to retinal images containing small disparities and these can be fused by the visual system into a single stereoscopic image. Such points are said to lie in 'Panum's area' – the size and shape of which changes with fixation distance. Points that lie outside this region are not fused into a single image – giving rise to double vision. Remarkably, in our everyday lives we are usually unaware of this double vision effect.

OTU Exercise 5.16: Fusing the Content of the Visual Field

Hold a pen or pencil vertically some 20 cm from your nose. Now hold another pen in your other hand, align it with the first and position it ~10 cm further away from you (for best results you may need to adjust these distances). Fixate on the pen that is closest and at the same time note your view of the second. (Initially this may prove to be a little difficult as it is important that you do not change your point of fixation when attempting to 'notice' what is happening with the second pen.) Now reverse the process, fixate on the pen that is the furthest away and note your view of the one that is closest (again remember not to change your point of fixation).

The above OTU Exercise is intended to demonstrate that we receive a fused view of the pen upon which we fixate and in the case of the other pen we see a 'double' image. In this context Aries Arditi writing in Boff *et al.* [1986] indicates:

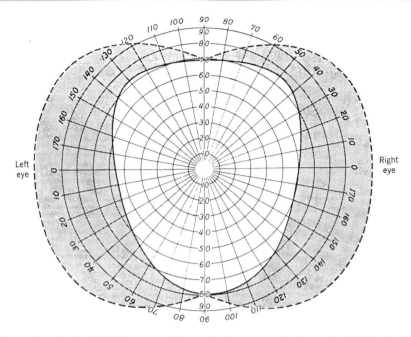

Figure 5.33 Here, we depict the visual field of the two eyes. The central region corresponds to the area in which the visual fields of both eyes overlap and so represents the region where binocular vision is supported. This has implications in, for example, the design of immersive virtual reality (IVR) headsets. (Reproduced by permission from Gibson [1950]: © 1950 Houghton Mifflin.)

'*Although geometrically double images abound in our visual worlds, we seldom notice them, even when the disparity between them is enormous . . . our failure to be confused by this conflicting information can be explained by the same mechanisms that underlie binocular suppression and rivalry and by our bias to judge the world as single.*'

In short, when we view our surroundings, a great deal of the visual field contains unfused (disparate) content – *and yet we are generally unaware of this and seldom perceive double vision.*

In the above discussion, we have referred to the 'theoretical horopter' and although as we have seen the Vieth-Müller circle defines (for a certain fixation distance) a set of points that each subtend the same angle at the two eyes, this does not guarantee that the retinal images will not contain disparities. In fact, horopters measured by experimental means differ from the theoretical form. One issue is how we define points of correspondence in the retinal image. For interesting discussion in this area see Howard and Rogers [2002] who, for example, describe physiological and geometrical corresponding points. The former are defined as projecting onto 'corresponding' binocular cells in the visual cortex and the latter as being located at congruent geometrical locations in the two eyes.

Finally in this brief discussion of binocular parallax, it is important to note that stereopsis is not supported across the entire visual field. By maintaining a constant point of fixation, and alternately closing one eye and then the other, we can readily confirm that parts of the visual field seen by one eye cannot be seen by the other. In Figure 5.33 we illustrate the visual field of the two eyes – the central region of this diagram corresponds to the region in which the visual field of each eye overlaps with the other and so corresponds to the region in which binocular parallax is supported. Outside this area (towards the periphery of our vision), we obtain a monocular view – however this is not usually apparent.

5.6.2 Motion Parallax

'And our knowledge will, we are easily persuaded,
appear in turn the merest ignorance to those who come after us.'[36]

The stereoscope that was invented in the 19th century by Charles Wheatstone and David Brewster (see Chapter 1) enables images depicted on a 2-D surface to appear to reside within a 3-D space. As we have seen, similar results may be achieved using the anaglyph technique. However, in their basic form, these methods provide us with only a single view onto an image scene, we cannot move our head from side to side and see the scene from a different viewpoint. In contrast when we view our surroundings and change our viewpoint, not only do we obtain a different view onto the scene under observation, but also objects appear to move relative to each other. (By way of example, as I look through a nearby open door, I am presented with a view of many trees – some very close and others more distant. Slight changes in head position result in apparent relative motion of the trees – both with respect to each other and with respect to the door frame through which I am looking). In more general terms, if the head is moved to the left, then objects that are closer than the point of fixation will appear to move to the right – and those that lie beyond the point of fixation will appear to move to the left.

OTU Exercise 5.17: Motion Parallax

Arrange three pens on a table so that they stand upright and lie in a straight line. Fixate on the middle pen and move the head slightly to the left. Note the apparent relative motion of the other two pens (remember to continue to fixate on the central pen). Repeat the exercise but fixate firstly on the closest pen and secondly on the pen that is furthest away.

In our everyday lives, such relative motion of objects within a 3-D space plays a critical role in depth perception. However, as with binocular parallax, motion parallax is not supported by the conventional computer flat screen display and this can negatively impact on our ability not only to accurately judge spatial relationships but also on the accuracy and ease with which we can perform interactive operations.

There are various forms of motion parallax – absolute parallax, linear parallax, looming and the kinetic depth effect (see Blundell [2007] for summary discussion or Howard and Rogers [2002] for a more detailed overview).

---

[36] *A Popular History of Astronomy During the Nineteenth Century*, by Agnes M. Clerke, Edinburgh: Adam & Charles Black (1887).

OTU Exercise 5.18: Use of Pictorial Cues

Consider the paintings that are reproduced in Figures 5.34–5.42. Discuss ways in which the artists have advantageously employed pictorial depth cues, textures etc. within their works. Here, you should consider the use of depth cues in combination and identify any inconsistencies.

5.7 Discussion

'A creative man is motivated by the desire to achieve,
not by the desire to beat others.'[37]

In this chapter we have introduced various facets of the human visual system and have highlighted important issues that should be considered when developing computer graphics and display technologies/techniques able to capitalise upon (rather than hamper) our remarkably powerful sense of sight. Unfortunately, limited space precludes more in-depth discussion and the interested reader is encouraged to peruse more specialised works. The books by Coren *et al.* [2004], Schiffman [1982], Purves and Lotto [2003] and Bruce *et al.* [2003] provide excellent starting points. In addition, the book by Boff *et al.* [1986] is a *tour de force* and is a vital source of essential information. Unfortunately, it is becoming increasingly difficult to buy copies of this book although it is still available in many libraries (Volume I focuses on the visual system).

Finally, it is important to bear in mind that nature has developed a diverse range of visual techniques of which the human eye represents only one particular instance. Further insight into the visual process can be obtained by examining other approaches and here, the fascinating book by Land and Nilsson [2002] is highly recommended[38].

5.8 Review Questions

1. Do changes in the size of the pupil account for the range of lighting conditions across which the human visual system is able to operate?
2. State the three categories of depth cues discussed in this chapter.
3. In the case of specular reflection, what determines the colour of the 'highlight'?
4. Approximately how many photoreceptors are located within the human eye?
5. The fovea is the region of the retina that supports super high resolution imaging. State the approximate density of photoreceptors in this region.
6. State three key parameters that are used in describing colour.
7. Distinguish between illuminance and luminance.

---

[37] Attributed to Ayn Rand (1905–1982) author of 'The Fountainhead'.

[38] Also see Cronly-Dillon and Gregory (Eds.) [1991] who refer to the copepod *Copilia quadrate*- '*a beautiful highly transparent pin-head size creature*'. It appears that rather than employ a retinal array of sensors, this creature has a single optic nerve for each eye. Incoming light is then scanned across the nerve (in a manner akin to a raster scan employed by CRT based displays)! Such is the diversity of the sense of sight.

'The heroine of Keats's poem is here seen contemplating the empty stand from which her brothers have taken the pot of sweet basil wherein she had placed the head of her murdered lover, Lorenzo. They are seen through the casement window bearing it away. In their hasty flight, scattered pieces of the plant have been dropped upon the marble floor.

'Piteous she looked on dead and senseless things,
Asking for her lost Basic amorously;
And with melodious chuckle in the strings
Of her torn voice, she oftentimes would cry
After the pilgrim in his wanderings,
To ask him where her Basil was; and why
'Twas hid from her. 'For cruel 'tis,' said she,
To steal my Basil-pot away from me."

Figure 5.34 'Isabella' by J.M. Strudwick (1849–1937). See OTU Exercise 5.18. (Image reproduced and description quoted from GPIPG [1905].)

'This careful student of Nature, who each year displays some truthful interpretation of English scenery, pays small regard to seasons in his choice of work, the leafy and the leafless tree being approached by him with equal devotion. Here it is the leafless tree, and in the amber glow of the wintry day there occur aspects and touches of Nature which strike us instantly as very true; such as the hard, frost-bound roadway, the bare and studiously drawn boughs and branches, the cold earth, unwarmed by the sky's glow, and the distant ridge, which will soon be merged into the winter dusk.'

Figure 5.35 'New Year's Eve' by Frank Walton (1840–1928). See OTU Exercise 5.18. (Image reproduced and description quoted from GPIPG [1905].)

'The picture is in illustration of Keat's poem of 'Endymion', and the painter has seized the moment when, at the conclusion of the poem, Endymion leaves his sister Peona, and vanishes far away with Cynthia, with the parting words:

'Peona, we shall range
These forests, and to thee they safe shall be
As was thy cradle; hither shalt thou flee
To meet us many a time".

The wonderment which the poet speaks of is still on the lovely face as she takes her way into the gloomy wood. With all his characteristic exactitude in every detail, the painter has made a beautiful interpretation of the mythological verse. It is one of his earlier works, but it differs in no respect in its general feeling and execution from his works of the present day, the utmost care being bestowed upon every part of the canvas.'

Figure 5.36 'Peona' by J.M. Strudwick (1849–1937). See OTU Exercise 5.18. (Image reproduced and description quoted from GPIPG [1905].)

'*The time of rest is at hand, and in the dim light cast by the low full moon the sheep have wended home to the comfortable enclosure where they will be in safety for the night. The old shepherd and his dog have seen that none are missing.*

It is the artist's aim in these pleasant English pastoral scenes to achieve the difficult task of obtaining absolute truthfulness of tone and colour in each object he introduces in its relationship to every other part of his picture. It will be observed in the present example that the eye rests, in the detection of this truth, with equal satisfaction on every object presented, whether it be the long, low roofing of the barns which come nearest to the nightly luminary, or the figures and sheep which are more or less shadowed, but which bring the charm of animation into the picture. One discordant note on such a sensitive canvas would take from the scene the solemnity of approaching night, given here with such fullness and accuracy.'

Figure 5.37 'Folding-Time' by Edward Stott (1859–1918). See OTU Exercise 5.18. (Image reproduced and description quoted from GPIPG [1905].)

'In the city of Verona in the sixteenth century there was a law that a man convicted of adultery should lose his head. Claudio, a youth of gentle birth, was convicted of the crime and condemned to death. His sister Isabella, virtuous and beautiful, begs his life of the Lord Deputy Angelo, who demands the forfeit of her honour as the price of Claudio's release. Abhorring both him and his suit, by no persuasion would she entertain this condition, and the execution is ordered. The picture represents the interview of Isabella with her imprisoned brother, to whom she is recounting the proposal made to her by Angelo. Claudio at first applauds her conduct, but, overcome by the fear of death, endeavours to persuade her towards dishonour.

'Claudio: "Ay! But to die, and go we know not where;
To lie in cold obstruction, and to rot.
This sensible warm motion to become
A kneaded cold...
Sweet sister, let me live".

Claudio's right hand catches absently at the iron fetter which chains him to the wall. His shoes are the long pointed ones of the period. Isabella's two hands are pressed to his heart in sisterly distress, and her right wrist is grasped tightly by Claudio. Her nun's apparel denotes the peaceful seclusion of the convent she has just left in the hope of saving her brother's life.'

Figure 5.38 'Claudio and Isabella' by W. Holman Hunt (1827–1910). See OTU Exercise 5.18. (Image reproduced and description quoted from GPIPG [1905].)

'No mere topographical transcript of the city's appearances is here, but the very spirit of the place, in the lurid light of those skies which, in the East, illuminate the land with fire and gold. Outside the city, the bare, unfruitful soil, scorched by the sun's heat, is formed into shallow hollows or ravines, where the sense of solitude is lightened only by the flocks of birds which here and there descend to find some prey.

This ancient city, so solemnly portrayed, is in the North-West Provinces of India, on a bend of the River Jumna, about 300 miles from its confluence with the Ganges, and 850 from Calcutta. It is a great grain market, but to Europeans its main speciality is its inlaid mosaic work, which is still as finely fabricated as in the time of the Munghal Emperors. Like Delhi and other cities in this part of India, Agra was the scene of much bloodshed at the time of the Indian Mutiny in 1857. The edifice in the distance, on the Delhi road, is the tomb of the Emperor Akbar.'

Figure 5.39 'Indian After-Glow, Agra' by Albert Goodwin (1845–1932). See OTU Exercise 5.18. (Image reproduced and description quoted from GPIPG [1905].)

'No home or resting place is found in the sea, even for the vessel it has wrecked, and it is tossed back on to the land. There the waves wash idly round it. Signs of the storm which has done its work are not wanting in the dark masses of angry cloud hurrying towards the right, or in the still agitated water and wind-blow sea-gulls that hover round. On such a scene the vivid lights disclosed in the sky by the departing clouds shed a sinister illumination.

It is the spirit of the sea in its vexed and destructive mood which the painter has so ably caught in this picture, and in interpreting it he has had the skill to import into the picture nothing which would have the effect of lessening the cheerless aspect, the loneliness, the immensity of the waste of waters.'

Figure 5.40 'The Homeless Sea', by Leslie Thomson (1851–1929). See OTU Exercise 5.18. (Image reproduced and description quoted from GPIPG [1905].)

'This is another of this notable painter's pieces of Welsh scenery; and the quick dexterity with which his practised hand deals with the masses of foliage, and the water which reflects them, can be plainly seen by the faithfulness of the brush and the manner of his working. No living painter has so entirely at his command these well-known mountain effects, where foliage softens the rugged hillsides, and the winding stream keeps ever fresh the meadows at their base.

In the present work the glimpse of high ground he gives us beyond the trees is suggestive of the lofty mountains of Moel Siabod or of the Snowdon Range being not far distant.'

Figure 5.41 'Near Capel Curig' by B.W. Leader (1831–1923). See OTU Exercise 5.18. (Image reproduced and description quoted from GPIPG [1905].)

'*Lucrezia is in the act of cleansing her hands of the poison she has been mixing with the wine of which one of the many victims of the Borgia family has just partaken. He is seen in the mirror in green, staggering up and down the room in company with her father, Pope Alexander VI, who is, undoubtedly, the main instigator of the crime. She turns and watches him. By the side of the decanter of poisoned wine lies a poppy, the emblem of sleep; and a rich blue vase to the right, with dark red ornamentation, and containing an orange tree laden with fruit, completes the rich harmony of this dramatic work.*'

Figure 5.42 'Lucrezia Borgia' by D.G. Rossetti (1828–1882). See OTU Exercise 5.18. (Image reproduced and description quoted from GPIPG [1905].)

8. What do you understand by the term 'grating acuity'?
9. Consider three orthogonal axes. Assume that the x and y axes lie in the plane of the page – with the positive x axis increasing to the right and the positive y axis increasing vertically. In the case of a right hand coordinate system, state the direction in which the positive z axis would increase.
10. Name four pictorial depth cues.

5.9 Feedback to Review Questions

1. No – under different lighting conditions, the area of the pupil only changes by a factor of ~9. However, between conditions of starlight and a bright sunny day, the photon flux changes by some eight orders of magnitude.
2. Pictorial, oculomotor and parallax cues.
3. This is determined by the colour of the light source – rather than the colour of the surface upon which the light impinges.
4. The human eye contains approximately 126 million photoreceptors.
5. The density of photoreceptors in the fovea is approximately $150,000\,\mathrm{mm}^{-2}$!
6. Brightness, saturation and hue.
7. Illuminance relates to light energy incident on a surface whereas luminance denotes light energy reflected by a surface.
8. Consider two line segments that are drawn end to end but which are misaligned. Grating acuity refers to the minimum misalignment that we are able to detect.
9. The positive z axis would increase 'out of the page' – i.e. towards the viewer.
10. Linear perspective, aerial perspective, height in the visual field and occlusion.

Into the Third Dimension: Transformations

'He never complained in words of our shifting habits, but curled his head round over his left paw and pressed his chin very hard against the ground whenever he smelled packing.'

6.1 Introduction

In Chapter 3 we considered the placement and manipulation of objects within a 2-D space and now extend these concepts to permit their application to three dimensions. We begin by introducing several 4 by 4 matrices that act on coordinates expressed in homogeneous form and achieve basic transformations (specifically, translation, scaling, reflection and rotation). In Section 6.3 we take a brief mathematical interlude ... and introduce the vector (cross) product which will be used here and in the following chapters. Subsequently, we show how transformations may be concatenated to allow more complex operations to be encapsulated within a single transformation matrix. This discussion is reinforced by means of two examples – in Section 6.4.1 we consider the rotation of an object about an axis that lies parallel to one of the axes of the coordinate system and in Section 6.4.2 we examine the slightly more complex situation in which an object is rotated about an arbitrarily positioned axis.

In Section 6.5 we revisit the formation of the perspective projection and show how this may be achieved by setting the values of certain elements within the transformation matrix. In previous sections of this book, we have highlighted the use of one or more vanishing points in the formation of a perspective representation and the projection of such a view onto a 2-D surface. In Section 6.5.2 we employ a simple example to demonstrate that the use of perspective

255

projection does not, in itself, guarantee that the resulting image will exhibit visual clarity. Within this context we emphasise the importance of judiciously defining object position and orientation with respect to the viewing location. Section 6.5.3 provides further discussion in relation to the centre of projection (COP) and vanishing point (VP). Here we consider the location of these two points relative to the projection plane.

Finally, in Section 6.6, we discuss the use of a virtual (synthetic) camera via which we can observe a selected portion of an image scene. Items comprising this scene are located within a 'world' coordinate system and the virtual camera is assigned its own 'viewing' coordinate system. To create a view from a certain vantage point it is necessary to map coordinates from the former coordinate system to the latter. The manner in which this transformation can be achieved is outlined in this section. This is intended to pave the way for more detailed discussion that is presented in Chapter 8.

Key Learning Outcomes: At the end of this chapter you should be able to:

- *Describe the use of 4 by 4 matrices for implementing basic transformations in 3-D – specifically translation, reflection, scaling and rotation.*

- *Concatenate a series of basic transformation matrices to encapsulate more complex transformations within a single matrix.*

- *Achieve perspective projection using a 4 by 4 matrix.*

- *Undertake basic operations using the vector (cross) product.*

- *Describe the relationship that exists between the location of the centre of projection (COP) and the vanishing point (VP).*

- *Discuss the use of a virtual (synthetic) camera for defining a vantage point onto a scene and transform between world and viewing coordinate systems.*

6.2 Basic Transformations in 3-D

'Take your life in your own hands, and what happens?
A terrible thing: no one to blame!' [1]

In Chapter 3 we described the use of matrices for effecting 2-D transformations and here we extend this discussion and consider the application of matrices to transformations within a 3-D space. As we have seen, multiple transformation can be encapsulated within a single matrix

---

[1] Attributed to Erica Jong (1942–).

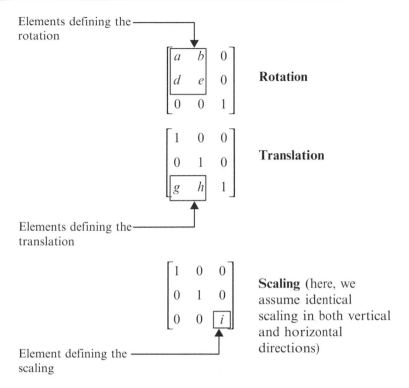

Figure 6.1 The groups of elements responsible for translation, rotation and scaling (see Section 3.5 for discussion).

comprising 3 rows and 3 columns. Such a matrix can act on points and vectors represented in homogeneous form.

> Recall that any point within a 2-D space does not have a single (unique) homogeneous representation. For example, consider a point with position vector (3 4). This can be represented in homogeneous form as [3 4 1], [6 8 2], [12 16 4] etc. In general a point (x,y) may be represented in homogeneous form as [wx wy w] where $w \neq 0$.

Let us begin by briefly reviewing the form of the basic 3 by 3 matrices responsible for performing rotation, translation and scaling within a 2 D space. These are summarised in Figure 6.1.

As discussed in Chapter 3, when we carry out a sequence of different transformations on an object, the overall result is generally decided by the order in which the transformations are applied. Furthermore, we can combine the three transformation matrices illustrated in Figure 6.1 into a single matrix (commonly referred to as concatenation). When these are combined in the order of rotation, followed by translation and then scaling, the resulting (composite) matrix operator retains the easily recognisable characteristics of the matrices from which it is formed. That is:

$$\begin{bmatrix} a & b & 0 \\ d & e & 0 \\ 0 & 0 & 1 \end{bmatrix} \begin{bmatrix} 1 & 0 & 0 \\ 0 & 1 & 0 \\ g & h & 1 \end{bmatrix} \begin{bmatrix} 1 & 0 & 0 \\ 0 & 1 & 0 \\ 0 & 0 & i \end{bmatrix} = \begin{bmatrix} a & b & 0 \\ d & e & 0 \\ g & h & i \end{bmatrix}.$$

Rotation   Translation   Scaling

However, if we change the order in which the operations are performed, then the result is not quite so well organised. For example, consider translation, followed by rotation, followed by scaling – that is:

$$\begin{bmatrix} 1 & 0 & 0 \\ 0 & 1 & 0 \\ g & h & 1 \end{bmatrix} \begin{bmatrix} a & b & 0 \\ d & e & 0 \\ 0 & 0 & 1 \end{bmatrix} \begin{bmatrix} 1 & 0 & 0 \\ 0 & 1 & 0 \\ 0 & 0 & i \end{bmatrix} = \begin{bmatrix} a & b & 0 \\ d & e & 0 \\ ag + dh & bg + eh & i \end{bmatrix}.$$

Translation   Rotation   Scaling

OTU Exercise 6.1: Combining Transformations

Determine a single matrix that corresponds to scaling, followed by rotation, followed by translation.

Let us now turn our attention to the use of transformations within a 3-D space. As we will see, this involves a simple extension of the techniques used for the manipulation of points on a 2-D plane. In Section 5.4.7, we outlined the representation of points within a 3-D space through the inclusion of a third axis which is orthogonal to both the x and y-axes. This is commonly referred to as the z-axis and as illustrated in Figure 5.25, we may adopt either a left-handed or right-handed coordinate system. Through until Section 6.5, we will make use of a right-handed coordinate system.

The location of a point may be specified by measuring its displacement in the x, y and z directions – thus the location of the point P illustrated in Figure 6.2 may be defined by the triple (3, 4, 5) and the length of the line segment from the origin to P is given by:

$$|OP| = \sqrt{3^2 + 4^2 + 5^2} = \sqrt{50}.$$

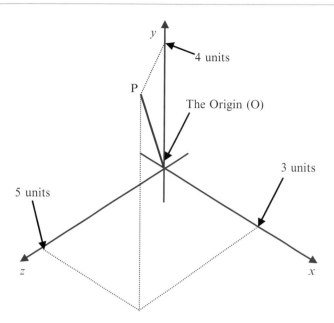

Figure 6.2 Representing a point in 3-D space. Here the position of the point P is given by the triple (3, 4, 5).

The vector from O to P may be represented in terms of three unit vectors: **i, j** and **k** where (as in the 2-D case) **i** and **j** are aligned with respect to the x and y axes and the additional unit vector (**k**) with the z-axis. Thus we would express the vector **OP** as:

$$\mathbf{OP} = 3\mathbf{i} + 4\mathbf{j} + 5\mathbf{k}.$$

OTU Exercise 6.2: Representing Points within a 3-D Space

Re-draw the three axes depicted in Figure 6.2. (Does this represent a left-handed or right-handed coordinate system?) Assign a scale to each axis and clearly show the location of a point P at (2, 0, 4) and a point Q at (1, 3, 2). Calculate the length of a line segment connecting these two points. If this is a type of calculation that you have not previously undertaken, note that the key issue in finding the solution is usually associated with the difficulty of visualising even a very simple 3-D geometry!!

As in the 2-D case, in order to readily accomplish transformations in 3-D, we make use of homogeneous coordinates. Conversion of Cartesian coordinates into homogeneous form is accomplished in the manner outlined in Section 2.2 although we now include the location of a point within the third dimension. For example, consider a point located at (3, 4, 5). We may represent this point in homogeneous form as [3 4 5 1], [6 8 10 2] etc (as with the 2-D case, a point in space can be represented by an infinite number of homogeneous coordinates – there is no unique representation).

Transformations in 3-D may be readily accomplished by means of 4 by 4 matrices acting on points or vectors that are represented in homogeneous form. In the subsections that follow we briefly summarise several transformations.

6.2.1 Translation

In order to achieve a translation operation within a 3-D space we make use of a matrix of the form:

$$\mathbf{T}(x, y, z) = \begin{bmatrix} 1 & 0 & 0 & 0 \\ 0 & 1 & 0 & 0 \\ 0 & 0 & 1 & 0 \\ D_x & D_y & D_z & 1 \end{bmatrix}.$$

Notice the use of the symbol $\mathbf{T}$ followed by (x, y, z) to denote a matrix responsible for translation (in the x, y and z directions). This provides a concise way of referring to a matrix of this form. By way of a simple example in connection with the use of this matrix, consider a point P that is located at $(3, 4, 5)$ – (this is the point depicted in Figure 6.2). Let us suppose that we wish to move this point 2, 4 units and 6 units in the x, y and z directions respectively. Firstly we represent P in homogeneous form – as, for example [3 4 5 1] and then use the transformation matrix with $D_x = 2$, $D_y = 4$ and $D_z = 6$:

$$\begin{bmatrix} 3 & 4 & 5 & 1 \end{bmatrix} \begin{bmatrix} 1 & 0 & 0 & 0 \\ 0 & 1 & 0 & 0 \\ 0 & 0 & 1 & 0 \\ 2 & 4 & 6 & 1 \end{bmatrix} = \begin{bmatrix} 3+2 & 4+4 & 5+6 & 1 \end{bmatrix} = \begin{bmatrix} 5 & 8 & 11 & 1 \end{bmatrix}.$$

Thus, in line with our objective, the x coordinate has been shifted by 2 units, the y coordinate by 4 units and z by 6 units.

6.2.2 Scaling

We can achieve scaling in the x, y and z directions using a matrix of the form:

$$\mathbf{S}(k, l, m) = \begin{bmatrix} k & 0 & 0 & 0 \\ 0 & l & 0 & 0 \\ 0 & 0 & m & 0 \\ 0 & 0 & 0 & 1 \end{bmatrix}.$$

Here, k, l and m represent the scaling factors applied respectively in the x, y and z directions and the letter S is used to denote the basic scaling matrix. As in the 2-D case, it is often convenient to apply the same scaling factor in each of the three orthogonal directions. In this case we define a single scaling parameter (s) such that $s = 1/k = 1/l = 1/m$. The above matrix may then be re-written as:

$$\mathbf{S} = \begin{bmatrix} 1 & 0 & 0 & 0 \\ 0 & 1 & 0 & 0 \\ 0 & 0 & 1 & 0 \\ 0 & 0 & 0 & s \end{bmatrix}.$$

However, as with the 2-D case, it is important to bear in mind that when $s < 1$ enlargement occurs and when $s > 1$ the result is a reduction in size. By way of a simple example, let us apply scaling to the vector **OP** (see Figure 6.2) so as to double its length ($s = 0.5$):

$$\begin{bmatrix} 3 & 4 & 5 & 1 \end{bmatrix} \begin{bmatrix} 1 & 0 & 0 & 0 \\ 0 & 1 & 0 & 0 \\ 0 & 0 & 1 & 0 \\ 0 & 0 & 0 & 0.5 \end{bmatrix} = \begin{bmatrix} 3 & 4 & 5 & 0.5 \end{bmatrix}.$$

To find the Cartesian coordinates of this point, we simply divide through by 0.5 – thereby obtaining (6, 8, 10).

6.2.3 Rotation About a Coordinate Axis

Consider the point P illustrated in Figure 6.2 and let us suppose that we wish to rotate it about either the x, y or z axes. If, for example, the point is rotated about the x-axis, then it is apparent from the illustration that the x coordinate of the point will not be changed. Similarly, when rotated about the y-axis the y coordinate will not be altered, and when the z-axis is the chosen axis of rotation the point's z coordinate will not be affected. Let us now consider the case that the point P is rotated through an angle α about the x-axis and for generality, we will assume that P is an arbitrary point with coordinates (x, y, z). Since the point's x-coordinate remains unaltered by the rotation, we can redraw Figure 6.2 as a view in the y-z plane (see Figure 6.3).

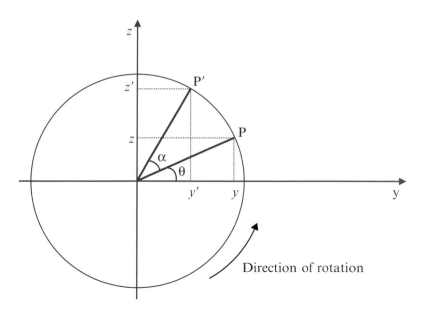

Figure 6.3 The point P is rotated through an angle α about the x-axis to position P' (the positive x-axis is assumed to be out of the page). The coordinates of P are given by (x, y, z) and those of P' are (x', y', z'). Note that the angle of rotation is assumed to be anti-clockwise (when considered from a perspective in which the rotation is viewed down the x-axis (from the positive end) – looking towards the origin).

The rotation matrix can be obtained by adopting the same approach as that used in Chapter 3 – and to recap, we can write:

$$\cos\theta = \frac{y}{|\mathbf{OP}|}, \qquad \sin\theta = \frac{z}{|\mathbf{OP}|},$$

$$\cos(\theta + \alpha) = \frac{y'}{|\mathbf{OP}|}, \qquad \sin(\theta + \alpha) = \frac{z'}{|\mathbf{OP}|}.$$

Using the sum and difference formulae (see Appendix A), we can expand the second pair of equations and then use the first two equations to eliminate θ. Thus we obtain:

$$y\cos\alpha - z\sin\alpha = y' \tag{6.1}$$

$$z\cos\alpha + y\sin\alpha = z'. \tag{6.2}$$

Bearing in mind that a rotation about the x-axis does not change a point's x coordinate, we can incorporate these equations within the 4 by 4 matrix as follows:

$$\begin{bmatrix} x & y & z & 1 \end{bmatrix} \begin{bmatrix} 1 & 0 & 0 & 0 \\ 0 & \cos\alpha & \sin\alpha & 0 \\ 0 & -\sin\alpha & \cos\alpha & 0 \\ 0 & 0 & 0 & 1 \end{bmatrix} = \begin{bmatrix} x' & y' & z' & 1 \end{bmatrix}.$$

We can use the same technique to produce rotations about the y and z-axes. For example, to obtain equations for rotation about the z-axis, we can use Eq.'s 6.1 and 6.2 and substitute x in place of y and y in place of z (in this case x' replaces y' and y' replaces z'). Thus we obtain:

$$x\cos\alpha - y\sin\alpha = x' \tag{6.3}$$

$$y\cos\alpha + x\sin\alpha = y'. \tag{6.4}$$

For rotation about the y-axis, we again use the 'cyclic substitution' approach and obtain:

$$z\cos\alpha - x\sin\alpha = z' \tag{6.5}$$

$$x\cos\alpha + z\sin\alpha = x'. \tag{6.6}$$

In Figure 6.4 we summarise the resulting matrices.

The terms roll, pitch and yaw are commonly used when referring to the three orthogonal directions in which an object can be rotated. For example, consider an aircraft in level flight. Roll corresponds to a rotation about a central axis running the length of the fuselage and results in one wing tip rising and the other falling. Pitch corresponds to a rotation about a horizontal axis that is at right-angles to the fuselage and causes the nose of the plane to rise or fall in height relative to the tail. Finally, yaw relates to rotation about a vertical axis that is again at right-angles to the fuselage. These three forms of rotation are illustrated in Figure 6.5(a). It is convenient to apply these terms to the rotation of any object about the three orthogonal axes and we will assume that as illustrated in Figure 6.5(b):

- Pitch corresponds to a rotation about the x-axis.
- Yaw corresponds to a rotation about the y-axis.
- Roll corresponds to a rotation about the z-axis.

Rotation about the x-axis:

$$R_x(\alpha) = \begin{bmatrix} 1 & 0 & 0 & 0 \\ 0 & \cos\alpha & \sin\alpha & 0 \\ 0 & -\sin\alpha & \cos\alpha & 0 \\ 0 & 0 & 0 & 1 \end{bmatrix}$$

Rotation about the y-axis:

$$R_y(\alpha) = \begin{bmatrix} \cos\alpha & 0 & -\sin\alpha & 0 \\ 0 & 1 & 0 & 0 \\ \sin\alpha & 0 & \cos\alpha & 0 \\ 0 & 0 & 0 & 1 \end{bmatrix}$$

Rotation about the z-axis:

$$R_z(\alpha) = \begin{bmatrix} \cos\alpha & \sin\alpha & 0 & 0 \\ -\sin\alpha & \cos\alpha & 0 & 0 \\ 0 & 0 & 1 & 0 \\ 0 & 0 & 0 & 1 \end{bmatrix}$$

Figure 6.4 Matrices for achieving rotation about the x, y or z coordinate axes. Here, α denotes the angle of rotation.

6.2.4 Reflection in a Coordinate Plane

'. . . the superman made the first aeroplane and the ape has got hold of it.'[2]

Consider a point that is reflected in, for example, the x–y plane. This reflection will have no effect on the point's x or y coordinates and will simply result in a change of sign in the z coordinate. Thus, if the point with coordinates (3, 4, 5) is reflected in this plane, a new point located at (3, 4, −5) will be obtained. Similarly, if a point is reflected in the y–z plane, the sign of the point's x coordinate will change and for a reflection in the x–z plane, the sign of the y coordinate will be flipped.

OTU Exercise 6.3: Matrices for Reflection

Write down the 4 by 4 matrices that will result in (a) reflection in the x–y plane, (b) reflection in the y–z plane and (c) reflection in the x–z plane.

---

[2] Attributed to Professor C.E.M. Joad, quoted in *The World of Wings and Things*, by Alliott Verdon-Roe. Originally published *c*.1938.

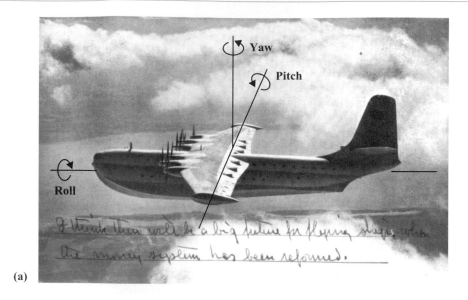

Figure 6.5 In (a) the use of the terms pitch, yaw and roll is illustrated in the context of an aircraft in flight[3]. In (b), we indicate a right-handed coordinate system and show the relation that we will assume between these axis and the terms pitch, yaw and roll.

---

[3] Hand-written comment added by A.V. Roe – aviation pioneer and aircraft engineer – a prophesy that was not fulfilled . . .

6.3 The Vector Product

'O! that a man might know
The end of this day's business, ere it come;
But it sufficeth that the day will end,
And then the end is known.'[4]

In this section we take the opportunity to introduce the 'vector product'. This is frequently used in computer graphics and we will be making use of this product in subsequent sections. The vector product is defined for vectors in a 3-D space. Consequently, it was not introduced in Chapter 2, where for simplicity, we confined our discussion to 2-D vectors. However, it is now appropriate to briefly introduce this powerful tool.

Recall that the 'scalar product' (discussed in Section 2.4.9 and Appendix C) is also referred to as the 'dot product'. This alternative name is commonly used because the product is indicated by a period between two vectors (e.g. $\mathbf{a} \cdot \mathbf{b}$). Similarly, the vector product is often referred to as the 'cross product' – a cross ('×') being used to denote the product (e.g. $\mathbf{a} \times \mathbf{b}$).

Consider two vectors $\mathbf{a}$ and $\mathbf{b}$ in 3-D space where $\mathbf{a} = a_1\mathbf{i} + a_2\mathbf{j} + a_3\mathbf{k}$ and $\mathbf{b} = b_1\mathbf{i} + b_2\mathbf{j} + b_3\mathbf{k}$ (here, as usual, $\mathbf{i}, \mathbf{j}$ and $\mathbf{k}$ denote the standard unit vectors that respectively lie along the x, y and z axes. Then the vector product of $\mathbf{a}$ and $\mathbf{b}$ is defined as:

$$\mathbf{a} \times \mathbf{b} = (a_2b_3 - a_3b_2)\,\mathbf{i} - (a_1b_3 - a_3b_1)\,\mathbf{j} + (a_1b_2 - a_2b_1)\,\mathbf{k}. \qquad (6.7)$$

Note that when we calculate the vector product, the result is a vector quantity (this is in contrast to the scalar product). This equation can be easily forgotten and so texts frequently provide an alternative form in which a 3 by 3 determinant representation is employed. In this case:

$$\mathbf{a} \times \mathbf{b} = \begin{vmatrix} \mathbf{i} & \mathbf{j} & \mathbf{k} \\ a_1 & a_2 & a_3 \\ b_1 & b_2 & b_3 \end{vmatrix}. \qquad (6.8)$$

Eq. 2.15 in Section 2.5.3 provides the means by which the determinant of a 3 by 3 matrix is calculated. Re-writing this equation in terms of the symbols used in Eq. 6.8 we obtain:

$$\mathbf{a} \times \mathbf{b} = \begin{vmatrix} \mathbf{i} & \mathbf{j} & \mathbf{k} \\ a_1 & a_2 & a_3 \\ b_1 & b_2 & b_3 \end{vmatrix} = \begin{vmatrix} a_2 & a_3 \\ b_2 & b_3 \end{vmatrix}\mathbf{i} - \begin{vmatrix} a_1 & a_3 \\ b_1 & b_3 \end{vmatrix}\mathbf{j} + \begin{vmatrix} a_1 & a_2 \\ b_1 & b_2 \end{vmatrix}\mathbf{k}. \qquad (6.9)$$

Recall from Section 2.5.3, that the determinant of a 2 by 2 matrix A which has the form:

$$A = \begin{bmatrix} a & b \\ c & d \end{bmatrix},$$

is obtained by calculating $ad–bc$. Thus Eq 6.9 can be re-written as:

$$\mathbf{a} \times \mathbf{b} = \begin{vmatrix} \mathbf{i} & \mathbf{j} & \mathbf{k} \\ a_1 & a_2 & a_3 \\ b_1 & b_2 & b_3 \end{vmatrix} = (a_2b_3 - a_3b_2)\,\mathbf{i} - (a_1b_3 - a_3b_1)\,\mathbf{j} + (a_1b_2 - a_2b_1)\,\mathbf{k}.$$

This is the same as Eq. 6.7 and so expressing the vector product in determinant form provides us with a convenient and simple way of remembering the manner in which the product is

---

[4] From 'Julius Caesar' (Shakespeare).

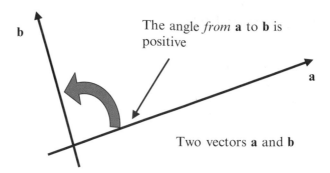

Figure 6.6 Here, we have two arbitrary vectors **a** and **b** arranged so that the angle from **a** to **b** is positive. In this case, the vector product **a** × **b** gives rise to a vector that points out of the page. Thus **a, b** and **a** × **b** form a right-handed set (cf Figure 5.25(a)). Contrawise, **a, b** and **b** × **a** form a left-handed set.

evaluated(but naturally necessitates remembering how the determinants of both 3 by 3 and 2 by 2 matrices are calculated!).

OTU Exercise 6.4: Calculating the Vector Product

Given the vectors **a** and **b** where **a** = **i** + 2**j** + 3**k** and **b** = 2**i** + **j** − **k** calculate:

1. **a** × **b**
2. **b** × **a**

On the basis of your answers, do you conclude that the vector product is commutative? If not, how are **a** × **b** and **b** × **a** related?

Let us suppose that we have two vectors, **a** and **b**, and that we calculate their vector product. The result is a vector that lies perpendicular to both **a** and **b**. This can be demonstrated by means of a simple example. We will assume that the vector **a** lies along the x-axis and arbitrarily suppose the vector to have a magnitude of 2 units. Thus it is given by **a** = 2**i** + 0**j** + 0**k**. Similarly, we assume the vector **b** lies along the y-axis and again is 2 units in length – therefore **b** = 0**i** + 2**j** + 0**k**. Using Eq. 6.7, the vector product of **a** and **b** is given by:

$$\mathbf{a} \times \mathbf{b} = (0 - 0)\,\mathbf{i} - (0 - 0)\,\mathbf{j} + (4 - 0)\,\mathbf{k} = 4\mathbf{k}.$$

Hence, we have generated a vector that lies along the z-axis and so it is at right-angles to both **a** and **b** (i.e. it lies at right-angles to the plane defined by **a** and **b**). The direction of this resulting vector is indicated in Figure 6.6.

In the case that we wish to calculate a unit vector that lies at right-angles to a plane, we simply calculate the vector product of the two vectors that define the orientation of the plane and divide the result by the vector product's magnitude. Thus the unit vector (which we will denote as **n̂**) is given by:

$$\hat{\mathbf{n}} = \frac{\mathbf{a} \times \mathbf{b}}{\left|\mathbf{a} \times \mathbf{b}\right|}. \tag{6.10}$$

The magnitude of the vector product may be expressed as follows:

$$|\mathbf{a} \times \mathbf{b}| = |\mathbf{a}||\mathbf{b}| \sin\theta,$$

where θ denotes the angle between vectors $\mathbf{a}$ and $\mathbf{b}$. It is instructive to spend a few moments justifying this useful expression.

Recall that:

$$\cos^2\theta + \sin^2\theta = 1,$$

Hence:

$$\sin\theta = \sqrt{1 - \cos^2\theta}.$$

Thus for two vectors $\mathbf{a}$ and $\mathbf{b}$ we can write that:

$$|\mathbf{a}||\mathbf{b}| \sin\theta = |\mathbf{a}||\mathbf{b}|\sqrt{1 - \cos^2\theta}, \tag{6.11}$$

where θ, denotes that angle between the vectors. Recall discussion presented in Chapter 2 (and in Appendix C) in relation to the scalar product and particularly Eq. 2.9. Re-writing this equation for vectors within a 3-D space:

$$\mathbf{a} \cdot \mathbf{b} = a_1 b_1 + a_2 b_2 + a_3 b_3 = |\mathbf{a}||\mathbf{b}| \cos\theta,$$

and so:

$$\cos\theta = \frac{\mathbf{a} \cdot \mathbf{b}}{|\mathbf{a}||\mathbf{b}|}.$$

Inserting this into Eq. 6.11, we obtain:

$$|\mathbf{a}||\mathbf{b}| \sin\theta = |\mathbf{a}||\mathbf{b}|\sqrt{1 - \left[\frac{\mathbf{a} \cdot \mathbf{b}}{|\mathbf{a}||\mathbf{b}|}\right]^2} = \sqrt{(|\mathbf{a}||\mathbf{b}|)^2 - (\mathbf{a} \cdot \mathbf{b})^2}. \tag{6.12}$$

However, from the above equation for the scalar product, we know that:

$$\mathbf{a} \cdot \mathbf{b} = a_1 b_1 + a_2 b_2 + a_3 b_3,$$

and also the magnitude of the vectors $\mathbf{a}$ and $\mathbf{b}$ are given by:

$$|\mathbf{a}| = \sqrt{a_1^2 + a_2^2 + a_3^2}, \quad |\mathbf{b}| = \sqrt{b_1^2 + b_2^2 + b_3^2},$$

Inserting these results into Eq. 6.12, we can write:

$$|\mathbf{a}||\mathbf{b}| \sin\theta = \sqrt{(|\mathbf{a}||\mathbf{b}|)^2 - (\mathbf{a} \cdot \mathbf{b})^2} = \sqrt{\left(a_1^2 + a_2^2 + a_3^2\right)\left(b_1^2 + b_2^2 + b_3^2\right) - (a_1 b_1 + a_2 b_2 + a_3 b_3)^2}.$$

If we now expand these brackets, several terms cancel and subsequently, we can factorise – so obtaining:

$$|\mathbf{a}||\mathbf{b}| \sin\theta = \sqrt{(a_2 b_3 - a_3 b_2)^2 + (a_1 b_3 - a_3 b_1)^2 + (a_1 b_2 - a_2 b_1)^2}. \tag{6.13}$$

In Eq. 6.7 we defined the vector product as:

$$\mathbf{a} \times \mathbf{b} = (a_2 b_3 - a_3 b_2)\,\mathbf{i} - (a_1 b_3 - a_3 b_1)\,\mathbf{j} + (a_1 b_2 - a_2 b_1)\,\mathbf{k}.$$

$$\mathbf{a} \times \mathbf{b} = (a_2 b_3 - a_3 b_2)\,\mathbf{i} - (a_1 b_3 - a_3 b_1)\,\mathbf{j} + (a_1 b_2 - a_2 b_1)\,\mathbf{k} = (|\mathbf{a}||\mathbf{b}|\sin\theta)\,\hat{\mathbf{n}}.$$

$$\mathbf{a} \times \mathbf{b} = \begin{vmatrix} \mathbf{i} & \mathbf{j} & \mathbf{k} \\ a_1 & a_2 & a_3 \\ b_1 & b_2 & b_3 \end{vmatrix} = \begin{vmatrix} a_2 & a_3 \\ b_2 & b_3 \end{vmatrix}\mathbf{i} - \begin{vmatrix} a_1 & a_3 \\ b_1 & b_3 \end{vmatrix}\mathbf{j} + \begin{vmatrix} a_1 & a_2 \\ b_1 & b_2 \end{vmatrix}\mathbf{k}$$

$$|\mathbf{a} \times \mathbf{b}| = |\mathbf{a}||\mathbf{b}|\sin\theta = \sqrt{(a_2 b_3 - a_3 b_2)^2 + (a_1 b_3 - a_3 b_1)^2 + (a_1 b_2 - a_2 b_1)^2}$$

$$\hat{\mathbf{n}} = \frac{\mathbf{a} \times \mathbf{b}}{|\mathbf{a} \times \mathbf{b}|}$$

Figure 6.7 A summary of several of the key equations introduced in relation to the vector (cross) product. See text for discussion.

Using Pythagoras' theorem, we can write down an expression for the magnitude of the vector product:

$$|\mathbf{a} \times \mathbf{b}| = \sqrt{(a_2 b_3 - a_3 b_2)^2 + (a_1 b_3 - a_3 b_1)^2 + (a_1 b_2 - a_2 b_1)^2}.$$

The right hand sides of this equation and Eq. 6.13 are identical and so we can write:

$$|\mathbf{a} \times \mathbf{b}| = |\mathbf{a}||\mathbf{b}|\sin\theta$$

If we define a unit vector ($\hat{\mathbf{n}}$) which lies normal to the plane defined by the vectors $\mathbf{a}$ and $\mathbf{b}$ such that $\mathbf{a}$, $\mathbf{b}$ and $\hat{\mathbf{n}}$ form a right handed set (recall Figures 5.25(a) and 6.6), then we can write:

$$\mathbf{a} \times \mathbf{b} = (|\mathbf{a}||\mathbf{b}|\sin\theta)\,\hat{\mathbf{n}}. \tag{6.14}$$

Including our previous definition for the vector product (Eq. 6.7), we can therefore write:

$$\mathbf{a} \times \mathbf{b} = (a_2 b_3 - a_3 b_2)\,\mathbf{i} - (a_1 b_3 - a_3 b_1)\,\mathbf{j} + (a_1 b_2 - a_2 b_1)\,\mathbf{k} = (|\mathbf{a}||\mathbf{b}|\sin\theta)\,\hat{\mathbf{n}}. \tag{6.15}$$

OTU Exercise 6.5: The Vector Product of Parallel Vectors

1. On the basis of Eq. 6.14, *state* the value of the vector product of two parallel vectors.
2. Consider the two vectors $\mathbf{a}$ and $\mathbf{b}$ where $\mathbf{a} = 2\mathbf{i} + 5\mathbf{j} - 3\mathbf{k}$ and $\mathbf{b} = 4\mathbf{i} + 10\mathbf{j} - 6\mathbf{k}$. Using Eq. 6.7, calculate $|\mathbf{a} \times \mathbf{b}|$ and so confirm your answer to the previous question.

For convenience, Figure 6.7 provides a summary of several of the equations introduced in this section and in Figure 6.8 various properties of the vector product are indicated.

- *The vector given by $\mathbf{a} \times \mathbf{b}$ is perpendicular to both a and b.*

- *The vector product is not commutative: $\mathbf{a} \times \mathbf{b} \neq \mathbf{b} \times \mathbf{a}$. In fact $\mathbf{a} \times \mathbf{b} = -(\mathbf{b} \times \mathbf{a})$.*

- *The vector product of two parallel vectors (i.e. two vectors which are scalar multiples of each other) is zero. For example, $\mathbf{a} \times \mathbf{a} = 0$.*

- *For three vectors a, b and c: $\mathbf{a} \times (\mathbf{b} + \mathbf{c}) = (\mathbf{a} \times \mathbf{b}) + (\mathbf{a} \times \mathbf{c})$.*

- *Given s represents a scalar value: $s(\mathbf{a} \times \mathbf{b}) = (s\mathbf{a}) \times \mathbf{b} = \mathbf{a} \times (s\mathbf{b})$.*

- *The quantity $|\mathbf{a} \times \mathbf{b}|$ equals the area of a parallelogram with sides given by the vectors a and b.*

Figure 6.8 A summary of some facets of the vector product.

OTU Exercise 6.6: Determination of the Surface Normal

The vector product provides a convenient way of determining the vector that is normal (lies at right angles) to a plane and in computer graphics, is commonly used for this purpose. Consider the plane whose orientation is defined by the vectors **a** and **b**, where **a** = 2**i** + 6**j** + 2**k** and **b** = 3**i** + 8**j** + 7**k**. Determine the unit vector ($\hat{\mathbf{n}}$) that is normal to this plane.

6.4 Combining Transformations

Here, we provide two examples demonstrating ways in which we can combine the basic transformations introduced in Section 6.2 thereby encapsulating more complex operations within a single matrix. In Figure 6.9(a) we summarise (in general terms) the role played by elements within the 4 by 4 matrix in achieving the basic transformations discussed previously. It is important to note that (as in the 2-D case), in order to achieve a specific result through the concatenation of basic transforms, we must carefully consider the order in which they are employed.

OTU Exercise 6.7: The Application of a 4 by 4 Matrix

Consider the position vector 3**i** + 4**j** + 5**k** to a point P in 3-D space – the location of this point is depicted in Figure 6.2. Apply the matrix indicated in Figure 6.9(b) and determine the location of the resulting vector.

6.4.1 Rotation about an Axis Parallel to a Coordinate Axis

In Section 6.2.3 we considered rotation about one of the three coordinate axes. In this subsection we describe the use of combined transformations so as to achieve rotation about an axis that lies

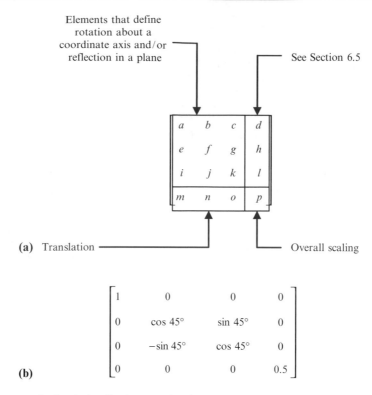

Elements that define
rotation about a
coordinate axis and/or
reflection in a plane

See Section 6.5

(a) Translation

Overall scaling

$$
\begin{bmatrix}
1 & 0 & 0 & 0 \\
0 & \cos 45° & \sin 45° & 0 \\
0 & -\sin 45° & \cos 45° & 0 \\
0 & 0 & 0 & 0.5
\end{bmatrix}
$$

(b)

Figure 6.9 In (a), we summarise the role played by elements within 4 by 4 matrices in achieving basic transformations. In connection with (b) see OTU Exercise 6.7.

parallel to a coordinate axis – see Figure 6.10. By way of an example we will assume, as indicated in the illustration, the chosen axis lies parallel to the x-axis.

To achieve our objective, we can first perform a translation operation to relocate the axis about which the rotation is to be performed so that it lies on the x-axis. We then carry out the rotation operation and finally reverse (undo) the previous translation operation. This sequence can be encapsulated using the following symbolic representation:

$$
\mathbf{R}(\alpha) = \mathbf{T}(y, z) \cdot \mathbf{R}_x(\alpha) \cdot \mathbf{T}^{-1}(y, z).
$$

Where $\mathbf{T}^{-1}(y, z)$ represents the inverse of the previous translation matrix. We will talk about the inverse matrix again shortly and for the moment we need simply remember that its purpose is to 'undo' the previous translation operation.

This series of operations may be achieved by concatenating the following three 4 by 4 matrices:

$$
\begin{bmatrix} x & y & z & 1 \end{bmatrix}
\begin{bmatrix}
1 & 0 & 0 & 0 \\
0 & 1 & 0 & 0 \\
0 & 0 & 1 & 0 \\
0 & -D_y & -D_z & 1
\end{bmatrix}
\begin{bmatrix}
1 & 0 & 0 & 0 \\
0 & \cos\alpha & \sin\alpha & 0 \\
0 & -\sin\alpha & \cos\alpha & 0 \\
0 & 0 & 0 & 1
\end{bmatrix}
\begin{bmatrix}
1 & 0 & 0 & 0 \\
0 & 1 & 0 & 0 \\
0 & 0 & 1 & 0 \\
0 & D_y & D_z & 1
\end{bmatrix}
= \begin{bmatrix} x' & y' & z' & 1 \end{bmatrix}
$$

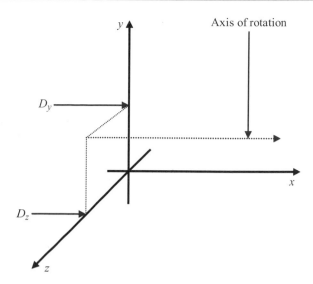

Figure 6.10 The rotation of an object about an axis that lies parallel to the x-axis. This is achieved by combining basic transforms – see text for discussion.

and so:

$$
\begin{bmatrix} x & y & z & 1 \end{bmatrix}
\begin{bmatrix}
1 & 0 & 0 & 0 \\
0 & \cos\alpha & \sin\alpha & 0 \\
0 & -\sin\alpha & \cos\alpha & 0 \\
0 & D_y(1-\cos\alpha)+D_z\sin\alpha & D_z(1-\cos\alpha)-D_y\sin\alpha & 1
\end{bmatrix}
= \begin{bmatrix} x' & y' & z' & 1 \end{bmatrix}
$$

6.4.2 Rotation about an Arbitrary Axis

We now turn our attention to a more interesting and slightly more challenging problem – the rotation of an object about an arbitrarily positioned axis (see Figure 6.11) and achieve this goal using the basic transformations previously introduced. The rotation may be achieved using five basic steps:

1. **Relocation:** Perform a translation operation so that the axis of rotation passes through the origin of the coordinate system. Thus, for example we could translate the axis so that the point (x_1, y_1, z_1) is shifted to the origin.

2. **Re-orientation:** Perform rotation operations so that the axis of rotation is coincident with one of the coordinate system's axes. Typically this involves two steps:
    (a) **Alignment with a Plane:** We perform a rotation operation so as to bring the axis of rotation into, for example, the x–z plane. This involves a rotation about the x-axis. (Equally we could use the y–z or x–y planes.)
    (b) **Alignment with Coordinate System Axis:** We perform a second rotation operation to align the axis of rotation with a particular axis of the coordinate system In the discussion that follows, we will assume that we align the axis of rotation so that it is coincident with the z-axis (an arbitrary choice). This involves a rotation about the y-axis.

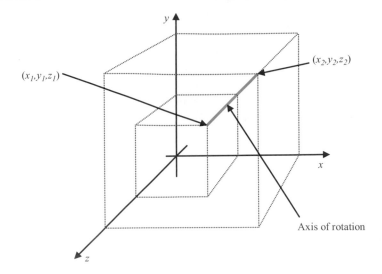

Figure 6.11 The rotation of an object about an arbitrarily positioned axis. We will define the location and orientation of this axis by assuming that it has end-points with coordinates (x_1, y_1, z_1) and (x_2, y_2, z_2).

3. **Rotation**: Perform the desired rotation operation (through an angle θ).

4. **'Undo' Re-orientation**: Perform rotation operations and so 'undo' step (2) thereby returning the axis of rotation to its original orientation.

5. **'Undo' Relocation**: Perform a translation operation to 'undo' step (1) and thereby return the axis of rotation to the original location.

In summary we can write:

$$\mathbf{R}(\theta) = \mathbf{T}(x, y, z) \cdot \mathbf{R}_x(\beta) \cdot \mathbf{R}_y(\chi) \cdot \mathbf{R}_z(\theta) \cdot \mathbf{R}_y^{-1}(\chi) \cdot \mathbf{R}_x^{-1}(\beta) \cdot \mathbf{T}^{-1}(x, y, z).$$

Below we outline how each of these steps may be achieved:

1. **Relocation**: In line with the above discussion we undertake a translation operation so that the point (x_1, y_1, z_1) on the axis of rotation is coincident with the coordinate system origin. Here, we simply use the basic translation matrix:

$$T(x, y, z) = \begin{bmatrix} 1 & 0 & 0 & 0 \\ 0 & 1 & 0 & 0 \\ 0 & 0 & 1 & 0 \\ -x_1 & -y_1 & -z_1 & 1 \end{bmatrix}.$$

2(a) **Re-orientation (Alignment with a Plane)**: Here, we determine the angle (β) through which the line segment must be rotated so that it lies in the x–z plane. It is instructive to consider two approaches that may be adopted in order to achieve this goal. We begin by

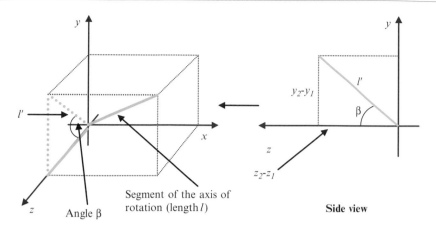

Figure 6.12 A segment of the axis of rotation of length l. On the right we depict the end elevation – such that the segment of the axis of rotation is projected onto the y–z plane. The projection of the line segment has a length l'.

considering the use of simple trigonometry and subsequently obtain the same result by means of a little vector algebra.

Method 1: In Figure 6.11 we indicate two points $((x_1, y_1, z_1)$ and $(x_2, y_2, z_2))$ that lie on the axis of rotation. Let us suppose that the distance between these points is l. Following Step (1), we will now project this line onto the y–z plane (see Figure 6.12). To determine the length of the projected line segment (l') we use Pythagoras' Theorem on the triangle shown in the side elevation view:

$$l' = \sqrt{(z_2 - z_1)^2 + (y_2 - y_1)^2}.$$

We can now rotate this projected line segment *about the x-axis* so that it lies in the x–z plane. This involves a rotation through an angle β (see diagram) – where:

$$\cos \beta = \frac{z_2 - z_1}{l'}, \text{ and } \sin \beta = \frac{y_2 - y_1}{l'}.$$

Thus:

$$\cos \beta = \frac{z_2 - z_1}{\sqrt{(z_2 - z_1)^2 + (y_2 - y_1)^2}}, \tag{6.16}$$

and

$$\sin \beta = \frac{y_2 - y_1}{\sqrt{(z_2 - z_1)^2 + (y_2 - y_1)^2}}. \tag{6.17}$$

We can insert these values into the basic transformation matrix for rotation about the x-axis. However, before forming this matrix operator, we turn our attention to a second approach by which we can determine $\sin \beta$ and $\cos \beta$.

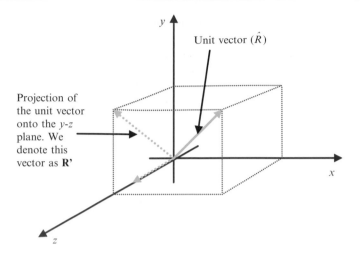

Figure 6.13 The unit vector $\hat{R}$ is projected onto the y–z plane giving a vector denoted as **R'**.

Method 2: Here, we use a similar approach to that outlined above but now make use of a little vector algebra.[5] Let us denote the axis of rotation by a vector **R** in which case we can define a unit vector in the direction of this rotational axis such that:

$$\hat{\mathbf{R}} = \frac{\mathbf{R}}{|\mathbf{R}|} = a\mathbf{i} + b\mathbf{j} + c\mathbf{k}.$$

To determine the angle (β) through which we must rotate the axis of rotation to cause it to lie in the x–z plane (this corresponds to a rotation about the x-axis), we first project $\hat{R}$ onto the y–z plane – see Figure 6.13. As indicated in this illustration we denote the vector produced by this projection as **R'** where:

$$\mathbf{R}' = b\mathbf{j} + c\mathbf{k}.$$

The angle of rotation (β) may now be obtained using the scalar product (recall Section 2.4.9) such that:

$$\mathbf{R}' \cdot \mathbf{k} = |\mathbf{R}'||\mathbf{k}| \cos \beta = |\mathbf{R}'| \cos \beta = \sqrt{b^2 + c^2} \cos \beta.$$

In addition, we can obtain the scalar product by multiplication of the vector components. The components of the vector **k** in the x or y directions are zero and so its scalar product with **R'** simply equals c. Thus we obtain the following expression for $\cos \beta$:

$$\cos \beta = \frac{c}{\sqrt{b^2 + c^2}}. \tag{6.18}$$

Recall that (as with Method (1) above) our objective is to find values for $\sin \beta$ and $\cos \beta$ that can be inserted into the basic rotation matrix. This equation provides an expression

---

[5] In the text that follows we loosely follow Hearn and Baker [1986].

for $\cos\beta$ which in turn allows us to determine the angle β and so compute $\sin\beta$. Thus we have – at least in principle attained our goal On the other hand we may seek a more computationally efficient solution – having obtained a simple expression for $\cos\beta$, can we employ a similar process and determine $\sin\beta$? In fact, this is easily achieved, and here it is convenient to employ the vector (cross) product – see Section 6.3. Below we briefly summarise the way in which we may obtain an expression for $\sin\beta$.

If we take the vector product of the vectors, $\mathbf{R}'$ and $\mathbf{k}$, then on the basis of Eq. 6.14, we obtain:

$$\mathbf{R}' \times \mathbf{k} = \mathbf{i}|\mathbf{R}'||\mathbf{k}|\sin\beta = \mathbf{i}\sqrt{b^2 + c^2}.\sin\beta$$

Where, as usual, $\mathbf{i}$ represents a unit vector in the x-direction. On the basis of Eq. 6.7 we can write:

$$\mathbf{R}' \times \mathbf{k} = (b - 0)\,\mathbf{i} + 0\cdot\mathbf{j} + 0\cdot\mathbf{k} = b\mathbf{i}.$$

Thus:

$$\sin\beta = \frac{b}{\sqrt{b^2 + c^2}}. \tag{6.19}$$

We can now insert Eq.'s 6.18 and 6.19 into the appropriate rotation matrix (for rotation about the x-axis) so obtaining:

$$\begin{bmatrix} 1 & 0 & 0 & 0 \\ 0 & \dfrac{c}{\sqrt{b^2 + c^2}} & \dfrac{b}{\sqrt{b^2 + c^2}} & 0 \\ 0 & \dfrac{-b}{\sqrt{b^2 + c^2}} & \dfrac{c}{\sqrt{b^2 + c^2}} & 0 \\ 0 & 0 & 0 & 1 \end{bmatrix}. \tag{6.20}$$

Recall Eq.'s 6.16 and 6.17 which were obtained using Method (1). Bearing in mind differences in symbols used, it is apparent that the results provided by these two approaches are identical. Although in the first instance, the vector technique may appear to be a little more complicated, the use of vectors often provides a way in which we may more readily tackle problems of greater complexity and in which more flexibility is required.

2(b) **Re-orientation (Alignment with Coordinate System Axis):** Here, we need to perform a rotation about the y-axis to make the axis of rotation coincident with the z-axis. Again we can use elementary trigonometry or the vector based approach. These are summarised below:

Method 1: In Figure 6.14(a), we provide a plane view onto Figure 6.12 and indicate the angle $-\chi$ that we wish to ascertain and which corresponds to the angle of rotation about the y-axis. For convenience we will assume a line segment that is located between points (x_1, y_1, z_1) and (x_2, y_2, z_2) and which is of unit length (this is the line segment that is depicted in bold within the illustration) and these coordinates correspond to points on the axis prior to Step (2). Here, an important point to note is that the previous rotation about the x-axis did not change the length of this line segment – nor does the rotation that we are now to perform about the y-axis.

As indicated in the illustration the x coordinate of the endpoint of the line segment is given by $x_2 - x_1$. The y coordinate of the endpoint is zero (as the line segment lies in the x–z plane) and the z coordinate is given by:

$$\sqrt{(y_2 - y_1)^2 + (z_2 - z_1)^2}.$$

Thus we can write:

$$\cos(-\chi) = \frac{\sqrt{(y_2 - y_1)^2 + (z_2 - z_1)^2}}{1},$$

and

$$\sin(-\chi) = \frac{x_2 - x_1}{1}.$$

Therefore:

$$\sin \chi = -(x_2 - x_1), \text{ and } \cos \chi = \sqrt{(y_2 - y_1)^2 + (z_2 - z_1)^2}. \qquad (6.21)$$

Method 2: Here we make use of Figure 6.14(b). Taking the scalar product of vectors $\mathbf{k}$ and $\mathbf{R}''$, we obtain:

$$\mathbf{k} \cdot \mathbf{R}'' = |\mathbf{R}''| \cos(-\chi),$$

and since the end points of $\mathbf{k}$ and $\mathbf{R}''$ are respectively given by $(0, 0, 1)$ and $(a, 0, \sqrt{(y_2 - y_1)^2 + (z_2 - z_1)^2})$, it is apparent that:

$$\mathbf{k} \cdot \mathbf{R}'' = \sqrt{(y_2 - y_1)^2 + (z_2 - z_1)^2}.$$

Combining these equations we obtain:

$$\cos \chi = \sqrt{(y_2 - y_1)^2 + (z_2 - z_1)^2}. \qquad (6.22)$$

To obtain an expression for $\sin \chi$, we can make use of the vector product (see Section 6.3). We can write:

$$\mathbf{R}'' \times \mathbf{k} = \mathbf{j}|\mathbf{R}''||\mathbf{k}| \sin(-\chi) = \mathbf{j} \sin(-\chi),$$

Inserting the components for vectors $\mathbf{k}$ and $\mathbf{R}''$ into Eq. 6.7, we obtain:

$$\mathbf{R}'' \times \mathbf{k} = a\mathbf{j}.$$

Combining these two equations we obtain:

$$\sin \chi = -a. \qquad (6.23)$$

Eq.'s 6.22 and 6.23 therefore correspond to those obtained using Method (1) – see Eq.'s 6.21. Inserting the values for $\sin \chi$ and $\cos \chi$ into the basic transformation matrix

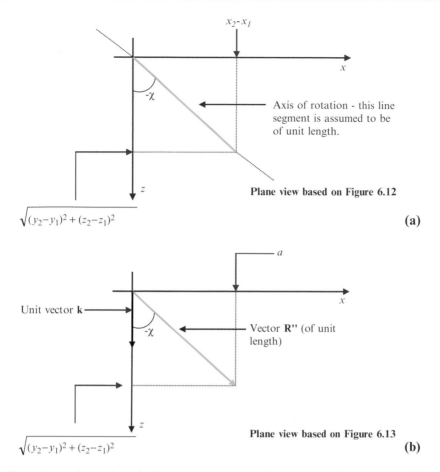

Figure 6.14 The angle $-\chi$ denotes the angle of rotation about the y-axis. The inclusion of the negative sign follows the convention previously adopted in which a positive rotational angle corresponds to an anti-clockwise rotation when we look along an axis (from the positive end) towards the origin. The diagram presented in (a) relates to 'Method 1' and diagram (b) to 'Method 2'. See text for discussion.

for rotation about the y-axis we obtain:

$$
\begin{bmatrix}
\sqrt{(y_2 - y_1)^2 + (z_2 - z_1)^2} & 0 & a & 0 \\
0 & 1 & 0 & 0 \\
-a & 0 & \sqrt{(y_2 - y_1)^2 + (z_2 - z_1)^2} & 0 \\
0 & 0 & 0 & 1
\end{bmatrix}. \tag{6.24}
$$

3. **Rotation**: The more taxing stage of this exercise is now behind us! Having made the axis of rotation coincident with one of the coordinate axes (we have arbitrarily chosen the z-axis), we now perform the desired rotation and simply use the basic transformation matrix that causes a rotation about this axis.

4.　**'Undo' Re-orientation**: Here, we 'undo' the previous rotations about the y and x axes. This involves using the inverse matrices. Finding the inverse of a matrix can be a tedious operation. However in the case of the affine transformation matrices that we are using here, determining the inverse is extremely simple. We simply need to remember that the purpose of the inverse matrix is to 'undo' a previous operation. Thus, for example if one matrix performs a rotation about the x-axis through an angle β, the inverse matrix must perform a rotation about the same axis through an angle $-\beta$. Hence to 'undo' the rotation about the y-axis (which was through an angle χ), we use the following matrix (which represents the inverse of the original):

$$\begin{bmatrix} \sqrt{(y_2-y_1)^2+(z_2-z_1)^2} & 0 & -a & 0 \\ 0 & 1 & 0 & 0 \\ a & 0 & \sqrt{(y_2-y_1)^2+(z_2-z_1)^2} & 0 \\ 0 & 0 & 0 & 1 \end{bmatrix}. \qquad (6.25)$$

OTU Exercise 6.8: The Inverse of a Matrix

(a)　Write down the inverse ($\mathbf{R}_z^{-1}(\alpha)$) of the matrix $\mathbf{R}_z(\alpha)$ which is given by:

$$\mathbf{R}_z(\alpha) = \begin{bmatrix} \cos\alpha & \sin\alpha & 0 & 0 \\ -\sin\alpha & \cos\alpha & 0 & 0 \\ 0 & 0 & 1 & 0 \\ 0 & 0 & 0 & 1 \end{bmatrix}.$$

Recall from Section 2.5.3 that the result of multiplying a matrix by its inverse, is to generate the identity matrix. Show that $\mathbf{R}_z(\alpha) \cdot \mathbf{R}_z^{-1}(\alpha)$ equals the identity matrix and hence confirm your result. **Hint:** $\cos(-\alpha) = \cos\alpha$ and $\sin(-\alpha) = -\sin\alpha$.

(b)　Multiply Eq. 6.24 by 6.25 and hence confirm that Eq. 6.25 is the inverse of Eq. 6.24. (To simplify the multiplication process you may wish to substitute a single symbol in place of $\sqrt{(y_2-y_1)^2+(z_2-z_1)^2}$.

5.　**'Undo' Relocation**: Finally, we must 'undo' the translation that was previously carried out in Step (1). This simply necessitates the application of the inverse translation matrix:

$$\mathbf{T}^{-1}(x,y,z) = \begin{bmatrix} 1 & 0 & 0 & 0 \\ 0 & 1 & 0 & 0 \\ 0 & 0 & 1 & 0 \\ x_1 & y_1 & z_1 & 1 \end{bmatrix}.$$

From the above discussion, it may appear that achieving the continuous rotation of an object about a fixed (but arbitrarily positioned) axis is, in terms of the number of steps involved, a little complex. However, from a computational point of view, the process is straight forward and the computational cost is quite low (recall that we have even avoided the need to calculate sines and cosines).

6.5 Perspective Revisited

'As far as the laws of mathematics refer to reality,
they are not certain, and as far as they are certain,
they do not refer to reality.'[6]

In Section 5.4.7 we discussed some issues relating to the formation of a perspective view and the projection of such a view onto a 2-D surface – the viewing/projection plane. Here, we extend this discussion and in the next subsection describe the way in which matrices can be used for perspective and projection operations. Subsequently, in Section 6.5.2, we briefly outline ways in which we can employ perspective drawing in a manner that more effectively conveys three-dimensionality. Finally, in Section 6.5.3 we briefly consider the significance of the vanishing point.

6.5.1 Perspective and Projection Operations

Recall Eq. 5.25 – which, for convenience, is given below:

$$L'_x = \frac{C_z L_x}{C_z - L_z}, \quad L'_y = \frac{C_z L_y}{C_z - L_z}, \quad L'_z = 0.$$

This refers to a point (L) located at coordinates (L_x, L_y, L_z) – as illustrated in Figure 6.15. The centre of projection (COP) is assumed to be located on the z-axis (at $0, 0, C_z$) and a projection plane is positioned in the plane $z = 0$. A line drawn from the point L to the COP intersects the projection plane at a point L' with coordinates (L'_x, L'_y, L'_z). The above equations can be re-written as:

$$L'_x = \frac{L_x}{1 - \frac{L_z}{C_z}}, \quad L'_y = \frac{L_y}{1 - \frac{L_z}{C_z}}, \quad L'_z = 0. \tag{6.26}$$

In the previous sections of this chapter, we have made no use of the upper three elements in final column of the 4 by 4 transformation matrix (see, for example, Figure 6.9). However, as we will now see these elements are able to play a key role in the production of a perspective view. For example, consider the following matrix acting on the point L (expressed in homogeneous form):

$$\begin{bmatrix} L_x & L_y & L_z & 1 \end{bmatrix} \begin{bmatrix} 1 & 0 & 0 & 0 \\ 0 & 1 & 0 & 0 \\ 0 & 0 & 1 & -1/C_z \\ 0 & 0 & 0 & 1 \end{bmatrix} = \begin{bmatrix} L_x & L_y & L_z & 1 - \frac{L_z}{C_z} \end{bmatrix}.$$

Dividing through by $1 - \frac{L_z}{C_z}$, we can obtain the Cartesian coordinates of the transformed point:

$$\left(\frac{L_x}{1 - \frac{L_z}{C_z}}, \quad \frac{L_y}{1 - \frac{L_z}{C_z}}, \quad \frac{L_z}{1 - \frac{L_z}{C_z}} \right). \tag{6.27}$$

---

[6] Attributed to Albert Einstein (1879–1955).

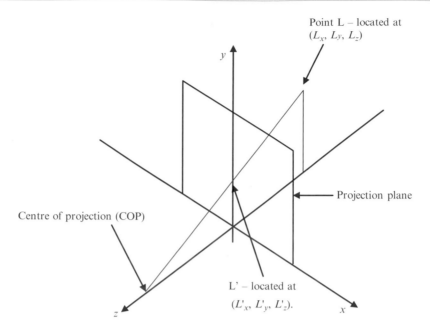

Figure 6.15 A line drawn from point L to the COP intersects the projection plane at L'. See text for discussion.

Recall that we have assumed that the projection plane is in the x–y plane (for which the z is zero). In this case, Eq. 6.27 gives the coordinates for L' indicated in Eq. 6.26. In fact, the following matrix will map any point onto the x–y plane:

$$\begin{bmatrix} 1 & 0 & 0 & 0 \\ 0 & 1 & 0 & 0 \\ 0 & 0 & 0 & 0 \\ 0 & 0 & 0 & 1 \end{bmatrix}. \tag{6.28}$$

It is convenient to combine this matrix with the perspective transformation[7] given above. Thus:

$$\begin{bmatrix} 1 & 0 & 0 & 0 \\ 0 & 1 & 0 & 0 \\ 0 & 0 & 1 & -1/C_z \\ 0 & 0 & 0 & 1 \end{bmatrix} \begin{bmatrix} 1 & 0 & 0 & 0 \\ 0 & 1 & 0 & 0 \\ 0 & 0 & 0 & 0 \\ 0 & 0 & 0 & 1 \end{bmatrix} = \begin{bmatrix} 1 & 0 & 0 & 0 \\ 0 & 1 & 0 & 0 \\ 0 & 0 & 0 & -1/C_z \\ 0 & 0 & 0 & 1 \end{bmatrix}. \tag{6.29}$$

OTU Exercise 6.9: Example Calculation

Consider a point L with Cartesian coordinates $(2, 2, -4)$ and let us suppose that we define a COP at $(0, 0, 10)$. Using Eq. 6.29, determine the location of the point L' which represents the perspective projection in the plane $z = 0$.

---

[7] Note: When we perform a perspective projection, lines that were previously parallel are made to converge to the vanishing point. Affine transformations retain parallel lines and so a perspective projection represents a non-affine operation.

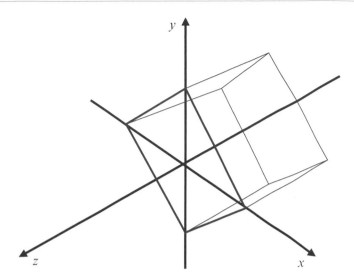

Figure 6.16 A cube located so that one face (for clarity, the edges of this face are depicted in bold) lies on the *x–y* plane (i.e. is coincident with the projection plane). The *z*-axis passes through the centre of the cube. See OTU Exercise 6.11.

OTU Exercise 6.10: The Perspective-Projection Matrix

Consider the perspective-projection matrix given in Eq. 6.29. Suppose that this matrix acts on a set of points (P) to produce a new set of points (P′). By generating the inverse of the matrix given in Eq. 6.29, can we subsequently apply this to the set of points denoted as P′ and so produce the original set (P) – i.e. can we 'undo' the original perspective projection? If not, why not?

6.5.2 Object Orientation and Location

The formation of a perspective projection does not in itself necessarily guarantee that an arbitrary 3-D object will appear to be three-dimensional. In fact, when working with wire-frame models the clarity of the perspective projection is strongly influenced by object orientation. This is illustrated in the following simple OTU Exercise.

OTU Exercise 6.11: The Perspective Projection – Object Orientation

Consider the formation of a perspective projection of a wire frame model of a cube. We assume that the cube is initially positioned as illustrated in Figure 6.16. As may be seen, one face of the cube is located in the *x–y* plane (i.e. in the projection plane) and the *z*-axis passes through the cubes centre. Assuming that the COP is located on the *z*-axis, draw a diagram showing the perspective projection of the cube that would be formed on the projection plane (i.e. the view seen when looking into the projection plane).

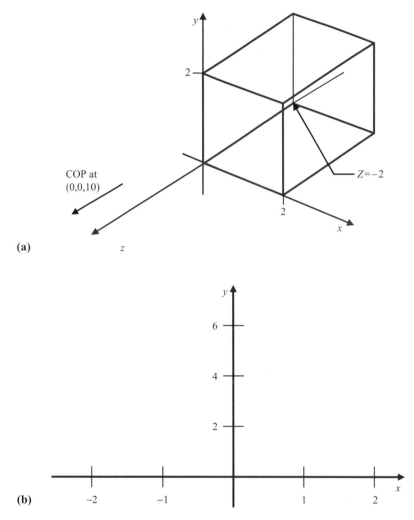

Figure 6.17 In (a) a cube with sides of length 2 units is depicted. One face is in the plane $z = 0$ (coincident with the projection plane). The cube is rotated and shifted prior to the formation of the perspective projection. Complete diagram (b): see OTU Exercise 6.12.

Clearly, the perspective projection of the cube referred to in the above OTU Exercise lacks clarity – and provides a sense of 'tunnel vision'. To obtain a better perspective view of the cube, we need to change the viewing geometry. Here, for example, we could move the cube so that it is no longer centred on the z-axis and also rotate it to ensure that none of its faces lie parallel to the projection plane. This will improve the visibility of all faces and give a better impression of the cube's three-dimensionality.

By way of an example suppose that we have a cube with edges of length 2 units that is positioned as indicated in Figure 6.17(a). We will assume that the projection plane is in the plane $z = 0$ and that the COP is located at (0, 0, 10). To enhance the 3-D appearance of the projected perspective view we will undertake the following steps:

Table 6.1 The creation of a perspective projection of a cube. The cube is rotated about the y-axis and shifted (in the y-direction).

Coordinates of vertices (original cube)	Coordinates of vertices (perspective projection)
$(0, 0, 0)$	$(0, 4, 0)$
$(2, 0, 0)$	$(0.9, 3.4, 0)$
$(2, 2, 0)$	$(0.9, 5.1, 0)$
$(0, 2, 0)$	$(0, 6, 0)$
$(0, 0, -2)$	$(-1.6, 3.6, 0)$
$(2, 0, -2)$	$(-0.6, 3.1, 0)$
$(2, 2, -2)$	$(-0.6, 4.7, 0)$
$(0, 2, -2)$	$(-1.6, 5.5, 0)$

1. Rotate the cube through an angle of $60°$ about the y-axis.
2. Translate the cube by 4 units in the y-direction.
3. Perform the perspective projection.

Using the basic transformations introduced previously in this chapter, we can form a single matrix that combines these operations:

$$\begin{bmatrix} \cos 60° & 0 & -\sin 60° & 0 \\ 0 & 1 & 0 & 0 \\ \sin 60° & 0 & \cos 60° & 0 \\ 0 & 0 & 0 & 1 \end{bmatrix} \begin{bmatrix} 1 & 0 & 0 & 0 \\ 0 & 1 & 0 & 0 \\ 0 & 0 & 1 & 0 \\ 0 & 4 & 0 & 1 \end{bmatrix} \begin{bmatrix} 1 & 0 & 0 & 0 \\ 0 & 1 & 0 & 0 \\ 0 & 0 & 1 & -1/10 \\ 0 & 0 & 0 & 1 \end{bmatrix} \approx \begin{bmatrix} 0.5 & 0 & 0 & 0.09 \\ 0 & 1 & 0 & 0 \\ 0.87 & 0 & 0 & -0.05 \\ 0 & 4 & 0 & 1 \end{bmatrix}. \quad (6.30)$$

We can now apply this result to each of the original cube's vertices and so obtain the coordinates of each vertex of the perspective projection – see Table 6.1.

OTU Exercise 6.12: The Perspective Projection

Use the axes presented in Figure 6.17(b) (or re-draw these axes) and depict the locations of each of the vertices of the cube's perspective projection. Vertex coordinates are provided in Table 6.1. Connect these vertices in the appropriate manner to depict the projection of the perspective view of the cube.

6.5.3 The Vanishing Point Revisited

In Section 1.3 we introduced vanishing points and briefly referred to the formation of diagrams using of one, two and three such points. In Section 5.4.7 we discussed linear perspective and our perception (arising as a direct consequence of the finite separation of the focusing system within the eye and the retina) that parallel lines appear to converge – to a distant vanishing point. Here it is appropriate to briefly consider the relationship between the location of the

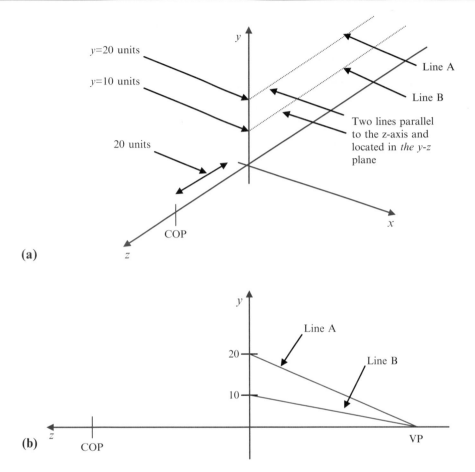

Figure 6.18 In (a) we illustrate two lines that lie parallel to the z-axis and that are located in the y–z plane. In (b) we indicate that when the perspective view is created, these lines converge on the z-axis at the vanishing point (VP). See the text for discussion.

centre of projection (COP) and the vanishing point (VP). We will examine this relationship on the basis of a simple numerical example.

In Figure 6.18(a) we indicate two lines that lie parallel to the z-axis and which are located in the y–z plane ($x = 0$). As usual, we will assume that the projection plane lies in the x–y plane and define the COP on the z-axis at a distance of 20 units from the origin. As we know, when we create the perspective view, these parallel lines will converge at the vanishing point – as illustrated in Figure 6.18(b). Here, we simply provide a 2-D view – which is appropriate since we are confining ourselves to lines within the y–z plane.

As indicated in the illustration, we assume that one of the parallel lines (denoted as line A) has a height above the z-axis of 20 units, and the second line (line B) a height of 10 units. As we have seen, when we form the perspective projection, the location of points that lie on the projection plane does not change. For example consider line A. The coordinates of the point at which this line meets the projection plane are (0, 20, 0). Expressing this in homogeneous form

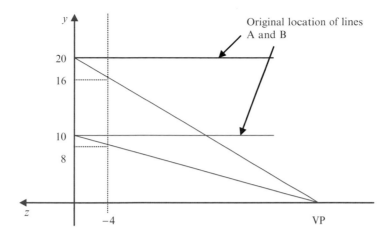

Figure 6.19 The location of points on the lines parallel to the z-axis and the perspective rendition of these lines – which converge at the vanishing point (VP). See the text for discussion.

and applying the perspective matrix, we obtain the following result:

$$\begin{bmatrix} 0 & 20 & 0 & 1 \end{bmatrix} \begin{bmatrix} 1 & 0 & 0 & 0 \\ 0 & 1 & 0 & 0 \\ 0 & 0 & 1 & -1/20 \\ 0 & 0 & 0 & 1 \end{bmatrix} = \begin{bmatrix} 0 & 20 & 0 & 1 \end{bmatrix}.$$

Thus the perspective matrix does not affect the location of this point and so line A passes through $(0, 20, 0)$ and line B through $(0, 10, 0)$. We can readily obtain equations for these two lines – we need to simply determine for each line a second point through which each passes. For example, suppose that we consider the point $(0, 20, -5)$ on line A and $(0, 10, -5)$ on line B. We now apply the perspective transformation matrix to these coordinates (expressed in homogeneous form). For line A:

$$\begin{bmatrix} 0 & 20 & -5 & 1 \end{bmatrix} \begin{bmatrix} 1 & 0 & 0 & 0 \\ 0 & 1 & 0 & 0 \\ 0 & 0 & 1 & -1/20 \\ 0 & 0 & 0 & 1 \end{bmatrix} = \begin{bmatrix} 0 & 20 & -5 & 1.25 \end{bmatrix}.$$

Similarly for line B, we obtain $\begin{bmatrix} 0 & 10 & 0 & 1.25 \end{bmatrix}$. Dividing through by 1.25, we obtain the location of these two points in 3-D space. For line A we have $(0, 16, -4)$ and for line B $(0, 8, -4)$. These points are indicated in Figure 6.19.

   We can obtain the point at which the two lines converge on the z-axis – either on the basis of similar triangles or by determining the equation for each. In the latter case, we can use the general equation for the straight line. Using Eq. 2.2, we obtain for line A:

$$y = z + 20,$$

and for line B:

$$y = 0.5z + 10.$$

Table 6.2 For various exemplar points located on the z-axis (at distance L_z from the origin), we indicate their individual locations (L'_z) after a perspective transformation. We assume that the COP is located at $(0, 0, 20)$.

L_z	L'_z
0	0
−10	−6.7
−20	−10
−30	−12
−40	−13.3
−50	−14.3
−100	−16.7
−1000	−19.6

Substituting into each $y = 0$, we obtain the point on the z-axis at which the two lines meet: $z = -20$. Thus the VP has coordinates $(0, 0, -20)$. Recall that the COP has coordinates $(0, 0, 20)$. Thus the VP is as far behind the projection plane as the COP is in front of it! Although we have shown this using a single numerical example, it is not a fluke – as we change the location of the COP, the VP will also change accordingly.

Let us now turn to a slightly different issue – although one that still relates to the VP. Suppose that the VP lies on the z-axis some 20 units behind the projection plane (with a corresponding COP at the same distance *in front* of the projection plane) and for a number of indicative points located along the z-axis, we calculate their location after the perspective transformation. Here, we make use of Eq. 6.27 – specifically:

$$L'_z = \frac{L_z}{1 - \frac{L_z}{C_z}}, \tag{6.31}$$

where L'_z represents the transformed coordinate along the z-axis.

As may be seen from Table 6.2, as the z coordinate values become larger, the transformed points get ever closer to the VP and as $L_z \to \infty$ (which reads as L_z 'tends to' (approaches) infinity), $L'_z \to$ VP. This is readily apparent when we examine Eq. 6.31. As L_z becomes increasingly negative, L_z/C_z also becomes more negative. Ultimately, the addition of 1 (which occurs in the denominator of Eq. 6.31 can be ignored – it has little effect on the overall value. Thus we can re-write the expression as:

$$L'_z \to \frac{L_z}{\frac{L_z}{C_z}} = \frac{C_z L_z}{L_z} = C_z$$

We have seen that the COP is as far in front of the projection plane as the VP is behind this plane. Thus, $L'_z \to$ VP.

One final point that should be noted. We have seen that three elements in the 4 by 4 transformation matrix play a key role in the creation of the perspective view. In this context, it is important to realise that when one of these elements is non-zero, we obtain a single point perspective and when two elements are non-zero, a two point perspective view is generated. Furthermore if all three elements are non-zero we can form a three-point perspective view.

6.6 Frames of Reference and the Virtual Camera

'Gentleman, much as we would like to help you by placing orders,
we cannot do this, as we are trustees of the public purse,
and we do not consider that aeroplanes
will be of any possible purposes for war purposes.'[8]

In the previous sections of this chapter, we have assumed that the plane onto which an image is projected lies in the x–y plane and that the COP is located on the z-axis. Thus we have anchored the projection plane to the coordinate system in which the locations of image components are defined. Consequently, when in Section 6.5.2 we sought to view an image component (in this case a cube) from a different vantage point, it was necessary to relocate and rotate the cube with respect to the 'world' coordinate system within which its position was defined. By way of analogy, this can be compared to a photographer who uses a fixed camera location to take photos of, for example, a group of people (e.g. traditional wedding photographs). Here, the people (representing the collection of objects within a space defined by a 'world' coordinate system) are positioned under the photographer's direction so as to be captured most advantageously on film. An alternative and more flexible approach is to move the position of the camera (this may be complemented by relocation of objects within the scene) to obtain the best possible vantage point. In computer graphics, we can achieve the same result by making use of a 'virtual' (synthetic) camera whose position and orientation can be changed relative to the world coordinate system. This technique has various advantages and permits a virtual camera to 'fly through' a scene (along a pre-defined track) capturing the image scene in a manner akin to the way in which we would employ a video camera when filming.

To employ a virtual camera we must define a viewing plane, a viewing window, a viewpoint and a coordinate system. Here, the coordinate system defines the location of the viewing plane, the viewing window and the viewpoint and is referenced to the origin of the world coordinate system. Below we summarise these key ingredients:

6.6.1 The Viewing Plane

This constitutes the plane onto which the image is projected and is equivalent to the projection plane that we have employed in our previous discussions. However, the key difference is that this plane is no longer anchored to a specific location within the world coordinate system – both its location and orientation can be changed.

6.6.2 Viewing Window

This defines the extent of the viewing plane onto which images are projected and by way of analogy can be thought of as a physical window casement or picture frame through which the

---

[8] Colonel F.E. Seely speaking on behalf of the Secretary of State for War in the UK in 1912. Quoted in *The World of Wings and Things*, by Alliott Verdon-Roe. Originally published c1938.

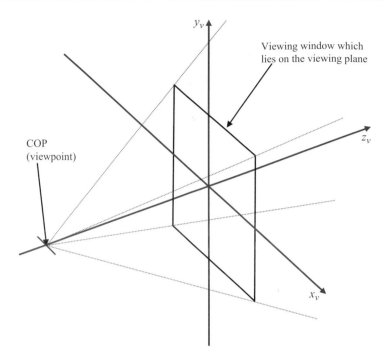

Figure 6.20 Here, we illustrate a rectangular 'viewing window' which lies in the viewing plane. The extent of this window coupled with the location of the COP defines four sides of a viewing volume (as indicated by the dashed lines). Image components within this 'viewing pyramid' may be projected onto the viewing plane. Any components within the image scene that lie outside of this region will not be visible at the viewpoint and 'clipping techniques' are used to clip the scene to the viewing pyramid. Note that the axes drawn here are associated with the virtual camera and are denoted x_v, y_v and z_v. This distinguishes this coordinate system from the world coordinate system whose axes will be labelled x_w, y_w and z_w. As may be seen from the illustration, for convenience we have adopted a left-hand coordinate system. See Chapter 8 for further discussion.

viewer looks onto a scene. In the case of a perspective projection, the dimensions of a rectangular viewing window coupled with the relative location of the COP define four sides of a 'viewing volume' – see Figure 6.20. As indicated in this illustration the location of the viewing window is typically centred about the origin of the viewing coordinate system – however, this is not a requirement (nor is there a requirement for the COP to be located on the z_v axis). The locations of both the viewing window and the COP are referenced with respect to the viewing coordinate system.

6.6.3 Viewing Coordinate System

In previous sections of this chapter we have consistently employed a right-handed coordinate system. However, in relation to the virtual camera, it is convenient to employ a left-handed coordinate system with the viewing plane lying within the x–y plane and positive z increasing with distance behind this plane (this provides an intuitive approach – the greater the depth of an object within the scene, the greater is its z coordinate value).[9] In the text that follows we shall denote the three axes of the viewing coordinate system as x_v, y_v and z_v. This allows us to

---

[9] The world coordinate system will continue to be treated as right-handed.

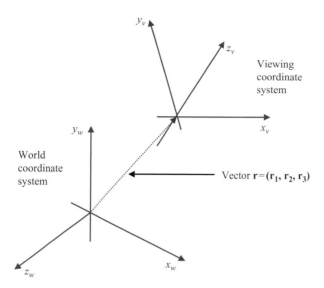

Figure 6.21 Here, the vector **r** denotes the locations of the viewing and world coordinate system. However, this vector does not give any information concerning the relative orientation of these two sets of axes.

readily distinguish this system from the axes employed in the world coordinate system that will be denoted x_w, y_w and z_w.[10]

As indicated in Figure 6.21 we can use a vector $\mathbf{r} = (r_1, r_2, r_3)$ to define the relative locations of the viewing and world coordinate systems. However, this vector does not give us any information concerning the orientation of the former relative to the latter. For this, we need to define other vectors – see Figure 6.22.

As may be seen from this illustration we define a unit vector **n** whose components are specified relative to the world coordinate system. This vector lies normal to the viewing window and defines the location of the z-axis (denoted z_v) of the viewing coordinate system. Although this vector defines the orientation of the z_v-axis, it does not provide a complete definition of the orientation of the viewing coordinate system (the x_v and y_v axes may rotate about the z_v axis). The locations of the remaining axes are therefore defined by means of two more vectors labelled **u** and **v** in Figure 6.22. These vectors lie at right-angles to the vector **n**, their components are specified with respect to the world coordinate system, and they lie in the viewing plane. Since all three vectors lie at right-angles to each other, once two of them are defined, the third (e.g. the vector **u**) has only two possible orientations. The choice of direction is determined by whether we adopt a left-handed or right-hand coordinate system. In the case that we employ the former, then the direction of **u** is given by the vector product (see Section 6.3) of **n** and **v**:

$$\mathbf{u} = \mathbf{n} \times \mathbf{v}.$$

---

[10] In some texts, the axes associated with the viewing coordinate system are labelled U, V and N. In this case the viewing coordinate system is referred to as the 'UVN system'. We adopt these labels for the three vectors that we will use to describe the orientation of the viewing coordinate system relative to the world coordinate system.

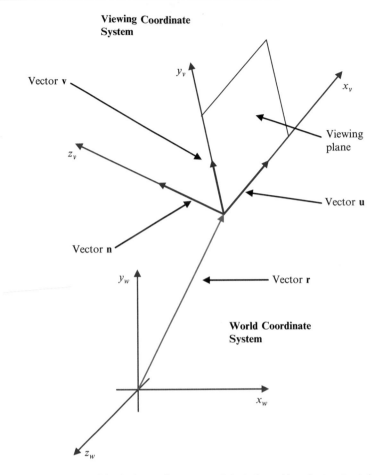

Figure 6.22 The location and orientation of the viewing coordinate system relative to the world coordinate system is described using the vectors **r, u, v** and **n**. We assume that the viewing plane is located in the plane $z_v = 0$.

Let us now suppose that for a given arbitrary location and orientation of the virtual camera we wish to generate the appropriate view of an image scene. The locations of all components within the scene are defined (in some way) relative to the world coordinate system. To create, for example, a perspective projection of various components within the scene in the viewing plane, we must define their location relative to the viewing coordinate system. In short, we must map world coordinates into viewing coordinates and this can be readily achieved by the concatenation of a series of basic transformations. Ultimately, we obtain a single transformation matrix that will map the axes used in relation to the viewing coordinate system onto those of the world coordinate system – aligning the two and making them coincident. Once we have obtained the values of the elements within the transformation matrix that are needed to achieve this objective, we can apply the same matrix to points specified within the world coordinate system and map them into the coordinate system employed by the virtual camera.

Steps used in this process are briefly summarised below:

Step 1: Reflection in the $z_v = 0$ plane: Recall that the world coordinate system is right-handed and the viewing coordinate system is left-handed. This is a somewhat arbitrary choice and, for example, we could have defined both as right-hand systems. However, transforming between the two systems is a trivial task requiring a single reflection operation – a reflection in $x–y$ ($z_v = 0$) plane. Thus positive values of z_v become negative and *visa versa*.

Step 2: A Translation Operation: We now make the origins of the two coordinate systems coincident. This involves a translation operation – the shift applied being defined by the vector **r** and being indicated symbolically as $\mathbf{T}(-r_1, -r_2, -r_3)$.

Step 3: Rotation about the x_w Axis: Once the origins of the two coordinate systems are coincident, we now perform a rotation about, for example, the x_w axis so as to bring the z_v axis onto the $x–z$ plane of the world coordinate system.

Step 4: Rotation about the y_w Axis: Following on from Step 3, we perform a rotation about the y_w axis so aligning the z-axes of the world and viewing coordinate systems.

Step 5: Rotation about the z_w Axis: Here, a rotation about the z_w axis is used to align the remaining axes.

Step 6: Scaling: Scaling may be used to adjust between the scales assigned to the world and viewing coordinate systems.

OTU Exercise 6.13: Transforming Between Coordinate Systems

(a) Draw two sets of axes the origins of which should be offset from each other and the axes arbitrarily oriented. One set of axis corresponds to the world coordinate system and the other to the viewing coordinate system. Appropriately label each axis. Using this diagram as a basis, draw separate sketches illustrating the progressive effect of each of the transformations undertaken in the six steps listed above.

(b) Determine a single transformation matrix that implements the six steps listed above.

6.7 Discussion

As we have seen, matrices provide a simple and logical tool by means of which we are able to perform transformations within both 2-D and 3-D space. The techniques outlined in this chapter are readily extended to the implementation of more complex operations in which, for example, we may wish to operate on a set of connected entities such as the limbs of an animated figure or the segments of a robotic arm. In addition, we have re-visited linear perspective and have discussed the use of matrices for the implementation of perspective transformations. Finally, we have introduced the concept of a virtual (synthetic) camera and the viewing coordinate system. Having laid these foundations, we are now able to consider other aspects of 3-D image formation and in the next chapter primarily focus on the modelling process whereby we describe the geometrical and spatial characteristics of objects that we wish to depict. This leads on to discussion in Chapter 8 in relation to the rendering process.

6.8 Review Questions

1. Consider two parallel vectors. What result do we obtain when we calculate their vector (cross) product?
2. In the case of non-parallel vectors, is the vector product commutative?
3. Suppose that we calculate the vector product of two vectors. What is the direction of the resulting vector?
4. What is the effect of the following matrix when it is applied to a point represented in homogeneous form:

$$\begin{bmatrix} 1 & 0 & 0 & 0 \\ 0 & 1 & 0 & 0 \\ 0 & 0 & 1 & 0 \\ D_x & D_y & D_z & 1 \end{bmatrix}.$$

5. What is the effect of the following matrix when it is applied to a point represented in homogeneous form:

$$\begin{bmatrix} 1 & 0 & 0 & 0 \\ 0 & \cos \alpha & \sin \alpha & 0 \\ 0 & -\sin \alpha & \cos \alpha & 0 \\ 0 & 0 & 0 & 1 \end{bmatrix}.$$

6. A vector is used to define the location of the origin of one coordinate system relative to another. Does this fully describe the relative relationships of the two coordinate systems?
7. State the underlying cause of our perception of linear perspective.
8. State the function of the viewing plane.
9. Discuss the replacement of the viewing plane by a non-planar viewing surface (e.g. a concave or convex surface).
10. Briefly describe the formation of a viewing volume.

6.9 Feedback to Review Questions

1. Their vector product will be zero.
2. Their vector product is not commutative – in fact $a \times b = -(b \times a)$.
3. The resulting vector is orthogonal to the plane containing the original two vectors.
4. This matrix will give rise to a translation operation.
5. This matrix will give rise to a rotation about the x-axis – the angle of rotation is denoted by α.

6. Additional vectors should be used – so enabling us to describe the relative orientations of the two coordinate systems.
7. Our perception of linear perspective arises as a result of the finite separation of the retina and the focusing system within the eye.
8. This represents the surface onto which the 3-D image is projected.
9. No feedback to this discussion question.
10. This may be formed by defining a viewing window. The extent of this window coupled with the location of the COP defines the four sides of the viewing volume. Any image components that lie outside this volume will not be visible from the COP.

3-D Graphics: Representation

'. . . and now and then heaving a great sigh.'

7.1 Introduction

In this chapter we primarily focus on the geometrical representation of objects. We begin by introducing the polygonal approach to object modelling via which objects are represented by means of a polygon mesh. Thus, for example, a sphere is modelled using a set of interconnected polygons so creating a multi-faceted (rather than a continuously smooth) approximation. Initially we consider the creation of wireframe models in which we form a skeletal outline of an object using a set of suitably interconnected line segments. In its most basic form, this provides us with a way of displaying an object's geometric and spatial form. Subsequently, we describe in general terms the 'boundary representation' (B-rep) approach via which we model an object in such a way as to embrace polygon *surfaces* so enabling objects to exhibit a 'solid' form.

In Section 7.4 we provide a review of some basic mathematics relating to the representation of a planar surface. The maths presented in this section is intended to give additional practice in the use and application of vectors. In Appendix D we provide related discussion and consider the intersection of a line with a plane of infinite extent and also with a triangular region. Additionally in this Appendix we discuss the intersection of two planes.

Various techniques may be used to define the geometrical form of objects and each approach has associated strengths and weaknesses. In Section 7.5 we briefly discuss some of the weaknesses of the polygonal approach and in Section 7.6 turn our attention to the formation of smoothly curving surfaces. Here, we confine ourselves to the production of Bézier surfaces and build on previous discussion provided in Section 4.4 relating to Bézier curves. In addition, we consider the formation of composite surfaces comprising a set of Bézier patches and explain the requirements for C^0 and C^1 continuity.

Finally, in Section 7.7 we briefly outline the Constructive Solid Geometry (CSG) approach where models are constructed using a set of basic object primitives. Whereas other techniques described in this chapter focus on the representation of an object's surface characteristics, the CSG approach treats objects as volumes – the objects comprising a set of points within a 3-D space. This approach is well suited to interactive design and for the production of models which are to be turned into physical entities using forms of automatic prototyping/manufacturing techniques.

Key Learning Outcomes: At the end of this chapter you should be able to:

- *Understand basic techniques used in the formation of polygonal meshes for model representation together with the strengths and weaknesses of this general approach.*

- *Describe a planar surface in mathematical terms and determine the surface normal vector.*

- *Form Bézier and composite surfaces comprising Bézier patches.*

- *Understand the requirements for C^0 and C^1 continuity in joining two or more Bézier patches.*

- *Outline the nature of the constructive solid geometry technique and identify key strengths and weaknesses.*

7.2 Polygonal Models

> *'How far that little candle throws his beams!*
> *So shines a good deed in a weary world.'* [1]

Suppose that you were asked to create a physical model of a cube or tetrahedron. Two general approaches may be adopted – one giving rise to a 'solid' cube (with each face comprising a planar surface formed using a piece of paper, card or the like), and the other representing the geometric outline of the cube. In this latter case we could join together pieces of rigid wire, rod etc. In computer graphics the depiction of the geometric and spatial outline of a shape (the shape's 'skeleton') using straight line segments is generally referred to as the generation of a 'wireframe model'.

---

[1] William Shakespeare (1564–1616).

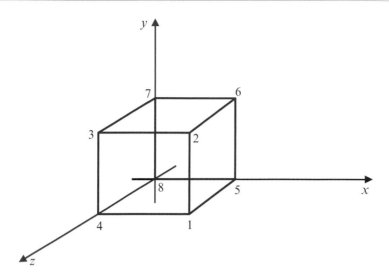

Figure 7.1 Here, we illustrate a cube with sides of unit length. Three edges of the cube each coincide with a coordinate axis. Each vertex is assigned a label and these labels are used in Table 7.1.

To produce such a model, we must specify the location in a 3-D space of each of the vertices (corners) – this takes the form of a vertex list. For example, consider a cube with edges of unit length and whose position and orientation relative to a right-hand coordinate system is as shown in Figure 7.1. The 'vertex list' for this cube is presented in Table 7.1(a). However, simply specifying within the model the location of the vertices for an object provides no indication as to which of these vertices should be directly connected via an edge. As indicated

Table 7.1 In (a), the vertex list for the cube illustrated in Figure 7.1 and in (b) a list indicating vertex connectivity. The labels assigned to the edges are shown in Figure 7.3.

Vertex	x	y	z
1	1	0	1
2	1	1	1
3	0	1	1
4	0	0	1
5	1	0	0
6	1	1	0
7	0	1	0
8	0	0	0

Edge	Vertex(a)	Vertex(b)
1	1	2
2	2	3
3	3	4
4	4	1
5	3	7
6	4	8
7	1	5
8	2	6
9	5	6
10	6	7
11	7	8
12	8	5

(a)   (b)

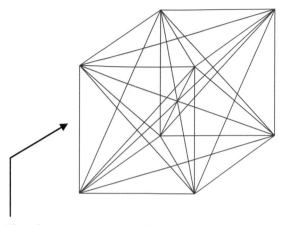

All vertices are connected to all other vertices

Figure 7.2 In order to generate a simple wireframe cube, we must not only define the location of each of the eight vertices but also specify their interconnectivity. In this diagram we illustrate the effect of simply allowing all vertices to be interconnected!

in Figure 7.2, simply connecting all vertices does not necessarily lead to the desired result! We must therefore provide connectivity information – an 'edge list' – as indicated in Table 7.1(b). Here, we reference each of the cube's edges using the labels assigned in Figure 7.3.

Equipped with information defining the location of the vertices and their interconnectivity, we have formed a wireframe model. In the case that we are employing a volumetric form of display (see Section 9.5), the perspective view is created automatically for us within the image space. Alternatively, in the more usual event that we are using a flat screen display, we may now wish to create a perspective view in which case, for a particular (desired) orientation of the cube, we project the coordinates of each of the vertices onto the viewing plane (see

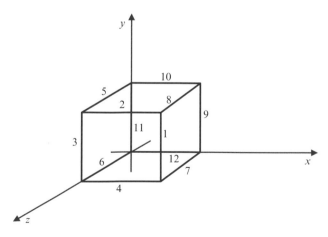

Figure 7.3 In this illustration we reproduce the cube depicted in Figure 7.1 and add labels to each of the twelve edges. These labels are used in Table 7.1.

Section 6.6). Straight line segments are created between the projected vertices in accordance with the connectivity information that we provide.

Wireframe models are often used to create polyhedra which are formed from a set of planar polygons. Although in general terms there is no restriction on polygon geometry, triangles are often employed (a shape defined by three vertices which are interconnected by straight line segments is inherently planar). This enables performance benefits to be derived from special purpose hardware and graphics accelerator cards. Although in some cases the wireframe technique will faithfully provide a true geometric representation of an object (e.g. in the case of the cube, tetrahedron and dodecahedron – whose faces are planar), curved surfaces can only be approximated (e.g. a sphere whose geometrical form is defined by a set of planar polygons).

Naturally, in the case that we are dealing with simple objects, it is very easy for us to manually define the locations of the various vertices and their interconnectivity. However, as we move to more complex objects (including the case that we wish to increase the accuracy with which we are to depict the geometry of curved surfaces), the manual approach becomes impractical. In the following two subsections, we consider the use of algorithmically based techniques via which wireframe models may be formed by computational means, and in Section 7.2.3 we briefly discuss the production of this type of model by means of a laser based scanning system.

7.2.1 An Extrusion Approach

Consider the formation of a wireframe model of a shape that has a uniform cross-section in at least one dimension (e.g. a prism[2] or cylinder). Such an object is illustrated in Figure 7.4 – where we arbitrarily locate the triangular 'base' in the x–z plane and assume that the direction of uniform cross-section lies in the y direction. Let us also assume that we wish to form a prism of length L. We begin the modelling process by defining the wireframe representation of the object's cross-section (which in this trivial example is a triangle) and locate this in the x–z plane. We then, in effect, 'extrude' this triangle in the y direction. This requires the determination of the coordinates of a triangle that lies at a distance L from the base triangle (we simply add L to the y coordinate of each vertex). In this way we have defined the location of the prism's six vertices. Finally, we generate the connectivity list which comprises the edges of the base triangle, the edges of the upper triangle and edges that connect corresponding vertices of the two triangles.

Naturally, this process can be applied to objects that have more complex cross-sections and in addition, the cross-section can vary during the extrusion process. In this latter case we begin by defining an initial cross-section (e.g. a circle) and as we perform the extrusion process we gradually vary the size of the cross-section (e.g. reduce the circle's radius – thereby forming a cone). The same general technique can be used to develop polygonal representations of more complex objects such as a wine bottle. Taking the technique one step further, we note that we are not limited to performing this so called extrusion process along a straight path but may do so along a curved track thereby forming representations of bananas, brief case carrying handles and the like. For related discussion see Watt [2000].

---

[2] A polyhedron having two congruent bases in the form of parallel polygons – all other faces being parallelograms.

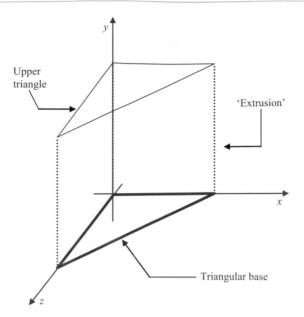

Figure 7.4 The formation of a model of a prism in which the vertices of the upper triangle are computed and edges are added that link these vertices with the corresponding vertices in the lower triangle.

7.2.2 Surface of Revolution

> *'Now here is the lake,*
> *and I still haven't changed.'*[3]

Unlike the approach outlined above, this technique is limited to the creation of models of objects that have a circular cross-section – although the cross-sectional radius need not be uniform throughout the length of the object. Thus it may be used to generate a cylinder, cone or more complex object: a wine bottle and glass provide classic examples. Suppose that we wish to produce a model of a funnel (that is, the type of funnel used to assist pouring a liquid into a container which has a narrow opening). We begin by defining the contour of the funnel – as shown in Figure 7.5(a). The profile is then rotated about an axis of symmetry (in the case of the example shown in the illustration – rotation is about the y axis).

We define the number of discrete steps that we wish to employ (n) during the rotation – as the number of steps is increased, the closer our wire frame model will come to approximating the geometrical curvature of the physical funnel. At each step we calculate the coordinates of the three points that are denoted as a, b and c in the illustration. These are given by:

$$a = \left(r_1 \cos\left(\frac{360}{n}\right), 0, r_1 \sin\left(\frac{360}{n}\right) \right), \quad b = \left(r_1 \cos\left(\frac{360}{n}\right), y_1, r_1 \sin\left(\frac{360}{n}\right) \right),$$

$$c = \left(r_2 \cos\left(\frac{360}{n}\right), y_2, r_2 \sin\left(\frac{360}{n}\right) \right).$$

[3] From 'The Life and Death of Colonel Blimp' (1942), Powell and Pressburger.

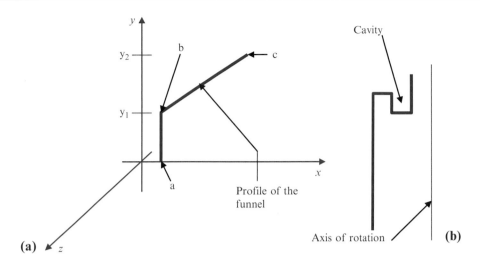

Figure 7.5 In (a) we define the profile of a funnel which is assume to comprise a cylinder joined to a truncated cone. The model is generated by rotating this profile about the y-axis. This results in the production of three circles – one defining the location of the top of the funnel (into which liquid is poured), a circle corresponding to the joining of the cone and cylinder) and a circle at the bottom of this cylinder. In (b) we illustrate a further profile – see text for discussion.

Where the integer $n \neq 0$ and r_1 denotes the radius of the cylinder and r_2 the maximum radius of the cone. In this way we are able to determine the coordinates of each vertex of our wireframe model. In addition, we must also generate the connectivity list and here, we specify the rules to be followed. For example, as we move between steps, current and previous vertices which have the same y-coordinate must be connected by an edge. Furthermore, at each of the step locations, the vertices a, b and c must be connected in the same way that they were connected in the original profile. Note that although we may obtain the vertical edges by connecting adjacent vertices (as defined by their y-coordinates) this may be undesirable as it would prevent the generation of certain models – such as the one arising from the rotation of the profile given in Figure 7.5(b) in which there is a 'cavity'.

The volume of revolution approach is not limited to the formation of wireframe models (in which vertices are interconnected via straight edges) – curves can be accommodated. In this case, we define the profile using a mathematical expression or set of expressions.[4]

Finally, in connection with the model of the funnel, we may enhance its visual appearance by increasing the number of points on the profile whose location we calculate during the rotation. Each of these will give rise to a horizontal polygon which connects the vertical lines within the wireframe mesh. However, as we will discuss later in this chapter, increasing the number of polygons that comprise a model is not necessarily advantageous.

---

[4] For example, if we were to model a parabolic dish (such as is used for satellite TV receivers), a single expression would be used. Alternatively, the modelling of more complex shapes would be most readily achieved using piecewise functions.

7.2.3 A Laser Based Scanning System

A number of techniques may be used for the capture of 3-D data relating to the geometric shape, spatial separation and motion of physical objects. This data may represent an object's surface characteristics, or may characterise the object throughout the volume in which it resides (e.g. data captured by means of various forms of medical scanner). In this latter case, the data is generally referred to as 'volumetric' or 'volume' data and takes the form of a set of points distributed within a 3-D space. Each point ('voxel') has associated x, y and z coordinates and may be assigned additional attributes – see Chapter 9.

Data relating to surface characteristics and to the spatial separation of a collection of objects may be obtained via a range of techniques. For example, it can be encapsulated within the disparities of two images comprising a stereopair. Alternatively, specialised hardware may be used – such as a laser based range measuring system. In one form, the object whose geometric shape is to be measured is placed on a rotating table. During each rotation, a laser beam is used to obtain a contour of the surface at a certain height above the rotating table. At the end of each rotation, the height of the object relative to the laser beam is changed. The result is a set of closely spaced horizontal contour scans ('slices'). A 'skinning' algorithm may then be used to create a polygon mesh of triangles between adjacent slices.

The selection of the technique used for the acquisition of 3-D data is often scene dependent – there is no single universal approach that will operate satisfactorily under all circumstances. For example in the case that we infer 3-D data from stereopairs, we are limited to a certain vantage point. Thus important data may not be available as, for example, objects within a scene may wholly or partially occlude one another. In the form outlined above, the laser range finding technique is most suited for operation with convex objects – data content relating to concave regions may not be easily acquired as the laser may fail to impinge on, and so be reflected by, such surfaces.

7.2.4 Interactive Formation

A polygonal mesh may be created using interactive design software. This enables designers to form and manipulate polygon meshes, add textures, establish lighting conditions and define object animation – without recourse to the underlying mathematics! Consequently, through the use of quite simple interactive operations, it is possible to build rich virtual scenes containing both static and animated objects. For further discussion see, for example, Gauthier [2005].[5]

7.3 The B-Rep Approach

'We do not remember days, we remember moments.'[6]

As we have discussed, in its most basic form, a wireframe (polygonal) model provides us with a skeletal outline of an object or structure. Although from a computational point of view such models can be efficiently displayed, the lack of object solidity negatively impacts on visual appearance (particularly when such images are presented on a conventional flat screen display). On the other hand, even in their simplest form such models can be extremely helpful and,

---

[5] This book includes a CD containing creative design software.
[6] Attributed to Cesare Pavese (1908–50).

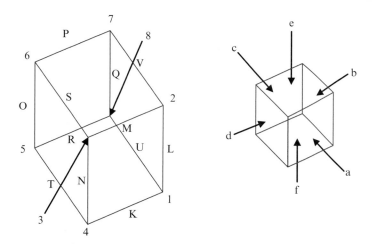

Figure 7.6 A cube with labels assigned to the vertices, edges and faces. The vertices are labelled 1–8 and edges K–V. To improve clarity, the diagram on the right shows the labels assigned to the faces: a–f.

for example, assist an animator wishing to interactively generate or fine-tune an animation sequence or during the interactive placement of objects within a scene. Such activities are not underpinned by surface realism/detail. Simple wire-frame images can also be used advantageously by several forms of creative 3-D display (e.g. the varifocal, volumetric and holographic approaches – see Chapter 9).

In addition to defining vertices and edges that comprise a model, we can supply additional information that will enable us to embrace and model surface characteristics thereby enhancing the visual appearance of the displayed image. Here, our focus is upon describing the boundary surfaces of objects – a boundary representation (B-rep) approach. This enables us to define the surface characteristics in such a way that we are able to generate models that appear to be solid and which can take on many of the visual characteristics of physical objects.

Recall that the wireframe technique described above employs a vertex list (in which the coordinates of vertices are defined) and an edge list (indicating their connectivity). In the case of the B-rep approach a polygon mesh is used to describe an objects surface or 'skin' and here, we include information (in the form of a 'face list') indicating the groups of vertices that define each polygon face. By way of a simple example, consider the cube illustrated in Figure 7.6.

The face list for this cube is presented in Table 7.2. We can distinguish between the inside and outside of a face by adopting a convention that relates to the order in which we list the vertices that define each face. For example, when we are looking onto a face from the outside, we list the vertices in an anticlockwise direction. Thus in the case of face a, since we are looking at the face from the outside, we list the vertices in an anticlockwise direction. The order in which we list vertices to define the 'sidedness' is arbitrary – although within an application we must be consistent. Alternatively, we can denote each circuit using edge vectors (recall previous discussion in Section 3.6) and adopt the convention that when we view a face from the *outside*, the face lies to the left of each bounding vector – which again corresponds to traversing the face in an anticlockwise direction.

Table 7.2 A 'face list' for the cube depicted in Figure 7.6. Thus face *a* is defined by the location of the vertices 1, 2, 3 and 4.

Face	Vertices
a	1 2 3 4
b	1 8 7 2
c	5 6 7 8
d	3 6 5 4
e	3 2 7 6
f	5 8 1 4

In Figure 7.7 we use a link list to represent the relationship between the vertices, edges and faces of the cube depicted in Figure 7.6 (pointers between elements in the list show the topological relationships). In the Activity that follows you are asked to complete the diagram.

OTU Exercise 7.1: Representation of Vertex, Edge and Face Lists

1. Complete the diagram presented in Figure 7.7 to show the relationship between the vertices, edges and faces of the cube depicted in Figure 7.6.
2. Draw a similar diagram for a tetrahedron.[7]

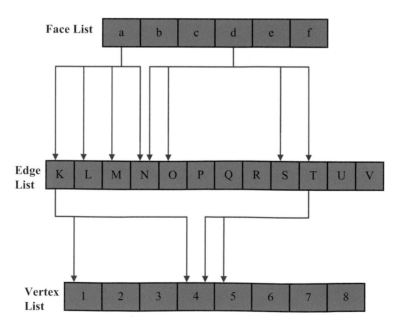

Figure 7.7 A partially completed diagram showing the relationship between vertices, edges and faces for the cube depicted in Figure 7.6. See OTU Exercise 7.1.

The scheme illustrated in Figure 7.7 can be extended by, for example, maintaining pointers from the edge list to the face list and from the vertex list to the edge list. Whilst this can improve flexibility, it also increases complexity. The Winged Edge data structure [Baumgart 1975] provides us with a further example of a representation scheme for polyhedra. This data structure is intended to provide a complete description via which reasonable queries may be supported. In this context Slater *et al.* [2002] provide a succinct summary of exemplar queries:

- *'For any face, find all of the edges, traversed in (counter)clockwise order.*
- *For any face, traverse all of the vertices.*
- *For any vertex, find all of the faces that meet at that vertex.*
- *For any vertex, find the edges that meet at that vertex.*
- *For any edge, find its two vertices.*
- *For any edge, find its two faces.*
- *For any edge, find the next edge on a face in a certain order (clockwise or counterclockwise).'*

For an introduction to this approach see, for example, Slater *et al.* [2002]. As we have indicated, a polyhedron is formed using an arrangement of polygons. In this context Mortenson [1985] writes:

'Polyhedron... an arrangement of polygons such that two and only two polygons meet at an edge, and it is possible to traverse the surface of the polyhedron by crossing its edges and moving from one polygonal face to another until all the polygons have been traversed by this continuous path.'

This may be readily understood by considering, for example, a cube or tetrahedron. These are examples of 'simple polyhedra' which, unlike 'non-simple polyhedra' have no holes. A toroidal polygon (doughnut) is an example of the latter. In fact, every convex polyhedron is classified as 'simple'.

The number of vertices, edges and faces that comprise a simple polyhedron are related according to an invariant relationship called 'Euler's formula for polyhedra'[8] such that:

$$V - E + S = 2, \tag{7.1}$$

where V represents the number of vertices, E the number of edges and S the number of surfaces. For example, in the case of a cube, there are 8 vertices, 12 edges and 6 surfaces – which is in agreement with the above equation. Similarly, for a tetrahedron, for which there are 4 vertices, 6 edges and 4 faces. 'Regular polyhedra' represent a particular form of simple polyhedra in which:

1. All faces have the same number of edges (e.g. a cube).
2. Every vertex has the same number of edges emanating from it (e.g. a cube).
3. Every edge has the same length.

---

[7] A tetrahedron comprises four triangular faces.

[8] Leonhard Euler: This remarkable and prolific mathematician was born in Basel, Switzerland in 1703 and published more than 500 books and papers. Writing about his later life, Boyer [1991] writes: '... *Euler spent almost all of the last seventeen years of his life in total darkness* [cataract condition]. *Even this tragedy failed to stem the flood of his research and publications, which continued unabated until 1783, at the age of seventy-six, he suddenly died while sipping tea and enjoying the company of one of his grandchildren.'*

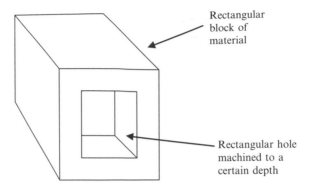

Rectangular
block of
material

Rectangular hole
machined to a
certain depth

Figure 7.8 A non-simple polyhedron. This comprises a cube into which a 'blind' hole has been cut. Euler's 'formula for polyhedra' as given in Eq. 7.1 is not valid for such objects. Instead we can use Poincaré's generalised version of Euler's equation. See text for details.

OTU Exercise 7.2: Regular Polyhedra

This exercise is an aside but can give useful insight into the form of regular polyhedra. Using Euler's formula for polyhedra (Eq. 7.1) and the first two characteristics of regular polyhedra that are given above, show that there are five regular polyhedra – state the characteristics of each in terms of the number of edges per face (e), the total number of edges emanating from each vertex (v) and the total number of edges (E) comprising the polyhedron. In each case state the name of the polyhedron.

As indicated above, Eq. 7.1 applies to 'simple polyhedra' – which contain no holes. By way of an example, consider the object depicted in Figure 7.8 comprising a cube into which a rectangular 'blind' hole has been machined (i.e. the hole does not pass all the way through the cube). This object has a total of 16 vertices, 24 edges and 11 faces. (Don't forget to count the face at the bottom of the blind hole!) Thus $V - E + S = 3$ – this does not agree with Euler's simple formula.

Poincaré[9] extended Euler's formula to take into account both holes that pass completely through an object and those that are of a limited depth:

$$V - E + S = 2(P - H) + H_B, \tag{7.2}$$

where H denotes the number of holes (which pass through the object), H_B the number of holes in faces and P the separate parts that comprise the object. Let us try this out on the object depicted in Figure 7.8. As indicated above, $V = 16$, $E = 24$ and $S = 11$. The object comprises a single part ($P = 1$), there are no holes passing completely through the object ($H = 0$) and there is a single blind hole ($H_B = 1$). Thus $V - E + S = 3$ and $2(P - H) + H_B = 2(1 - 0) + 1 = 3$. Thus the above equation is valid for this object.

---

[9] Jules Henri Poincaré (1854–1912).

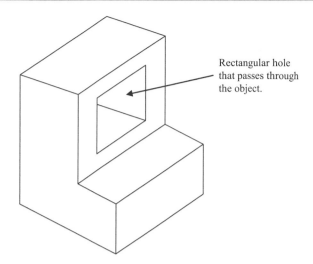

Rectangular hole
that passes through
the object.

Figure 7.9 A 'non-simple' polyhedron which includes a rectangular hole that passes through to the rear surface. See OTU Exercise 7.3 for discussion.

OTU Exercise 7.3: The Euler – Poincaré Equation

Consider the object illustrated in Figure 7.9 and that includes a hole that passes from one side to the other. Verify that the Euler – Poincaré equation applies to this object.

B-rep models are often difficult to generate and care has to be taken in order to avoid the creation of invalid models. Equations 7.1 and 7.2 provide us with a means of gaining confidence in a model. However, although these equations provide us with necessary conditions, they do not in themselves guarantee validity. Thus, for example, Eq. 7.1 provides us with a necessary condition that must be met in order for a model to represent a simple polyhedron. However, consider the object depicted in Figure 7.10 comprising a cube together with an extra surface that is sticking out from it (akin to a flap of a box). This object has 10 vertices, 15 edges and 7 surfaces. Inserting these values into Eq. 7.1 indicates that this is a valid 'simple polyhedron'. On the other hand, because of the presence of the additional surface, the overall set of surfaces do not bound a volume. Since a bounding volume is a characteristic of simple polyhedra, we need to include additional checks that will confirm validity (or otherwise). In this context Foley *et al.* [1990] indicate:

1. Each edge must connect two vertices.
2. Each edge must be shared by exactly two faces.
3. At least three edges must meet at each vertex
4. Faces must not interpenetrate.

The object shown in Figure 7.10 violates the second and third of these constraints. In the case of 'non-simple' polyhedra, Eq. 7.2 is also a necessary condition to validity – but it is not a guarantee – additional constraints must be applied.

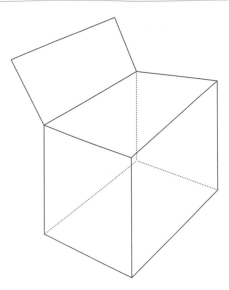

Figure 7.10 A solid cube with an extra surface that sticks out from it. Does 'Euler's formula for polyhedra' validate this as a simple polyhedron? See text for discussion.

7.4 A Little Maths: The Plane

> *'When you have flown halfway across a desert,*
> *you experience the desperation of a sleepless man*
> *waiting for dawn which only comes when*
> *the importance of its coming is lost.'* [10]

In previous chapters, we have discussed the representation and manipulation of points and lines in both 2-D and 3-D space. In this section we turn our attention to the representation of a plane within a 3-D space. We begin by considering the 'general form' of the equation for a plane based on the location of three 'non-collinear' points that lie on the plane. Subsequently, in Section 7.4.2, we represent a plane by considering a point on the plane and a vector that lies at right-angles to the plane (the 'surface normal'). In Section 7.4.3 we revisit the discussion presented in Section 7.4.1 – but adopt a vector based approach. Subsequently in Section 7.4.4 and 7.4.5 we represent a plane in parametric form and by means of a scalar product. For further related discussion see Appendix D.

7.4.1 Plane Representation Based on Three Points

Consider three points that are located within a 3-D space and which are not collinear (i.e. they do not lie on a straight line but rather represent the vertices of a triangle). Using three such points we are able to define the location and orientation of a plane – each point lying on the plane. Here, it is important to note that a triangle is by definition planar whereas polygons with a greater number of vertices can be either planar or non-planar. Consequently, if a B-rep model

---

[10] Beryl Markham, 'West With The Night', 1942.

comprises only triangular faces, we are able to guarantee that each of these faces will be planar – whereas in the case of other forms of face, errors may result in the unintentional generation of non-planar faces.

The general form of the equation for a plane (based on the location of three points that lie within the plane) may be written as:

$$Ax + By + Cz + D = 0, \tag{7.3}$$

where A, B, C and D are constants relating to the particular plane under consideration (we discuss there significance in the next sub-section). Their values may be found by considering the three points (mentioned above) which lie within the plane and may, for example correspond to three of the vertices of a face within a B-rep model. Let us suppose that these points have the following coordinates: (x_1, y_1, z_1), (x_2, y_2, z_2), (x_3, y_3, z_3). We can insert these coordinates into Eq. 7.3 and this results in the production of three equations as indicated below (in each case we have divided through by D):

$$\left(\frac{A}{D}\right)x_1 + \left(\frac{B}{D}\right)y_1 + \left(\frac{C}{D}\right)z_1 = -1$$

$$\left(\frac{A}{D}\right)x_2 + \left(\frac{B}{D}\right)y_2 + \left(\frac{C}{D}\right)z_2 = -1$$

$$\left(\frac{A}{D}\right)x_3 + \left(\frac{B}{D}\right)y_3 + \left(\frac{C}{D}\right)z_3 = -1.$$

We can represent these three equations in matrix form:

$$\begin{bmatrix} x_1 & y_1 & z_1 \\ x_2 & y_2 & z_2 \\ x_3 & y_3 & z_3 \end{bmatrix} \begin{bmatrix} A/D \\ B/D \\ C/D \end{bmatrix} = \begin{bmatrix} -1 \\ -1 \\ -1 \end{bmatrix}. \tag{7.4}$$

Recall summary discussion in Section 2.5.6 concerning the use of matrices for solving simultaneous equations. If we represent the left most matrix in the above expression as K, the column matrix on the left-hand side as L and the right-hand matrix as M, then we can express Eq. 7.4 as:

$$K \cdot L = M.$$

When we multiply through by the inverse of K (K^{-1}), we obtain:

$$L = K^{-1}M. \tag{7.5}$$

Consequently, we can readily solve Eq. 7.4 and so find the values A, B, C and D by obtaining the inverse matrix (K^{-1}). In Chapter 2 we limited discussion to the determination of the inverse of a 2 by 2 matrix. In the case of a 3 by 3 matrix, the process is a little more complicated and is briefly summarised below (for more detailed discussion see, for example, Jordan and Smith [2002] or Jeffrey [2002].

Suppose that we have a matrix Q with the following elements (recall the use of two subscripts to denote the row and column positions of each element):

$$Q = \begin{bmatrix} a_{11} & a_{12} & a_{13} \\ a_{21} & a_{22} & a_{23} \\ a_{31} & a_{32} & a_{33} \end{bmatrix}.$$

In order to obtain the inverse matrix (Q^{-1}) we undertake the following steps.[11]

1. **Find the Determinant of the Matrix**: The determinant of a matrix Q is generally referred to as detQ. In the case of a 3 by 3 matrix, the determinant is obtained using Eq. 2.15.

2. **Find the Adjoint**[12] **of the Matrix**: The 'adjoint' of a matrix is generally abbreviated to 'adj' (e.g. adjQ). This is achieved by calculating:

$$adjQ = \begin{bmatrix} a_{22}a_{33} - a_{32}a_{23} & -(a_{12}a_{33} - a_{32}a_{13}) & a_{12}a_{23} - a_{22}a_{13} \\ -(a_{21}a_{33} - a_{31}a_{23}) & a_{11}a_{33} - a_{31}a_{13} & -(a_{11}a_{23} - a_{21}a_{13}) \\ a_{21}a_{32} - a_{31}a_{22} & -(a_{11}a_{32} - a_{31}a_{12}) & a_{11}a_{22} - a_{21}a_{12} \end{bmatrix}. \quad (7.6)$$

3. **Calculate the Inverse Matrix**: We now determine the inverse matrix (Q^{-1}) by calculating:

$$Q^{-1} = \left(\frac{1}{\det Q}\right).adjQ. \quad (7.7)$$

Returning to the problem in hand, we need to calculate the inverse of the left-most matrix in Eq. 7.4 (in keeping with the above, we will denote this matrix as Q). Following the process outlined above, we begin by finding the determinant. Using Eq. 2.15, we can write:

$$\det Q = x_1(y_2z_3 - z_2y_3) - y_1(x_2z_3 - z_2x_3) + z_1(x_2y_3 - y_2x_3).$$

Using Eq. 7.6 we can find adjQ:

$$adjQ = \begin{bmatrix} y_2z_3 - z_2y_3 & -(y_1z_3 - y_3z_1) & y_1z_2 - y_2z_1 \\ -(x_2z_3 - x_3z_2) & x_1z_3 - x_3z_1 & -(x_1z_2 - x_2z_1) \\ x_2y_3 - x_3y_2 & -(x_1y_3 - x_3y_1) & x_1y_2 - x_2y_1 \end{bmatrix}.$$

We can now re-write Eq. 7.5 as:

$$\begin{bmatrix} A/D \\ B/D \\ C/D \end{bmatrix} = Q^{-1} \begin{bmatrix} -1 \\ -1 \\ -1 \end{bmatrix}, \quad (7.8)$$

where Q^{-1} is given by Eq. 7.7. If we now multiply the first row of elements in Q^{-1} by -1, we obtain an expression for A/D. Thus:

$$\frac{A}{D} = \frac{-(y_2z_3 - z_2y_3) + (y_1z_3 - y_3z_1) - (y_1z_2 - y_2z_1)}{x_1(y_2z_3 - z_2y_3) - y_1(x_2z_3 - z_2x_3) + z_1(x_2y_3 - y_2x_3)}.$$

---

[11] Here, we assume that the matrix that we are dealing with does indeed have an inverse. Such a matrix is said to be 'nonsingular'.

[12] Also referred to as the 'adjugate'.

Finally, we can rearrange this equation to give:

$$\frac{A}{D} = \frac{y_1(z_2 - z_3) + y_2(z_3 - z_1) + y_3(z_1 - z_2)}{-x_1(y_2z_3 - z_2y_3) - x_2(z_1y_3 - y_1z_3) - x_3(y_1z_2 - y_2z_1)}.$$

Thus the top line (numerator) of this equation gives us an expression for A and the bottom line (denominator) an expression for D. So as to obtain expressions for B and C we repeat this process – using the second and third rows of elements in the inverse matrix (Q^{-1}) in accordance with Eq. 7.8. In the next subsection, we consider the connection between these values and the components of the vector that lies at right-angles to a surface (the 'surface normal' vector).

7.4.2 The Normal Vector

'I've had a wonderful evening, but this wasn't it.'[13]

Consider a plane within a 3-D space which contains a point P whose location relative to the origin is given by the vector $\mathbf{p}$ such that $\mathbf{p} = x_1\mathbf{i} + y_1\mathbf{j} + z_1\mathbf{k}$. Let us also define a vector $\mathbf{n}$ that lies at right-angles to the plane. This vector is called the 'surface normal' and is orthogonal to any vector contained *within* the plane – such as a vector drawn from P to an arbitrary point, in the plane, Q (where the location of Q is defined by the position vector $\mathbf{q} = x\mathbf{i} + y\mathbf{j} + z\mathbf{k}$). These vectors are illustrated in Figure 7.11.

We will denote the surface normal vector as $\mathbf{n} = a\mathbf{i} + b\mathbf{j} + c\mathbf{k}$. A vector from P to Q (and which lies within the plane) can be expressed as $-\mathbf{p} + \mathbf{q}$ which equals:

$$-\mathbf{p} + \mathbf{q} = -(x_1\mathbf{i} + y_1\mathbf{j} + z_1\mathbf{k}) + (x\mathbf{i} + y\mathbf{j} + z\mathbf{k}) = (x - x_1)\mathbf{i} + (y - y_1)\mathbf{j} + (z - z_1)\mathbf{k}.$$

Since this vector is at right-angles to the surface normal, it follows that the scalar product of the two vectors is zero. That is:

$$\mathbf{n} \cdot (-\mathbf{p} + \mathbf{q}) = (a\mathbf{i} + b\mathbf{j} + c\mathbf{k}) \cdot ((x - x_1)\mathbf{i} + (y - y_1)\mathbf{j} + (z - z_1)\mathbf{k}) = 0.$$

Thus:

$$a(x - x_1) + b(y - y_1) + c(z - z_1) = 0. \tag{7.9}$$

This equation is generally referred to as the 'standard form' of expression for a plane in 3-D space. Expanding the terms in this equation gives:

$$ax + by + cz + (-ax_1 - by_1 - cz_1) = 0. \tag{7.10}$$

This is known as the 'general form' of equation for a plane in a 3-D space. This is equivalent to Eq. 7.3.

> Given the 'general form' of equation for a plane, the coefficients of x, y and z correspond to the components of the vector that lies at right-angles to plane.

---

[13] Attributed to Groucho Marx (1890–1977).

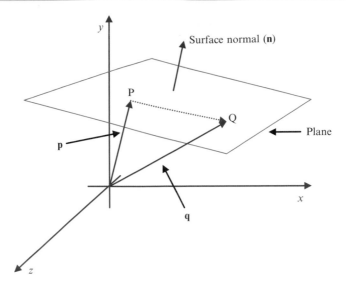

Figure 7.11 A plane in a 3-D space. P and Q are two points that are located on the plane and their respective position vectors are denoted by **p** and **q**. The broken arrowed line represents a vector drawn from P to Q. This vector lies in the plane and so lies at right-angles to the 'surface normal' vector (**n**). See text for discussion.

OTU Exercise 7.4: The Normal Vector

Determine the unit vector that lies at right-angles to the surface of the plane which is given by:

$$3x + 2y + 4z - 12 = 0.$$

7.4.3 Plane Representation Using Three Vectors

Recall that in Section 7.4.1 we developed an equation for a plane based on three non-collinear points. It is instructive to re-visit this discussion – but this time we will adopt a vector-based approach. This will lead us to the same result but will provide additional experience in vector operations.

Consider three points P, Q and R with respective position vectors **p, q** and **r**. We assume that these points lie on the plane whose equation we wish to determine. As indicated in Figure 7.12, we draw two vectors: one from P to Q and the other from P to R. We will denote these vectors as **e** and **f**. Recall discussion in Section 6.3 concerning the vector product – particularly OTU Exercise 6.6. In summary when we calculate the vector product of two vectors that lie in a plane, we obtain a new vector that lies at right-angles to the original pair. This provides us with a convenient means of determining the 'normal vector' to a plane. Thus if we calculate the vector product of **e** and **f** we obtain a vector that is orthogonal to both of them – as indicated in Figure 7.12, we denote this vector as **n**.

Therefore, assuming that vector **e** has components $x_e\mathbf{i} + y_e\mathbf{j} + z_e\mathbf{k}$ and those of vector **f** are $x_f\mathbf{i} + y_f\mathbf{j} + z_f\mathbf{k}$, we can write:

$$\mathbf{n} = \mathbf{e} \times \mathbf{f} = (x_e\mathbf{i} + y_e\mathbf{j} + z_e\mathbf{k}) \times (x_f\mathbf{i} + y_f\mathbf{j} + z_f\mathbf{k}).$$

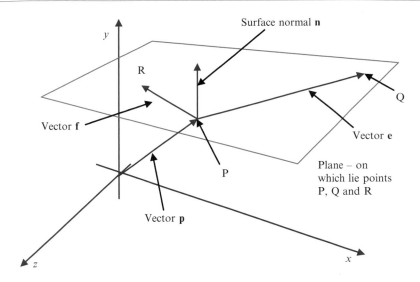

Figure 7.12 Points P, Q and R lie on the plane whose equation we wish to determine. We draw a vector from P to Q (labelled **e**) and a vector from P to R (labelled **f**). These two vectors lie in the plane. The vector **n** which lies at right-angles to the plane is determined by taking the vector (cross) product of vectors e and **f**. On the basis of discussion in Section 6.3, confirm the direction of vector **n**.

And on the basis of Eq. 6.15:

$$\mathbf{n} = (y_e z_f - z_e y_f)\mathbf{i} - (x_e z_f - z_e x_f)\mathbf{j} + (x_e y_f - y_e x_f)\mathbf{k}. \tag{7.11}$$

As an aside, recall that we can also write this in a more compact form – using Eq. 6.8:

$$n = \begin{vmatrix} \mathbf{i} & \mathbf{j} & \mathbf{k} \\ x_e & y_e & z_e \\ x_f & y_f & z_f \end{vmatrix}.$$

In turn this can be written as:

$$\mathbf{n} = \begin{vmatrix} y_e & z_e \\ y_f & z_f \end{vmatrix}\mathbf{i} - \begin{vmatrix} x_e & z_e \\ x_f & z_f \end{vmatrix}\mathbf{j} + \begin{vmatrix} x_e & y_e \\ x_f & y_f \end{vmatrix}\mathbf{k}. \tag{7.12}$$

Continuing with our derivation, let us introduce another point (S) that is positioned at an arbitrary location within the 3-D space with coordinates (x_s, y_s, z_s). If this point lies within the plane illustrated in Figure 7.12, then it follows that a vector drawn between S and any other point within the plane will lie at right-angles to the surface normal vector (**n**). Let us therefore suppose that we draw a vector from S to P – thereby generating a vector which we will denote **t**. We will assume that this vector has components given by $\mathbf{t} = x\mathbf{i} + y\mathbf{j} + z\mathbf{k}$. From previous discussion of the scalar product (Section 2.4.9) we know that when any two vectors are orthogonal, their scalar product is zero. Thus:

$$\mathbf{t} \cdot \mathbf{n} = 0,$$

and so:

$$\mathbf{t} \cdot \mathbf{n} = (x\mathbf{i} + y\mathbf{j} + z\mathbf{k}) \cdot ((y_e z_f - z_e y_f)\mathbf{i} - (x_e z_f - z_e x_f)\mathbf{j} + (x_e y_f - y_e x_f)\mathbf{k}) = 0,$$

– if, and only if, the point S lies on the plane defined by points P, Q and R. Consequently, this equation defines all points in the plane – i.e. the plane itself. Calculating this scalar product, we obtain:

$$\mathbf{t} \cdot \mathbf{n} = x(y_e z_f - z_e y_f) - y(x_e z_f - z_e x_f) + z(x_e y_f - y_e x_f) = 0.$$

We can write this in a more compact form using three, 2 by 2 determinants:

$$\mathbf{t} \cdot \mathbf{n} = x\begin{vmatrix} y_e & z_e \\ y_f & z_f \end{vmatrix} - y\begin{vmatrix} x_e & z_e \\ x_f & z_f \end{vmatrix} + z\begin{vmatrix} x_e & y_e \\ x_f & y_f \end{vmatrix} = 0.$$

Consider the middle determinant which equals $x_e z_f - z_e x_f$. We can re-write this as $-(z_e x_f - x_e z_f)$. This enables us to change the sign of this central term – in which case the equation becomes:

$$\mathbf{t} \cdot \mathbf{n} = x\begin{vmatrix} y_e & z_e \\ y_f & z_f \end{vmatrix} + y\begin{vmatrix} z_e & x_e \\ z_f & x_f \end{vmatrix} + z\begin{vmatrix} x_e & y_e \\ x_f & y_f \end{vmatrix} = 0.$$

So far we have not assigned to points P, Q and R actual coordinates (thereby specifying their locations relative to the origin) – we assume these are (x_p, y_p, z_p), (x_q, y_q, z_q) and (x_r, y_r, z_r) respectively. Consider x, y and z in the above equation. These values correspond to the respective magnitudes of the x, y and z components of the vector $\mathbf{t}$. Therefore, since this vector has end points at x_s and x_p, we can write $x = x_s - x_p$. We can do likewise for y and z and for all the other vector component magnitudes appearing in the above equation. Consequently, the equation for the scalar product of $\mathbf{t}$ and $\mathbf{n}$ becomes:

$$(x_s - x_p)\begin{vmatrix} y_q - y_p & z_q - z_p \\ y_r - y_p & z_r - z_p \end{vmatrix} + (y_s - y_p)\begin{vmatrix} z_q - z_p & x_q - x_p \\ z_r - z_p & x_r - x_p \end{vmatrix} + (z_s - z_p)\begin{vmatrix} x_q - x_p & y_q - y_p \\ x_r - x_p & y_r - y_p \end{vmatrix} = 0$$

By expanding the brackets, we can re-arrange this equation:

$$x_s\begin{vmatrix} y_q - y_p & z_q - z_p \\ y_r - y_p & z_r - z_p \end{vmatrix} + y_s\begin{vmatrix} z_q - z_p & x_q - x_p \\ z_r - z_p & x_r - x_p \end{vmatrix} + z_p\begin{vmatrix} x_q - x_p & y_q - y_p \\ x_r - x_p & y_r - y_p \end{vmatrix} + D = 0, \qquad (7.13)$$

where D is given by:

$$D = -x_p\begin{vmatrix} y_q - y_p & z_q - z_p \\ y_r - y_p & z_r - z_p \end{vmatrix} - y_p\begin{vmatrix} z_q - z_p & x_q - x_p \\ z_r - z_p & x_r - x_p \end{vmatrix} - z_p\begin{vmatrix} x_q - x_p & y_q - y_p \\ x_r - x_p & y_r - y_p \end{vmatrix}.$$

Notice that Eq. 7.13 has the same form as Eq. 7.3 (the general form of equation for a plane in a 3-D space):

$$Ax + By + Cz + D = 0.$$

Consequently, we can relate each of the three determinants given above to the corresponding coefficients – A, B and C. For example, A is given by:

$$A = \begin{vmatrix} y_q - y_p & z_q - z_p \\ y_r - y_p & z_r - z_p \end{vmatrix} = (y_q - y_p)(z_r - z_p) - (z_q - z_p)(y_r - y_p).$$

Multiplying the brackets and simplifying we obtain:

$$A = y_q z_r - y_q z_p - y_p z_r - z_q y_r + z_q y_p + z_p y_r.$$

Factorising this expression yields:

$$A = y_p(z_q - z_r) + y_q(z_r - z_p) + y_r(z_p - z_q).$$

Disregarding the different symbols that are used, this equation is identical to the equation for A that is presented at the end of Section 7.4.1. Similarly, and as we would expect, the two approaches are in agreement in the equations that they give for B, C and D.

7.4.4 Plane Representation: Parametric Form

We can represent a plane by specifying the location of a point on the plane and two non-collinear vectors which lie in the plane – see Figure 7.13. Here, we define the location of a point C (with position vector $\mathbf{c}$) which lies on the plane. In addition, two vectors (denoted $\mathbf{a}$ and $\mathbf{b}$) are also specified. Clearly, we can reach any point on the plane by adding to the vector $\mathbf{c}$ (which takes us to the plane) certain proportions of vectors $\mathbf{a}$ and $\mathbf{b}$. If we denote the 'amounts' of the vectors $\mathbf{a}$ and $\mathbf{b}$ needed to reach an arbitrary point P (with position vector $\mathbf{p}$ and vector components $x\mathbf{i} + y\mathbf{j} + z\mathbf{k}$) on the plane by λ and ε respectively, then we can write:

$$\mathbf{p} = \mathbf{c} + \lambda\mathbf{a} + \varepsilon\mathbf{b}. \tag{7.14}$$

Thus λ and ε are scalar quantities which are used to provide a linear combination of vectors $\mathbf{a}$ and $\mathbf{b}$. Note that if we fix one of these values (e.g. $\lambda = 1$) then we obtain:

$$\mathbf{p} = (\mathbf{c} + \mathbf{a}) + \varepsilon\mathbf{b}.$$

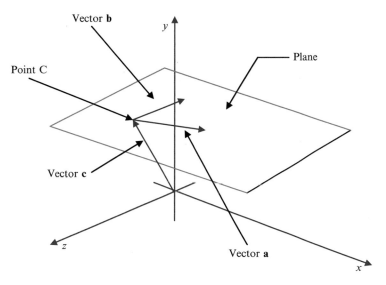

Figure 7.13 Here we represent a plane using a point on the plane (C) and two non-collinear vectors (**a** and **b**) which lie in the plane. We can reach any point on the plane by adding to vector **c** appropriate proportions of vectors **a** and **b**. This allows us to represent the plane using a parametric equation.

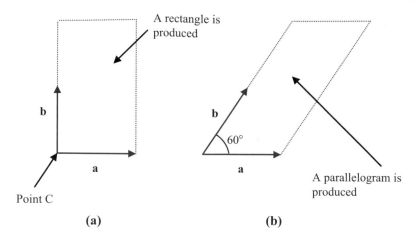

Figure 7.14 The generation of two different shapes. In (a) the two vectors are orthogonal and in (b) the angle between them is $\approx 60°$.

This represents the parametric equation for a straight line (recall Section 2.3.1) with ε representing the 'parameter'.

Frequently, we need to specify not only the plane's location and orientation but also its actual extent. In the case that $-\infty \leq \lambda \leq \infty$ and $-\infty \leq \varepsilon \leq \infty$, then the plane has no boundaries – it has an infinite extent. On the other hand, we can restrict the extent of the plane by placing limitations on the range of values that may be assigned to these two parameters. By way of example, suppose that the vectors **a** and **b** have the same magnitude and are arranged to lie at right-angles to each other. If we now limit the parameters to $0 \leq \lambda \leq 1$, $0 \leq \varepsilon \leq 2$ a rectangle will be produced – see Figure 7.14(a). In the case that we change the angle between the vectors (e.g. to $60°$) and maintain the same range of values for the parameters, a parallelogram will be formed (Figure 7.14(b)).

OTU Exercise 7.5: A Triangular Surface

On the basis of the above discussion how would you arrange vectors **a** and **b** and define the values of parameters λ and ε to generate a right-angle triangle?

Hint: Would the values of the parameters be related in some way?

7.4.5　Plane Representation: Scalar Product Form

Recall from Section 7.4.1 that the general form of the equation for a plane is given by:

$$Ax + By + Cz + D = 0.$$

Here, x, y and z represent the coordinates of an arbitrary point on the plane. Let us denote this point as P and represent its location by the position vector **p** where $\mathbf{p} = x\mathbf{i} + y\mathbf{j} + z\mathbf{k}$. In Section 7.4.2, we demonstrated that the coefficients of x, y and z in the above equation correspond to the components of the vector that lies at right-angles to the plane – i.e. the surface normal vector (**n**). Thus:

$$\mathbf{n} = A\mathbf{i} + B\mathbf{j} + C\mathbf{k}.$$

Recall from Section 2.4.9 that the scalar product of two vectors (say, $\mathbf{a} = a_x\mathbf{i} + a_y\mathbf{j} + a_z\mathbf{k}$ and $\mathbf{b} = b_x\mathbf{i} + b_y\mathbf{j} + b_z\mathbf{k}$) is given by:

$$\mathbf{a} \cdot \mathbf{b} = a_x b_x + a_y b_y + a_z b_z = |\mathbf{a}||\mathbf{b}| \cos\theta,$$

where θ denotes the angle between the two vectors ($0 \le \theta \le 180°$). Thus we can re-write the general equation for a plane in terms of the scalar product of the surface normal vector and the position vector to point P:

$$Ax + By + Cz + D = \mathbf{n} \cdot \mathbf{p} + D = 0.$$

Thus we can represent the plane in terms of a scalar product:

$$\mathbf{n} \cdot \mathbf{p} + D = 0. \tag{7.15}$$

In addition, from the above expression for the scalar product we can write:

$$Ax + By + Cz + D = |\mathbf{n}||\mathbf{p}| \cos\theta + D = 0.$$

If we divide all the terms in this equation by $|\mathbf{n}|$ we obtain:

$$\frac{Ax}{|\mathbf{n}|} + \frac{By}{|\mathbf{n}|} + \frac{Cz}{|\mathbf{n}|} + \frac{D}{|\mathbf{n}|} = |\mathbf{p}| \cos\theta + \frac{D}{|\mathbf{n}|} = 0.$$

In the case that $|\mathbf{n}| = 1$ (i.e. that we are dealing with a unit vector – in which case $\sqrt{A^2 + B^2 + C^2} = 1$) then we can re-write the right-hand part of the above equation as:

$$|\mathbf{p}| \cos\theta = -D. \tag{7.16}$$

In the case that the angle (θ) between vectors **n** and **p** is zero then this equation becomes:

$$|\mathbf{p}| \cos 0° = |\mathbf{p}| = -D$$

Thus, under these circumstances, the magnitude of the vector **p** equals the magnitude of D. Since the angle between the vectors **p** and **n** is zero, it follows that both vectors lie at 90° to the surface of the plane. This situation is illustrated in Figure 7.15 – where for clarity we illustrate the plane in cross-section.

> The magnitude of the term D in the general equation for a plane cor-
> responds to the length of the line drawn from the origin to a point
> on the plane such that it meets the plane at 90°. This is referred to as
> the perpendicular distance of the plane from the origin. This applies as
> long as the coefficients A, B and C in the general equation for the plane
> represent the components of a surface normal of unit length.

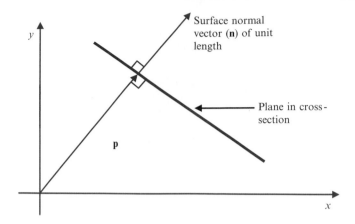

Figure 7.15 Here, for clarity, a plane is drawn in cross-section. By definition the surface normal vector (**n**) lies at right-angles to the plane. Since in the situation shown here, the angle between the normal vector and the position vector (**p**) is zero, it follows that the vector **p** is also orthogonal to the plane. See text for discussion.

OTU Exercise 7.6: Determining the Plane Equation and Perpendicular Distance

Consider a plane for which the normal vector is given by $\mathbf{n} = \mathbf{i} + \mathbf{j} + \mathbf{k}$ and on which a point P is located. The location of this point is given by the position vector $\mathbf{p} = 2\mathbf{j} + \mathbf{k}$. Determine an equation for this plane and the perpendicular distance of the plane from the origin.

7.5 Polygonal Representation: Some General Remarks

'If we knew what it was we were doing,
it would not be called research, would it?'[14]

In this section we briefly discuss issues concerning the use of a mesh of polygons for object representation and aspects of the modelling process in general.

7.5.1 Purpose

In previous sections we have considered the production of the visible image to be the *raison d'etre* for the creation of the model describing an object's basic geometry. Indeed the overall modelling process provides the fundamental spatial, geometric and surface characteristics upon which we draw when generating an image for depiction on some form of display. However, this often represents only one aspect of the model's purpose. For example, in the case of computer-aided design (CAD), an operator may interact with the system to construct the model of a

---

[14] Attributed to Albert Einstein (1879–1955).

component that is to be turned into a physical entity using an automated or semi-automated process. Thus, for example output from a computer system may be applied to a 'numerically controlled' machine via which a physical rendition of the object is created. In this case, when considering the level of accuracy needed to describe an object, we cannot simply concern ourselves with the level of accuracy required to produce a visually satisfactory image but must also consider the accuracy demanded in the fabrication process. By way of a simple example, consider the production of a crankshaft. Here, the machined bearing surfaces must exhibit a smooth (continuous) curvature and must have dimensions within required tolerance. Although from a visualisation point of view, a polygonal representation of the bearing surfaces may be satisfactory, the use of a physical multi-faceted surface would in practice be disastrous!

In many situations an image scene does not comprise a collection of static entities – but rather objects that move, and with which the operator can interact. In this context, object collision is of vital interest and we must not only be able to detect when collisions take place but also, for example, determine the trajectories of objects following a collision. The inclusion of haptic feedback (see Chapter 10) places additional demands on the overall representation process. For example, we may wish to assign to different objects (or to different regions of an object) specific frictional properties and thereby enable a user employing a haptic probe to 'feel' different forms of surface. Furthermore, although the approximation of a curve by a mesh of planar surfaces may be satisfactory from a visual perspective, it may negatively impact on the haptic experience – geometrical discontinuities being revealed through our sense of touch.

In summary, the information that must be included in the representation of object geometry and the scene as a whole is not solely governed by our wish to generate a visually acceptable image but also by issues such as the ways in which we may wish to interact with the image scene, animation and the ultimate purpose of the system – e.g. the production of a design that can be directly manufactured by automated machinery.

7.5.2 Interaction

Consider that we use a mesh of polygons to represent an object comprising several planar and curved surfaces. We could define each planar surface by a single polygon. If we assume that in our representation we use triangles, then each rectangular surface could be formed using two triangles. Here, we note that the number of triangles needed is not necessarily defined by the size of each surface. On the other hand, in the case of the curved surfaces, the number of triangles required relates (or should relate) to the degree of surface curvature – the greater the curvature, the larger is the number of triangles that are needed to produce a smooth representation. The use of polygons for the modelling of curved surfaces represents a 'piecewise linear approximation'. Consequently, should we attempt to represent a highly curved surface using only a small number of polygons, we can expect there to be a lack of accuracy – the polygonal representation of the surface differing significantly from the continuously curving surface that we are modelling. On the other hand if we use a larger number of smaller polygons then the accuracy of the piecewise linear approximation is improved. However, as discussed in Section 8.7, shading techniques are available via which we can reduce the visibility of the geometrical discontinuities that exist between adjacent polygons – hence we can in effect blend polygons thereby reducing the visible impact of the discrete nature of the polygonal representation.

Suppose that we wish to create and display a model of a rectangular block. As indicated above, we could represent each face using a single rectangle or, for example, two triangles. We now interact with this block in such a way as to deform its shape. For example, we could apply a force between two opposite surfaces so as to compress the block (and so cause the other four surfaces to 'bulge') or apply a torque so as to twist the block. If we wish to realistically depict the resulting deformation, it is clear that we now need to display an object that no longer comprises six planar faces – we have introduced a curved geometry – but will the polygons used in defining the initial geometrical shape of the block accommodate the depiction of curved surfaces?

In fact even changing the location of a single vertex within a polygon mesh can cause difficulty. For example, suppose that we have a curved surface represented by polygons and that via an interaction process we are able to increase its curvature (by selecting and dragging an appropriate vertex). Although we are able in this way to change the curvature, the visual result may be far from satisfactory – the 'polygon resolution' may no longer properly support the degree of curvature of the manipulated surface.

7.5.3 Number of Polygons

It is by no means unusual for the polygonal representation of an object to comprise hundreds of thousands of polygons. The larger the number of polygons employed, the larger is the data structure used to store the geometric model and the greater the time required to render the object and produce each different frame of the visible image (in the case of animated image sequences and real-time interaction scenarios this can be particularly important). Consequently increasing the number of polygons used to enhance the geometric accuracy of the polygonal model (in as much as it matches the 'true' representation) is not necessarily desirable. In fact, it may be a pointless undertaking as we need to also consider the actual size at which an object is to be displayed. By way of a simple example consider a bird in flight. At a distance the bird is simply perceived as a dark dot or a very small and indistinct entity. It is only as the bird gets closer that we are able to perceive its form in greater detail. This type of situation applies in computer graphics – there is little point in rendering large numbers of polygons if the results of this process are to be displayed by only a small number of screen pixels. Conversely, when initially defining an object's geometric model, we will often not know the actual size at which it is to be displayed (and hence the number of pixels that will be devoted to its depiction). Furthermore, in the case that an operator has the ability to interactively zoom, display size cannot be pre-defined.

This type of problem occurs in various applications such as computer games, flight simulators and the like. Consider the case of a commercial flight simulator. As with the bird mentioned above, an approaching aircraft may when represented at a distance via an (electronic) cockpit window, simply appear as a dark dot against a blue or white background. Creating a model to represent this distant view is therefore trivial. However, as the aircraft moves closer, it will occupy a greater portion of the cockpit window and we expect a gradual increase in the level of visible detail. In the extreme situation (corresponding to a near collision!), we would expect the approaching aircraft to be represented in great detail – its representation filling the window. Given that the simulator must operate in real time and that increasing the number of polygons used to represent an object increases the rendering time (needed to create the visible image), we are left with a dilemma – how do we best match the changing level of visible image content to make most efficient use of processing resources? One approach is to use several different geometrical models to describe an object – each comprising a different number of polygons and thereby a different level of detail. In this way we can ensure that the number of polygons is not overly excessive – especially when considered in terms of the actual visible image size and hence the number of pixels that will be employed in its depiction. However, this approach may result in visible image disturbance as we simply switch from one model to another. This is obviously undesirable as it may interrupt an operator's concentration and hence the sense of immersion. In short, this simple approach fails to encourage (and is in fact contrary to) the 'suspension of disbelief' (recall Section 1.2). Clearly, it is preferable to arrange for a non-abrupt transition such that one model gradually 'blends' into another.

7.6 Surface Construction Using Bézier Patches

In this section we briefly consider the formation of space curves using 'Bézier patches'. Recall previous discussion in Section 4.4 in relation to the formation of Bézier curves in which they are described using the following compact expression:

$$\mathbf{p}(t) = \sum_{k=0}^{n-1} \mathbf{p}_k h_k(t). \tag{7.17}$$

Here, $\mathbf{p}(t)$ represents a position vector to points on the curve and n the number of points that we are employing to define the curve. Thus if we employ four points, their respective position vectors are given by $\mathbf{p}_0$, $\mathbf{p}_1$, $\mathbf{p}_2$ and $\mathbf{p}_3$. The 'blending functions' are represented by $h_k(t)$ and as we previously explained, these functions scale the contribution that the position vectors ($\mathbf{p}_0$ to $\mathbf{p}_3$) make in defining the overall shape of the curve. For example, in the case that $n = 4$, $\mathbf{p}(t)$ is given by:

$$\mathbf{p}(t) = (1 - t)^3 \mathbf{p}_0 + 3t(1 - t)^2 \mathbf{p}_1 + 3t^2(1 - t)\mathbf{p}_2 + t^3\mathbf{p}_3.$$

We can readily use Bézier curves to form smoothly curving surfaces whose 3-D shape can be adjusted by the manipulation of control points. To provide an insight into how this can be achieved, it is convenient to employ a simple analogy. Let us suppose that we take a number of strips of elastic material and lay these out to form a regular mesh. At each point at which one elastic strip crosses another we apply some glue and in addition, we attach the ends of the strips to a rigid frame (see Figure 7.16). Thus the mesh is initially planar. In this analogy, each place at which one strip crosses another is intended to represent some form of 'control point' and by pushing or pulling at these points, we can create a space curve. A key point is that as we move the position of a control point we modify the curvature of the entire mesh – each point acts on the mesh as a whole.

In a similar way (although it is important not to take our analogy too far), we can create a complex smoothly curving surface patch using two sets of Bézier curves (cubic Bézier curves are commonly employed (recall these are defined by two end points and two additional control points)) – one set being equivalent to the horizontal lengths of elastic material indicated in Figure 7.16 and the other corresponding to the vertical strips. The two sets of curves are not independent of each other and the location of a point on a bi-cubic[15] Bézier surface is defined by the parametric vector function:

$$\mathbf{p}(u, v) = \sum_{j=0}^{3} \sum_{k=0}^{3} \mathbf{p}_{j,k} h_j(v) h_k(u). \tag{7.18}$$

---

[15] Bi-cubic indicates that cubic Bézier curves are used for both sets of curves.

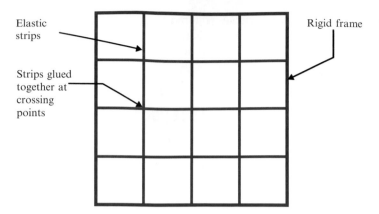

Figure 7.16 A simple analogy in which a mesh is formed using lengths of an elastic material. We consider each place at which these strips cross to represent some form of control point. By pushing or pulling at these points (i.e. by applying a force that is at right-angles to the surface of the planar mesh), we can change the shape of the mesh and so create a curved surface. Note that the applied force has an effect across the entire mesh.

At first glance this equation may appear a little complicated (!) and so it is worth briefly examining its foundations and significance. Let us consider that we have a set of cubic Bézier curves (returning to our analogy, we will assume that these loosely correspond to the vertical strips of elastic material depicted in Figure 7.16). We denote the locations of the control points on the first of these curves by the position vectors $\mathbf{p}_{0,0}$, $\mathbf{p}_{0,1}$, $\mathbf{p}_{0,2}$, and $\mathbf{p}_{0,3}$ (thus, for example, the position vector $\mathbf{p}_{0,0}$ defines the location of the control point $P_{0,0}$ shown in Figure 7.17). The position vector defining the location of an arbitrary control point may be denoted $\mathbf{p}_{j,k}$. where j denotes a particular Bézier curve and k the actual control point on the curve.

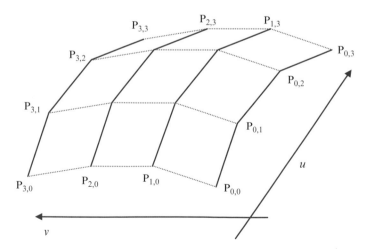

Figure 7.17 Here, we show the control points for a set of four cubic Bézier curves. The four control points corresponding to each individual curve are connected by the lines denoted in bold typeface. For clarity, we have only labelled the control points that lie on the periphery of the patch. In general terms we denote an arbitrary control point as $P_{j,k}$ (with position vector $\mathbf{p}_{j,k}$) where in this example j and k may have the values 0, 1, 2, 3. Each of these curves is a function of the parameter u.

We assume that the set of Bézier curves referred to in Figure 7.17 are each a function of the parameter u and so on the basis of Eq. 7.17, we can express the location of points on this set of curves in the following way:

$$\mathbf{p_j}(u) = \sum_{k=0}^{3} \mathbf{p}_{j,k} h_k(u), \quad \text{where} \quad j = 0, 1, 2, 3 \quad \text{and} \quad 0 \le u \le 1 \tag{7.19}$$

If, for example, we are referring to the curve created by the right-hand set of control points indicated in Figure 7.17, we would set j to zero and would therefore obtain:

$$\mathbf{p}(u) = \mathbf{p}_{0,0} h_0(u) + \mathbf{p}_{0,1} h_1(u) + \mathbf{p}_{0,2} h_2(u) + \mathbf{p}_{0,3} h_3(u).$$

The values of the blending functions ($h_k(u)$) are given in Table 4.3.

In order to create a surface, we could use an interpolation technique to define the surface profile between the set of Bézier curves that we have formed. By way of an analogy consider the construction of the wing of a model aeroplane. The set of Bézier curves could represent the wing ribs and we may use a covering of tissue, fabric etc. to form the actual wing surface. In this case, we are effectively interpolating the curvature of the wing on the basis of the shape and relative locations of the set of wing ribs that are in place. However, in the case of a Bézier surface, the initial set of Bézier curves is used to define the location of the control points of a Bézier curve (which lies at right-angles to the initial set of curves) and this curve is used to sweep-out and so define the surface.

When encountered for the first time, this can sound a little confusing so let's take a simple example of how this process may work. Assuming that we know the position vectors that define the location of the control points illustrated in Figure 7.17, we can select a particular value for the parameter u (remember that this parameter is in the range $0 \le u \le 1$) and calculate the location of a 'corresponding' point on each of the Bézier curves. These four points are then used as control points for a new Bézier curve. If we repeat this process for different values of u, we can create a set of such curves. Looking at this from another viewpoint, we take a single Bézier curve and sweep out the profile of the surface. During the sweep process, the shape of this curve is likely to continuously change – it being determined by the instantaneous position of its control points (which are defined by the original set of curves!). Slater *et al.* [2002] describe this succinctly:

'Hence the Bézier surface may be thought of as a Bézier curve of Bézier curves.'

If we assume that the swept curve is a function of a parameter v (see Figure 7.17), then the location ($\mathbf{p}'(v)$) of the set of points which comprise this curve is given by:

$$\mathbf{p}'(v) = \sum_{j=0}^{3} \mathbf{p}_j h_j(v).$$

Inserting Eq. 7.19 into this equation allows us to eliminate $\mathbf{p}_j$:

$$\mathbf{p}'(u, v) = \sum_{j=0}^{3} h_j(v) \sum_{k=0}^{3} \mathbf{p}_{j,k} h_k(u).$$

By making one small adjustment to the equation, we obtain Eq. 7.18. Notice that $h_j(v)$ is not effected by the right-hand summation operation (which operates on different vales of k and not on values of j). Consequently, we can re-write this equation as:

$$\mathbf{p}'(u, v) = \sum_{j=0}^{3} \sum_{k=0}^{3} \mathbf{p}_{j,k} h_j(v) h_k(u),$$

which corresponds to Eq. 7.18. The depiction of a Bézier surface using a mesh is quite a straightforward undertaking and is based on the judicious use of the two parameters u and v. Referring to Figure 7.17, in order to create curved mesh lines in the direction of the original set of Bézier curves we know that each line will have a certain (constant) value of v. In short, for this set of lines v determines the location of the curve and u defines points on the curve. Similarly in the case of mesh curves that are to run in the direction of the 'swept' Bézier curve, the location of each is determined by the parameter u and v defines points on a particular curve.

Finally, note that in order to create a bi-cubic Bézier surface, we have employed 16 control points (if we were to form a bi-quadratic surface, nine control points would be needed). In addition, we can employ curves of different order in the two directions (e.g. a set of cubic curves and a forth order 'swept' curve). The above equation can readily handle changes in the order of the curves used – we simply need to alter the limits in of the summations.

7.6.1 Using Matrices to Represent Bézier Curves and Surfaces

'Many people hear voices when no-one is there.
Some of them are called mad and are shut up in rooms
where they stare at the walls all day.
Others are called writers and they do pretty much the same thing.'[16]

It is often convenient to describe Bézier curves and surfaces using a matrix notation. Consider the case of a cubic curve. As indicated at the beginning of this section the position vector $\mathbf{p}(t)$ to points on a cubic Bézier curve is given by:

$$\mathbf{p}(t) = (1 - t)^3 \, \mathbf{p}_0 + 3t \, (1 - t)^2 \, \mathbf{p}_1 + 3t^2 \, (1 - t) \, \mathbf{p}_2 + t^3 \mathbf{p}_3,$$

where t denotes the parameter. If we expand each of these terms, we obtain:

$$\mathbf{p}(t) = \left(-t^3 + 3t^2 - 3t + 1 \right) \mathbf{p}_0 + \left(3t^3 - 6t^2 + 3t \right) \mathbf{p}_1 + \left(-3t^3 + 3t^2 \right) \mathbf{p}_2 + t^3 \mathbf{p}_3.$$

We can express these four terms as the product of three matrices:

$$\begin{bmatrix} t^3 & t^2 & t & 1 \end{bmatrix} \begin{bmatrix} -1 & 3 & -3 & 1 \\ 3 & -6 & 3 & 0 \\ -3 & 3 & 0 & 0 \\ 1 & 0 & 0 & 0 \end{bmatrix} \begin{bmatrix} \mathbf{p}_0 \\ \mathbf{p}_1 \\ \mathbf{p}_2 \\ \mathbf{p}_3 \end{bmatrix}.$$

This provides us with a compact expression for the terms used to describe the curve.

---

[16] Attributed to Meg Chittenden.

OTU Exercise 7.7: Matrix Representation of a Quadratic Bézier Curve

Produce a matrix expression for the terms that describe the position vector to points on a quadratic Bézier curve.

Hint: You may wish to look back to Section 4.4.

We can also use matrices to describe a Bézier surface. For example in the case of a bi-cubic Bézier surface we could use the following expression:

$$\begin{bmatrix} v^3 & v^2 & v & 1 \end{bmatrix} \begin{bmatrix} -1 & 3 & -3 & 1 \\ 3 & -6 & 3 & 0 \\ -3 & 3 & 0 & 0 \\ 1 & 0 & 0 & 0 \end{bmatrix} \begin{bmatrix} p_{0,0} & p_{0,1} & p_{0,2} & p_{0,3} \\ p_{1,0} & p_{1,1} & p_{1,2} & p_{1,3} \\ p_{2,0} & p_{2,1} & p_{2,2} & p_{2,3} \\ p_{3,0} & p_{3,1} & p_{3,2} & p_{3,3} \end{bmatrix} \begin{bmatrix} -1 & 3 & -3 & 1 \\ 3 & -6 & 3 & 0 \\ -3 & 3 & 0 & 0 \\ 1 & 0 & 0 & 0 \end{bmatrix} \begin{bmatrix} u^3 \\ u_2 \\ u \\ 1 \end{bmatrix}$$

Notice that when multiplied, the two right-hand matrices provide us with the terms in the Bernstein Polynomial relating to curves with the parameter u – in Eq. 7.18 these terms are denoted $h_k(u)$ Similarly the two left-hand matrices generate the terms in a Bernstein Polynomial (denoted $h_j(v)$) relating to the parameter v. The central matrix represents position vectors $\mathbf{p_{j,k}}$ in Eq. 7.18.

This matrix form of representation is convenient and given position vectors to the 16 control points we can readily determine the position vector to any point on the Bézier surface. For related discussion see Mortenson [1985].

7.6.2 Joining Bézier Surfaces

Complex surface geometries may be formed by joining together a number of Bézier patches. Recall previous discussion concerning connecting Bézier curves (Section 4.6). As we indicated, when two curves are joined we usually require a smooth (seamless) transition from one to the other. This is achieved by ensuring that the end point of one curve coincides with the end point of the second curve (thus there is no sudden break in the composite curve (C^0 continuity)) and by arranging that the endpoint and adjacent control point of each of the two curves lie on a straight line (C^1 continuity). As we have seen, these requirements arise because:

1. A Bézier curve passes through the two endpoints.
2. At the endpoint, the line connecting the endpoint to the adjacent control point forms a tangent to the curve.

We can apply similar conditions to two Bézier patches that are to be joined and so ensure C^0 and C^1 continuity. Specifically:

1. **Zero Order Continuity**: This is achieved by ensuring that the control points located along the joining boundaries are coincident – see Figure 7.18.
2. **First Order Continuity**: Here, a sufficient condition is that at the joint, the lines connecting the endpoints with the adjacent control points are collinear.

This second requirement imposes quite a severe constraint and may negatively impacts on the designer's freedom to manipulate surfaces. In this context Watt [2000] writes:

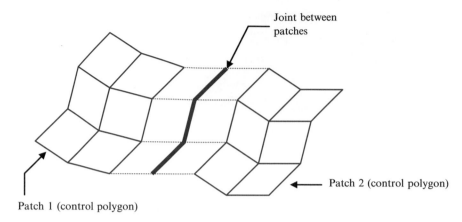

Figure 7.18 The joining of two Bézier patches. In order to obtain C^0 and C^1 continuity we ensure that the control points along the joining boundary (denoted by the bold line segments) are coincident and that at the joint, the lines connecting the endpoints to the adjacent control points (these are indicated by the broken lines) are collinear.

'*Faux, in 1979, pointed out that in CAD contexts, this constraint is severe, if a composite surface is constructed from a set of Bézier patches. For example, a composite surface might be designed by constructing a single patch and working outwards from it. Joining two patches along a common boundary implies that eight of the control points for the second patch are already fixed, and joining a patch to two existing patches implies that 12 of the control points are fixed.*

A slightly less restrictive joining condition was developed by Bézier in 1972. In this patch, corners have positional but not gradient continuity. However, tangent vectors of edges meeting at a corner must be co-planar. Even with this marginally greater flexibility, there are still problems with the design of composite surfaces.'

Surface patches may also be formed using B-splines – see, for example, texts such as Watt [2000], Hill [1990], Newman and Sproull [1981], Slater *et al.* [2002] – this latter book provides an interesting discussion concerning the formation of triangular Bézier patches.

7.7 Constructive Solid Geometry

'*I shall be telling this with a sigh somewhere ages and ages hence:*
Two roads diverged in a wood, and I –
I took the one less travelled by, and that has made all the difference.'[17]

In the case of 'constructive solid geometry' (CSG), an operator is provided with a set of primitive components (such as a cube, cylinder, cone, sphere etc.) from which more complex objects may be formed. An important difference between the B-rep approach and the CSG technique is that in the case of the former we model only surface characteristics whereas in the case of CSG we consider objects as volumes – each object comprises a set of points within a 3-D space. Consequently, in the case that we wish to bring together a number of primitives, we simply unite the points used in their representation.

---

[17] Robert Lee Frost (1874–1963).

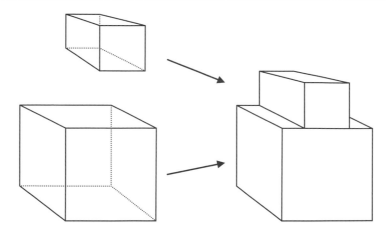

Figure 7.19 The formation of an object by bringing together two primitive elements. In this simple case we amalgamate two rectangular blocks. This is referred to as a Boolean 'union' operation.

For example, consider a trivial situation in which we wish to create a model of an object comprising two rectangular blocks – as shown in Figure 7.19. By means of an interactive design interface we can specify the dimensions of these two blocks together with their relative position and orientation. Once we have defined these parameters, we can employ Boolean operations to create the set of points that represent the overall object.

Let us briefly consider the nature of such operations. Suppose that we have two sets of elements that we will refer to as set A and set B. We will assume that set A has three members – the numbers 1, 2 and 3 and that set B has 4 members: 3, 4, 5 and 6. We can represent these sets as:

$$A = \{1, 2, 3\}, \quad B = \{3, 4, 5, 6\}.$$

Of course these two sets can comprise anything – types of car, types of fruit, points in a 3-D space – the members of a set need not be numerical elements. If we now wish to form a new set (let's denote this as set C) which represents the set of elements that belong to either set A or set B, we undertake a Boolean 'union' operation. This is generally denoted by means of the symbol '∪' and we would therefore represent this operation by:

$$A \cup B = C.$$

Note that when we perform this operation we are creating a set that comprises the members of A and the members of B – but elements that are common to both sets are included only one. Thus in case of this example:

$$C = \{1, 2, 3, 4, 5, 6\}.$$

In the case of CSG, the union operation enables us to join together object primitives and so construct more complex objects.

When machining physical objects, we often need to cut away bulk material, create holes – and the like. In Figure 7.20 we illustrate a scenario in which we wish to cut a rectangular hole within a rectangular block. In CSG this can be achieved by taking the Boolean difference between two primitives. The difference between two sets is generally indicated using '−' symbol. If we introduce set D which is given by D = {4, 5}, the difference between sets B and D could be

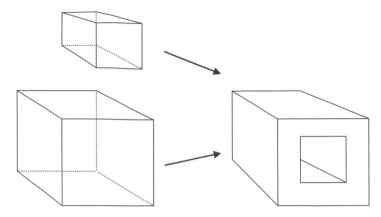

Figure 7.20 The formation of an object by means of two primitive elements. In this simple case we use the smaller of the blocks to define the shape and extent of a region that is to be cut out of the larger block. This is referred to as a Boolean 'difference' operation.

expressed as:

$$B - D = C.$$

In this case set C would be given by: $C = \{3, 6\}$. By way of a further example, we may wish to create a length of tube with a certain diameter and wall thickness. This can be easily achieved by using a cylindrical object primitive. We simply specify two cylinders of different radii, locate these about a common central axis and perform a Boolean difference operation!

Another Boolean operation is referred to as the 'intersection' of two sets (denoted '∩'). In this case we identify the elements that are common to the sets. For example, $A \cap B = \{3\}$ – as this is the only element contained in both sets.

In the above discussion we have overlooked a problem that can occur when we apply basic mathematical set operators. Consider the situation indicated in Figure 7.21 in which we wish to determine the intersection of two shapes – which, for simplicity we will assume are two-dimensional. On the left hand side we depict the two shapes (labelled A and B) separately and in the central illustration we show their position relative to one another. Here, for clarity, shape B is depicted with a stronger outline. On the right of the illustration we show the results of the Boolean intersection operation. As may be seen, an unexpected 'dangling edge' has been generated. This sort of problem can occur when all or part of the boundary of one object coincides with all or part of the boundary of another object. For related discussion see, for example, Slater *et al.* [2002].

Clearly the CSG approach strongly supports important aspects of interactive design. In addition, this technique enables us to not only define the geometric shape and form of an object but also to create a modelling history containing the sequence of tasks that we have employed during the process. This may relate to the sequence of operations that must be performed when producing the physical entity.

As indicated above, the CSG approach represents objects as points within a 3-D space. Consequently each object is defined in terms of its spatial occupancy. For example, consider the case of a sphere (which is likely to be available to the designer as an object primitive). Its spatial occupancy may be defined using a single inequality:

$$x^2 + y^2 + z^2 \leq r^2.$$

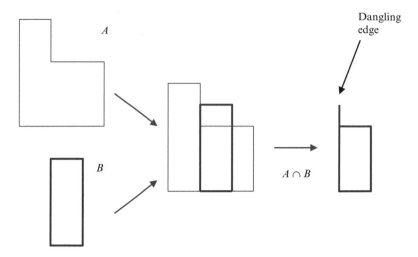

Figure 7.21 Here, we depict two simple objects labelled A and B. In the central illustration we show their relative positions and on the right-hand side indicate the result of performing a Boolean intersection operation. This leads to the formation of an undesirable 'dangling edge'.

Where r denotes the radius and the sphere is centred on the origin. Thus given an arbitrary point with coordinates (x_1, y_1, z_1), we can readily determine whether or not the point lies within or outside the volume occupied by the sphere.

Below we present inequalities that describe the spatial occupancy of some other simple objects:

1. **A Cylinder**: Consider the case of a cylinder that is centred about the y-axis (an arbitrary choice) and whose base is located in the x–z plane. Given that the cylinder has a height h and a radius r, we can represent its spatial occupancy using three inequalities:

$$y \geq 0, \quad y \leq h, \quad x^2 + z^2 \leq r^2.$$

   If a point satisfies all three of these inequalities then it lies within the volume occupied by the cylinder.

2. **A Cube**: We can define a cube in terms of the region that is enclosed by six planes. Consider the case of a cube whose base lies in the x–z plane and for which three edges coincide with the positive x, y and z axes. Six inequalities can be used to specify the region occupied by the cube (to lie within or on the surface of the cube, the coordinates of a point must satisfy all these inequalities). Assuming that the sides of the cube are of unit length, these inequalities are:

$$x \geq 0, \quad x \leq 1, \quad y \geq 0, \quad y \leq 1, \quad z \geq 0, \quad z \leq 1.$$

   which can be presented as:

$$0 \leq x \leq 1, \quad 0 \leq y \leq 1, \quad 0 \leq z \leq 1.$$

   Note that given a primitive element in the form of a cube, we can represent any rectangular block. This is achieved by applying different scaling factors along each of the cubes three dimensions. Similarly in the case of a sphere: by applying different scaling factors along three orthogonal directions, we are able to generate an ellipsoid.

OTU Exercise 7.8: The Spatial Occupancy of a Cone

Consider a cone whose radius and height are of unit length and whose base lies in the $x - z$ plane. Assuming that the y axis forms the central axis of the cone, use three inequalities to define its spatial occupancy.

A binary tree structure may be used to represent an object formed by means of a number of primitive elements. Consider the elementary example depicted in Figure 7.19 in which two rectangular blocks are joined together. A binary tree representation is presented in Figure 7.22. Here, the root represents the object model and the leaf nodes detail the primitives that have been used together with parameters concerning their size, location and orientation. The internal nodes detail the Boolean operations that are carried out between primitives. In the case of this particular example, the leaf nodes define two rectangular blocks and the internal node indicates a union operation.

By interrogating the data structure we can easily determine whether or not a particular point lies within or outside an object. To do this we begin with the leaf nodes and establish if the point lies within any of the primitives used in the formation of the object. Here, for example, we can signify that a point lies within a primitive by setting a flag to a binary 1 – otherwise the flag is a zero. We then pass these values up to the appropriate internal nodes and apply the specified Boolean operations. The final binary value that we obtain when we reach the root node indicates the presence (or otherwise) of the point within the object. Note that simply determining that a point lies within the volume encompassed by one of the primitive elements does not in itself indicate that the point lies within the overall object formed from the primitives. This is because a primitive may, for example not be used to add to the volume occupied by the object but may be used to remove 'material' from the object (via, for example, a Boolean difference operation).

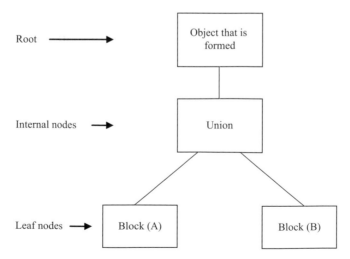

Figure 7.22 Here, a binary tree structure is used to represent the formation of the simple model depicted in Figure 7.19. The root indicates the object that is modelled, the leaf nodes define the primitives that are used together with parameters indicating their size, location and orientation. Internal nodes define the Boolean operations that are carried out between primitives.

To illustrate the basic application of this process let us consider the elementary example depicted in Figure 7.20. If we replace the internal node indicated in Figure 7.22 with a Boolean difference operation then this provides us with the binary tree describing the model. Let us suppose that the rectangular block denoted as A is the larger of the two and we begin by assuming that we wish to determine if an arbitrary point P lies within the overall object formed from the two blocks. Below we examine two possible scenarios:

1. **P lies in block A and not in block B**: Thus for the leaf corresponding to block A we set a flag to a binary 1 and for the other leaf we set a flag to zero. These values are passed to the internal node and the Boolean operation is performed. This results in a binary 1. If at the top of the hierarchy we obtain a binary 1, this is assumed to indicate that the point lies within the volume occupied by the object.

2. **P lies in block A and also in block B**: Here for both leaf nodes a binary 1 is generated. These values are passed to the internal node and the Boolean difference is determined. The result is not a binary 1 and therefore the point is assumed to lie outside the volume occupied by the object. Indeed, this is the case as the point P lies in the hole that we have created in the larger block!

Although this is a very simple example, these ideas can be readily applied to more complex binary tree structures.

OTU Exercise 7.9: Modelling a Simple Object

Suppose that we are to use the CSG approach to model a simple object. This consists of a sphere through which three orthogonally positioned holes (circular) are to be machined. Thus one hole passes from the front to the back of the sphere, another from the top to the bottom, and a third between the left and right hand sides (these holes all meet at the centre of the sphere).

1. On the basis of sphere and cylinder primitives, write an expression indicating the Boolean operations that you would perform to form a model of this object.
2. Describe this process using a binary tree structure.

As we have previously mentioned there is no modelling process that provides a Utopian technique – each has associated strengths and weaknesses and CSG is no exception. The ability to accommodate intuitive user interaction within the design process represents a key advantage of this general technique. Here, as we have seen, we are able to use a set of basic primitives for object formation and each primitive may be used to add or remove material. We can therefore view CSG as a user centred design technique although, when it comes to creating complex objects the design process is generally far from simple (but this is true of all modelling techniques).

A further advantage of CSG is its suitability for use with automated prototyping/manufacturing equipment. The shapes of all surfaces are exactly defined through the mathematical equations that are employed within the modelling process and inherently associated with each of the primitive elements used in the formation of a model. On the other hand, the depiction of CSG models can be computationally expensive. As indicated earlier in this section, a CSG model represents an object in terms of its occupancy of space – i.e. a volume representation is used. This contrasts with the B-rep approach – in the case of CSG there is no explicit information stored in the data structure relating to an object's surfaces. As we generally depict opaque objects, the visible image is formed by consideration of the size, form, orientation, location and visible properties of surfaces – because the interior of an opaque solid is not visible, it is not directly relevant to the rendering process. Two effective strategies for creating an image of a CSG model are:

1.   **Ray Casting:** See Section 8.8 for brief discussion of this approach.

2.   **Conversion to B-rep Form:** In this case, once the model has been converted, it may be rendered using standard techniques. In addition the CSG model remains available for use in the production of the physical artefact.

7.8 Discussion

> *'How is it that little children are so intelligent and men so stupid?*
> *It must be education that does it.'*[18]

In this chapter we have briefly introduced several techniques that may be used to represent an objects geometrical form. No single approach provides a Utopian solution – all have associated strengths and weaknesses. The boundary representation technique is the approach most commonly used for the production of high quality images. However, as we have seen, this modelling technique has associated weaknesses and these can lead to implementation issues.

In the next chapter we turn our attention to outlining rendering techniques used in generating the visual image of an object or collection of objects represented within the computer system. Here, we limit discussion to applications in which the conventional flat screen display is employed.

7.9 Review Questions

1.   State three key characteristics of 'regular polyhedra'.
2.   State Euler's formula for simple polyhedra.
3.   State the general form of equation for a plane.
4.   Indicate the significance of the coefficients employed in the general form of equation for a plane.
5.   State the significance of the fourth term in the general equation for a plane (i.e. the term which does not include x, y or z – and to which in the text we have assigned the symbol D).
6.   In the case that we join Bézier surfaces, how do we ensure C^0 and C^1 continuity?
7.   State one key difference between the B-rep and CSG approaches.
8.   Give an equation that describes the spatial occupancy of a sphere of radius r.
9.   Given the determinant of a matrix Q and its adjoint, how would you determine the inverse of Q?
10.   State one restriction associated with the basic surface of revolution approach to object representation.

---

[18] Attributed to Alexandre Dumas (1802–1870).

7.10 Feedback to Review Questions

1. 'Regular polyhedra' represent a particular form of simple polyhedra in which:
    a. All faces have the same number of edges (e.g. a cube).
    b. Every vertex has the same number of edges emanating from it (e.g. a cube).
    c. Every edge has the same length.
2. $V - E + S = 2$.
    Where V represents the number of vertices, E the number of edges and S the number of surfaces.
3. $Ax + By + Cz + D = 0$.
4. Given the 'general form' of equation for a plane, the coefficients of x, y and z correspond to the components of the vector that lies at right-angles to plane – the 'surface normal vector'.
5. The magnitude of this term in the general equation for a plane corresponds to the length of the line drawn from the origin to a point on the plane such that it meets the plane at 90°. This is referred to as the perpendicular distance of the plane from the origin. This applies as long as the coefficients A, B and C in the general equation for the plane represent the components of a surface normal of unit length.
6. C^0: This is achieved by ensuring that the control points located along the joining boundaries are coincident.
    C^1: A sufficient condition is that at the joint, the lines connecting the endpoints with the adjacent control points are collinear.
7. In the case of the B-rep approach surface properties are represented. In contrast, in the case of CSG objects are modelled as volumes (they are described by a set of points occupying a 3-D space).
8. $x^2 + y^2 + z^2 \le r^2$.
9. Simply multiply the adjoint by the reciprocal of the determinant – that is:

$$Q^{-1} = \left(\frac{1}{\det Q} \right) \cdot adjQ.$$

10. The model that is formed should have a circular cross-section.

3-D Graphics: Mainly Rendering 8

'It was high autumn; there had been frost already, for the ground was fine with red and yellow leaves; and presently we saw himself coming, professionally questing among those leaves.'

8.1 Introduction

In the previous chapter we outlined several techniques that may be used in the modelling process and here we turn our attention to steps that may be followed in forming a visible image comprising one or more of the entities that we have modelled. Figure 8.1 summarises some of the stages that we will consider.

In the next section we discuss the placement of objects within a common framework and defining their spatial relationships etc. Subsequently we consider setting up a virtual camera in order that we can specify the viewpoint from which the scene will be observed (Section 8.3). This leads on to discussion concerning clipping and culling together with further examination of perspective projection. In Section 8.7 we consider how the sources of illumination will impact on our view of the various objects that comprise the scene.

The processes that we outline are entirely logical and easily understood – it is as if we are managing a film set – placing props and people in appropriate positions, managing the lighting, and ensuring that the camera will capture the scene from an optimal viewing position. Although this is a meaningful and valid way to describe the stages that we may work through in order to successfully create a 3-D computer graphics image, it is important to remember that within the computer we are simply manipulating data structures and carrying out mathematical and geometric operations.

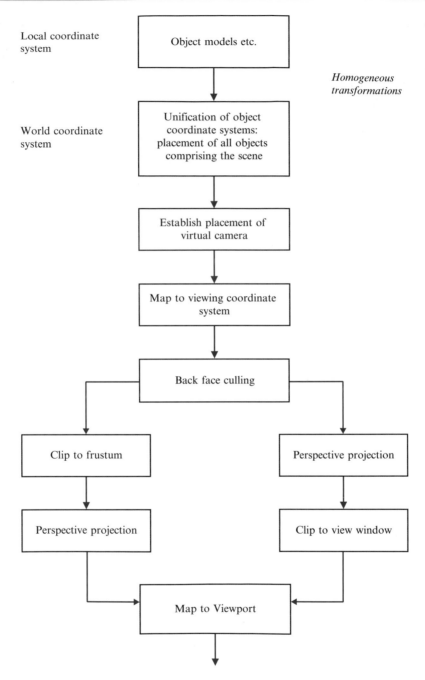

Figure 8.1 From the model to the image. A conceptualised outline of some of the key steps that may be followed in depicting an image scene. These processes are outlined in Sections 8.2 to 8.5. Subsequently we briefly consider clipping, shading and colour.

As discussed in the previous chapter, objects are represented using data structures and when we place objects within a scene we are inter-relating key information contained in separate object data structures – such as the relative location of vertices. In establishing the location of the virtual camera we are defining the relationship of objects relative to the virtual camera's frame of reference. In short, whilst it is extremely convenient to use the analogy of establishing a film set, adjusting the illumination, camera position and the like, within the digital world the processes occurring are rather complex.

Within the available space, we can do little more than provide an insight into some of the techniques that may be employed. For brevity, we confine our discussion to static images and the formation of a perspective view. Additionally, we generally assume the use of B-rep models.

Key Learning Outcomes: At the end of this chapter you should be able to:

- *Outline key steps needed to transform a collection of object representations into a visual image.*

- *Understand the use of a world coordinate system.*

- *Discuss the use of culling and clipping processes.*

- *Discuss features of the view volume including the use of back and front clipping planes.*

- *Describe features of the Gouraud and Phong interpolative shading techniques.*

- *Describe the synthesis of shadows.*

- *Outline aspects of ray tracing and ray casting techniques.*

8.2 Unification: The World Coordinate System

'From the solemn gloom of the temple children run out to sit in the dust,
God watches them play and forgets the priest.'[1]

Typically a computer graphics scene will comprise a collection of objects, each of which may have been formed using the techniques outlined in the previous chapter. Individually, objects will often be represented in terms of 'local' coordinate systems. For example, we may have conveniently positioned a cube so that one of its vertices is coincident with the origin of a local coordinate system, and a cylinder may be located so that its central axis is coincident with one of the axes of another local coordinate system. In this way we may more readily (and intuitively) support local transformations.

To construct the computer graphics scene we must place the constituent objects within a unified coordinate system, so enabling their relative locations to be defined within a common

---

[1] Attributed to Rabindranath Tagore (1861–1941).

framework (a world coordinate system). Here, we make use of the homogeneous transformation matrices outlined in Chapter 6 which enable us to map between two arbitrarily positioned sets of coordinate axes. In addition to placing object components within a scene, we must also define the location of 'light sources' that will be used to simulate illumination.

During this process, we essentially define the objects that comprise the scene and their spatial relationships. Some volumetric display technologies (see Chapter 9) permit 3-D images to be depicted within a transparent cylinder or sphere. In principle, such systems impose very little restriction on viewing freedom and an observer can move around the display vessel and view the scene from practically any orientation. However, in the case that we employ a more conventional form of display it is necessary to define the location of a 2-D 'viewing window' via which the scene will ultimately be viewed and by means of which we can define the part of a scene that is to be depicted. This denotes the next key task to be carried out.

8.3 The Viewing Volume

Recall previous discussion presented in Section 6.6 in which we introduced the virtual camera, view plane, viewing window and viewpoint (centre of projection (COP)). These are associated with a viewing coordinate system which is referenced to the world coordinate system. The location and orientation of former may be freely changed relative to the latter and this enables us to define any desired vantage point onto a scene. In Figure 8.2 we summarise key elements used to define a 'viewing volume'.

As may be seen, this diagram builds on Figure 6.20 and indicates a viewing volume that is a 'frustum' (a truncated pyramid). Here, we have added front and back clipping planes (these are also referred to by the much more pleasing titles of 'hither' and 'yon' planes). Both planes are parallel to the view plane and their presence enables the elimination (on the basis of depth) of unnecessary/unwanted scene content:

1. **Back Clipping Plane:** In the case of a perspective projection, the more distant an object is from the observer (centre of projection (COP)), the smaller it appears to be. Thus an object within the scene that is at a great distance may ultimately project onto only a single display pixel. By means of the back clipping plane we can eliminate such objects from the scene thereby saving processing time and avoiding cluttering the displayed image with undistinguishable background content.

2. **Front Clipping Plane:** Similarly, as objects get closer to the COP, they may take on huge proportions thereby either dominating the scene and so obscuring other objects of interest, or even extending far beyond the bounds of the displayed image. In this latter case, the observer would only see a part of such an object and this may make the object unrecognisable.

From the above, it is apparent that the inclusion of back and front clipping planes increases our control of what is displayed and in addition can reduce computational cost.

OTU Exercise 8.1: The Location of the View Plane

What is the effect of moving the location of the view plane – away from, or towards the centre of projection?

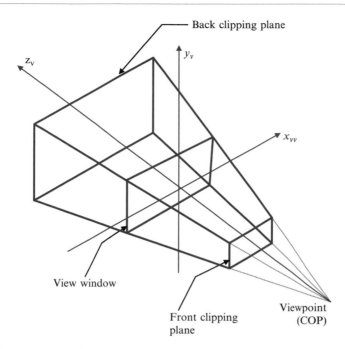

Figure 8.2 The view volume may be defined by six planes. Here we illustrate the front and back clipping planes. The viewing coordinate system (a left handed coordinate system) has axes denoted x_v, y_v and z_v. Objects or parts of objects that lie outside this view volume are not visible from the COP.

As discussed, the image scene is defined in terms of a world coordinate system and we now need to map between this system and that of the viewing coordinate system. The individual sequence of steps involved in this process was outlined in Section 6.6 and will not be described further here (for further details of the maths, see texts such as Jones *et al.* [2001], and Hill [1990]).

8.4 Culling, Clipping and the Perspective Projection

Once the image scene is described in terms of the viewing coordinate system, we are in a position to form the 2-D rendition of the 3-D scene. This involves projecting the scene content onto the viewing window – a process that was outlined in general terms in Section 6.5. However, before we undertake the projection operation, we need to consider whether or not it should be carried out on all content comprising the image scene – can we improve efficiency be eliminating portions of the scene that will not be visible from our defined vantage point.

By way of example, let's consider so-called 'back face culling' which is used to remove polygons that are directed away from the view point. Here it is important to distinguish between two terms:

1. **Culling**: This refers to removing non-visible polygons in their entirety and is particularly effective when working with convex polygonal representations.
2. **Clipping**: This refers to the removal of non-visible *portions* of polygons and can be non-trivial.

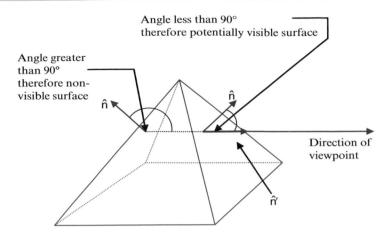

Figure 8.3 A simple example of back face culling. If the angle between the surface normal vector and a vector from the surface to the view point is greater than 90° then the surface is not visible. However, if the angle is less than 90° then the surface may be visible (actual visibility may be defined by other factors – see text for discussion).

Recall from the previous chapter that in a B-rep model we included surface normal vectors ($\hat{\mathbf{n}}$) for each polygon – each vector being oriented to point outwards from the object. To implement back face culling we may create a vector $\mathbf{n}'$ from the polygon under consideration to the viewpoint – see Figure 8.3. In the case that the angle between this vector and the surface normal vector is greater than 90°, the entire polygon is invisible to the observer. However, if the angle is less than 90°, the polygon may be visible. If we are dealing with a scene comprising a single convex polyhedron, then back face culling will eliminate the hidden faces and providing the object lies completely within the viewing frustum, the remaining faces will be entirely visible. If a scene comprises several objects, then one object may obscure a part of another and in the case that we are dealing with a non-convex polyhedron, one portion of an object may be partially occluded by another part – see Figure 8.4. These are not situations that can be dealt with by means of back face culling.

In order to carry out back face culling, we simply calculate the scalar product of the unit normal surface vector and the unit vector from the surface to the viewpoint. Since both vectors have

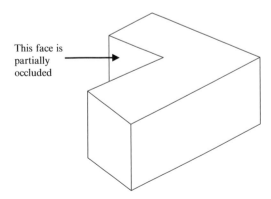

Figure 8.4 In the case that we are dealing with a non-convex polyhedron, one portion of the object may be partially occluded by the object itself.

a magnitude of unity, the scalar product equals the cosine of the angle (θ) between the vectors:

$$\hat{\mathbf{n}} \cdot \hat{\mathbf{n}}' = \cos \theta.$$

Hence if the scalar product is positive this must indicate that θ is less than 90°, otherwise it is greater than 90°. As indicated above, in the case of the former the surface may be visible and in the case of the latter the surface is not visible and can therefore be culled. By means of this technique, we can reduce the number of polygons that must be considered further.

One of the next tasks to be performed is to determine the parts of the image scene that will lie within the view window. Here, we may consider the use of two approaches – the first involves clipping/culling before undertaking the perspective projection (whereby the 3-D scene is mapped onto the 2-D view plane) whereas in the case of the second method clipping/culling occurs during or subsequent to the projection process. In the subsections that follow, we briefly introduce these two approaches.

Clipping/culling techniques are commonly classified according to whether they act directly on data pertaining to each object or on the image formed when objects are projected onto a 2-D surface. Within this context the terms 'object space' and 'image space' are often used:

An object space technique: Here the clipping/culling technique acts directly on objects contained within the 3-D scene. Back face culling is an example of an object space technique.

An image space technique: In this case, the clipping/culling technique acts on the planar rendition of the objects that comprise a scene. The z-buffer technique that will be described shortly (see Section 8.6.1) is an example of an image space technique.

8.4.1 Clipping to the View Frustum

The viewing frustum may contain the entire collection of objects that we have previously placed within the image scene, or may contain only a part of the scene. In this latter case, it is possible that only a very small portion of the overall image scene will ultimately be displayed and so projecting all scene content onto the view plane will not make efficient use of computer resources. In short it may be desirable to identify and discard those parts of the scene that do not lie within the frustum prior to undertaking the projection of the scene onto the view plane. This requires us to carry out operations on the objects themselves and consequently, in line with the terminology introduced above, this is referred to as an object space technique.

The view frustum comprises six planes (recall Figure 8.2) and by inserting the coordinates of the endpoints of each line segment comprising the scene into the equation for each of these planes, we can readily determine if the point lies within or outside the frustum. Consider, for example, the left and right hand walls of the frustum. If a point lies to the left of the left-hand wall *or* to the right of the right-hand wall, then it lies outside the view frustum. Conversely if the point lies to the right of the left-hand wall *and* to the left of the right-hand wall it may lie within the frustum (the final decision depends on the point's location relative to the other four walls). However, this procedure is not quite as straightforward as it may initially appear. For example, if both the end-points of a line lie outside the frustum, this does not necessarily mean that the entire line segment lies outside the frustum – a part of the line may pass through the frustum! Recall previous discussion (relating to the 2-D case) presented in Section 3.7. For details of algorithmic techniques see texts such as Watt and Watt [1992] and Foley *et al.* [1990] and for our purposes, it is sufficient to note that once we have determined the image scene content that lies within the view frustum, we can perform the perspective projection[2] thus mapping this content onto the view window.

8.4.2 Clipping to the View Window

In the case that most of the overall image scene is located within the view frustum, performing the perspective projection on the scene as a whole (and subsequently clipping against the view window) is likely to be more efficient than clipping against the view frustum and then performing the perspective projection. These two scenarios are summarised in Figure 8.1. To determine the most efficient approach we need to consider the cost associated with clipping to the view frustum and balance this against the cost of the projection calculations and the number of these calculations that will simply be discarded (in the event that they produce results that lie outside the view window).

Assuming that we decide to project the overall image scene onto the view plane, we need to examine the results of the projection operations and deal with content that can be culled (because it lies completely outside the view window) or that must be clipped (in the case that it lies partially within the view window).

8.5 Mapping to a Viewport

Once the image scene has been projected onto the view window we are, in principle, in a position to undertake the mapping of the scene onto the viewport of the display. In short, we now need to determine correspondence between the spatial content of the view window and the 2-D array of pixels that will be used for image depiction. Here, we may transform view window coordinates into intermediate normalised device coordinated (NDC) and subsequently transform these to viewport (pixel based) coordinates. Alternatively we may carry out the process directly and omit the NDC step. The use of NDC is outlined in Section 3.2.

Consider the view window and viewport illustrated in Figure 8.5. In this diagram we indicate a point P with view window coordinates (x, y) which we wish to map onto the viewport (point P' which we assume has coordinates (x', y')). Consider the mapping of the x coordinate. The ratio of the size of the two ports (in the x direction) is given by:

$$\frac{x'_{max} - x'_{min}}{x_{max} - x_{min}}.$$

This represents the factor that is used to scale the x coordinate of the point P. The distance of this point from the left-hand boundary of the view window is $x - x_{min}$. In the viewport, this distance is scaled to:

$$\frac{(x - x_{min})\left(x'_{max} - x'_{min}\right)}{x_{max} - x_{min}}.$$

---

[2] Or parallel projection.

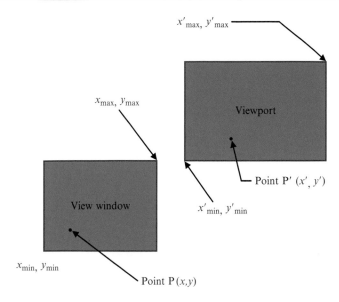

Figure 8.5 Mapping between the view window and viewport. See text for discussion.

Hence the absolute location of the point in the viewport (relative to the origin) is given by:

$$x' = x'_{min} + \frac{(x - x_{min})\left(x'_{max} - x'_{min}\right)}{x_{max} - x_{min}}.$$

Similarly, the mapping for the y coordinate of P is given by:

$$y' = y'_{min} + \frac{(y - y_{min})\left(y'_{max} - y'_{min}\right)}{y_{max} - y_{min}}.$$

8.6 Clipping for Opacity

'The true harvest of my life is intangible –
a little star dust caught,
a portion of the rainbow I have clutched.'[3]

In the above sections we have outlined some of the key steps that may be used in the depiction of polygonal representations. As you may have noticed, our overview is far from complete. In the case that we omit back face culling then our discussion embraces the majority of the tasks needed to depict wireframe images (recall Section 7.2 – a wireframe representation depicts the geometric and spatial outline of a shape (the shape's 'skeleton')). However, even in the case of wireframe image depiction, there are additional problems that must be addressed. For example – consider the issue of aliasing which can occur when we employ a display comprising a matrix of discrete elements. As indicated in Figure 8.6, this can result in the depiction of

---

[3] Attributed to Henry David Thoreau (1817–1862).

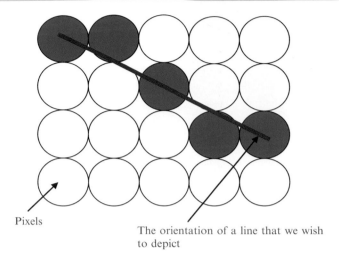

Pixels

The orientation of a line that we wish
to depict

Figure 8.6 A simple example of aliasing in relation to the depiction of a line. Here we greatly magnify the size of pixels and assume that in each column of pixel elements, the pixel closest to the line is illuminated. These selected pixels are indicated by shading. As can be seen this will lead to the production of a jagged line – often referred to as a 'staircase' effect.

lines that comprise a series of jagged steps. Anti-aliasing techniques are used to ameliorate this effect – see for example discussion of the Bresenham line drawing algorithm, the Pitteway-Watkinson algorithm etc in texts such as Hill [1990], Hearn and Baker [1986] and Foley *et al.* [1990].

With the exception of back face culling, the stages that we have described so far do not accommodate image opacity – hence they are appropriate to basic wire frame image depiction. In this section we briefly turn our attention to exemplar techniques that can be used for clipping (commonly referred to as 'hidden line/surface removal') thereby enabling components within the image scene to obscure or partially obscure others. In this way an image scene is able to provide an impression of object solidity. Within this context we outline the z-buffer and the so-called painter's techniques.

8.6.1 The Z-Buffer Technique

This approach is also referred to as the 'depth buffer' technique and represents an image space method (recall summary of image and object space methods provided in Section 8.4). Consider the diagram presented in Figure 8.7 in which we show two surfaces located at different depths within the image scene. The dashed line can be thought of as denoting the 'line of sight' of a pixel into the image scene and passes through these two surfaces (thus along this 'line of sight' one surface lies behind the other). The pixel should depict an element of the surface that lies closest the view plane – i.e. the surface that has (along the line of sight) the smallest z coordinate.

We assume the use of two memory arrays – as depicted schematically in Figure 8.8. The first array acts as the frame buffer and stores the colour/grey scale of each pixel and the second (the z-buffer) stores the z-coordinate of the point within the image scene that each individual the pixel represents. Let us begin by setting the frame buffer contents to represent the scene background (e.g. in the simplest case a single colour) and set all the values in the z-buffer to

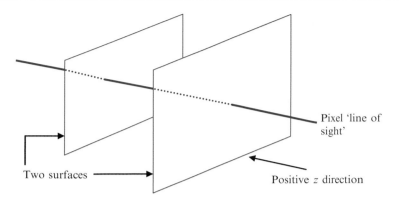

Figure 8.7 Two surfaces and a pixel 'line of sight'. The pixel should represent an element on the surface which lies closest to the view plane. See text for discussion.

the maximum depth of the scene content. For each pixel, we then examine all polygons that lie along its direct 'line of sight' and determine the polygon with the smallest z-coordinate (each time a smaller intersection value is identified the appropriate entry in the z-buffer is updated). The corresponding location in the frame buffer will then be set to represent the colour of this polygon at the point at which it intersects the line of sight. For further introductory discussion see Hill [1990].

8.6.2 The Painter's Technique

This approach broadly mimics a technique that may be used by artists in painting a scene. Here, the artist begins by applying a background colour to a canvas. The most distant objects within the scene are then added. The process continues with addition of objects that are less distant – and as these object are included, parts of more distant objects may be over-painted and hence obscured.

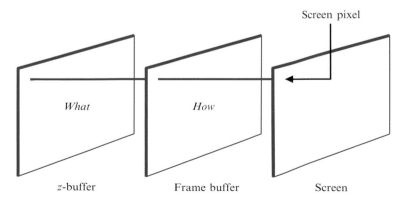

Figure 8.8 Correspondence between a screen pixel and entries in the z and frame buffers. The former denotes the z coordinate defining *what* is displayed by a pixel and the latter defines *how* items are to be displayed (e.g. colour).

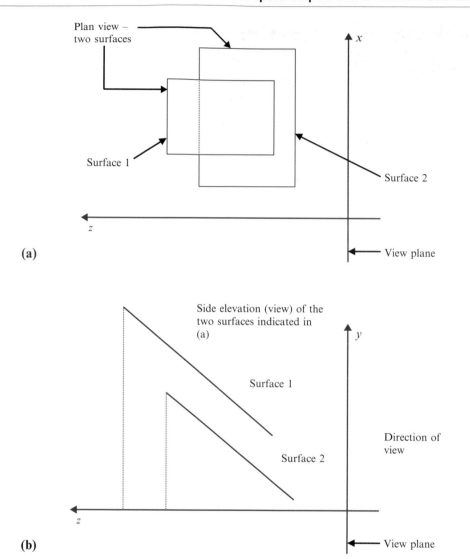

Figure 8.9 The use of the painter's technique. In (a) we illustrate (in plan view) two surfaces. As can be seen from (b), the surfaces are not horizontal but slope 'uphill' with distance from the view plane. Surface 1 is assumed to have a vertex with the greatest z value. The Painter's technique is used to perform hidden surface removal. See OTU Exercise 8.2 for details.

To apply this approach to computer graphics it is necessary to order polygon surfaces (according to depth within the scene) – once the most distant surface has been identified it may be 'painted' into the appropriate area of the frame buffer. Gradually other less distant surfaces are identified and added – and where there are areas of overlap, a new surface will overwrite a part of a surface that has already been added.

The decision on the most distance surface is based on the surface which has the vertex with the greatest z coordinate. Although this may appear to be a safe approach, in the case of overlapping surfaces it can lead to unexpected results.

OTU Exercise 8.2: The Painter's Technique

Consider the scenario indicated in Figure 8.9. In (a) we show (in plan view) two surfaces of differing size. The surfaces are not horizontal – as indicated in (b) they slope 'uphill' with distance from the view plane (and hence distance from the viewer). Here, it is helpful to envisage the situation using two pieces of paper or two books that may be to hand. As can be seen Surface 1 is furthest away from the view plane and so has the vertex with the greatest z coordinate.

Consider the use of the Painter's technique for hidden surface removal. Would this lead to the expected occlusion? If not – what would be indicated?

Now let us suppose that we adjust the placement of the surfaces so that Surface 2 now has a vertex with the greatest z coordinate. How would this effect the result derived from the Painter's technique?

For further introductory discussion in relation to the Painter's algorithm and other hidden surface techniques, see texts such as Hearn and Baker [1986], Foley *et al.* [1990] and Cooley [2001].

8.7 Shading and Colour

> ' "*Our second experiment. "The Professor announced . . .*"
> *is the production of that seldom-seen-but-greatly-to-be-admired phenomenon,*
> *Black Light! . . . This box . . . is quite full of it. The way I made it was this –*
> *I took a lighted candle into a dark cupboard and shut the door.*
> *Of course the cupboard was then full of Yellow Light.*
> *Then I took a bottle of Black Ink, and poured it over the candle:*
> *and, to my delight, every atom of the Yellow Light turned Black!*" '[4]

Having created a perspective projection of the part of the scene that is to be viewed and having removed hidden surfaces, thereby introducing a sense of object solidity, we move on to consider the way we are going to illuminate the scene and the manner in which we wish to synthesise the interaction between objects and light. A simple approach is to employ constant intensity shading (also referred to as 'flat shading'). In this case a uniform luminance is assigned to each face of a polygonal representation. This is a computationally undemanding approach and so yields rapid results. Naturally, this technique results in the geometrical discontinuities between adjacent polygons being visible. However, when rapid results are needed or in the case that we are not attempting to depict a continuously curving surface, this flat shading technique may well be satisfactory.

In the next subsection we briefly summarise previous discussion presented in Section 5.4 concerning aspects of diffuse and specular reflection. Subsequently we consider the Gouraud and Phong interpolative shading techniques and the formation of shadows within a scene.

---

[4] Lewis Carroll, *Sylvie and Bruno*. Dover Publications, 1988.

8.7.1 Diffuse and Specular Reflection

In the case of a matte surface, light is scattered equally in all directions and so luminance (brightness) does not vary with viewing angle. However, as we discussed in Section 5.4.5, consider the case that a surface is illuminated with a point source. The luminance (l) of the surface will then vary as we change the angle of the source relative to the surface. This leads to Lambert's Law:

$$l = \frac{IK_d}{r^2}\hat{\mathbf{n}}\cdot\hat{\mathbf{s}},$$

where, I denotes the luminous intensity of a source at a distance r, k_d the coefficient of diffuse reflectance (a property of the surface), $\hat{\mathbf{s}}$ a unit vector in the direction of the light source and $\hat{\mathbf{n}}$ the surface normal. Since we are dealing with unit vectors, the scalar product $\hat{\mathbf{n}} \cdot \hat{\mathbf{s}}$ provides us with the cosine of the angle between the surface normal (this vector being included within the B-rep model (or being derived from other information within the model)) and the unit vector in the direction of the source of illumination. As mentioned previously, this shading model does not provide optimal results and typically the denominator is replaced with a distance term (d) that may for example represent the distance of a surface from the COP – so that:

$$l = \frac{IK_d}{d + \eta}\hat{\mathbf{n}}\cdot\hat{\mathbf{s}}.$$

Here, η is assigned an arbitrary value and ensures that the denominator cannot approach zero as the value of d is reduced. Of course, the location of the lighting source may be such that portions of an object that are within an observer's line of sight receive no illumination and so are, in fact invisible. To avoid this situation we need to include ambient lighting that illuminates the scene as a whole. In this case the luminance of a surface will be given by:

$$l = \frac{IK_d}{d + \eta}\hat{\mathbf{n}}\cdot\hat{\mathbf{s}} + I_a K_d,$$

where, I_a represents the level of ambient lighting. So far we have made no allowance for the colour spectrum of the lighting source(s) or for the colour of the surface. For example, if we illuminate a red surface using green light, then the surface will appear to be black – irrespective of the level of illuminance (assuming no specular reflection). This increases the complexity of the model and we must now consider the reflectance characteristics of the surface with reference to the red, green and blue content represented within the lighting source.

As discussed in Section 5.4.5 specular reflection relates to smooth surfaces which exhibit angular directionality in their reflection of incident light. The classic Phong reflection model accounts for both diffuse and specular reflection and is widely used in computer graphics. In the next subsection we consider the Gouraud and Phong interpolative shading schemes which are able to reduce/eliminate the multifaceted appearance of polygonal object representations.

8.7.2 Gouraud and Phong Interpolative Shading

As discussed in the previous chapter, the geometrical discontinuities that exist between adjacent polygons in a polygonal representation can have a significant (and usually undesirable) visual impact. Fortunately, this problem may be greatly ameliorated by using Gouraud and Phong interpolative shading techniques. Below we begin by outlining the former approach which is less computationally demanding than the Phong scheme but yields lower quality results.

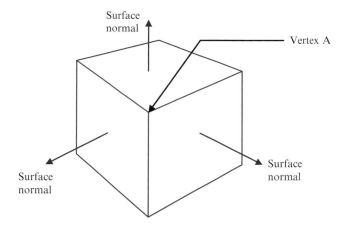

Figure 8.10 The vertex normal is calculated by averaging the orientation of the adjacent surface normal vectors. Here, the three surface normal vectors that are adjacent to the vertex are indicated. The resulting vertex normal vector is out of the page.

1. *Gouraud Interpolative Shading*

This approach requires the determination of the vertex normal vector for each vertex in our polygonal model. These vectors are readily found by calculating the average of the surface normal vectors for all surfaces that share a common vertex. This is perhaps most easily explained by referring to a simple example. Consider the cube depicted in Figure 8.10. In the case of vertex A, we determine the vertex normal vector by averaging the three surface normal vectors indicated in the diagram.

We can represent this process by means of the following equation:

$$\hat{\mathbf{n}}_{\mathbf{v}} = \frac{\sum\limits_{s=1}^{k} \hat{\mathbf{n}}_{\mathbf{s}}}{\left| \sum\limits_{s=1}^{k} \hat{\mathbf{n}}_{\mathbf{s}} \right|}.$$

Here, we assume that k surfaces share a common vertex, that the surface normal for the sth surface is denoted $\hat{\mathbf{n}}_{\mathbf{s}}$ and the unit vertex normal vector is $\hat{\mathbf{n}}_{\mathbf{v}}$. Using a shading model we can now calculate the luminance at each vertex. Recall from the summary discussion provided in the previous section, the use of the scalar product between a unit vector in the direction of the light source and the unit surface normal vector (for which we now use the unit vertex normal vector). It is important to note that all polygons sharing a vertex will be assigned the same level of luminance at the vertex. We now use a linear interpolation technique which interpolates the luminance along each edge of each polygon and determines the luminance of points within each polygon. For example, consider the square depicted in Figure 8.11 that represents one of the faces of the cube shown in Figure 8.10. The luminance at each of the four vertices (labelled I_a to I_d) having been determined, we now find luminance values at points on the left and right-hand edges. In the illustration we have included a 'scan line' with vertical coordinate y_s. Thus the luminance at the point at which this line intersects the left edge of the square (I_m) is given by:

$$I_m = \frac{y_2 - y_s}{y_2 - y_1} I_d + \frac{y_s - y_1}{y_2 - y_1} I_a. \tag{8.1}$$

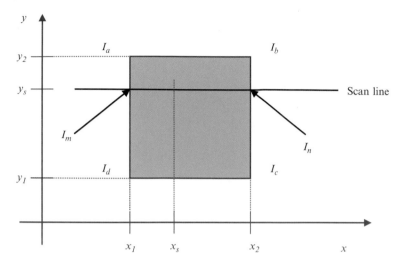

Figure 8.11 Here we illustrate one of the faces of the cube depicted in Figure 8.10. The luminance of each vertex has been determined (these are denoted I_a through to I_d). In addition we show a horizontal 'scan line' and begin the linear interpolation process by determining the luminance at the two points at which the scan line intersects the edges of the square. Subsequently we repeat this process for scan lines positioned at different vertical heights (by analogy, the positioning of the scan line is akin to the raster scan employed by a Cathode Ray Tube (see Chapter 1)).

We can readily verify this equation. In the case that the y coordinate of the scan line equals y_2, the first term is zero and $I_m = I_a$. Similarly if the scan line has a y coordinate of y_1, the second term becomes zero and $I_m = I_d$. If the line is equidistant from the two vertices, then as we would expect, $I_m = I_a/2 + I_d/2$. We can write a similar equation for the luminance (I_n) at the point at which the scan line meets the right hand edge. Subsequently, we can again use linear interpolation to determine the luminance at points along the scan line – i.e. within the square. Thus for a point with coordinates (x_s, y_s) we can express the luminance (I_p) as:

$$I_p = \frac{x_s - x_1}{x_2 - x_1} I_n + \frac{x_2 - x_s}{x_2 - x_1} I_m. \tag{8.2}$$

In fact we can simplify matters by determining the edge luminance values for one scan line on the basis of those obtained for the previous scan line. By way of a simple example suppose that over the height of the square depicted in Figure 8.11 we space scan lines at a distance d. Thus if one scan line has a y coordinate of y_s, the next line is at $y_s + d$. Substituting this into Eq. 8.1 and re-arranging the expression, we obtain:

$$I'_m = I_m + \frac{d\,[I_a - I_d]}{y_2 - y_1}.$$

Similarly we can calculate the luminance of points along each scan line by basing our calculation for the next point on the luminance of the previous point.

In connection with the Gouraud interpolative shading technique, we note the following:

1. Adjacent (shared) polygon edges are merged – they share the same luminance and colour. As a result, the visual impact of the geometric discontinuities that exist between adjacent polygons over the surface of a polyhedron are removed In the case of colour shading, the

levels of each of the colour components are calculated at the vertices and interpolated across the surfaces.

2. This approach can give rise to the illusionary appearance of undesirable 'Mach bands'[5] – of which Foley *et al.* [1990] write:

'At the border between two facets, the darker facet looks darker and the lighter facet looks lighter.'

In relation to this, Watt and Watt [1992] write:

'If we consider the intensity change across a boundary between polygons, this will exhibit a piecewise linear profile – there is no first order continuity.[6] The human visual system enhances the second derivative of intensity changes – reputedly of our need to detect and enhance edges – and the discontinuity at the shared edges of polygons results in these apparent bands.'

OTU Exercise 8.3: Interpolative Shading

Consider the interpolative shading technique discussed above. To what extent do you believe that this approach will ameliorate the geometric discontinuities between adjacent polygons around the silhouette of a polygonal representation?

2. *Phong Interpolative Shading*

As we have seen, in the case of Gouraud interpolative shading, a local reflection model is employed at the vertices of each polygon and the results obtained are linearly interpolated across the polygons surface. In contrast, in the case of the Phong[7] technique the vertex normal vectors themselves are interpolated across the surface of each polygon and for each pixel, the shading model is applied in such a way that it operates with the local interpolated vertex normal vector.

The Phong technique greatly reduces the Mach band effect mentioned above – but there is a penalty in terms of the computational overhead – as compared to the Gouraud approach. However, there are various ways in which the processing requirements may be reduced – for example, instead of applying the shading model to each pixel, it can be applied to every other pixel. In this case the intermediate pixels are set by taking the average of the values assigned to immediate neighbours. Watt and Watt [1992] provide interesting discussion on techniques that can be used to reduce the overheads associated with the Phong technique and also highlight a number of weaknesses of this approach.

OTU Exercise 8.4: Interpolation of Vertex Normal Vectors

Consider the cube depicted in Figure 8.10. If the vertex normal vectors are interpolated across a face of this cube, what would be the orientation of the interpolated vector at the centre of a face?

---

[5] Named after their discoverer Ernst Mach who uncovered this effect in ~1865.
[6] Recall previous discussion concerning orders of continuity in relation to Bézier curves and splines.
[7] Developed by Phong Bui Tuong.

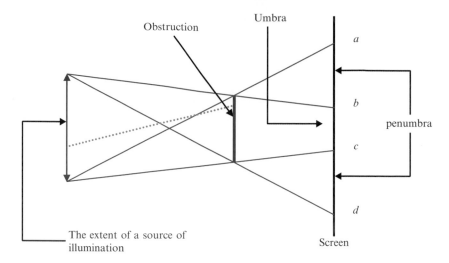

Figure 8.12 The passage of light from an extended source is obstructed. This leads to the formation of a shadow on the screen. The shadow comprised a penumbra and umbra. The broken line denotes a ray whose passage is blocked and which cannot reach the region between points *a* and *b*.

8.7.3 A World Without Shadows

In computer graphics we are given great freedom – we can develop scenes in which the fundamental laws of physics that we associate with our surroundings are followed or we can adjust, change and even disregard such laws. For example, in the case of animated images we need not adhere to Newton's Laws of motion – we can create scenes in which action and reaction are not equal and opposite (however, the repercussions may be somewhat surprising . . .).

The formation of scenes in which the fundamental laws of physics apply can be a very challenging and computationally expensive task. Furthermore, as we have seen (in the case of Lambert's Law) the direct application of equations that model real world behaviour to the graphics domain may not lead to optimal results. Consider the case of shadows. Under natural conditions, shadows do not usually have sharply defined edges and we associate with them umbra and penumbra regions that directly arise as a consequence of the finite extent of sources of illumination – see Figure 8.12. Here, an opaque object blocks the passage of light from the source. From the construction rays indicated in the illustration, it is apparent that light emanating from any part of the source may reach points on the screen that are beyond *a* and *d*. However, between points *a* and *b* and between *c* and *d* the obstruction partially blocks the passage of light. This is illustrated by the ray which is denoted by a broken line and which cannot reach the region of the screen between points *a* and *b*. Consequently these two regions are partially shadowed – penumbra. No light can pass directly from the source to the region between points *b* and *c* and in the case that we employ only the single source and there is no ambient illumination, this region will lie in total darkness – the umbra.

Thus real world shadows formed by extended light sources or, for example, by diffuse lighting that enters via a window do not have sharply defined edges.

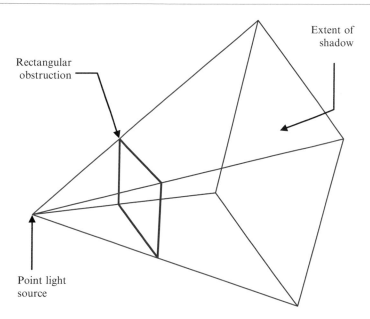

Rectangular obstruction

Extent of shadow

Point light source

Figure 8.13 Here, a point light source is employed and a shadow is cast by the rectangular obstruction. The extent of the shadow can be determined by tracing lines (construction rays) from the source to the vertices of the obstruction. By extending these lines to the point at which each intersects objects in the scene, we can determine the size and shape of the shadow cast by the rectangle. In this diagram the construction rays are assumed to intersect with a plane whose orientation is slightly inclined from the vertical.

> It is important to bear in mind that the texture of the surface onto which a shadow is cast can also play a pivotal role in defining shadow sharpness. Consider, for example a shadow cast onto a gravel path or onto mown grass. In both cases, texture is the predominant factor that determines the nature of the shadows silhouette.

In fact, when the source of illumination is direct sunlight, the sharpness of the silhouette is largely determined by the texture of the surface on which the shadow is cast – possibly coupled with the texture of the object responsible for the formation of the shadow.[8] In this latter respect, consider the shadow cast by a furry creature such as a dog. Here, the texture of the fur is likely to play a major role in defining the sharpness of the shadow formed.

For simplicity, in computer graphics, we often assume the illumination of a scene by means of a point source. In the case that the viewpoint and location of the point source coincide, no shadows would be visible (here we assume the use of a single source). This is because all points within the scene that can be illuminated are the very same points that are visible from this vantage point. Thus visible shadows occur when the location of the lighting source does not correspond to the location of the view point.

We can locate the position of shadows by extending lines from the point light source through the scene such that these lines intersect with and extend beyond vertices of objects comprising the scene. Take the simple case of a rectangular surface – as illustrated in Figure 8.13. In

---

[8] Colour and degree of opacity may also be considerations.

this example we draw lines from the source to each vertex of the rectangular obstruction. The lines are then extended and are assumed to intersect with a plane which is slightly inclined from the vertical position. In this way we determine both the size and shape of the shadow. Since we have made use of a point light source, there is no penumbra and a shadow with a sharp silhouette is formed. By using an array of closely spaced light sources we can attempt to simulate an extended light source – although this will in effect simply create a set of overlaid shadows and of course the computational overheads increase as we add more sources.

Recall that hidden surface removal allows us to eliminate parts of a scene that should not be visible to an observer from the chosen viewpoint. We can employ a similar technique to determine the shadows that are created by a point source – after all, these shadows represent scene content that cannot be 'seen' by the light. Of course some or all of these shadows may not be visible from the observer's vantage point.

In the case of conventional computer graphics, shadows are synthesised by geometric calculations. An alternative approach is to use a volumetric display system (see Chapter 9) which supports image opacity. This may permit shadows to be inherently (and automatically) associated with the image scene. For further details see Blundell and Schwarz [2000] and Blundell [2007].

8.8 Ray Casting and Ray Tracing

In this section we briefly outline the ray casting and ray tracing techniques and provide references for additional reading. We begin with the simpler of the two – ray casting:

1. **Ray Casting**: This name is commonly used in relation to a ray tracing technique in which we wish to determine visible surfaces. Let us suppose that we cast a ray from the centre of projection through a particular pixel location and identify the closest object within the scene with which the ray impinges. The colour of the pixel may then simply be set to the defined surface colour of the object at the point of intersection – or an appropriate illumination model may be applied. Naturally, we repeat this process for all pixel positions and in each case fire rays from the COP through the centre of the appropriate pixel. Notice that it is as if we are firing rays from the eye into the scene and for each ray the visible surface is the one which intersects the ray at the least distance.

2. **Ray Tracing**: This is more correctly referred to as 'recursive ray tracing' and is able to embrace hidden surface removal, shadow formation, refraction, reflection, etc. As with ray casting, rays are fired from the COP into the image scene – each ray passing through the centre of a pixel – i.e. the number of rays corresponds to the number of pixels. We identify the intersection of rays with objects in the scene – the shortest intersection distance indicating the point within the image scene that is to be depicted by the pixel. However, depending on the location of the light source, the point may be in a shadowed region. To test for this, secondary rays are spawned to each of the point sources illuminating the scene. If any of these rays intersect an opaque object, then we know that the light source with which they are associated cannot directly illuminate the point on the original object.

Various forms of secondary rays are employed. For example, in the case of a perfectly mirrored surface, a secondary ray is spawned in such a way that the angle of incidence and the angle of reflection are equal. In the case of a refractive surface then we spawn both reflected and refracted rays. In turn, each of these secondary rays may spawn other rays and so the process continues with each level making an ever-diminishing contribution to the colour of the associated pixel. The number of levels of contribution that we employ can be determined by various factors – such as when a set of secondary rays fail to reach some defined contribution threshold.

OTU Exercise 8.5: Ray Tracing

As indicated above, conventional ray tracing follows the paths of rays in a direction that is opposite to the propagation of light – it is as if rays travel from the eye into the scene. What key problem would you associate with the opposite technique – tracing the paths of rays from the point light sources through the image scene and ultimately to display pixels?

Ray tracing may give rise to glossy – perhaps overly shiny – images with very sharp shadow silhouettes. One potential difficulty concerns the treatment of diffuse surfaces – which, as we have seen scatter incident light in all directions. Thus the intersection of a ray with a diffuse surface can result in spawning a large number of rays and naturally, this can lead to a rapid growth in computational cost.

Interestingly, ray tracing is by no means a recently discovered technique – in the 17th century this approach was employed by René Descartes to model the refraction of light in rain droplets and this allowed him to explain the shape of the rainbow.[9] General aspects of ray tracing are discussed in most introductory computer graphics texts – such as Hill [1990]. See also Watt and Watt [1992]. Whitted [1980] describes pioneering work in relation to recursive ray tracing – see also Cook, Porter and Carpenter [1984].

8.9 Discussion

> *'I have learned that if you must leave a place that you have lived in and loved*
> *and where all your yesterdays are buried deep –*
> *leave it any way except a slow way,*
> *leave it the fastest way you can.'*[10]

In this chapter we have introduced a few of the underlying techniques that are used in transforming object representations into the visible image. In many respects we have done

---

[9] In this context, Watt and Watt [1992] write: '*An observer looking away from the sun sees a rainbow formed by '42°' rays from the sun. The paths of such rays form a 42° 'hemicone' centred on the observer's eye. (An interesting consequence of this model is that each observer has his own personal rainbow.)*'
[10] Beryl Markham, 'West With The Night', 1942.

little more than scratch the surface of this fascinating area of activity and hopefully the reader will feel encouraged to study these topics further. Texts such as Watt and Watt [1992], Watt [2000] and Foley *et al.* [1990] provide more advanced coverage whilst Hearn and Baker [1986], Hill [1990] and Jones [2001] are invaluable resources at the more introductory level.

8.10 Review Questions

1. Distinguish between clipping and culling.
2. Explain issues that may influence/determine the sharpness of a shadows silhouette.
3. Explain one potential weakness associated with Gouraud's interpolative shading technique.
4. What is the underlying approach adopted in Phong's interpolative shading technique?
5. Distinguish between object space and image space techniques.
6. How does back plane clipping increase efficiency?
7. State one way of reducing the computational cost associated with Phong's interpolative shading technique.
8. Investigate the use of Radiosity techniques within the context of computer graphics. Identify key strengths and weaknesses.
9. Investigate the use of texture mapping. Include so-called 'bump mapping' within your study – how can this be readily incorporated within the Phong shading process?
10. Use software such as Maya to create 3-D scenes. This will give you a sound insight into the application of some of the techniques that we have briefly considered here and in previous chapters.

8.11 Feedback to Review Questions

1. Culling refers to removing non-visible polygons in their entirety and is particularly effective when working with convex polygonal representations. Clipping refers to the removal of non-visible *portions* of polygons and can be non-trivial.
2. The nature of the illumination – e.g. the use of a point source or extended source (in the case of the latter we may also consider its distance). In addition sharpness is influenced by the texture of the surface onto which the shadow is cast and perhaps even by the texture of the source of the shadow.
3. The undesirable appearance of Mach bands.
4. The vertex normal vectors are interpolated across the surface of each polygon. The shading model is applied so that it operates with these interpolated vectors.
5. In the case of an object space technique the clipping/culling processes act directly on objects contained within the 3-D scene – e.g. back face culling. In contrast, in the case of an image space technique, the clipping/culling processes act on the planar rendition of the objects that comprise a scene. The z-buffer technique is an example of an image space technique.

6. As a consequence of linear perspective, an object within the scene that is at a great distance may ultimately project onto only a single display pixel. By means of the back clipping plane we can eliminate such objects from the scene thereby saving processing time and avoiding cluttering the displayed image with undistinguishable background content.

7. Various approaches may be adopted. For example, instead of applying the shading model to each pixel, it can be applied to every other pixel. In this case the intermediate pixels are set by calculating the average of the values assigned to immediate neighbours.

8–10. No feedback to these Review Questions.

Creative 3-D Display Techniques 9

'...we heard a bark which meant:
"Here is a door I cannot open!".'

9.1 Introduction

In this chapter we provide a brief introduction to a range of emerging 3-D display techniques that are not only able to support various pictorial depth cues but in addition the parallax and, in some instances, oculomotor cues. In line with previous works (e.g. Blundell and Schwarz [2006], Blundell [2007]), we will refer to these systems as 'creative 3-D displays'. For current purposes, it is sufficient to assume that such displays possess one or more of the following characteristics:

- The ability to satisfy a range of pictorial depth cues, binocular and motion parallax and in some instances the oculomotor cues (recall previous discussion concerning depth cues – see Chapter 5).
- There is some degree of uncertainty about the technologies and techniques that are best employed in their implementation.
- There is some uncertainty as to the optimal form of the 3-D tableau in which images reside or appear to reside (we will discuss various forms of 3-D tableaux shortly).
- Such displays offer to support alternative and more intuitive interaction techniques. This may include bi-manual interaction and/or haptic feedback (see Chapter 10).
- There is uncertainty as to the optimal ways of using these systems and their ultimate impact on working practices.

In short, there is a great deal of scope for creativity in the design, implementation and application of such systems. Creative 3-D display systems have been the subject of on-going research for many decades and various commercial systems are currently available. One difficulty that researchers have faced (and continue to face) relates to the diversity of approaches that may be adopted in their implementation coupled with the lack of standard metrics by which display performance can be measured (so enabling different display techniques to be compared in a meaningful and non-subjective manner).

In this chapter, we can do little more than provide a brief insight into creative 3-D techniques. However, where appropriate we provide details of references that contain additional and useful information. In the next section, we present a simple scheme for the characterisation of different forms of creative 3-D displays in accordance with their ability to support different types of depth cue. This leads on to discussion concerning different forms of image space (display tableaux) within which images may be placed. Here, we identify the planar image space that is associated with the conventional flat screen display, together with the physical, free, virtual and apparent forms which are supported by the various creative display technologies.

In Section 9.3, we focus on creative 3-D display systems whose principle of operation is fundamentally based on that of the stereoscope (recall that this was pioneered by both Charles Wheatstone and David Brewster in the 19th century). Here, we introduce four general approaches that may be used for the inclusion of the binocular parallax cue – specifically: the non-coded, chromatically coded, temporally coded and spatially coded techniques. This leads on to discussion in Section 9.4 of ways in which we can incorporate support for motion parallax and so enable a user to move from side to side (or up and down) to see an image from a different vantage point. Within this context we briefly consider issues relating to head tracking.

Volumetric display systems are introduced in Section 9.5. This class of display enables 3-D images to be depicted within a physical transparent volume. Since images may occupy three physical dimensions, a range of depth cues (including the oculomotor cues) are satisfied in a natural manner. Our discussion involves both swept volume and static volume systems and we highlight a number of strengths and weaknesses of this general technique by introducing several exemplar technologies.

In Section 9.6 we describe the varifocal display technique (which also supports the oculomotor cues) and finally, in Section 9.7, outline aspects of the holographic approach.

Key Learning Outcomes: At the end of this chapter you should be able to:

- *Identify the general characteristics of creative 3-D display systems.*

- *Discuss the classification of a range of creative 3-D display system technologies and the characteristics of five key forms of image space in which images may be depicted.*

- *Describe techniques that are used in the implementation of display systems that are based on the principle of the stereoscope and discuss the extension of this technique in support of motion parallax.*

- *Discuss the volumetric, varifocal and computational holography approaches.*

- *Describe the strengths and weaknesses of various forms of stereoscopic and autostereoscopic display systems.*

9.2 Creative 3-D Display Systems: General Characteristics

'Great spirits have always encountered violent opposition from mediocre minds.'[1]

Many methods and techniques may be applied to the implementation of creative 3-D display systems and these often give rise to systems that exhibit markedly different characteristics. To most readily compare and contrast such systems, it is useful to develop a classification or categorisation scheme whereby displays may be grouped according to one or more criteria. Unfortunately, the development of precise schemes is by no means a trivial undertaking – displays can differ in so many ways and there are many 'maverick' displays that represent exceptional cases and cannot easily be encompassed within a simple and straightforward classification framework. Even agreeing upon the criteria on which a categorisation system should be based is by no means a simple task. For example, should we adopt a 'bottom up' approach – so focusing on the fundamental principles of operation and the technologies employed in display system implementation? Alternatively, should we adopt a 'top down' scheme thereby classifying systems according visual image attributes (if so, which attributes do we deem to be of the greatest importance)? Furthermore, since the display forms a focal point for interactive operations, should we not embrace issues that relate to a display's ability to support different forms of interaction device?

In the next subsection we present a rudimentary scheme which focuses on the ability of display technologies to present to the human visual system pictorial, oculomotor and binocular depth cues. Although this scheme focuses almost exclusively on one aspect of display system performance, it does provide a simple and useful framework. Subsequently, in Section 9.2.2 we turn our attention to the different forms of image space that may be produced by creative 3-D display systems, and here we identify five key types of image space. This discussion draws on a previous work (Blundell [2007]) and provides us with a useful insight into the nature and characteristics of the different types of image that can be formed through the use of creative display systems.

9.2.1 A General Classification

Creative 3-D display systems can be categorised in a number of ways. For example, they may be distinguished and grouped according to the technologies used in their implementation; in accordance with inherent attributes of the visible image; or on the basis of the characteristics of the region in which the image resides (the 'image space'). One simple and commonly used scheme is illustrated in Table 9.1 and is in essence based on the ability of a display paradigm to support various types of depth cue. As may be seen from this diagram, the conventional flat screen display (in its basic form) via which we interact with the digital world usually provides support for only the pictorial depth cues (see Section 5.4). However, this display modality can be advanced to provide support for binocular parallax (stereopsis). This enables images to appear to reside within a 3-D space but in its basic form does not allow us to move our head from side to side (or upwards and downwards) to view an image from a different vantage point (the motion parallax cue – see Section 5.6.2). Through the incorporation of additional techniques, stereoscopic systems can often be made to support this cue. This may, for example, involve the tracking of an observer's vantage point (see Section 9.4) – although

---

[1] Attributed to Albert Einstein (1879–1955).

Table 9.1 A simple categorisation of various types of creative 3-D display. The arrows loosely indicate techniques that can be extended to form the basis for another class of technology. Two classes of autostereoscopic system are included to distinguish between systems that do not support oculomotor cues and those which do. However, in the main publications do not make this distinction.

Monocular	Stereoscopic	Autostereoscopic (Class I)	Autostereoscopic (Class II)
The conventional flat screen display	Chromatically coded (anaglyph)		Volumetric
	Non-coded	Immersive/augmented virtual reality	Varifocal
	Temporally coded		Holographic
	Spatially coded		
Support for only pictorial depth cues	*Support for pictorial depth cues and binocular parallax*	*Support for pictorial depth cues, binocular and motion parallax*	*Support for pictorial depth cues, binocular and motion parallax and oculomotor cues*
Direct viewing	*Direct or indirect viewing (via glasses)*	*Direct or indirect viewing (via glasses or other headgear)*	*Direct viewing*
No head tracking	*No head tracking*	*May or may not require head tracking*	*No head tracking required*

in general only horizontal parallax is supported.[2] We categorise display systems that are able to support the pictorial cues together with binocular and motion parallax as 'autostereoscopic systems'.

Generally, autostereoscopic displays are assumed to support both pictorial and binocular cues. However, as may be seen in Table 9.1 we indicate two classes of autostereoscopic system – these differ in terms of their ability to support the oculomotor cues (see Section 5.5). Techniques listed in the first of these two columns (Class I), do not support oculomotor cues and in fact depth cue conflict may exist in relation to the breakdown of the visual system's accommodation and convergence. (Recall that when we view our surroundings, the eyes focus on – and their optical axes converge on – the object on which we fixate. However, when we regard images depicted on displays based on the stereoscope, this no longer happens – these two processes no longer operate in synchronism). Techniques listed in the right-hand column of Table 9.1 (Class II) support (at least in principle) pictorial, parallax and oculomotor cues. Volumetric, varifocal and holographic systems represent the main form of display paradigms that fall into this category. These approaches will be introduced later in the chapter.

When comparing and contrasting display techniques according to their ability to support different types of depth cue, caution needs to be exercised – a display should not necessarily be deemed superior simply because it is able to support a greater number of depth cues.

---

[2] In the case that only horizontal parallax is supported ('horizontal parallax only' is often given the acronym HPO), an observer may move the head from side to side and obtain a different vantage point onto an image scene. However, in this case moving the head in a vertical direction will not give rise to a different view onto a scene.

> When viewing our surroundings, the relative emphasis that we place on different depth cues varies according to the scene under observation and the way in which we may wish to interact with it. In some situations the inability of a display to support one or more cues may not be problematic. On the other hand, for some applications, the lack of support for particular depth cues may hamper the visualisation and/or interaction processes.

9.2.2 Forms of Image Space

In the previous subsection, we presented a general categorisation scheme based on the ability of each display paradigm to satisfy a range of depth cues. However, as mentioned previously we can categorise creative display technologies according to other criteria – such as the form of image space that is associated with a technique. The most straightforward way of defining an image space is to say that it represents the 2-D or 3-D region within which images may be placed. Unfortunately, this definition is a little too restrictive – an image space does not necessarily represent a physical 3-D region in space. For example, consider the stereograms depicted in Figure 1.32. When these are correctly viewed (i.e. by means of the viewing glasses provided with this book or by directly fusing the stereopair (by slightly 'crossing' the eyes)) a 3-D image is observed. This image appears to reside in a 3-D space – however this is an impression that is formed within the human visual system. In this scenario, the actual image (i.e. the stereopair) resides on a 2-D surface. Only when these images are viewed in the correct manner do we perceive an image that *appears* to occupy three physical dimensions (and hence assume the formation of a 3-D image space). However, this is a perception of (and within) the visual system and is not based on any physical reality. Consequently, for the purposes of this book we will define an image space as follows:[3]

> An image space denotes a region within which image components may be placed or within which they appear to be located.

In Figure 9.1 we summarise five general forms of image space (these are based on a classification scheme previously introduced in Blundell [2007]) and each is briefly discuss each below:

9.2.2.1 *The Planar Image Space*

This type of image space is associated with the conventional flat screen display. Here, image components are positioned on a planar (2-D) surface and only pictorial depth cues are made available to the visual system (as previously discussed, oculomotor and binocular cues are absent). The extent of such an image space is defined by the dimensions of the display and in the case of today's computer displays, the planar image space is divided into two general regions – the workspace and the menu system. The former represents the region in which the results of the computational process are displayed and in which we can undertake creative activity, whereas the latter comprises the icons etc which form the event driven user interface.

---

[3] This definition does not encompass all possible scenarios but is sufficient for our purposes.

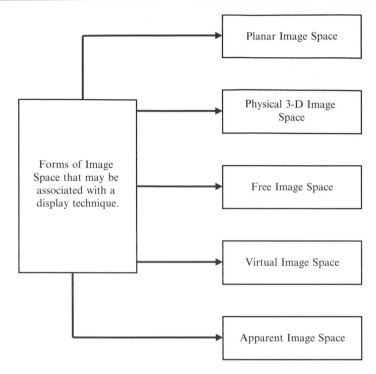

Figure 9.1 A summary of the different forms of image space that may be associated with various classes of display technology. The characteristics of the image space not only impact on the visualisation opportunities offered by a display but also on the interaction techniques that may be most effectively employed.

9.2.2.2 *The Physical 3-D Image Space*

In the case of volumetric display systems (these will be introduced shortly – see Section 9.5) the image space comprises a transparent physical 3-D volume within which images may be depicted. For the moment, it is sufficient to compare this volume to a goldfish bowl or tropical fish tank within which the fish (representing image components) are free to move. When we view fish in a bowl or tank, the visual system is presented not only with a range of pictorial depth cues but also, since the fish occupy three physical dimensions, both binocular and oculomotor cues are present. Any display system that permits images to be depicted within a physical image space is by definition categorised as autostereoscopic (Class II) – recall Table 9.1. In the case that the physical volume in which images are depicted has physical boundaries (e.g. glass or plastic walls) or materials within the volume itself which prevent the insertion of the hand or an interaction tool, then we will refer to this as a 'physical' image space.

9.2.2.3 *The Free Image Space*

As we have just indicated, image scenes depicted within a physical image space present the observer with pictorial, oculomotor and binocular cues. In addition, a physical image space is assumed to be contained within a solid vessel – the presence of which prevents the insertion of the hand or interaction tools (such as a pointer).[4] However, in some applications, it is advantageous for a user to be able to 'touch' image components and so the presence of materials which exclude the insertion of physical objects into an image space may be undesirable. Thus, we introduce the 'free' image space in which the image scene appears to be suspended within a 3-D space into which physical objects may be inserted.

In popular literature, the ability of creative 3-D display technologies to produce 'free space' images is sometimes misrepresented – with writers preferring to overlook fundamental science in order to portray futuristic displays that enable images to appear to be suspended in space. In this respect, great care has to be exercised. By way of example, consider the diagram presented in Figure 9.2(a).

Here, our aim is to generate a free space image in Region A and with this in mind, we use some form of projection system to cast an image vertically upwards. The observer at Location B will not see any image – the projected light will continue to travel in a straight path – upwards! Alternatively, if (as indicated in Figure 9.2(b)) Region A contains particles able to scatter the projected light (recall Section 5.4.3), then light will reach the observer (although in practise producing high quality images by this approach may be problematic). Interestingly, the use of scattering centres to produce an image that appears to reside within free space was first employed many years ago and underpinned the operation of a projection device known as the Phantasmagoria. Dating back to the 18th century, in its basic form this device enabled lantern slides to be cast into a cloud of smoke particles. This gave rise to ghostly images that appeared to be suspended in space and it is claimed that this was put to military use during the French Revolution as a means of terrifying combatants at night-time![5] In a more refined form, the smoke particles were replaced with a cloud of fine barium oxide particles. Under normal lighting conditions this cloud may not have been particularly visible – but when illuminated with ultraviolet light the particles would have glowed and the cloud would have appeared to shimmer.

The nature of the free-space image is summed up in Halle [1997] where the 'projection constraint' is defined as follows:

'A display medium or element must always lie along a line of sight between the viewer and all parts of a spatial [free space] *image.'*

This situation is illustrated in Figure 9.2(b). Here, we assume that a medium able to scatter the light (introduced from below) exists and is in the line of sight of the observer. Halle goes on to write:

'Photons must originate in, or be redirected by, some material. The material can be behind, in front of, or within the space of the image [image space], *but it must be present. All claims to the contrary violate what we understand of the world ... Technologies lavished with claims of mid-air projection should always be scrutinized with regard to the fundamental laws of physics.'*

In principle, an optical arrangement can be used to convert a physical image space into a free image space and this may also offer image magnification. Thus an image created within a volume that has solid boundaries can be magnified and repositioned so that it appears to be suspended in space. However, any such arrangement must meet the 'projection constraint' mentioned above. For related discussion see Blundell [2007].

---

[4] The actual material(s) or arrangement of the materials that form the image space may also make it impossible to insert physical objects into the image space.

[5] The authenticity of this claim is uncertain – perhaps it is no more than an amusing possibility.

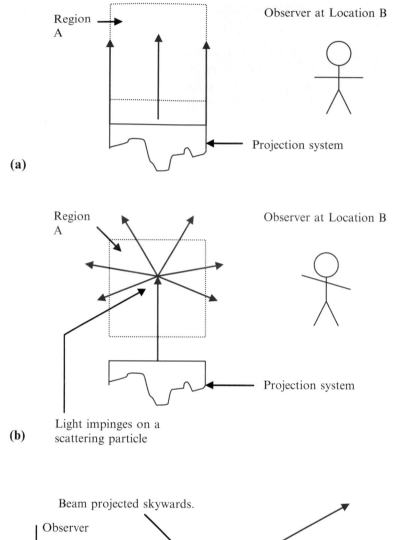

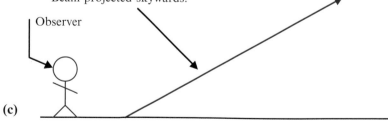

Figure 9.2 In (a) some form of beam is projected vertically in an effort to create a free space image in Region A. In (b) we introduce into Region A particles able to scatter the projected beam. In (c) some form of beam is projected into the air in an attempt to generate a free space image that appears to be suspended in the sky — see OTU Exercise 9.1.

OTU Exercise 9.1: The 'Free Space' Image

Consider the diagram presented in Figure 9.2(c). Here, in an attempt to generate images that appear to be suspended in the sky, some form of powerful beam (which may either be scanned or spatially modulated – this issue need not concern us) is projected upwards. How effective will this approach be – how does your answer conform to the comments that are reproduced above from Halle [1997]?

9.2.2.4 *The Virtual Image Space*

When we look into a planar mirror, the reflected image appears to reside behind the mirror. If we back away from the mirror, the reflected image moves away from us – in fact, the image lies as far behind the mirror as an object is in front of it. This is illustrated in Figure 9.3(a). Here, an object is placed at a distance d_1 in front of the mirror. Two rays of light are shown emanating from the object. As indicated in the illustration, at the point at which one of these rays impinges on the mirror the angle between the ray and the surface normal (the angle of incidence) is i. A basic law of reflection is that the angle of incidence and the angle of reflection are equal, thus angles i and r are of the same size. Applying this law to both of the rays incident on the mirror, the paths traversed by the reflected rays are immediately evident. To an observer, the image appears to be located at the point at which the reflected rays appear to meet. This occurs at a location behind the mirror such that distances d_1 and d_2 are equal.

The image produced by a plane mirror is said to be a 'virtual image' since it cannot be cast onto a screen. Some forms of creative 3-D display system are able to produce a virtual image space which we define as one which appears to be located *behind* the optical component via which the image space is made visible to the observer. This is clarified in Figure 9.3(b).

The virtual image technique has been employed in theatrical productions for many decades and dates back at least as far as the 1860s. Interestingly, the technique that was developed at that time underpins the operation of at least one form of creative 3-D display. It is therefore instructive to briefly outline the manner in which virtual images were generated and employed for the formation of theatrical illusions.

The basic technique appears to have been devised by Henry Dircks (although within literature credit is often incorrectly attributed to John Pepper) and is an advancement of the Phantasmagoria technique mentioned above. In the 1860s 'Pepper's (Dircks') Ghost' made a sensational appearance on the London stage. One form of this illusion is depicted in Figure 9.4. In this illustration, the audience can be seen to the left hand side and interposed between these spectators and the actors (to the right) is a large glass plate which is tilted towards the audience. A phantom (physical actor) is located below the stage and is not directly visible to the audience. However due to reflection in the glass plate, the audience see a virtual rendition of the phantom – who appears to coexist within the space occupied by the actors. The optical arrangement is summarised in Figure 9.5(a).

In Figure 9.5(b) we depict the basic process whereby light is reflected in the glass plate. In this illustration the plate is shown in cross section and a ray of light impinges on this plate from the left. When light travels between materials that have different optical densities, it undergoes refraction – the direction of propagation of a ray (or group of rays) changes. This is caused by the speed of propagation of the light changing – a property of a material known as the refractive

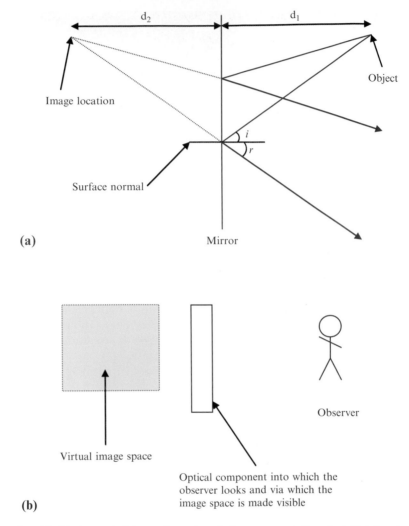

Figure 9.3 As indicated in (a) when we look into a planar mirror, the image appears to lie as far behind the mirror as the object is in front of it. Thus distances d_1 and d_2 are equal. In (b) we illustrate the concept of a virtual image space. Here, the observer looks into some form of optical component (or arrangement of components). In the case of a free image space, the image space would reside *between* the observer and optical component – however in the case of a virtual image space, the image appears to reside *behind* the optical component.

index provides us with a measure of the speed at which light will travel in a particular medium as compared to its speed in 'free space'. The amount by which the direction of propagation changes at the interface between two materials is given by Snell's Law:

$$n_1 \sin \theta_1 = n_2 \sin \theta_2. \tag{9.1}$$

Figure 9.4 The use of Pepper's Ghost (or more accurately Dircks' Ghost) as a theatrical illusion. This same technique is used in the implementation of a creative 3-D display able to produce a virtual image space – see Figure 9.7. (Image reproduced from Low, A.M., *Popular Scientific Recreations*, Ward, Lock and Co (1933).)

The meaning of the various symbols may be readily understood from Figure 9.5(c). Let us now consider the case that light passes from an optically dense to a less optically dense material (e.g. from glass to air). As indicated in Figure 9.5(c), the light will be bent away from the normal (i.e. $\theta_2 > \theta_1$). When $\theta_2 = 90°$, the emerging light will simply travel along the surface of the glass block and when $\theta_2 > 90°$, the light will no longer emerge from the block but will be reflected back into it – this is known as total internal reflection and in this case the glass is acting as a mirror. Thus, on the basis of Eq. 9.1, for total internal reflection to occur we require that:

$$\frac{n_1}{n_2} \sin \theta_1 > \sin 90°,$$

and so:

$$\sin \theta_1 > \frac{n_2}{n_1}. \tag{9.2}$$

OTU Exercise 9.2: Total Internal Reflection

Assuming that the refractive index of air is ~1.003 and that of glass is ~1.52, calculate the minimum angle of incidence at the glass to air boundary that will result in total internal reflection.

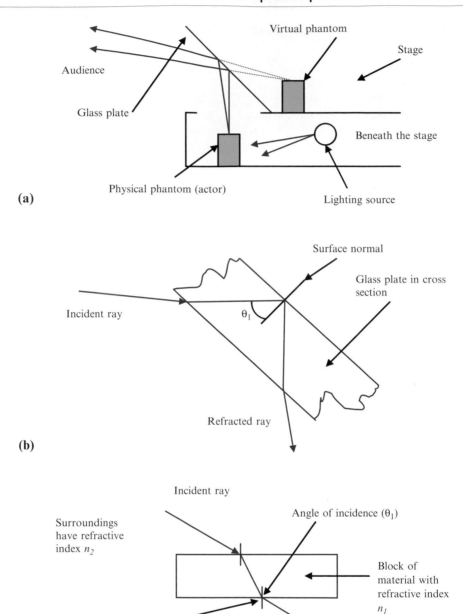

(a)

(b)

(c)

Figure 9.5 In (a) we illustrate the optical arrangement that underpins Pepper's (Dircks') Ghost. Here, the physical phantom is located beneath the stage and cannot be directly viewed by the audience. However, due to reflection in the glass plate (see Figure 9.4) the audience sees a virtual image of the ghost that appears to coexist in the space in which the actors move. In (b) we illustrate the reflection within the glass plate. This is caused by total internal reflection (based on refraction at the glass to air interface). In (c) a ray of light travels through a block of material and undergoes refraction.

This equation is used in determining the angle at which the glass plate employed in the so called Pepper's Ghost illusion should be tilted. In terms of total internal reflection in general, it is important to note that:

> Total internal reflection can occur when light passes from a dense to a less optically dense medium – i.e. in the case of the plate used in the Pepper's Ghost illusion when light attempts to emerge from the plate. Total internal reflection does not occur as the light enters the glass – i.e. when light travels from a less dense to a more optically dense medium.

In appreciating the power of the 'Pepper's' Ghost illusion, it is important to bear in mind that from the perspective of an audience, the phantom appears to exist in the same space as that occupied by the actors (however the phantom is not visible to the actors). Thus as long as the actors are able to note the location at which the phantom will appear to be positioned (as far as the audience is concerned), they are able to apparently make contact with it, do battle, threaten it with cloves of garlic (if indeed garlic works with phantoms...) etc. Under such duress, the phantom may choose to flee in which case, in the true tradition of spectres, it can pass through solid objects located on the stage!

The relevance of this theatrical illusion to today's creative 3-D display technologies is readily apparent when we consider the display technique shown in Figure 9.7.

Here, a flat screen display is inclined relative to a horizontal glass plate. The observer does not directly view the images depicted on the display but rather views the image reflected in the glass plate. Consider the point on the display screen labelled 'A' in Figure 9.6 and that corresponds to a picture element (pixel). As indicated by the two rays, when we view the reflection of this point, it will appear to be located beneath the glass plate. In fact, the display screen taken as a whole will appear to lie in the approximate location indicated by the bold dashed line that is shown in the diagram. If we were to depict stereoscopic images on the display screen (recall from Section 1.6 the chromatic and temporal coding techniques that can be used in the implementation of such a display), then the 3-D image would appear to lie within a volume beneath the glass plate. This represents a virtual image space.

The technique illustrated in Figures 9.6 and 9.7 is particularly effective when considered from the point of view of interaction. An operator can reach around the glass plate and so place the hand (together with an interactive pointer) within the space in which the image appears to reside. The hand and interaction tool are directly visible through the glass and by analogy represent the on-stage actors employed in the Pepper's Ghost illusion (the 3-D image representing the spectre). If the interaction tool supports haptic (in this case force feedback – see Chapter 10) then the operator can 'touch' the image – the ghost appears to have substance – the 3-D image seems to be a solid entity.

9.2.2.5 The Apparent Image Space

This form of image space was briefly introduced at the beginning of this subsection. However, in the light of the above discussion concerning other forms of image space, a brief review of this image space modality is worthwhile.

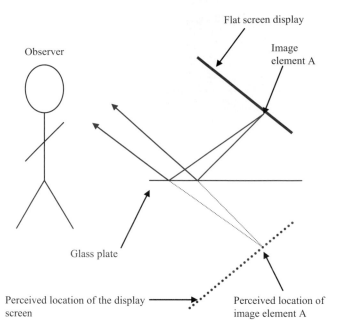

Figure 9.6 A Display technique based on the Pepper's (Dircks') Ghost illusion. In this embodiment, a flat screen display depicting stereoscopic images is inclined above a horizontal glass plate. The observer views the image reflected in the plate (i.e. does not directly view the image depicted on the display screen). The image appears to reside beneath the glass plate – i.e. within a virtual image space. Also see Figure 9.7.

In the case of the virtual image space, the image space location and extent is defined by the geometry of the optical system employed within the display system, and in the case that binocular parallax is supported, by the disparity of the two retinal images. These two ingredients lead to the formation of an image space that lies behind the optical element via which the observer views an image scene. However, an apparent image space is primarily formed on the basis of binocular parallax – there is no fundamental requirement for an optical component to be interposed between the observer and image space, and our perception of an image space is not defined by the geometry of light entering the eyes. In some embodiments such an optical component may exist and this complicates our explanation. However, for the moment we shall put this complication to one side and consider the most straightforward case. Take another look at the stereograms presented in Figure 1.32 and the additional stereograms reproduced in Figure 9.8. As indicated previously, although a stereoscope or the type of viewing glasses included with this book facilitate fusing the pair, they are not an essential requirement and most people can (after a little practice) fuse such images by slightly crossing the eyes. The result is a 3-D image that appears to reside behind, in front of, or which spans the stereo plane (this is the surface on which the stereopair is depicted). We refer to this as an apparent image space – the depth and location of which is wholly illusionary. The sensations of depth and location are perceived *within* the visual system from disparities that are encoded in the pair of images (the image space has no physical basis – its existence is solely based on our perception).

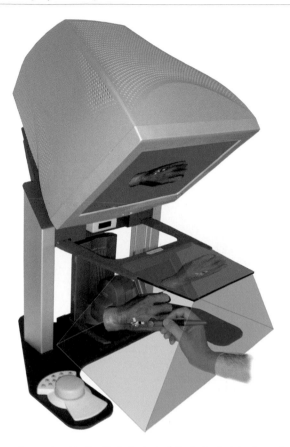

Figure 9.7 A commercial display system produced by Reachin Technologies.[6] The basic principle of operation of this system is based on the Pepper's (Dircks') Ghost illusion which dates back to the 1860s. As can be seen, from this artist's rendition, the reflected image appears to reside behind the glass plate. Thus the users hand and interaction tool appear to coexist exist within the same virtual image space. This system employs a 19 inch CRT based display (1024 by 768 pixels) that is refreshed at 120 Hz (giving a 60 Hz refresh frequency for each eye). The stereo viewing glasses are of the shutter type and are connected by means of a wireless link. (Image kindly supplied by and reproduced by permission of Reachin Technologies AB.)

> In the context of display system technologies, it is very important to use the term 'illusionary' with caution. Here, we must be clear – the images depicted by all display system technologies are, to a greater or lesser extent, illusionary. This is not very surprising since our visual perception of the physical world is also largely illusionary (recall discussion in Chapter 5). Thus the 'illusion' of the existence of an apparent image space is no more remarkable than our sensing different wavelengths of light via an experience of colour.

---

[6] Reachin Technologies AB, Formansvagen 11, 117 43 Stockholm, Sweden (www.reachin.se).

(a)

Figure 9.8 Two stereopairs. As with those presented in Figure 1.32, these may be viewed using the glasses provided with this book or with a little practice, crossing the eyes slightly will enable them to be fused directly – without recourse to glasses. Should you experience difficulty in fusing these images without recourse to glasses try photocopying/scanning this page and reduce the size of the stereopair.

(b)

Figure 9.8 *Continued*

Rather than fusing the images by slightly crossing the eyes, the stereograms presented in Figures 1.32 and 9.8 may be viewed using an optical device such as the stereoscope. In this case an optical arrangement lies between the observer and the image space. However, this arrangement simply aids the viewing process and is not a requirement. Consequently we still refer to the formation of an apparent image space. On the other hand, the viewing system may relocate the image space so, for example, making it appear to be further away. In this case the decision as to whether an apparent or virtual image space is formed is often ambiguous and so it is necessary to consider such systems on a case-by-case basis.

9.3 Stereoscopic Techniques

> *'If we wish to know the force of human genius we should read Shakespeare.*
> *If we wish to see the insignificance of human learning*
> *we may study his commentators.'*[7]

Creative 3-D display systems which employ the stereoscopic technique are fundamentally based on the stereoscope, which was independently developed by both Charles Wheatstone and David Brewster in the mid-nineteenth century. Here, as indicated in Chapter 1, a 3-D scene is depicted on a 2-D medium. These views are presented in such a way that one view is visible to one eye, and the other view to the other eye. Disparities in these views (see Section 5.6.1) are interpreted by the human visual system as providing an indication of depth and so we perceive a three-dimensional image. In the original form, pairs of stereoscopic images were hand-drawn but this approach was rapidly superseded with the development of stereo photography.

Before moving on to discuss stereoscopic techniques in a little more detail, it is worth mentioning the so-called and somewhat ammusing 'Chimenti controversy'. The mid 19th century denoted a period of great scientific and engineering advancement – an age of industrial revolution. Scientists were often strong, flamboyant and legendary characters funded by a personal income or by a wealthy patron. Wheatstone and Brewster were well known members of this scientific community and for reasons that will perhaps be never fully understood, Brewster appears to have decided that he would go to practically any length to deny Wheatstone the credit for the invention of stereoscopic imaging. It was certainly not that he sought the credit for himself – he was simply keen to demonstrate that Wheatstone was not the first pioneer of this field and so he attempted to place the credit elsewhere. This led to an acrimonious exchange of Letters in the 'Times' newspaper and what joy Brewster must have experienced when, in 1859, he learnt that a student – Alexander Crum Brown – had reported viewing two rediscovered images created by Jacopo Chimenti da Empoli some 300 years earlier. These were displayed side by side in the Musée Wicar in Lille and according to Crum Brown formed a stereopair (see Figure 9.9).

Brewster was perhaps a little rash in accepting (apparently without question) Crum Brown's opinion on the stereoscopic nature of the pair of images – perhaps it would have been more prudent to view the images for himself… However, in his enthusiasm to deny Wheatstone the credit for this invention, Brewster chose to promote the images sight unseen and over the intervening decades, the Chimenti drawings have continued to attract attention and claims that they provide evidence that stereoscopic techniques were mastered in the 16th century.

---

[7] Attributed to William Hazlitt (1778–1830).

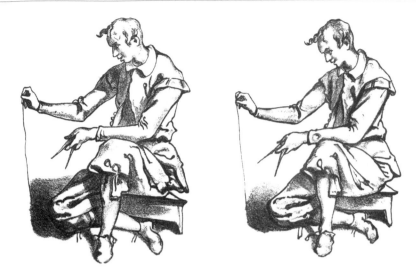

Figure 9.9 The two Chimenti images. Differences are readily apparent – but do they really represent a stereopair? See text for discussion and also OUT Exercise 9.3. (Supplied by and reproduced with the kind permission of Professor Nicholas Wade.)

OTU Exercise 9.3: The Chimenti Drawings

Once you have practiced fusing stereograms such as those presented in Figures 1.32 and 9.8 directly (without recourse to a stereoscope or other viewing glasses), investigate the stereoscopic nature of the Chimenti drawings presented in Figure 9.9. You may wish to photocopy and enlarge these drawings so that they are viewed under the conditions favoured by Alexander Crum Brown. He indicated that in their original form each drawing measured ~30 cm by 22 cm, and they were best observed from a distance of 4–5 yards (although he does not appear to have specified their separation). You may wish to fix the drawings to a wall and experiment with different separations. In addition, perhaps exchange the 'left' and 'right' views.

The author is able to discern relief from *limited* regions of the Chimenti drawings – overall relief is not apparent and certainly, if Chimenti were experimenting with stereoscopic techniques, it would seem natural to have chosen a subject of far less complexity (perhaps a simple cube, cylinder or cone). It is unlikely that we will ever know why Chimenti created these two images but it is doubtful that they were intended to represent a stereopair. However, it is evident that in his promotion of these images, David Brewster should have exercised far greater caution. The debate continues and even recent publications propagate claims that are not backed by fact. For example, in an excellent book published in 1976 in the area of 3-D display systems [Okoshi 1976] (which continues to act as a standard work although it has been out of print for many years and so is unfortunately becoming increasingly difficult to obtain), the author writes:

'*The first trial of artificial three-dimensional imaging was a stereoscopic drawing technique devised by Giovanni Battista della Porta around the year 1600. It is a technique for drawing two precise pictures of an object observed from two different viewing directions. His drawings do not exist today. Similar stereoscopic pictures, however, were drawn by many people for more than 200 years since della Porta.'*

In fact, David Brewster also credited della Porta with the invention of the stereoscope and it is perhaps on the basis of Brewster's comments that this claim continues to appear in publications. Certainly della Porta wrote about the possible reasons for nature providing us with two eyes, but the thoughts that he expressed in his 1593 publication do not inspire one to the belief that he had any insight into binocular vision. For example, he writes:

'If someone places a staff in front of himself and sets it against some obvious crack in the wall opposite, and notices the place, then when he shuts the left eye he will not see the staff to have moved from the crack opposite. The reason is that one sees with the right eye, just as one uses the right hand and foot and someone using the left eye or hand or foot is considered a monster. But if the observer closes the right eye, the staff immediately shifts to the right side. There is a third argument – that nature made two eyes, one beside the other, so that one may defend a man from attackers from the right and the other from the left. This is more obvious in animals, for their eyes are separated by half a foot, as is seen in cattle, horses and lions. In birds one eye is opposite the other, consequently, if things must be seen both on the right and on the left, the power of seeing must be engaged very quickly for the mind to be able to accomplish its function. For these reasons the two eyes cannot see the same thing at the same time.' (Translation by Helen Ross from della Porta [1593].)

In the next subsection we briefly discuss the way in which a virtual camera may be used to create stereo-views of a computer generated scene, and subsequently summarise and build on discussion previously presented in Section 1.6.2 in relation to stereoscopic coding techniques.

9.3.1 Creating Stereo-views

In Section 6.6 we discussed the use of a virtual camera comprising a viewing plane, viewing window, viewpoint and viewing coordinate system. We adopted a left-handed coordinate system, placed the viewing plane in the plane $z_v = 0$ and positioned the viewpoint on the z_v axis.[8] By forming two perspective projections – each corresponding to a different viewpoint location – we can create a virtual stereo-camera and so provide stereo-views of a scene. In Figure 9.10, we illustrate appropriate viewpoint positions and as may be seen each of these locations is offset by a distance x_e from the z_v axis (these correspond to the left and right eye views).

In forming the stereo-views, we would typically set y_e to zero thereby locating the viewpoints in the x–z plane. We then set x_e to $\sim$ one half of the interocular distance and undertake a perspective projection for both $+x_e$ and $-x_e$ locations (one location corresponding to the left eye view and the other to the right).

Four fundamental ways of encoding stereoscopic images for presentation to the human visual system are summarised in Figure 9.11. Here we adopt the same terminology as used in previous books [Blundell and Schwarz 2006, Blundell 2007] and refer to these techniques as non-coded, chromatically coded, temporally coded, and spatially coded. These approaches were briefly introduced in Section 1.6.2 and in the subsections that follow we revisit each and provide references for further reading.

---

[8] Recall that the axes of the coordinate system were ascribed a subscript 'v' to distinguish them from those of the world coordinate system which were given a subscript 'w'.

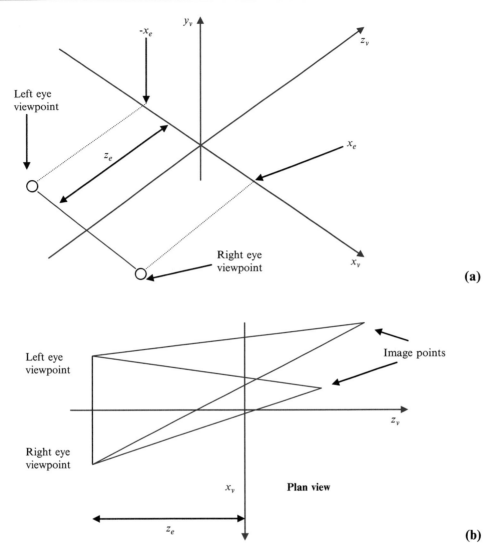

Figure 9.10 In (a) we illustrate the two viewpoints used to create a stereopair. Here, the interocular distance corresponds to $2x_e$. In (b), diagram (a) is re-drawn in plan view and two points of the image are indicated.

9.3.2 Non-coded Stereoscopic Techniques

As indicated in Section 1.6, this approach closely mimics the techniques pioneered by Wheatstone and Brewster in the mid-nineteenth century. In its original form two hand-drawn images corresponding to slightly different viewpoints onto a 3-D scene are placed side by side and are viewed so that each image is directed to the appropriate eye. In the 1940s research was undertaken into replacing the two drawings/photographs which form a stereopair, with electronic display screens based on CRT technology. This pioneering work developed over the subsequent twenty years and in the 1960s led to the form of headset which we now associate with immersive virtual reality (IVR) systems.

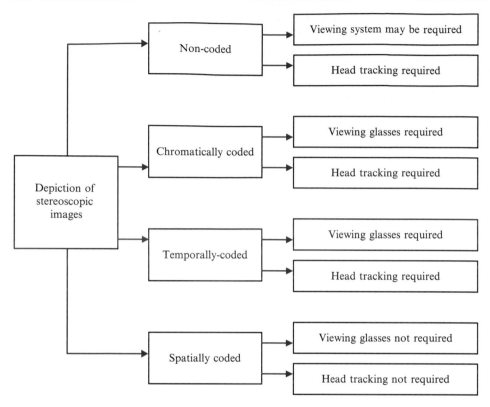

Figure 9.11 Summarising the four general types of coding technique that can be used in connection with stereoscopic display system implementations. On the right-hand-side we indicate whether or not each general approach demands the use of viewing glasses or other forms of viewing system and also the requirement for head tracking. In this latter respect, we are considering natural support for motion parallax and as may be seen, only the spatially coded approach can support this cue without the need to track the observer's view point[9].

From our present perspective, it is instructive to identify the strengths and weaknesses of each of the four general techniques that are identified in Figure 9.11. As summarised in Table 9.2, key strengths of this approach are the avoidance of cross-talk (the images presented to the two eyes are completely segregated), and the suitability of this technique for use in immersive virtual reality (IVR) and augmented (mixed) reality headsets. In Section 1.6.2 we referred to the implementation of the immersive virtual reality (IVR) headset, and here it is worth briefly examining the augmented reality approach.

This technique enables real and synthetic images to be combined and in the case that a headset is employed, the user can view real world images which are overlayed with computer generated (synthetic) content. By way of a simple example of this type of application, consider the situation that a technician is undertaking fault-finding on a complex system of electronic circuits, pipework or the like. Naturally, a system that can reliably assist the technician in identifying the function of cables, groups of cables or pipes could be a great asset – particularly if this circumvents the need to continuously consult extensive manuals or other forms of documentation.

---

[9] Frequently, spatially coded systems support only horizontal parallax. Additional support for vertical parallax may necessitate tracking the observers vantage point.

Table 9.2 Summary of the strengths and possible weaknesses/complications of various general forms of stereoscopic technique.

Technique	Key Advantages	Potential Difficulties
Non-coded	Elimination of cross-talk. Suitability for IVR. Suitability for augmented reality.	The use of two display screens. Motion parallax requires head tracking. Screens and optics must match the requirements of the human visual system.
Chromatic coding	Simple and cost effective. Well suited to wire-frame image depiction.	Viewing glasses are required. Limited ability to depict multi-colour images. Motion parallax requires head tracking. Cross-talk should be minimised.
Temporal coding	The colour pallet of the display is not compromised.	Viewing glasses are required. Motion parallax requires head tracking. Display must support a high refresh frequency. Cross-talk should be minimised.
Spatial coding	Viewing glasses are not required. Motion parallax does not require head tracking. The colour pallet of the display is not compromised.	As the number of views are increased, there is a corresponding decrease in the number of pixels per view.

In such a scenario, the augmented (mixed) reality technique may be beneficial; as the observer looks at the wiring etc, computer generated labels are overlaid on the visible scene. However, to operate successfully, it is pivotally important that the computer is able to identify the items within the operator's visual field. It appears that Ivan Sutherland may well have been the first person to investigate this display modality [Sutherland 1968]. In relation to the head mounted display (HMD) which he developed, he writes:

'*Half-silvered mirrors in the prisms through which the user looks allow him to see both the images from the cathode-ray tubes* [as with the original IVR headsets, two cathode ray tubes were used for the depiction of the binocular pair] *and objects in the room simultaneously. Thus displayed material can be made either to hang disembodied in space or coincide with maps, desk tops, walls, or the keys of a typewriter.*'

He goes on to discuss the issue of position sensing (see Section 9.4) and describes the use of both a system comprising mechanical linkages and a wireless technique employing ultrasonic transmitters and receivers.

In comparing the IVR and augmented reality approaches, there is one important issue that should not be overlooked. In the case of IVR, the user is immersed within a virtual space – the physical world is no longer visible. This can lead to disorientation – especially if the IVR application demands that the user be able to move around. Although one or more senses may be supplied with wholly artificial content, gravity is ever present and the human sense of balance can readily become confused when faced with conflicting sensory input. In short, a traveller in cyberspace must still take into account their physical surroundings – to trip and fall in the physical world can quickly bring a cyber voyage to an abrupt end!!

> An IVR headset disconnects the user's sense of sight from the physical world. This can result in disorientation and sensory conflict. The augmented (mixed) reality approach (employing a headset) enables physical and synthetic content to be overlayed and unlike the IVR approach, the user is not visually disconnected with the physical world.

Returning to the strengths and possible weaknesses of the non-coded technique as summarised in Table 9.2, in the case that a headset is used, key weaknesses (or perhaps it may be better to say complexities) of this approach are:

1. The need to employ separate display screens for the left and right views on the stereopair.
2. The need to interpose an optical arrangement between each display screen and the eye.
3. If the motion parallax depth cue is to be supported (enabling the user to view images from different orientations simply by moving the head position) then a head tracking system must be included.
4. The visual and temporal characteristics of the display screens must match the requirements of the human visual system.
5. In the case of the IVR embodiment of this technique, the user may become disoriented and sensory conflict may be problematic.

9.3.3 Chromatically Coded Images

Recall the section of anaglyph images presented earlier in this book. Here, the two different viewpoints onto a 3-D scene are each depicted in a different colour. By using the filtered glasses provided with this book, each eye is only able to see one of these two colours. Thus the image depicted in red is seen by one eye, and the image depicted in green by the other eye. The images are fused within the visual system and disparities within the views give rise to our perception of three-dimensionality. Typically, glasses employing green and red or green and blue filters are used – this provides strong wavelength separation of the two views and thereby enables the use of lower quality filters.

The colour of the background on which anaglyph line drawing are created can impact on the production of an anaglyph image. By way of example, let us suppose that an anaglyph drawing is created in red and green and is viewed using glasses with corresponding filters. When green lines are viewed through the red filter, they will appear to be black (as the red filter passes only red (or close to red) light and the green does not contain wavelengths close to red). Similarly, when red lines are viewed through the green filter, they will also appear to be black. Now let us suppose that as illustrated in Figure 9.12(a), the lines are depicted on a black background. Since the green line appears to be black when viewed through the red filter, it will merge with the black background and so be non-visible (or practically so). Similarly the red line appears black through the green filter and therefore will again merge with the background. Confirm this using the anaglyph glasses supplied with this book – as you will observe, the red line is visible only through the red filter and the green line only through the green filter. Now use the glasses to view the diagram presented in Figure 9.12(b). You will see that the red line is now visible through the green filter and the green line through the red filter: because of the reversal in the background colour, line visibility has also reversed! Finally, in Figure 9.12(c), the two coloured lines are printed on a grey background. When this diagram is viewed using the anaglyph glasses, each line can be seen through the two filters. Consequently, not only do the colours of the lines and

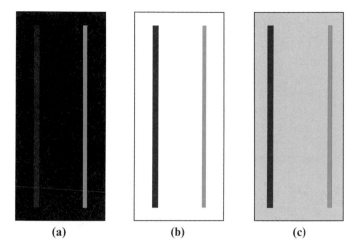

Figure 9.12 When (a) is viewed using the anaglyph glasses supplied with this book, the red line is visible through the red filter and the green line through the green filter. In contrast when (b) is viewed in the same manner, the red line is visible though the green filter and the green line through the red filter. In (c), as a result of the background colour, the extent of the cross-talk is increased.

the characteristics of the filters impact on the extent of the cross-talk – but also the background colour plays a key role.

Let us now turn our attention to the possible strengths and weaknesses of the anaglyph approach – see Table 9.2 for summary information. In terms of the former, the images are easily created and can be particularly useful in the formation of three-dimensional wireframe representations. In addition, this is perhaps the simplest and cheapest approach to the formation of stereoscopic images. The main disadvantage relates to the inability of this technique to support full colour depiction. As will be apparent during the course of this chapter, support for the inclusion of the third dimension allways has associated costs and may create problems. In terms of the anaglyph approach, restrictions in the extent of the colour pallet denotes the 'Achilles' heel' of this technique. On the other hand this does not imply that this technique is without merit since in many situations full-colour image depiction is unnecessary and in some applications sound benefits can be derived from the depiction of images composed of a single, or several, colours and which appear to reside in three-dimensional space.

9.3.4 Temporally Coded Images

Recall from our previous discussions that images depicted on a computer display comprise a series of frames that are re-written at regular intervals. In the case of temporal coding the left and right views of a stereopair are depicted in alternate frames, and viewing glasses are used to provide a means by which these alternate frames are visible only to the appropriate eye. As indicated in Section 1.6.2, these glasses can be either active or passive. Active glasses act as shutters and here, for example, liquid crystal eye pieces can be used (although in the early days of exploration of this technique, mechanical shutters were employed [Hammond 1924, 1928, US Patent 2,273,512]). When active glasses are employed, synchronisation signals must be transmitted from the display to the glasses via either a cable or wireless link. In contrast, passive glasses require no such connection and offer a lower cost solution.

Cross-talk can be associated with systems that employ either active and passive glasses. For example, in the case that active glasses are used in conjunction with a CRT based display, the characteristics of the display itself (specifically the persistence of the phosphors) can lead to cross-talk. The issue here is that following their stimulation by the electron beams, the light output from the phosphors gradually decays – but the red, green and blue phosphors do not decay at the same rate – green tends to decay the least rapidly. As a result, when the active glasses switch visibility from one eye to the other, the green phosphor may still be visibly emitting light – and this light is then presented to the 'wrong' eye. The use of passive glasses based on the linear polarization of light can also result in cross-talk – although for a somewhat different reason. Recall Figure 1.34; as the head is tilted, the extent of the cross-talk increases – until when the head has been rotated by 90° the incorrect view is presented to each eye.[10]

Finally, as indicated in Section 1.6.2, the temporal coding technique places increased demands on the performance of the display – specifically in terms of the frame refresh frequency.

9.3.5 Spatially Coded Images

In Section 1.6.2 we briefly introduced the spatial coding technique which enables 3-D images to be viewed directly (without recourse to viewing glasses) and that is fundamentally based on the 'parallax stereogram' approach devised by F.E. Ives at the beginning of the 20th century. Recall Figure 1.35 in which we show a plate (parallax barrier) containing a set of vertical slits that is placed in front of a display screen or specially prepared stereo photograph. The stereoscopic image comprises a set of interleaved strips and this embodiment assumes a viewing zone such that the strips corresponding to the left and right-eye views are visible only to the appropriate eye. As we mentioned, this approach has several weaknesses – particularly limited freedom in viewing position and the loss of image intensity because a significant portion of the light output from the displayed image is blocked by the presence of the barrier.

In the case that a parallax barrier is used to depict a single view onto a scene the observer's lateral location should remain close to the intended viewing position. As the observer moves away from this region, both eyes may be presented with the same left or right view of the stereo pair (and so the binocular cue will be lost) or a pseudoscopic image may be observed (here, the left eye is presented with the right-hand stereo image and the right eye with the left-hand image).[11]

This display paradigm may be used to encompass the motion parallax cue. Here, multiple stereo views onto a scene are interleaved – one view being visible from each of a number of adjacent viewing locations. Thus as the observer changes position a new view becomes visible. However, as with all 3-D techniques, there is a penalty associated with the encapsulation of the third dimension. Let us suppose that a display is able to depict n_h pixels in the horizontal direction and n_v pixels vertically and that we employ some form of barrier to create a spatially coded 3-D display that supports n views in the horizontal direction. In this case, the number of pixels that can be associated with each view is given by:

$$\frac{n_h \cdot n_v}{n}.$$

Thus as we increase the number of views there is a corresponding reduction in the number of pixels from which each view can be formed. Furthermore, even in the case that we support

---

[10] An extreme problem that would only affect those who prefer to watch films while lying on a sofa . . .

[11] In the case that a pseudoscopic view is presented, what would the observer perceive?

only a single view, the inclusion of binocular parallax reduces the conventional horizontal pixel resolution by 50%.[12] Support for motion parallax also increases the demands placed on the parallax barrier – increasing the number of views requires a corresponding reduction in the barrier pitch and in turn this negatively impacts on image brightness.

Fortunately, spatially coded systems are not limited to the parallax barrier approach. For example, the barrier may be replaced by 2-D array lenses which direct light into the designated viewing zones. This technique was devised in the early 20th century by Lippmann [1908] who developed the use of a 'fly's eye' array of lenses in support of full parallax (both vertical and horizontal). Today this method is commonly encountered on novelty postcards (often of a fairly dubious nature...) – the different views being used to encode either changes in the subjects that are depicted or image animation (in which case as the observer changes viewing location the image content appears to move). Display systems that employ this general approach often make use of a set of cylindrical lenses (these lenses being referred to as a lenticular sheet). The central axis of each lens usually lies in a vertical direction and so they act to support only horizontal parallax. Since the lenticular sheet is completely transparent there is no occlusion of light emitted from the display screen and therefore the image brightness issues that are associated with the parallax barrier method are no longer an issue.

For further introductory detail see Okoshi [1976] and for interesting discussion concerning alternative techniques that may be employed in the development of spatially coded systems see, for example, Collender [1967], Tilton [1988], Travis [1990], Lang *et al.* [1992], and Dodgson *et al.* [1999]. In addition, details of a number of commercial systems are readily available via the Internet.

9.4 Stereoscopic Systems: Supporting Motion Parallax

'Those are my principles.
If you don't like them I have others.'[13]

As indicated in the previous section, in their basic form the non-coded, anaglyph and temporally coded systems do not support motion parallax. Consequently, we cannot move our head from side to side or up and down to produce a different view onto a scene. Similarly, when we reposition our head we do not experience the relative motion of objects which lie at different depths. However, a brief re-examination of Figures 1.32 and 9.8 reveals the vital importance of the motion parallax cue – we quickly become frustrated by not being able to change our head position (and hence viewpoint) relative to the scene. In fact we extract a great deal of information about the spatial form of a scene by slight adjustments in vantage point and so when we view 3-D images, we instinctively wish to change our view point – but in their basic form, these techniques do not allow us to do so.

One solution is to incorporate head-tracking by which the computer system is able to monitor an operator's vantage point and as this changes the position of, for example, the virtual camera is modified accordingly. This is by no means a new idea and in the seminal paper written by Parker and Wallis in the 1940s [Parker and Wallis 1948] the authors write:

---

[12] However, despite this reduction, support for binocular parallax ensures that the visual system is presented with additional and important information.
[13] Attributed to Groucho Marx (1890–1977).

'Since the use of parallax in everyday life most commonly occurs when one is moving relative to a large number of stationary objects, it may be preferable for the operator to move his head rather than give him aspect controls to turn manually. The aspect controls would then be operated by movements of the operator's head, a joystick device being used as a coupling, for example. The operator will then move his head around to look into an apparently stationary three-dimensional volume. In order to remove any ambiguity and improve realism, the perspective and/or perspective shading described previously could be added to the display. This could be made adjustable, arranged to follow automatically any head movements, by the incorporation of a telescopic device in the above mentioned joystick. It is clear, however, that this could be arranged for only one observer at each display.'

The precise details of this quotation need not concern us – it is sufficient to note that the writers were suggesting the use of a system employing mechanical linkages via which an operator's vantage point was to be monitored. Changes in position would then result in an update of the image scene with an appropriate modification of the perspective view (by calculating this for the new centre of projection) and/or changes in perspective shading. Since in the 1940s these authors did not have access to digital computers (analogue computation was employed), this was indeed a remarkable achievement.[14]

In Section 9.3.2 we referred to the work undertaken in the 1960s by Ivan Sutherland in relation to augmented reality. This system also employed head-tracking and he describes two approaches [Sutherland 1968]. The first paralleled the technique described some 20 years earlier by Parker and Wallis and employed a system of mechanical linkages – with one end being attached to the operator's headset and the other to the ceiling. The joints were equipped with digital position encoders so that the computer responsible for image generation could monitor the user's location (both translational and rotational motion are reported as having been measured). Naturally, such a system would have been a little cumbersome and Sutherland also described the use of ultrasound for position sensing. In fact, this approach was the precursor to the head-tracking systems that are often used today. This (and other) head tracking techniques are described by Burdea and Coiffet [2003] and summary discussion is presented in Blundell [2007].

Position tracking can be achieved in various ways – in the case of systems implemented using optical, magnetic and ultrasound techniques, there is no requirement for a physical connection between the operator and the static tracking hardware. Below we briefly consider one approach to the implementation of an ultrasound system.

Ultrasonic waves propagate in air at a speed (v) that is approximately given by:

$$v \sim 331 + 0.6\,T \tag{9.3}$$

where T denotes the temperature measured in °C.

OTU Exercise 9.4: Head Tracking

Using Eq. 9.3 determine the time taken for an ultrasonic wave to travel a distance of 80 cm – assuming a temperature of 27 °C.

---

[14] The Parker and Wallis publication is extensive and rich in content. Unfortunately, there is often insufficient clarification as to the extent to which displays and associated devices (such as the head-tracking system) were actually implemented.

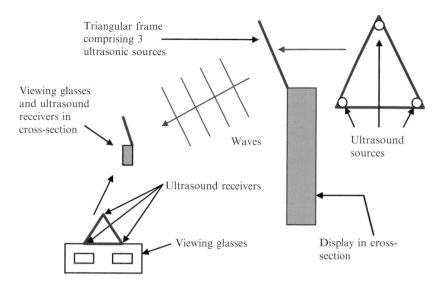

Figure 9.13 A head tracking arrangement. Three ultrasound sources are mounted at the corners of a triangular frame. This is typically attached to the top of the display. Three ultrasound receivers are mounted at the corners of a triangular frame that is fixed to the viewing glasses worn by the observer. See text for discussion.

In one embodiment, three sources of ultrasonic sound are mounted at the corners of a triangular frame. This is typically positioned above the computer display. The operator dons stereoscopic viewing glasses that are equipped with three ultrasonic detectors – again these are mounted at the corners of a triangular support (although for convenience, this triangle is somewhat smaller than the one that supports the ultrasonic transmitters – see Figure 9.13).

In the case of one approach, each transmitter broadcasts a short burst of ultrasound in turn. Each transmission is detected by the three receivers and so once all three transmitters have broadcast, nine position measuring signals have been acquired. By means of this temporal data we can determine the relative location of the two triangular frames and in turn this enables us to track the position of the observer.

As we know from OTU Exercise 9.4, the ultrasound signal will take $\sim 2.3 \times 10^{-3}$ seconds to travel a distance of 80cm. Thus the set of three transmissions may occupy $\sim 6.9 \times 10^{-3}$ s. In addition after each transmission it is necessary to pause to ensure that all extraneous echoes have died away (these may be caused by a signal bouncing off objects within a room (or off the walls) and subsequently impinging on the detectors). If, for example, we pause for a period of 20×10^{-3} seconds between each transmission then a set of three will be completed in $\sim 47 \times 10^{-3}$ s. This represents a basic position sensing latency – this time must elapse before a complete position measurement can be obtained.[15] Subsequently the computer must perform calculations on the basis of the new viewpoint and update the display. In short, the update of the display will lag (to a greater or lesser extent) behind the movements of the observer. In some scenarios this lag may be readily apparent and can detract from the usability of a technique. In Figure 9.14, we indicate the various sources of latency that may be associated with the head-tracking display technique. For further discussion of various approaches to head tracking and motion capture in general, see Burdea and Coiffet [2003].

---

[15] We have assumed that each transmitter broadcasts in sequence. However, if an approach supports parallel transmission, the latency can be reduced.

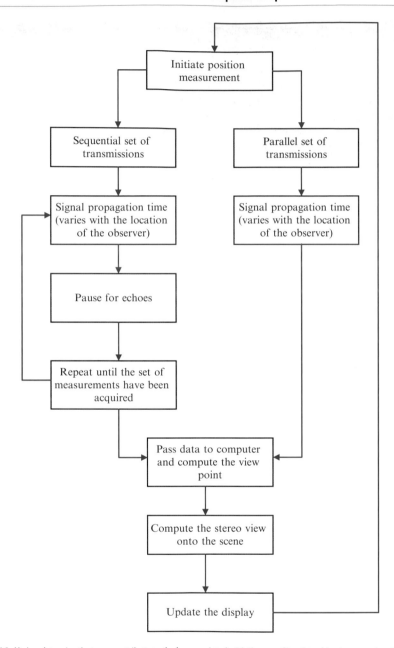

Figure 9.14 Various latencies that *may* contribute to the lag associated with the use of head-tracking to support motion parallax.

OTU Exercise 9.5: The CAVE and RAVE

The CAVE provides us with an example of an immersive 3-D environment based on temporally coded stereoscopic techniques and that employs head-tracking. Research the history, principles of operation and applications of this approach. Identify at least one major advantage and one major drawback of this display paradigm. The RAVE is a display system that represents a derivative of the CAVE and was also pioneered at the Electronic Visualization Laboratory (at the University of Illinois). Research this technique. Hint: information concerning the CAVE may be found on-line and, for example, in Burdea and Coiffet [2003] and Blundell and Schwarz [2006]. Also see Defanti *et al.* [1992] and Cruz-Neira [1993].

OTU Exercise 9.6: The Cybersphere

The Cybersphere provides us with an example of a radical approach to the implementation of a projection-based display. Research the principles of operation of this system. Identify at least one major advantage and one major drawback of this display paradigm. Hint: sources for information include Fernandes *et al.* [2003] and Blundell and Schwarz [2006].

OTU Exercise 9.7: Stereoscopic Workbench Technologies

Research the implementation of stereoscopic workbench technologies which enable stereo images to be positioned above a horizontal surface. Identify key strengths and weaknesses. Details of commercially available systems may be found on-line. Also see Burdea and Coiffet [2003].

9.5 Volumetric Display Techniques

'Go confidently in the direction of your dreams.
Live the life you have imagined'[16]

As we have seen, in the case of the stereoscope the two different views on an image scene are directed so that only one of these is visible to either eye, and the majority of creative 3-D display techniques are fundamentally based on this principle. Volumetric systems adopt a somewhat different approach. Here, images are depicted within a transparent physical *volume* and since an image is able to occupy three spatial dimensions, it is inherently three-dimensional.

In Figure 9.15 several simple volumetric images are presented (also see Figure 9.22). Unfortunately, it is impossible to do true justice to a volumetric image when it is captured by conventional photography. As soon as the volumetric image is photographed, all but the pictorial depth cues are lost and it is the combined presence of pictorial, oculomotor and parallax

---

[16] Attributed to Henry David Thoreau (1817–1862).

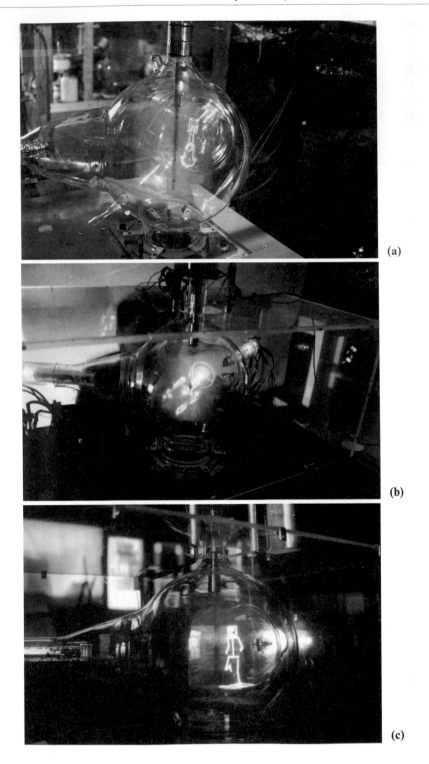

(a)

(b)

(c)

 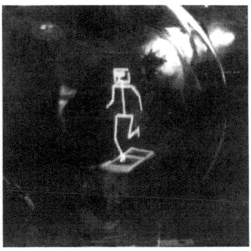

(d)

Figure 9.15 Here, we illustrate several very simple volumetric images depicted on an early Cathode Ray Sphere prototype (see Section 9.5.2). Unfortunately when volumetric images are captured on conventional photographs the oculomotor and parallax cues are lost. This problem is exacerbated by the fact that most volumetric display technologies generate translucent images. In (a) we show an animated piston, crankshaft and connecting rod, (b) depicts a wireframe model of the 'Starship Enterprise' and (c) shows an animated stick figure that walks in a natural manner around the display volume. This same figure is depicted as a stereogram in (d). When correctly fused, the natural three-dimensionality of the figure is readily apparent. (Original images © B.G. Blundell 2005.)

cues that make volumetric images (when viewed directly) so visually captivating. However, in Figure 9.15(d) a volumetric image is captured as a stereopair – and so the binocular parallax cue is preserved. When this pair of images is fused either by direct viewing or by means of the stereo viewing glasses provided with this book, the inherent three-dimensionality of this simple stick figure is readily apparent.

Volumetric images are depicted within a transparent physical volume and by way of analogy this can be compared to fish swimming in a goldfish bowl or tank. The fish, water-weeds, and other objects in the bowl represent image components. Each fish occupies three physical dimensions and the spatial separation of the fish (and any other items within the volume) is immediately apparent. Furthermore, as with fish swimming in a bowl volumetric images may be fully animated and many technologies allow practically unrestricted freedom in viewing orientation. In this latter respect, a number of observers can look into the volume in which the images are depicted and simultaneously observe the image scene from different orientations. Additionally, viewing glasses or other viewing headgear are not required.

The volume within which volumetric images are depicted, is generally referred as an 'image space', and images are usually constructed from voxels.

A voxel (volume element) is the three-dimensional equivalent of the pixel and has various associated attributes. Whereas in the case of a pixel we simply define position on a 2-D surface, a voxel's position is described as a triple with x, y, and z coordinates being specified. As with a pixel, voxels have associated colour and intensity descriptors and can either emit or scatter incident light.

In the text that follows we briefly summarise some of the general characteristics of volumetric display systems:

1. **Support for depth cues**: Since volumetric images occupy three physical dimensions, they are inherently three dimensional. Various pictorial and non-pictorial depth cues are satisfied. However, in the case of practically all volumetric embodiments developed to date the depth cue of occlusion is absent. Thus images take on a ghostly translucent appearance. For some applications this 'see-through' characteristic can be advantageous and ensures that from any particular viewing direction one image component cannot occlude another. Furthermore, the ability of volumetric displays to naturally support accommodation and convergence compensates (to some extent) for the absence of occlusion. Unfortunately in literature it is often claimed that volumetric systems are inherently unable to satisfy occlusion – this is not correct (see, for example Blundell and Schwarz [2000] and Blundell [2007]).

   Volumetric systems naturally satisfy a wide range of depth cues and this interfaces well with the expectations of the human visual system. On the other hand, it is important to note that the ability of volumetric systems to satisfy depth cues is generally limited by the physical dimensions of the image space. For example, consider the depth cue of accommodation. Volumetric image components can be located at different depths within an image space and so, as we direct our attention to different image components, the eyes automatically refocus and their convergence distance changes. The extent to which the accommodation and convergence distances change is usually limited by the physical depth of the image space.

2. **Image space characteristics**: Let us continue for a moment with the goldfish in a bowl analogy. If the water is not clear the clarity of our view of the goldfish will obviously be affected. Furthermore, since water has a higher refractive index than air, as light emerges from the goldfish bowl it undergoes refraction (we will refer to this as 'boundary refraction') and this leads to a distorted view not only of the shape and size of individual goldfish but also of their spatial separation and of the depth of the goldfish bowl. These are important issues that we must consider when developing a volumetric architecture. The image space should not only be transparent but should also exhibit a uniform refractive index. In addition, to avoid (or minimise) boundary refraction we require that the refractive index of the image space is as close as possible to the air that surrounds it. Failure to meet these conditions can considerably detract from the usability of volumetric displays.

> Let us suppose that a volumetric technology allows us to accurately position well-defined voxels within an image space in such a way that we are able to create superb, high quality images. This in itself by no means guarantees that we will perceive such images as being of a high quality. Components within the image space that obstruct the passage of light or variations in the refractive index of the image space medium will strongly impact upon the quality of the perceived image. In addition, boundary refraction may cause image distortion, making it difficult to, for example, accurately gauge the separation of image components within a scene and accurately navigate a cursor so as to interact with these components.

3. **Viewing freedom**: Display systems based upon the stereoscopic approach generally provide one window onto the 3-D scene.[17] Some volumetric embodiments provide a single window onto a 3-D scene, other approaches provide two windows enabling observers to look into the 3-D scene from both the front and rear, and other systems provide essentially unrestricted freedom in viewing the 3-D scene. In this latter respect, an image space may take the form of a sphere (e.g. the Cathode Ray Sphere – see Section 9.5.2), hemisphere or cylinder, and observers can look onto the scene from practically any orientation. In addition, volumetric displays support natural motion parallax. Consequently, an observer gains a different vantage point onto a 3-D scene not only by moving from side to side, but also by moving in any other direction.

   For certain applications, unrestricted viewing freedom can be advantageous and in other situations can be problematic. Consider, for example, a volumetric system employed for air traffic control and which imposes no restriction on viewing freedom. The controller can be positioned at any location around the image space – there is no defined vantage point. This can lead to disorientation.

9.5.1 Display Subsystems

It is convenient to describe volumetric displays in terms of three key subsystems. These are summarised in Figure 9.16 and the function of each is briefly discussed below:

1. **The Image Space Creation Subsystem**: This subsystem relates to the techniques used for the formation of the image space within which volumetric images are depicted. Two general approaches are adopted. Firstly, an image space may be formed through the rapid cyclic motion of a surface or structure. In line with previous discussion [Blundell and Schwarz 2000] we will refer to this as the 'swept volume' approach. Alternatively, an image space may be formed without recourse to mechanical motion (e.g. a gaseous medium may be employed). We will refer to such systems as employing a 'static volume' approach.

2. **The Voxel Generation Subsystem**: This relates to the underlying physical processes used in the production of visible voxels and may be readily understood by reference to the conventional flat screen display based on, for example, CRT technology (see Section 1.5.1). In this case, phosphor particles are stimulated to emit visible light by a process known as cathodoluminescence. This denotes the underlying physical process that causes pixel visibility and so by analogy represents the voxel generation subsystem.

3. **The Voxel Activation Subsystem**: This relates to the technique(s) that we employ to stimulate the voxel generation process. Again returning to the CRT analogy, whilst cathodoluminescence denotes the voxel generation subsystem, visible pixel formation is achieved by means of one or more electron beams that are swept across the surface of the screen. In this case, we would say that the activation subsystem is implemented using electron beam technologies. Usually, once we have defined the nature of the voxel generation subsystem,

---

[17] One of the great difficulties in discussing emerging creative 3-D display technologies is in making generalised statements that apply without exception. Whilst in the main, systems based on the stereoscopic approach do provide a single window through which the 3-D scene can be viewed, there are exceptions (e.g. the CAVE – referred to in OTU Exercise 9.5).

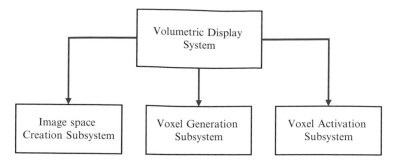

Figure 9.16 Any volumetric display can be described in terms of three key subsystems. These relate to the formation of the image space, the fundamental process that is used for the generation of visible voxels and the way in which voxels are activated so as to change between non-visible and visible states.

we have only a limited number of choices as to the ways in which the voxel activation may be implemented.

In the two subsections that follow, we provide a brief introduction to several exemplar volumetric display system architectures. For more detailed discussion on display subsystems see Blundell and Schwarz [2000], and Blundell [2007].

9.5.2 Swept Volume Volumetric Displays

As indicated above all swept volume display units are based on the rapid cyclic motion of a surface or structure. Either rotational or translational (reciprocating) movement[18] may be adopted and in Figure 9.17 we indicate several exemplar techniques that are briefly reviewed below. However, before we begin it is important to note that during the last 75 years, a great range of swept volume systems have been proposed and constructed. In fact it appears that John Logie Baird (the inventor of television) was probably the first to undertake research in this area – and in 1931 he filed a remarkable patent (British Patent Number 373,196) the significance of which has, until recently, been largely overlooked. Work in connection with this patent must have been carried out some five years after he gave the first demonstration of practical television and this provides us with a clear indication that Baird very quickly realised the limitations of the flat screen display and the potential benefits of 3-D systems. For a review of Baird's work in connection with volumetric systems see Blundell [2006(a), 2007].

One of the difficulties faced in considering the swept volume approach is in coming to terms with the great range of possible techniques that can be used in the implementation of the three display unit subsystems. The exemplar systems introduced below are simply intended to provide an insight into general techniques – references are supplied for further reading.

1. **A Swept Volume Display Employing Translational Motion**: Consider the arrangement illustrated schematically in Figure 9.18. Here, a rectangular planar screen equipped with a 2-D array of light emitting elements moves back and forth so sweeping out a cubic volume (image space). The 3-D image that we wish to depict is processed to comprise a set of parallel slices and the volume swept out by the screen is also divided into a corresponding set of slices (the slices being located at right angles to the direction of screen motion). As the

---

[18] Occasionally a combination of these two forms of motion may be employed.

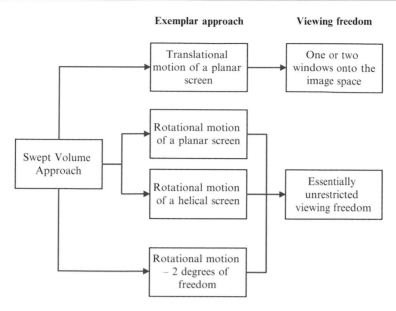

Figure 9.17 Four exemplar swept volume techniques that are briefly reviewed in the text.

screen passes through each slice position, the corresponding image slice is made visible by illuminating the appropriate light emitting elements. By way of a simple example, suppose that we wished to depict an open cylinder whose axis lies parallel to the direction of screen movement (this represents the simplest case). The slicing (ordering) of the data set gives rise to a set of image slices each of which depicts the circular cross section of the image. As the screen passes through each corresponding slice position, the appropriate light emitting elements are illuminated. (On the basis of the coordinate system indicated in Figure 9.18, the z direction is represented in terms of the screen's temporal position.)

The frequency at which the screen must sweep out the image space is determined by our need to avoid image flicker and in practice this means that the screen must complete a full cycle of motion (comprising the forward and backward sweep) in no more than ~40 ms (corresponding to 25 Hz).

Typically, a display employing translational motion provides one or two windows onto the image space – corresponding to the front and rear. Side views are generally highly restricted because of the presence of the mechanical components that support the screen and generate its movement.

In the late 1950s a display called the Peritron was developed [Withey 1958]. This used the translational motion of a planar phosphor coated screen and an electron beam for voxel activation. This was therefore a hybrid form of CRT – the CRT screen moving forwards and backwards. In fact, the Peritron provides us with an example of a simple and effective implementation of a swept volume display employing translational movement. One of the key difficulties to development of displays of this type centres on the generation of screen motion. Ideally, the depth of the image space should correspond to the part of the screen's motion in which it is moving with constant speed.[19] In turn, it is naturally desirable

---

[19] For discussion on screen update, linear motion and sinusoidal motion see Blundell and Schwarz [2000] and Blundell [2007].

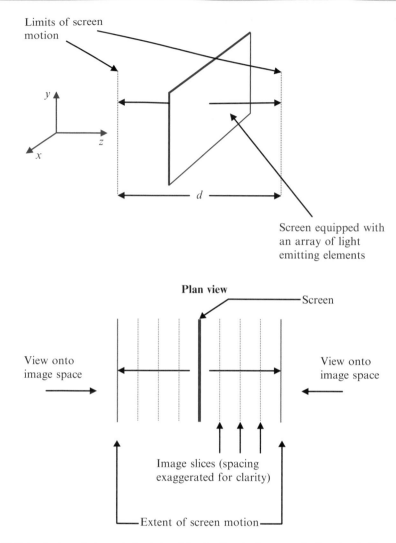

Figure 9.18 A simple swept volume display employing the translational motion of a planar screen that is equipped with an array of light emitting elements.

that the screen's acceleration and deceleration (at either extreme of its motion) should be maximised. In the case of the Peritron, the screen, mechanical drive system, and electron beam were housed within an evacuated vessel. This would have effectively eliminated air resistance to screen motion and so would have allowed the use of a light-weight screen and drive system. For a summary of key advantages and potential problems associated with the translational motion approach see Table 9.3.

2. **A Swept Volume Display Employing the Rotational Motion of a Planar Screen**: The majority of swept volume display systems developed to date have employed rotational motion. Here we will briefly discuss one particular embodiment which for a number of

Table 9.3 A summary of various characteristics associated with the exemplar swept volume displays that are introduced in the text.

Exemplar Swept Volume System	General Strengths	Potential or Inherent Weaknesses
Translational Motion of a Planar Screen	1. Voxels may be positioned within a regular 3-D lattice. 2. Light passing through the image space is not subjected to absorption or refraction. 3. No boundary refraction. 4. Light-weight display. 5. Overall simplicity.	1. Implementation of the screen drive. 2. Ultimately the motion limits the dimensions of the image space.
Rotational Motion of a Planar Screen	1. Simplicity of the mechanical system responsible for screen rotation. 2. Light passing through the image space is not subjected to absorption or refraction. 3. Minimal boundary refraction. 4. Voxel generation and activation subsystems may be implemented in a number of ways. 5. Light-weight display. 6. Viewing freedom.	1. Screen strength and rigidity are likely to limit image space volume. 2. Uniformity of voxel density and placement may be an issue.
Rotational Motion of a Helical Screen	1. Support for large volume image space generation. 2. Light passing through the image space is not subjected to absorption or refraction. 3. Minimal boundary refraction. 4. Light-weight display. 5. Viewing freedom.	1. Gradient of helix increases towards the axis of rotation. 2. Uniformity of voxel density and placement may be an issue.

years formed a focal point to the author's research into volumetric displays.[20] The display is named the Cathode Ray Sphere (CRS) and some simple images depicted on CRS prototypes were previously presented in Figure 9.15. A diagram showing some of the key components within an early CRS prototype is provided in Figure 9.19.

As may be seen from this illustration, CRS prototypes employ a rectangular glass plate that rotates in such a way that the axis of rotation lies in the plane of the screen. This plate is coated with one or more phosphors and two stationary electron guns are used for voxel activation. Naturally, as the screen rotates, the geometry between the screen and the electron guns continuously varies and when the plane of the screen lies at more acute angles to an electron gun axis (see Figure 9.20(b) and (c)) problems occur in screen addressing. For example:

- Voxels become increasingly elongated – see Figure 9.20(b).
- A small deflection of the electron beam causes an unacceptably large displacement of the beam on the screen – see Figure 9.20(c).

---

[20] See US Patents 5,703,606 and 6,054,817.

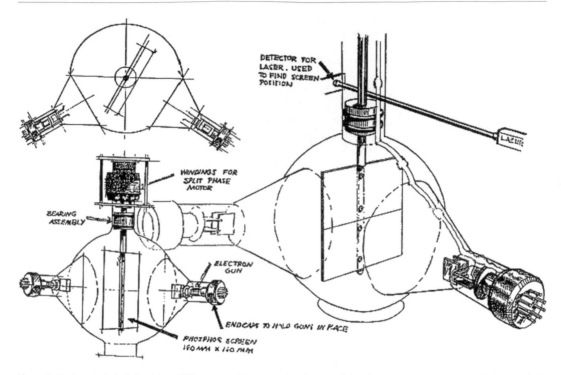

Figure 9.19 An early Cathode Ray Sphere (CRS) prototype. Here, a thin phosphor coated glass plate rotates within an evacuated glass vessel. The voxel activation subsystem comprises two electron guns. (Original drawing by Warren King.)

Figure 9.20 In (a) we show in plan view the region swept out by the rotating planar screen and the use of a single electron gun. This diagram provides a general overview and in (b) and (c) we illustrate types of difficulty that can occur as the plane of the screen lies at an increasingly acute angle to the electron beam axis. In (b), to the left we illustrate the screen lying at 90° to the electron gun axis (for clarity, the diameter of the beam is exaggerated). In this situation a circular region of phosphor is excited. To the right we illustrate the situation in which the plane of the screen lies at an acute angle to the electron gun axis. Here, the region of phosphor that is excited is no longer circular – this leads to voxel elongation. In (c) we illustrate a further problem that arises. On the left hand side, we show the screen at 90° to the electron gun axis. Two beam positions are indicated – the angle between these lines is intended to denote the smallest angle through which the controlling hardware can deflect the beam (for clarity this angle is exaggerated). This results in a displacement of the beam on the screen which is denoted as η. On the right hand side, we show the situation that occurs when the plane of the screen lies at an acute angle to the electron gun axis. Again the diagram indicates the smallest beam deflection angle that can be achieved by the controlling hardware. The displacement on the screen is now denoted as η' where $\eta' > \eta$. Gradually, as the screen lies at an increasingly acute angle with respect to the electron gun axis, we lose accuracy in voxel placement.

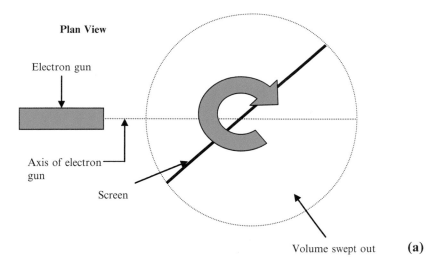

Plan View

Electron gun

Axis of electron
gun

Screen

Volume swept out   **(a)**

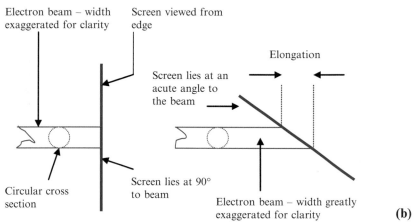

Electron beam – width
exaggerated for clarity

Screen viewed from
edge

Elongation

Screen lies at an
acute angle to
the beam

Circular cross
section

Screen lies at 90°
to beam

Electron beam – width greatly
exaggerated for clarity   **(b)**

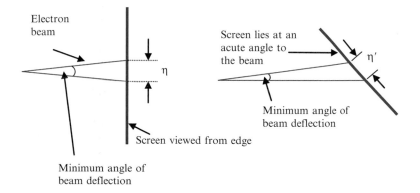

Electron
beam

Screen lies at an
acute angle to
the beam

η'

η

Minimum angle of
beam deflection

Screen viewed from edge

Minimum angle of
beam deflection   **(c)**

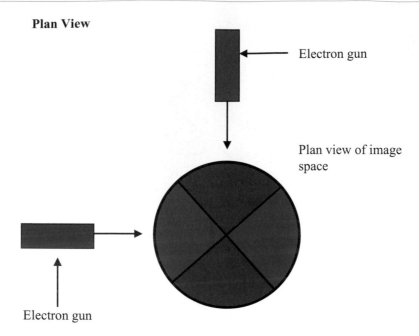

Plan View

Electron gun

Plan view of image space

Electron gun

Figure 9.21 One simple approach that ameliorates the distortional and voxel placement dead zones. Here, two electron guns are used and each is responsible for voxel activation within a limited region of the image space. Thus the gun that is denoted in red, is responsible for voxel activation when the screen lies within the portion of the image space that is highlighted in red. Similarly, the gun depicted in blue writes to the region of the image space that is shaded in this colour.

We refer to the first of these problems as giving rise to a distortional dead zone and the second as the voxel placement dead zone[21]. Within this context, a dead zone may be defined in the following way:

> **Dead Zone:** A region of an image space within which image quality is compromised by a reduction in one or more image space characteristics.

Distortional and voxel placement dead zones may be resolved in various ways. In the case of the CRS, a 'brute force' approach has generally been adopted and this involves using two or three electron guns. These are arranged around the image space and each is responsible for writing to a limited portion of this display volume. In short, each gun only writes to the screen when the geometry between the screen and electron gun axis is favourable – see Figure 9.21. Other approaches may be adopted. See, for example, the work of Max Hirsch (US Patent Number 2,967,905) who in 1958 described two techniques. On of these represents a truly radical approach – Hirsch maintained fixed geometry between the electron guns and the screen by simply co-rotating the screen and electron guns! A

---

[21] In fact various dead zones may be associated with both swept and static volume displays. For further discussion see [Blundell and Schwarz 2000, Blundell 2007] and for more in depth analysis [Schwarz and Blundell 1994a, 1994b, 1994c].

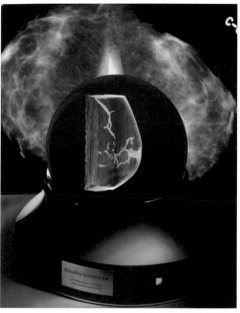

(a)

(b)

Figure 9.22 The Perspecta Spatial 3-D Display developed by Actuality Systems. In (a) a previous version of the display is shown projecting a 25 cm diameter volumetric image of an aeroplane over fractally-generated terrain. The image is visible from any angle around or above the display. Actuality Systems Inc.'s founder Gregg Favalora is in the background. In (b) a segmented MRI scan of a cancerous lesion within a breast is displayed. The various anatomical regions of interest are depicted using different colours. For example, the tumour is shown in purple, while the blood vessels are illustrated in red and blue. The image data is courtesy of U. Penn. Radiology (Phila., Penn., USA) and Brigham and Women's Hospital's Surgical Planning Laboratory (Boston, Mass., USA). (Images kindly supplied by, and reproduced by permission of Gregg Favalora, Actuality Systems Inc.)

publication in relation to a display system called the 3D-Rotatron [Shimada 1993] describes an interesting optical arrangement, and a commercially available swept volume system (the Perspecta) provides an excellent example of a further technique[22] – see Figure 9.22 and Table 9.4. A display described in a 1977 patent (US Patent Number 4,160,973) provides us with another example of techniques that can be used in the implementation of the planar screen swept volume display. Here, the rotating screen is equipped with a 2-D array of light emitting elements and so beam sources are unnecessary.

As described previously, in the case that an image space is generated by the translational motion of a planar screen, the data set is processed to generate a series of parallel slices through the image scene and these are output to corresponding locations within the image space. However, in the case that the rotational motion of a planar screen is employed, the image space is divided into a number of sectors (see Figure 9.23) to which corresponding radial slices of the image data set are output. The screen must rotate with sufficient rapidity so that image flicker is not problematic. As with the display outlined previously (using translational motion) this implies that the screen rotates at a frequency in excess of 25 Hz. However, there is the possibility of obtaining two image refreshes during each cycle of screen rotation and this therefore enables (at least in principle) the frequency of rotation to be halved.

---

[22] The Perspecta is produced by Actuality Systems Inc., 213 Burlington Road, Suite 105, Bedford, Massachusetts 01730. (http://www.actualitysystems.com)

Table 9.4 Some general details of the Perspecta display produced by Actuality Systems. (Reproduced by kind permission of Gregg Favalora, Actuality Systems Inc.)

The Perspecta 3-D System v1.9:

Image space: 25 cm diameter.
Field of view: 360° horizontal, 270° vertical.
Resolution: 198 slices (~1 slice per degree), 768 by 768 pixels per slice.
Display dimensions: 48″ high by 31″ wide by 22.25″ deep.
Graphics engine NVIDIA GPU, 2.2 GHz 64-bit AMD Athlon CPU.
Interface: Dual Gigabit Ethernet.

Full colour with 2-D and 3-D OpenGL texture-mapping support.

Key strengths and potential weaknesses of the planar screen approach are summarised in Table 9.3.

OTU Exercise 9.8: Image Refresh

As indicated above, swept volume displays employing the rotational motion of a planar screen may, at least in principle, support two image refreshes during each cycle of screen motion. With reference to the CRS illustrated in Figure 9.19 suggest how you would obtain this objective. Additionally, in the case that we assume only one image refresh during each cycle of screen motion, how would you arrange for the CRS to generate multi-colour images?

---

3. **A Swept Volume Display Employing the Rotational Motion of a Helical Screen**: In the case that a planar screen is employed in conjunction with rotational motion, it is likely that the mechanical rigidity and stability of the screen will set an upper limit on the dimensions

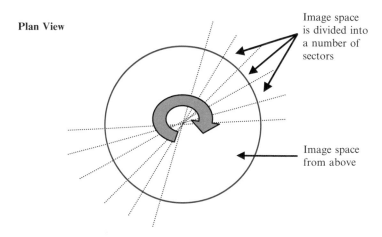

Plan View

Image space is divided into a number of sectors

Image space from above

Figure 9.23 Plan view of the image space. This is divided into a number of sectors and as the screen passes through each sector, a corresponding slice of the image data set is output to it.

of the image space.[23] A helical screen offers greater mechanical rigidity than its planar equivalent and is therefore better suited to the implementation of 'large volume' displays.

A patent filed in 1976 by Rüdiger Hartwig (German Patent Number DE 26 22 802 C2), describes a swept volume display system based on a rotating helix and using directed laser beams for the formation of voxels on the helical surface. Systems of this type are generally referred to as HL3D (helix-laser-3-D) based technologies. Various forms of helix may, in principle, be used – such as the single bladed configuration illustrated in Figure 9.24.

The original HL3D system employed a cylindrical image space measuring 60 cm in diameter and 40 cm in height which was formed using a single bladed helix constructed from a white plastic. Over the years considerable work has been undertaken in relation to helical based displays – including research at Texas Instruments (see, for example, Williams and Garcia [1988]) and by the US Navy[24] (Soltan et al. 1992, 1994).

One further point to note concerning the use of a rotating helix relates to the ease by which Cartesian coordinates may be mapped into the image space. Let us suppose that we wish to map a set of points whose coordinates are denoted (x, y, z). We must define the orientation of a corresponding image space coordinate system and then map our set of points onto the rotating helix. We will assume that the image space coordinate system is as indicated in Figure 9.24 – with the z-axis coincident with the axis of rotation. In principle, when we map our set of points onto the helix, we need not modify the x and y values (although in practice we would, for example, apply scaling). As far as the z coordinates are concerned this is easily dealt with and is defined by the time (during each cycle of motion) at which we write each point onto the helix. Due to the geometry of the helix, the height of a point within the image space is directly proportional to the time at which it is illuminated (where time is measured from the start of each rotational cycle).

4. **A Swept Volume Display Employing Two Degrees of Rotational Freedom**: The approach illustrated in Figure 9.25 is included to prove a simple example of the ingenuity that has been directed to the implementation of swept-volume systems. This display is described in a patent filed in 1991 (European Patent Number 0 418 583 A2) and employs a planar screen (10) that is housed within a transparent sphere (15). Two drive systems ((16) and (19)) are employed – these being at right-angles to each other. Thus one drive provides horizontal motion and the other supports vertical movement. Consequently, by adjusting their relative speeds of motion the sphere (and screen) may be moved through a complex motion cycle. The screen is constructed from a material able to scatter incident light and a number of scanned laser sources are placed around the sphere – these are responsible for voxel activation.

OTU Exercise 9.9: A Display Employing Two Degrees of Freedom

Consider the swept volume display illustrated in Figure 9.25. Discuss its operation – what are the main strengths and weaknesses of this approach?

---

[23] Other factors may also play a part – e.g. in the case of the CRS, the maximum achievable deflection of the electron beams is an important issue.

[24] One prototype system provided a cylindrical image space measuring 36 inches in diameter and 18 inches in height. This provided support for colour image depiction (by means of three directed laser beams) and an image refresh frequency of 40 Hz.

(a)

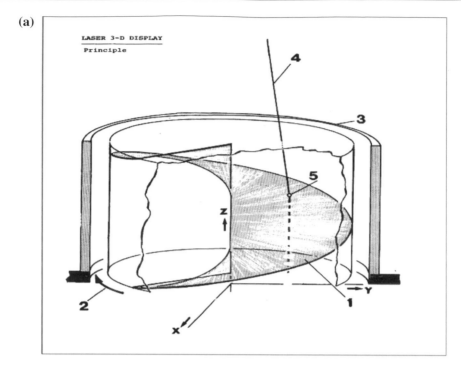

(b)

Figure 9.24 In (a) a single bladed helix – as described in the original Hartwig 1976 patent. In (b) a prototype of the Helix3D display unit employing the helical screen invented by Rüdiger Hartwig in 1976. This shows Prof. Hartwig at the first public presentation of his Helix3D display technology at the University of Heidelberg, Germany 1982. The rotational axis which is clearly visible was used only in this first prototype. Due to another aspect of the Hartwig invention, the Helix3D can be built without the need for such an axis and this eliminates the visual disturbance that its presence can cause. For further information see US Patent 6,958,837, European Patents DE2622802C2 and DE10047695, also Hartwig [1982]. (Reproduced by kind permission of Professor R. Hartwig.)

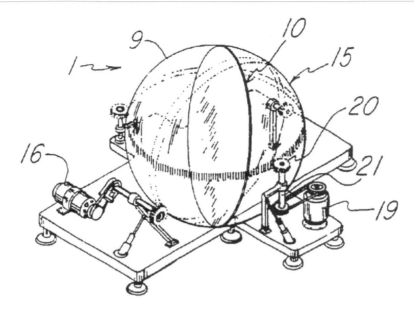

Figure 9.25 A swept volume display employing two degrees of freedom. The transparent sphere contains a semi-transparent screen. Several scanned laser sources are used for voxel activation. (Reproduced from European Patent Number 0 418 583 A2.)

9.5.3 Static Volume Volumetric Displays

Research into the development of static volume systems has an even longer history than the swept volume approach and dates back at least as far as 1912 (see French Patent Number 461600). Many techniques have been evaluated and as with swept volume research, some of the early designs (prior to the late 1960s) simply failed because workers did not have access to the necessary computer systems and required technologies.

Perhaps the simplest and most direct approach to the implementation of a static volume display involves the use of a 3-D array of light emitting elements located within some form of supporting structure. However, this method has a number of major disadvantages. For example:

1. Consider a cubic volume (image space) comprising an array of n by n by n light emitting elements. If we were to double the length of side of this volume (and were to maintain the same spacing between the light emitting elements) then there would be an 8-fold increase in the total number of elements in the 3-D array). Thus doubling the length of side would increase the number of elements from n^3 to $8n^3$!

2. Even in the case of a small image space, to support a *tolerable* inter-voxel spacing, a large number of elements are required. For example consider a cubic image space with sides of length 20cm and an inter-voxel spacing of 1mm (which is quite coarse). Some 8 million light emitting elements would be required and from (1) above, doubling the length of side of the volume would increase this number to 64 million!

3. Naturally the presence of such an enormous number of light emitting elements (together with the associated connections) would impact on image space transparency and would therefore detract from image visibility, clarity, and the like.

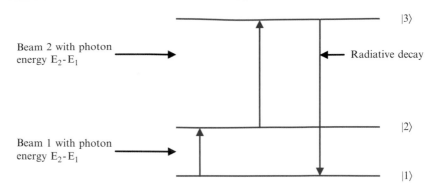

Figure 9.26 Here we consider a simple model of a fluorescent centre comprising three electronic energy levels. Two non-visible beams may be used to excite the fluorescent centre from state $|1\rangle$ to $|3\rangle$ (via intermediate state $|2\rangle$). Subsequent radiative decay to the ground state may result in the emission of a photon of visible light.

4. Due to the incorporation of enormous number of elements, interconnections and the necessary supporting structure, any image space of useful dimensions is likely to have quite a high mass and this may well impact on portability.

The above points highlight some of the weaknesses associated with employing a 3-D array of light emitting elements – an approach that is likely to be unsuccessful.

Having put to one side an obvious method for implementing a static volume display, let us now consider by way of example a more practical approach. Here, we will assume that an image space is formed by means of a suitable gas held at an appropriate pressure within a transparent container. Voxel generation may be achieved by a process known as the two-step (stepwise) excitation of fluorescence – in which case the voxel activation subsystem usually employs two beams of radiation. These are directed into the image space and a visible voxel is formed in the region at which the beams intersect. In Figure 9.26, we provide a simple (idealised) model that demonstrates the manner in which this process operates. Here we consider three quantised atomic electronic energy levels – denoted $|1\rangle$, $|2\rangle$ and $|3\rangle$. Following previous publications (e.g. Lewis *et al.* [1971], Blundell and Schwarz [2000]), we will refer to this atom as a 'fluorescent centre' – which is defined in the following way:

> **A fluorescent centre may be defined as an atom, ion or molecule that directly contributes to the production of light and hence the formation of the visible voxel.**

As indicated in Figure 9.26, we assume that the energy difference between states $|1\rangle$ and $|2\rangle$ is $E_2 - E_1$ and between states $|2\rangle$ and $|3\rangle$ is $E_3 - E_2$. Let us now suppose that a beam of radiation with a frequency f impinges on the fluorescent centre. Basic physics allows us to relate the frequency of radiation to the energy (E) of the photons that comprise the beam:

$$E = hf, \qquad (9.4)$$

where h denotes Planck's constant.[25] Furthermore, the frequency (f) and wavelength (λ) of a wave are related by the following expression:

$$c = f\lambda,$$

where c represents the speed of electromagnetic radiation in the medium through which the radiation is travelling. Thus we can write:

$$E = hf = \frac{hc}{\lambda}. \tag{9.5}$$

Returning now to the fluorescent centre: if a beam of radiation comprising photons with energy $E_2 - E_1$ (i.e. a beam whose frequency (f_1) is resonant with the $|1\rangle$ and $|2\rangle$ transition), then energy absorption will occur and the fluorescent centre will undergo excitation from state $|1\rangle$ to state $|2\rangle$. Under natural conditions this 'excited' fluorescent centre will decay and so return to the 'ground state'. However, if we also apply a second radiation beam with frequency f_2 (which is resonant with the energy difference between the $|2\rangle$ to $|3\rangle$ levels), the fluorescent centre will undergo a further excitation from state $|2\rangle$ to state $|3\rangle$. Subsequently, the fluorescent centre will return directly to the ground state.[26] This will be accompanied by the emission of radiation with photon energy E such that:

$$E = E_3 - E_1 = h(f_1 + f_2).$$

Thus, in this simple model, the frequency of the radiation emitted is greater than that of either of the beams used in the excitation process and so, in principle, this approach may be implemented using two infrared (non-visible beams). However, in practice other intermediate energy levels are usually involved in both the excitation and decay processes and the model illustrated in Figure 9.26 represents a simple (conceptualised) scenario.

A number of gases may be employed in the implementation of a gaseous image space able to support voxel formation by means of the two-step excitation process. Those interested in learning more about this technique will find useful information a range of publications such as Blundell [2007] (a general overview, analysis and references), Zito and Schraeder [1963(a), (b)] (concerning the use of mercury vapour) and US Patent Number 4,881,068 (containing extensive discussion including the use of rubidium vapour). Also in connection with the use of a solid image space medium (rather than a gas) see Lewis et al. [1971], Soltan et al. [1992], Chinnock [1994], Downing et al. [1994], Glanz [1996], Soltan and Lasher [1996], Nayar and Anand [2007].

Many other techniques have been applied to the implementation of static volume systems (see Blundell [2007]) and for our present purposes, it is instructive to mention two of these:

1. In two (practically identical) patents filed in 1968 (US Patent Numbers 3,609,706 and 3,609,707) the development of static volume systems employing photochromic and thermochromic materials is considered. It is not necessary to describe here the physical processes by which these materials are able to support the production of visible voxels (for relevant discussion see Blundell and Schwarz [2000] and Blundell [2007]). However, the use of such materials offers to support the formation of voxels that scatter (rather than emit) light.

---

[25] Planck's constant (h) $\sim 6.63 \times 10^{-34}$ Js.

[26] Or indirectly via some intermediate state that we have not included within our simple model.

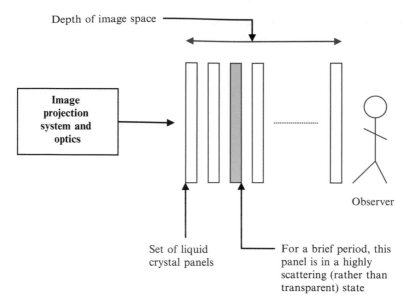

Figure 9.27 A simplified drawing showing the basic principle of operation of the DepthCube display manufactured by LightSpace Technologies. The image space comprises a set of liquid crystal panels which are individually switched between transparent and scattering states. A high-speed optical projection system casts a series of image slices into the display volume – to make a particular slice appear visible at a certain depth, the corresponding liquid crystal panel is placed in a scattering state (all other panels being transparent). In effect, this approach represents the 'solid state' rendition of a swept volume display employing translational motion.

> **Voxels that scatter incident light are optically opaque or semi-opaque. This enables images to take on a solid appearance and hence the depth cue of occlusion is satisfied. Furthermore, shadows may be created naturally through the use of external light sources. This opens up many interesting opportunities and enables the volumetric image to more closely represent the electronic equivalent of the traditional sculpted object.**

2.   LightSpace Technologies Inc. manufactures a static volume display system known as the DepthCube™. The image space comprises a set of liquid crystal panels that are stacked so as to lie parallel to each other (see Figure 9.27), and each may be individually switched between transparent and strongly scattering states.[27] The control hardware addresses the panels in sequence and so the depth at which scattering occurs continuously varies. An optical image projection system is used to output a series of image slices into the image space. In Figure 9.27, we indicate a panel at a particular depth within the image space that for a brief period is in a scattering state. At this time, the optical projection system outputs the image slice that is to appear at this depth. Subsequently, the panel is returned to a transparent state and an adjacent panel is switched into a scattering state. Another

---

[27] Note: each panel is switched in its entirety between these two states – limited parts of each panel are not addressed.

image slice is then output etc. For further discussion see Sullivan [2003], US Patent Number 6,100,862 and the LightSpace Technologies website.[28]

9.6 Varifocal Systems

*'Until a man duplicates a blade of grass,
nature can laugh at his so called scientific knowledge.'*[29]

We now briefly turn our attention to an autostereoscopic display paradigm that received particular attention in the mid to late 1960s and 1970s. It is interesting to note that most of the work that was undertaken in relation to this display technique was directed to medical applications and some excellent results were obtained.

As the name implies, the varifocal mirror approach is based on a curved mirror whose focal length continuously changes. In a particularly simple form this is achieved by stretching a highly reflective flexible membrane (e.g. aluminised Mylar) across the cone of a loudspeaker – see Figure 9.28. A sinusoidal signal is then applied to the 'speaker and this causes the flexible membrane to continuously vary between concave and convex states. The well known mirror equation provides us with a relationship between the position of an object (u), the focal length of the mirror (f) and the location of the image that is produced (v):

$$\frac{1}{u} + \frac{1}{v} = \frac{1}{f}.$$ (9.6)

Furthermore, suppose that an object has a height denoted as h_o and the image a height h_i, then the lateral magnification produced by a curved mirror is given by:

$$Magification = \frac{h_i}{h_o} = \frac{v}{u}.$$ (9.7)

Alternatively, combining this with Eq. 9.6, we can write:

$$Magnification = \frac{v}{f} - 1.$$ (9.8)

In applying Eq.'s 9.6 through to 9.8, we need to adopt a sign convention that distinguishes between concave (converging) and convex (diverging) mirrors and that enables us to distinguish between real and virtual objects and images.[30] Such a convention is as follows:

---

[28] http://www.lightspacetech.com.
[29] Attributed to Thomas Edison (1847–1931).
[30] In standard elementary optics/physics texts, a real image is one that is brought to focus in the region between the observer and the mirror. This contrasts with a virtual image which appears to lie behind the mirror. In the context of the forms of image and image space introduced earlier in this chapter, we refer to the former as a 'free' image and continue to use the term 'virtual' for the latter.

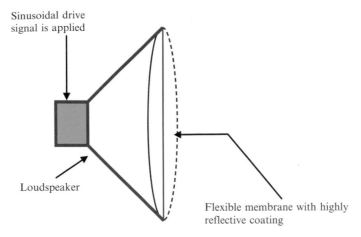

Sinusoidal drive signal is applied

Loudspeaker

Flexible membrane with highly reflective coating

Figure 9.28 A simple implementation of a varifocal system. A flexible membrane (with mirrored coating) is attached to the front of a conventional loudspeaker. A sinusoidal signal is applied to the 'speaker and this causes the flexible mirror to continuously vary between concave and convex states.

> **Real is Positive:**
> - Real objects and real images are said to be located at positive distances from the mirror.
> - Virtual objects and virtual images are said to be located at negative distances from the mirror.
> - A concave (converging) mirror is said to have a positive focal length.
> - A convex (diverging) mirror is said to have a negative focal length.

OTU Exercise 9.10: Locating the Size and Position of an Image Formed by Curved Mirrors

1. Consider a concave (converging) mirror with a focal length of 20 cm. An object of height 2 cm is placed 10 cm from the mirror. Determine the location and size of the final image. Is this image located in front of, or behind the mirror (i.e. in terms of the forms of image identified earlier in this chapter, does this constitute a free space or virtual image)?
2. Repeat question (1) but this time assume the use of a convex mirror.

Hint: Remember to adopt the sign convention indicated above!

As the radius of curvature of the varifocal mirror changes, so too does its focal length. Consequently, on the basis of Eq. 9.6, it is apparent that as the mirror moves through a cycle of its vibration, the image of an object that is placed in front of the mirror will appear to change in position. Furthermore, only a small change in mirror curvature is needed to generate a large change in image location. This is demonstrated by the following equation in which the image position (denoted as $v(t)$ (indicating the v is a function of time)) is related to the mirror diameter (d), the object location (u), the maximum mirror displacement (x_{max}) and the frequency of the sinusoidal waveform that is applied to the mirror ($\omega = 2\pi f$):

$$v(t) \sim \frac{d^2 u}{16u\,|x_{max}|\sin\omega t - d^2}.$$

(9.9)

For a simple derivation of. this equation, see Appendix B.

OTU Exercise 9.11: The Curvature of a Varifocal Mirror

Consider that an object is placed 80 cm in front of a varifocal mirror which has a diameter of 30 cm. Assuming that the peak to peak amplitude of motion of the mirror is 4 mm and considering only the portion of the mirror's motion for which it is convex, determine the depth of the image space (i.e. the range of image location).

As is apparent from OTU Exercise 9.11, a small change in mirror curvature has a considerable impact on the location of the image and so the varifocal approach supports (in principle) the formation of an image space which has significant depth. However, we should also bear in mind that the changing curvature of the mirror also impacts on magnification. For example continuing with the scenario described in the previous OTU Exercise, we can use Eq. 9.8 to determine the magnification at the two locations that correspond to the extremes of the mirror's convex cycle. In the case that $t = 0$, we know that the object and image distances are equal and therefore the magnification is unity. On the other hand, when $t = 3T/4$, the magnification is approximately $51/80 \sim 0.6$.

The issue of the continuously varying magnification associated with a varifocal mirror means that when a series of image slices are computed for output to the mirror, each must be suitably scaled. In this way, we can resolve the variable magnification issue.

Naturally, so that images depicted by means of a varifocal based display are perceived as being free from flicker, the mirror must vibrate with sufficient rapidity. As with the swept volume volumetric system employing translational motion, this means that the mirror must vibrate at a frequency in excess of 25 Hz. In the case that the display is based on the simpler loudspeaker approach summarised in Figure 9.28, this leads to undesirable acoustic noise (the lower bound to human hearing is in the range 16–32 Hz). Unfortunately, in literature, the issue of acoustic noise is often cited as representing a fundamental flaw associated with this approach and this is said to negate the usefulness of this technique. However, this is not correct and a number of techniques can be used to either ameliorate or completely eliminate this problem. For example:

1. Lawrence Sher undertook a great deal of research in connection with varifocal systems and in a patent filed in 1977 (US Patent Number 4,130,832) he describes a system that was intended to overcome the problem of acoustic noise.

2. Alternative designs place the mirror within an evacuated vessel and this completely eliminates the issue of acoustic noise. For example, see UK Patent Application Number GB 0700505.1.

Figure 9.29 A stereoscopic photograph of simulated air traffic control data depicted on a varifocal system prototyped by Alan Traub in the 1960's. The image is depicted on an oscilloscope and is reflected by the varifocal mirror (which appears on the right hand side of each of the stereo images). This simple varifocal system employed a loudspeaker drive (part of which can be seen on the extreme right). The images may be fused using the stereo glasses supplied with this book or simply by slightly 'crossing' the eyes. Notice that when viewed as a stereopair, the varifocal image appears to lie behind the varifocal mirror and so this represents a virtual image space. (Reproduced from Traub [1967], by kind permission, © 1967 Optical Society of America).

> **Acoustic noise is not an inherent problem of the varifocal technique, but is rather a problem that is associated with certain varifocal architectures. With judicious design a silent varifocal system can be implemented and this enables the refresh rate to be increased beyond 30 Hz.**

Without doubt the varifocal technique offers many interesting opportunities and represents a low cost autostereoscopic display modality. In Figure 9.29, a stereoscopic photograph of a varifocal image is reproduced. For further reading see, for example, Blundell [2007], McAllister [1993][31], Traub [1967], Rawson [1968, 1969], King and Berry [1970], Harris *et al.* [1986], Kennedy and Nelson [1987], Sher [1988] and US Patents 3,493,290 and 4,130,832.

9.7 Holographic Techniques

'Each of us visits the Earth involuntarily and without an invitation. For me, it is enough to wonder at its secrets.'[32]

Researchers working on the development of creative 3-D display systems often regard an electronic display able to depict animated holographic images in real time as the ultimate (although somewhat elusive) display technique. Holographic images are able to support the pictorial, oculomotor and parallax depth cues and so they are well suited for the natural requirements of

---

[31] In Chapter 11, Lawrence Sher discusses varifocal systems.
[32] Attributed to Albert Einstein (1879–1955).

the human visual system. On the other hand, in its truest form, computed holography (which is also called electroholography or holographic video) has extreme computational overheads and places stringent requirements on the display hardware. Shortly, we will briefly discuss the computational requirements of this technique but before doing so we provide some general background detail.

9.7.1 General Issues

Detailed discussion on holographic techniques is beyond the scope of this book and our purpose is simply to present some general information and references for further reading.

The basic concept of holography was first described in a one-page article written by Denis Gabor that was published in 'Nature' in the late 1940s [Gabor 1948][33]. At that time Gabor was primarily interested in using holography to advance electron microscopy; the development of optical holographic techniques represented a secondary objective. Despite his remarkable publication, some years were to pass before interest in optical holography really gained momentum. The implementation of practical holographic recording and display techniques requires access to a coherent high-intensity monochromatic (single wavelength) light source. These are characteristics of laser radiation and so with the advent of the laser in the early 1960s, optical holography became a practical proposition (see, for example, [Leith and Upatnieks [1962, 1963, 1964]]).

Conventional photography captures on film the amount of light reflected by the objects that comprise the scene. Furthermore, there is a one-to-one correspondence between points within the scene and points on the photographic film. In contrast, a holographic image is created by capturing not only the amplitude of reflected light, but also its phase. In short:

> When an object scatters incident light, the scattering process is described by the strength and phase of the waves emanating from the surface. This information can be used to capture the three-dimensional form of an object and enables (at least in principle) pictorial, oculomotor and parallax cues to be supported.

Furthermore, as we have just mentioned, in the case of conventional photography each 'point' within an image scene is mapped onto a corresponding point on the photographic film. In contrast, in the case of a holographic recording, there is no such one-to-one mapping – each point within the scene is mapped to a wide area of the hologram. Thus, if the holographic recording is scratched or even if a fragment is removed, this does not mean that a corresponding part of the image scene will be lost!

A holographic recording takes the form of an interference pattern and in brief, this can be obtained by taking a laser and splitting the beam so that light travels along two paths – see Figure 9.30. Light traversing one of these paths impinges on the object (or collection of objects) whose holographic image is to be recorded. Light scattered by the object then interferes with the second (reference) beam and the interference pattern is captured on film. Subsequently, when the holographic recording is re-illuminated with the laser source used in the recording process, the original object (or collection of objects) appears in 3-D form.

---

[33] Additionally, a review paper written by Gabor in the early 1970s is well worth reading – it provides a wealth of important information [Gabor 1972].

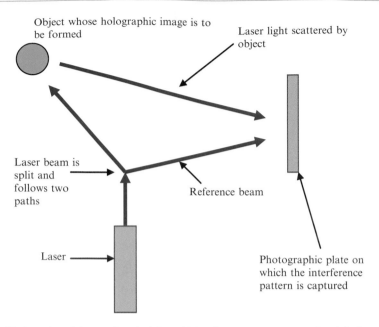

Object whose holographic image is to be formed

Laser light scattered by object

Laser beam is split and follows two paths

Reference beam

Laser

Photographic plate on which the interference pattern is captured

Figure 9.30 A simplified overview of the recording of a holographic interference pattern. Here, we show light from a laser split into two beams that traverse separate paths. One of these beams forms a 'reference' and the other impinges on the object whose holographic image is to be recorded. Subsequently, the light scattered by the object and the reference beam combine to produce an interference pattern on the recording medium. In this way it is possible to record not only the amplitude of the waves scattered by the object but also their phase.

9.7.2 Computed Holography

In the above discussion, we have outlined a general technique for capturing a holographic fringe pattern that contains both amplitude and phase information. Naturally, we can also generate such a fringe pattern on the basis of mathematical calculations and in this way may make holographic recordings of virtual objects and scenes. In one scenario, once the fringe pattern has been computed, it is imprinted on a suitable medium and when illuminated in an appropriate manner the 3-D scene may be viewed. However, this approach does not support interaction nor does it enable image animation. Consequently, an ultimate goal is to display holographic images in real time (i.e. at video refresh rates) and thereby allow both animation and interaction. Unfortunately, this is a daunting task. Within this context, Blundell and Schwarz [2006] write:

'... *in order to diffract visible light, the fringe pattern needs a resolution on the order of the wavelength of light* (~400–700 nm). *The digital fringe pattern must therefore be displayed at a spatial resolution of around 2000 pixels/mm.*'

Recall junior level science lessons in which plane waves are generated in a water tank (the so called 'ripple tank'). When these waves pass through an opening whose width is larger than the wavelength of the waves – plane waves will emerge. On the other hand, if they pass through a narrower opening (i.e. one whose width is less than or approximately equal to the wavelength

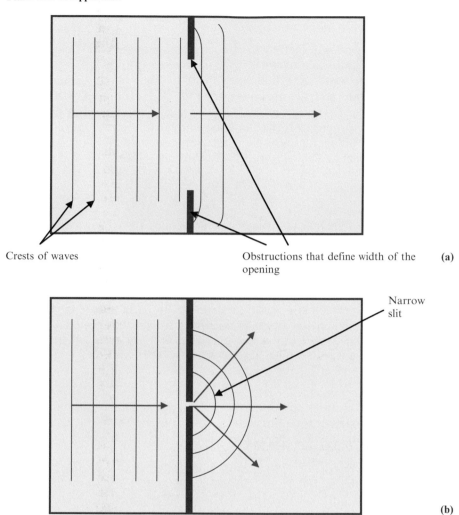

Figure 9.31 Here, we illustrate (in plan view) a ripple tank. Planar waves in water are generated on the left hand side and propagate to the right. In (a) these waves pass through a gap (wide slit) whose width is considerably greater than their wavelength. Consequently, after passing through the gap, the waves continue to be essentially planar. This contrasts to the situation illustrated in (b). The width of the slit is now less than the wavelength of the waves. As a result, the waves subsequently spread out and exhibit semicircular wavefronts. This process is known as diffraction.

of the incident waves) semi-circular waves will emerge – see Figure 9.31. This 'spreading out' of the waves is known as diffraction. In this context Nelkon and Parker [1995] write:

'...*when a wave is incident on a narrow opening whose width is of comparable order to the wavelength. The wave now spreads out or is 'diffracted' after passing through the slit. If the width of the slit, however, is large compared with the wavelength, the wave passes straight through the opening without any noticeable* *diffraction. This is why visible light, which has wavelengths of the order of 6×10^{-7} m, passes straight through wide openings and produces sharp shadows; whereas sound which has wavelengths over a million times longer and of the order of say 0.5 m can be heard round corners.'*

Returning now to the previous quotation. Let us consider light with a wavelength of 500nm. It follows that in order for diffraction to occur when light passes through a fringe pattern that we have created, the fringe pattern must exhibit 'detail' with spacings on the order of 500×10^{-9} m. Thus within the fringe pattern we require on the order of $1/0.5 \times 10^{-6} = 2 \times 10^{6}$ 'elements' per metre. This is equal to a spatial resolution of 2000 'elements' per mm. A more accurate estimate of the number of digital samples (N) that must be computed so as to generate a full parallax (vertical and horizontal) hologram is given by St. Hilaire *et al.* [1992]. If we assume that we are to generate a hologram that has a height h and width w, then:

$$N = \frac{4wh\sin^2\theta}{\lambda^2}. \tag{9.10}$$

Where λ represents the wavelength of the light and θ the range of viewing angle.

OTU Exercise 9.12: Computing a Holographic Fringe Pattern

On the basis of Eq. 9.10 determine the approximate number of digital samples that must be calculated to generate a square holographic image with sides of length 20 cm and that supports a viewing angle of 30°. Assume that the wavelength of the light is 500 nm.

The above OTU Exercise indicates a need to compute $\sim16 \times 10^{10}$ digital samples per holographic frame. For any real-time application this is a daunting task. Furthermore, if we assume that each fringe pattern sample is represented by eight bits and that we wish to have a frame update frequency of 30 Hz, then the digital bandwidth to the display device is $\sim38 \times 10^{12}$ bits per second.

Certainly, when we consider the generation and depiction of computed holograms for real time applications, the problems are daunting. Not only must we be able to compute the digital samples with sufficient rapidity, but also the graphics pipeline must be able to handle their throughput and the display system must be able to support their depiction. Unfortunately, popular literature often overlooks these fundamental issues, and accounts of stylistic display technologies based on holographic techniques are presented as accomplished fact. In addition, some workers in the area of creative 3-D display technologies have exploited the general popularity of the holographic technique by implying (in some way) that their display products are based on holographic principles when in actual fact this is by no means the case. Thus in the case that a real-time display product has a name (or the like) which implies that it is based on a holographic approach, caution should be exercised...

Returning to Eq. 9.10 we can use a number of strategies for reducing the number of digital samples that comprise the fringe pattern. For example, we can reduce the size of the holograph, reduce the extent of viewing freedom and support only horizontal parallax. This latter approach has a significant impact and in this case Eq. 9.10 reduces to:

$$N = \frac{2wh\sin\theta}{\lambda}.$$

OTU Exercise 9.13: Viewing Freedom

Suppose that in an attempt to reduce the overheads associated with the computed hologra-phy technique, we support only horizontal parallax and reduce θ from 45° to 25°.

1. Estimate the impact this would have on the lateral extent of the viewing zone. Assume a typical viewing distance of 50 cm.

2. Estimate the effect this would have on the number of digital samples comprising the fringe pattern (as with OTU Exercise 9.12, assume $\lambda = 500$ nm and that the hologram is a square with sides of length 20 cm).

Other techniques are summarised in Blundell and Schwarz [2006]. For more detailed discussions also see, for example, Okoshi [1976], Lucente [1993, 1994, 1996], Ritter *et al.* [1997, 1998] and Halle [1996].

9.8 Discussion

'Il y en a toujours l'un qui baise, et l'un qui tourne la joue.' [34]

Despite the considerable length of this chapter, we have been able to do little more than provide a brief insight into the technologies and techniques that may be used in the implementation of creative 3-D display technologies and have identified various general characteristics. Certainly there is no 'perfect' 3-D display – they all possess (to a greater or lesser degree) limitations and undesirable characteristics. On the other hand these must be balanced against the inherent limitations of the conventional flat screen display – and for certain key applications, the inability of today's standard computer display to support the parallax depth cues has a negative impact on the visualisation and interaction processes.

At present there is a significant and growing interest in the development of creative 3-D display and interaction technologies. For example, in Figure 9.32 we reproduce two stereopairs showing an image depicted on a 3-D display system that is under development at the University of Southern California. Observers are able to move around the image space and view displayed images from any orientation. Horizontal parallax is inherently associated with this display technique and in addition head tracking can be used to support vertical parallax. Interestingly this approach fundamentally builds on both volumetric and multi-view techniques. However, unlike the majority of volumetric architectures the depth cue of occlusion is supported thereby allowing images to exhibit a 'solid' appearance. Voxels are emissive and so external lighting cannot be used to form natural shadows. For further details of this exciting technology see Jones *et al.* [2007] [35] – the Abstract from which is reproduced below:

'We describe a set of rendering techniques for an autostereoscopic light field display able to present interactive 3D graphics to multiple simultaneous viewers 360 degrees around the display. The display consists of a high-speed video projector, a spinning mirror covered by a holographic diffuser, and FPGA circuitry to decode

---

[34] Quoted from Monsarrat, N., 'The Cruel Sea', Cassell and Co (1953). Translation: *'There is always one who kisses and the other who turns the cheek.'*

[35] A preprint of this publication together with a video download are available via the following URL: http://gl.ict.usc.edu/Research/3DDisplay/ (date last visited: December 2007).

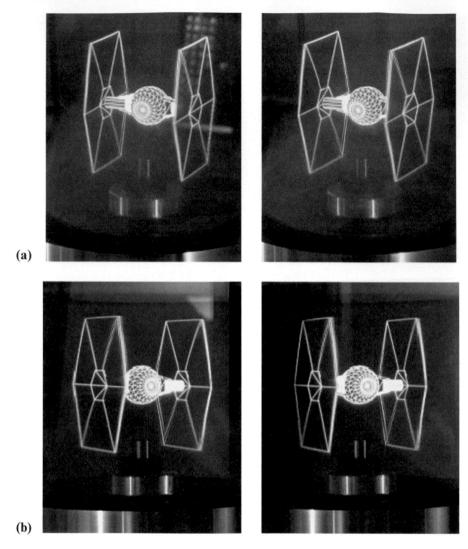

(a)

(b)

Figure 9.32 Stereo pairs of an image depicted on the Light Field display developed by Andrew Jones *et al*. These stereopairs have been captured at different viewpoints around the display. In connection with these images the researchers write: '*The two stereo viewpoints sample the 360° field of view around the display. The right pair* [Figure a] *is from a vertically-tracked camera position and the left pair* [Figure b] *is from an untracked position roughly horizontal to the centre of the display.*' [Jones *et al*. 2007]. (Images kindly provided by Mark Bolas, reproduced with permission.)

specially rendered DVI video signals. The display uses a standard programmable graphics card to render over 5,000 images per second of interactive 3D graphics, projecting 360-degree views with 1.25 degree separation up to 20 updates per second. We describe the system's projection geometry and its calibration process, and we present a multiple-center-of-projection rendering technique for creating perspective-correct images from arbitrary viewpoints around the display. Our projection technique allows correct vertical perspective and parallax to be rendered for any height and distance when these parameters are known, and we demonstrate this effect with interactive raster graphics using a tracking system to measure the viewer's height and distance. We further apply our projection technique to the display of photographed light fields with accurate horizontal and vertical parallax. We conclude with a discussion of the display's visual accommodation performance and discuss techniques for displaying color imagery.'

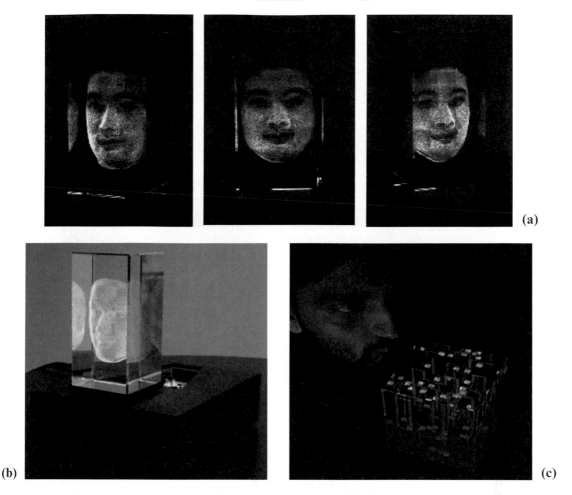

Figure 9.33 Images depicted on the display technology developed by Shree K. Nayar and Vijay N. Anand. Image (a) shows a 3-D avatar photographed from three different viewpoints. This avatar is also depicted in (b) and is reported to comprise 127,333 points. In (c) 3-D Pac-Man is depicted on the display. (Images kindly provided by Shree Nayar, reproduced with permission).

A further example of ongoing development work is described in an excellent publication by Nayar and Anand [2007]. This relates to a volumetric technique in which images are formed within a solid transparent medium. In Figure 9.33 we reproduce several images displayed using this system. In describing this technology, the researchers write:

'*Systems for displaying images and videos have become part of our everyday lives. However, most systems in use today can only display 2D images. Since we live in a 3D physical world, a system that can display static and dynamic 3D images would provide viewers with a more immersive experience...*

Our displays use a simple light engine and a cloud of passive optical scatterers. The basic idea is to trade off the light engine's 2D spatial resolution to gain resolution in the third dimension. One way to achieve such a tradeoff is to use a stack of planar grids of scatterers where no two stacks overlap each other with respect to the light engine's projection rays.

Such a semiregular 3D grid suffers from poor visibility. As the viewer moves around the point cloud, the fraction of visible points varies dramatically and is very small for some viewing directions. However, randomizing the point cloud in a specific manner consistent with the light engine's projection geometry produces a remarkably stable visibility function.

We used a technology called laser induced damage…that can efficiently, precisely, and at a very low cost embed a desired point cloud in a solid block of glass or plastic. Each scatterer is a physical crack in the block that is created by focusing a laser beam at a point. When such a crack is lit by ambient light it is barely visible, but when it is lit by a focused source it glows brightly.

To illuminate the scatterers, we developed an orthographiclight engine that uses an off-the-shelf digital projector and inexpensive optics to create parallel rays with a large footprint. While orthographic projection isn't required, it allows us to use point clouds without resolution biases and with relatively straightforward calibration of the display.

We developed several versions of our volumetric display, each designed to meet the needs of a specific class of objects or a specific application…' [Nayar and Anand [2007]

In the next chapter we turn our attention to issues relating to interaction, and introduce haptic interaction techniques which are ideally suited for use with various forms of creative 3-D display. In fact many of the underlying software techniques used in the implementation of haptic systems closely parallel those used in 3-D computer graphics.

OTU Exercise 9.14: Constructing a Simple Varifocal Display System

In a most interesting publication, Professor Fuchs *et al.* [1982] describe the implementation of a varifocal display system. Two illustrations from this publication are reproduced in Figure 9.34. In recent correspondence with the author of this book, Professor Fuchs summarised a highly practical approach to the implementation of such a display. This does not require access to specialised equipment and is presented in slightly edited form below. This provides an excellent opportunity for project activity.

1) Buy a drum head with a shiny surface from a music store (or a piece of aluminised mylar stretched tightly across an embroidery hoop).
2) Place this very close (<1″) to a large (12″) speaker.
3) Attach a sine-wave generator (set to 30 Hz) to the speaker.
4) Take the RGB component outputs of a video card from your PC to an oscilloscope monitor's raw inputs (red to x-deflection, green to y-deflection, blue to intensity (z-modulation)).[36]
5) Attach the vertical sync output of the video card to the trigger input of the sine-wave generator.
6) Set the video card to 30 Hz output rate, 24 bit RGB (8 bits per colour).
7) Load the 3D points you want to display on this varifocal mirror into the graphics card. Note that the video card's pixels will be output to the varifocal mirror display once every 1/30 of a second in synchrony with the vibrating movements of the drum-head mirror. Thus the pixels will be in depth order, the pixels nearer the top of the 'image' in the video card, will be scanned out before the ones farther down the 'image'.

Professor Fuchs adds *'My impression is that people have made this kind of desktop varifocal display within a day. It's the easiest demonstration of a true 3d display I know of. The images are pretty dramatic, they float in space and people can walk around them.'*

---

[36] Naturally due care should be taken so as to avoid causing any damage to the PC or video card!

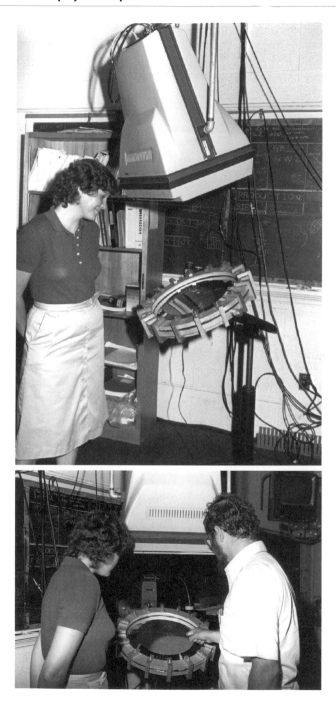

Figure 9.34 These illustrations are reproduced from the most interesting publication by Fuchs *et al*. [1982] and show the projection arrangement used in the implementation of a varifocal system. The display (in this case CRT based) may be seen towards the top of the illustrations and from this, image slices are cast onto the varifocal mirror (into which the viewers are looking). Note that each viewer will see a slightly different perspective view of the image scene. See OTU Exercise 9.14. (Images kindly supplied by Professor Henry Fuchs.)

9.9 Review Questions

1. Recall that various types of image space were introduced in Section 9.2.2. In general, what type of image space is generated by volumetric display systems?
2. In the context of volumetric systems, what do you understand by the term 'dead zone'?
3. Consider the case of a stereoscopic display that employs temporal coding. What is the key penalty that is associated with this coding technique?
4. Consider the case of a stereoscopic display that employs chromatic coding. What is the key penalty that is associated with this coding technique?
5. Consider the case of a stereoscopic display that employs spatial coding. What is the key penalty that is associated with this coding technique?
6. State the three key subsystems that comprise a volumetric display.
7. What additional depth cues are supported by holographic, varifocal and volumetric display systems?
8. State the five forms of image space that we have identified in this chapter.
9. Consider the case of standard stereograms – such as those presented in Figure 1.32. What form of image space is associated with this approach?
10. When does total internal reflection occur?

9.10 Feedback to Review Questions

1. The volumetric display technique usually gives rise to a physical image space.
2. A dead zone represents a region of an image space within which image quality is compromised by a reduction in one or more image space characteristics.
3. Each eye only receives alternate frames. Therefore, to avoid image flicker the frame refresh rate must be increased by a factor of approximately two.
4. Such an approach is limited in its ability to support multicolour imaging – the colour pallet is greatly reduced – often to only two colours.
5. The total pixel bandwidth of the display is distributed across the number of stereo views that are generated. Naturally, this results in a reduction in the number of pixels that comprise each view.
6. The image space creation subsystem, the voxel generation subsystem and the voxel activation subsystem.
7. The oculomotor cues – accommodation and convergence.
8. Planar image space, physical image space, free image space, virtual image space and apparent image space.
9. An apparent image space.
10. Total internal reflection can occur when light travels from a dense to a less optically dense medium.

Interaction and Haptic Feedback

10

'. . . and consoled himself with pastimes
such as cricket, which he played in a
manner highly specialised, following
the ball up the moment it left the
bowler's hand, and sometimes
retrieving it before it reached the
batsman.'

10.1 Introduction

The mouse is the tool most commonly used for interaction with both graphical images and
the event driven user interface. Despite its simplicity and intuitive functionality, this device is
uni-directional – enabling us to input to the computer but not, in itself, providing us with
any sensation of the results of the interaction activity. In this sense the conventional mouse
is passive and the only haptic feedback[1] that we receive during the interaction process is
generated by the friction between the mouse and the surface on which it is moved, resistance
to finger pressure as we press its buttons, etc. In this context, it is important to appreciate
that unlike our other sensory systems the haptic channel is bi-directional – enabling us to
sense and act upon our surroundings. However, in terms of our interaction with computer
systems, traditional interaction devices do not capitalise on the bi-directional capabilities of the
human haptic system – we output to the computer but do not receive input (via this sensory
modality) relating to the results of our interaction activities. In this context, Kim *et al.* [2003a, b]
write:

'*Imagine trying to tell Michel Angelo to sculpt David within the confines of the computer interface. This would
be equivalent to restricting him to the use of only one eye since the monitor only provides 2-D images and to
the use of only one arm since he works through the mouse. It would be necessary to disengage his nerve endings*

---

[1] Haptics – derived from the Greek – *haptesthai* – meaning to come into contact with. Here, we use the
term 'haptic feedback' in its broadest sense to encompass both touch and force feedback.

because the mouse provides no force feedback and his arm must be confined so that it can only move in one plane at a time.'

Clearly, impairing the human sensory systems can greatly detract from our natural dexterity – thereby increasing task difficulty and in some cases making it impossible for us to perform tasks within the digital domain which, within the physical world, would be relatively straightforward. Consideration of simple and even rudimentary everyday tasks reveals the critical reliance that we place on haptic feedback. For example:

1. Testing soft fruit (e.g. peaches) for ripeness. Can we place total confidence on the visual system? To what extent is this seemingly simple task facilitated by bringing several of our senses to bear?

2. Threading a nut onto a bolt or inserting a key into a lock – such tasks are made much more difficult when our hands are numb from cold and thereby our tactile sense is impaired.

3. Working with materials such as wood, plastics and metals in situation in which we need to gauge the amount of force that we are applying when, for example, bending or cutting.

4. Reaching for and grasping a wine glass whilst distracted by conversation. Here, we need to sense initial contact and in addition gauge the pressure applied as we grasp the glass.

To date, the standard computer interface does not incorporate haptic capabilities and for certain applications this can negatively impact on our ability to make optimal use of computer technologies. However, there is a growing recognition that as computer applications continue to increase in complexity there is a need to advance computer display technologies (by supporting, for example, the parallax depth cues) and also to incorporate some form(s) of haptic feedback.

> **The development of the computer interface in support of three-dimensional tactile images should be driven by a wish to advance key applications that can really benefit from such capabilities and should be underpinned by practical technologies.**

Within this context, when considering the practicality of technologies, we must give careful attention to their ability to effectively (harmoniously) interface with the human sensory systems and the associated computational costs – especially in relation to real time applications. Below we briefly consider two indicative areas of application in which haptic technologies are playing an increasingly important role:

10.1.1 Medical Training

There are many situations in which our activities can have potentially harmful consequences. In such cases, simulation systems play a vital role during the training process, enabling, for example, the trainee to make mistakes without undesirable physical consequences. In addition, it is possible for the trainee to view the results of actions which in real world situations could have serious consequences, and to particularly focus on more demanding aspects of procedures. In the case of surgery and the like, simulation systems will often enable a significant portion of the training process to be carried out on virtual objects, which reduces the undesirable reliance that is traditionally placed on animal subjects or human volunteers. Surgery places tremendous demands on a surgeon's tactile senses and any surgical simulation system that does not incorporate support for haptic feedback is likely to have only limited application (as critical information will be absent) and will not best support a 'suspension of disbelief' (recall discussion in Chapter 1).

Typically, surgical simulation systems make use of specially designed surgical tools via which the operator interacts with computer generated images – the virtual patient (for interesting discussion, see for example, Hinckley and Pausch [1998]). Consider, for example, 'minimally invasive surgery'. Here, surgical instruments located on the end of a thin tube (a laparoscope) are inserted through a small incision – a so-called 'keyhole'. A small camera attached to the end of the laparoscope provides the surgeon with vital visual cues and procedures are underpinned by haptic cues that occur during the insertion and manipulation processes. It has been found that 'mentor based' training procedures (of the type used in traditional 'open surgery') are less suited to the remote laparoscope based approach, and here simulation plays a crucial role (see, for example, Seymour *et al.* [2002] and Schijven and Jakimowicz [2003]). Similarly, the administration of an epidural anaesthetic to the spine places critical reliance on human dexterity and tactile sensation since the needle encounters several soft tissue layers (exhibiting different levels of resistance) during the insertion process. Here, any lack of skill or concentration on the administrator's part (resulting, for example, in the penetration of the dura) can cause pain to the patient and may have long term repercussions. Again this is an area where simulation can play a vital role in the training process, although great reliance is placed on the fidelity haptic feedback system and requires that it is able to signal delicate changes in haptic sensation.[2] This contrasts with, for example, a flight simulator where haptic signals are stronger and changes in signal occur at a coarser level.

10.1.2 Creative Design

There is increasing recognition that human creative activities that are supported by digital technologies can be advanced through the incorporation of appropriate haptic systems. These offer to provide the artist and designer with a better sensation of material properties, surface textures etc. and enable interaction operations to more closely mimic traditional methods (e.g. the tactile sensations derived when using a brush on canvas or when cutting and forming materials). Indeed the sculptor may be presented with virtual clay which can not only take on the properties of its physical counterpart but may also be assigned additional properties, thereby opening up new opportunities.[3] Furthermore, it is possible to assign haptic properties to the 3-D space in which interaction occurs (in contrast to assigning the haptic properties to objects within the space). For example, a three-dimensional grid of 'force grooves' can be created thus facilitating the guidance of the interaction tool (and so, for example, assisting in the formation of straight lines). In addition, researchers report that this form of grid encourages users to move the interaction tool *into* the interaction space [Snibbe *et al.* [1998].

In this chapter we briefly discuss aspects of the interaction process and haptic feedback in general. We begin by considering interaction in the context of visual and proprioception cues. Here we refer to both uni-manual and bi-manual interaction and emphasise the critical role played by the latter as we interact with our surroundings, and which can be clearly demonstrated by unscrewing the cap from a bottle of ketchup (or the like) when using only one hand! In

---

[2] For a video download describing a epidural simulation system that incorporates haptic feedback see http://www.yantric.com (date last visited, 2nd September 2007).

[3] For excellent video downloads showing exemplar applications see http://www.sensable.com/industries-video-gallery.htm (date last visited, 4th September 2007).

Section 10.3 we focus on somatosensory perception which relates to the wide-ranging sensations we derive from both internal sensory receptors, and from the vast network of receptors located within the structure of the skin. Here, we also briefly consider the frequency characteristics of the human haptic channel and consider the demands that this can place on the haptic rendering process.

In Section 10.4 we summarise issues relating to traditional human computer interaction tools and again refer to uni-manual and bi-manual interaction. Finally, in Section 10.5 we focus on the implementation of haptic systems and provide a number of references that provide more in-depth discussion.

> **Key Learning Outcomes**: At the end of this chapter you should be able to:
>
> - *Discuss issues relating to our interaction with digital systems.*
>
> - *Describe aspects of the human haptic system.*
>
> - *Discuss key issues relating to the incorporation of haptic feedback within the human-computer interaction interface.*
>
> - *Appreciate the synergy that can be derived through bi-manual interaction.*

10.2 Concerning Interaction

> *'What we embed in the computer is the inert and empty shadow, or abstract reflection of the past operation of our own intelligence.'*[4]

The keyboard and mouse provide the means by which the majority of today's computer users undertake interactive operations. Interestingly, these two interaction modalities are somewhat dissimilar in the demands that they place on our sensory and motor systems. Consider the keyboard, which a touch typist with sufficient skill may rapidly operate with little if any recourse to visual cues. Here, reliance is placed on an intuitive (largely subconscious) ability to accurately judge both the relative and absolute locations of the hands/fingers and the force applied to the keys. Only an occasional glance at the keyboard will be needed and visual feedback is continually provided via the display screen. However, even if we break this feedback loop (e.g. by turning off the screen) the typing process can continue in a reasonably successful way (although the frequency of errors is likely to increase). This compares to other situations in which tasks are strongly underpinned by our ability to judge the absolute and relative locations of the hands – even when, as with the keyboard, such tasks require the cooperation of both hands. For example, consider the skilled pianist. Only occasionally will he or she glance at the keys – the sheet of music usually being the primary focus of attention. This process is in fact far more demanding than is the rapid use of a keyboard by a touch typist because, for example, although both situations require an accurate knowledge of the location of hands and fingers, the use of the

---

[4] Source: Talbott, S.L., *'The Future Does Not Compute'*, O'Reilly & Associates, Inc., (1995).

keyboard requires relatively little arm movement whereas the pianist must maintain the high accuracy of hand and finger placement across larger distances. This necessitates a continual shift in the location of the arms (and even changes in body posture). The pianist receives continual feedback (primarily of an audible nature)[5] and as with the visual feedback provided to the typist via the computer screen, if the cues supplied by audible feedback loop are in some way severed, the musician can still continue to play.

In summary, the efficient use of the keyboard is strongly underpinned by our ability to accurately judge the location of the hands and fingers and through the sense of touch by which we determine the force imparted by the fingers. This is demonstrated in the brief sample of text presented below and that was dictated to a touch typist able to type at 110 words to minute:

> **This text is being dictated to a touch typist at normal talking speed. However, the computer display is turned off and so the only feedback received by the typist is from her view of the keyboard.**
>
> **This is being dictated not only wi th the computer display turned off, but also with the typist not looking at the keyboard. In short, this text is being typed with the typist only employing her intuitive knowledge of the relative and absolute positions of her fingers together with tactile feedback.**

Although these represent only brief fragments of text, it is apparent that the lack of visual feedback has had little impact on the typist's ability to enter text into the computer (the first fragment contains no errors and the second has a single error: '*wi th*').

Now let us turn our attention to the mouse. The operation of this device is underpinned by hand-eye coordination and certainly, if we were to turn off the computer display there would be little chance of our being able to employ the mouse in a useful manner. It is helpful to assign to an interaction tool an 'interaction space' – this representing the physical region within which the interaction tool operates. For example, a joystick may operate by the motion of the 'stick' and in this case, the extent of the interaction space corresponds to the range of possible movement. When the device is used to navigate a cursor on a conventional flat screen display, there is a one-to-one mapping (via a suitable scaling factor) between the movement of the joystick and the displacement of the cursor. In the case of a mouse, the extent of the interaction space is not limited by the device itself (after all we can define any scaling factor that we deem appropriate for the mapping between the interaction and image spaces), but rather by the practicalities of using the device. In fact, we often employ a very small interaction space and adopt a scrolling action (involving the continual lifting and repositioning of the mouse).

Although the mouse provides us with a simple, effective and intuitive means of navigating a cursor on a conventional flat screen display, its usefulness can be somewhat eroded when we consider the issue of cursor navigation in a 3-D space. Let us suppose the use of a simple mouse in which the motion of the cursor in the third dimension is effected by pressing (and holding down) a mouse button. Furthermore let us suppose that we wish to navigate the cursor so that it becomes coincident with an image component that is located within a 3-D space and that motion parallax is not supported by the display technology. In such a scenario, we are likely to encounter difficulties in judging the depth of the cursor relative to the image component under consideration. This is easily demonstrated in the following OTU Exercise.

---

[5] Although, of course should an error occur, the pianist does not have access to a 'delete' facility!

OTU Exercise 10.1: Object Alignment in a 3-D space

1. Position your left hand so that your first finger is pointing vertically upwards and is about 40cm in front of you. Close both of your eyes. Now point the first finger of your right hand vertically downwards and attempt to align the two fingers so that the finger of the left hand is directly below that of the right hand (the fingers should not touch). Open your eyes and determine how well you have succeeded in this alignment task.
2. Repeat (1) but instead of using your fingers, hold a pointer (e.g. a pen or pencil) in the left hand and another in the right. Again one pointer should be held vertically upwards and the other vertically downwards and the objective is to align the two.
3. If you are still in any doubt as to the ease and accuracy with which the fingers or pointers can be aligned (and which is underpinned by the accurate knowledge of the orientation and position of our limbs) repeat (1) and (2) but now with your hands behind your back! (Although you will now need to select a more convenient distance!)
4. Now for a more demanding task. Stand a pointer (e.g. pen, pencil or the like) vertically upwards on a tabletop. Crouch down so that your head is at approximately the same height as the pointer and so that it lies at a distance of ~40cm. Hold a second pointer in either your left or right hand. Orientate this pointer so that it points vertically downwards, close one of your eyes and keeping your head absolutely still, move the pointer held in the hand so that it is aligned with (i.e. is vertically above) the static pointer positioned on the tabletop. Open both eyes and move your head to determine how well/accurately you were able to achieve alignment.

> Consider two objects (such as the pointers referred to in the above OTU Exercise) which are misaligned so that, for example, one pointer is not directly above the other. In this case, when we shift our viewpoint in a horizontal direction the pointers appear to move relative to each other. This movement is referred to as parallax (hence the associated depth cue is called 'motion parallax'). Alternatively, if the two pointers are properly aligned, shifting the viewing position will not result in our perception of relative motion. This is referred to as a state of 'no parallax'.

In carrying out the above OTU Exercise, it is likely that you will have been able to undertake the first three tasks without any difficulty and that you will have accurately aligned your fingers or pointers. However, in the case of the fourth task, achieving accurate alignment is a little more problematic. In this scenario, since you are not in physical contact with the pointer that has been placed on the tabletop, you are unable to benefit from the cues that were present in the previous tasks in which you grasped both pointers. Consequently, cues based on proprioception provide you with no information concerning the location of the desktop pointer and you are now dependent on visual cues. By using only one eye and ensuring that your head does not move, the parallax cues are absent (as is the case when we employ a conventional computer display). In the case that the two pointers are identical (or if you have prior knowledge of their relative sizes) linear perspective is likely to represent an important visual cue. In addition, the oculomotor cues are also likely to assist. (Can you suggest any other cues that may play a useful role?) The accuracy with which you were able to achieve alignment may be disappointing – especially in view of the conscious effort applied to the task.

Consider a further scenario in which one pointer continues to rest on a tabletop and the second is held in some form of clamp which is suspended and is moved by means of a system of pulleys and strings (again we assume that the parallax cues are disabled – throughout the alignment task the head does not move and one eye is closed). This represents an even more difficult case – as neither pointer is held and so cues based on proprioception are entirely absent. However, if we restore the parallax cues, the alignment process is greatly facilitated (for this task motion parallax is particularly important).

Let us now return to the original scenario in which we seek to navigate a cursor through a 3-D scene using a conventional mouse (recall we assumed that motion of the cursor in the third dimension would be affected by holding down one of the mouse buttons). In the case that we are using a conventional flat screen display, both the parallax and oculomotor cues are absent and so too are cues that we may derive on the basis of proprioception (thus this parallels the alignment scenario outlined in the previous paragraph). Indeed achieving accurate navigation and the alignment of the cursor with image components is far from easy. We can of course adopt strategies that will ameliorate the difficulty. For example:

- *We can align the cursor in the x–y plane with an image component. Subsequently, we rotate the image scene so that the display screen coincides with the y–z plane and now perform alignment in the third dimension. Some degree of iteration may be necessary and this approach parallels the incorporation of motion parallax.*
- *As we navigate the cursor, the object (or image component) that is in closest proximity to it may be made to change colour. In this way we reduce the level of accuracy that is needed to successfully align the cursor with an entity in the image scene – once the intended target changes colour we need simply press a predefined key and so dock the cursor with the target.*

Various other strategies may be employed some of which are entirely software based and can be adopted for use with the conventional computer interface and others require the incorporation of additional hardware. In general terms software based approaches that operate with the standard flat screen display serve to simply ameliorate the difficulties associated with interacting with a 3-D scene and do not allow us to make full use of our sensory systems. Alternative approaches that necessitate hardware changes include the following:

(1) **Support for the Parallax and Perhaps Oculomotor cues**: This enables us to make full use of our binocular vision and allows the interaction process to be carried out in a manner that more closely follows the intuitive ways in which we interact with our surroundings. The display techniques introduced in the previous chapter provide us with examples of systems that may be used. However, it is important to note the key role played by the motion parallax cue – a system that supports binocular parallax but which fails to embrace motion parallax may be advantageous as far as visualisation is concerned but may not necessarily advance the interaction process. Furthermore, in the case that support for the motion parallax cue is based on the head tracking technique, latencies (representing the delay that occurs between head movement and the update of the displayed image) must be minimised. Ideally, the display system should support both horizontal and vertical parallax (although in the case of real time applications, this may be precluded by the associated computational cost or by limitations of the display technology).

(2) **Interaction and Image Space Mapping**: Here we consider the use of interaction tools for cursor navigation that support a 3-D interaction space and that provide an intuitive and direct mapping between movements in the interaction space and the corresponding motion of a cursor in image space. When coupled with (1) above, this can lead to significant advantages.

(3) **Haptic Feedback**: The incorporation of haptic feedback so that it is possible to 'feel' ones way through the image space – apparently touching and so sensing the proximity of objects within a scene. Within this context it is appropriate to quote Hermann Helmholtz (1821–1894):

'*The sense of touch, it is true, can distinguish relations in space, and has the special power of judging of all matter within reach, at once as to resistance, volume, and weight; but the range of touch is limited, and the distinction it can make between small distances is not nearly so accurate as that of sight. Yet the sense of touch is sufficient, as experiments upon persons born blind have proved, to develop complete notions of space. This proves that the possession of sight is not necessary for the formation of these conceptions, and we shall soon see that we are continually controlling and correcting the notions of locality derived from the eye by the help of the sense of touch, and always accept the impressions on the latter sense as decisive. The two senses, which really have the same task, though with very different means of accomplishing it, happily supply each other's deficiencies. Touch is a trustworthy and experienced servant, but enjoys only limited range, while sight rivals the boldest flights of fancy in penetrating to illimitable distances*'[6]

There can indeed be little doubt that faced with one of today's computers, Helmholtz would have been quick to identify weaknesses in the interface and ways in which it could be developed so as to make better use of our sensory and motor systems. Perhaps he would have particularly appreciated the importance of supporting both pictorial and non-pictorial cues and of exploiting the synergy that occurs when the visual and haptic channels are simultaneously (and harmoniously) brought to bear on a common task.

10.3 Somatosensory Perception

> '*No reader of this book will need to ask why I have dedicated it to Helmholtz. There is no one else to whom one can owe so completely the capacity to write a book about sensation and perception. If it be objected that books should not be dedicated to the dead, the answer is that Helmholtz is not dead. The organism can predecease its intellect, and conversely. My dedication asserts Helmholtz's immortality – the kind of immortality that remains the unachievable aspiration of so many of us.*'[7]

Somatosensory perception is the title given to the wide-ranging sensations that we derive from both internal sensory receptors and from the vast network of receptors that are located within the structure of the skin. As indicated in Figure 10.1, these give rise to five general modalities of sensation and because of the range of receptors involved, it is convenient to group receptors according to their general function. For example, we can identify:

---

[6] Quoted from the 19th century writings of Hermann Helmholtz. Appearing in Warren and Warren (eds.) [1968].

[7] Warren and Warren (eds.) [1968] quoting from Boring, E.G., 'Sensation and Perception in the History of Experimental Psychology'.

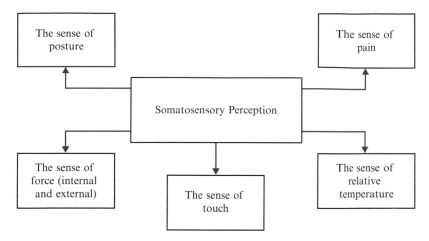

Figure 10.1 Somatosensory perception embraces five general types of sensation. See text for discussion.

- *Mechanoreceptors*: These convey mechanical deformations of the skin (these receptors are also present in joints and muscles).
- *Thermoreceptors*: These convey changes in temperature of the skin.
- *Nocioceptors*: These convey sensations of pain.

However, although grouping receptors according to their function offers a seemingly tidy solution, it presupposes that they each respond to only one form of stimulus. This is not always the case – as demonstrated by the following OTU Exercise.

OTU Exercise 10.2: The Functionality of Receptors

Here, you will need somebody to assist.

1. Ask the person to lie down and place a warm coin on his or her forehead. Subsequently replace the coin with one that is cold – but otherwise identical. Do not mention that you are using identical coins. Ask them to indicate which coin is the heavier.
2. Repeat the above experiment but this time place the coins on the forearm. However, now make use of coins that are at three temperatures – warm, cold and skin temperature.

For the purposes of our present discussions, it is the senses of posture, force and touch that can play an important part within the interaction process and so it is the mechanoreceptors that are of primary interest. These receptors play a key role in cutaneous sensitivity (our sense of touch) and also in our sense of proprioception (recall Section 5.3.1 and especially Figure 5.9 in which different facets of proprioception are summarised). In the following subsection, we briefly discuss issues relating to our sense of touch and subsequently turn our attention to proprioception.

10.3.1 Cutaneous Sensitivity

As indicated above, our sense of touch (by which, for example, we are able to determine the surface texture and relative temperature of objects) is underpinned by the various types of receptor that lie within the skin. Five main types of mechanoreceptor are involved – these are:

1. **Meissner's Corpuscles**: These lie close to the surface of the skin and have a small well-defined receptive field (the median extent being $\sim 13mm^2$ [Kaczmarek *et al.* 1991]). These receptors are said to be 'rapidly adapting' because for a sustained (constant) level of input, their firing rate rapidly decays. Consequently, they respond to *changes* in input stimulus.

2. **Merkel's Disks**: As with the Meissner's Corpuscles, these receptors also lie close to the surface of the skin and have a small well-defined receptive field (the median field being $\sim 11mm^2$ [Kaczmarek *et al.* 1991]). They are 'slowly adapting' and are therefore able to detect sustained (constant) pressure. It appears that these receptors play a particularly important role is our detection of surface roughness [Blake *et al.* 1997].

3. **Pacinian Corpuscles**: These are rapidly adapting and therefore, as with Meissner's Corpuscles, do not signal a constant level of stimulus but rather rapid variations. The receptive field of these detectors is large and indistinct (the median extent being $\sim 101 \, mm^2$ [Kaczmarek *et al.* 1991]).

4. **Ruffini Endings**: These are slowly adapting receptors that are particularly able to detect the stretching of the skin. As with Pacinian Corpuscles, they exhibit a large and rather indistinct receptive field (the median receptive field being $\sim 59 \, mm^2$ [Kaczmarek *et al.* 1991]).

5. **Basket Ending**: These are associated with 'hairy' skin[8] and are located at the roots of hairs. They are extremely sensitive to hair displacement.

OTU Exercise 10.3: Spatial Resolution of Receptors

The spatial distribution of the mechanoreceptors that lie close to the surface of the body varies with location and the 'two point threshold' technique may be used to provide an indication of the spatial density of receptors.

Hold two pointers (e.g. pencils) in one hand (grasping them as 'chopstick' so that you are able to adjust the separation of their two tips). Investigate the spatial distribution of receptors on, for example the hands (e.g. palms and finger-tips), arms and legs. This is most easily done with the help of another participant. For example, grasp the pointers so that their tips are $\sim$1cm apart and bring the two into contact with the arm (it is important for both pointers to come into contact with the skin simultaneously). Exert light pressure and ask the participant how many points of contact he/she can feel. In the case that only one point of contact is sensed, increase the separation of the pointers and repeat the process until the participant is just able to detect two points of contact – the 'two point threshold'.

Hint: In the case of the fingertips, the pointers will need to be in quite close proximity.

---

[8] This contrasts with the mucous membrane that is found internally, mucocutaneous skin which interfaces between hairy and mucous membrane and glabrous skin which is found on parts of the fingers, on the soles of the feet and on the palms.

10.3.2 Proprioception

As we have discussed, proprioception[9] is multifaceted (recall Figure 5.9). It not only provides us with a certain (and quite accurate knowledge) of the position and spatial orientation of our limbs but also with information concerning their motion and the means by which we are able to determine the force we exert as we interact with objects (or, conversely, the force that objects exert on us). The mechanisms via which such information is derived have been the subject of considerable debate and in the nineteenth century the widely held view was that such information was provided by means of a sense of 'innervation'. In brief, researchers believed that rather than employing feedback from detectors able to measure the position and orientation of joints, the body places reliance on a knowledge of the signals being issued by the brain. Hermann Helmholtz was a keen advocate of this view and in this context, Sherrington [1900] writes:

'A phenomenon cited by Helmholtz is the following: "When the right external rictus is paralysed, the right eye can no longer rotate to the right. So long as it turns only to the nasal side it makes regular movements, and the correct position of objects is perceived. When it should be rotated outwardly, however, it stays still in the primary position, and the objects appear flying to the right, although the position of eye and retinal image are unaltered". The left sound eye is covered. "In such a case", Helmholtz goes on to say, "the exertion of the will is followed neither by actual movement of the eye, nor by contraction of the muscle in question, nor even by increased tension in it. The act of will produced absolutely no effect beyond the nervous system, and yet we judge of the direction of the line of vision, as if the will had exercised its normal effects. We believe it to have moved to the right, and, since the retinal image is unchanged, we attribute to the object the same movement we have erroneously ascribed to the eye... These phenomena leave no room for doubt that we only judge the direction of the line of sight by the effort of will with which we strive to change the position of our eyes ... We feel, then what impulse of the will, and how strong a one, we apply to turn the eye into a given position".'

The opposing (and current understanding) is that we place great reliance on the feedback that we receive from muscle receptors – specifically 'muscle spindles' and 'Golgi organs':

- **Muscle Spindles**: *These are arranged in parallel to the main muscle fibres and are able to detect changes in length (and the rate of change of length). In addition to their action as receptors they also perform a motor function, and this duality of purpose is likely to have hampered our understanding of the important role that they play in the feedback process.*
- **Golgi Organs**: *These are located in series with the muscle fibres and provide feedback in connection with the tension of the muscle.*

Over the years, the 'innervationists' were able to strengthen their case by means of the 'phantom limb phenomenon'. In this context, Clark and Horch (writing in Boff *et al.* [1986]) write:

'After an amputation, many persons have powerful illusions that the amputated limb or portions of it, still exists, and they feel they can move the missing limb... These illusions may come from abnormal activity arising from the neuroma, or tumor, that forms on the stump of a severed nerve as the fibres attempt to regrow, but more likely, the phantom from some internal schema the brain has. Any kinesthetic sensations associated with attempts to flex or extend a phantom joint voluntarily would clearly need to arise internally because no sensory receptors remain to provide a sensation.'

Of course, the fact that patients report such sensations following an amputation (and the consequent removal of receptors) provides a powerful argument in relation to the sense of innervation and the relative unimportance of receptor based feedback. Clark and Horch (citing the work of others) continue:

---

[9] Proprioception is also referred to as 'kinesthesis'.

'*However, . . . when speaking of movement of a phantom limb, one must distinguish between a movement of a phantom as a whole, because the remaining stump moved, and a "bending" of a non-existing joint within the phantom . . . Only the latter situation would involve the generation of new signals related to the phantom . . . amputees feel that they can bend a non-existent joint only when some portion of the muscles that once moved the joint remains in the stump. Eliminate these bits of muscle and the sensory receptors they contain, and the person loses this sense of feeling.*'

Perhaps it will ultimately be demonstrated that both feedback from muscle receptors and a sense of innervation provide complementary data via which the brain is able to deduce a wealth of vital information in a seemingly effortless manner.

10.3.3 The Frequency Characteristics of the Human Haptic System

In developing interaction tools – and particularly tools that are able to effectively operate with the human haptic channel – it is important to consider the frequency characteristics of the relevant sensory systems.

As discussed, in the case that a display employs transient optical phenomena (i.e. displays where the light output is not continuous and falls away in the intervals between image refresh), it is necessary for the display to be refreshed at a frequency equal to or greater than the critical flicker frequency. Consequently, a display must be refreshed at a frequency of no less than 30 Hz.[10] On the other hand, smooth image animation can be achieved with an image update frequency of ~ 10Hz. This denotes the time available for the computation of image frames and their output to the display.

In contrast, the mechanoreceptors within the skin are sensitive to a wide range of vibrational frequencies. In this context, Burdea [1996] writes:

'. . . *tactile sensing has a 0 to 400 Hz bandwidth. Very fine feature recognition, such as surface textures with small rugosities, requires a much higher bandwidth (up to 5,000 to 10,000 Hz).*'

Here, it is interesting to pause for a moment and run the fingertips across different types of surface texture (e.g. wood, plaster or the bark of a tree). Notice that even as the fingers are moved more rapidly across the surface, it is still possible to sense characteristics of the texture quite accurately. The realistic simulation of such a seemingly simple process demands a high tactile update frequency and this places great demands on the computer system and on the hardware responsible for the provision of the tactile sensation.

Consider the much simpler situation in which we simply seek to simulate steady contact with a surface (i.e. the finger tips 'touch' but do not move across the surface). Should the refresh frequency be insufficient, one would experience vibration rather than steady pressure (the tactile equivalent of image flicker). In addition, constant pressure contact does not enable us to readily distinguish between hard and soft surfaces – here we are more reliant on changes in pressure. As a result, the tactile update frequency plays a key role in determining the ability of a haptic system to realistically simulate surfaces which exhibit different levels of rigidity.[11]

---

[10] As previously indicated, to eliminate the problem of subliminal flicker the refresh frequency is significantly greater than this.

[11] It is interesting to consider the way we evaluate fruit for ripeness. Consider the case of a pear. Usually, in order to determine the hardness of the fruit, we don't simply prod it with a fingertip but rather hold the pear in the hand. Peter Cahusac writing in Roberts [2002] describes this as 'active' – as opposed to 'passive' – touch (where we simply prod an object), and writes: '*Our hands are most suitably adapted to perform active touch as they work together to grasp, palpate, prod, press, rub and heft the tested object.*'

OTU Exercise 10.4: Tactile Update Frequency

Consider the simulation of (a) a hard (rigid) surface such as a metallic plate, and (b) a deformable (soft) surface such as rubber, or a human limb. Discuss the demands that these two situations place on the *tactile* update frequency.

The update frequency needed to effectively support the simulation of force feedback is somewhat less demanding, and 20–30 Hz may be sufficient for the human sensory system but may not necessarily result in realistic simulation. By way of a simple example, consider the scenario in which some form of haptic probe (which supports force feedback) is rapidly moved through an image scene that comprises a number of 'solid' objects. In the case that the force update frequency is insufficient, the probe may not provide feedback to the user that it has contacted an object until the probe itself has been moved some distance beneath the object's surface. If we suppose that a probe is moved at a speed of 20 cm.s^{-1} and we assume a force update frequency of 20Hz, then it is possible for the probe to have penetrated 1cm beneath the object's surface before a haptic force is experienced!

Consider the case of a physical 'soft ball'. If we hold the ball in the hand and apply a pressure with the thumb, the ball will be deformed and the thumb will 'penetrate' a certain distance. In accordance with the third of Isaac Newton's Laws of motion[12] a state of equilibrium will be reached in which the 'action' (corresponding to the force applied by the thumb ($\mathbf{f_t}$)) and 'reaction' (the restoring force resulting from the deformation of the ball ($\mathbf{f_b}$)) are in balance. In the simplest case, the reaction increases linearly with the amount ($\mathbf{d}$) by which the thumb deforms the ball. Thus, $\mathbf{f_b} = -k\mathbf{d}$ – where k is a constant of proportionality and accounts for the stiffness of the material from which the ball is fabricated (see Section 10.5). We can therefore write that when in a state of balance:

$$\mathbf{d} = \frac{-\mathbf{f_t}}{k}$$

Let us now consider the equivalent deformation of a virtual 'soft ball'. As we have already mentioned, if the haptic force update frequency is not able to properly support the speed at which the haptic probe is moved, the probe may penetrate some distance beneath the surface of the ball before the system responds. In fact, if we are simulating a ball that has a high rigidity (represented by k in the above equation), then the depth of penetration ($\mathbf{d}$) may be one that would, in practical terms, correspond to a very large force. Unless we design the simulation system with care, this could result in the user suddenly experiencing a high haptic feedback force that would result in the probe being ejected from the ball (being bounced out of it) – see Figure 10.2. Naturally, this contrasts with the real world scenario in which we would expect to experience a gradual increase in the reaction force as the ball is deformed.

The issue of an insufficient force update rate also impacts on our perception of the work done and energy released during the deformation of a soft 'springy' surface. Continuing with the example of the 'soft ball'; in a real-world situation when we apply a force and deform the ball, we are doing work and this results in energy being stored in the ball. Upon the removal of

---

[12] The three laws of motion were published by Newton in 1687 in his classic work '*Principia Mathematica Philosophiae Naturalis*' (Mathematical Principles of Natural Philosophy). These laws are given in Section 10.5.

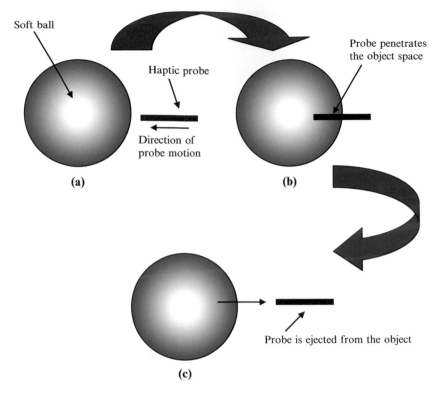

Figure 10.2 Here, a haptic probe encounters a virtual 'soft ball'. In (a), we assume that the haptic force update occurs *just before* the probe encounters the space occupied by the ball. No contact force is therefore experienced. The next haptic force update occurs when the probe is in the location indicated in (b). Here, the probe has penetrated the space occupied by the ball but up until this point the user has experienced no haptic force. As indicated in (c), a sudden (high) haptic force is fed back to the user and the probe is ejected from the ball. Various techniques can be used to circumvent this problem and it is important to ensure that the system supports an adequate haptic force update frequency.

the external force the ball releases this energy and returns to its undeformed shape. As discussed above, in the case that we are dealing with the simulation of a virtual ball and have an insufficient haptic force update frequency, the probe is able to penetrate the ball without work having been done. Subsequently, following a force update the probe experiences a strong restoring force and is ejected – a situation corresponding to a release of energy. In the real-world scenario, the mechanical energy released is, to a close approximation, equal to the work done in deforming the ball.[13] However, in the case of the simulation, energy release can occur even though work has not been done!

It is also important to note that if the haptic force update frequency is insufficient, the haptic probe may not only penetrate the space occupied by virtual objects but even worse – it may pass completely through them. This situation is illustrated in Figure 10.3.

In the above discussion we have focused on issues that relate to the output of signals from the machine to the human operator. It is also important to note the frequency response of the

---

[13] The mechanical energy released cannot be greater than the work done on the soft ball and in practice is a little less. This is due to the generation of heat as the ball is deformed and when it is returning to its undeformed shape.

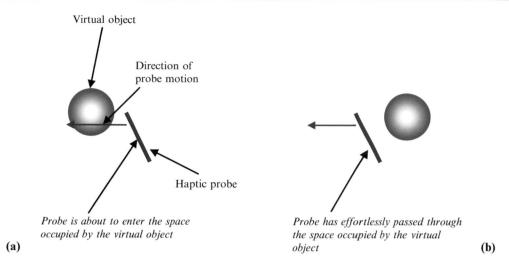

Virtual object

Direction of
probe motion

Haptic probe

*Probe is about to enter the space
occupied by the virtual object*

(a)

*Probe has effortlessly passed through
the space occupied by the virtual
object*

(b)

Figure 10.3 In (a) we assume that the haptic probe is about to enter the space occupied by a virtual ('solid') object. At this instant the haptic force is updated and since the probe has not yet encountered the object, no force is registered. The next haptic force update occurs *after* the probe has passed through the space occupied by the object (as indicated in (b)). Naturally, this situation is problematic and highly undesirable.

human system in its ability to issue force and motor commands. In this context, the human finger can comfortably operate up to ∼5–10 Hz [Burdea 1996].

10.4 Traditional Interaction

*'The true harvest of life is intangible –
a little star dust caught, a portion of the rainbow I have clutched.'*[14]

The vast majority of users interact with the computer by means of the keyboard and mouse. Seldom do they have the opportunity of employing other forms of interaction modality, and interactive operations are largely accomplished in a uni-manual manner. Both the keyboard and mouse have a long history – the former dating back to the 19th century and the latter to the 1960s. In many countries the 'QWERTY' keyboard layout is used, and it is interesting to note that this was originally devised to *reduce* (rather than increase) typing speed. This layout is in fact a legacy of the days of the early mechanical typewriter when weaknesses in the design of the mechanical components would, if particular character sequences were entered too rapidly, cause the mechanism to 'jam'. The 'QWERTY' layout was therefore devised to increase the distance between certain keys and so force the fingers to travel further when selecting particular keystroke combinations. This inserted small delays into the speed at which a typist could select the 'rogue' keystroke combinations and so reduced the frequency with which typewriters faltered. Despite the fact that mechanical components have been eliminated from today's computer keyboards,

---

[14] Attributed to Henry David Thoreau (1817–1862).

we still live with the legacy of the past – a keyboard layout that is designed to reduce the speed at which we are able to effect communication![15]

In fact, the efficiency of the standard keyboard has little relevance to computer graphics applications and, in this context, the mouse plays a much more important role. This device was prototyped in ~1964 for use in a study concerning the relative merits of various forms of interaction tool. In its original form, the mouse was somewhat different to the device so widely used today. The original mouse was housed in a wooden case and used two orthogonally positioned wheels. Motion of the mouse resulted in differences in the rates of rotation of the wheels and in turn this motion was captured by potentiometers[16] one of which was connected to each wheel.

The study referred to above evaluated the use of not only the mouse, but also the lightpen, joystick, a knee control (via which a cursor could be navigated by movements of the knee) and a curious device called a 'Grafacon'. This study is reported in English *et al.* [1967] and for summary discussion, see Blundell and Schwarz [2006]. In essence, English and his co-workers used the interaction device to navigate a cursor and 'acquire' a target on a conventional 2-D screen. Acquisition time and acquisition accuracy were measured. For experienced users, the mouse demonstrated the shortest acquisition time and lowest error rate, whereas when novice users were tested, the lightpen, knee control and mouse exhibited similar acquisition times – the mouse exhibiting the lowest error rate. Of course, the results of any such trial must be interpreted with considerable care as these are likely to be linked to the nature of the application. Furthermore, it is also necessary to consider the impact of the tool on the human operator (e.g. in terms of fatigue and RSI). Additionally, the trial was specifically based on the navigation of a cursor (the researchers referred to this as a 'bug') in a 2-D space – issues become much more complex when we consider navigation in three spatial dimensions.[17] Certainly English *et al.* were aware that it was unrealistic to make an unequivocal statement indicating the superiority of any one particular interaction device, and within this context they write:

'*Thus it seems unrealistic to expect a flat statement that one device is better than another. The details of the usage system in which the device is to be embedded make too much difference. Irrespective of the speeds with which one can make successive display selections with a given device, the tradeoffs for the characteristics of fatigue, quick transfer to and from the keyboard, etc., will heavily weight the choice amongst the devices. And these tradeoffs, and the possibilities for designing around them, are not apparent until after a good deal of design and analysis has been done for the rest of the system.*'

In the 1970s, workers at Xerox PARC developed the Alto and Xerox 800 series workstations. These were the precursors of today's desktop machines and incorporated many advanced

---

[15] One key issue is the number of touch typists who are trained in the use of the conventional keyboard layout. The adoption of any other layout would involve re-training and this can only be justified if there is clear evidence that an alternative layout is significantly better. Despite attempts that have been made over the years to develop more logical keyboard layouts, it has been difficult to clearly demonstrate that they offer greater efficiency.

[16] A potentiometer is a variable resistor. Rotation of a shaft causes the resistance of the potentiometer to change. The prototype mouse was an analog (rather than a digital) device – mouse motion giving rise to a change in the magnitude of analog signals.

[17] English *et al.* did not separately measure the time taken to reach for the interaction device and the subsequent time required for cursor navigation – these two times were compounded within a single measurement. Naturally, this would have influenced the results they obtained. For related discussion see Card *et al.* [1978] who recorded these times separately.

features that we now take for granted.[18] In 1971, Xerox licensed the mouse from Stanford Research Institute and subsequently incorporated it within its workstation technologies. By the mid 1980s, personal computers and workstations were proliferating at a dramatic pace; the graphical user interface (with its icons and menus) was a standard feature of these machines, and so too was the mouse.

It is readily apparent that the mouse is a uni-manual device – supporting input from the 'preferred' hand. In contrast, it may initially seem that the keyboard is a bi-manual device. In the context of our current discussions we assume that a bi-manual activity is one where the two hands are simultaneously and synergistically brought to bear on a common task, and so advance human dexterity. Although the keyboard enables us to employ both hands, the hands essentially act independently – and in the main only one key is pressed at any instant.[19] Thus, a touch typist uses both hands to simply increase the speed of throughput and not to increase dexterity. We therefore view the keyboard as an essentially uni-manual input device. In the next sub-section, we briefly review aspects of synergistic bi-manual interaction – a technique which is likely to play a critical role in our interaction with emerging creative 3-D display systems.

10.4.1 Synergistic Bi-manual Interaction

In Figure 10.4 we identify various forms of bi-manual activity and illustrate these by reference to some simple tasks. As may be seen, we broadly define two types of bi-manual activity in accordance with whether the hands undertake a task in a cooperative or independent manner. In addition we consider actions undertaken by the hands as being either symmetrical or asymmetrical. For example, consider the case that we use the hands to simultaneously trace out two similar shapes such as circles. If the hands are moving in the same direction then they are both executing the same task (symmetrical) in an independent manner. Alternatively, tasks such as knitting, using a knife and fork, or knotting a shoe-lace would be classed as cooperative asymmetrical activities.

In many situations we derive great benefit by bringing the two hands to bear in a synergistic manner on a common task (try knotting a shoe-lace or tie using only one hand ...). Dexterity is increased, the effort that must be applied to the task is reduced, and the overall accuracy of the resulting interactive operation is improved. In contrast, when we attempt to simultaneously perform two independent tasks with our hands, cognitive effort is increased. For example, trace out a circle with one hand and a square with the other, or try to tap out separate rhythms with the two hands.[20] Despite the difficulty that we experience, such tasks are relatively simple when compared to the intricate movements associated with knitting, and this provides a simple demonstration of the effectiveness of synergistic bi-manual interaction as compared to bi-manual independent action.

In discussing synergistic bi-manual interaction, Blundell and Schwarz [2006] write:

---

[18] In relation to this fascinating history (which includes the development of the event driven user interface and WYSIWYG ('what you see is what you get') document editor) see Smith and Alexander [1999], and summary discussion in Blundell and Schwarz [2006].

[19] In some instances, two (or even three) keys are simultaneously pressed (e.g. 'the use of the shift key for letter capitalisation and the use of 'shift'+'alt'+'del'). However, in the main only one key is pressed at any one time.

[20] Referred to as a polyrhythm: '... *a polyrhythm: two conflicting but isochronous sequences. Most people have great difficulty in coordinating the two hands in such tasks in which two rhythms are not integer multiples of each other.*' [Leganchuk *et al.* 1998].

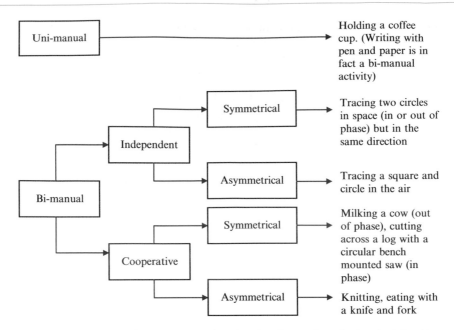

Figure 10.4 Bi-manual activities can be either cooperative or independent. In each case tasks can be viewed as being either symmetrical or asymmetrical. On the right of the illustration we provide simple examples of associated activities. See text for further discussion.

'The non-preferred hand provides a dynamic frame of reference for the preferred hand. Finer granularity of motion is achieved with the preferred hand – the two hands exhibit "asymmetric temporal-spatial scales of motion". The non-preferred hand leads the sequence of actions.'

Thus the actions of the preferred hand are referenced to the non-preferred hand. This is readily evident from our everyday experience. For example, the buttons of a small calculator are generally more easily (rapidly) selected when we hold the calculator in the non-preferred hand rather than when we simply rest it on a table top. Similarly, writing on paper is facilitated by resting the non-preferred hand on the paper (even under circumstances where the paper is unlikely to shift position as we write). In an excellent publication, Hinckley *et al.* write:

'... two hands do more than just save time over one hand. Users have a keen sense of where their hands are relative to one another, and this can be used to develop interaction techniques which are potentially less demanding of visual attention. Using both hands helps users to ground themselves in a body-relative interaction space as opposed to requiring consciously calculated action in an abstract environment-relative space ... Using both hands alters the syntax of the manual tasks which must be performed, which influences a user's problem-solving behaviour and therefore has a direct influence on how users think about a task.'

Interestingly, a study conducted by Leganchuk *et al.* [1998] indicates that the benefits offered by bi-manual activity increase with task complexity:

'For the cognitively less demanding tasks ... we see the performance of the two-handed technique was similar or even inferior to that of the one-handed technique. However as the tasks become more cognitively demanding ... we see that two-handed [interaction] has a significant performance gain.'

The conventional flat screen display severely restricts the opportunities for synergistic bi-manual interaction. Indeed the effectiveness of such interaction modalities is strongly reliant on the display paradigm permitting the interaction tools to enter the image space in which an image resides (or in which it appears to reside).[21] Furthermore, it is not necessarily advantageous to force particular interaction techniques upon the user. In this context Blundell and Schwarz [2006] summarise the work of Cutler *et al.* [1997] as follows:

'*A publication by Cutler et al. [1997] reinforces this point. This describes a bi-manual interaction paradigm used in conjunction with the "Responsive Workbench" display system. In brief this display projects high-quality temporally coded stereoscopic images onto the table-top. Head tracking is supported, and a user is able to move around the table and "touch" the images that appear above its surface. Interaction is reported as being effected via Fakespace's PINCH gloves (equipped with six-degrees-of-freedom (DOF) position sensors) that can detect the pinching together of different fingers and a Polhemus stylus (being pen-like in form and tracked by a 6-DOF position sensing system and having a single interaction button). Here the stylus represents the more accurate interaction tool, and the user is free to either use the gloves (continually worn) for interaction or pick up and use the stylus. By providing this flexibility, it is possible for the operator to naturally select the most intuitively appropriate manipulator. A set of tools are described, these being categorized as either uni-manual (e.g. "one-handed grab" – pick up and move a single object), bi-manual symmetric (e.g. "turntable" – enabling an object to be rotated about a fixed axis), or bi-manual asymmetric (e.g. "zoom"). The researchers report:*

"*During our observations we also found that users often picked up two seemingly independent one-handed tools and used them together in a coordinated fashion ... One of the more surprising results was that the asymmetric combination of a PINCH glove for the left hand and stylus for the right hand worked much better in many situations than the two PINCH gloves, especially for asymmetric tasks.*"

In their summary, they add:

"*When beginning this work we thought that all the two-handed input techniques would need to be explicitly designed and programmed. However, when using the system we found that perhaps the most interesting tasks emerged when the user combined two otherwise independent uni-manual tools.*" [Cutler *et al.* 1977]

Advantages may therefore be obtained by providing a set of interaction tools within an environment that is able to support different interaction modalities. In this way, the system does not force a specific interaction technique onto the user, but is adaptive to human problem solving skills and our natural interactive dexterity.

10.5 Haptic Feedback

'*The system of nature, of which man is a part, tends to be self-balancing, self-adjusting, self-cleansing. Not so with technology.*'[22]

Today, a diverse range of haptic interaction systems are available. These range from full-body or arm exoskeletons, ceiling or floor mounted haptic 'arms', through to haptic gloves and desk mounted interaction probes (for more detailed discussion see Burdea [1996]). In the discussion that follows we focus on the use of the use of a haptic probe (a pen-like interaction paradigm) of the general type illustrated in Figure 10.5. In its simplest form, this is used to manipulate a virtual point within a 3-D space and the haptic sensation is derived from the interaction tool's ability to output a force vector of appropriate magnitude. Since this vector has three orthogonal

---

[21] See, for example, the video clip concerning suturing that is available via the following URL: http://www.medicvision.com.au/simulators.htm (date last visited 5th September 2007).
[22] Attributed to E.F. Schumacher (1911–1977).

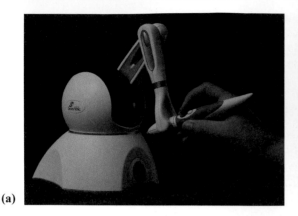 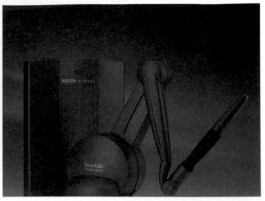

(a)   **(b)**

Figure 10.5 Exemplar desktop haptic interaction tools (force feedback). In (a) the PHANTOM Omni™ 6-DOF device and in (b) the PHANTOM Desktop™ which also offers 6-DOF. For technical details see Table 10.1. (Images supplied by, and reproduced with the permission of SensAble Technologies Inc.®.)

components, the haptic tool is referred to as a 3-DOF (degrees of freedom) device. This is in contrast to an interaction tool that is able to provide both force and torque sensations – a 6-DOF device.

Although a simple 3-DOF pen-like interaction tool provides only a very limited haptic experience (and does not, for example, make use of the delicate sense of touch supported by our fingertips), it can be used advantageously in the interaction process. Furthermore, the implementation of this approach is relatively straightforward as we need only concern ourselves with the motion of the tip of the probe (or its virtual representation) within a 3-D space. Thus the problem is reduced to a simulation of a point in space. In contrast, although a glove based interaction tool can increase the sense of realism and enhance interaction dexterity (by supporting force and possibly tactile feedback), implementation issues are somewhat more complex. Such gloves typically support the application of forces to the fingertips relative to the palm, back of the hand or forearm. Thus, for example, a user can experience haptic sensations in relation to picking up and squeezing objects. In order to provide a realistic sensation of an object's weight, it is necessary 'ground' the haptic device – thereby enabling a vertical force to be supplied to, and experienced by, the user.

> In some situations (such as the provision of a synthetic gravitational force) the 'grounding' of a haptic device is necessary. This enables the device to exhibit the fundamental characteristic that we associate with Newton's third Law of Motion (see below). Although in principle a haptic glove offers greater mobility (in terms of the extent of the interaction space) than do various other haptic interaction modalities, mobility can be lost as a consequence of the need to 'ground' the interaction tool.

Newton's Laws of Motion provide a succinct description of the movement of objects in situations where forces are either present or absent. They are therefore of pivotal importance in the

Table 10.1 Technical specifications for the PHANTOM Omni and PHANTOM Desktop haptic interaction devices that are illustrated in Figure 10.5. (Technical data kindly supplied by SensAble Technologies Inc, who indicate 'SensAble PHANTOM product specifications are subject to change without notice. SensAble shall not be liable for technical or editorial errors or omissions contained herein. PHANTOM, PHANTOM Desktop, PHANTOM Omni, SensAble, and SensAble Technologies, Inc., are trademarks or registered trademarks of SensAble Technologies, Inc.')

Model	The PHANTOM Desktop Device	The PHANTOM Omni Device
Force feedback workspace	~6.4 W x 4.8 H x 4.8 D in > 160 W x 120 H x 120 D mm	~6.4 W x 4.8 H x 2.8 D in > 160 W x 120 H x 70 D mm
Footprint Physical area the base of device occupies on the desk	5 5/8 W x 7 1/4 D in ~143 W x 184 D mm	6 5/8 W x 8 D in ~168 W x 203 D mm
Weight (device only)	6 lb 5oz	3 lb 15 oz
Range of motion	Hand movement pivoting at wrist	Hand movement pivoting at wrist
Nominal position resolution	> 1100 dpi ~ 0.023 mm	> 450 dpi ~ 0.055 mm
Backdrive friction	< 0.23 oz (0.06 N)	<1 oz (0.26 N)
Maximum exertable force at nominal (orthogonal arms) position	1.8 lbf. (7.9 N)	0.75 lbf. (3.3 N)
Continuous exertable force (24 hrs.)	0.4 lbf. (1.75 N)	> 0.2 lbf. (0.88 N)
Stiffness	X axis > 10.8 lb/in (1.86 N/mm) Y axis > 13.6 lb/in (2.35 N/mm) Z axis > 8.6 lb/in (1.48 N/mm)	X axis > 7.3 lb/in (1.26 N/mm) Y axis > 13.4 lb/in (2.31 N/mm) Z axis > 5.9 lb/in (1.02 N/mm)
Inertia (apparent mass at tip)	~0.101 lbm. (45 g)	~0.101 lbm. (45 g)
Force feedback	x, y, z	x, y, z
Position sensing ••••••••••••••••••••••••••••••• [Stylus gimbal]	x, y, z (digital encoders) ••••••••••••••••••••••••••••••• [Pitch, roll, yaw (± 3% linearity potentiometers)]	x, y, z (digital encoders) ••••••••••••••••••••••••••••••• [Pitch, roll, yaw (± 5% linearity potentiometers)]
Interface	Parallel port	IEEE-1394 FireWire® port
Supported platforms	Intel-based PCs	Intel-based PCs
GHOST® SDK compatibility	Yes	No
OpenHaptics™ toolkit compatibility	Yes	Yes
Applications	Selected Types of Haptic Research FreeForm® Modeling™ system FreeForm® Modeling Plus™ system	Selected Types of Haptic Research FreeForm® Concept™ system ClayTools™ system

creation of models that are intended to represent dynamic scenes (such as a set of objects that occasionally collide). Furthermore, as indicated above, Newton's third Law of Motion[23] must be considered when we endeavour to support various forms of force feedback. For convenience Newton's three laws are stated below:

---

[23] In relation to Isaac Newton, Margaret A. Boden [2006] sheds some light on one of the quotations that is widely attributed to him – *'If I have seen further it is by standing on the shoulders of Giants.'* She writes, *'Sir Isaac Newton was not a nice man. His personal unhappiness often fuelled intemperate attacks on others including his social inferiors. One such was his Royal Society colleague, Robert Hooke. Although Hooke was a scientific rival (with a competing theory of light), and the first to suggest (in 1679) that the planets move under some influence inversely proportional to the square of their distance from the sun, he was menially employed as a technician. Newton rarely minced his words in criticising him . . . Yet Newton is now regarded*

Newton's Three Laws of Motion

1. Every body continues in a state of rest or uniform motion in a straight line, unless compelled by an external force to do otherwise.
2. The rate of change of momentum of the body is directly proportional to the applied force and takes place in the direction in which the force acts.
3. Action and reaction are equal and opposite.

(Momentum is a vector quantity that is given by the product of mass and velocity.)

In the next subsection, we briefly outline several key stages within the haptic interaction loop.

10.5.1 Support for Haptic Feedback

In this subsection we limit our discussion to the use of a 3-DOF 'pen-like' interaction probe and so simply deal with the movement of a point (corresponding to the tip of the probe) in a 3-D space. In the text that follows, we loosely follow Blundell and Schwarz [2006] where more detailed discussion is presented. Several key steps within the haptic pipeline are summarised in Figure 10.6 and these are outlined below:

1. **Model Formation**: Here we assign haptic properties to objects within the image scene. In the simplest case we may indicate that the point representing the tip of the haptic probe cannot enter the space occupied by an object. Naturally this gives rise to a rigid (non-deformable) representation that we would associate with, for example, a billiard ball. Alternatively, we may wish to model an elastically deformable object such as a soft ball. Here, we can make use of Hooke's Law (recall mention of Robert Hooke in the previous footnote) in which the reaction force ($\mathbf{F}$) increases linearly with the extent of the deformation ($\mathbf{d}$). For example, suppose that we wish to model an elastically deformable sphere of radius r. In general terms, Hooke's Law is given by:

$$\mathbf{F} \propto -\mathbf{d},$$

---

as a model of magnanimity because of his oft-quoted remark: "If I have seen further it is by standing on the shoulders of Giants." He said this in a letter to Hooke, one of several written at that time in which he fulsomely complimented his long-term adversary. These comments weren't intended seriously, however, indeed Newton's apparent modesty contained a venomous personal insult. His remark was a commonplace, dating back five centuries to John of Salisbury, for whom it was already second hand: 'Bernard of Chartres used to compare us to [puny] dwarfs perched on the shoulders of Giants. He pointed out that we see more and further than our predecessors not because we have keener vision or greater height, but because we are lifted up and borne aloft on their gigantic stature.' John's words had often been quoted ... so Newton's contemporaries, including Hooke himself, would inevitably be reminded of puniness and dwarves. And the punchline? The unfortunate Hooke was a tiny hunchback, described by an acquaintance as '[physically] but despicable, being very crooked ... [and] but low of Stature, tho' by his limbs he shou'd have been moderately tall'. Magnanimity this was not.'

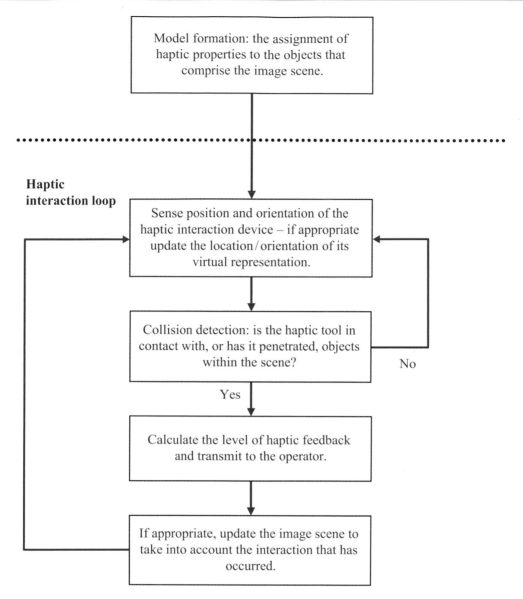

Figure 10.6 A simplified overview summarising key stages in relation to the generation of haptic output. See text for discussion.

and so:

$$\mathbf{F} = -k\mathbf{d}.$$

where the constant of proportionality is referred to as the elastic constant associated with a particular material and represents the resistance of the material to a force of deformation. In the case of the sphere referred to above, we may model its elastic properties using an equation of the form:

$$|\mathbf{F}| = k(r - d_p),$$

where d_p represents the distance of the point that represents the tip of the haptic probe from the centre of the sphere and $0 \leq d_p \leq r$. Thus an elastic force is indicated when the probe enters the space occupied by the sphere, and gradually increases as the probe moves closer to the sphere's centre. Such a model is somewhat naïve in that, in the case of physical objects, Hooke's Law is only applicable over a certain deformation range. If an 'elastic' object is subjected to too great a deformation (denoted by the object's 'elastic limit') then, when the force is removed, the object will not return to its original form – it will remain deformed. In addition, we should also consider the inclusion of a surface friction model – in the absence of which the haptic probe will tend to slip along convex surfaces into concavities. Realism may be further enhanced through the inclusion of a surface texture model which can be achieved by allowing frictional parameters to vary over short distances (for related discussion see, for example, Minsky *et al.* [1990] and Mark *et al.* [1996]).

The haptic properties that we associate with a scene can be static or dynamic. In this latter respect we may, for example, model a scene in which the temperature gradually changes over time causing objects to become more (or less) elastic and even undergoing changes in state (such as a liquid freezing). Naturally such temporal changes must be incorporated within the model.

2. **Device Location**: In the case that we are using a 3-DOF interaction probe, we must determine the location of the probe's tip within 3-D space (in the case of a 6-DOF interaction tool that is able to support both force and torque feedback we must also determine orientation). In the most basic scenario we obtain Cartesian coordinates defining the location of the tip of the probe, and use these coordinates to determine its position relative to objects that comprise the image scene. This is achieved by forming a virtual representation of the interaction device which in the case of the 3-DOF probe referred to above is simply a point (sometimes referred to in literature as the 'haptic interaction point' (HIP)). This representation may be used to generate visible cues on the display screen through the formation of an appropriate 'cursor', although in the case that the interaction tool and image are able to occupy the same space (recall discussion in Section 9.2.2) the creation of a visible cursor is unnecessary.

3. **Collision Detection**: Here, we determine whether or not a 'spatial collision' has occurred between the HIP and the scene contents. In the case that the haptic probe is not in touch with any of the objects that comprise the image scene (and assuming that the virtual medium within which the objects reside has zero density[24]), then movement of the haptic probe should not give rise to any sensation of force. The development of efficient collision detection algorithms is of great importance in the formation of dynamic computer graphics scenes and also in robotics. Collision detection within the context of haptic feedback draws on this work and can be approached in various ways. If, for example the shape and volume of objects that comprise a scene are represented using simple analytic expressions (recall Section 7.7), then in the case of a 3-DOF haptic probe we simply determine if the HIP has entered the space occupied by each object. Alternatively, if we are dealing with other

---

[24] Here we are assuming that the objects are located in free space and are not, for example, immersed in a liquid.

representations (e.g. polyhedra) the task is somewhat more complicated – see, for example, Lin and Gottschalk [1998], Watt [2000], Jimenez [2001], Lin *et al.* [2004] and Foley *et al.* [1990].

4. **Generation of Haptic Feedback**: This stage involves the calculation of the haptic force and its output to the operator. When a 3-DOF probe is employed, the force vector corresponding to the most recent HIP location is determined and transmitted to the interaction device. The use of a 6-DOF probe necessitates the calculation of both force and torque vectors and this increases the computational cost.

5. **Update of the Image Scene**: Finally, we must update the image scene to take into account changes that have been made as a result of user interaction. For example, this may include imparting (or modifying) object motion, the results of object deformation etc.

10.6 Discussion

> '*Imagination was given to man to compensate him for what he is not;*
> *a sense of humour to console him for what he is*'.[25]

In this, the final chapter, we have briefly considered aspects of the interaction process. In this context we have considered traditional and emerging interaction modalities and have alluded to the complex human haptic systems. It is hoped that this discussion will encourage the reader towards further studies in this area, and in the context of human haptic systems the book by Kandel *et al.* [2000] provides an excellent starting point. Burdea [1996] provides sound coverage of basic haptic interaction tools and gives extensive references for further reading. A number of excellent publications discuss collision detection, and Watt [2000] is a good starting point.

In the case that a haptic probe is used in connection with objects that are represented in polyhedral form, the operator is likely to sense the discontinuities that exist between polygons. 'Force shading' techniques (analogous to Phong shading) can be employed to reduce perceived force discontinuities – see, for example Zilles and Salisbury [1994] and also Morgenbesser and Srinivasan [1996]. For readers interested in the application of haptic interaction tools to volumetric data, Blundell and Schwarz [2006] provides a useful introduction and contains references for further reading.

> '*After long storms and tempests over-blown*
> *The sun at length his joyous face doth clear:*
> *So whenas fortune all her spite hath shown,*
> *Some blissful hours at last must needs appear . . .*
> *In which captiv'd she many months did mourn,*
> *To taste of joy, and to wont pleasures to return.*'[26]

---

[25] Francis Bacon (1561–1626).
[26] Edmund Spenser, *The Faerie Queene*, Canto III.

Appendix A
Maths: Some Useful Results

'He was asleep, for he knew not remorse.'

1. **Equation for a Straight Line:**

$$y = mx + c.$$

Here, m denotes the gradient and c the y intercept (the point at which the line crosses the y-axis).

2. **Parametric Equations for a Line Segment:**

$$x = x_1 + (x_2 - x_1)\,t$$
$$y = y_1 + (y_2 - y_1)\,t.$$

The line connects points (x_1, y_1) and (x_2, y_2). The parameter is denoted by t.

3. **Parametric Vector Equation for a Line:**

$$\mathbf{r}(u) = \mathbf{a} + u(\mathbf{b} - \mathbf{a}).$$

Here, the parameter is denoted by u.

4. **Identity Matrix for Multiplication:**
   (a) Two by two:

$$\begin{bmatrix} 1 & 0 \\ 0 & 1 \end{bmatrix}.$$

   (b) Three by three:

$$\begin{bmatrix} 1 & 0 & 0 \\ 0 & 1 & 0 \\ 0 & 0 & 1 \end{bmatrix}.$$

5. **Determinant of a 3 by 3 Matrix**

$$a_{11} \begin{vmatrix} a_{22} & a_{23} \\ a_{32} & a_{33} \end{vmatrix} - a_{12} \begin{vmatrix} a_{21} & a_{23} \\ a_{31} & a_{33} \end{vmatrix} + a_{13} \begin{vmatrix} a_{21} & a_{22} \\ a_{31} & a_{32} \end{vmatrix}.$$

6. **Scalar Product:**

$$\mathbf{a} \cdot \mathbf{b} = a_1 b_1 + a_2 b_2 = |\mathbf{a}||\mathbf{b}| \cos \theta.$$

7. **Equations for a Parabola:**
   (a) For a parabola created about the vertical axis:

$$(x - h)^2 = 4p\,(y - k).$$

   Where the vertex is located at (h, k) and p denotes the vertical distance of the focus from the vertex.
   (b) For a parabola created about the horizontal axis:

$$(y - k)^2 = 4p\,(x - h).$$

8. **The Circle:**

$$(x - a)^2 + (y - b)^2 = r^2.$$

   Where r denotes the radius and the circle is centred on the point (a, b).

9. **The Ellipse (centred on the origin):**

$$\frac{x^2}{a^2} + \frac{y^2}{b^2} = 1.$$

10. **Pythagorean Identities:**

$$\cos^2 \theta + \sin^2 \theta = 1$$
$$1 + \tan^2 \theta = \sec^2 \theta = \frac{1}{\cos^2 \theta}$$
$$1 + \cot^2 \theta = \operatorname{cosec}^2 \theta = \frac{1}{\sin^2 \theta}$$

11. **Sum and Difference Formulae**

$$\sin(a+b) = \sin a \cos b + \cos a \sin b$$
$$\sin(a-b) = \sin a \cos b - \cos a \sin b$$
$$\cos(a+b) = \cos a \cos b - \sin a \sin b$$
$$\cos(a-b) = \cos a \cos b + \sin a \sin b$$

12. **Differentiation – The Product Rule:**

$$\frac{d(uv)}{dx} = u\frac{dv}{dx} + v\frac{du}{dx}.$$

13. **Differentiation – The Chain Rule:**

$$\frac{dy}{dx} = \frac{dy}{dt} \cdot \frac{dt}{dx}.$$

14. **Pascal's Triangle:**

```
                    1
                 1     1
              1     2     1
           1     3     3     1
        1     4     6     4     1
     1     5    10    10     5     1
   1    6    15    20    15     6    1
 1    7    21    35    35    21    7    1
```

15. **Vector (Cross) Product**

$$\mathbf{a} \times \mathbf{b} = (a_2b_3 - a_3b_2)\,\mathbf{i} - (a_1b_3 - a_3b_1)\,\mathbf{j} + (a_1b_2 - a_2b_1)\,\mathbf{k} = (|\mathbf{a}||\mathbf{b}|\sin\theta)\,\hat{\mathbf{n}}.$$

$$\mathbf{a} \times \mathbf{b} = \begin{vmatrix} \mathbf{i} & \mathbf{j} & \mathbf{k} \\ a_1 & a_2 & a_3 \\ b_1 & b_2 & b_3 \end{vmatrix} = \begin{vmatrix} a_2 & a_3 \\ b_2 & b_3 \end{vmatrix}\mathbf{i} - \begin{vmatrix} a_1 & a_3 \\ b_1 & b_3 \end{vmatrix}\mathbf{j} + \begin{vmatrix} a_1 & a_2 \\ b_1 & b_2 \end{vmatrix}\mathbf{k}.$$

$$\mathbf{a} \times \mathbf{b} = (|\mathbf{a}||\mathbf{b}|\sin\theta)\,\hat{\mathbf{n}}.$$

$$|\mathbf{a} \times \mathbf{b}| = |\mathbf{a}||\mathbf{b}|\sin\theta = \sqrt{(a_2b_3 - a_3b_2)^2 + (a_1b_3 - a_3b_1)^2 + (a_1b_2 - a_2b_1)^2}.$$

$$\hat{\mathbf{n}} = \frac{\mathbf{a} \times \mathbf{b}}{|\mathbf{a} \times \mathbf{b}|}.$$

Appendix B
The Curvature of a Varifocal Mirror

*'On the whole, perhaps his life was uneventful
for so far-travelling a dog, though it held its
moments of eccentricity . . .'*

In this Appendix we present a brief derivation of Eq. 9.10 – an equation which provides us with the location of the image generated by a varifocal mirror as a function of the mirror's curvature. For convenience Eq. 9.10 is given below and the meanings of the various symbols are summarised in Figure B.1.

$$v(t) \sim \frac{d^2 u}{16u|x_{\mathrm{max}}|\sin \omega t - d^2}.$$

On the basis of the right-angle triangle (denoted ABC) in Figure B.1, we can write:

$$\left(\frac{d}{2}\right)^2 + (R(t) - x(t))^2 = R(t)^2.$$

Re-arranging this expression for $R(t)$ we obtain:

$$R(t) = \frac{1}{2x(t)}\left[x(t)^2 + \frac{d^2}{4}\right].$$

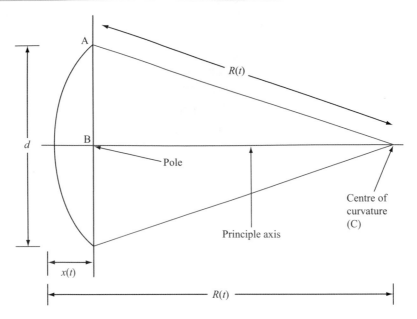

Figure B.1 The varifocal mirror (shown here in cross section) has a maximum displacement in its curvature of x_{max}. $R(t)$ denotes the mirror's radius of curvature (when concave) and this distance is twice the mirror's focal length. The mirror's diameter is d.

It is reasonable to assume that the mirror's diameter is very much greater than the maximum mirror deformation (i.e. $d \gg x_{max}$) and so we may re-write the above expression as:

$$R(t) \sim \frac{d^2}{8x(t)}. \tag{B.1}$$

Given that the deformation of the mirror varies in a sinusoidal manner (e.g. in the case that we use the loudspeaker and silvered Mylar membrane arrangement and apply a sinusoidal wave to the 'speaker'), then we can express $x(t)$ as:

$$x(t) = |x_{max}| \sin \omega t,$$

where, $\omega = 2\pi v = 2\pi/T$ (v denotes the frequency of vibration and T the periodic time of vibration). Hence we can re-write Eq. B.1 as:

$$R(t) \sim \frac{d^2}{8\,|x_{max}| \sin \omega t}. \tag{B.2}$$

Finally, we make use of the basic formula for curved mirrors.[1]

$$\frac{1}{u} + \frac{1}{v(t)} = \frac{1}{f(t)},$$

---

[1] This equation is derived in most basic physics and optics textbooks. See, for example, Nelkon and Parker [1995].

and since the focal length is one half of the radius of curvature (i.e. $f(t) = R(T)/2$):

$$\frac{1}{u} + \frac{1}{v(t)} = \frac{2}{R(t)}.$$

Using Eq. B.2 to eliminate $R(t)$ and re-arranging for $v(t)$, we obtain:

$$v(t) \sim \frac{d^2 u}{16u \, |x_{\mathrm{max}}| \sin \omega t - d^2}.$$

Note that at $t = 0$, this equation reduces to $v(0) \sim -u$. This corresponds to the time at which the varifocal mirror is planar. A virtual image is formed – this lies as far behind the mirror as the object is in front of it.

Appendix C
The Scalar Product

'And how a battle cheered his spirit! He was certainly no Christian; but, allowing for essential dog, he was very much a gentleman.'

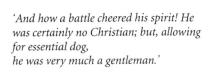

Given two vectors $\mathbf{a} = a_1\mathbf{i} + a_2\mathbf{j} + a_3\mathbf{k}$ and $\mathbf{b} = b_1\mathbf{i} + b_2\mathbf{j} + b_3\mathbf{k}$, their scalar (dot) product is given by:

$$\mathbf{a} \cdot \mathbf{b} = a_1b_1 + a_2b_2 + a_3b_3 = |\mathbf{a}||\mathbf{b}| \cos\theta, \qquad (C.1)$$

where θ denotes the angle between the vectors such that $0 \leq \theta \leq 180°$. The fact that the scalar product is equal to the sum of the products of the corresponding components of the two vectors $(a_1b_1 + a_2b_2 + a_3b_3)$ is simply based on the definition of the scalar product. However, it is both interesting and instructive to understand how this product relates to the angle between the two vectors – i.e. to verify the right hand side of the above expression.

Here, it is necessary to use the 'Cosine Rule'. Recall that Pythagoras' theorem allows us to relate the lengths of the sides of a right-angle triangle. The Cosine Rule goes one step further – it can be used on any triangle – the rule is not limited to the right-angle variety. Consider the triangle depicted in Figure C.1 and which has sides of length A, B and C and internal angles a, b and c (note that angle a is opposite side A, angle b opposite side B etc.). The Cosine Rule indicates that:

$$A^2 = B^2 + C^2 - 2BC \cos a. \qquad (C.2)$$

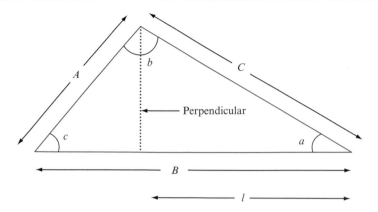

Figure C.1 To readily obtain the Cosine Rule, we use a perpendicular to divide the arbitrary triangle ABC into two right-angled triangles.

In fact, in the case that angle a is 90°, the right-hand term is zero and the equation reduces to a statement of Pythagoras' theorem. The Cosine Rule can be derived by including a perpendicular that splits the arbitrary triangle illustrated in Figure C.1 into two right-angled triangles.

Consider the right-hand triangle. The length of the perpendicular (x) is given by:

$$x = C \sin a.$$

In addition, the length of the base of this triangle (l) is:

$$l = C \cos a.$$

Thus the base of the left-hand triangle may be expressed as:

$$B - C \cos a.$$

We now know the lengths of the three sides of the left-hand triangle and apply Pythagoras' theorem:

$$A^2 = (C \sin a)^2 + (B - C \cos a)^2.$$

Expanding the right-hand bracket and re-arranging we obtain:

$$A^2 = B^2 + C^2(\sin^2 a + \cos^2 a) - 2BC \cos b.$$

Recall that $\sin^2 \theta + \cos^2 \theta = 1$ (see Figure C.2) and so this expression reduces to the Cosine Rule presented above.

Let us now return to our original goal concerning the expression of the scalar product given at the beginning of this Appendix (Eq. C.1). On the basis of the definition of the scalar product, and for a vector $\mathbf{a} = a_1\mathbf{i} + a_2\mathbf{j} + a_3\mathbf{k}$ we can write:

$$\mathbf{a} \cdot \mathbf{a} = a_1a_1 + a_2a_2 + a_3a_3 = a_1^2 + a_2^2 + a_3^2 = |\mathbf{a}|^2.$$

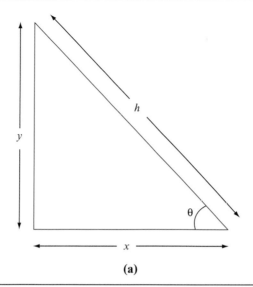

(a)

For the triangle: $\sin\theta = y/h$, $\cos\theta = x/h$.

Thus $y = h\sin\theta$, $x = h\cos\theta$.

Using Pythagoras' theorem: $x^2 + y^2 = h^2$,

and so: $(h\cos\theta)^2 + (h\sin\theta)^2 = h^2$

Thus $\cos^2\theta + \sin^2\theta = 1$.

(b)

Figure C.2 The right-angled triangle depicted in (a) is used to show that $\cos^2\theta + \sin^2\theta = 1$.

Consider the vectors **a**, **b** and **b**−**a** illustrated in Figure C.3. Based on the above equation, we can write:

$$(\mathbf{b} - \mathbf{a}) \cdot (\mathbf{b} - \mathbf{a}) = |\mathbf{b} - \mathbf{a}|^2.$$

We can expand the terms on the left hand side so that we can write:

$$\mathbf{b} \cdot \mathbf{b} - \mathbf{a} \cdot \mathbf{a} - \mathbf{a} \cdot \mathbf{b} - \mathbf{b} \cdot \mathbf{a} = |\mathbf{b} - \mathbf{a}|^2.$$

The scalar product is commutative (i.e. $\mathbf{a} \cdot \mathbf{b} = \mathbf{b} \cdot \mathbf{a}$) and so:

$$\mathbf{b} \cdot \mathbf{b} - \mathbf{a} \cdot \mathbf{a} - \mathbf{a} \cdot \mathbf{b} - \mathbf{b} \cdot \mathbf{a} = |\mathbf{b} - \mathbf{a}|^2 = \mathbf{b} \cdot \mathbf{b} - \mathbf{a} \cdot \mathbf{a} - 2\mathbf{a} \cdot \mathbf{b}.$$

and since $\mathbf{b} \cdot \mathbf{b} = |\mathbf{b}|^2$ and $\mathbf{a} \cdot \mathbf{a} = |\mathbf{a}|^2$, we can write:

$$|\mathbf{b} - \mathbf{a}|^2 = |\mathbf{b}|^2 + |\mathbf{a}|^2 - 2\mathbf{a} \cdot \mathbf{b}. \tag{C.3}$$

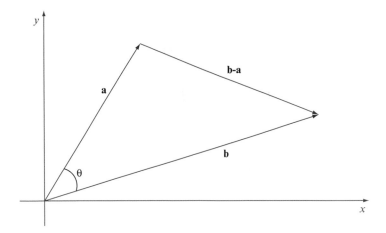

Figure C.3 Illustrating three vectors – **a**, **b** and **b**–**a**. See text for discussion.

Returning to Figure C.3, we can use apply the Cosine Rule to this triangle and so:

$$|\mathbf{b} - \mathbf{a}|^2 = |\mathbf{b}|^2 + |\mathbf{a}|^2 - 2|\mathbf{a}||\mathbf{b}|\cos\theta,$$

Equating this equation with Eq. C.3, we obtain:

$$|\mathbf{b}|^2 + |\mathbf{a}|^2 - 2\mathbf{a}\cdot\mathbf{b} = |\mathbf{b}|^2 + |\mathbf{a}|^2 - 2|\mathbf{a}||\mathbf{b}|\cos\theta,$$

and so:

$$\boxed{\mathbf{a}\cdot\mathbf{b} = |\mathbf{a}||\mathbf{b}|\cos\theta.}$$

Appendix D
Concerning the Plane

*'How many thousand walks
did we not go together,
so that we still turn to see
if he is following at his padding gait,
attentive to the invisible trails'*

D.1 Introduction

*'Nothing in education is so astonishing as the amount of ignorance
it accumulates in the form of facts.'*[1]

In this Appendix we introduce some basic mathematics relating to the plane. We begin by considering the intersection of a line with a plane. Here we represent the line in parametric form and determine the coordinates of the point at which the line and an arbitrarily oriented plane intersect (if indeed they do). Initially we consider the case of an unbounded plane and subsequently describe the intersection of a line with a finite (triangular) region. In Section D.3, we turn our attention to the intersection of two planes. The techniques used here provide useful practice in the application of elementary vector techniques.

---

[1] Attributed to Henry Brooks Adams (1838–1918).

D.2 Determining the Intersection of a Line with a Plane

In computer graphics there is a frequent need to efficiently determine whether a line that has a particular location and orientation intersects with planar surfaces comprising objects within a scene. By way of a simple analogy, suppose that you are presented with a laser pointer and planar surface (such as a white board). Naturally, you can direct the pointer so that it impinges on the surface – or otherwise. Given a surface that has an infinite extent, the column of light emitted from the laser will impinge on the surface unless: (1) the laser emits light in a direction that is parallel to the plane of the surface, or (2) the laser is oriented away from the surface, or (3) the laser is aligned in the plane of the surface ('edge on').

In the case that the surface has a finite extent (e.g. a whiteboard), the laser may fail to impinge upon the surface for any of the above reasons, and in addition may simply be oriented so as to intersect the plane containing the surface at a point that is outside the boundary of the actual surface.

Clearly, if a scene contains multiple objects, one object may obstruct all or part of our view of another. Thus, for example, although I may aim a laser pointer in the direction of a whiteboard (or the like), the passage of light may be blocked by the presence of my computer – which lies between the board and the pointer. Given a computer graphics scene comprising a number of objects, it is vital that we are able to determine the parts of each object that are visible from a certain viewpoint. Let us therefore consider the way in which we are able to determine the coordinates of the point at which a line (corresponding to the column of light emitted by the laser in the above analogy) intersects a planar surface.

Recall from Section 2.4.11 that we can represent a line using a parametric equation in which we define a position vector to a point on the line together with a vector that lies along the line. Thus if we define two position vectors ($\mathbf{a}$ and $\mathbf{b}$) to points on the line, we can define the location of any other point on the line ($\mathbf{r}(u)$) as:

$$\mathbf{r}(u) = \mathbf{a} + u(\mathbf{b} - \mathbf{a}), \tag{D.1}$$

where u denotes the parameter, and in the case that vectors $\mathbf{a}$ and $\mathbf{b}$ define the end-points of a line segment, $0 \le u \le 1$. We can re-write this expression in terms of the vector components in the x, y and z directions. Thus:

$$\mathbf{r}(u) = (a_x + u(b_x - a_x))\,\mathbf{i} + (a_y + u(b_y - a_y))\mathbf{j} + (a_z + u(b_z - a_z))\,\mathbf{k},$$

where we assume that vector $\mathbf{a}$ has components $a_x\mathbf{i} + a_y\mathbf{j} + a_z\mathbf{k}$ and similarly vector $\mathbf{b}$ has components $b_x\mathbf{i} + b_y\mathbf{j} + b_z\mathbf{k}$. Recall Eq. 7.3 – the general form of equation for a plane:

$$Ax + By + Cz + D = 0.$$

At the point at which the line and plane intersect (if indeed they do intersect) both line and plane have the same coordinates. Thus we can insert the components of the vector $\mathbf{r}(u)$ into the above expression for the plane. This gives:

$$A\,(a_x + u(b_x - a_x)) + B(a_y + u(b_y - a_y)) + C\,(a_z + u(b_z - a_z)) + D = 0.$$

Expanding the brackets and re-arranging:

$$Aa_x + Ba_y + Ca_z + D + u(A(b_x - a_x) + B(b_y - a_y) + C(b_z - a_z)) = 0.$$

We can re-arrange this further and so obtain an expression for the parameter u:

$$u = \frac{Aa_x + Ba_y + Ca_z + D}{A(a_x - b_x) + B(a_y - b_y) + C(a_z - b_z)}.$$

Recall from Section 7.4 that in the case of the 'general form' of equation for a plane, the coefficients A, B and C correspond to the components of the vector that lies at right-angles to plane (the surface normal). Bearing this in mind (and denoting this normal as $\mathbf{n}$), we can write the above equation in a more compact manner:

$$u = \frac{(\mathbf{a} \cdot \mathbf{n}) + D}{\mathbf{n} \cdot (\mathbf{a} - \mathbf{b})}. \tag{D.2}$$

Once we have determined the parameter u, this value can be inserted into Eq. D.1 so providing us with the position vector of the point of intersection. The sign of the calculated value of the parameter provides useful information. Let us suppose that we are located at the point on the line whose location is defined by position vector $\mathbf{a}$ – thus we are looking 'down' the line towards the point defined by position vector $\mathbf{b}$. A negative value of u indicates that the surface is 'behind' us and therefore it is not in our line of sight – from a practical point of view there is no intersection (this is akin to the laser pointer mentioned earlier being oriented so as to emit light in a direction that is away from the whiteboard).

As mentioned at the beginning of this subsection, a line may lie parallel to the surface of the plane in which case the two will not intersect. In this scenario, the line is oriented at right-angles to the surface normal in which case the scalar product $\mathbf{n} \cdot (\mathbf{a} - \mathbf{b})$ is zero – thus Eq. D.2 will indicate that u becomes infinitely large – implying that the line and plane never meet.

So far in our analysis we have assumed that the plane has an infinite extent – we have not considered the intersection of a line with a finite plane. To illustrate this scenario, we will consider that the surface is a triangle with vertices P, Q and R. The position vectors to these three vertices will be denoted $\mathbf{p}$, $\mathbf{q}$ and $\mathbf{r}$ respectively – as indicated in Figure D.1. We now consider a point (labelled L in the diagram and with position vector $\mathbf{l}$), the coordinates of which have been obtained using the analysis presented above – point L corresponds to the point at which a line intersects the plane containing triangle PQR. Our task is to find out whether or not this point lies inside the triangle.

This may be achieved by representing the position of point L in terms of the vectors $\mathbf{p}$, $\mathbf{q}$ and $\mathbf{r}$. Consider a line that is drawn from L to one of the sides of the triangle – the line being drawn in such a way that it lies parallel to one of the other sides (PR). In the illustration this line is shown for one particular position of L. In Figure D.2 an alternative scenario is depicted. In this case, we have created a line that is parallel to edge PQ. However given the position of L relative to the triangle, intersection with an edge of the triangle will now only occur if the edge is extended.

Thus the line that we have created is arranged to be parallel to one side of the triangle and intersects another side – or an extended side. We can express the sides of the triangle in terms of the position vectors $\mathbf{p}$, $\mathbf{q}$ and $\mathbf{r}$. Thus $\mathbf{PQ} = \mathbf{q} - \mathbf{p}$ and $\mathbf{PR} = \mathbf{r} - \mathbf{p}$. Now let us define the location of L in terms of the known vectors (this parallels previous discussion presented in Section 7.4.4). This is readily achieved by considering the path we can traverse to move from the origin to L. We begin by using vector $\mathbf{p}$ – this gets us to point P. We then move some certain distance along vector $\mathbf{PQ}$ – this gets us to the location at which the dashed line from L intersects the edge of the triangle. Finally we must move in the direction of the dashed line. Since this line is parallel to vector $\mathbf{PR}$, we need simply move a certain distance in this specified direction. This may be

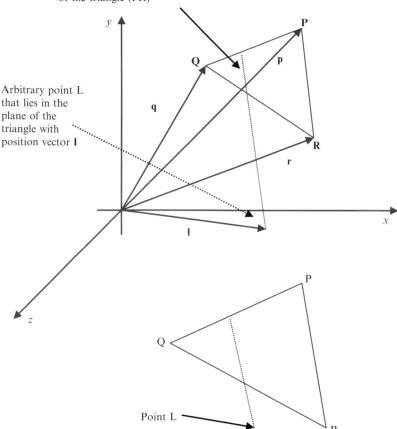

This dashed line is in the plane of the triangle and is parallel to one edge of the triangle (PR)

Arbitrary point L that lies in the plane of the triangle with position vector **l**

Point L

Figure D.1 Here we illustrate a triangle with vertices P, Q and R. L represents a point that lies in the plane of the triangle. We begin our analysis by drawing a line from L to an edge of the triangle in such a way that the line is parallel to one of the triangle's edges. In this case we have drawn the line from L to side PQ in such a way that it is parallel to side PR. See text for discussion.

expressed as:

$$\mathbf{l} = \mathbf{p} + \lambda\mathbf{PQ} + \varepsilon\mathbf{PR} = \mathbf{p} + \lambda\,(\mathbf{q} - \mathbf{p}) + \varepsilon\,(\mathbf{r} - \mathbf{p}),$$

where λ and ε are fractional distances respectively indicating the distance moved in the direction of vectors **PQ** and **PR**.

Finally, we need to specify some conditions that will determine whether or not point L lies within the triangle.

1. Both λ and ε must be equal to, or greater than, zero. If, for example, λ were to be negative, then this would mean that we were not moving along the relevant edge of the triangle – but rather in the opposite direction – away from the triangle – in which case L obviously cannot be within the triangle.

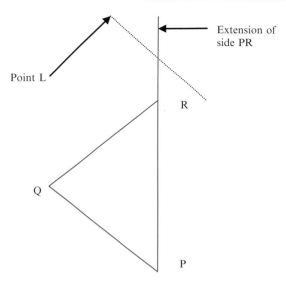

Figure D.2 In this case we have chosen to consider a line from point L that is parallel to PQ. To obtain an intersection between this line and one of the sides of the triangle, we must extend the side – otherwise there will be no intersection.

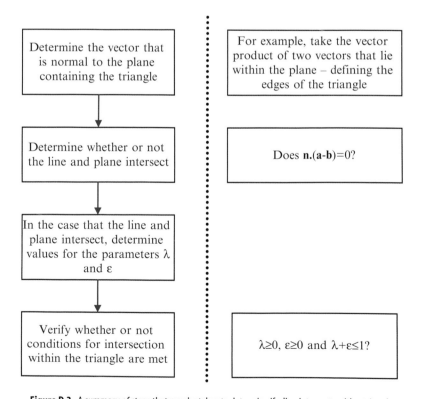

Determine the vector that is normal to the plane containing the triangle	For example, take the vector product of two vectors that lie within the plane – defining the edges of the triangle
Determine whether or not the line and plane intersect	Does $n.(a-b)=0$?
In the case that the line and plane intersect, determine values for the parameters λ and ε	
Verify whether or not conditions for intersection within the triangle are met	$\lambda \geq 0$, $\varepsilon \geq 0$ and $\lambda + \varepsilon \leq 1$?

Figure D.3 A summary of steps that may be taken to determine if a line intersects with a triangle.

2. Recall OTU Exercise 7.5 in which we considered the production of a right-angle triangle. Given two orthogonal vectors (**a** and **b**) the hypotenuse of the triangle may be defined by 'mixing' together **a** and **b** in the appropriate proportion – that is to say:

$$\lambda\mathbf{a} + \varepsilon\mathbf{b} = \lambda\mathbf{a} + (1 - \lambda)\,\mathbf{b}.$$

Thus for the triangle illustrated in Figure D.1, in the case of the locus of points defining the edge connecting vertices Q and R:

$$\lambda + \varepsilon = \lambda + (1 - \lambda) = 1,$$

and so for points that lie on, or inside this edge:

$$\lambda + \varepsilon \leq 1.$$

In summary, we require both parameters to be greater than or equal to zero and the sum of the parameters must be less than or equal to one. In Figure D.3, we summarise the steps that we may carry out in order to establish if an arbitrary line intersects with the interior of a triangular region.

D.3 The Intersection of Two Planes

'Great God! this is an awful place and terrible enough for us to have laboured to it without the reward of priority.'[2]

The intersection of two planes occurs along a straight line which lies in both planes (see Figure D.4(a)). In contrast, in the case of a cube, the mutual intersection of three planes occurs at a point (at each vertex of the cube). In this subsection, we confine our discussion to the intersection of two planes – the basic approach used here can be extended to encompass the three-plane situation.

We can represent the line of intersection (**L**) using a parametric equation in which, as usual, we define a vector ($\mathbf{a} = a_x\mathbf{i} + a_y\mathbf{j} + a_z\mathbf{k}$) in the direction of the line and a position vector ($\mathbf{p} = p_x\mathbf{i} + p_y\mathbf{j} + p_z\mathbf{k}$) to a point on the line (P):

$$\mathbf{L} = \mathbf{p} + u\mathbf{a}$$

It is easy to define the vector **a**. Consider the diagram presented in Figure D.4(b). Here, we show the surface normal vectors for the two planes (denoted $\mathbf{n}_1$ and $\mathbf{n}_2$). Taking their vector product, we obtain a vector that lies at right-angles to the two normal vectors and which lies in the direction of the line that denotes the intersection of the two planes. Thus:

$$\mathbf{n}_1 \times \mathbf{n}_2 = \mathbf{a}.$$

Determining the position vector to a point on the line is a little more taxing. Using the general equation for a plane (Eq. 7.3) we can write for Plane 1:

$$A_1 p_x + B_1 p_y + C_1 p_z + D_1 = 0, \tag{D.3}$$

---

[2] Captain Robert Falcon Scott (1868–1912).

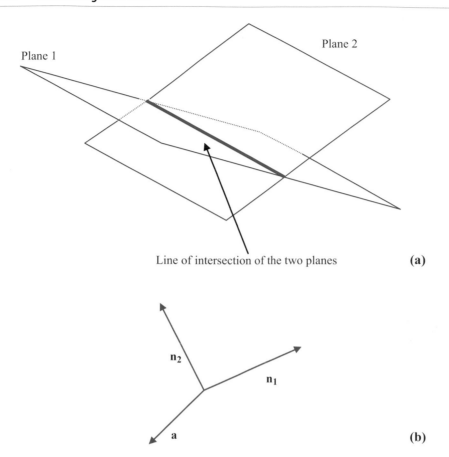

Plane 1

Plane 2

Line of intersection of the two planes   **(a)**

$\mathbf{n_2}$

$\mathbf{n_1}$

$\mathbf{a}$ **(b)**

Figure D.4 In (a) we illustrate the intersection of two non-parallel planes. Intersection takes place along a line that lies in both planes. Diagram (b) shows the surface normal vectors (denoted $\mathbf{n_1}$ and $\mathbf{n_2}$) for the two planes. These vectors are drawn from a point along the line at which the planes intersect. Their vector product results in a vector along the line of intersection (denoted $\mathbf{a}$ in the text).

and for Plane 2:

$$A_2 p_x + B_2 p_y + C_2 p_z + D_2 = 0. \tag{D.4}$$

Where A_1, B_1 and C_1 denote the components of the surface normal vector $\mathbf{n_1}$ and A_2, B_2 and C_2 are those associated with $\mathbf{n_2}$. (Do you recall the physical significance of the fourth term in these equations?) Clearly any particular point along the line on which the planes intersect has the same coordinates in both planes – once we have the coordinates of P, we can insert it into the two plane equations and will find that it satisfies each of them. In order to determine the three coordinates of the point P algebraically we need an additional equation.[3] Such an equation can be obtained by defining that the point P be positioned such that the angle between the vector $\mathbf{p}$ and the line is 90° (this does not limit the validity of the result). Thus we can write:

$$\mathbf{a}\cdot\mathbf{p} = 0.$$

_____
[3] Also see Jones _et al._ [2007] who discusses a simple and direct approach to determining the coordinates of P.

From which it follows that:

$$a_x p_x + a_y p_y + a_z p_z = 0. \tag{D.5}$$

We can express Eq.'s D.3–D.5 in matrix form:

$$\begin{bmatrix} A_1 & B_1 & C_1 \\ A_2 & B_2 & C_2 \\ a_x & a_y & a_z \end{bmatrix} \begin{bmatrix} p_x \\ p_y \\ p_z \end{bmatrix} = \begin{bmatrix} -D_1 \\ -D_2 \\ 0 \end{bmatrix}. \tag{D.6}$$

We can now solve this equation and obtain expressions for p_x, p_y and p_z.

OTU Exercise D.1: Finding the Coordinates of a Point on the Line of Intersection

On the basis of Eq. D.6, obtain equations for the coordinates of the point P which lies on the line denoting the intersection of two planes.

Hint: You may wish to glance back to the strategy used in Section 7.4.1.

Feedback to Selected OTU Exercises

Chapter 1

1.5: Cross-Sections

Diagram (a) could, for example represent a cross-section through a block of material within which three circular holes have been cut.

Diagram (b) cannot represent a cross-section of a physical object. The two 'circuits' (here, we use the term 'circuits' in the context of 'graph theory' to indicate a closed path containing at least one edge) are non-disjoint. This contrasts with the situation depicted in (a) and (c) in which the circuits are disjoint.

Diagram (c) could, for example represent a horizontal cross-section through a chair or table – each of the circles representing a single leg.

1.6: Vector and Scalar Quantities

Mass – scalar, Velocity – vector, Distance – vector, Density – scalar, Time – scalar, Temperature – scalar, Acceleration – vector, Force – vector.

1.7: Video Memory Access Time

Using Eq. 1.1, we obtain an access time of ~18 ns (ns denotes nanoseconds (1 ns $= 10^{-9}$ s)). Note the refresh period is $1/70 \sim 0.014$ s.

1.8: Passive Polarizing Glasses

If the head is tilted, this will result in increased cross-talk. This problem can be overcome by using circularly polarized filtering – see, for example, Walworth [1984].

Chapter 2

2.1: Conversion from Rectangular to Polar Coordinates

(a) The value of r is calculated using Pythagoras: $\sqrt{3^2 + 3^2} \approx 4.2$. The value of θ may be determined from Eq. 2.1:

$$\vartheta = \arctan\left(\frac{y}{x}\right) = \arctan\left(\frac{3}{3}\right) = \arctan 1 = 45°$$

Thus the coordinates of P are given by $(4.2, 45°)$

(b) The value of r is calculated using Pythagoras: $\sqrt{(-3)^2 + 3^2} \approx 4.2$
The value of θ is found using by Eq. 2.1:

$$\vartheta = \arctan\left(\frac{y}{x}\right) = \arctan\left(\frac{3}{-3}\right) = \arctan(-1) = -45°$$

However, it is important to recall that θ is measured in an anticlockwise direction from the positive x-axis. If you plot the location of P in Figure 2.1 you will see that it lies in Quadrant II and so θ is in the range $90° \le \theta \le 180°$. In fact, the angle that we have calculated is measured from the negative x-axis. Thus to determine the correct value of θ we must subtract this angle from $180°$. This gives $135°$.

Thus the coordinates of P are given by $(4.2, 135°)$

2.2: The Equation of a Line

The line passes through these two points and it may be helpful to begin by sketching the line. Since the line passes through the point $(2,1)$ we can use Eq. 2.2 and write $1 = 2m + c$. Similarly for the *point (3,2) we can write $2 = 3m + c$. Solving these equations for m and c, we obtain m = 1 and c = -1*. Thus the equation for the line is $y = x - 1$.

2.3: The Parametric Form

Rearrange the two equations:

$$t = \frac{x - x_1}{x_2 - x_1} \qquad t = \frac{y - y_1}{y_2 - y_1}.$$

We can now equate these two equations and so eliminate t:

$$\frac{x - x_1}{x_2 - x_1} = \frac{y - y_1}{y_2 - y_1}.$$

Rearranging gives Eq. 2.3.

2.4: Parametric Form and Mid-Point of a Line Segment

Inserting the end point values into Eqs. 2.3 and 2.4, we obtain:

$$x = 1 + (3 - 1)t$$
$$y = 2 + (4 - 2)t$$

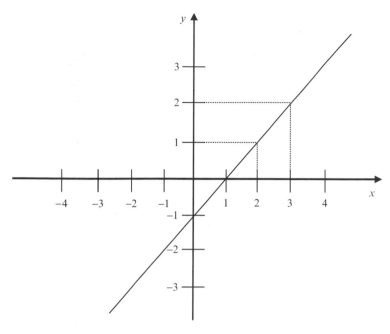

Figure OTU 2.2 The Equation of a Line.

Thus:

$$x = 1 + 2t$$
$$y = 2 + 2t$$

The mid-point of the line segment is at $t = 0.5$. Substituting this value into the above two parametric equations we obtain $x = 2$ and $y = 3$. Thus the coordinates of the mid-point are $(2,3)$.

2.6: Expressing a Vector in Terms of Orthogonal Unit Vectors

$$\mathbf{OQ} = 6\mathbf{i} + 9\mathbf{j}.$$

2.7: Addition and Subtraction of Vectors

$$\mathbf{p} + \mathbf{q} = 6\mathbf{i} + 14\mathbf{j}.$$
$$\mathbf{p} - \mathbf{q} = -2\mathbf{i} + 4\mathbf{j}.$$

2.8: Reversing the Direction of a Vector

$$\mathbf{d} = 4\mathbf{i} - 2\mathbf{j}.$$

2.9: Using the Scalar Product

1. Find the magnitude of **a** and **b**: $|\mathbf{a}| = \sqrt{2^2 + 3^2} = \sqrt{13}$ and $|\mathbf{b}| = \sqrt{4^2 + 1^2} = \sqrt{17}$.
    Determine the dot product: $\mathbf{a}\cdot\mathbf{b} = 2\cdot 4 + 3\cdot 1 = 11$.
    Now use Eq. 2.7 to find the angle between the vectors: $11 = \sqrt{13} \cdot \sqrt{17} \cos\theta$
    Thus $\cos\theta \sim 0.74$ and so $\theta \sim 42°$.
2. Determine the dot product: $\mathbf{p}\cdot\mathbf{q} = 0$
    Thus $\mathbf{p}\cdot\mathbf{q}/|\mathbf{p}||\mathbf{q}| = 0$ (irrespective of vector magnitudes). Hence $\cos\theta = 0$ and so $\theta = 90°$.

2.10: Potting Lines Using the Vector Equation

Choose some exemplar values for t (we will select 0, 1, 2) and for both vector equations we determine vector values. We subsequently draw and compare the two graphs.

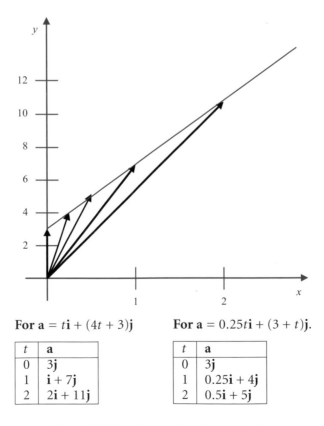

For a $= t\mathbf{i} + (4t + 3)\mathbf{j}$

t	**a**
0	$3\mathbf{j}$
1	$\mathbf{i} + 7\mathbf{j}$
2	$2\mathbf{i} + 11\mathbf{j}$

For a $= 0.25t\mathbf{i} + (3 + t)\mathbf{j}$.

t	**a**
0	$3\mathbf{j}$
1	$0.25\mathbf{i} + 4\mathbf{j}$
2	$0.5\mathbf{i} + 5\mathbf{j}$

Figure OTU 2.10 Plotting Lines Using the Vector Equation.

2.11: Locating the Point at which Two Lines Intersect

1. As indicated in Eq. 2.11: $\mathbf{r} = \mathbf{a} + t\mathbf{d}$. Here, d represents the direction vector – this defines the slope (gradient) of the line. Thus for two lines to be parallel, their direction vectors ($\mathbf{d_1}$ and $\mathbf{d_2}$) must be parallel. In turn, this means that $\mathbf{d_1} = k\mathbf{d_2}$ where k denotes a scaling factor (the vectors may be of different length but must be parallel in their orientation). The direction vectors of the two lines are: $-\mathbf{i} + 2\mathbf{j}$ and $2\mathbf{i} + \mathbf{j}$. By inspection, it is clear that we cannot multiply one of these equations by a number (k) so as to obtain the other. Consequently, it follows that the lines are not parallel.

2. To find the point of intersection, we must appreciate that we need to locate a point on both lines that is defined by the same position vector. Clearly if a point on one line is given by a position vector $\mathbf{p}$ and a point on the other line is given also defined by the same position vector, then the two points must occupy the same location in space and this by definition corresponds to the point at which the lines intersect.

We begin by expressing the two vector equations in the form $\mathbf{r} = x\mathbf{i} + y\mathbf{j}$. By rearranging the terms, the first line may be expressed as:

$$\mathbf{r_1}(t) = (1 - t)\mathbf{i} + (3 + 2t)\mathbf{j},$$

and the second line:

$$\mathbf{r_2}(s) = (1 + 2s)\mathbf{i} + (-2 + s)\mathbf{j}.$$

At the point at which the lines intersect $\mathbf{r_1} = \mathbf{r_2}$. We can therefore equate the horizontal and vertical components of these two vectors:

$$1 - t = 1 + 2s, \; 3 + 2t = -2 + s.$$

Thus from the first equation we know that $t = -2s$. Inserting this into the second equation gives $s = 1$, and so $t = -2$. To obtain the position vector for the point of intersection, we insert either the value of t into the above equation for $\mathbf{r_1}$ or the value of s into the other. (Using both substitutions we can check our answer – both position vectors should be the same at the point of intersection!). We obtain $\mathbf{r} = 3\mathbf{i} - \mathbf{j}$.

2.12: The Multiplication of Matrices

1. $\begin{bmatrix} 1 & 2 \\ 2 & 3 \end{bmatrix} \begin{bmatrix} 1 & 1 \\ 3 & 2 \end{bmatrix} = \begin{bmatrix} 1 \times 1 + 2 \times 3 & 1 \times 1 + 2 \times 2 \\ 2 \times 1 + 3 \times 3 & 2 \times 1 + 3 \times 2 \end{bmatrix} = \begin{bmatrix} 7 & 5 \\ 11 & 8 \end{bmatrix}.$

2. $\begin{bmatrix} 2 & 1 \\ 3 & 2 \end{bmatrix} \begin{bmatrix} 2 \\ 1 \end{bmatrix} = \begin{bmatrix} 2 \times 2 + 1 \times 1 \\ 3 \times 2 + 2 \times 1 \end{bmatrix} = \begin{bmatrix} 5 \\ 8 \end{bmatrix}.$

3. $\begin{bmatrix} 1 & 2 \\ 3 & 4 \end{bmatrix} \begin{bmatrix} 1 & 0 \\ 0 & 1 \end{bmatrix} = \begin{bmatrix} 1 & 2 \\ 3 & 4 \end{bmatrix}.$

In the case of the third question, multiplication by $\begin{bmatrix} 1 & 0 \\ 0 & 1 \end{bmatrix}$ has no effect.

2.13: An Identity Matrix

$$\begin{bmatrix} 1 & 2 & 1 \\ 2 & 1 & 0 \\ 2 & 0 & 3 \end{bmatrix} \begin{bmatrix} 1 & 0 & 0 \\ 0 & 1 & 0 \\ 0 & 0 & 1 \end{bmatrix} = \begin{bmatrix} 1+0+0 & 0+2+0 & 0+0+1 \\ 2+0+0 & 0+1+0 & 0+0+0 \\ 2+0+0 & 0+0+0 & 0+0+3 \end{bmatrix} = \begin{bmatrix} 1 & 2 & 1 \\ 2 & 1 & 0 \\ 2 & 0 & 3 \end{bmatrix}.$$

2.14: Calculating an Inverse Matrix

The determinant is: -10

Thus the inverse is given by: $\begin{bmatrix} -1/10 & 4/10 \\ 3/10 & -2/10 \end{bmatrix}$.

2.16: The Parabola

Let $y = u$, then $x = u^2$. Thus:

$$\mathbf{r}(u) = u^2\mathbf{i} + u\mathbf{j}.$$

u	-3	-2	-1	0	1	2	3
$\mathbf{r}(u)$	$9\mathbf{i} - 3\mathbf{j}$	$4\mathbf{i} - 2\mathbf{j}$	$\mathbf{i} - \mathbf{j}$	$0\mathbf{i} + 0\mathbf{j}$	$\mathbf{i} + \mathbf{j}$	$4\mathbf{i} + 2\mathbf{j}$	$9\mathbf{i} + 3\mathbf{j}$
x	9	4	1	0	1	4	9
y	-3	-2	-1	0	1	2	3

2.17: The Circle

Rearranging the equation for the circle we obtain:

$$y = \sqrt{9 - x^2}.$$

We use x values in the range $-3 \le x \le 3$. For example:

x	-3	-2	-1	0	1	2	3
y	0	+2.2 or −2.2	+2.8 or −2.8	+3 or −3	+2.8 or −2.8	+2.2 or −2.2	0

Chapter 3

3.1: Scaling the Dimensions of a Shape

Here, the horizontal and vertical components are each scaled by a different amount. In this sense the scaling is said to be unbalanced.

3.2: Rotation About the Origin

In both cases, we insert the relevant angle into Eq. 3.5. Thus:

1. $\begin{bmatrix} 0 & 1 \\ -1 & 0 \end{bmatrix}$.

2. $\begin{bmatrix} -1 & 0 \\ 0 & -1 \end{bmatrix}$.

3.4: Combining Transformations

Here, we reverse the order of the two left most matrices in Eq. 3.7 – the rotation matrix now comes first.

$$\begin{bmatrix} 0 & 1 \\ -1 & 0 \end{bmatrix} \begin{bmatrix} -1 & 0 \\ 0 & 1 \end{bmatrix} = \begin{bmatrix} 0 & 1 \\ 1 & 0 \end{bmatrix}.$$

Applying this to the position vectors that define the location of the vertices of the rectangle ABCD that was used in OTU Exercise 3.3 confirm this result.

3.5: A Translation Operation

$$\mathbf{p} = 2\mathbf{i} + 4\mathbf{j}$$
$$\mathbf{q} = 4\mathbf{i} + \mathbf{j}$$

Expressing these as homogeneous vectors:

$$\mathbf{p} = \begin{bmatrix} 2 & 4 & 1 \end{bmatrix}$$
$$\mathbf{q} = \begin{bmatrix} 4 & 1 & 1 \end{bmatrix}$$

We now apply the shift operation to these two homogeneous vectors. Using Eq. 3.13, we obtain:

$$\begin{bmatrix} 2 & 4 & 1 \end{bmatrix} \begin{bmatrix} 1 & 0 & 0 \\ 0 & 1 & 0 \\ 4 & 2 & 1 \end{bmatrix} = \begin{bmatrix} 6 & 6 & 1 \end{bmatrix},$$

and

$$\begin{bmatrix} 4 & 1 & 1 \end{bmatrix} \begin{bmatrix} 1 & 0 & 0 \\ 0 & 1 & 0 \\ 4 & 2 & 1 \end{bmatrix} = \begin{bmatrix} 8 & 3 & 1 \end{bmatrix}.$$

Thus the coordinates of P′ and Q′ are (6,6) and (8,3) respectively.

Chapter 4

4.1: Derivatives

1. $f'(x) = 9x^2 + 12x - 4,$ $f''(x) = 18x + 12.$

2. $\dfrac{dy}{dx} = 36x^3 - 12x^2 + 4x + 5,$ $\dfrac{d^2y}{dx^2} = 108x^2 - 24x + 4.$

3. $y = x(4x + 3) = 4x^2 + 3x.$ $\dfrac{dy}{dx} = 8x + 3,\ \dfrac{d^2y}{dx^2} = 8.$

4. $y = \sqrt{x} = x^{1/2}.$ $\dfrac{dy}{dx} = \dfrac{1}{2} \cdot x^{-1/2} = \dfrac{1}{2.x^{1/2}} = \dfrac{1}{2\sqrt{x}}.$

    $\dfrac{d^2y}{dx^2} = \dfrac{1}{2} \cdot \dfrac{-1}{2} x^{-3/2} = -\dfrac{1}{4x^{3/2}}$

4.2: Further Derivatives

1. $dy/dx = 5(6x + 3)^4 \cdot 6 = 30(6x + 3)^4$
2. $dy/dx = 6(1 - 3x)^1 \cdot -3 = -18(1 - 3x) = 54x - 18.$
    Alternatively, we can begin by expanding the equation – giving: $y = 3 + 27x^2 - 18x.$ If we now differentiate, we obtain $dy/dx = 54x - 18.$
3. $y = 3x(1 - x)^2.$ Here we can use the Product Rule – let $u = 3x$ and $v = (1 - x)^2.$

$$\frac{dy}{dx} = 3x \cdot \frac{d}{dx}(1 - x)^2 + (1 - x)^2 \cdot \frac{d}{dx}3x = -6x(1 - x) + 3(1 - x)^2.$$

4.3: Determining the Coordinates of a Turning Point

$$\frac{dy}{dx} = 12x - 6 = gradient$$

At the turning point, the gradient equals zero and so: $12x - 6 = 0.$ Thus $x = 0.5.$ Inserting this value into the Cartesian equation for the curve, we obtain y $= -3.5.$ Thus the coordinates of the turning point are $(0.5, -3.5).$

4.4: Summation Notation

$$x = \sum_{j=2}^{4} 2^j = 2^2 + 2^3 + 2^4 = 28$$

4.10: Sketching a Bézier Curve

Table of values for the graph is as follows:

t	x	y
0	1	1
0.2	3.6	3.24
0.4	5.8	4.36
0.6	7.6	4.36
0.8	9	3.24
1.0	10	1.0

4.11: Sketching a Piecewise Polynomial

Tables of values for the graphs are as follows:
   For $a(t)$:

t	y
0	0
0.2	0.02
0.4	0.08
0.6	0.18
0.8	0.32
1.0	0.5

For $b(t)$:

t	y
1.0	0.5
1.2	0.66
1.4	0.74
1.6	0.74
1.8	0.66
2.0	0.5

For $c(t)$:

t	y
2.0	0.5
2.2	0.32
2.4	0.18
2.6	0.08
2.8	0.02
3.0	0

4.12: A Spline Function

(a)   Differentiating the three equations gives:

$$a'(t) = t$$
$$b'(t) = -2(t - 1.5)^1 = 3 - 2t$$
$$c'(t) = -1(3 - t)^1 \cdot -1 = t - 3$$

At the point at which the first two functions join, $t = 1$. At this point, $a'(t) = 1$ and $b'(t) = 1$. Thus at this point the gradients of the two functions are the same. At the point at which the second and third functions meet, $t = 2$. Here, $b'(t) = -1$ and $c'(t) = -1$. Thus at the point at which these two curves meet, they have the same gradient.

(a)   Taking the second derivative, we obtain:

$$a''(t) = 1$$
$$b''(t) = -2$$
$$c''(t) = 1$$

Clearly, for $a(t)$ and $b(t)$, the rate of change of gradient is different. Similarly, $b(t)$ and $c(t)$ have a different rate of change of gradient.

4.14: Polynomials – Order and Degree

The polynomial has a degree of 5 and an order of 6.

Chapter 5

5.1: The Density of Pixels on a Standard Computer Display

Let's suppose that a monitor offers 1000 by 800 pixels per frame and let us assume a screen measuring 400 by 300 mm. Thus the density of pixels (assuming that they are equally spaced in both the vertical and horizontal directions) is $8 \times 10^5 / 12 \times 10^4 \sim 7 \, \text{mm}^{-2}$. In this respect, the image acquisition characteristics of this central region of the eye far surpass the displays image depiction capabilities!

5.4: Photon Energy

Combining Eqs. 5.1 and 5.2 we obtain:

$$E = \frac{hc}{\lambda}.$$

The wavelength $\lambda = 550 \, \text{nm} = 550 \times 10^{-9} \, \text{m}$. Assuming $c \sim 3 \times 10^8 \, \text{ms}^{-1}$ and $h \sim 6.6 \times 10^{-34} \, \text{J.s}$. Thus:

$$E \approx \frac{6.6 \times 10^{-34} \times 3 \times 10^8}{550 \times 10^{-9}} = 0.36 \times 10^{-18} \, \text{J}.$$

5.6: Perceived Brightness

On the basis of Eq. 5.3, approximately eight lamps would be required.

5.7: Detection Acuity

(a)   Let the diameter of the wire be denoted by D. Then:

$$\tan 1' = \tan 1/60° = \frac{D}{2}. \quad \text{Thus: } D \approx 0.6\,\text{mm}.$$

Let the horizontal extent of the retinal image be denoted as d. Then:

$$\tan 1' = \frac{d}{20}. \quad \text{Thus: } d \approx 0.006\,\text{mm}.$$

(b)   Assume, for example, a screen that measures 35 cm horizontally and which depicts 1000 pixels along this length. In this case we can estimate pixels that are $\sim$0.3 mm in diameter (here, we make a small allowance for the inter-pixel separation). Assuming a viewing distance of 50 cm = 500 mm, then:

$$\tan \theta = \frac{0.3}{500} = 6 \times 10^{-4}. \quad \text{Thus } \theta \approx 0.03° = 1.8'.$$

5.14: Convergence Angle

Equation 5.26 relates the distance (d) with the angle of convergence (β):

$$\tan \frac{\beta}{2} = \frac{I}{2d},$$

where I is the interocular distance that we assume $\sim$6.3 cm. Thus when $d = 400$ cm:

$$\beta = 2 \tan^{-1} \frac{3.15}{400} \approx 0.902°,$$

and when $d = 500$ cm:

$$\beta = 2 \tan^{-1} \frac{3.15}{500} \approx 0.722°.$$

The angle of convergence changes by approximately 0.18°. For the second part of this exercise, we can write:

$$0.18° \approx 2 \tan^{-1} \frac{3.15}{20} - 2 \tan^{-1} \frac{3.15}{x},$$

where x represents the distance that we wish to determine. Evaluating this expression we obtain:

$$0.18° \approx 17.9 - 2 \tan^{-1} \frac{3.15}{x},$$

and so the *change* in distance is $\sim$0.2 cm.

Chapter 6

6.1: Combining Transformations

$$\begin{bmatrix} 1 & 0 & 0 \\ 0 & 1 & 0 \\ 0 & 0 & i \end{bmatrix} \begin{bmatrix} a & b & 0 \\ d & e & 0 \\ 0 & 0 & 1 \end{bmatrix} \begin{bmatrix} 1 & 0 & 0 \\ 0 & 1 & 0 \\ g & h & 1 \end{bmatrix} = \begin{bmatrix} a & b & 0 \\ d & e & 0 \\ gi & hi & i \end{bmatrix}.$$

6.3: Matrices for Reflection

(a) Reflection in the x–y plane:

$$\begin{bmatrix} 1 & 0 & 0 & 0 \\ 0 & 1 & 0 & 0 \\ 0 & 0 & -1 & 0 \\ 0 & 0 & 0 & 1 \end{bmatrix}.$$

(b) Reflection in the y–z plane:

$$\begin{bmatrix} -1 & 0 & 0 & 0 \\ 0 & 1 & 0 & 0 \\ 0 & 0 & 1 & 0 \\ 0 & 0 & 0 & 1 \end{bmatrix}.$$

(c) Reflection in the x–z plane:

$$\begin{bmatrix} 1 & 0 & 0 & 0 \\ 0 & -1 & 0 & 0 \\ 0 & 0 & 1 & 0 \\ 0 & 0 & 0 & 1 \end{bmatrix}.$$

6.4: Calculating the Vector Product

Eq. 6.7 provides an expression for the vector product:

$$\mathbf{a} \times \mathbf{b} = (a_2 b_3 - a_3 b_2)\,\mathbf{i} - (a_1 b_3 - a_3 b_1)\,\mathbf{j} + (a_1 b_2 - a_2 b_1)\,\mathbf{k}.$$

Thus

1. $\mathbf{a} \times \mathbf{b} = (-2 - 3)\,\mathbf{i} - (-1 - 6)\,\mathbf{j} + (1 - 4)\,\mathbf{k} = -5\mathbf{i} + 7\mathbf{j} - 3\mathbf{k}$
2. $\mathbf{b} \times \mathbf{a} = (3 + 2)\,\mathbf{i} - (6 + 1)\,\mathbf{j} + (4 - 1)\,\mathbf{k} = 5\mathbf{i} - 7\mathbf{j} + 3\mathbf{k}$

Hence $\mathbf{a} \times \mathbf{b} \neq \mathbf{b} \times \mathbf{a}$ and hence the operation is not commutative. However on inspection of the results, it is apparent that $\mathbf{a} \times \mathbf{b} = -(\mathbf{b} \times \mathbf{a})$. Thus the resulting vectors are of the same magnitude but point in directly opposite directions.

6.5: The Vector Product of Parallel Vectors

1. In the case that two vectors are parallel, $\theta = 0°$ and so $\sin\theta = 0$. As a result, the vector product is zero.

2. Using Eq. 6.7, we can write:

$$\mathbf{a} \times \mathbf{b} = (a_2b_3 - a_3b_2)\,\mathbf{i} - (a_1b_3 - a_3b_1)\,\mathbf{j} + (a_1b_2 - a_2b_1)\,\mathbf{k}$$
$$= (-30 + 30)\,\mathbf{i} + (-12 + 12)\,\mathbf{j} + (20 - 20)\,\mathbf{k}.$$

Hence $\mathbf{a} \times \mathbf{b} = 0$.

6.6: Determination of the Surface Normal

Using Eq. 6.7, we can write:

$$\mathbf{n} = \mathbf{a} \times \mathbf{b} = (a_2b_3 - a_3b_2)\,\mathbf{i} - (a_1b_3 - a_3b_1)\,\mathbf{j} + (a_1b_2 - a_2b_1)\,\mathbf{k}$$
$$= (42 - 16)\,\mathbf{i} - (14 - 6)\,\mathbf{j} + (16 - 18)\,\mathbf{k}.$$

Thus:

$$\mathbf{n} = 26\mathbf{i} - 8\mathbf{j} - 2\mathbf{k}.$$

This vector is perpendicular to the plane defined by $\mathbf{a}$ and $\mathbf{b}$. It has a magnitude determined by the magnitudes of both $\mathbf{a}$ and $\mathbf{b}$ and also by the angle between these two vectors. To convert the vector $\mathbf{n}$ into a unit vector, we need to calculate the magnitude of $\mathbf{a} \times \mathbf{b}$. This is given by:

$$|\mathbf{n}| = |\mathbf{a} \times \mathbf{b}| = \sqrt{26^2 + 8^2 + 2^2} = \sqrt{744}.$$

Eq. 6.10 now allows us to obtain the unit vector:

$$\hat{\mathbf{n}} = \frac{\mathbf{a} \times \mathbf{b}}{|\mathbf{a} \times \mathbf{b}|} = \frac{\mathbf{n}}{|\mathbf{n}|} = \frac{26\mathbf{i} - 8\mathbf{j} - 2\mathbf{k}}{\sqrt{744}} = \frac{26\mathbf{i}}{\sqrt{744}} - \frac{8\mathbf{j}}{\sqrt{744}} - \frac{2\mathbf{k}}{\sqrt{744}}.$$

6.7: The Application of a 4 by 4 Matrix

$$\begin{bmatrix} 3 & 4 & 5 & 1 \end{bmatrix} \begin{bmatrix} 1 & 0 & 0 & 0 \\ 0 & \cos 45^\circ & \sin 45^\circ & 0 \\ 0 & -\sin 45^\circ & \cos 45^\circ & 0 \\ 0 & 0 & 0 & 0.5 \end{bmatrix} \approx \begin{bmatrix} 3 & -0.7 & 6.4 & 0.5 \end{bmatrix}.$$

Thus the point is approximately located at $(6, -1.4, 12.8)$.

6.8: The Inverse of a Matrix

(a)

$$\mathbf{R}_z^{-1}(\alpha) = \begin{bmatrix} \cos\alpha & -\sin\alpha & 0 & 0 \\ \sin\alpha & \cos\alpha & 0 & 0 \\ 0 & 0 & 1 & 0 \\ 0 & 0 & 0 & 1 \end{bmatrix}.$$

and,

$$\begin{bmatrix} \cos\alpha & \sin\alpha & 0 & 0 \\ -\sin\alpha & \cos\alpha & 0 & 0 \\ 0 & 0 & 1 & 0 \\ 0 & 0 & 0 & 1 \end{bmatrix} \begin{bmatrix} \cos\alpha & -\sin\alpha & 0 & 0 \\ \sin\alpha & \cos\alpha & 0 & 0 \\ 0 & 0 & 1 & 0 \\ 0 & 0 & 0 & 1 \end{bmatrix} = \begin{bmatrix} \cos^2\alpha + \sin^2\alpha & 0 & 0 & 0 \\ 0 & \sin^2\alpha + \cos^2\alpha & 0 & 0 \\ 0 & 0 & 1 & 0 \\ 0 & 0 & 0 & 1 \end{bmatrix}$$

Recall that $\cos^2\alpha + \sin^2\alpha = 1$ and so the above result is the identity matrix for multiplication.

6.9: Example Calculation

The point L can be represented in homogeneous form as $[2\ 2\ -4\ 1]$. Thus the coordinates of L′ may be determines as follows:

$$[2\ 2\ -4\ 1]\begin{bmatrix} 1 & 0 & 0 & 0 \\ 0 & 1 & 0 & 0 \\ 0 & 0 & 0 & -1/10 \\ 0 & 0 & 0 & 1 \end{bmatrix} = [2\ 2\ 0\ 0.4+1].$$

The coordinates of L′ are therefore:

$$\left(\frac{2}{1.4},\ \frac{2}{1.4},\ 0\right) \approx \left(1.43,\ 1.43,\ 0\right).$$

6.11: The Perspective Projection: Object Orientation

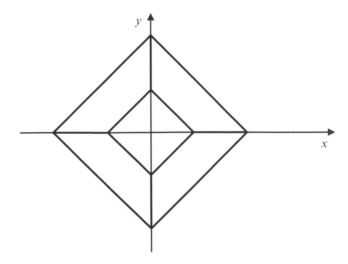

Figure OTU 6.11 The Perspective Projection – Object Orientation.

Chapter 7

7.2: Regular Polyhedra

The number of edges per face is represented by e and the total number of faces by S. Thus, we can write, $eS = 2E$ where E represents the total number of edges forming the polyhedron (note the factor of two arises because each edge is 'shared' between two adjacent faces). We can also write that $Vv = 2E$, where v denotes the number of edges emanating from each vertex. Thus:

$$V = \frac{2E}{v} \text{ and } S = \frac{2E}{e}.$$

Substituting into Eq. 7.1, we obtain:

$$\frac{2E}{v} - E + \frac{2E}{e} = 2.$$

Dividing through by $2E$ gives:

$$\frac{1}{v} + \frac{1}{e} - \frac{1}{2} = \frac{1}{E}.$$

Obviously, the total number of edges comprising the polyhedron (E) must be greater than zero. Thus:

$$\frac{1}{E} > 0, \text{ and so } \frac{1}{v} + \frac{1}{e} - \frac{1}{2} > 0.$$

For a polyhedron, it is apparent that both e and v must be equal to or greater than three (e.g. a face bounded by only two faces would not make particular sense ...). In the case that *both e* and *v* equal four, the left hand side of the above equation equals zero and when *both e* and *v* are greater than four, the left hand side of the equation becomes negative – implying that E is negative – which is not the case! We can therefore conclude that *both e* and *v* cannot be greater than three. Thus if we assume that e equals three, then to satisfy the above inequality, $3 \le v \le 5$. Similarly, if we assume that v equals three, then $3 \le e \le 5$.

We can conclude that valid combinations for e and v (denoted as an ordered pair (e, v)) are $(3,3), (3,4), (3,5), (4,3), (5,3)$. Inserting these values, we can determine corresponding values for E. These are presented below:

Edges per face (e)	Edges from each vertex (v)	Total number of edges (E)	Polyhedron
3	3	6	Tetrahedron
3	4	12	Octahedron
3	5	30	Icosahedron
4	3	12	Cube
5	3	30	Dodecahedron

7.3: The Euler-Poincaré Equation

For this polyhedron there are 20 vertices (V), 30 edges (E) and 12 surfaces (S). There is a single component ($P = 1$), one hole passes through the object ($H = 1$) and a total of two holes ($H_B = 2$ – corresponding to either end of the hole that passes through the object). Eq. 7.2 indicates:

$$V - E + S = 2(P - H) + H_B.$$

Using this data, both the left and right hand sides of this equation equate to two.

7.4: The Normal Vector

The normal vector ($\mathbf{n}$) is given by $3\mathbf{i} + 2\mathbf{j} + 4\mathbf{k}$. The question requires us to find the unit vector – hence we must calculate the magnitude of $\mathbf{n}$. This is given by:

$$|\mathbf{n}| = \sqrt{3^2 + 2^2 + 4^2} = \sqrt{29}.$$

Thus the unit vector is given by:

$$\hat{\mathbf{n}} = \frac{1}{\sqrt{29}}(3\mathbf{i} + 2\mathbf{j} + 4\mathbf{k}).$$

7.6: Determining the Plane Equation and Perpendicular Distance

The general equation for the plane is:

$$Ax + By + Cz + D = 0.$$

The values of the coefficients A, B and C are given by the vector components of the surface normal. Inserting these values we obtain:

$$x + y + z + D = 0.$$

We are told that the plane passes through a point P with position vector $\mathbf{p} = 2\mathbf{j} + \mathbf{k}$. Inserting these values we find that $D = -3$. Thus the equation for the plane is given by:

$$x + y + z - 3 = 0.$$

The magnitude of the normal vector is given by $|\mathbf{n}| = \sqrt{1^2 + 1^2 + 1^2} = \sqrt{3}$. The perpendicular distance from the origin is given by:

$$\frac{|D|}{|\mathbf{n}|} = \frac{3}{\sqrt{3}}.$$

7.8: The Spatial Occupancy of a Cone

$$y \geq 0, \quad y \leq 1, \quad x^2 + z^2 \leq (1 - y)^2.$$

Chapter 9

9.2: Total Internal Reflection

Using Eq. 9.2:

$$\sin\theta_1 > \frac{n_2}{n_1} \sim \frac{1.003}{1.52}$$

Thus

$$\theta_1 > 41.3°$$

9.4: Head Tracking

Given a temperature of 27 °C, the velocity of the wave is:

$$v \sim 331 + 0.6T = 331 + 0.6 \times 27 \sim 347\,\text{ms}^{-1}$$

$$\text{Speed} = \frac{\text{Distance traveled}}{\text{Time taken}}$$

Hence, time = $0.8/347 \sim 2.3 \times 10^{-3}$ seconds.

9.10: Locating the Size and Position of an Image Formed by Curved Mirrors

(1) $f = 20$ cm, $u = 10$ cm. Using Eq. 9.7:

$$\frac{1}{10} + \frac{1}{v} = \frac{1}{20},$$

thus $v = 20$ cm. Further, the answer is negative indicating that the image is behind the mirror (virtual).

Using Eq. 9.8:

$$Magnification = \frac{v}{u} = \frac{20}{10} = 2.$$

(2) In the case of the convex mirror, we denote the focal length as being negative. Thus $f = -20$ cm, $u = 10$ cm. Again using Eq. 9.7, we now obtain $v \sim 6.67$ cm. The calculated distance is negative and so again the image is virtual. Note that whatever the location of a real object placed in front of a convex mirror, the image is always virtual.

Using Eq. 9.8: we obtain a magnification of 2/3 – indicating that the image is diminished in size.

Chapter 10

10.2: The Functionality of Receptors

1. This is known as the 'Weber Illusion' (after the 19th century German physiologist). The cold coin is perceived as being the heaviest. This indicates the presence of receptors that respond to both temperature and pressure.
2. The warm and cold coins are now likely to be perceived as being heavier than the coin at skin temperature. We may conclude that the sensation provided by the receptors varies with location on the body.

References

NOTE: Within the body of the text, dates cited in relation to patents indicate the year when the patents were filed. In the references below, we provide the year when the patents were granted. From an historical perspective, the filing date is naturally of primary importance.

US Patents

US1,506,524 Hammond, L. (1924), 'Stereoscopic Motion Picture Device'.

US1,658,439 Hammond, L. (1928), 'Stereoscopic Picture Viewing Apparatus'.

US1,876,272; Bayer, J.V. (1932), 'Fog Penetrating Televisor'.

US2,273,512 Caldwell, G.D., and Hathorn, G.M. (1942), 'Viewing Instruments for Stereoscopic Pictures and the Like'.

US2,967,905; Hirsch, M. (1961), 'Three Dimensional Display Apparatus'.

US3,050,870 Heilig, M. (1962), 'Sensorama Simulator'.

US3,493,290; Traub, A.C. (1970), 'Three-Dimensional Display'.

US3,609,706; Adamson, A.W. (1971), 'Method and Apparatus for Generating Three-Dimensional Patterns'.

US3,609,707; Lewis, J.D. (1971), 'Method and Apparatus for Generating Three-Dimensional Patterns'.

US4,130,832; Sher, L.D. (1978), 'Three-Dimensional Display'.

US4,160,973; Berlin, E.P. (1979), 'Three-Dimensional Display'.

US4,881,068; Korevaar, E.J., and Spivey, B. (1989), 'Three Dimensional Display Apparatus'.

US5,703,606; Blundell, B.G. (1997), 'Three-Dimensional Display'.

US6,054,817; Blundell, B.G. (2000), 'Three Dimensional Display System'.

US6,100,862; Sullivan, A. (2000), 'Multi-Planar Volumetric Display System and Method of Operation'.

US6,958,837 Hartwig, R. (2004), 'Method of Producing Picture Element Groups by Means of Laser Rays in Space on a Plane'.

UK Patent Application

GB0700505.1, Blundell, B.G. (2007), 'A Varifocal Display Technique'.

European Patent

DE2622802C2, Hartwig, R. (1976), 'Helix Laser 3D Display'.
DE10047695, Hartwig, R. (2002), 'Method of Producing Picture Element Groups by Means of Laser Rays in Space on a Plane'.
EP 0 418 583 A2; Garcia Jr, F. (1991), 'Real Time Three Dimensional Display'.
FR461 600; Luzy, E., and Dupuis, C. (1914), 'Procédé Pour Obtenir des Projections en Relief'.

Publications

Abramson, A., *The History of Television, 1880 to 1941*, McFarland and Co. (1987).
Agoston, M.K., *Computer Graphics and Geometric Modeling: Implementation and Algorithms*, Springer-Verlag London (2005).
Baumgart, B.J., 'A Polyhedron Representation for Computer Vision', in *44th AFIPS National Computer Conference*, pp. 589–596 (1975).
Berkley, C., 'Three-Dimensional Representation on Cathode-Ray Tubes', *Proceedings of the IRE – Waves and Electrons Section*, pp. 1530–1535 (December 1948).
Bickley, W.G., and Thompson, R.S.H.G., *Matrices: Their Meaning and Manipulation*. The English Universities Press Ltd (1964).
Blake, D.T., Hsaio, S.S., and Johnson, K.O., 'Neural Coding Mechanisms in Tactile Pattern Recognition: The Relative Contributions of Slowly and Rapidly Adapting Mechanoreceptors to Perceived Roughness', *Journal of Neuroscience*, **17** (19), pp. 7480–7489 (1997).
Blundell, B.G., '3-D Display Systems: Myth and Reality', *ITNow*, **48** (1), pp. 32–33 (2006a).
Blundell, B.G., 'Baird and the Volumetric Display', *IET Engineering and Technology*, pp. 36–40 (August 2006b).
Blundell, B.G., *Enhanced Visualization: Making Space for 3-D Images*, John Wiley & Sons Inc (2007).
Blundell, B.G., and Schwarz, A.J., *Creative 3-D Display and Interaction Interfaces: A Trans-Disciplinary Approach*, John Wiley & Sons Inc (2006).
Blundell, B.G., and Schwarz, A.J., *Volumetric Three-Dimensional Display Systems*, John Wiley & Sons Inc (2000).
Blundell, B.G., Daskalakis, C.N., Heyes, N.A.E., and Hopkins, T.P., *An Introductory Guide to Silvar Lisco and HILO Simulators*, Macmillan Education (1987).
Boden, M.A., *Mind as Machine: A History of Cognitive Science*, Vol. 1, Oxford University Press (2006).
Boff, K.R., Kaufman, L., and Thomas, J.P. (eds.), *Handbook of Perception and Human Performance, Volume I, Sensory Processes and Perception*, John Wiley & Sons Inc (1986).
Boyer, C.B. (Revised by Merzbach U.C.), *A History of Mathematics* (2nd edn.), John Wiley & Sons Inc (1991).
Brown, S.F., 'Seeing Triple', *Scientific American*, pp. 88–89 (June 2007).
Bruce, V., Green P.R., and Georgeson M.A., *Visual Perception: Physiology, Psychology and Ecology* (4th edn.), Psychology Press (2003).
Burdea, G.C., *Force and Touch Feedback for Virtual Reality*, John Wiley & Sons Inc (1996).
Burdea, G.C., and Coiffet, P., *Virtual Reality Technology* (2nd edn.), John Wiley & Sons Inc (2003).
Campbell Swinton, A.A., 'Presidential Address', *The Journal of the Röntgen Society*, **VIII** (30), pp. 1–13 (January 1912).
Card, S.K., English, W.K., and Burr, B.J., 'Evaluation of Mouse, Rate-Controlled Isometric Joystick, Step Keys and Text Keys for Text Selection on a CRT,' *Ergonomics*, **21** (8), pp. 601–613 (1978).
Chinnock, C., 'Researchers Demonstrate 3-D Volumetric Images', *Laser Focus World*, pp. 28–32 (November 1994).
Clements, A., *Principles of Computer Hardware* (4th edn.), Oxford University Press (2006).

Coleridge, S.T., *Biographia Literaria: Biographical Sketches of my Literary Life and Opinions*, Princeton University Press (1985).

Collender, R.B., 'The Stereoptiplexer: Competition for the Hologram', *Information Display* 4 (6), pp. 27–31 (1967).

Comninos, P., *Mathematical and Computer Programming Techniques for Computer Graphics*, Springer-Verlag London Ltd (2006).

Cook, R.L., Porter, T., and Carpenter, L., 'Distributed Ray Tracing', *Computer Graphics* **18**(3), pp. 137–145 (1984).

Cooke, R., *The History of Mathematics: A Brief Course*, John Wiley & Sons Inc (2005).

Cooley, P., *The Essence of Computer Graphics*, Pearson Education Limited (2001).

Coren, S., Ward, L.M., and Enns, J.T., *Sensation and Perception* (4th edn.), Harcourt Brace & Company (1994).

Cossairt, O.S., Napoli, J., Hill, S.L., Dorval, R.K., and Favalora, G.E., 'Occlusion-Capable Multiview Volumetric Three-Dimensional Display', *Applied Optics*, **46**(8), pp. 1244–1250 (10 March 2007).

Cronly-Dillon, J.R., and Gregory, R.L. (eds.), 'Evolution of the Eye and Visual System', in *Vision and Visual Disfunction*, Vol. 2, The Macmillan Press Ltd (1991).

Cruz-Neira, C., Sandin, D.J., and DeFanti, T.J., 'Virtual Reality: The Design and Implementation of the CAVE', *Proceedings SIGGRAPH 93 Computer Graphics Conference*, ACM SIGGRAPH, pp. 135–142 (1993).

Cutler, L.D., Froehlich, B., and Hanrahan, P., 'Two-Handed Direct Manipulation on the Responsive Workbench', *1997 Symposium on Interactive 3D Graphics, Providence RI, USA*, ACM, pp. 107–114 (1997).

Cyrus, M. and Beck, J., 'Generalized Two- and Three-Dimensional Clipping', *Computers and Graphics*, **3**(1), pp. 23–28 (1978).

Davies, A.G.J., *Solid Geometry in 3-D*, Chatto and Windus (1967).

DeFanti, T., Cruz-Neira, C., Sandin, D., Kenyon, R., and Hart, J., 'The CAVE: Audio Visual Experience Automatic Virtual Environment', *Communications of the ACM* **35**(6), pp. 64–72 (June 1992).

Della Porta, G., *De Refractione Optices Parte* (1593).

Dodgson, N.A., Moore, J.R., and Lang, S.R., 'Multi-View Autostereoscopic 3D Display', *Proceedings International Broadcasting Convention* (September 10–14, Amsterdam), pp. 497–502 (1999).

Downing, E., Hesselink, L., Macfarlane, R.M., and Barty, C.P.J., 'Solid-State Three-Dimensional Computer Display', *CLEO '94* (1994).

Eberly, D.H., *Game Physics*, Elsevier Inc (2004).

Edgerton, S.Y., *The Heritage Of Giotto's Geometry – Art And Science On The Eve Of The Scientific Revolution*, Cornell University Press (1991).

Edgerton, S.Y., *The Renaissance Rediscovery Of Linear Perspective*, Harper and Row (1976).

Egerton, P.A., and Hall, W.S., *Computer Graphics: Mathematical First Steps*, Pearson Education Limited (1999).

Elkins, J., *How to Use Your Eyes*, Routledge (2000).

Encarnacao, J., and Schlechtendahl, E.G., *Computer Aided Design: Fundamentals and System Architectures*, Springer-Verlag (1983).

English, W.K., Engelbart, D.C., and Berman, M.L., 'Display-Selection Techniques for Text Manipulation', *IEEE Transactions on Human Factors in Electronics*, **HFE-8** (1) (March 1967).

Fernandes, K.J., Raja, V., and Eyre, J., 'Cybersphere: The Fully Immersive Spherical Projection System', *Communications of the ACM*, **46** (9ve), pp. 141–146 (September 2003).

Foley, J.D., van Dam, A., Feiner, S.K., and Hughes, J.F., *Computer Graphics: Principles and Practice*, 2nd edn., Addison-Wesley Publishing Company (1990).

Gabor, D., 'A New Microscopic Principle', *Nature*, **161**, pp. 777–778 (May 1948).

Gabor, D., 'Holography, 1948–1971', Proc. IEEE, **60** (6) (1972).

Gauthier, J-M., *Building Interactive Worlds in 3D: Virtual Sets and Pre-Visualization for Games, Film & the Web*, Focal Press (2005).

Geddes, K., and Bussey, G., *The Setmakers: A History of the Radio and Television Industry*, The British Radio & Electronic Equipment Manufacturers' Association (1991).

Gibson, J.J., *The Perception of the Visual World*, Houghton Mifflin (1950).

Girling, A.N., *Stereoscopic Drawing: A Theory of 3-D Vision and its Application to Stereoscopic Drawing*, Arthur Girling (1990).

Glanz, J., 'Three-Dimensional Images are Conjured in a Crystal Cube', *Science* **273**, p. 1172 (August 1996).

GPIPG: Great Pictures in Private Galleries, Cassell and Company Ltd (1905).

Halle, M., 'Autostereoscopic Displays and Computer Graphics', *Computer Graphics (ACM SIGGRAPH)* **31** (2) pp. 58–62 (1997).

Halle, M., 'Multiple Viewpoint Rendering', *Proceedings SIGGRAPH '96* (1996).

Harris, L.D., Camp, J.J., Ritman, E.L., and Robb, R.A., 'Three-Dimensional Display and Analysis of Tomographic Volume Images using a Varifocal Mirror', *IEEE Transactions on Medical Imaging*, **MI-5** (2), pp. 67–72 (June 1986).

Hartwig, R., 'The Helix3D – A Three Dimensional Computer Display', invited presentation and demonstration, TELI – European Union of Science Journalists Association, German Study Tour, Heidelberg (November 5, 1982).

Hearn, D., and Baker, M.P., *Computer Graphics*, Prentice-Hall Inc (1986).

Hecht, S., and Mintz, E.U., 'The Visibility of Single Lines at Various Illuminations and the Retinal Basis of Visual Resolution', *Journal of General Physiology*, pp. 593–612 (1939).

Hecht, S., Shlaer, S., and Pirenne, M.H., 'Energy Quanta and Vision', *Journal of General Physiology*, **25**, pp. 819–840 (1942).

Helmholtz, H.H., *Popular Lectures on Scientific Subjects* (English Translation by Atkinson, E.), Longmans, Green, and Co. (1873).

Hill Jr., F.S., *Computer Graphics*, Macmillan Publishing Company (1990).

Hinckley, K., and Pausch, R., Two-Handed Virtual Manipulation', *ACM Transactions on Computer-Human Interaction*, **5** (3), pp. 260–302 (September 1998).

Howard, I.P., and Rogers, B.J., *Seeing in Depth*, Vol. II Depth Perception, I. Porteous (2002).

Jiménez, P., Thomas, F., and Torras, C., '3D Collision Detection: A Survey', *Computers and Graphics*, **25**, pp. 269–285 (2001).

Jones, A., McDowall, I., Yamada, H., Bolas, M., Debevec, P., 'Rendering for an Interactive 360° Light Field Display'. *ACM Trans. Graph.* **26**(3), Article 40 (July 2007).

Jones, G., Lee, D., Holliman, N., Ezra, D., 'Controlling Perceived Depth in Stereoscopic Images', *Proceedings SPIE (Stereoscopic Displays and Virtual Reality Systems VIII)*, **4297**, pp. 42–53 (2001).

Jordan, D.W., and Smith, P., *Mathematical Techniques: An Introduction for the Engineering, Physical, and Mathematical Sciences* (3rd edn.), Oxford University Press (2002).

Kaczmarek, K.A., Webster, J.G., Bach-y-Rita, P., and Tompkins, W.J., 'Electrotactile and Vibrotactile Displays for Sensory Substitution Systems', *IEEE Transactions on Biomedical Engineering*, **38** (1), pp. 1–16 (1991).

Kamm, A., and Baird, M., *John Logie Baird: A Life*, National Museums of Scotland Publishing Ltd (2002).

Kandel, E.R., Schwartz, J.H., and Jessell, T.M., *Principles of Neural Science* (4th edn.), McGraw-Hill (2000).

Kemp, M., 'Science, Non-Science and Nonsense: the Interpretation of Brunelleschi's Perspective', *Art History*, **1** (2), pp. 134–161 (1978).

Kennedy, D.N., and Nelson, A.C., 'Three-Dimensional Display from Cross-Sectional Tomographic Images: An Application to Magnetic Resonance Imaging', *IEEE Transactions on Medical Imaging*, **MI-6** (2), pp.134–140 (1993).

Kim, S., Berkley, J.J., and Sato, M., 'A Novel Seven Degree of Freedom Haptic Device for Engineering Design', *Virtual Reality*, **6** (4), pp. 217–228 (2003a).

Kim, Y.J., Otaday, M.A., Lin, M.C., and Manocha, D., 'Six-Degree-of-Freedom Haptic Rendering using Incremental and Localised Computations', *Presence*, **12** (3), pp. 277–295 (2003b).

Kubovy, M., *The Psychology of Linear Perspective and Renaissance Art*, Cambridge University Press (1986).

Land, M.F., and Nilsson, D.-E., *Animal Eyes*, Oxford University Press (2002).

Lang, S.R., Travis, A.R.L., Castle, O.M., and Moore, J.R., 'A 2nd Generation Autostereoscopic 3-D Display', *Proceedings 7th Eurographics Workshop on Graphics Hardware (Cambridge, UK, 5–6 September 1992)*, Lister, P.F. (ed.), pp. 53–63 (1992).

Larson, R.E., Hostetler, R.P., and Edwards, B.H., *Calculus: With Analytic Geometry* (6th edn.), Houghton Mifflin Company (1998).

Leganchuk, A., Zhai, S., and Buxton, W., 'Manual and Cognitive Benefits of Two-Handed Input: An Experimental Study', *ACM Trans. On Computer-Human Interaction*, **5** (4), pp. 326–359 (December 1998).

Leith, E.N., and Upatnieks, J., 'Reconstructed Wavefronts and Communication Theory', *J. Opt. Soc. Am.*, **52**, pp. 1123–1130 (1962).

Leith, E.N., and Upatnieks, J., 'Wavefront Reconstruction with Continuous-Tone Objects', *J. Opt. Soc. Am.*, **53**, pp. 1377–1381 (1963).

Leith, E.N., and Upatnieks, J., 'Wavefront Reconstruction with Diffused Illumination and Three-Dimensional Objects', *J. Opt. Soc. Am.*, **54**, pp. 1295–1301 (1964).

Lewis, J.D., Verber, C.M., and McGhee, R.B., 'A True Three-Dimensional Display', *IEEE Transactions on Electron Devices*, **ED-18** (9), pp. 724–732 (September 1971).

Liang, Y-D., and Barsky, B., 'A New Concept and Method for Line Clipping', *ACM TOG*, **3**(1), pp. 1–22 (January 1984).

Lin, M.C., and Gottschalk, S., 'Collision Detection Between Geometrical Models: A Survey', *Proceedings IMA Conference on Mathematics of Surfaces* (1998).

Lin, M.C., Manocha, D., 'Collision and Proximity Queries', in *Handbook of Discrete and Computational Geometries* (2nd edn.), O'Rourke, J., and Goodman, E. (eds.), Ch. 35, pp. 787–808, CRC Press (2004).

Lindsay, P.H., and Norman, D.A., *Human Information Processing: An Introduction to Psychology*, Academic Press (1972).

Lippman, G., 'Epreuves Reversibles Donnant la Sensation du Relief', *Journal of Physics*, **7** (4th series), pp. 821–825 (November 1908).

Low, A.M., *Popular Scientific Recreations*, Ward, Lock and Co. (1933).

Lucente, M., *Diffraction-Specific Fringe Computation for Electro-Holography*, Ph.D. Thesis, Massachussetts Institute of Technology (1994).

Lucente, M., 'Holographic Bandwidth Compression using Spatial Subsampling', *Optical Engineering*, **35** (6), pp. 1529–1537 (1996).

Lucente, M., 'Interactive Computation of Holograms using a Look-Up Table', *Journal of Electronic Imaging*, **2** (1), pp. 28–34 (1993).

Lynes, J.A., 'Brunelleschi's Perspectives Reconsidered', *Perception*, **9**, pp. 87–99 (1980).

MacDonald, L.W., and Lowe, A.C. (eds.), *Display Systems: Design and Applications*, John Wiley & Sons Ltd (1997).

MacKay, D.M., 'Projective Three-Dimensional Displays, Part I', *Electronic Engineering* (July 1949).

MacKay, D.M., 'Projective Three-Dimensional Displays, Part II', *Electronic Engineering* (August 1949).

Mark, W., Randolph, S., Finch, M., van Verth, J., and Taylor, R., 'Adding Force Feedback to Graphics Systems: Issues and Solutions', *Proceedings SIGGRAPH '96 (New Orleans)*, pp. 447–452 (1996).

McAllister, D.F. (ed.), *Stereo Computer Graphics and Other True 3D Technologies*, Princeton University Press (1993).

Minsky, M., Ming, O., Steele, F., Brook, F.P., and Behensky, M., 'Feeling and Seeing: Issues in Force Display', *Proceedings Symposium on 3D Real-Time Interactive Graphics*, **24**, pp. 235–243 (1990).

Morgenbesser, H.B., and Srinivasan, M.A., 'Force Shading for Haptic Shape Perception', *Proceedings ASME Dynamic Systems and Control Division*, **58**, pp. 407–412 (1996).

Mortenson, M.E., *Geometric Modeling*, John Wiley & Sons (1985).

Nayar and Anand, V.J., '3D Display Using Passive Optical Scatterers', *IEEE Computer*, pp. 54–63 (July 2007).

Necker, L.A., *The London & Edinburgh Philosophical Magazine and Journal of Science*, **1**, pp. 329–337 (1832).

Nelkon and Parker, P., *Advanced Level Physics* (7th edn.), Heinemann Educational Publishers (1995).

Newman, W.M., and Sproull, R.F., *Principles of Interactive Computer Graphics* (2nd edn.), McGraw-Hill (1981).

Okoshi, T., *Three-Dimensional Imaging Techniques*, Academic Press (1976).

Parker, M.J., and Wallis, P.A., 'Three-Dimensional Cathode-Ray Tube Displays', *Journal of the IEE*, **95**, pp. 371–390 (September 1948).

Purves, D., and Lotto, R.B., *Why We See What We Do: An Empirical Theory of Vision*, Sinauer Associates Inc (2003).

Rawson, E.G., '3D Computer-Generated Movies using a Varifocal Mirror', *Applied Optics*, **7** (8) pp. 1505–1511 (1968).

Rawson, E.G., 'Vibrating Varifocal Mirrors for 3D Imaging', *IEEE Spectrum*, pp. 37–43 (September 1969).

Ritter, A.O., Bottger, J., Deussen, O., and Strothotte, T., '*Fast Texture-Based Interference for Synthetic Holography*', Technical Report 3/98, Fakultät für Informatik, Otto-von-Guericke-Universität Magdeburg, Germany (1998).

Ritter, A.O., Wagener, H., and Strothotte, T., 'Holographic Imaging of Lines: a Texture Based Approach', *Proceedings International Conference on Information Visualization IV '97*, London, August, pp. 272–278 (1997).

Rivlin, R., *The Algorithmic Image: Graphic Visions of the Computer Age*, Microsoft Press (1986).

Roberts, D. (ed.), *Signals and Perception: The Fundamentals of Human Sensation*, Palgrave Macmillan (2002).

Rooney, J., and Steadman, P. (eds), *Principles of Computer-Aided Design*, Pitman/The Open University (1987).

Salisbury, J.K., Conti, F., and Barbagli, F., 'Haptic Rendering: Introductory Concepts', *IEEE Computer Graphics and Applications*, **24** (2), pp. 24–32 (2004).

Salmon, R., and Slater, M., *Computer Graphics: Systems and Concepts*, Addison-Wesley (1987).

Schiffman, H.R., *Sensation and Perception* (2nd edn.), John Wiley & Sons Inc (1982).

Schiffman, H.R., *Sensation and Perception* (3rd edn.), John Wiley & Sons Inc (1990).

Schijven, M., and Jakimowicz, J., 'Virtual Reality Surgical Laparoscopic Simulators', *Surgical Endoscopy*, **17**, pp. 1943–1950 (2003).

Schmitt, O.H., 'Cathode-Ray Presentation of Three-Dimensional Data', *J. Appl. Phys.*, **18**, pp. 819–829 (September 1947).

Schwarz, A.J., and Blundell, B.G., 'Considerations for Accurate Voxel Positioning on a Rotating-Screen Volumetric Display System', *IEE Proceedings on Optoelectronics*, **141** (5), pp. 336–344 (1994a).

Schwarz, A.J., and Blundell, B.G., 'Optimising Dot-Graphics for Volumetric Displays', *IEEE Trans. on Computer Graphics and Applications*, pp. 72–78 (1997).

Schwarz, A.J., and Blundell, B.G., 'Regions of Extreme Image Distortion in Rotating-Screen Volumetric Display Systems', *Computers and Graphics*, **18** (5), pp. 643–652 (1994b).

Schwarz, A.J., and Blundell, B.G., 'Regions of Extreme Image Distortion in Rotating-Screen Volumetric Graphics Displays', *IEEE Computer Graphics and Applications*, **17** (3), pp. 72–88 (1994c).

Seymour, N.E., Gallagher, A.G., Roman, S.A., O'Brien, M.K., Bansal, V.K., Andersen, D.K., and Satava, R.M., 'Virtual Reality Training Improves Operating Room Performance: Results of a Randomized, Double-Blinded Study', *Annals of Surgery*, **236** (4), pp. 458–464 (2002).

Sher, L.D., 'SpaceGraph, a True 3-D PC Peripheral', *SPIE* **902** *Three-Dimensional Imaging and Remote Sensing Imaging*, pp. 10–17 (1988).

Sherman, W.R., and Craig, A.B., *Understanding Virtual Reality: Interface, Application and Design*, Morgan Kaufmann (2003).

Sherr, S., *Applications for Electronic Displays: Technologies and Requirements*, John Wiley & Sons Inc (1998).

Sherrington, C.S., 'The Muscular Sense', in *Textbook on Physiology*, Schaefer, E.A. (ed.), Macmillan (1900).

Shimada, S., 'A New Approach to the Real-Image 3D Globe Display', *SID 93 Digest*, pp. 1001–1004 (1993).

Slater, M., Steed, A., and Chrysanthou, Y., *Computer Graphics and Virtual Environments: From Realism to Real-Time*, Pearson Education Limited (2002).

Smith, D.K., and Alexander, R.C., '*Fumbling the Future: How Xerox Invented, Then Ignored, the First Personal Computer*', toExcel (1999).

Snibbe, S., Anderson, S., and Verplank, B., 'Springs and Constraints for 3D Drawing', *Proceedings Third PHANToM User's Group Workshop (October 3–6)* (1998).

Soltan, P., and Lasher, M., 'Non-Moving 3D Volumetric Display using Upconversion Materials', *NRaD Report* (11 April 1996).

Soltan, P., Trias, J., Dahlke, W., Lasher, M., and MacDonald, M., 'Laser-Based 3D Volumetric Display System (2nd generation)', *SID '94 Proceedings* (1994).

Soltan, P., Trias, J., Robinson, W., and Dahlke, W., 'Laser Based 3D Volumetric Display System', *SPIE* **1664**, pp. 177–192 (1992).

St. Hilaire, P., Benton, S., and Lucente, M., 'Synthetic Aperture Holography: a Novel Approach to Three-Dimensional Displays', *J. Opt. Soc. Am. A.* **9** (11), pp. 1969–1977 (1992).

Sullivan, A., 'A Solid-State Multiplanar Volumetric Display', *Proceedings SID '03 Digest* (2003).

Sutherland, I.E., 'A Head-Mounted Three Dimensional Display', *AFIPS Conf.Proceedings*, **33**, pp. 757–764 (1968).

Sutherland, I.E., 'Sketchpad: A Man-Machine Graphical Communication System', in *SJCC*, Spartan Books, Baltimore, MD (1963).

Sutherland, I.E., and Hodgman, G.W., 'Reentrant Polygon Clipping', *CACM*, **17**(1), pp. 32–42 (January 1974).

Tilton, H.B., 'Nineteen-Inch Parallactiscope', *Proceedings SPIE* **902**, pp. 17–23 (1988).

Torrance, K.E., and Sparrow, E.M., 'Theory for Off-Specular Reflection from Roughened Surfaces', *J. Opt. Soc. Am.* **57** (9), pp. 1105–1114 (September 1967).

Traub, A.C., 'Stereoscopic Display Using Rapid Varifocal Mirror Oscillations', *Applied Optics*, **6** (6), pp. 1085–1087 (June 1967).

Travis, A.R.L., 'Autostereoscopic 3-D Display', *Applied Optics*, **29** (29), pp. 4341–4342 (1990).

Troland, L.T., *The Principles of Psychophysiology*, Van Nostrand (1930).

Vince, J., *Mathematics for Computer Graphics*, Springer (2005).

Wade, N.J. (ed.), *Brewster and Wheatstone on Vision*, Academic Press (1983).

Walworth, V., 'Three-Dimensional Projection with Circular Polarizers', *Proceedings SPIE 462 (Optics in Entertainment II)* (1984).

Ware, C., *Information Visualization: Perception for Design*, Morgan Kaufman (2000).

Warren, R.M., and Warren, R.P., (eds.), 'Helmholtz on Perception: Its Physiology and Development', John Wiley (1968).

Watt, A., *3D Computer Graphics*, Addison-Wesley (2000).

Watt, A., and Watt., M., *Advanced Animation and Rendering Techniques*, Addison-Wesley Professional (1992).

Weiler, K., and Atherton, P., 'Hidden Surface Removal Using Polygon Area Sorting', *Computer Graphics*, **11**(2), pp. 214–222 (1977).

Whitted, T., 'An improved Illumination Model for Shaded Display', *Communications of the ACM* **23**(6), pp. 343–349 (1980).

Williams, R.D., and Garcia, F., 'A Real Time Autostereoscopic Multiplanar 3D Display System', *SID'88 Digest*, **19**, pp. 91–94 (1988).

Withey, E.L., 'Cathode-Ray Tube Adds Third Dimension', *Electronics (Engineering Edition)*, pp. 81–83 (23 May 1958).

Zilles, C.B., and Salisbury, J.K., 'A Constraint-Based God-Object Method for Haptic Display', *Proceedings ASME Haptic Interfaces for Virtual Environment and Teleoperator Systems, Dynamic Systems and Control 1994 (Chicago)*, **1**, pp. 146–150 (1994).

Zito Jr., R., 'Rate Analysis of Multiple-Step Excitation in Mercury Vapor', *J. Appl. Phys.* **34** (5), pp. 1535–1543 (May 1963).

Zito, R., and Schraeder, A.E., 'Optical Excitation of Mercury Vapour for the Production of Isolated Fluorescence', *Applied Optics*, **2** (12), pp. 1323–1328 (December 1963).

Index

Printed in the United States of America